THE LIBERAL ARTS TRADITION

A Documentary History

Bruce A. Kimball

*Published in cooperation with the Association for
Core Texts and Courses*

University Press of America,® Inc.
Lanham · Boulder · New York · Toronto · Plymouth, UK

Copyright © 2010 by
University Press of America,® Inc.
4501 Forbes Boulevard
Suite 200
Lanham, Maryland 20706
UPA Acquisitions Department (301) 459-3366

Estover Road
Plymouth PL6 7PY
United Kingdom

Library of Congress Control Number: 2010924017
ISBN: 978-0-7618-5132-5 (paperback : alk. paper)
eISBN: 978-0-7618-5133-2

To the professors, deans, and students,
fellow laborers in the vineyard at colleges near and far,
who have read and discussed these texts with me
and have deepened and troubled our understanding
over the past twenty-five years,
this enchiridion is affectionately dedicated.

Table of Contents

Preface

The origins of this collection lie in 1986 when I began to lead an annual seminar for professors and deans based upon a selection of original, translated documents from the history of the liberal arts. My intent has been to read and discuss together some of the significant writings that have informed the meaning of liberal education in the past. This documentary history represents my effort to codify the selected documents, which I have whittled down from some 1,500 pages.

During the long development of this work, I have become indebted to many people in a number of ways. In the early 1980s my colleagues on the faculty of the University Honors Program at the University of Houston were deeply influential, particularly Ted Estess, Jack McNees, John Bernard, John Ettling, and John Danford. Acting on the kind recommendation of Sheldon Rothblatt of the University of California, Berkeley, Vice President Ralph Lundgren of the Lilly Endowment invited me in 1986 to offer a seminar on the history of liberal education as part of the summer institute on liberal education that the Lilly Endowment sponsored annually in Colorado Springs until 1994. I am grateful for their support and counsel during those years. My colleagues on the faculty of that institute provided important insights that contributed significantly to the evolution of that seminar and, ultimately, this anthology: Herman Blake, Mary Burgan, Elof Carlson, Jerry Gaff, George Lopez, Phil Moots, Frank Newman, Herman Sinaiko, David Smith, Martha Sullivan, Virginia Wright Wexman, and Margaret Wilkerson.

Subsequent to 1994 I offered that seminar at my own university and, upon invitation, at various other colleges and universities, including, particularly, St. Mary's College of California, Westmont College in California, and St. Norbert's College in Wisconsin. I am grateful to the sponsors of those seminars and particularly to Bill Hynes and Robert Orrill for their support of this project over many years. My former colleagues at the University of Rochester helped me at various points with learned suggestions: Mark Motley, Randall Curren, Tyll Van Geel, Lynn Gordon, and Harold Wechsler. Over the years, many research assistants have been immensely helpful: Kathleen Mahoney, Eleanor Rosenfield, Kevin O'Brien, John Barker, Jason Blokhuis, and Ben Johnson. J. Albert Dragstedt and Frances M. Sweeney, of St. Mary's College, California, participated in my seminar in 1995 and 1996; and I am appreciative of their learned comments and their permission to pubish their translations that have contributed significantly to this project. Helpful criticism and suggestions about the manuscript at various stages have been received from Eva Brann, Hugh Hawkins, Stanley Katz, Herman Sinaiko, John d'Arms, and Frank Oakley.

In addition, I would like to thank the Association of Core Texts and Courses and its executive director Scott Lee for their endorsement and sponsorship of this project. I am also extremely grateful for financial support of the research underlying this work, which has been received at various points from the Spencer Foundation, the American Philosophical Society, the Carnegie Corporation of New York, and the College Board. The opinions and conclusions of the research are my own and do not necessarily reflect the positions or policies of those institutions.

Throughout the selections, the spelling, punctuation, paragraphing, and, occasionally, syntax have been modernized.

"As plants in gardens excel those that grow wild,
or as brutes by due management . . . are much altered,
so [we] by liberal education are much bettered
as to intellectuals and morals."

—Bathsua Makin (1673)

Introduction

The Disputed Origins

The meaning and nature of the liberal arts have been fiercely contested during certain epochs in the past, and intense debate has once again erupted in recent decades. We will be in a better position to understand this debate if we know the history of the liberal arts. Yet, that history is also contested, and the historiographical dispute is manifested in the conflicting proposals that have been advanced for the origins of liberal education. Consequently, this documentary history begins by examining the variety of conflicting starting points that recent scholars have adopted in analyzing the history of liberal education. In this way, we will see the roots of prominent contrasting views of liberal education that have been advanced over the last century.[1]

Certainly the best-known claim is that the liberal arts originated in ancient Greece during the fifth and fourth centuries B.C. Though often regarded as monolithic, this view actually comprehends at least three competing propositions. One was famously expressed early in the twentieth century by the distinguished scholar Werner Jaeger, who in 1933 published the first volume of his influential work, *Paideia*.[2] This Greek term may be translated either as "culture" or "education," and in his work Jaeger made a breathtaking claim on behalf of the originality, the priority, and the truth of the ancient Greek view of culture and education. Jaeger wrote, "We are accustomed to use the word culture . . . to denote something inherent in every nation of the world, even the most primitive. We use it for the entire complex of all the ways and expressions of life, which characterize any one nation. Thus the word [culture] has sunk to mean a simple anthropological concept, not a concept of value, a consciously pursued ideal. In this vague [anthropological] sense, it is permissible to talk of Chinese, Indian, Babylonian, Jewish or Egyptian culture, although none of these nations has a word or an ideal which corresponds to real culture. Of course every highly organized nation has an educational system; but the law and the prophets of the Israelites, the Confucian system of the Chinese, the Dharma of the Indians are in their whole intellectual structure fundamentally and essentially different from the Greek ideal of culture."[3]

---

1. This introduction draws from Bruce A. Kimball, "The Disputed Origins of Liberal Education and the Origin of Recent Disputes," Henry Crimmel Lecture on Liberal Education (18 Oct. 2001), St. Lawrence University, Canton, New York; Bruce A. Kimball, "A Historiographical Fresco of the Liberal Arts" (9 Feb. 2002), Institute of the Liberal Arts, Westmont College, Santa Barbara, California.

2. Born in Germany in 1888, Jaeger completed the *gymnasium* in 1907, and received the Ph.D. from the University of Berlin in 1911. Between 1914 and 1936, he taught at a number of German universities and wrote *Paideia: The Ideals of Greek Culture* in the mid-1930s before fleeing Nazi Germany in 1936 and joining the faculty at the University of Chicago. In 1939 he was appointed to one of the newly instituted University Professorships at Harvard University, where he remained for the rest of his career, widely influencing conceptions of Western culture and liberal education in the United States. Jaeger died in 1961 in Massachusetts.

3. Jaeger's quotations are drawn from *Paideia: The Ideals of Greek Culture* (1933), tr. Gilbert Highet, 2nd English ed. (New York: Oxford University Press, 1945), v. 1, pp. xiii–xviii.

And what was that distinctive Greek meaning of "real culture"? As Jaeger went on to assert, "Greece is in a special category. From the point of view of the present day, the Greeks constitute a fundamental advance on the great peoples of the Orient, a new stage in the development of society. [The Greeks] established an entirely new set of principles for communal life. However highly we may value the artistic, religious, and political achievements of earlier nations, the history of what we can truly call civilization—the deliberate pursuit of an ideal—does not begin until Greece."

Jaeger thus maintained that the Greeks invented the notion of "pursuing an ideal conception of the human being," and this pursuit is what he called "culture." By the same token, Jaeger asserted that the Greeks invented the idea of education, by which he meant that they originated the idea of purposefully training youths to pursue an ideal conception of the human being. In general terms, this understanding of education is what, for Jaeger, becomes liberal education. More specifically, Jaeger turned to Plato to fill in the particulars of that higher type of person and cultural ideal, as well as to provide the philosophical justification for the entire framework. The choice of Plato was perfectly consistent, inasmuch as Plato is one of the thoroughly idealistic theorists of education.

While Jaeger enshrined the idealistic philosophy of Plato as the source of liberal education, another eminent scholar, Ernst Curtius, attributed the origins to Isocrates, a rhetor whose school competed with Plato's Academy.[4] In 1948 Curtius published his masterpiece, *European Literature and the Latin Middle Ages*, which was translated into English in 1953, as well as Spanish, French, and Portuguese, and reissued as recently as 1990. Curtius's interests were no less universalistic than Jaeger's, but he located the "universal standpoint" in the study of literature, language, and rhetoric, rather than philosophy.

Curtius granted that "the Liberal Arts . . . go back to ancient Greece," where liberal education was "called *encyclios paideia* which means 'the customary, ordinary education.'"[5] But Curtius deprecated Jaeger's hero, Because "Plato, we know, wanted philosophy alone to serve as the means of education. [He] not only fought against Homer, and drove the poets from his [ideal] state, but also rejected "general [literary] education." The dictatorial claim, which is inherent in every philosophy, has never been so passionately and bluntly asserted as it was by the greatest of Greek thinkers, [Plato]. But his pedagogics suffered the same shipwreck as his politics. His contemporary, the orator Isocrates, intervened in the conflict between philosophy and general education, recognizing that both educational forces were justified. . . . Despite sporadic theoretical opposition, Isocrates's standpoint remained authoritative in practice for the whole of Antiquity."[6]

Consequently, in the view of Ernst Curtius and a number of historians of antiquity, Isocrates originally established the normative interpretation of liberal education. Isocrates's school established language, literature, and rhetoric as the core of liberal education and attracted more students than Plato's idealistic and contemplative program.

---

4. Ernst Curtius was born in 1886 in Alsace, on the border of France and Germany, and studied comparative philology at the universities of Berlin and Strasbourg. Specializing in Romance languages and literatures, he taught at the Universities of Bonn, Marburg, and Heidelberg, and died in Rome in 1956.

5. The term *encyclios paideia* did not begin to acquire its current sense of "encyclopedia" until after the beginning of the Christian era. Through the end of antiquity, the term predominantly denoted "general education." Curtius interprets the sense of "general" to refer to the breadth of the population who received the education; but "general" may also refer to the breadth of the curriculum, in keeping with the modern ambiguity of "general education" discussed in selections #53 and #54.

6. Ernst R. Curtius, *European Literature and the Latin Middle Ages* (1948) adapted from the translation by W. R. Trask (1953; Princeton, NJ: Princeton University Press, 1990), pp. 36–9.

The third prominent appeal to ancient Greece for the origins of liberal education stands much closer to Jaeger's attribution to Plato than Curtius's attribution to Isocrates. Quintessentially expressed in *The Idea of a University* by the English Catholic churchman, John Henry Newman, this third version assigns primacy in founding liberal education to Plato's student, Aristotle.[7] In Newman's words, "While the world lasts, will Aristotle's doctrine on these matters last, for he is the oracle of nature and of truth. While we are men, we cannot help, to a great extent, being Aristotelians for the great Master does but analyze the thoughts, feelings, views, and opinions of humankind. He has told us the meaning of our own words and ideas, before we were born. In many subject matters, to think correctly, is to think like Aristotle; and we are his disciples whether we will or no, although we may not know it."

Based upon this authority, Newman maintains, "Now, as to the particular instance before us, the word "liberal" as applied to Knowledge and Education, expresses a specific idea, which ever has been, and ever will be, while the nature of man is the same, just as the idea of the Beautiful is specific, or of the Sublime, or of the Ridiculous, or of the Sordid. It is in the world now, it was in the world then; and, as in the case of the dogmas of faith, it is illustrated by a continuous historical tradition, and never was out of the world, from the time it came into it. There have indeed been differences of opinion from time to time, as to what pursuits and what arts came under that idea, but such differences are but an additional evidence of its reality. That idea must have a substance in it, which has maintained its ground amid these conflicts and changes, which has ever served as a standard to measure things withal, which has passed from mind to mind unchanged, when there was so much to color, so much to influence any notion or thought whatever, which was not founded in our very nature. Were it a mere generalization, it would have varied with the subjects from which it was generalized; but though its subjects vary with the age, it varies not itself."

Ultimately, then, "I am chargeable with no paradox, when I speak of a Knowledge which is its own end, when I call it a liberal knowledge, or a gentleman's knowledge, when I educate for it, and make it the scope of a University. And still less am I incurring such a charge, when I make this acquisition consist, not in Knowledge in a vague ordinary sense, but in that knowledge which I have especially called Philosophy or, in an extended sense of the word, Science; for whatever claims Knowledge has to be considered as a good, these it has in a higher degree when it is viewed not vaguely, not popularly, but precisely and transcendently as Philosophy. Knowledge, I say, is then especially liberal, or sufficient for itself, apart from every external and ulterior object, when and so far as it is philosophical, and this I proceed to show."[8]

Newman concluded, "All that I have been now saying is summed up in a few characteristic words of [Aristotle]. 'Of possessions,' he says, 'those rather are useful, which bear fruit; those liberal, which tend to enjoyment. By fruitful, I mean, which yield revenue; by enjoyable, where nothing accrues of consequence beyond the using.'"[9] In these words appear again some of the themes found in Jaeger's

---

7. Born into an evangelical Anglican family in Birmingham, England, in 1801, Newman graduated from Oxford University with a B.A. in 1820. Ordained to the clergy in 1824, Newman ascended to the pulpit of the University Church of Oxford four years later. In 1845 Newman concluded that Roman Catholicism was the true descendant of ancient Christianity and therefore converted. In 1852 he issued the collection of lectures that, revised and supplemented by other essays, was published in 1873 as *The Idea of a University*. In 1858 Newman returned to Birmingham, and in 1879 was named a Cardinal of the Catholic Church. He died in Birmingham in 1890.

8. Newman's quotations are drawn from John Henry Newman, *The Idea of a University, Defined and Illustrated* (1852, 1873), with an introduction and notes by Martin J. Svaglic (Notre Dame, IN: University of Notre Dame Press, 1982), Discourse V, part. 5.

9. Here Newman draws from Aristotle's *Rhetoric* 1361a16–19. See Aristotle's *Politics* in selection #3.

invocation of Plato: appeals to eternal verities and to philosophy. But such distinctions as that in metaphysics between Plato's idealism and Aristotle's hylemorphism, or as that in epistemology between Plato's rationalism and Aristotle's empiricism, entail significantly different implications for the meaning of liberal studies. Newman thus presented a third, distinct claim for the origin of liberal education.

All these attributions to ancient Greece have recently been challenged, as discussed in Section X, but the challenge was expressed long ago. Among the first to do so were certain sophisticated and classically educated leaders of the early Christian church, including Augustine.[10] Composed early in the fifth century, his work *On Christian Learning* had more intellectual influence in Western Europe for the next 800 years than any other writing by a Church Father. At one point in this treatise, Augustine adopted from his mentor, Bishop Ambrose of Milan, the argument that the ancient Greeks borrowed from the Egyptians all their learning, including the liberal arts. The next step in this gambit was to claim that the Egyptians received their learning from the Hebrews and, hence, finally to assert that all of Greek learning, along with liberal education, had Judaeo-Christian origins. This argument was directed both to Christian rigorists who scorned pagan learning, fearing the temptation to indulge in worldly things, and to pagans who dismissed even the Christian doctrines they admired as being derivative of Greek philosophy.

Augustine made the argument in regard to the doctrine of monotheism in these words: "What a question our Ambrose solved after . . . the readers and admirers of Plato . . . dared to say that all the lessons of our Lord Jesus Christ, which they were forced to admire and to teach, were learned from the writings of Plato, since it cannot be denied that Plato lived long before the advent of the Lord! Did not the famous bishop [Ambrose], when he had considered the history of the pagans and found that Plato had traveled in Egypt during the time of Jeremiah, show that Plato had probably been introduced to our literature by Jeremiah so that [Plato] was able to teach or to write doctrines that are justly commended [by the Church]? Pythagoras himself did not live before the literature of the Hebrew nation, in which the [doctrine] of [monotheism] took its origin. . . . And from the disciples of Pythagoras . . . Plato learned theology. Thus from a consideration of [history] it becomes more credible that the Platonists took from our literature whatever they said that is good and truthful than that Our Lord Jesus Christ learned from [Plato]. To believe the latter view is the utmost madness."[11]

Madness or not, Augustine appreciated that the argument claiming Christian origins for Greek learning and liberal education was rather forced. In fact, Augustine later retracted this view. Nevertheless, the argument remained popular for the next thousand years, partly due to the authority of Augustine's text, and it was still being credited by learned individuals as late as the fifteenth century in Western Europe. Despite his retraction, Augustine never relinquished his steadfast defense of the appropriateness of secular learning and the liberal arts for Christians.

Augustine's argument on behalf of the Judaeo-Christian origins of the liberal arts may seem naive or contrived, particularly given his later retraction. Yet, an analogous contention for a fifth different starting point for liberal education attracted considerable attention in the late twentieth century. This argument on behalf of "The Afroasiatic Roots of Classical Civilization" was advanced by Martin Bernal, who published the first volume of *Black Athena: The Afroasiatic Roots of Classical Civilization*

10. See the introduction to Augustine (354–430) in selection #7. Ambrose (c. 340–397), theologian and bishop of Milan, was the mentor of Augustine.

11. Augustine, *On Christian Learning*, tr. D. W. Robertson, Jr. (Indianapolis, IN: Bobbs-Merrill, 1958) II xxviii 43–44.

in 1987.[12] This book argued that much of Greek civilization originated in Middle Eastern cultures and that racism and cultural chauvinism explain the ignorance of these origins.

Bernal wrote that the "Aryan" model of Greek history viewed Greece "as essentially European or Aryan" and was "developed only during the first half of the nineteenth century." A competing "Ancient Model" of Greek history was "the conventional view among the Greeks in the Classical and Hellenistic Ages. According to it, Greek culture had arisen as the result of colonization, around 1500 B.C., by Egyptians and Phoenicians who had civilized the native inhabitants. Furthermore, Greeks had continued to borrow heavily from Near Eastern cultures."

Bernal presented evidence on behalf of the Ancient Model and concluded, "If I am right in urging the overthrow of the Aryan Model and its replacement by the Revised Ancient one, it will be necessary not only to rethink the fundamental bases of "Western Civilization" but also to recognize the penetration of racism and 'continental chauvinism' into all our . . . writing of history. The Ancient Model . . . was overthrown for external reasons. For eighteenth- and nineteenth-century Romantics and racists it was simply intolerable for Greece, which was seen not merely as the epitome of Europe but also as its pure childhood, to have been the result of the mixture of native Europeans and colonizing Africans and Semites. Therefore the Ancient Model had to be overthrown, and replaced by something more acceptable."[13]

In striking contrast to Jaeger and Newman, Bernal thus maintained that Greek culture did not transcend the earlier eastern civilizations, but rather relied upon them. In addition, Bernal's emphasis upon "external reasons" for historical explanation contradicted others, such as Paul Kristeller, who argued "that education and culture are autonomous . . . and are not merely the by-products of social and political forces that happen to prevail at a given time."[14] Consequently, Bernal's assertions generated great controversy amid the arguments over Afrocentric perspectives that became increasingly intense at the beginning of the twenty-first century.[15] Sometimes lost in this controversy was the similarity of Bernal's view to that of Ambrose, Augustine, and other early Christians on behalf of the Judaeo-Christian origin of Greek learning and, concomitantly, the liberal arts.

Also analogous to the argument in *Black Athena* was a sixth claim for the origins of liberal education, advanced with less notoriety two decades earlier in *History of the Islamic Origins of Western Education* by Mehdi Nakosteen.[16] Although scholars had long studied the process whereby Western

---

12. In 1937 Martin Bernal was born in London, the son of J. D. Bernal, a social non-conformist and ardent Marxist from Ireland who became a world renowned professor of physics and crystallography at the University of London. Martin completed his undergraduate and graduate degrees at King's College, Cambridge University, in Chinese studies. From 1962 to 1965 he held a post-graduate appointment at the University of California, Berkeley, and then joined the faculty of Cornell University. In 1975 he shifted his research from Chinese studies to Ancient Eastern Mediterranean history and retired from Cornell as a professor in the latter field.

13. Martin Bernal, *Black Athena: The Afroasiatic Roots of Classical Civilization*, v. 1 of *The Fabrication of Ancient Greece, 1785–1985* (New Brunswick, NJ: Rutgers University Press, 1987), pp. 1–2. Bernal's emphasis.

14. Paul O. Kristeller, "Liberal Education and Western Humanism," *Liberalism and Liberal Education*, v.5, no.1, *Seminar Reports, Program of General Education in the Humanities, Columbia University* (Fall 1976), pp. 15–6.

15. For example: Jacques Berlinerblau, ed., Heresy in the University: The "Black Athena" Controversy and the Responsibilities of American Intellectuals (New Brunswick, NJ: Rutgers University Press, 1999); Martin Bernal, Black Athena Writes Back (Durham, NC: Duke University Press, 2001).

16. Born in Tehran, Iran, in 1906, Nakosteen emigrated to the United States, became a citizen and raised his family. In 1929 he graduated with a B.A. degree from the College of Wooster in Ohio and then earned an M.A. from Columbia University and a Ph.D. in philosophy of education from Cornell University in 1933. Entering the professoriate in the midst of the Depression, Nakosteen joined the faculty at the University of Colorado in 1938 and

Europe received logic, mathematics, and other liberal arts and sciences from Middle Eastern sources during the high middle ages,[17] Nakosteen's textbook extended that understanding by explaining the process from the viewpoint of the Islamic scholars transmitting their knowledge. Beyond the shift in perspective, Nakosteen called into question scholars' longstanding treatment of this Islamic contribution as merely the "Arabic bonus"[18] to a purely western tradition.

Given that the liberal arts were thoroughly reconstructed following the reception of Islamic learning, a claim can be made, as Nakosteen's title suggests, on behalf of the Islamic origins of the liberal education that was incorporated into European universities. In his words, "The eighth and ninth centuries, particularly the period between 750 and 900, saw the introduction of [Greek] classical learning, education, and refinement into the Islamic culture and schools. . . . The tenth and eleventh centuries—the golden age of Islamic scholarship—were centuries of interpretation of classical thought . . . [S]uccessful modifications of, and new and significant additions to, important areas of this classical cultural heritage were achieved. . . . The results of translations of Muslim works upon the curriculum of Western Europe were revolutionary. . . . In the [European] universities of the twelfth and thirteenth centuries scholarship was based almost entirely on the writings of the Muslim and Greek authors as translated from Arabic or Greek sources. Muslim-Aristotelian science remained the core of the curriculum of the University of Paris until the sixteenth century."[19]

Nakosteen therefore concluded, "Islam had given the West the best of what it had learned from classical cultures and what it had added by its own creative genius. Europe took over where Islam left off. . . . Only one debt remains partially unpaid. The Western mind, so generously enriched by the creative toil of five hundred years of Muslim scholarship, has been too slow, perhaps too reluctant, to acknowledge this indebtedness and render unto its givers an overdue expression of thanks." In this fashion, Mehdi Nakosteen made in 1964 what would today be considered a modest claim on behalf of the non-Western origins of the liberal education that was incorporated into the universities of Europe in the thirteenth and fourteenth centuries.

Even as Mehdi Nakosteen published his views, a different claim for the origins of liberal education was advanced by Harold Taylor, who became the youngest college president in the country when he was chosen in 1945 to lead Sarah Lawrence College.[20] Near the end of his presidency, Taylor was invited to participate in a lecture series held at Swarthmore College. Notwithstanding the chilling climate of McCarthyism, Taylor advanced a staunchly "progressive idea" of liberal education, of which "John Dewey stands as the pre-eminent exponent."[21] Taylor declared, "Liberal education is the intellectual and cultural instrument through which the basic ideas of liberalism are transmitted and devel-

---

remained there for the rest of his career. His scholarship straddled the two worlds of his personal life, for he studied and wrote both on Persian literature and on the history and philosophy of education in the West.

17. See selection #16 by John of Salisbury.

18. Claudia Kren, "Astronomy," in *The Seven Liberal Arts in the Middle Ages*, ed. David L. Wagner (Bloomington: Indiana University Press, 1983), p. 245.

19. Quotations here and below are adapted from Mehdi Nakosteen, *History of Islamic Origins of Western Education A.D. 800–1350, with an Introduction to Medieval Muslim Education* (Boulder: University of Colorado Press, 1964), pp. 173–5, 190–5. Cf. John Freely, *Aladdin's Lamp: How Greek Science Came to Europe Through the Islamic World* (New York: Knopf, 2009).

20. See Harold Taylor in selection #62.

21. Quotations are from Willis D. Weatherford, Jr., "Introduction," in *The Goals of Higher Education*, ed. Willis D. Weatherford, Jr. (Cambridge, MA: Harvard University Press, 1960), pp. 3–5.

oped. . . . Throughout the history of Western society, liberal education has been both the institutional expression of liberalism as a philosophy and the intellectual force which helped to create the political and social changes of liberalized societies. The central idea of liberal education is therefore the idea of individualism and individual freedom. . . . The idea of liberalism and of liberal education is a fairly recent one and a local one. It has its origin in the Western world, in political and social changes which began in the seventeenth century with the discovery of a new universe and a new world, with a new mercantile class and the growth of common law."[22]

In sharp contrast to Taylor's view, yet another starting point for the liberal arts was identified by the distinguished scholar of the Italian Renaissance, Paul Kristeller. In a faculty seminar at Columbia University in 1976 he dismissed the idea "that liberalism and liberal education are related or interdependent." In fact, "liberal education in a broad sense existed for many centuries before political liberalism was even heard of," maintained Kristeller, while identifying ancient Greek roots for the "humanities" curriculum that he implicitly identified with liberal education. Furthermore, he associated liberal education most closely with the study of language and literature, as Ernst Curtius proposed. However, for Kristeller it was during the Renaissance that liberal education first appeared. During the fourteenth and fifteenth centuries, he argued, the long lost classical letters were reborn and gradually formalized into the humanities curriculum that served both a professional and a humanizing, or socializing, role in subsequent colleges and universities.[23]

Diverging from both Taylor and Kristeller, Elizabeth Kamarck Minnich subsequently presented still another interpretation and located the origins of liberal education in "Old Class, Race, and Gender Hierarchies."[24] In her writing and lecturing, Minnich devoted a great deal of attention to feminist scholarship and women's studies, and this interest naturally appeared in her book *Transforming Knowledge*, published in 1990 and awarded the Frederic W. Ness Book Award by the Association of American Colleges and Universities.[25] Addressing the "liberal arts," Minnich maintained that "conceptions of the liberal arts themselves tend to hide . . . the articulated hierarchy from which they sprang. In liberal arts institutions, studio courses—doing courses of any kind—are barely recognized or, if recognized, are often not given full liberal arts standing. Technical schools are considered intellectually inferior, and illiberal. These divisions reflect the privileged, male, Greek (largely Athenian) division between those who use reason and lead a life devoted to it . . . and those who should be ruled by the reasoning few. The standards of what is and what is not liberal arts are used to justify themselves, and with them the class as well as gender hierarchies of old."

These invidious origins and characteristics of liberal education prompted Minnich to challenge the link between "liberation" and "liberal education" posited by Harold Taylor: "It is assumed that the

---

22. Harold Taylor, "Individualism and the Liberal Tradition" (1958), in *The Goals of Higher Education*, pp. 9–12, 24–5.

23. See Paul Kristeller in selection #63. His quotations here are drawn from Paul O. Kristeller, "Liberal Education and Western Humanism," in *Liberalism and Liberal Education*, v. 5, no. 1, *Seminar Reports, Program of General Education in the Humanities, Columbia University* (Fall 1976), pp. 15–22.

24. Born in 1943, Minnich matriculated at Sarah Lawrence College two years after the departure of President Harold Taylor, and graduated with a Bachelor of Arts degree in 1965. Following a year of study in India, she earned a Ph.D. in social and political philosophy from the New School for Social Research, where Harold Taylor had gone on to teach. In 1977 she became Associate Dean of Faculty in Barnard College at Columbia University and in 1980 Professor of Philosophy and Women's Studies at the Union Institute and University in Cincinnati. Currently, she serves as a Senior Fellow at the Association of American Colleges and Universities.

25. The following quotations are drawn from Elizabeth Kamarck Minnich, *Transforming Knowledge* (Philadelphia: Temple University Press, 1990), pp. 116–9.

liberal arts liberate, that they counter human limitations, enrich human abilities. But can they do so while we retain the old . . . [dichotomies of] . . . mind and body, knowledge and action, theory and practice . . . in which all that has to do with the "lower" human activities is defined as appropriate to women and lower-caste men, and so as 'improper' for the educated "free man"[?] The "liberal" in liberal arts was never intended to mean "liberating" except insofar, as the arts . . . "liberated" some men from concern for mundane, useful, care-taking concerns, ostensibly so they could give their full attention to "higher" things. . . . The liberal arts that descended from the education of gentlemen still carry within them all the errors that exclusiveness [and] snobbishness, built into them—and yet, it is to the liberal arts that we turn today to show and promote concern for the enduring questions of human life and meaning." In this way, Minnich explicitly attributed the origins of liberal education and its continuing characteristics to "Old Class, Race, and Gender Hierarchies."

Complementary to Minnich's analysis is the view of Jane Roland Martin, who attributed the origin of liberal education to a "male Cognitive Perspective."[26] In a Presidential address to the Philosophy of Education Society, Martin stated about "liberal education" that "the disciplines into which a person must be initiated to become a educated person exclude women and their works, construct the female to the male image of her, and deny the truly feminine qualities she does possess." Thus, "consider the traits or characteristics . . . attributed to the educated person. Feelings and emotions only enter into the makeup of the educated person [in the sense of] being committed to the standards of a theoretical pursuit such as science. . . . Concern for people and for interpersonal relationships has no role to play: the educated person's sensitivity is to the standards immanent in activities, not to other human beings; nor is the educated person thought to be empathetic or supportive or nurturing. Intuition is also neglected. Theoretical knowledge and . . . "reasoned understanding" are the educated person's prime characteristics." Hence, "this educated person . . . coincides with our cultural stereotype of a male human being . . . [universities] set forth an ideal for [liberal] education which embodies just those traits and dispositions our culture attributes to the male sex and excludes the traits our culture attributes to the female sex."[27] This exclusion thus caused harm to women, to men, and to liberal education, Martin argued.

§ § §

Given this range of starting points and allegations of associated interests, it is obviously perilous to identify significant documents that have informed the meaning of liberal education at its origins or throughout its history. Nevertheless, since beginning to study the history of liberal education in the mid-1970s, I have maintained that a helpful way to proceed in examining this topic is to follow the usage of the terms "liberal education" and "liberal arts" and their direct Latin antecedents (*artes liberales, disciplinae liberales*, and so forth).

Needless to say, this simple approach rapidly becomes complicated because influential, ancillary documents that do not mention "liberal arts" soon appear, and because the etymological antecedents of the Latin terms are not nearly so direct as those of the English. Yet, by adhering closely to the line

---

26. Jane Roland Martin was born in 1929 in New York City and in 1951 completed the B.A. at Radcliffe College, the women's college incorporated within Harvard University. After teaching elementary school, she returned to Harvard for graduate study, and in 1961 completed a Ph.D. degree in philosophy of education, which was awarded by Radcliffe because Harvard still refused to grant graduate degrees to women. In 1972, Martin joined the philosophy department at the Boston campus of the University of Massachusetts, where she spent her career.

27. Jane Roland Martin, "The Ideal of the Educated Person" (1981), in *Changing the Educational Landscape: Philosophy, Women, and Curriculum* (New York: Routledge, 1994), pp. 70–87.

of writings that explicitly address "liberal education" or "liberal arts" or their antecedents or synonyms, it is possible to identify a historical tradition without relying as much upon an *a priori* or arbitrary definition as has often been the case in the historiography of liberal education. Underlying this approach is the effort to be descriptive rather than prescriptive, and this intention, too, will perhaps appear naively pre-postmodern to some. Nevertheless, documents from the history of what has been called "liberal education" can be collected and studied in the same way as they can about what has been called "Christianity" or "democracy," regardless of what one thinks about the benefits or ills of these institutions.

This documentary history therefore presents significant or exemplary documents that are intended to instruct and to prompt discussion about the history of the liberal arts. After the introduction of the printing press, the literature becomes so vast that some kind of winnowing is necessary. The second half of the volume therefore focuses upon the American experience by presenting documents written almost exclusively in the United States or the antecedent colonies.

The introductions and footnotes to the Sections and individual selections are intended to provide background for understanding, to raise points for discussion, or to indicate certain cross references among the documents. Throughout the introductions and the notes, I have minimized citations to the voluminous secondary literature, referencing only quotations and points of particular interest. While the introductions and notes attempt to aid consideration and discussion of significant issues in each section and selection, I have not tried to employ an overall interpretation as a mold or sieve for the collection, although my own interpretation of the history of liberal education has inevitably influenced the selection and arrangement of documents. Consequently, it may be helpful to present at the outset a synopsis of my interpretation.[28]

The central thesis is that the history of what has empirically been called "liberal arts" or "liberal education" can be understood in terms of two basic traditions: one emphasizing "reason," including its various denotations of a rationale, a faculty of thinking, and an act of thinking; and another emphasizing "speech," including its meanings of the pronouncing of words, the faculty of talking, and a formal act of communication. "Reason" and "speech" are the two semantic branches of *logos*, the term that the Greeks applied to the human faculty that was thought to be the source of learning and civilization, as illustrated in selection #2 by Isocrates. On one branch were orators and rhetors, who emphasized the newly invented arts of grammar and rhetoric and the skills of composing, delivering, and analyzing a speech. These skills were paramount in a democratic city-state or a republic where persuasion determined the outcome of every question arising in the political and judicial assemblies. On the other branch were those who regarded rhetoric as an imprecise and practical tool constituting but a shadow of the nature of *logos*. These others, including Plato and Aristotle, searched for a precise, rational method of pursuing knowledge, and regarded the new arts of mathematics and logic as most closely approximating the nature of *logos*.

The debate between advocates of mathematics and logic, on one side, and grammar and rhetoric, on the other, passed to the Romans, who, as did Cicero, felt most sympathetic toward a theory of education emphasizing public expression, political and legal discourse, and general and ethical training in the literary tradition that prescribed the noble virtues and orderly society of the past. The literary and rhetorical Roman liberal arts eventually deteriorated toward sophistry, but were then adopted and reinvigorated by Christian scholars and educators, who observed that classical learning was refracted into "oratory and philosophy," as did Paul in his first letter to the *Corinthians*. Faced with the choice between speech and reason, Christians such as Jerome and Augustine embraced the pagan liberal arts that were concerned with interpreting and expounding the meaning of normative texts. They made the

28. See Bruce A. Kimball, *Orators and Philosophers: A History of the Idea of Liberal Education* (1986; New York: College Board, 1995).

study of grammar and rhetoric preeminent in the *artes liberales*, regarded logic as an adjunct to rhetoric, and studied music primarily in its sonorous dimensions. They treated mathematical and scientific disciplines as bodies of facts providing technical information useful for exegesis. Specialization and advanced study were not encouraged by the Christians and were even criticized as leading to self-indulgence—the same criticism that the orators Cicero and Isocrates had expressed about Plato's vision of a philosophical education extending into adulthood and about Aristotle's idea of liberal education as the pursuit of inquiry during "leisure" or free time.

As invasions and turmoil brought an end to the period now called Antiquity, the Christian philosopher Boethius tried to recover the Platonic and Aristotelian view of the liberal arts, which emphasized the study of mathematics and logic to train the mind in critical analysis and speculative thought. Boethius died at a relatively young age, however, and his influence was not as great as that of three other writers who adopted the practical, literary, and rhetorical model of liberal education: Martianus Capella, Cassiodorus, and Isidore of Seville. In the fifth and sixth centuries, they each wrote handbooks codifying liberal education into a program of seven liberal arts: grammar, logic, rhetoric, arithmetic, geometry, music, and astronomy. Appearing in selections below, the three handbooks served as textbooks for the Christian medieval schools throughout Western Europe.

In the twelfth and thirteenth centuries, the rhetorical model of liberal education was challenged when the newly recovered texts of Aristotle and of Islamic philosophers and mathematicians prompted a revival of critical and speculative thought on the part of the scholastics at the newly arising medieval universities. In 1159 John of Salisbury observed the challenge when writing that "*logos* means both 'word' and 'reason.'" The outcome of this renewed confrontation was that the theoretical and rationalistic orientation of these university scholastics, or professors, such as Thomas Aquinas, transformed the meaning and content of the liberal arts. Logic emerged preeminent as a refined analytic tool, and mathematics and logic increasingly addressed abstract number rather than practical matters. Rhetoric almost dropped from sight, while grammar was transmuted into linguistic analysis and stripped of its association with literature and texts. Overall, the liberal arts became narrow and relatively cursory *scientiae speculativae* intended to prepare students for advanced and specialized study in the graduate faculties of the universities.

During the fourteenth and fifteenth centuries, the provocative logical disputations that represented the core of the scholastic liberal arts degenerated into sophistry. At the same time, the Ciceronian conception of liberal education, along with the works of Cicero, were being rediscovered by the humanists of the Renaissance. The humanist movement began outside of the universities and gradually infiltrated those institutions through the efforts of individuals such as Pier Paolo Vergerio, who wrote in his fifteenth-century treatise: "There are two kinds of liberal ways of life: one which is totally composed of leisure and contemplation, and a second which consists in activity and affairs."

Inclining toward the latter, the humanist model of rhetorical and literary learning was amplified with Christian ethics and with notions of courtesy derived from the medieval tradition of knighthood. These three normative traditions—the humanist model of learning, the social etiquette of courtesy, and Christian ethics—coalesced to yield the ideal of Christian gentility, which became the archetype of a liberally educated person in sixteenth- and seventeenth-century England. Treatises addressing liberal education during this period proclaimed the orator, the statesman, or what Sir Thomas Elyot in 1531 called the "governor," as the model for a student engaged in liberal education. At the same time, the fundamental tension between reason and speech was recalled, for example, by Bathsua Makin in the first English-language treatise arguing on behalf of higher education for women. Makin wrote, "There was a Contest between twenty Grecian and twenty Roman Ladies, which were most excellent in learning. The Roman Dames were the best Oratours; But the Grecian Ladies the best Philosophers."

The model of Christian gentility was endorsed by the founders of Harvard College in 1636, as well as in the eight other colleges subsequently established in the American colonies. The bulk of the curriculum leading to the B.A. degree was devoted to rhetoric and grammar, and to reading, memorizing, and interpreting literary and theological texts that defined the virtues of a citizen in God's commonwealth. These characteristics persevered in the American experience of liberal education, even as leaders of the seventeenth-century Scientific Revolution and eighteenth-century Enlightenment resurrected the philosophical tradition with its commitment to mathematical laws and Socratic inquiry. The ideas of scientists and *philosophes* began to inform discussion about liberal education in the late eighteenth and early nineteenth centuries, as can be seen in the writings of the Unitarian chemist Joseph Priestley, and in the essay of Samuel Smith, in selection #34, which won a contest in 1795 calling for descriptions of "the best system of liberal education and literary instruction, adapted to the genius of the government of the United States."

Conflict inevitably developed between the rhetorical and philosophical models of liberal education, just as it had in the medieval universities and in Athens in the fifth and fourth centuries B.C. During the 1880s, the literary critic and essayist Matthew Arnold and the Darwinian scientist Thomas Henry Huxley toured the United States lecturing on diametrically opposed conceptions of liberal education. Contemporaneously, James McCosh, Presbyterian minister and President of Princeton, and Charles Eliot, chemist and President of Harvard, were engaged in the same debate, which appears in selections #47 and #48. Each of these confrontations repeated the centuries-old debate as to which pole of *logos*—reason or speech—should predominate in culture and in the liberal arts.

Even as Arnold and McCosh spoke, however, Huxley, Eliot and their allies carried the day in the United States. A new generation of scholastics established a flock of universities devoted to advanced and specialized research, including Cornell in 1868, Johns Hopkins in 1876, Clark in 1889, Stanford in 1891, and Chicago in 1892. The devotion of the new universities to the scientific method and to specialized research transformed liberal education once again into preparation for graduate study and the pursuit of knowledge.

Defenders of the rhetorical, practical, and textual liberal arts were not easily brushed aside, however, particularly at the small, special-interest colleges that emerged to serve religious sects, women, or African-Americans. A vigorous debate ensued in the late nineteenth and early twentieth centuries and became as acrimonious as those of the thirteenth century and the fourth century B.C. Sectarian colleges and universities clung to the humanist program of studies with its emphasis on literary and rhetorical training that could be traced back through the Renaissance colleges to Cicero and Isocrates. That program was amplified by the teaching of divinity and scholastic theology in order to mold the Christian citizen. At the same time, many of the universities, encouraged by the scientific emphasis on value-free research, abandoned the idea of training the virtuous citizen. Commensurately, as William Foster describes below, these universities introduced the undergraduate major, a specialized preparation for the pursuit of truth that was modeled on graduate study and grounded in precise, rational method guiding inquiry.

Through the beginning of the twentieth century, this two-fold tradition of what has been called "liberal education" thus persevered, rooted in what Friedrich Paulsen in 1906 called: "A kind of undulatory movement . . . perceptible in the history of intellectual life. Periods of logical-philosophical ascendancy alternate with periods of poetical-literary interest."[29] Over the course of this history, advocates of the two traditions have generally not appreciated each other's position. Proponents of the rational and precise philosophical tradition often criticize the rhetorical tradition for

29. Friedrich Paulsen, *The German Universities and University Study*, tr. Frank Thilly and William W. Elwang (London: Longmans Green, 1906), p. 31.

relying on crude generalizations about knowledge and, therefore, about liberal education. Conversely, advocates of the oratorical tradition claim that emphasis on a putatively neutral, rational method artificially narrows the scope and meaning of knowledge because language is the primary conduit of knowledge and the foundation of the commonweal, and, therefore, lies at the heart of liberal education. Proponents of each tradition hold a diminished view of the other because each makes different assumptions about the nature of reason, language, knowledge, and value.

During the twentieth century, the philosophical, rationalist tradition of liberal education, enshrined in the American research university, became increasingly dominant, until it was challenged in the final third of the century by new social forces and by the "rhetorical" turn in scholarship. This challenge was accompanied by reconsideration of the nature and the role of the received textual sources in the liberal arts tradition. Some of these later developments are addressed in Section X, "Approaching the Past in the New Millennium."

Section I

Debates in Antiquity

The multifarious historiography concerning liberal education might induce skepticism about studying its history at all. Notwithstanding "the circular reasoning to which almost all historical thought is liable,"[1] it is possible to make headway in this study by examining the historical usage of the terms "liberal education" and "liberal arts" and their direct antecedents, such as *artes liberales*. Whatever the universality or contingency of the "liberal arts," there is a record of discussion and reflection explicitly employing this term, and that record can be followed and studied like that of any other cultural tradition and social practice. The usage of the term, in lieu of an *a priori* definition, thus serves as the empirical basis for the study. Furthermore, whether or not liberal education originated in ancient Greece, it is clear that the Greeks formulated certain issues and tensions that informed the subsequent understanding of liberal arts. From those Greek foundations, the Romans drew the arts and sciences that were gradually codified as the *artes liberales*. The selections in Section I are drawn from Greek and Roman writings conveying the nature of those tensions and debates that reverberated in discussion explicitly about liberal arts during the following centuries.

The background to these selections lies in the culture of the heroic warrior portrayed in the epic poems of Homer and still found among the Greek ruling class of the seventh and sixth centuries B.C. In this traditional "Homeric" view, *paideia*[2] meant the inculcation of *areté* (excellence, virtue) defined in terms of a code of military honor. In practice, this meant training a ruling, warrior elite, who exercised and perpetuated military, political, and religious leadership among themselves. These three kinds of leadership were closely related: the military to secure and maintain power, the political to exercise power through offices in the clan or the nascent city-state, and the religious to legitimate power by invoking divine authority through performing the rites of the patron diety of the clan or state cultus.

A twofold program of education gradually became conventional for youth preparing for such leadership, as Plato and Aristotle mention in selections #1 and #3 from the fourth century B.C. The two branches of the conventional program were "gymnastic" and "music." The former apparently included the physical training needed for military leadership and for performing the sacred dance and rites in the state cultus. The latter referred generally to the "arts of Muses" but, above all, to the recitation of Homeric epic poetry which provided technical instruction in speech-making and inculcated the knightly mores and noble ethic of the warrior culture.

In the late sixth and early fifth centuries political and cultural transformations outmoded the purpose and rationale of that traditional Homeric education. On the one hand, Greek culture flowered in all dimensions: sculpture, architecture, philosophy, literature, mathematics, natural sciences. On the other hand, the democratic city-state began to displace rule by the noble, warrior families, as a class of free citizens emerged and constituted popular assemblies to make legislative and judicial decisions. These developments, particularly evident in Athens, stimulated debate about the nature of education

---

1. Werner Jaeger, *Paideia: The Ideals of Greek Culture* (1933), tr. Gilbert Highet, 2nd English ed. (New York: Oxford University Press, 1945), v. 1, p. xviii..

2. That is, education or culture. See the note on the meaning of *paideia* in the Introduction.

that could best prepare those who had both the free time and the political freedom to exercise the new responsibilities of governing the city-state and advancing the cultural achievements. In Greek, the adjective *eleutheros* expressed this twofold sense of "freedom," which was conveyed into Latin as *liberalis*. In its most general and literal sense, then, the meaning of liberal education introduced by the Greeks and transmitted to the Romans was the education particularly suited to the youth who is free. Specifying the precise nature of this kind of education stimulated a continuing debate, for, as Aristotle tells us below, there was no agreement even in the fourth century B.C. about a new curriculum to replace the inherited program of gymnastic and music. The disagreement over the nature of this kind of education came to focus upon *logos*, the term employed by the Greeks to denote the human faculty providing both the principle and the source of culture or civilization. Understanding *logos* was the key to explain the new developments in arts, learning, and politics. But the meaning of *logos* was profoundly ambiguous, as seen in the passage from Isocrates below. To some, it signified "reason," including its various denotations of a rationale, a faculty of thinking, and an act of thinking; to others, it meant "speech" with all of its meanings: the pronouncing of words, the faculty of talking, and a formal act of communication.

Those in the latter camp included orators and rhetors, who emphasized the newly invented arts of grammar and rhetoric and the skills of composing, delivering, and analyzing a speech. These skills were paramount in a democratic city-state or a republic where persuasion determined the outcome of every question arising in the political and judicial assemblies. The former group were those who regarded rhetoric as an imprecise and practical craft, perhaps useful in politics and trade, but devoid of any fundamental knowledge grounded in the nature of human *logos* and its true purposes. This group, including Plato and Aristotle, searched for reliable, exact modes of inquiry and regarded mathematics and logic as the arts most securely founded in the nature of *logos*.

The debate between advocates of mathematics and logic, on one side, and grammar and rhetoric, on the other, passed to the Romans, who introduced the terms *ratio* and *oratio*. This terminology reflected both the connection and the tension between reason and speech that were expressed by Cicero in the excerpt below from his major treatise on education. The Romans, being engineers, lawyers, and administrators of an emerging empire, felt most sympathetic toward a theory of education emphasizing public expression, political and legal discourse, and general and ethical training in the literary tradition that described the noble virtues and orderly society of the past. The Roman *artes liberales* were therefore founded in the study of "grammar," which included literature, as well as language, and was pursued throughout the course of education. Meanwhile, a modicum of attention was occasionally given to arithmetic, geometry, and astronomy, which were regarded as bodies of facts, useful for speeches, but not as theoretical and axiomatic disciplines in the way that Plato and Aristotle had understood them. Music was sometimes studied as practical training for the ear and voice and as an aid to appreciating poetry, but not as one of the theoretical and axiomatic sciences. Logic, or dialectic, was offered as a means of providing the skeletal arguments for public speeches, while rhetoric became the crowning art, which taught the methods of constructing a persuasive discourse on any topic, be it political, religious, military, aesthetic, or legal. This Roman preference for rhetorical, public, practical, prescriptive, and literary education over the precision and clarity of logic and mathematics is exactly what Plato, Aristotle, and many of their students had found objectionable, centuries earlier, in the orators' interpretation of the liberal arts.

Resonating with echoes of the Homeric background, this debate unfolds in the following selections and sets in opposition the ideals of reason and speech, along with their concomitant tensions in epistemology, psychology, ethics, and politics, as well as in educational models of teaching, curriculum, and institutional organization.

Reason and Speech

1. Plato, *Republic* (370s B.C.)

INTRODUCTION

Plato (428–348 B.C.) was born into a leading Athenian family soon after the beginning of the Peloponnesian War (431–404) in which Sparta and its allies fought Athens and its league. When the war ended with the defeat and humiliation of Athens, an oligarchy usurped the power of the democratic leaders of Athens whose extreme policies had contributed to the defeat. The excesses of the oligarchics provoked a reaction in 403 that restored the democratic government, which put Socrates on trial in 399. Plato does not record when or how he met Socrates, but he was clearly a follower and interlocutor of the Socratic inner circle by age 28, when he witnessed Socrates's trial and offered a bond on his behalf.

The execution of Socrates, culminating the tragic events from 404 to 399, appears to have turned Plato away from a career in politics toward one in philosophy, writing, and teaching. During the first decade after Socrates's death, Plato composed what are now considered his "early" dialogues, such as the *Apology* and the *Euthyphro*. These dialogues offer a vivid portrayal of Socrates challenging his fellow citizens to formulate and adhere to a deliberate and reasoned conception of virtue. Brilliantly posing the kinds of questions that this formulation entailed, these early dialogues implicitly criticized the social and political ethos; and it is not difficult to see how persistent inquiry along these lines, during a period of intense political and social upheaval, would provoke a popular reaction against the inquirer. After visiting Italy and Syracuse, possibly to meet with the Pythagorean philosophers there, Plato returned to Athens and founded his Academy in about 385. The Academy trained youths from all over Greece in political philosophy and constitution making and also supported advanced investigation, especially in mathematics, astronomy, and a kind of philosophical inquiry that Plato called dialectic. Plato described his ideal curriculum in the seventh book of the *Republic*, one of the "middle dialogues," written between the mid-380s and mid-360s, from which selection #1 is drawn.

Scholars have debated the significance of these curricular recommendations. Some have suggested that Plato was offhandedly sketching an educational program that should not be given much weight; but most say that he surely regarded this large section of the *Republic*, his masterpiece, with great seriousness. Drawn from Book VII, selection #1 is preceded by the famous metaphor of the Cave, posing the question as to what kind of studies would lead someone from the shadows of mere appearance to the clear light in which reality is truly seen. The selection itself presents a dialogue between Socrates and Glaucon in which they discuss the education of future leaders up to about age twenty. This educational program is thus analogous to, as it was influential upon, what were subsequently called the "liberal arts."

Not long after completing the *Republic*, Plato twice visited Syracuse during the 360s in order to advise the young autocrat Dionysius II on statecraft. However, the studies of mathematics, dialectic, and philosophy did not deter Dionysius II from irrational and short-sighted policies. Repelled by the corrupt politics in Syracuse, Plato returned to Athens, completed the so-called "late" dialogues, begun in the 360s, and died in 348.

SELECTION[3]

[521 c] "Do you want us now to consider in what way such men will come into being and how one will lead them up to the light, just as some men are said to have gone from Hades up to the gods?"[4]

"How could I not want to?" he said.

"Then, as it seems, this wouldn't be the twirling of a shell[5] but the turning of a soul around from a day that is like night to the true day; it is that ascent to what *is* which we shall truly affirm to be philosophy."

"Most certainly."

[521d] "Then mustn't we consider what studies have such a power?"

"Of course."

"What then, Glaucon, would be a study to draw the soul from becoming to being?[6] And, as I speak, I think of this. Weren't we saying that it's necessary for these men to be champions[7] in war when they are young?"

"Yes, we were saying that."

"Then the study we are seeking must have this further characteristic in addition to the former one."

"What?"

"It mustn't be useless to warlike men."

"Of course, it mustn't," he said, "if that can be."

"Now previously they were educated by us in gymnastic and music."

[521e] "That was so," he said.

"And gymnastic, of course, is wholly engaged with coming into being and passing away. For it oversees growth and decay in the body."

"It looked that way."

"So it wouldn't be the study we are seeking."

[522a] "No, it wouldn't."

"And is music, so far as we described it before?"

"But it," he said, "was the antistrophe[8] to gymnastic, if you remember. It educated the guardians through habits, transmitting by harmony a certain harmoniousness, not knowledge, and by rhythm a certain rhythmicalness. And connected with it were certain other habits, akin to these, conveyed by

---

3. Plato, *The Republic*, tr. Allan Bloom (New York: Basic Books, 1968), bk. 7, 521c–533d. Bloom's translation is among the most faithful to the Greek, because a given Greek word is almost always translated into the same English word and because Bloom tries to render an English sentence for each Greek sentence, although this is difficult given the enormous length (by English standards) of some of Plato's sentences. Reprinted by permission of Basic Books, a member of Perseus Books Group.

4. The analogy is to the preceding metaphor Simile of the Cave in which the educated person moves from shadowy ignorance to illuminating truth.

5. The reference is to a children's game.

6. This ontological contrast between becoming and being, between the temporal or contingent and the permanent, is repeated by Plato, as in 525b, 526e, 527b.

7. The Greek is *athlètés*, a competitor or champion in athletics.

8. "This is a term that refers to drama, in particular to the chorus. It is either a movement of the dancers from left to right, corresponding to a previous movement from right to left (the *strophé*), or the song they sing while performing their movement." Translator's note, p. 465n.

speeches, whether they were tales or speeches of a truer sort.[9] But as for a study directed toward something of the sort you are now seeking, there was nothing of the kind in it."

[522b] "Your reminder to me is quite precise," I said. "For, really, it had nothing of the sort. But Glaucon, you demonic man, what could there be that is like this? For all the arts surely seemed to be mechanical."[10]

"Certainly they were. And, yet, what other study is left now that music, gymnastic, and the arts are excluded?"

"Come, then," I said, "if we have nothing left to take besides these, let's take something that applies to them all."

"What kind of thing?"

[522c] "For example, this common thing that all kinds of art, thought, and knowledge use as a supplement to themselves, a thing that it is necessary for everyone to learn among his first studies."

"What's that?" he said.

"The lowly business," I said, "of distinguishing the one, the two, and the three. I mean by this, succinctly, number and calculation.[11] Or isn't it the case with them that every kind of art and knowledge is compelled to participate in them?"[12]

"Very much so," he said.

"The art of war too?" I said.

"Most necessarily," he said.

[522d] "At all events," I said, "in the tragedies Palamedes is constantly showing up Agamemnon as a most ridiculous general. Or haven't you noticed that he says that by discovering number he established the dispositions for the army at Illium and counted the ships and everything else, as though before that they were uncounted and Agamemnon didn't know how many feet he had, if he really didn't know how to count?[13] And, if this is the case, what kind of general do you suppose he was?"

"A strange one," he said, "if this was true."

[522e] "Shall we not then," I said, "set down as a study necessary for a warrior the ability to calculate and to number?"

"Most of all," he said, "if he's going to know anything whatsoever about the order of the army, and, what's more, if he's to be a human being."

"Do you," I said, "notice the same thing I do in this study?"

"What?"

---

9. "Music" thus refers to the nine arts of the Muses in general. Compare the appraisal here with Isocrates's views of these arts of speech in the following reading.

10. "Mechanical" is the translation of *banausos*, connoting low, mean, infra dig, and often translated as "philistine."

11. "In Greek mathematics the study of numbers and their attributes (*arithmétiké*) is distinguished from that of calculation (*logistiké*), which involves operations with numbers (addition, subtraction, etc.)." Translator's note, p. 465n. Both are subsequently subsumed under "arithmetic" in the liberal arts tradition.

12. From 522c to 526b, Plato incorporates the Pythagorean doctrine that abstract number is "this common thing" manifested in "all kinds of art, thought, and knowledge." Number is thus the beginning, or *arché*, of all intellection. See 530d.

13. Agamemnon, legendary Greek hero, led the Greek army against Troy in the Trojan War (c. 1200s B.C.), as described in the *Iliad* of Homer. Palamedes was a lesser-known, legendary hero of the Trojan War.

[523a] "It probably is one of those things we are seeking that by nature lead to intellection; but no one uses it rightly, as a thing that in every way is apt to draw men toward being[14]. . . . [525b] Therefore, as it seems, they would be among the studies we are seeking. It's necessary for a warrior to learn them for the sake of his dispositions for the army, and for a philosopher because he must rise up out of becoming and take hold of being or else never become skilled at calculating."

"That's so," he said.

"And our guardian is both warrior and philosopher."[15]

"Certainly."

[525c] "Then it would be fitting, Glaucon, to set this study down in law and to persuade those who are going to participate in the greatest things in the city to go to calculation and to take it up, not after the fashion of private men, but to stay with it until they come to the contemplation of the nature of numbers with intellection itself, not practicing it for the sake of buying and selling like merchants or tradesmen, but for war and the ease of turning the soul itself around from becoming to truth and being."[16]

"What you say is very fine," he said.

[525d] "And further," I said, "now that the study of calculation has been mentioned, I recognize how subtle it is and how in many ways it is useful to us for what we want, if a man practices it for the sake of coming to know and not for trade."

"In what way?" he said.

"In the very way we were just now saying. It leads the soul powerfully upward and compels it to discuss numbers themselves. It won't at all permit anyone to propose for discussion numbers that are attached to visible or tangible bodies. For surely, you know the way of men who are clever in these things. If in the argument someone attempts to cut the one itself, they laugh and won't permit it. [525e] If you try to break it up into small coin, they multiply, taking good care against the one's ever looking like it were not one but many pieces."

"What you say is very true," he said.

[526a] "What, Glaucon, do you suppose, would happen if someone were to ask them, 'you surprising men, what sort of numbers are you discussing, in which the one is as your axiom claims it to be—each one equal to every other one, without the slightest difference between them, and containing no parts within itself?' What do you suppose they would answer?"

"I suppose they would answer that they are talking about those numbers that admit only of being thought and can be grasped in no other way."[17]

---

14. The passage omitted is the subject of some debate among commentators. The basic point is that comparative judgments made by the senses, such as about the relative size (e.g. large, small) of objects, stimulate the mind to seek invariable standards that can be found in numerical quantities underlying the physical objects apparent to the senses. Thus, the mind rises above the senses by solving the contradictions of sensory perceptions.

15. By guardian, Plato refers to a member of the ruling elite, whom he wishes to educate properly. Below he also uses the term "lawgiver."

16. Why does Plato exempt warfare from his repeated derogation of utilitarian rationales for learning the arts and sciences (525c, 527d, 531c)?

17. The reference may be to pure numbers, apart from the entities being counted. Plato may also be referring to irrational numbers, such as the square root of two, which cannot be expressed as a ratio of whole integers and can be prehended only in geometrical terms, such as the diagonal of an Isosceles triangle. To the Pythagoreans, the discovery of irrational numbers challenged their doctrine that abstract numerical law provides the norms of reality; and they treated this discovery as a veritable "mystery" of their philosophico-religious sect. While Plato does not quite embrace the Pythagorean mystification of irrational numbers, he does believe that they evidence a higher plane of intelligible reality. Victor J. Katz, *A History of Mathematics* (New York: Harper Collins, 1993), pp. 47ff.

[526b] "Do you see, then, my friend," I said, "that it's likely that this study is really compulsory for us, since it looks as if it compels the soul to use the intellect itself on the truth itself?"[18]

"It most certainly does do that," he said.

"What about this? Have you already observed that men who are by nature apt at calculation are, in a word, naturally quick in all studies,[19] while those who are slow, if they are educated and given gymnastic in it, all make progress by becoming quicker than they were, even if they are benefited in no other way?"

"That's so," he said.

[526c] "And, further, I don't suppose you would easily find many studies that take greater effort in the learning and in the practice than this."[20]

"Certainly not."

"Then, for all these reasons this study shouldn't be neglected, and the best natures must be educated in it."

"I join my voice to yours," he said.

"Therefore we have settled on this one," I said. "And let's consider whether the study adjoining this one is in any way suitable."

"What is it?" he said. "Or do you mean geometry?"[21]

"That's exactly it," I said.

[526d] "As much of it as applies to the business of war is plainly suitable," he said. "In pitching camp, assaulting places, gathering the army together and drawing it up to the line, and in all other maneuvers armies make in the battle itself and on marches, it would make quite a difference to a man whether he were skilled in geometry or not."

"However," I said, "for such things only a small portion of geometry—as of calculation—would suffice. It must be considered whether its greater and more advanced part tends to make it easier [526e] to make out the *idea*[22] of the good. And we say that this tendency is possessed by everything that compels the soul to turn around to the region inhabited by the happiest part of what it is, which is what the soul must by all means see."

"What you say is right," he said.

"Then if geometry compels one to look at being, it is suitable; if at becoming, it is not suitable."

"That is what we affirm."

[527a] "Well, then," I said, "none of those who have even a little experience with geometry will dispute it with us: this kind of knowledge is exactly the opposite of what is said about it in the arguments of those who take it up."[23]

"How?" he said.

---

18. Compare the view of Robert Hutchins in selection #58.

19. Plato's point here and his claim for the unique stimulus provided by the difficult study of mathematics is perhaps confirmed by the experience of Emma Willard and Mary Fairfax Somerville in reading Euclid, as recorded in selections #35 and #45. The implied social distinction is echoed below by a contrast between the many and the few (527d–528a) and is correlated with the ontological and epistemological distinctions noted above.

20. If turning the soul toward truth is a difficult task, then should liberal education focus upon the most difficult studies? And if that is true, then should mathematics be the core of liberal education?

21. Geometry is a second, mathematical liberal art, according to the subsequent tradition.

22. *Eidos* (also translated as "form") comes from *eido* ("I see"), cognate with the Latin *video*, and originally denoted "the look" or "the face" of a thing. Plato is here transmuting the meaning of the physical representation of a thing into the intelligible abstract being of the thing.

23. Compare the view of Robert Hutchins in selection #58.

"In that what they say is quite ridiculous and constrained. They speak as though they were men of action and were making all the arguments for the sake of action, uttering sounds like 'squaring,' 'applying,' 'adding,' and everything of the sort, whereas the whole study is surely pursued for the sake of knowing."

[527b] "That's entirely certain," he said.

"Mustn't we also come to an agreement about the following point?"

"What?"

"That it is for the sake of knowing what is always, and not at all for what is at any time coming into being and passing away."

"That may well be agreed," he said. "For geometrical knowing is of what is always."

"Then, you noble man, it would draw the soul toward truth and be productive of philosophic understanding in directing upward what we now improperly direct downward."

"It does so," he said, "to the greatest extent possible."

[527c] "Then to the greatest extent possible," I said, "the men in your beautiful city must be enjoined in no way to abstain from geometry. For even its by-products aren't slight."

"What are they?" he said.

"What you said about war, of course," I said, "and, in addition, with respect to finer reception of all studies, we surely know there is a general and complete difference between the man who has been devoted to geometry and the one who has not."

"Yes, by Zeus," he said, "the difference is complete."

"Then, shall we set down as the second study for the young?"

"Yes," he said, "we shall set it down."

[527d] "And what about this? Shall we set astronomy down as the third? Or doesn't it seem to be the thing?"

"It does, at least to me," he said. "A better awareness of seasons, months and years is suitable not only for farming and navigation, but no less so for generalship."

"You are amusing," I said. "You are like a man who is afraid of the many in your not wanting to seem to commend useless studies.[24] It's scarcely an ordinary thing, rather it's hard, to trust that in these studies [527e] a certain instrument of everyone's soul—one that is destroyed and blinded by other practices—is purified and rekindled, an instrument more important to save than ten thousand eyes. For with it alone is truth seen. To those who share your opinion about this, what you say will seem indescribably good, while all those who have had no awareness at all of it can be expected to believe you are talking nonsense. They see no other benefit from these studies worth mentioning. [528a]. . . . Well, then," I said, "retreat a way. What we took up as following geometry just now wasn't right."

"Where was the mistake?" he said.

[528b] "After a plane surface," I said, "we went ahead and took a solid in motion before taking it up by itself. But the right way is to take up the third dimension[25] next in order after the second, and this is surely the dimension of cubes and what participates in depth."

"Yes, it is," he said. "But, Socrates, . . . tell me more clearly what you meant just now; you presumably set geometry down as that which treats of the plane."

"Yes," I said.

"Then," he said, "at first you set down astronomy after geometry, but later you withdrew."

---

24. The pejorative social distinction is correlated with the distinction between rationales.

25. Socrates says that they made a mistake by skipping three-dimensional (solid) geometry, which should follow two-dimensional (plane) geometry and precede astronomy.

"My haste to go through everything quickly is the cause of my being slowed down,"[26] I said. "The investigation of the dimension with depth was next in order, but, due to the ridiculous state of the search for it, I skipped over it after geometry and said astronomy, which treats the motion of what has depth."

[528e] "What you say is right," he said.

"Well, then," I said, "as the fourth study let's set down astronomy,[27] assuming that the study that is now being left aside will be present if a city pursues it."

"That's likely," he said. "And on the basis of the reproach you just made me for my vulgar praise of astronomy, Socrates, now I shall praise it in the way that you approach it. [529a] In my opinion, it's plain to everyone that astronomy compels the soul to see what's above and leads it there away from the things here."

"Perhaps it's plain to everyone except me," I said. "In my opinion, that's not the way it is."

"Then how is it?" he said.

"As it is taken up now by those who lead men up to philosophy, it has quite an effect in causing the soul to look downward."

"How do you mean?" he said.

"In my opinion," I said, "It's no ignoble conception you have for yourself of what the study of the things above is. [529b] Even if a man were to learn something by tilting his head back and looking at decorations on a ceiling, you would probably believe he contemplates with his intellect and not his eyes. Perhaps your belief is a fine one and mine innocent. I, for my part, am unable to hold that any study makes a soul look upward other than the one that concerns what *is* and is invisible. And if a man, gaping up or squinting down, attempts to learn something of sensible things, I would deny that he ever learns—for there is no knowledge of such things—or that his soul looks up, rather than down, even if he learns while floating on his back on land or sea."[28]

[529c] "I am paying the just penalty," he said. "You are right in reproaching me. But just what did you mean when you said that astronomy must be studied in a way contrary to the one in which they now study it, if it's going to be studied in a way that's helpful for what we are talking about?"

"As follows," I said. "These decorations in the heaven, since they are embroidered on a visible ceiling, may be believed to be the fairest and most precise of such things; but they fall far short of the true ones, [529d] those movements in which the really fast and the really slow—in true number and in all the true figures—are moved with respect to one another and in their turn move what is contained in them. They, of course, must be grasped by argument and thought, not sight. Or do you suppose otherwise?"

"Not at all," he said.

"Therefore," I said, "the decoration in the heaven must be used as patterns for the sake of learning these other things, just as if one were to come upon diagrams exceptionally carefully drawn and worked out [529e] by Daedalus or some other craftsman or painter. A man experienced in geometry would, on seeing such things, presumably believe that they are fairest in their execution but that it is ridiculous to consider them seriously as though one were to grasp the truth about equals, doubles, or any other proportion in them."

---

26. Might this paradoxical aphorism apply to liberal education?

27. After geometry is astronomy, the study of number applied to three-dimensional figures set in motion. Because plane and solid geometry are not separated in the subsequent tradition of the liberal arts, astronomy is considered not the fourth, but the third mathematical art, as Plato does at 527d.

28. The contrast here and in the following passages (530a, 532a) between vision and intellection, as well as between hearing and intellection (531a), establishes a psychological distinction between body and mind that is correlated with the ontological and epistemological distinctions noted earlier.

[530a] "How could it be anything but ridiculous?" he said.

"Then," I said, "don't you suppose that a man who is really an astronomer will have the same persuasion in looking at the movements of the stars? He will hold that the craftsman[29] of heaven composed it and [all that's] in it as beautifully as such works can be composed. But as for the proportion of night to day, of these to a month, of a month to a year, and of the rest of the stars to these and to one another, don't you think he will consider strange the man who holds that these are always the same and deviate in no way at all? [530b] For these things are connected with body and are visible. Hence won't he consider it strange to seek in every way to grasp their truth?"

"That is my opinion," he said, "at least now that I am listening to you."

"Therefore," I said, "by the use of problems, as in geometry, we shall also pursue astronomy; and we shall let the things in the heaven go, if by really taking part in astronomy we are going to convert the prudence by nature in the soul from uselessness to usefulness."

[530c] "The task you prescribe," he said, "is many times greater than what is now done in astronomy."

"And," I said, "I suppose our prescriptions in the rest will also be of the same kind, if we are to be of any help as lawgivers. But have you any suitable study to suggest?"

"No, I haven't," he said, "at least not right now."

"However," I said, "motion presents itself not in one form but several, as I suppose. [530d] Perhaps whoever is wise will be able to tell them all, but those that are evident even to us are two."

"What are they?

"In addition to astronomy," I said, "there is its antistrophe."

"What's that?"

"It is probable," I said, "that as the eyes are fixed on astronomy, so the ears are fixed on harmonic movement,[30] and these two kinds knowledge are in a way akin, as the Pythagoreans say and we, Glaucon, agree.[31] Or what shall we do?"

"That," he said.

[530e] "Then," I said, "since it's a big job, we'll inquire of the Pythagoreans what they mean about them and if there is anything else besides them. But throughout all of this we shall keep a guard over our interest."

"What's that?"

"That those whom we shall be rearing should never attempt to learn anything imperfect, anything that doesn't always come out at the point where everything ought to arrive, as we were just saying about astronomy. [531a] Or don't you know that they do something similar with harmony too? For, measuring the heard accords and sounds against one another, they labor without profit, like the astronomers."[32]

---

29. "The word is *demiurge*, meaning 'a man who practices an art for the public.' In the exalted sense of this passage, he becomes the craftsman of the *cosmos*." Translator's note, p. 466n.

30. Harmony, or music, becomes the fourth mathematical liberal art in the subsequent tradition.

31. Plato explicitly associates his views with the Pythagoreans, whose doctrine underlies much of this discussion.

32. "Ancient musicians measured the concordant intervals (for example, fourth, fifth, and octave) and gave them mathematical proportions on the basis of the length of the strings required to produce them." Translator's note, p. 466n. The harmonic characteristic is commensurability: the two things could be measured in terms of integral units of each other.

"Yes, by the gods," he said, "and how ridiculous they are. They name certain notes 'dense'[33] and set their ears alongside, as though they were hunting a voice from the neighbors' house. Some say they distinctly hear still another note in between and that this is the smallest interval by which the rest must be measured, while others insist that it is like those already sounded. Both put ears before their intelligence."

[531b] "You mean," I said, "those good men who . . . do the same thing the astronomers do. They seek the numbers in these heard accords and don't rise to problems, to the consideration of which numbers are concordant and which not, and why in each case."

"The thing you speaking of," he said, "is demonic."

"Useful, rather, for the quest after the fair and the good," I said, "but pursued in any other way it is useless."

"That's likely," he said.

"And I suppose," I said, "that if the inquiry into all the things we have gone through arrives at their community and relationship with one another, [531d] and draws conclusions as to how they are akin to one another, then the concern with them contributes something to what we want, and is not a labor without profit, but otherwise it is."

"I, too, divine that this is the case," he said. But it's a very big job you speak of, Socrates."

"Do you mean the prelude or what?" I said. "Or don't we know that all of this is a prelude[34] to the song itself which must be learned? For surely it's not your opinion that the men who are clever at these things are dialecticians."

[531e] "No, by Zeus," he said, "with the exception of a very few whom I have encountered."

"But," I said, "was it ever your opinion that men who are unable to give an account and receive one will ever know anything of what we say they must know?"

"To this question too," he said, "the answer is no."

[532a] "Glaucon," I said, "isn't this at last the song itself that dialectic performs? It is in the realm of the intelligible, but it is imitated by the power of sight. We said that sight at last tries to look at the animals themselves and at stars themselves and then finally at the sun itself. So, also, when a man tries by discussion—by means of argument without the use of any of the senses—to attain to each thing itself that *is* and [532b] doesn't give up before he grasps by intellection itself that which is good itself, he comes to the very end of the intelligible realm just as that other man was at the end of the visible."[35]

"That's entirely certain," he said.

"What then? Don't you call this journey dialectic?"[36]

---

33. "A technical term in music, here probably meaning notes the intervals of which are so small as to be almost inaudible; condensed or combined notes. The word in its original sense refers to cloth which has tightly woven threads." Translator's note, p. 466n.

34. Plato's prelude consists, then, of five mathematical arts: arithmetic (number in itself), two-dimensional geometry (numerical law of shape), three-dimensional geometry (numerical law of solids), astronomy (numerical law of bodies in motion), and harmony (numerical commensurability). These five become four in the subsequent tradition, as the two branches of geometry are treated together. Although this account describes geometry in terms of number, it is important to note that the Greeks viewed numerical operations in terms of geometrical figures.

35. See 529b, 530a, 531a.

36. Dialectic is a complex term that denoted "conversation" or "discussion," as well as the formal sense of "debate." It was adopted by Plato to refer to a systematic inquiry that could be conducted within one's own mind; and Aristotle formalized the rules of this investigation, which he sometimes called "logic," but also "dialectic." In addition, Aristotle employed "dialectic" to mean, among other things, a particular kind of investigation and reasoning conducted in the "practical" or human sciences. In the subsequent tradition of the liberal arts, "dialectic" and "logic" are frequently, though not always, employed interchangeably.

"Of course."

"Then," I said, "the release from the bonds and the turning around from the shadows to the phantoms and the light, the way up from the cave to the sun; and, once there, the persisting inability to look at the animals and the plants and the sun's light, and [532c] looking instead at the divine appearances in water and at shadows of the things that *are*, rather than as before at shadows of phantoms cast by a light that, when judged in comparison with the sun, also has the quality of a shadow of a phantom—all this activity of the arts, which we went through, has the power to release and leads what is best in the soul up to the contemplation of what is best in the things that *are*, just as previously what is clearest in the body was led to the contemplation of what is brightest in the region of the bodily and the visible."[37]

[532d] "I accept this as so," he said. "It seems to me extremely hard to accept, however, but in another way hard not to accept. All the same—since it's not only now that these things must be heard, but they must all be returned to many times in the future—taking for granted that this is as has now been said, let's proceed to the song itself and go through it just as we went through the prelude. So tell what the character of the power of the dialectic is, and then, into exactly what forms it is divided; and finally what are its ways. [532e] For these, as it seems, would lead at last toward that place which is for the one who reaches it a haven from the road, as it were, an end of his journey."

[533a] "You will no longer be able to follow, my dear Glaucon," I said, "although there wouldn't be any lack of eagerness on my part. But you would no longer be seeing an image of what we are saying, but rather the truth itself, at least as it looks to me. Whether it is really so or not can no longer be properly insisted upon. But that there is some such thing to see must be insisted on. Isn't it so?"

"Of course."

"And, also, that the power of dialectic alone could reveal it to a man experienced in the things we just went through, while it is no other way possible?"

"Yes," he said, "it's proper to insist on that too."

[533b] "At least," I said, "no one will dispute us when we say that some other inquiry methodically attempts with respect to everything to grasp—about each several thing itself—what each *is*. For all the other arts are directed to human opinions and desires, or to generation and composition, or to the care of what is grown or put together. And as for the rest, those that we said do lay hold of something of what is—geometry and the arts following on it—we observe that they do dream about what *is*; but they haven't the capacity to see it in full awakeness so long as they use hypotheses and, [533c] leaving them untouched, are unable to give an account of them. When the beginning is what one doesn't know, and the end and what comes in between are woven out of what isn't known, what contrivance is there for ever turning such an agreement into knowledge?"

"None," he said. "Then," I said, "only the dialectical way of inquiry proceeds in this direction, destroying the hypotheses, to the beginning itself in order to make it secure; and when the eye of the soul is really buried in a barbaric bog, dialectic gently draws it forth and leads it up above, using the arts we described as assistants and helpers in the turning around."[38]

---

37. The normative and ethical distinction between worse and better, which has been implicit, now becomes explicit.

38. In the subsequent discussion, Plato clarifies the chronological organization of the liberal disciplines of arithmetic, geometry, astronomy, music, and dialectic: "As children, future leaders will learn [arithmetic] and geometry through play, not compulsion. During their late teens they will . . . pursue physical training exclusively. At twenty, those suited to be rulers will be selected and given education in those sciences that will show them how they are akin to each other and to the nature of reality, an education also designed to test their steadfastness. At thirty the best will be selected again and will be taught dialectic and tested in it, to see that they are interested in truth and are by nature orderly and steady. (For when it is taught under the wrong circumstances, and to the wrong sort of people, dialectic has a way of removing one's earlier beliefs and leaving one with the tendency to dispute simply for the sake of producing contradictions, and not for the sake of truth.) At thirty-five, they will be

2. Isocrates, *Antidosis* (340s B.C.)

INTRODUCTION

Isocrates (c. 436–338 B.C.) was born into a prosperous, Athenian family a few years before the outbreak of the Peloponnesian War in 431. The military and political destruction of that war dominated his youth, instilling in him a lifelong desire for unity and peace among the city-states of Greece which was strengthened by the expropriation of his inherited wealth by the end of the war in 404. Forced to support himself and draw upon his education received under some of the most prominent sophists and teachers of the day, Isocrates began to earn his livelihood through writing judicial speeches. He did not deliver the speeches but sold them to others to present in court because he lacked a strong voice and the personal presence necessary for public oratory. Paradoxically, his speechwriting thus contributed to the invention of prose writing, which is sometimes credited to Isocrates. In about 393 he relinquished professional speechwriting and opened a school.

For the next forty years, Isocrates developed this school into the most successful educational institution of its day, as indicated by Ernst Curtius in the introduction. The fees were heavy, and the overarching purpose was to prepare students for a successful career in public affairs. His two-fold program involved, on the one hand, elevating the arts of speech, especially rhetoric, above the arts championed by others, such as mathematics and dialectic by Plato or logic by Aristotle. But Isocrates did not exclude other arts, as was common among the leaders of rival schools in his day. In addition, Isocrates required that persuasive and eloquent speech be joined to the high-minded ethical tradition that he derived through a commonsensical appeal to the models of the great Athenian statesmen of the past, such as Pericles. This second characteristic also stood in distinct contrast to the practice of certain sophistic teachers who conveyed the same arts of speech as did Isocrates, but without any moral teaching.

Near the end of his career as an educator, perhaps in the early 340s, Isocrates composed the *Antidosis*. Modeled on Plato's *Apology*, the *Antidosis* is written in the form of a speech presenting his defense at a fictional trial in which Isocrates recounts his life's work as a teacher while rebutting the capital charge against him. Scholars over the past century have generally been unsympathetic to Isocrates's approach to teaching what the Romans later called the *artes liberales*. Isocrates's commonsensical appeal to a moral tradition, his suspicion of unrelenting analysis, and his faith in the transformative power of sincere speech are generally treated as evidence of his intellectual limitations by recent scholars, who prefer what they see as the greater sophistication of Plato and Aristotle.[39] Whether this preference is the expression of "most learned men abounding in excessive leisure and wealth of intellect," to whom Cicero replies in selection #4, is worth pondering.

While his school flourished, Isocrates wrote, but still did not deliver, occasional speeches expressing his aspirations for political unity and peace among the Greek city-states. In the last decade of his life, when his hopes for the realization of these ideals faded, he addressed his works to King

---

compelled to take on the task of ruling in matters concerning war and the young, and in this they will be tested again for fifteen years. At fifty, they will be led to a knowledge of the good itself, and they will spend a great deal of time in philosophical activity. But they will be compelled to take their turns ruling for the sake of the city, using the good as a paradigm, and regarding the activity of ruling not as something fine and splendid but as something necessary, until they depart life for the Isles of the Blessed." Nicholas P. White, *A Companion to Plato's Republic* (Indianapolis, IN: Hackett, 1979), p. 202.

39. This preference, associating Isocrates with Aristotle and the philosophers and distinguishing Isocrates from Cicero and Quintilian, may be found in Janet M. Atwill, *Rhetoric Reclaimed: Aristotle and the Liberal Arts* (Ithaca, NY: Cornell University Press, 1998), p. 5. See also Takis Poulakos, *Speaking for the Polis: Isocrates's Rhetorical Education* (Columbia: University of South Carolina Press, 1998).

Philip of Macedon, envisioning that an outside autocrat might achieve the Panhellenism that the Greeks themselves could not. Had Isocrates lived even longer than his 98 years, he no doubt would have applauded the unification wrought by Alexander the Great, for he celebrated the defeat of the Greeks by Philip in 338, the final year of his life.

SELECTION[40]

[253] Accordingly, one must think about *logos*, in fact, quite similarly as one thinks about other human capacities, and not come to contrary conclusions concerning things that are similar, nor show hostility towards that capacity which is responsible for most of the goods that fall within the scope of human nature! In our other capacities, as I have already remarked in an earlier work,[41] we do not excel the animals, but prove to be inferior to many of them in speed, strength, and other active endowments. [254] Yet, by having been endowed with the power of persuading one another and revealing clearly to each other our purposes, we not only freed ourselves from living in a bestial manner, but we united in founding cities, established laws for ourselves, and invented arts. *Logos* is what allowed us to succeed in all these endeavors.

[255] For it is *logos* that established norms to distinguish the just and the unjust, the noble and the shameful—distinctions which must be properly made if we are to be able to live with one another. It is really by *logos* that we challenge the base and praise the good. And it is through *logos* that we educate the witless and put the intelligent to the test, for we rate sound speech as the greatest evidence of cogent deliberation, and genuinely lawful and just *logos* is the indication of a good and trustworthy soul. [256] It is with the aid of *logos* that we dispute contested matters and scrutinize the unknown; for it is by employing the very same arguments by which we persuade others when we speak that we engage in our own deliberations.[42] Thus, we call eloquent those who are capable of speaking before the crowd, and we assess as judicious those who converse best in their own minds concerning affairs.

[257] If we may speak in a summary way about this capacity, we shall find that nothing that is done judiciously is done without *logos*, and that *logos* is the leader of all our actions and thoughts, and that those who use it most are the ones with most intelligence.[43]

Without considering any of these points, Lysimachus audaciously accused those who attend to this capacity that is responsible for goods in such number and of such quality![44] [258] But why should one be surprised at this accusation when even some who study the art of disputation blaspheme similarly the art of speaking on generally useful themes[45] (just like the cheapest sort of men do), though aware of the power of speech and that they will render their own art most estimable if they slander this other.[46] [259] I could speak much more sharply against them than they against us, but I do not suppose there is any need either to become similar to those who are corrupted by jealousy, or to blame those who are not actually harming their followers, even if they are less able to benefit them

---

40. Adapted from a new, unpublished translation by J. Albert Dragstedt.

41. *Panegyricus* 48, written in about 380 B.C.

42. Compare Isocrates's linguistic behaviorism—denying "mentalisms" or abstract intelligible essences—with Plato's distinctions between speech and reason, between the public forum and philosophy, and between rhetoric and philosophy.

43. These paragraphs (253–257) are identical to *Nicocles* 5–9, written in about 370 B.C.

44. This Lysimachus appears to be the immoral son of the Athenian general and statesman Aristides the Just or Elder (d. c. 468 B.C.).

45. Isocrates may be resenting the criticisms of the followers of Aristotle.

46. The teachers compete, as do their interpretations of the arts of *logos*.

than others are. Nevertheless, I shall remark briefly on their account, mostly because they have done so on ours, and so that you may be better situated to view each of us justly, through being more clearly aware of their capabilities, [260] and, in addition, so that I make perfectly clear that we who cultivate political *logos* (whom they term disputatious) prove to be much gentler than they. For, though they are constantly saying insults about us, I would not utter that sort of thing, having truth to employ in their regard.

[261] And I believe that even the dynasts of disputation and the advocates of astronomy, geometry, and such like sciences[47] do not harm their followers but benefit them, less than they promise but more than others suppose. [262] The majority of mankind believes that such sciences are pastimes and distinction-mongering; because nothing about them is useful either in public or private affairs or is even remembered for any time by those who learn them, since these sciences are not a continuing part of life and do not bear upon its necessities. As for me, I neither adopt this view nor completely set it aside: those who judge this education to be of no use in affairs seem to me to understand correctly, and those who praise it seem to speak truth.

[263] The reason for this contradiction is that these sciences have a different nature from the others we are taught. For these latter naturally assist us once we have seized the knowledge of them, but the former sciences do not aid those who have deepened their knowledge [264] beyond the discipline that the sciences provide in studying them, unless the students elect to make their livelihood from these sciences. The fact is that when one passes time at the details and precise calculations of astronomy and geometry, being compelled to concentrate one's mind upon subjects difficult to learn [265] and also to habituate oneself to a sustained effort without one's mind wandering, one is able, being exercised and sharpened in these things, to accept and learn more easily and rapidly those matters which are more important and worthwhile.[48]

[266] So, I certainly do not think it fitting to dignify with the name "philosophy" a study which now is of use neither for speaking nor for acting, and I call such a study a gymnastic of the mind and a *preparation* for philosophy—more adult than the one that children ply in the school rooms, but mostly resembling it.[49] [267] After all, those children who exert themselves in grammar, music and the rest of the curriculum[50] have not yet developed to the point of speaking or deliberating better about affairs, but do improve in their preparation to learn the greater and more significant branches of knowledge. [268] Therefore, I would advise the youth to spend a certain amount of time on all the arts, but not to permit their nature to dry up in such fields or run aground on the studies made by the scientists of old by means of *logos*. One of these said that things are the sum of infinite elements, while Empedocles said there were four, including strife and love. But Ion said there were no more than three, Alcmaeon only two, Parmenides and Melissus one, and Gorgias that there was absolutely nothing at all.[51] [269] I consider that such exaggerated pronouncements are like magic tricks that confer no benefit and are applauded by fools. Those who wish to do some good must give no attention to all such empty arts and activities that confer nothing towards the affairs of life.

---

47. Likely a reference to Plato and the Academy.

48. Compare Isocrates's rationale for studying mathematics with the justification for studying Latin and Greek in the Yale Report of 1828 in selection #37.

49. Said to be coined by Pythagoras or members of his school, the Greek word *philosophia* is derived from *philos* ("loving") and *sophia* ("knowledge" or "wisdom"). In its original sense, *philosophia* denotes the desire for, or pursuit of, wisdom, rather than a formal body of acquired knowledge. What does Isocrates mean by the term here and below?

50. Compare this view with Plato's interpretation of the conventional "musical curriculum" in *Republic* 522a.

51. These "scientists of old" were pre-Socratic philosophers and sophists who speculated about metaphysics.

[270] I have now spoken and advised about these things sufficiently for the present purpose. As to what regards wisdom and philosophy, it would hardly behoove someone arraigned on other particulars[52] to speak on these terms, alien as they are to each and every legal action. But since I am under indictment concerning such things and I say that what some call "philosophy" does not exist, I ought to delimit and explain to you what would rightly be called "philosophy."

[271] I happen to entertain a straightforward view about these things. Since it is not within the nature of men to acquire a science whereby we would *know* what must be done or said, I count as wise those who are able to hit generally upon the best course through their opinions, and I hold as philosophers those who spend their time in studies through which they will most speedily acquire this kind of prudence.[53] [272] Just which studies have this power I can say, but I hesitate to speak out, for they are so violently contrary and distant from the way of thinking of others, that I fear you will fill the entire law court with commotion and shouting once I begin to say them. Despite this trepidation, I shall attempt to speak about them, for I am ashamed to seem to anyone to betray the truth out of fear stemming from my old age and little life remaining. [273] But I do ask that you not charge me with the perverse courage of deliberately choosing to utter views contrary to yours while in the midst of danger, for I speak only because I judge that my views follow from my previous statements and believe that I have true and clear proofs to support them.

[274] I consider that the sort of art that would inculcate modesty and justice in those badly endowed by nature with regard to virtue has never existed, and that those who make promises concerning these things should cease and desist from their raving until such an education can be found.[54] [275] Nevertheless, people would become better and worthier, if they would devote themselves with honorable ambition towards speaking well, develop a passion for the capacity to persuade their listeners, and furthermore desire to become superior[55]—not in the way sought by the mindless,[56] but genuinely superior.

[276] I believe that I shall readily show that these things are in the natural order. First, when someone has decided to speak or write speeches worthy of praise and honor, it is impossible for him to take as his subject causes that are unjust, trivial, or parochial; rather the speaker must choose great, noble, and philanthropic ones, and ones concerning public affairs. If he cannot find any, he will accomplish nothing of what he seeks. [277] In addition, among the circumstances relevant to his subject, he will select the most morally suitable and apposite ones. Now the man habituated to scrutinizing and assessing such subjects will retain this same capacity not only with reference to the speech, which is the task before him, but also concerning the other affairs he encounters, with the result that both speaking well and thinking rightly will appear together in those whose discourse is imbued with love of wisdom and of honor.

---

52. A reference to the fictional indictment that serves as the literary occasion for the *Antidosis*.

53. Are morals improved, then, not by studying moral philosophy, but by acquiring a general orientation and a rough calculus that is rapidly employed as countless ethical decisions confront us?

54. Another aspersion directed at the Socratic schools' inquiry into the meaning of virtue and their belief that this knowledge will necessarily lead to practicing virtue.

55. The belief that imitation of fine language implies imitation of high-minded virtue persevered among the proponents of rhetorical and humanistic studies.

56. This apparently refers to the sophists for whom superiority meant winning a debate regardless of the validity of one's argument.

Intellectual Inquiry and Social Engagement

3. Aristotle, *Politics* (c. 330 B.C.)

INTRODUCTION

Aristotle (384–322 B.C.) was born in the town of Stagira in northern Greece, where his father served as physician and advisor to King Philip of Macedon. At age seventeen Aristotle was sent to Athens to be educated and may have initially enrolled in Isocrates's school, but soon found his way to Plato's Academy where he apparently began to write compelling dialogues, though only fragments of these have survived. In about 347 Aristotle left Athens to escape the rising antipathy toward Macedon, whose power was growing under Philip. After spending five years in Asia Minor, Aristotle traveled to Macedon at the invitation of Philip to tutor his son, Alexander the Great, who was then about thirteen years old. After a few years of intermittent tutoring, Aristotle returned to Stagira and then to Athens, where he opened his school, the Lyceum, in 335.

The subsequent decade was relatively uneventful in the political life of Athens due to the circumscribed autonomy that the city enjoyed within the Macedonian empire, which Alexander was rapidly expanding eastward. At the Lyceum Aristotle took advantage of this calm to pursue disciplined inquiry into virtually every field of knowledge. To convey his findings, Aristotle customarily lectured to his students while strolling in the covered walk-way (*peripatos*) of the Lyceum, a practice that gave the name "Peripatetics" to Aristotle's school. In 323 the sudden death of Alexander precipitated a revolt throughout Greece against Macedonian rule. In the midst of this resurgent antipathy against Macedon, Aristotle was indicted for impiety and fled lest the Athenians "sin twice against philosophy," as he reportedly said, mindful of the death of Socrates. Aristotle died in 322.

Selection #3 is drawn from the *Politics*, Book 8, which Aristotle wrote during his Lyceum period. Addressing, in part, the role and nature of education in the state, Book 8 opens with the words: "No one will doubt that the legislator should direct his attention above all to the education of youth; for the neglect of education does harm to the constitution. The citizen should be molded to suit the form of government under which he lives. For each government has a peculiar character which originally formed and which continues to preserve it. The character of democracy creates democracy, and the character of oligarchy creates oligarchy; and always the better the character, the better the government."[57] These observations lead rapidly to this selection, which became the *locus classicus* within the liberal arts tradition for authorizing a distinction between useful and liberal education, as famously expressed by John Henry Newman in the introduction. Why, how, and even whether Aristotle asserts this distinction are worth careful consideration.

Nevertheless, Aristotle's argument that leaders should be educated liberally, rather than practically or technically, prevailed. By the time that the *artes liberales* were codified in the Roman world and adopted by Christians, the cultural elite took for granted the necessity of educating future leaders in the liberal arts, however defined.[58]

---

57. Aristotle, *Politics* 1337a10–19. Stanford professor Edgar E. Robinson seems to concur in selection #55.

58. Compare the debate on this point between Booker T. Washington and W. E. B. Du Bois in selections #50 and #51.

SELECTION[59]

[Bk. 8, ch. 2; 1337a33] That education should be regulated by law and should be an affair of state is not to be denied, but what should be the character of this public education, and how young persons should be educated, are questions which remain to be considered.

[1337a36] As things are, there is disagreement about the subjects. For men are by no means agreed about the things to be taught, whether we look to excellence or the best life. Neither is it clear whether education is more concerned with intellectual or with moral excellence. The existing practice is perplexing; no one knows on what principle we should proceed—should the useful in life, or should excellence, or should the higher knowledge, be the aim of our training?—all three opinions have been entertained. Again, about the means there is no agreement;[60] for different persons, starting with different ideas about the nature of excellence, naturally disagree about the practice of it.

[1337b3] There can be no doubt that children should be taught those useful things which are really necessary, but not all useful things; for [pursuits] are divided into liberal and illiberal; and to young children should be imparted only such kinds of knowledge as will be useful to them without making mechanics of them. And any occupation, art, or science, which makes the body, soul or mind of the freeman less fit for the practice or exercise of excellence, is mechanical;[61] wherefore we call those arts mechanical which tend to deform the body,[62] and likewise all paid employments, for they absorb and degrade the mind.

There are also some liberal arts quite proper for a freeman to acquire, but only in a certain degree, and if he attends to them too closely, in order to attain perfection in them, the same harmful effects will follow. The object also which a man sets before him makes a great difference; if he does or learns anything for his own sake or for the sake of his friends, or with a view to excellence, the action will not appear illiberal; but if done [at the behest] of others, the very same action will be thought menial and servile. The received subjects of instruction, as I have already remarked, are partly of a liberal and partly of an illiberal character.

[ch. 3, 1337b23] The customary branches of education are in number four; they are—reading and writing, gymnastic exercises, and music, to which is sometimes added drawing. Of these, reading and writing and drawing are regarded as useful for the purposes of life in a variety of ways, and gymnastic exercises are thought to infuse courage. Concerning music a doubt may be raised—in our day most men cultivate it for the sake of pleasure, but originally it was included in education, because nature herself, as has often been said, requires that we should be able, not only to work well, but to use leisure well; for, as I must repeat once again, the first principle of all action is leisure.[63] Both are

---

59. Quotation is drawn the translation by Benjamin Jowett revised by Jonathan Barnes, in *The Complete Works of Aristotle*, ed. Jonathan Barnes (Princeton, NJ: Princeton University Press, 1984), v. 2, pp. 2121–3. Copyright 1984 by The Jowett Copyright Trustees. Reprinted by permission of Princeton University Press.

60. Contrary to a common view that there existed harmony among Greek views about liberal education, Aristotle observes that disagreement prevails over what to teach ("the subjects"), why to teach ("on what principle"), and how to teach ("the means").

61. The semantic contrast here is between *eleutheros* ("liberal") and *banausos*, which could also be translated as "vulgar."

62. What are some arts, or pursuits, that deform or break the body? By the same token, might there be studies that deform the mind—studies whose nature is such that the more one pursues them the less the mind is fitted for that which it naturally does?

63. Leisure is the translation of *scholé*, which might be more literally rendered "free time." Why is this "the first principle of all action?"

required, but leisure is better than occupation and is its end; and therefore the question must be asked, what ought we to do when at leisure?

[1337b36] Clearly, we ought not to be playing, for then play would be the end of life. But if this is inconceivable, and play is needed more amid serious occupations than at other times (for he who is hard at work has need of relaxation, and play gives relaxation, whereas occupation is always accompanied with exertion and effort), we should introduce amusements only at suitable times, and they should be our medicines, for the emotion which they create in the soul is a relaxation, and from the pleasure we obtain rest.[64] But leisure of itself gives pleasure and happiness and enjoyment of life, which are experienced, not by the busy man, but by those who have leisure. For he who is occupied has in view some end which he has not attained; but happiness is an end, since all men deem it to be accompanied with pleasure and not with pain.

This pleasure, however, is regarded differently by different persons, and varies according to the habit of individuals; the pleasure of the best man is the best, and springs from the noblest sources. [1338a10] It is clear then that there are branches of learning and education which we must study merely with a view to leisure spent in intellectual activity,[65] and these are to be valued for their own sake; whereas those kinds of knowledge which are useful in business are to be deemed necessary, and exist for the sake of other things. And therefore our fathers admitted music into education, not on the grounds either of its necessity or utility, for it is not necessary, nor indeed useful in the same manner as reading and writing, which are useful in money-making, in the management of a household, in the acquisition of knowledge and in political life, nor like drawing, useful for a more correct judgment of the works of artists, nor again like gymnastic, which gives health and strength; for neither of these is to be gained from music. There remains, then, the use of music for intellectual employment in leisure;[66] which is in fact evidently the reason of its introduction, this being one of the ways in which it is thought that a freeman should pass his leisure. . . .

[1338a31] It is evident, then, that there is a sort of education in which parents should train their [children], not as being useful or necessary, but because it is liberal or noble.[67] Whether this is of one kind only, or of more than one, and if so, what they are, and how they are to be imparted, must hereafter be determined.[68] This much we are already in a position to say; for the ancients bear witness to us—their opinion may be gathered from the fact that music is one of the received and traditional branches of education. Further, it is clear that [youths] should be instructed in some useful things— for example, in reading and writing—not only for their usefulness, but also because many other sorts of knowledge are acquired through them. With a like view they may be taught drawing, not to prevent their making mistakes in their own purchases, or in order that they may not be imposed upon in the buying or selling of articles, but perhaps rather because it makes them judges of the beauty of the human form. To be always seeking after the useful does not become free and exalted souls.[69]

---

64. If leisure (scholé) is neither play nor relaxation, then what does Aristotle mean by it?

65. Why are happiness, leisure, and intellectual activity said to coincide?

66. Aristotle's discussion of the origins of the inclusion of gymnastics and music in the curriculum is anachronistic, as indicated in the introduction to Section I.

67. Some have objected that Aristotle's formulation of liberal education requires unjust or invidious social distinctions. What may be said about this?

68. Aristotle never returned to these studies.

69. Robert Hutchins echoes this view in selection #58, while Bathsua Makin expresses a similar view in selection #30: "when [other] things are competently cared for and where there are endowments of nature and leisure, then higher things ought to be endeavored after."

4. Cicero, *On the Orator* (55 B.C.)

INTRODUCTION

Marcus Tullius Cicero (106–43 B.C.) was born into a prosperous, land-owning family in central Italy and provided with an excellent education at schools in Rome, Greece, and Rhodes. After serving in the military in his early twenties, Cicero began arguing legal cases in court and by 80 B.C. established his reputation as one of the most promising, young advocates of his day. In the following decade, he advanced his legal reputation, and entered politics by assuming a prominent position in the financial administration of Sicily.

During the 60s his political career ascended rapidly as he allied himself closely with the general and statesman Pompey, achieving a lifetime ambition by becoming a consul in 63. In 60, however, Cicero refused to support the First Triumvirate of Julius Caesar, Marcus Licinius Crassus, and Gnaeus Pompeius Magnus on the principled grounds that their military and political alliance was unconstitutional. As a result, Cicero was forced into exile in 58 when one of his political enemies became tribune and Pompey did not step forward to protect him. Returning from exile in 57, Cicero had to ally himself with the triumvirate, and this humiliation led him to retire from public life for about the next six years. During this retirement, Cicero wrote many of his philosophical and rhetorical treatises that attempted to introduce Greek learning into the Latin language and culture. This longstanding interest extended back to his earliest works in as much as the first recorded use of the Latin term *artes liberales* is found in Cicero's youthful treatise *On Discovery*.[70] This transmission was not uncreative, because Cicero selected and adapted Greek learning in order to fit the Roman situation. Nowhere is this more apparent than in his masterpiece, *On the Orator*.

Written during the 50s, this dialogue presents two idealized Roman statesmen, Crassus (d. 53 B.C.) and Marcus Antonius (d. 30 B.C.), discussing the qualifications and the education of an orator. Selection #4 is drawn from *On the Orator*, which, for the next two millennia, became the classic expression of liberal education understood as a preparation for someone seeking to lead the political and social affairs of a republic.

In 51 B.C. Cicero reentered public life shortly before the civil war commenced between Julius Caesar and Pompey, then retired again after the defeat of the latter in 48. Following the assassination of Caesar in 44, Cicero once more entered politics, making the mistake of attacking Marc Antony and underestimating the capability of Caesar's adopted son, Augustus. In 43 these two, as members of the Second Triumvirate, had Cicero hunted down and executed. His head and hands were cut off and brought back to Rome and displayed on the speaker's platform at the Forum where he had become renowned as a statesman and orator.

SELECTION[71]

[52] "Well, Antonius," Crassus replied, "those two points which I just ran through—or, better, which I almost ignored—are easy to treat of: namely, good Latinity and clarity of style. The other points are important, complicated, diverse, and weighty; and it is on them that all admiration of one's genius and all applause for one's eloquence depend. For no one has ever admired an orator for speaking grammatically. If he fails at this, people mock him and not only do not rate him an orator, but scarcely a human being. Nobody heaps praises upon one who merely speaks well enough to be understood by

---

70. Cicero, *On Discovery* I xxv 35.

71. Adapted from a new, unpublished translation by J. Albert Dragstedt of Book III 52–81. Cf. Cicero, *On the Ideal Orator (de Oratore)*, tr. James M. May and Jakob Wisse (New York: Oxford University Press, 2001).

those present, but rather regards with contempt those who fall short of this. [53] So who is it who thrills his audience? Who reduces them to stupefied awe? Whom do they reckon a god, so to speak, among all? It is the one whose style has variety, precision, and scope, and who knows how to set forth thoughts and words into the light, and who though speaking in prose creates a kind of poetic rhythm and cadence. That is the style I term 'artistic.' And if he controls it with due regard to the varied claims of circumstances and persons, he will deserve to be praised for the kind of excellence I call the apt and fitting style.

[54] "Antonius has declared that he has never yet seen anyone speaking at that level, and has said that the title 'eloquent' must be attributed to them alone. Have a laugh then, I urge you, and sneer at all those characters who judge that they have mastered the entire oratorical faculty through the precepts of these so-called rhetoricians, but do not understand what role they are playing, nor what obligations their profession imposes.[72] For the genuine orator, since the entirety of human life is, after all, his domain, must have examined, understood, read, discussed, treated and acted upon all the questions that are involved in it.[73] [55] Eloquence is actually a certain ultimate virtue. All virtues are equal and of the same value, I grant you, yet some seem to have a greater external beauty and luster. Such is this faculty we are speaking of, which embraces all knowledge and then explicates the sentiments and thoughts of the mind with such words that it can compel those who listen in any direction it applies itself. But the greater its power is, by just so much is there the greater necessity of it being conjoined with integrity and the highest wisdom.[74] If we find we have handed on the power of eloquence to people who lack the virtues, we shall not have rendered them orators but shall have given virtual weaponry to madmen.

[56] "Yes, this method of reflecting and articulating, this power of speech is what the ancient Greeks called 'wisdom.' It was the source of those like . . . Solon, and it was from something similar that came our men like . . . Cato [the Elder] and Scipio—not so learned, perhaps, but characterized by a similar impulse and will of the mind.[75] There were, however, others of the same wisdom, but with a different conception in respect of the purposes of life, who followed a life of calm retreat, like Pythagoras, Democritus and Anaxagoras, and who renounced the governance of states to apply themselves totally to the study of nature. And this way of life due to its tranquility and due to the charm of science in itself—a charm sweeter than anything for men—attracted more of them than was useful for the commonweal.[76]

[57] "You see, as these men of outstanding genius gave themselves over to study, profiting from being free of material care and from having their time at their disposal, these most learned of men abounding in excessive leisure and wealth of intellect considered that they had to have as objects of inquiry and investigation many more things than were really necessary. In the past, at least, the same instruction fostered right conduct as well as good speech. Nor were the teachers distinct, but the preceptors of ethics were preceptors of rhetoric, such as that figure Phoenix in Homer who says he was

---

72. Cicero is opposing teachers who claimed to teach oratory by conveying a few rhetorical techniques and strategies.

73. The Ciceronian recommendation of a broad, general education—repeated throughout this selection and echoed by Pier Paolo Vergerio in selection #25—may be compared to the approach to general education introduced at Columbia University in the 1920s, described in Section VIII.

74. The theme of wedding eloquence with learning and virtue is echoed below at para. 61 and subsequently in the tradition of liberal education, particularly after the lost Latin text of *On the Orator* was recovered in 1422.

75. Solon (c. 639–c. 559 B.C.) Athenian statesman; Africanus Minor Scipio (c. 185–129 B.C.), Roman general and patron of learning. Ironically, Cicero associates Cato and Scipio here, although the ancient Roman family of Scipio was patrician and detested by the family of Cato the Elder, who embraced rustic conceits.

76. Here begins the charge of reclusiveness, even self-indulgence, against scholarly specialists.

assigned to the youthful Achilles by his father Peleus to accompany him in the war, and render him 'an orator of words and a doer of acts.'[77]

[58] "But just as men who are accustomed to hard, daily labor betake themselves, at times when they are kept from work by inclement weather, to ball, dice or board games, or even think up some new game for themselves in their leisure, so these philosophers, either excluded from public affairs (as if from labor) by circumstances or having chosen to go on vacation, betook themselves the ones to the poets, some to geometers and others to musicians, while yet others as dialecticians begat a new study and amusement for themselves, and used up all their time and their lives in these arts which have been discovered for the molding of the minds of the young humanely and virtuously.

[59] "But while there were some men—even a great number of them—who flourished in public life through this dual wisdom of acting and speaking, which cannot be separated,[78] (such as Themistocles, Pericles and Theramenes)[79] or others who were less engaged in public affairs but were, nevertheless, teachers of this two-fold wisdom (such as Gorgias, Thrasymachus, and Isocrates), there were men to be found who, through abounding in learning and talent, yet avoided civic affairs and business deliberately and on principle, and denounced oratory and rejected it.

[60] "The leader of these men was Socrates. By the testimony of all the erudite, and in the judgment of all Greece, he was a man who easily led the rest both in prudence, penetration, grace and finesse, as well as in eloquence, variety and abundance regarding whatever subject he addressed. Before his time, those who treated, discussed and taught those things that concern us now were all spoken of with one name, since the knowledge and the practice of the most exalted subjects was named philosophy. But Socrates wrested this name away, and separated two things that had been until then conjoined: judging wisely and speaking elegantly, though they together have a real coherence. Plato has passed on the genius of Socrates and his various conversations to immortality by means of his own writings, since Socrates himself did not leave a scrap of writing.

[61] "This is the point from which there arose that severance of tongue and brain—shocking, injurious and condemnable though it be—resulting in a situation where it is one group who teaches us to judge and another group who teaches us to speak. Furthermore, though the greatest number of philosophical schools, you see, virtually owed their existence to Socrates, each attached itself to some particular idea out of his varied and diverse discussions inquiring in all directions as they were, and a whole series of virtual doctrinal families were disseminated, becoming far apart and disparate and warring amongst themselves, even as all in their role as philosophers wished to be called and considered Socratic.

[62] "And first, it was from Plato himself that Aristotle and Xenocrates derived, the former establishing the name of Peripatetics for his school; the latter, that of the Academy. It was next from Antisthenes, who fell in love chiefly with the lessons in patience and firmness in Socratic conversation, that the Cynics and then the Stoics derived. Then the Cyrenaic philosophy derived from Aristippus,[80] who was seduced more by those discussions about pleasure, which he and his followers defended in a straightforward way, whereas, those who nowadays measure everything by pleasure, while doing so

---

77. Homer, *Iliad* IX 443.

78. In the following paragraphs Cicero explicitly begins denying the dualistic distinctions enshrined by Plato above: thinking and speaking-60; tongue and brain-61; rhetoric and philosophy-61, 72; thought and action-62–4, 72.

79. Themistocles (c. 525–c. 460 B.C.), Athenian statesman; Theramenes, Greek rhetorician of the fifth century B.C.

80. Xenocrates (396–314 B.C.) became head of the Academy. Antisthenes (c. 444–c. 370) and Aristippus (c. 435–c. 360 B.C.) were heads of Greek philosophical schools.

more timidly, do not do enough to satisfy the demands of *reputation* (a thing which they do not reject), nor yet protect *pleasure* (the thing they intend to embrace).

"There were, in addition, other sects of philosophers,[81] roughly all of which tried to say they were Socratic: Eretrians, Erillians, Megarians, and Pyrhhonians; but they have long been broken up and quenched by the force of the discussions of the aforementioned philosophers. [63] Of these schools which remain, however, the philosophy that has undertaken to plead for pleasure—though some may think it genuine—is yet far distant from the kind of man we seek, and whom we wish as initiator of public policy, executor of civic governance, and leader in ideas and eloquence whether in the senate, among the people, or in political trials. And yet we shall commit no injustice against that philosophy, for we shall not be barring it from a place to which it will seek access. Rather, it will reside quietly in the little gardens where it wishes, where still reclining it summons us with gentle charm away from the rostrum, the courts, the senate house: a wise plan, perhaps, considering the present state of the republic. [64] . . .

"Wherefore . . . [69] just like rivers from the Apennine peaks, so the stream of learning from the common watershed of wisdom divides, with the result that philosophers flow into the upper sea, Greek and rich in harbors, while orators slide down into this barbarous Tuscan sea with its dangerous rocks in which even Ulysses[82] went astray.[83] [70] Hence, for you to content yourselves with the kind of eloquence taught at present and the kind of orator who knows [merely rules of pleading in court]. . . . in a word, if you are content with this view of the orator, even adding to it what you have wished to hear from me, then you are forcing the orator back from a huge and boundless field into a truly paltry little rink. [71] But if you wish to follow the famous Pericles or even your Demosthenes, who is more familiar to us owing to the number of his writings, and if you have fallen in love with the glittering and outstanding image of the complete orator and with its beauty, then you must embrace this recent power of Carneades or that earlier method of Aristotle.

[72] "For as I have said, those masters of old right down to Socrates used to join with the art of speech, all knowledge and understanding of all things appertaining to the customs of men, to their ways of life, to virtue and to the republic. After they were dissociated by Socrates, as I have laid out, and then by all the Socratics in a similar way, philosophers came to despise eloquence and orators, wisdom. Nor was there the least contact among them except to the extent that the former borrowed from the latter, and the latter from the former; whereas they would be drawing from the same source, if they had chosen to maintain their pristine community. [73] But just as the priests of old were led by the great number of sacrifices to designate three men to be in charge of the public banquets, even though by [traditional] regulations the banquet which accompanied the games was also part of their job, in a similar way the Socratics separated practicing advocates from their ranks and from the name of philosophy common til then, although the masters of old had wished for a remarkably close alliance between speaking and reasoning.

[74] "Since this is the situation, I shall briefly beg your leave and ask that you take what I say as spoken not with regard to myself but with regard to the orator. For if in my youth my father presided over my instruction with the greatest of zeal and if I brought to the forum as much talent as I am

---

81. In Cicero's day, philosophy was broken into competing sects, some of which adopted arcane terminology and peculiar dress, as Quintilian notes in selection #6. This development influenced Cicero's critique of Socrates and Greek philosophy, as well as the view of the philosophical schools conveyed by Martianus Capella's description of Lady Logic in selection #8 and Boethius's description of the robe of Lady Philosophy in selection #9.

82. Ulysses (in Greek, Odysseus) is the ancient Greek leader portrayed in Homer's epic *Odyssey*.

83. This oft-stated distinction between Greek and Roman culture, conceded here by Cicero, is repeated in the subsequent tradition of liberal education, including Martianus Capella in selection #8 and Bathsua Makin in selection #30.

aware of and not all that which you perhaps suppose me to have, I would not be able to claim that I have learned these matters now in view as well as I believe they must be learned. In point of fact, I presented myself to plead political cases younger than anyone else, and I was just twenty-one years old when I arraigned a man of great ancestry and eloquence before the bar of justice. I have had no school other than the forum, no teachers other than experience, laws, and institutions of the Roman people and the custom of our ancestors. [75] Despite my thirst for these arts of which I am speaking, I have tasted of them but little. . . .

"And so, as to the fact that I uphold such great science and power of doctrine, it not only is not special pleading on my behalf but is far more directed against myself and against all these ridiculous characters who profess arts of rhetoric, for I am not talking about what capacity I have, but what the orator has. Those characters write only about their technical precepts about the classification of litigation and rules of narrative; [76] yet that power of eloquence is so great that it controls the origin, nature and modifications of the totality of reality, of all virtues and duties of all nature regarding the characters, emotions and conduct of men. It goes on to determine customs, laws and covenants; to rule the republic; and to articulate everything with brilliance and abundance on whatever subject they address."[84]

---

84. Compare Cicero's claim for the most demanding liberal art with that of Plato (526c) in selection #1.

Liberal Arts and Moral Improvement

5. Seneca the Younger, "On Liberal and Vocational Studies" (c. A.D. 63)

INTRODUCTION

Lucius Annaeus Seneca (c. 4 B.C.– A.D. 65), also called Seneca the Younger or Seneca the Philosopher, was born into a distinguished and well-to-do family in Spain. His father (known as Seneca the Elder) was an imperial Roman official who became a noted authority on forensic and political rhetoric. Though suffering from ill health throughout his life, the son traveled to Rome to study law, politics, and philosophy and to Egypt to study geography and natural science. Honed by this education, his natural speaking talent and mental acumen enabled Seneca to rise rapidly through the imperial bureaucracy; and he became a leading figure in the Senate by A.D. 37. But in 41 the consort to the new emperor Claudius (10 B.C.– A.D. 54)arranged to have him banished to Corsica, where he spent the next eight years writing works in Stoic philosophy and circulating them to a small group of friends and acquaintances. Among these was a letter that Seneca wrote to his mother, Helvia, telling her to comfort herself in his absence by returning to her liberal studies.[85]

In 49 Agrippina, wife of Claudius, arranged for Seneca to be recalled to Rome, inducted into high office, and appointed tutor of her twelve-year-old son, the future emperor Nero (A.D. 37–68) Upon the poisoning of Claudius and accession of Nero, Seneca became one of the most influential advisors to the teenage emperor. For five years he exercised a beneficent influence, and public government enjoyed a period that Emperor Trajan (c. A.D. 53–117) later called the finest in the history of imperial Rome. Nevertheless, Seneca made significant compromises in the severe Stoic morality expressed in much of his writings, sacrificing principle to political expediency and acquiring great wealth at the same time.

Beginning in the late 50s, the inconsistency between his practice and his philosophical teachings became the basis of a campaign of denunciations by jealous competitors for Nero's favor, who encouraged the emperor to shake loose from his boyhood tutor. Sensing that his position was rapidly eroding, Seneca requested, and was granted, imperial permission to retire to the countryside. There he spent his last three years composing various works of philosophy, literature, and drama that influenced many subsequent writers, including Peter Abelard and numerous humanists of the Renaissance. Most significant among these late writings are the *Moral Letters to Lucilius*, which have often been credited with inventing the "essay" form. The following letter has been considered "a *locus classicus*" for the form and for liberal studies.[86]

In 65 Seneca was implicated—perhaps justifiably—in a conspiracy upon the life of Nero. In the frenzied purge that followed, he obeyed the order of the emperor, his former tutee, to commit suicide.

---

85. Bathsua Makin recalls this letter in selection #30.

86. In selection #67, Martha Nussbaum gives prominence to Seneca's letter while seeking to reconcile him with Socrates through a formulation of "Socratic liberal education." Quotation is from Ernst R. Curtius, *European Literature and the Latin Middle Ages* (1948) tr. W. R. Trask (1953; Princeton, NJ: Princeton University Press, 1990), pp. 36–7.

SELECTION[87]

[1] Health to you, Lucilius: You want to know what I feel about liberal studies. I don't admire or count as worthwhile any study which aims at making money. Such studies are just hiring out our talents and are only of value if they train the mind and do not pre-occupy it. We should only spend time on them as long as the mind has nothing better to do, as they form our apprenticeship, not our proper work.[88] [2] You can see why liberal studies are so called: they are worthy of a free man.[89] But only one study is truly liberal in making a man free, and that is the study of wisdom, with its strength of purpose and its noble and exalted ideals. All the others are trivial and childish. Do you think there can be anything of value in those subjects which are expounded by the most disgraceful and outrageous teachers you could find?[90] We should have finished learning such things, not still be learning them.

Some people have thought it worth asking whether liberal studies create the good man. Well, they do not even undertake to do this and they do not claim the requisite knowledge. [3] The study of grammar[91] is concerned with the correct use of language; if it branches out a bit it deals with points of subject matter; at its widest range, the rules governing poetry. Which of these topics paves the way to virtue? Analysis of syllables, careful attention to words, the recording of stories, the laws of scansion—which of these banishes fear, gets rid of desire, or curbs passion?[92] [4] Let us turn to geometry and music: you'll find nothing in them to bid us stop being afraid and stop being covetous. And if a man doesn't know these things all his other knowledge is useless. The point is whether or not these scholars are teaching us virtue. If they are not teaching it, they are not even imparting it indirectly; if they are teaching it, they are philosophers. If you want to know how far they are from formally teaching virtue consider how very disparate are all the things they study: if they were teaching the same thing they would show some shared characteristic.

[5] Unless perhaps they persuade you that Homer was a philosopher, although they [refute] this conclusion by the very passages from which they derive it. For at one time they make him out to have been a Stoic, approving of virtue alone, rejecting pleasures and refusing even immortality if the price was dishonorable. At other times they claim him as an Epicurean, praising the condition of tranquility in a state which spends its days in banqueting and song. Now he is a Peripatetic, dividing benefits into three classes; now an Academic, stating that nothing is certain. It is quite clear that none of these doctrines is in Homer because they all are, and they are mutually incompatible. Even granting that Homer

---

87. Drawn from the translation in *Seneca 17 Letters*, tr. C. D. N. Costa (Warminister, United Kingdom: Aris and Phillips, 1988), Letter 88, pp. 71–86. Reprinted by permission of Oxbow Books Ltd.

88. Lucilius, the procurator of Sicily at the time, was a native of Pompeii who had worked his way up the civil service and was moderately educated in literature and philosophy. Seneca interchanges "studies" and "arts" throughout the text.

89. "A free man" is the translation of *liber*, the root of the adjective *liberalis*. This phrasing that ("liberal studies . . . are worthy of a free man") was frequently echoed by Renaissance humanists beginning in the fourteenth century, when Seneca began to exercise significant influence upon the study of moral philosophy, or ethics, in what came to be called "humanistic studies." See Pier Paolo Vergerio in selection #25.

90. Such statements drawing attention to the divergence between people's professions and practice is what has long led Seneca himself to be charged with hypocrisy.

91. The study of "grammar," the term employed by Seneca, customarily included "literature," which is the rendering given by the translator.

92. "Fear, desire, and passion were three of the emotions that Stoic teaching aimed chiefly to curb." Translator's note, p. 192n3.

was a philosopher, he surely acquired his wisdom before he mastered any of his songs. [6] So let us learn those things which made Homer wise. . . .

[9] Turning to music, I say that you teach me how treble and bass notes harmonize, and how a concord is produced from strings that give dissimilar sounds. I would rather learn how to harmonize my mind and stop my purposes being out of tune. You show me which are the plaintive melodies: show me instead how not to utter a plaintive cry in times of trouble.

[10] A geometrician teaches me to measure my estates rather than how to measure the amount that is enough for a man. He teaches me to do sums and put my fingers to the service of greed, instead of teaching me that those calculations have no importance, that a man is not the happier for having properties which tire out his accountants—in fact that possessions are superfluous if the owner is plunged in misery at the thought of having to calculate them all by himself. [11] What's the good of my knowing how to divide a plot of land into sections if I don't know how to divide it with my brother? What's the good of carefully computing the units of an acre, including even the bits which have escaped the measuring rod, if I get upset by an arrogant neighbor who encroaches on my land? The geometrician teaches me how to keep my boundaries intact, but what I want to learn is how to lose the whole lot cheerfully. . . .

[14] I come now to the man who prides himself on his knowledge of the heavens[93]: "On which side Saturn's icy star retreats, And in what orbits blazing Mercury roams."[94] What will be the benefit of this knowledge? To make me feel worried when Saturn and Mars are in opposition, or when Mercury sets in the evening in view of Saturn, rather than helping me to learn that these planets are propitious whatever their position and cannot change?[95] [15] They are driven on in unalterable courses by a fixed sequence of destined events;[96] they reappear in established cycles and they either cause or signalize all the operations of the universe. But if they cause everything that happens, what will be the use of knowing about an unchangeable process? And if they signalize events, what is the point of foreseeing what you cannot avoid? . . .

[18] You must bear with me if I do not stick to the regular program of studies. I refuse utterly to include painters in the list of liberal arts[97] any more than sculptors or marble-masons or the other panders to luxury. Equally I reject wrestlers and the oil-and-mud artists from our liberal studies,[98] or else I must accept perfumers and cooks and all the others who devote their skills to our pleasures. [19] What, I ask you, is liberal about those people who vomit after drinking on an empty stomach, whose bodies are stuffed while their minds are starved and sluggish? Can we think of that as a liberal study for our youth—the youth whom our ancestors trained to stand up straight and throw javelins, hurl

---

93. Seneca writes "knowledge of the heavens," which the translator renders as "knowledge of astrology," but could just as easily be "knowledge of astronomy" because the modern distinction between "astronomy," study of the stars, and "astrology," conjuring their influences on human life, was not firm at this time.

94. Vergil, *Georgics* I 336–7.

95. "The context of these lines is advice to farmers to take warning of approaching storms from weather signs in the sky. . . . [A] planet is in opposition when it is exactly opposite to the sun in the sky. Saturn and Mars were regarded as unfavorable planets, and Mercury (a favorable planet) is here thought to be adversely affected by Saturn." Translator's note, p. 196n14.

96. "This is a fundamental Stoic dogma, often endorsed by Seneca." Translator's note, p. 196n15.

97. Having listed grammar, music, geometry, and astronomy, Seneca makes an unusually explicit remark showing that he is consciously deciding which arts are "liberal." What are the criteria that he employs?

98. Wrestlers were anointed with oil and became covered with mud.

staves, manage horses and handle weapons? They taught their children nothing which had to be learned lying down. But neither these nor the other forms of training teach or foster virtue. For how does it benefit you to control a horse and restrain him with a bridle, if you yourself are swept away by unbridled emotions? How does it benefit you to overcome lots of opponents in wrestling or boxing, if you are overcome by your own temper?

[20] "Well, then," you say, "do we gain nothing at all from liberal studies?" Regarding other things we gain a lot; regarding virtue, nothing. So too, those admittedly inferior manual skills contribute a great deal to life's amenities but have no relevance to virtue. "Why then do we educate our sons in liberal studies?" Not because they can confer virtue but because they prepare the mind to receive it. Just as what long ago used to be called basic grammar, by which children acquire the rudiments of their education, does not teach the liberal arts but prepares the ground for them to be acquired in due course, so the liberal arts themselves do not lead the mind to virtue but clear the way for it. . . .

[23] The arts relating to children, which are somewhat like the liberal arts, are those which the Greeks call "encyclic" and we call "liberal."[99] But the only liberal arts or, to speak more accurately, the only ones worthy of free men are those whose concern is virtue. . . .

The mind achieves its highest excellence in one sphere only, the unalterable knowledge of good and evil, and no other art shows any interest in good and evil. [29] I would like to take a look at individual virtues.

Bravery treats with contempt things that fill us with dread, despising and challenging and destroying all that makes us slaves to terror. Can we then say that bravery is strengthened by liberal studies? Loyalty is the most sacred virtue of the human heart, never forced to deceive by any compulsion, never corrupted by a bribe. "Burn, beat, kill me," it says, "I shall not betray. The more the agony searches out my secrets, the deeper I shall hide them." Can we say that liberal studies create this sort of courage? Moderation controls our pleasures, hating and banishing some, regulating others and reducing them to healthy limits, and never approaching them for their own sake: she knows that the best limit for our desires is not how much you want but how much you ought to have. [30] Kindness stops us being arrogant towards our fellows, or bad-tempered. In words, deeds and feelings she shows herself obliging and good-natured to all, regarding other people's troubles as her own and valuing her own blessings in particular because they can be blessings to somebody else. Can we say that liberal studies teach these attitudes? Not any more than they teach candor, or modesty and self-control, or thrift and frugality, or mercy that spares another's blood as if it were its own, and knows that no human being should make wasteful use of another human, being.

[31] Some may object here: "When you people say that virtue cannot be attained without liberal studies how can you also say that they offer no assistance to virtue?" The answer is that virtue cannot be attained without food either, but there is no connection between virtue and food. Timbers offer no assistance to a ship even though a ship cannot be created without them. I repeat that you must not think that anything comes into being through the assistance of something without which it cannot come into being.[100] [32] Indeed you can even argue that wisdom can be achieved without liberal studies: for although virtue has to be learnt, it is not learnt through these. Anyway, why should I imagine

---

99. "Encyclic" is drawn from the Greek term *encyclios paideia*, which, in general modern accounts of ancient education, is often said to have circulated among the Greeks (such as Plato or Socrates) in the fifth century B.C. or earlier as the equivalent of the later Latin *artes liberales*. However, the earliest preserved texts that actually employ the term were written in Alexandria in the first century B.C. and first century A.D. The later dating fits this reference by Seneca, who speaks in the present tense and had visited Egypt in his youth.

100. What exactly is Seneca's view of the relationship between liberal studies and virtue? Compare the discussion of Seneca by Martha Nussbaum in selection #67.

that a man who is ignorant of books will not become wise, seeing that wisdom does not lie in books? Wisdom hands down deeds, not words, and I rather think that the memory is more reliable when it has nothing external to help it. . . .

[36] [Others may object,] "but knowledge of many subjects is a real source of pleasure." In that case let us only retain as much of them as we need. Do you regard one man as blameworthy who equates superfluous things with useful ones and sets out a display of costly objects in his house, and not another one who is engrossed in a superfluous quantity of the furniture of learning? To wish to know more than is sufficient is a kind of extravagance. [37] Observe too how that obsession with the liberal arts makes people tiresome, long-winded, tactless and self-satisfied, not learning what they need to because they have spent their time learning what is useless.[101] The grammarian Didymus wrote four thousand books: I would be sorry for him if he had only read so many useless works. In these books he discusses Homer's birthplace, who was Aeneas's real mother, whether Anacreon lived the life of a lecher or of a drunkard, whether Sappho was a whore, and other things you would want to unlearn if you knew them.[102] Go on, tell me life isn't long enough! . . .

[42] Measure your life: it simply has no room for . . . liberal studies.

---

101. Seneca's objections to "useless" learning may be compared to those of Cicero in the reading above.

102. Didymus Chalcenterus, Greek grammarian of the first century B.C.; Aeneas, legendary founder of the Roman race, according to Vergil's epic poem, *Aeneid*; Anacreon, Greek lyric poet of the late sixth century B.C.

6. Quintilian, *Education of the Orator* (c. A.D. 95)

INTRODUCTION

Born and raised in Spain, Marcus Fabius Quintilianus (c. 40–c. 100) traveled to Rome during his teenage years to study rhetoric and the practice of the law courts. After returning to Spain in about 60, likely with the intention of becoming an advocate in the provincial courts, Quintilian went back to Rome and founded a school of rhetoric. He also served as a pleader in the courts, organizing the technical legal material obtained from jurisconsults, delivering speeches on behalf of his client, and cross-examining witnesses. But his school increasingly occupied his attention and brought him fame; he was likely the first professor of rhetoric to receive a salary from public funds, which was provided by Emperor Vespasian during the 70s.

In this prominent chair of rhetoric, Quintilian replaced the popular, epigrammatic style of Seneca with that of the mellifluous, classical style of Cicero, while reasserting the synthesis of virtue, eloquence, and learning that Cicero had regarded as the essence of the orator. In so doing, Quintilian became the only ancient writer, Greek or Roman, to give serious attention to education in early childhood.[103] All these purposes appear in his greatest written work: *Education of the Orator*, which was widely quoted and admired by those who developed the "humanistic studies" of the Renaissance, as will be seen in Section IV below. Quintilian wrote the twelve books of *Education of the Orator* between A.D. 88 and 95, and died near the turn of the century.

SELECTION[104]

[9] We are trying to form, then, the perfect orator, who cannot exist except he be a good man; and we accordingly demand that there be in him not merely the rarest talent for speaking but all the moral virtues.[105] [10] For I would not grant the necessity, as some have had it, of relegating the method of living rightly and honestly to philosophers. The kind of man who is a true citizen and fit to assume the guidance of affairs both public and private, who can direct cities with his policies, found them with his legislation and correct them with his exercise of justice, would not—I can assure you—be anyone other than the orator. [11] For that reason, though I allow that I shall make use of certain principles which are contained in the books of philosophers, still I would openly declare that these principles belong by right and truth to my domain and properly pertain to the art of oratory. [12] After all, considering how often the discussion will turn to justice, courage, temperance and the like (to the point that one could scarcely find a case in which some inquiry relevant to these matters does not appear and require development through invention and eloquence), is there any doubt that the role of the orator is decisive wherever the force of mind and abundance of speaking are required?

[13] These two things have been, as Cicero makes abundantly clear, somehow joined in their very nature and inseparable in practice to the point that the wise and eloquent were held to be the same people. Subsequently, a separation developed in this study due to neglect by its professors, and as a result there seemed to be a plurality of arts; for, once words began to be a source of livelihood and

---

103. Quintilian's unusual attention to the issue led subsequent humanist educators to attend to it as well. See Pier Paolo Vergerio in selection #25.

104. Adapted from a new, unpublished translation by J. Albert Dragstedt of the preface of Book I.

105. Attributed to Cato the Elder, the standard, epigrammatic definition of the Ciceronian orator ("a good man, skilled in speaking") was quoted by Quintilian (*Education of the Orator* XII i 1), and in selection #10 by Cassiodorus (II ii 1) and in selection #11 by Isidore (II 3), and is mentioned by Francesco Petrarca in selection #24.

people began abusing the benefits of eloquence, those who were held to be eloquent abandoned the stewardship of morality. [14] Then, neglected as it was, morality fell prey to more mediocre talents, as certain others turned, out of a contempt for the effort required to speak well, to the task of forming minds and establishing rules of living, and kept the most important part (I grant you) of philosophy for themselves (assuming it could be divided into parts). Meanwhile, they arrogated to themselves the most pretentious of names entailing that they alone be called friends of wisdom or philosophers; a title that neither the most illustrious princes nor those occupying themselves with greatest distinction in the governance or the most important affairs and administration of the entire republic have had the audacity to claim at any time. For they preferred to perform rather than promise great deeds.

[15] In sum, I would agree that, among those who professed to teach wisdom in times past, there were many who gave noble precepts and lived in conformity with their precepts; but in our day, truth to say, it is the greatest vices that lurk under this label of philosophy, for the most part. For it was not through virtue and earnest study that this group strove to be considered philosophers; rather their severe facial expression and unique external appearance have served to mask their most corrupt of characters.

[16] These questions, moreover, to which philosophy lays claim, as if they were her exclusive terrain, are all dealt with at times by all of us. For who does not have occasion to refer to the just, the fair and the good, except a man of the worst sort? Who is there, even among the farmers, who does not raise some question about natural causes? And the propriety and distinctness of terms ought to be held in common as a study by all who care about their language. [17] But all these subjects are what the orator will know and articulate best,[106] and if the orator had achieved perfection, then one would not seek precepts of virtue from the philosophers' schools. As matters stand, it is necessary to have recourse to these authors who have seized this most valuable part of the art of oratory (after its abandonment by the orators, as I have said) and to demand its return, so to speak—not so that we employ their inventions but so that we instruct them that they have made use of things that do not belong to them.

[18] Let the orator, therefore, be a man such as could be addressed as a genuinely wise man; and he is not to be complete only in his character (for that is not enough in my opinion, although there are those who disagree), but he is to be complete in the knowledge and entire capacity for speaking, such as perhaps no one up to now has attained. [19] But that is no reason for us to exert ourselves less for the highest goals. And that is what most of the ancients did, who handed down the precepts of wisdom despite their not believing that any wise man had yet been discovered. [20] For a consummate eloquence is certainly something real, and does not stand beyond the reach of human endowment. Even if one should fail to attain it, nevertheless one will climb higher if one strives toward the peaks than if one stops right at the foothills out of a despair at making the ascent.

---

106. Following Cicero, Quintilian argues that the liberally educated orator must have a broad, general education.

Section II

Late Antiquity and Middle Ages:
Christian Appropriation, Codification, and Female Imagery

After surviving persecutions during the first and second centuries, adherents of Christianity, who at the outset belonged predominantly to the poor and uneducated classes of society, rose to the most powerful offices in the Roman Empire during the third and fourth centuries. Their new authority and status prompted questions about the nature of Christians' relationship to classical culture in general and to the liberal arts in particular. No longer was it possible for Christians to follow the Apostle Paul saying, "As for me brothers, when I came to you, it was not with any display of oratory or philosophy, but simply to tell you what God has guaranteed" [1 *Corinthians* 2: 1.] Many pagan citizens, educated in the classical tradition, regarded the upstart gospel as coarse and simplistic; and when the invaders from the east appeared on the horizon, they charged Christianity with undermining the moral strength and vigor of Roman civilization. Conversely, certain church leaders despised classical culture due to past persecutions and because pagan mythology offended them both morally and theologically.

This tension between Graeco-Roman and Judaeo-Christian traditions was experienced and addressed by many Church Fathers, such as Jerome, who feared that his love of classical letters would subject him to the divine condemnation "you are a Ciceronian, not a Christian."[1] Other leaders of the Latin church invoked pagan and Jewish accounts of Plato visiting Egypt, as seen in Augustine's selection, in order to support their claim that the liberal arts and all classical learning derived either directly from their Scriptures or from the Egyptians, who had learned it from the Hebrews. It was Augustine who expressed what would become the medieval resolution of this question in *On Christian Learning* by adopting the forms of classical erudition and legitimating their use for Christians at the same time that he met pagan critics on their own ground. The work was widely cited in the subsequent centuries and is included below.

By the close of antiquity at the end of the fifth century, church leaders had appropriated classical learning and were engaged in reconciling it with Christian doctrine. Through this effort at formalization and codification, a consensus was reached upon the number, identity, and general order of the *septem artes liberales*,[2] as was expressed in three encyclopedic handbooks written by Martianus Capella, Cassiodorus, and Isidore of Seville. The latter two were church leaders, while the treatise of the first was a pagan work that Christians nonetheless purged, cited, taught, and finally claimed as their own. All three handbooks became textbooks in the schools as learning declined amid the political and social turmoil during invasions and migrations in the subsequent centuries.

Already in the fifth century, Jerome observed about the carnage: "If a few of us survive to this point, it is not to our merits but to the mercy of God that we owe it. Countless, savage barbarians have occupied all of Gaul. Everything between the Alps and the Pyrenees, the Rhine and the ocean has

---

1. Jerome, *Letters* VI xxii 30. Jerome (c. 347–c. 420) was Christian scholar and editor

2. The gradual codification of the "seven liberal arts" is evidenced by the tables in Henri I. Marrou, "Les arts libéraux dans l'antiquité classique," in *Arts libéraux et philosophie au Moyen Âge* (Montréal: Institut d'études médiévales, Universitéde Montréal, 1969), pp. 5–27.

been destroyed by the barbarians. . . . Time has dried our tears, and everyone, apart from a few old men not born into captivity and warfare, no longer mourns the freedom that they never knew. For, who could believe what I say: that Rome no longer fights for glory, but for survival; in fact, not even fights, but ransoms her life with gold and jewels?"[3]

As a result, liberal education gradually retreated into private tutorials in the homes of noble families who still remembered the ideal of eloquent and virtuous learning; into parish and episcopal schools, though these flickered on and off; and above all, into monasteries which, being small, self-sufficient, and enclosed, were best suited to preserve liberal education during a period of political unrest and military invasion. In these sanctuaries, Christians transmitted the "seven liberal arts" over the next six centuries. At the same time, they adopted the representation of the arts in female form, and this representation had a variety of significations. Underlying all these significations, however, was the irony that women were largely excluded from liberal education at the same time that they were being portrayed as personifying the liberal arts. The countervailing implications of the female imagery of the liberal arts are found in the selections from Martianus Capella, Boethius, and Christine de Pizan.

---

3. Jerome, *Letters* CXXIII 15–16. Translation adapted from St. Jerome, *Lettres* (Paris: Société d'Édition Les Belles Lettres, 1961), v. 7.

Christian Appropriation of the Liberal Arts

7. Augustine, *On Christian Learning* (396, 426)

INTRODUCTION

Aurelius Augustinus (354–430) was raised as a Christian by his mother, Monica, in northern Africa, but gave up his religion when he went to school in Carthage, near present-day Tunis. As a student, he chose the conventional route to a successful career—the study of rhetoric—and indulged in a carefree social life, fathering a son out of wedlock. These events and his youthful conversion to Manichaeanism are recounted in his *Confessions*. Moving to Rome in 383, he became a successful master, or teacher, of rhetoric, and went to Milan in 384 to assume an imperial appointment to teach rhetoric. Despite this success in his secular career, he fell into great anxiety and mental unrest over the next two years. Growing doubts about Manichaeanism were heightened by studies of Platonism, Stoicism, and Skepticism and by the fervent preaching of Bishop Ambrose of Milan. The result was that Augustine had a conversion experience and was baptized as a Christian in 387. Returning to his birthplace, he formed a monastic community with a number of friends; and in 391, during a visit to the city of Hippo in present-day Algeria, he reluctantly agreed to be ordained as a priest to serve the Christians there. Four years later he was consecrated Bishop of Hippo and remained in this office until his death during the siege of the city by the Vandals.

Selection #7 is drawn from *De Doctrina Christiana*, which is variously translated as "On Christian Learning," "On Christian Education," or "On Christian Teaching." Less studied today than his *Confessions* or his explicitly theological works, Augustine's *On Christian Learning* became during the middle ages the most important and widely cited authority on behalf of the Christian appropriation of pagan culture and the liberal arts. Some even maintain that the Puritan's first curriculum of Harvard College was "directly or indirectly derived from St. Augustine's *On Christian Learning*,"[4] although others have questioned its influence on later programs of study and argued that the purpose and audience of the work are uncertain.[5] Nevertheless, scholars still affirm that Augustine's "program of the liberal arts . . . is the cardinal theme of the work and . . . represents its central importance for the history of Christian thought."[6]

The background of this treatise lies in the cultural conflict between Christians and educated pagans in the Roman Empire, outlined above. In 396 Augustine addressed that controversy when writing the first three books of *On Christian Learning*, which defend pagan learning as necessary for Biblical hermeneutics or "discovery." This defense involves the claim that classical learning was not invented by pagans, but discovered in the divinely created nature of things. In these three books,

---

4. Arthur O. Norton, *Harvard Text-Books and Reference Books of the Seventeenth Century* (Boston: Colonial Society of Massachusetts, 1935), p. 8n. See selection #29 from Harvard College, *New England's First Fruits* (1643).

5. Christoph Schäublin, "*De Doctrina Christiana*: A Classic of Western Culture?" in *De Doctrina Christiana: A Classic of Western Culture*, ed. Duane W. H. Arnold and Pamela Bright (Notre Dame, IN: University Notre Dame Press, 1995), pp. 47–55; Edmund P. Hill, "Introduction," in Augustine, *Teaching Christianity, De Doctrina Christiana*, tr. Edmund P. Hill (New York: New City Press, 1996), p. 95.

6. Frederick Van Fleteren, "St. Augustine, Neoplatonism, and the Liberal Arts: The Background to *De Doctrina Christiana*," in *De Doctrina Christiana*, pp. 14–5.

Augustine was elaborating the view, first made by Clement of Alexandria, that the liberal arts and secular philosophy are gifts of God.[7]

Returning to *On Christian Learning* in 426, Augustine completed Book IV, addressing primarily the role of rhetoric—the art of preaching and teaching what one has discovered—which crowned the liberal arts both in his own education and in that of leading Roman citizens. As with the other liberal arts, he justified the study of rhetoric for Christians not only by his analysis, but also by quoting the works of Vergil and Cicero, the leading figures of Roman letters anathematized by Christian rigorists. In this fashion, Augustine adopted the forms of classical erudition, thus legitimating their use by other Christians, at the same time that he met pagan critics on their own ground. He also implied, as argued in the *City of God*, that Christianity had not caused the decline of the empire. Rather, pride and love of praise—the antithesis of the Christian virtue of humility—had rotted out the civilization. At the same time, he admonished Christians that their faith and classical culture shared certain values, and for this reason the latter could not be completely condemned. Augustine in this way laid the foundation for the accommodation between Christianity and liberal education.

SELECTION[8]

Book II
xxviii

[43] With reference to the usefulness of history, if I may omit the Greeks, what a question our Ambrose solved after the calumnies of the readers and admirers of Plato, who dared to say that all the lessons of our Lord Jesus Christ, which they were forced to admire and to teach, were learned from the writings of Plato, since it cannot be denied that Plato lived long before the advent of the Lord! Did not the famous bishop, when he had considered the history of the pagans and found that Plato had traveled in Egypt during the time of Jeremiah, show that Plato had probably been introduced to our literature by Jeremiah so that he was able to teach or to write doctrines that are justly commended? Pythagoras himself did not live before the literature of the Hebrew nation, in which the cult of one God took its origin and from which Our Lord came "according to the flesh" [*Romans* 9: 5], was written. And from the disciples of Pythagoras these men claim that Plato learned theology. Thus from a consideration of times it becomes more credible that the Platonists took from our literature whatever they said that is good and truthful than that Our Lord Jesus Christ learned from them. To believe the latter view is the utmost madness. . . .[9]

---

7. In his *Miscellanies*, the Christian theologian and educator Clement of Alexandria (A.D. 150–215) attempted to synthesize Platonic and Christian doctrine and declared that the liberal arts and secular philosophy were gifts of God acquired through the Holy Spirit.

8. D. W. Robertson, Jr., tr., *Augustine: On Christian Doctrine* (Indianapolis, IN: Bobbs-Merrill, 1958), pp. 64, 67–75, 136–8, 142–3. Reprinted by permission of Pearson Education, Inc.

9. Augustine thus endorses the argument of Bishop Ambrose on behalf of the Egyptian, Hebraic, and therefore Judaeo-Christian origins of Greek learning. This argument was directed both to Christian rigorists who scorned pagan learning, fearing the temptation to indulge in worldly things, and to pagans who dismissed even the Christian doctrines they admired as being derivative of Greek philosophy. Augustine later retracted his endorsement of Ambrose's view (which was still widely credited as late as the fifteenth century, but he never relinquished his steadfast defense of the appropriateness of secular learning and the liberal arts for Christians.

xxxi

[48] There remain those [arts][10] which do not pertain to the corporal senses but to the reason, where the sciences of disputation and number hold sway.[11] The science of disputation is of great value for understanding and solving all sorts of questions that appear in sacred literature. However, in this connection the love of controversy is to be avoided, as well as a certain puerile ostentation in deceiving an adversary.[12] There are, moreover, many false conclusions of the reasoning process called sophisms, and frequently they so imitate true conclusions that they mislead not only those who are slow but also the ingenious when they do not pay close attention. For example, a man holding a discussion with another submits the proposition: "What I am, you are not." The other, because it is true in part, or because the speaker is deceitful and he is simple, agrees. Then the first adds, "I am a man." When this too is agreed upon, he concludes, saying, "Therefore you are not a man." As I see it, the Scripture condemns this kind of captious conclusion in that place where it is said, "He that speaketh sophistically is hateful." [*Ecclesiastes* 37: 23] At times a discourse which is not captious, but which is more abundant that is consistent with gravity, being inflated with verbal ornament, is also called sophistical.

[49] There are also valid processes of reasoning having false conclusions which follow from the error of the disputant. An error of this kind may be led to its conclusions by a good and learned man so that the disputant, being ashamed of them, relinquishes his error. For if he maintains it, he will also be forced to maintain conclusions which he himself condemns. . . . Since [valid] inferences may be made concerning false as well as true propositions, it is easy to learn the nature of valid inference even in schools which are outside of the Church. But the truth of propositions is a matter to be discovered in the sacred books of the Church.[13]

xxxii

[50] However, the truth of valid inference was not instituted by men; rather it was observed by men and set down that they might learn to teach it. For it is perpetually instituted by God in the reasonable order of things. Thus the person who narrates the order of events in time does not compose that order himself; and he who shows the location of places or the natures of animals, plants, or minerals does not discuss things instituted by men; and he who shows the location of places or the natures of animals, plants, or minerals does not discuss things instituted by men; and he who describes the stars or their motions does not describe anything instituted by himself or by other men. In the same way, he who describes the stars or their motions does not describe anything instituted by himself or by other men. In the same way, he who says, "When a consequent is false, it is necessary that the antecedent upon which it is based be false also," speaks very truly; but he does not arrange matters so that they are this way. Rather, he simply points out an existing truth. . . . The principle that if the consequent is false the antecedent must also be false was not instituted by men, but discovered. And this rule applies to the validity of inferences, not to the truth of propositions. . . .

---

10. Having addressed other kinds of arts, Augustine begins a discussion of the liberal arts that ends at II xxxix.

11. According to the Stoic usage that influenced Augustine, *dialectica*, translated here as "disputation," refers to grammar, rhetoric, and logic. Understood in this way, "disputation," together with "number," refers to the two hemispheres of the liberal arts: language and mathematics.

12. Note here and below Augustine's wariness of the temptation of sophistry, reminiscent of Isocrates's warning in selection #2.

13. Here and below, Augustine's distinction between the validity of logical inferences (which are based upon the rules of a pagan liberal art) and the truth of such inferences (which depend upon the nature of their premisses) exemplifies his strategy of reconciling pagan and Christian cultures. In the words of a later scholastic aphorism, classical learning and Christian doctrine "are different but not contradictory."

xxxiv

[52] In this way it is one thing to know the rules of valid inference, another thing to know the truth of propositions. Concerning inferences, one learns what is consequent, what is inconsequent, and what is incompatible. It is logical that "If one is an orator, he is a man"; it is illogical that "If one is a man, he is an orator"; and the parts of "If one is a man, he is a quadruped" are incompatible. In these instances, the inferences themselves are judged. Concerning the truth of propositions, however, the rules of inference are not relevant and the propositions are to be considered in themselves. But when true and certain propositions are joined by valid inferences to propositions we are not sure about, the latter, also, necessarily become certain. There are those who boast when they have learned the rules of valid inference as if they had learned the truth of propositions. And on the other hand, there are some who know many true propositions but think ill of themselves because they do not know the rules of inference. But he who knows that there is a resurrection of the dead is better than another who knows that it follows from the proposition that there is no resurrection of the dead that "then Christ is not risen." . . .

xxxvi

[54] There are, moreover, certain precepts for a more copious discourse which make up what are called the rules of eloquence, and these are very true, even though they may be used to make falsehoods persuasive.[14] Since they can be used in connection with true principles as well as with false, they are not themselves culpable, but the perversity of ill using them is culpable. Men did not themselves institute the fact that an expression of charity conciliates an audience, or the fact that it is easy to understand a brief and open account of events, or that the variety of a discourse keeps the auditors attentive and without fatigue. There are other similar principles which may be employed either in false or in true causes, but which are themselves true in so far as they cause things to be known or to be believed, or move men's minds either to seek or to avoid something. And these are rather discovered than instituted.[15]

xxxxvii

[55] But when these precepts are learned they are to be applied more in expressing those things which are understood than in the pursuit of understanding. However, a knowledge of inference, definition, and division aids the understanding a great deal, provided that men do not make the mistake of thinking that they have learned the truth of the blessed life when they have learned them. Moreover, it frequently happens that men more easily learn the things themselves on account of which these principles are learned than the very knotty and spiny precepts of these disciplines. It is as if one should wish to give rules for walking and admonishes that the rear foot is not to be raised until the first foot is put down, and then goes on to describe in detail how the hinges of the joints and knees are to be moved. He speaks truly, nor is it possible to walk in any other way. Yet men more easily do these things when they walk than pay attention to them while they are doing them or understand them when they are described. And those who cannot walk care about the rules much less, since they cannot try them by experience. In the same way an ingenious person more easily discerns a false conclusion than he learns the rules governing it. And a stupid person who does not discern it is much less apt to understand the rules.[16] And in all of these things the semblances of truth more frequently delight us than

---

14. Having addressed the art of logic (II xxxi–xxxiv), Augustine now turns to rhetoric, his specialty, which occupies the bulk of his attention.

15. This contrast between "discovered" and "instituted" is another distinction frequently employed by Augustine in order to reconcile pagan and Christian cultures.

16. In his dialogue *The Teacher*, Augustine challenges the efficacy of relying not only on rules, but even on teaching at all as a means to learn how to act.

prove themselves helpful to us in disputing or judging. They make men's discernment more alert, but they may also make men malign and proud so that they love to deceive with specious arguments and questions these things and therefore place themselves above good and innocent people.

xxxviii

[56] It is perfectly clear to the most stupid person that the science of numbers was not instituted by men, but rather investigated and discovered. Vergil did not wish to have the first syllable of *Italia* short, as the ancients pronounced it, and it was made long.[17] But no one could in this fashion because of his personal desire arrange matters so that three threes are not nine, or do not geometrically produce a square figure, or are not the triple of the ternary, or are not one and a half times six, or are evenly divisible by two when odd numbers cannot be so divided. Whether they are considered in themselves or applied to the laws of figures, or of sound, or of some other motion, numbers have immutable rules[18] not instituted by men but discovered through the sagacity of the more ingenious.

[57] But whoever delights in these things in such a way that he boasts among the unlearned, and does not seek to learn the source of the truths which he has somehow perceived and to know whence those things are not only true but immutable which he has seen to be immutable, and thus, arising from corporal appearances to the human mind, when he finds this to be mutable since it is now learned and now unlearned, does not come to understand that it is placed between immutable things above it and other mutable things below it, and so does not turn all his knowledge toward the praise and love of one God from whom he knows that everything is derived—this man may seem to be learned. But he is in no way wise.

xxxix

[58] Thus it seems to me that studious and intelligent youths who fear God and seek the blessed life . . . should not neglect those human institutions helpful to social intercourse in the necessary pursuits of life. Among other teachings to be found among the pagans, aside from the history of things both past and present, teachings which concern the corporal senses, including the experience and theory of the useful mechanical arts, and the sciences of disputation and of numbers, I consider nothing to be useful. And in all of these, the maxim is to be observed, "Nothing in excess." And this is especially true with reference to those arts pertaining to the corporal senses, since they are limited by times and places. . . .

xl

[60] If those who are called philosophers, especially the Platonists, have said things which are indeed true and are well accommodated to our faith, they should not be feared;[19] rather, what they have said should be taken from them as from unjust possessors and converted to our use. Just as the Egyptians had not only idols and grave burdens which the people of Israel detested and avoided, so also they had vases and ornaments of gold and silver and clothing which the Israelites took with them secretly when they fled, as if to put them to a better use. They did not do this on their own authority but at God's commandment, while the Egyptians unwittingly supplied them with things which they themselves did not use well. [*Exodus* 3: 22, 11: 2, 12: 35] In the same way all the teaching of the pagans contain not

---

17. Vergil, *Aeneid* I 2. Here and below the citations and translations are given by the translator.

18. Here the Platonic understanding of the mathematical liberal arts is simplified to a formula that is being handed on: "numbers have immutable rules . . . considered in themselves [arithmetic] or applied to the law of figures [geometry], or of sound [music], or of some other motion [astronomy]." The surviving remnants of the treatises that Augustine wrote addressing each of the four mathematical arts indicate that he understood little of the underlying principles and interpreted these arts in a practical and mundane fashion, as compared to Plato's understanding.

19. Augustine is known for favoring Plato and neo-Platonic philosophy.

only simulated and superstitious imaginings and grave burdens of unnecessary labor, which each one of us leaving the society of pagans under the leadership of Christ ought to abominate and avoid, but also liberal disciplines more suited to the uses of truth, and some most useful precepts concerning morals. Even some truths concerning the worship of one God are discovered among them. These are, as it were, their gold and silver, which they did not institute themselves but dug up from certain mines of divine Providence, which is everywhere infused, and perversely and injuriously abused in the worship of demons. When the Christian separates himself in spirit from their miserable society, he should take this treasure with him for the just use of teaching the gospel. . . .

Book IV

[1] This work of ours entitled *On Christian Learning* was at the beginning divided into two parts. For after the Prologue in which I replied to those who would criticize it, I wrote, "There are two things necessary to the treatment of the Scriptures: a way of discovering those things which are to be understood, and a way of teaching what we have learned. We shall speak first of discovery and second of teaching." Since we have already said much concerning discovery and devoted three books to that one part, with the help of God we shall say a few things concerning teaching, so that, if possible, we shall conclude everything with one book and thus complete the whole work in four books. . . .[20]

ii

[3] For since by means of the art of rhetoric both truth and falsehood are urged, who would dare to say that truth should stand in the person of its defenders unarmed against lying, so that they who wish to urge falsehoods may know how to make their listeners benevolent, or attentive, or docile in their presentation, while the defenders of truth are ignorant of that art? Should they speak briefly, clearly, and plausibly while the defenders of truth speak so that they tire their listeners, make themselves difficult to understand and what they have to say dubious? Should they oppose the truth with fallacious arguments and assert falsehoods, while the defenders of truth have no ability either to defend the truth or to oppose the false? Should they, urging the minds of their listeners into error, ardently exhort them, moving them by speech so that they terrify, sadden, and exhilarate them, while the defenders of truth are sluggish, cold, and somnolent? Who is so foolish as to think this to be wisdom? While the faculty of eloquence, which is of great value in urging either evil or justice, is in itself indifferent, why should it not be obtained for the uses of the good in the service of truth if the evil usurp it for the winning of perverse and vain causes in defense of iniquity and error?

iii

[4] But whatever observations and rules concerning this matter there may be, in accordance with which one acquires through exercise and habit a most skillful use of vocabulary and plentiful verbal ornaments, are established by what is called eloquence or oratory. Those who are able to do so quickly, having set aside an appropriate period of time, should learn them at a proper and convenient age outside of these writings of mine. For the masters of Roman eloquence themselves did not hesitate to say that, unless one can learn this art quickly, he can hardly learn it at all. Why should we inquire whether this is true? For even if these rules can sometimes be learned by those who are slow, we do not hold them to be of such importance that we would wish mature and grave men to spend their time learning them. It is enough that they be the concern of youths; nor should they concern all of those

---

20. This is a succinct summary of Augustine's, twofold defense for the verbal arts of grammar, logic, and rhetoric. As recounted in the first three books, written some thirty years earlier, grammar and logic serve Christians in the interpretation of sacred texts. The second service is to train Christians in preaching the truth that they learn from interpretation. Hence, the focus of Book IV is primarily upon rhetoric, the most "dangerous" of the liberal arts.

whom we wish to educate for the utility of the Church, but only those who are not pursuing some more urgent study, or one which obviously ought to take precedence over this one.

For those with acute and eager minds more readily learn eloquence by reading and hearing the eloquent than by following the rules of eloquence.[21] There is no lack of ecclesiastical literature, including that outside of the canon established in a place of secure authority, which, if read by a capable man, even though he is interested more in what is said than in the eloquence with which it is said, will imbue him with that eloquence while he is studying. And he will learn eloquence especially if he gains practice by writing, dictating, or speaking what he has learned according to the rule of piety and faith. But if capacity of this kind to learn eloquence is lacking, the rules of rhetoric will not be understood, nor will it help any if they are in some small measure understood after great labor. Even those who have learned these rules and speak fluently and eloquently cannot be aware of the fact that they are applying them while they are speaking unless they are discussing the rules themselves; indeed, I think that there is hardly a single eloquent man who can both speak well and think of the rules of eloquence while he is speaking. And we should beware lest what should be said escape us while we are thinking of the artistry of the discourse. Moreover, in the speeches and saying of the eloquent, the precepts of eloquence are found to have been fulfilled, although the speakers did not think of them in order to be eloquent or while they were being eloquent, and they were eloquent whether they had learned the rules or never come in contact with them. They fulfilled them because they were eloquent; they did not apply them that they might be eloquent. . . .

iv

[6] Thus the expositor and teacher of the Divine Scripture, the defender of right faith and the enemy of error, should both teach the good and extirpate the evil.[22] And in this labor of words, he should conciliate those who are opposed, arouse those who are remiss, and teach those ignorant of his subject what is occurring and what they should expect. But when he has either found his listeners to be benevolent, attentive, and docile, or has caused them to be so, other aims are to be carried out as the cause requires. If those who hear are to be taught, exposition must be composed, if it is needed, that they may become acquainted with the subject at hand. In order that those things which are doubtful may be made certain, they must be reasoned out with the use of evidence. But if those who hear are to be moved rather than taught, so that they may not be sluggish in putting what they know into practice and so that they may fully accept those things which they acknowledge to be true, there is need for greater powers of speaking. Here entreaties and reproofs, exhortations and rebukes, and whatever other devices are necessary to move minds must be used. . . .

v

But since some do these things dully, unevenly, and coldly, while others do them acutely, ornately, and vehemently, he should approach this work about which we are speaking who can dispute or speak wisely, even though he cannot do so eloquently, so that he may be of benefit to his hearers, even though he benefits them less than he would if he could also speak eloquently. But he who is foolish and abounds in eloquence is the more to be avoided the more he delights his auditor with those things to which it is useless to listen so that he thinks that because he hears a thing said eloquently it is true. This lesson, moreover, did not escape those who thought to teach the art or rhetoric. They granted that "wisdom without eloquence is of small benefit to states; but eloquence without wisdom is often ex-

---

21. Compare II xxxvii above with the judgment in selection #16 by John of Salisbury (I 1).

22. This chapter provides "an outline of the *officia*—dialectical and rhetorical—of the Christian orator. . . . The foundation of Augustine's office is entirely classical; the spirit is wholly Christian; the result is a new rhetorical ideal." Thérèse Sullivan, *Doctrina Christiana, Liber Quartus, A Commentary and Translation* (Washington, DC: Catholic University of America, 1930), p. 44n1.

tremely injurious and profits no one."[23] If those who taught the rules of eloquence, in the very books in which they did so, were forced by the power of truth to confess this, being ignorant of that true wisdom which descends supernal from the Father of Lights, how much more ought we, who are the sons and ministers of this wisdom, to think in no other way? . . .

xii

[27] Therefore a certain eloquent man said, and said truly, that he who is eloquent should speak in such a way that he teaches, delights, and moves. Then he added, "To teach is a necessity, to please is a sweetness, to persuade is a victory."[24] Of the three, that which is given first place, that is, the necessity of teaching, resides in the things which we have to say, the other two in the manner in which we say it. . . .

[28] But if they still do not know this, instruction should come before persuasion. And perhaps when the necessary things are learned, they may be so moved by a knowledge of them that it is not necessary to move them further by greater powers of eloquence. But when it is necessary, it is to be done, and it is necessary when they know what should be done but do not do it. And for this reason teaching is a necessity. But men may act and still not act in accordance with what they know. But who would tell them to do something in accordance with what they do not know? And therefore persuasion is not a necessity because it need not always be applied if the listener consents through teaching and even through delight also. But it is also true that persuasion is victory, for people may be taught and pleased and still not consent. And of what use are the first two if the third does not follow? But delight is not a necessity either. . . .

xiii

[29] It is necessary therefore for the ecclesiastical orator, when he urges that something be done, not only to teach that he may instruct and to please that he may hold attention, but also to persuade that he may be victorious.[25] For it now remains for that man, in whom the demonstration of truth, even when suavity of diction was added, did not move to consent, to be persuaded by the heights of eloquence. . .

xvii

[34] He who seeks to teach in speech what is good, spurning none of these three things, that is, to teach, to delight, and to persuade, should pray and strive that he be heard intelligently, willingly and obediently. When he does this well and properly, he can justly be called eloquent, even though he fails to win the assent of his audience. To these three things—that he should teach, delight, and persuade—the author of Roman eloquence himself seems to have wished to relate three other things when he said, "He therefore will be eloquent who can speak of small things in a subdued manner, of moderate things in a temperate manner, and of grand things in a grand manner."[26] It is as though he had added these to the three mentioned previously and said, "He is therefore eloquent who in order to teach, can speak of small things in a subdued manner, and in order to please, can speak of moderate things in a temperate manner, and in order to persuade, can speak of great things in a grand manner."

23. Cicero, *On Discovery* I 1. Augustine's quoting of Cicero inaugurates the practice by Church leaders.

24. Cicero, *Orator* 21, 69.

25. The telling phrase "ecclesiastical orator" expresses the reconciliation of Christian and classical cultures that is being advanced here.

26. Cicero, *Orator* 29, 101. See Martianus Capella (V 428) in selection #8.

Codification of the Liberal Arts and and their Female Images

8. Martianus Capella, *The Marriage of Philology and Mercury* (c. 425)

INTRODUCTION

For more than a millennium, Martianus Capella's only extant work, *The Marriage of Philology and Mercury* (c. 425), was among the most popular books in western Europe.[27] In the first two chapters, *The Marriage* relates the story, told by an old man to his son, of how the god Mercury chooses Philology, an erudite young woman, to be his bride. At the wedding banquet in the heavens, Mercury presents his bride with seven learned handmaids personifying the seven liberal arts. In each of the final seven chapters, one of the seven learned women is introduced and describes her art. Extolling Cicero and drawing upon a lost encyclopedia of Marcus Terentius Varro (116–c. 27 B.C.), Martianus warns against too intensive or lengthy study of dialectic, and presents the mathematical arts as compilations of factual information. Fundamentally, the nuptial allegory teaches the Ciceronian lesson embraced by Augustine: the liberal arts provide the means for joyfully attaining the divinely sanctioned goal of uniting eloquence (Mercury) and learning (Philology).

Aside from the wish to display his scanty learning drawn from handbooks and encyclopedias of the time, Martianus's intentions are often understood in two ways. In one respect, *The Marriage* can be taken as a textbook for the preparatory education of the citizen having leisure to study; in another respect, when the description of liberal arts in the last seven books is combined with the allegorical mélange of metaphysics and theology in the first two books, it can be regarded as a compilation of knowledge. Neither interpretation is wholly satisfactory, however, because the scope of the work is too wide for a school text and too narrow for an encyclopedia. Taken together, these two interpretations suggest that *The Marriage* presents the sum total of education necessary for the citizen with leisure to study. Confirmation lies in the fact that Martianus stopped at seven liberal arts and explicitly excluded the practical and technical arts of medicine and architecture that Varro had included.[28]

Whatever Martianus's intentions, Christians, after excising the first two books of pagan mythology, began to cite, teach, copy, and finally claim *The Marriage* as their own. Thus, Gregory of Tours in the sixth century urged leaders of the Church to study the "seven disciplines" of "our Martianus."[29] In this way, the treatise became renowned among teachers of the liberal arts during the middle ages, and its themes and motifs reappeared in the treatises, literature, sculpture, and painting of Western Europe.[30] The notoriety of *The Marriage* extended into the early modern era. The Dutch jurist Hugo Grotius (1583–1645) published a new edition, and the German philosopher Gottfried Wilhelm Leibniz (1646–1716) planned a translation. Nevertheless, by the twentieth century, readers

27. William H. Stahl, "Introduction," in *Martianus Capella and the Seven Liberal Arts*, v. 1, p. 21. Very little is known about Martianus Minneus Felix Capella, however. Some phrases within the nine mythological chapters of *The Marriage* suggest that he was a non-Christian lawyer who lived in north Africa near Carthage, making him a neighbor and contemporary of Augustine.

28. See IX 891 in this selection.

29. *History of the Franks*, bk. X, pts. 18, 31, by Gregory of Tours (538–594), French historian and bishop.

30. Philippe M. Verdier, "L'iconographie des arts libéraux dans l'art du moyen âge jusqu'à la fin du quinzième siècle" in *Arts libéraux et philosophie au Moyen Âge* (Montréal: Institut d'études médiévales, Universitéde Montréal, 1969), pp. 305–54.

often found it arcane if not "insipid."[31] The authors of the modern critical translation and commentary of *The Marriage* observe, "the reader is immediately at a loss to explain how a book so dull and difficult could have been one of the most popular books of Western Europe."[32]

More recently, questions have been raised about the ironical personification of the liberal arts as women, who were often thought to be incapable of studying the arts and excluded from study of them. Martianus's *The Marriage* and the subsequent selections pose graphically the question of how to interpret the female representation of the liberal arts.

SELECTION[33]

I. The Betrothal

[5] [Mercury], then, was moved . . . by the reciprocity of love among the gods; at the same time he saw what was clear to many people—love and marriages being universally celebrated. He too decided to get married. His mother had encouraged him in this inclination when, on his yearly journey through the zodiac, he greeted her in the company of the Pleiades. She was concerned about him, especially because his body, through the exercise of wrestling and constant running, glowed with masculine strength and bore the muscles of a youth perfectly developed. Already with the first beard on his cheeks, he could not continue to go about half naked, clad in nothing but a short cape covering only the top of his shoulders—such a sight caused [Venus] great amusement. With all this in mind he decided to marry.

[6] Because of the importance of the venture, he pondered a great deal on whom he ought to marry. He himself ardently desired Wisdom, because she was prudent and holy, and purer and fairer than the other maidens. However, she was his sister's [Athena] foster sister and seemed to be inseparably devoted to her, and seemed therefore to have espoused virginity herself; he accordingly decided not to marry her, as this would offend [Athena]. In the same way, the splendid beauty of Prophecy inflamed his desires. She was nobly born, being the eldest daughter of Forethought, and her farsighted and penetrating wisdom commended her to him. But at that very time, as it happened, she went of her own accord to young Apollo and, unable to endure her inordinate passion, she became his lover.

[7] He wanted then to ask Psyche, the daughter of Entelechia and Sol, because she was extremely beautiful and the gods had taken great care over her education. . . . [After considering several possible brides, Mercury settles on *Philologia*,[34] who agrees to marry him and to live among the gods.]

II. The Marriage

[99] At length, when she learned the decrees of the gods, Philology, wakeful though the night was now far advanced, pondered long and anxiously with great concern. First she must enter the heavenly assembly, and she must be examined by [Jupiter] without preparation, and she must migrate to the

31. Ernst R. Curtius, *European Literature and the Latin Middle Ages* (1948) tr. W. R. Trask (1953; Princeton, NJ: Princeton University Press, 1990), pp. 37–8.

32. Stahl, "Introduction," v. 1, p. 21.

33. Drawn from the transation of William H. Stahl and Richard Johnson with E. L. Burge, in *Martianus Capella and the Seven Liberal Arts*, 2 vols. (New York: Columbia University Press: 1977), v. 2, pp. 3–7, 34–5, 62–7, 106–11, 155–9, 218–20, 290–2, 314–7, 345–9. Reprinted by permission of Columbia University Press.

34. *Philologia* at this time denoted learning in general, rather than either the meaning implied by the "philologi-cal theses" in the Harvard College curriculum of 1642 in selection #29 or the modern sense of "philology" as the study of the linguistic aspects of written texts.

heavens and to the gods' way of life. [100] Then again, she was to be united to [Mercury], whom admittedly she had always desired with a remarkable passion, but whom she had barely glimpsed while she was picking blooms amongst certain select little herbs[35] and he was running back after being anointed for exercise. What is this? Was she anxiously wondering whether this grand marriage was in her own interest? She had a fear, not without substance, that after she had ascended to the sky, she would forgo altogether the myths and legends of mankind, those charming poetic diversities of the Milesian tales. . . . [Ultimately, Philology decided to marry Mercury.]

[209] Jupiter was now sitting there with Juno and all the gods, on white benches placed on a great dais, waiting for the nuptial party to approach. He heard the voices of the Muses and the sweet strains of varied songs as the maiden drew near, and so he ordered [Mercury] to come forward. [210] [Bacchus] and [Phoebus],[36] [Mercury's] fondest and loyal brothers, and . . . all the divine progeny of [Jupiter] were in attendance on him. [211] The guardians of the elements followed the progress of [Mercury], as did a glorious assembly of angelic beings and the souls of the ancients who attained celestial bliss and had earned temples in heaven.[37] [212] Linus, Homer, and [Vergil] were to be seen there, wearing crowns and chanting their poems; Orpheus and Aristoxenus were playing their lyres; Plato and Archimedes made golden spheres rotate. [213] Heraclitus was afire, Thales was soaked with moisture,[38] and Democritus appeared surrounded with atoms. Pythagoras of Samos was cogitating certain celestial numbers. Aristotle with the utmost care was seeking Entelechia throughout the heights of heaven.[39] Epicurus was carrying roses mixed with violets and all the allurements of pleasure. Zeno was leading a woman who practiced foresight, Arcesilaus was examining the neck of a dove,[40] and a whole crowd of Greeks were singing discordantly; yet, loud as they were, they could not be heard through the harmonious songs of the Muses.

[214] As [Mercury] approached and entered, the whole senate of the gods rose in honor, to his exaltation. Jupiter himself sat him down next to himself, with [Athena] on Mercury's right. [215] After a brief interval, Philology was brought in, surrounded by the Muses, with her mother walking ahead of her. . . . [217] Then her mother arose and asked of [Jupiter] and all the gods that whatever [Mercury] had prepared in the way of a dowry should be handed over in the sight of all, and then that

---

35. According to the Carolingian commentator Remigius of Auxerre (c. 841–908), the meaning of this scene "is that Philology beholds Mercury, or eloquence, while she is engaged in mastering the rudiments of grammar and literary studies; in other words, we discover and attain eloquence only through the study of the basic liberal arts." Translator's note, p. 34n. See Remigius's interpretation of selection #9 by Boethius, noted in the introduction below.

36. Phoebus, meaning "brilliant or "shining" in Greek, was another name for Apollo, Greek god of light, arts, muses, medicine, and prophecy. Martianus employs a euphemism here, and routinely employs "Phoebus" below.

37. Belief that leading intellectuals were gathered together in paradise was common in the fourth century A.D.; the ancient philosophers and scientists are accompanied here by symbols of their doctrines. Translator's note, p. 62n. These points held throughout the Middle Ages. See Verdier, "L'iconographie des arts libéraux," pp. 305–54.

38. Linus, legendary son of the Greek god Apollo and a Muse, is said to have taught music to Hercules or Orpheus; Aristoxenus was a Greek theorist of music of the fourth century B.C. Heraclitus (c. 535–c. 475 B.C.), Greek philosopher from Ephesus, believed that all things were in a continual state of flux because fire was the basic substance of the cosmos. Thales (c. 636–c. 546 B.C.), Ionian philosopher and physicist, maintained that water was the basic substance of the universe.

39. Aristotle made an important distinction between *entelecheia* (fulfillment, completion) and *energeia* (actuality).

40. Arcesilaus (c. 316–c. 241 B.C.) was a Greek philosopher whose views resembled those of the Skeptics.

a gift should be given by the maiden, and after that, let them permit the recital of the [marriage] laws. [218] In reply to this most reasonable plea, the senate of the gods decreed that the offerings should be approved in the full assembly of heaven. Now Phoebus arose, without usurping his brother's duty, and he began to bring forward, one by one, chosen members of [Mercury's] household, women who shone with a beauty in every way equal to their raiment.

III. Grammar

[223] So [Apollo brought] forward from her former place one of the servants of Mercury, an old woman indeed but of great charm, who said that she had been born in [Egypt]⁴¹ when Osiris was still king;⁴² when she had been a long time in hiding, she was found and brought up by [Mercury] himself. This woman claimed that in Attica, where she had lived and prospered for the greater part of her life, she moved about in Greek dress; but because of the Latin gods and the Capitol and the race of Mars and the descendants of Venus, according to the custom of Romulus, she entered the senate of the gods dressed in a Roman cloak. She carried in her hands a polished box, a fine piece of cabinetmaking, which shone on the outside with light ivory, from which like a skilled physician the woman took out the emblems of wounds that need to be healed.

[224] Out of this box she took first a pruning knife with a shining point, with which she said she could prune the faults of pronunciation in children; then they could be restored to health with a certain black powder carried through reeds, a powder which was thought to be made of ash or the ink of cuttlefish. Then she took out a very sharp medicine which she had made of fennelflower and the clippings from a goat's back, a medicine of purest red color, which she said should be applied to the throat when it was suffering from bucolic ignorance and was blowing out the vile breaths of corrupt pronunciation. She showed too a delicious savory, the work of many late nights and vigils, with which she said the harshness of the most unpleasant voice could be made melodious. [225] She also cleaned the windpipes and the lungs by the application of a medicine in which were observed wax smeared on beechwood and a mixture of gallnuts and gum and rolls of [papyrus]. Although this poultice was effective in assisting memory and attention, yet by its nature it kept people awake. [226] She also brought out a file fashioned with great skill, which was divided into eight golden parts joined in different ways,⁴³ and which darted back and forth—with which by gentle rubbing she gradually cleaned dirty teeth and ailments of the tongue and the filth which had been picked up in the town of Sol [solecisms].

[227] She is reckoned to know by the effort of frequent calculations these arcane poems and manifold rhythms. Whenever she accepted pupils, it was her custom to start them with the noun. She mentioned also how many cases could cause faults or could be declined accurately. Then, appealing to her pupils' powers of reasoning, she firmly held the different classes of things and the words for them, so that the pupils would not change one name for another, as often happens with those who need her attention. Then she used to ask them the moods of the verbs and their tenses and the figures, and she ordered others, on whom complete dullness and inert laziness had settled, to run through the steps and to climb upon as many works as possible, treading on the prepositions or conjunctions or participles, and to be exercised to exhaustion with every kind of skill.

---

41. "The old woman is *Grammatikē* (Grammar). Mercury is said to have invented languages for mankind. His Greek name Hermes is taken to be akin to *hermeneutes* (an interpreter); hence, the idea that he 'found and brought up' Grammar. The idea that various disciplines originated in Egypt was common." Translator's note, pp. 64–5n.

42. Osiris, legendary Egyptian king and god of the underworld.

43. The conventional "parts" of speech in ancient manuals.

[228] . . . So she was asked for her name and her profession and an explanation of her whole field of study. [229] As if it was normal for her to explain what had been asked and easy to tell what was wanted of her, she modestly and decently folded back her cloak from her right hand and began: "In Greece I am called *Grammatiké*, because a line is called *grammé* and letters are called *grammata* and it is my province to form the letters in their proper shapes and lines. For this reason Romulus gave me the name *Litteratura*, although when I was a child he had wanted to call me *Litteratio*, just as amongst the Greeks I was at first called *Grammatistiké*; and then Romulus gave me a priest and collected some boys to be my attendants. Nowadays my advocate is called *Litteratus*, who was formerly called *Litterator*. . . . Such a man was called by the Greeks *Grammatodidaskalos*.

[230] My duty in the early stages was to read and write correctly, but now there is the added duty of understanding and criticizing knowledgeably.[44] These two aspects seem to me to be shared with the philosophers and the critics. . . .

IV. Dialectic

[327] Into the assembly of the gods came Dialectic, a woman whose weapons are complex and knotty utterances.[45] Without her, nothing follows, and likewise, nothing stands in opposition. She brought with her the elements of speech; and she had ready the school maxim which reminds us that speech consists in words which are ambiguous, and judges nothing as having a standard meaning unless it be combined with other words. Yet, though Aristotle himself pronounce his twice-five categories and grow pale as he tortures himself in thought; though the sophisms of the Stoics beset and tease the senses, as they wear on their foreheads the horns they never lost;[46] though Chrysippus heap up and consume his own pile, and Carneades match his mental power through use of hellebore,[47] no honor so great as this has ever befallen any of these sons of men, nor is it chance that so great an honor has fallen to your lot; it is your right, Dialectic, to speak in the realms of the gods, and to act as teacher in the presence of [Jupiter].

[328] So at [Phoebus'] summons this woman entered, rather pale but very keen-sighted.[48] Her eyes constantly darted about; her intricate coiffure seemed beautifully curled and bound together, and descending by successive stages,[49] it so encompassed the shape of her whole head that you could not have detected anything lacking, nor grasped anything excessive. She was wearing the dress and cloak of Athens, it is true, but what she carried in her hands was unexpected, and had been unknown in all

---

44. In line with the predominant Ciceronian view of the time, "grammar" includes the study of literature, rather than merely forms and rules of language and syntax.

45. In the original Latin, several chapters begin with a hymn in verse.

46. "This refers to the common, ancient sophism: 'What you have not lost, you have; you have not lost horns from your head, therefore you have horns on your head.'" Translator's note, p. 106n.

47. "Chrysippus was a celebrated, Stoic philosopher [c. 280–c. 207 B.C.] who 'heaped' up a 'pile' of sorites in a book on logic. . . . Carneades, a skeptic philosopher [213–129 B.C.], is said to have used hellebore, a purgative drug, to make his mind keener and more subtle before disputing with Chrysippus." Translator's note, p. 106n.

48. This forbidding image of the liberal art of logic was well known in subsequent centuries. Attavante degli Attavanti (1452–c. 1517), an Italian illustrator and miniaturist, painted a portrait of this liberal art of logic in a manuscript of the *Marriage of Philology and Mercury* written for the King of Bohemia and reposited today in the St. Mark's Library of Venice. The coiled snake was embroidered on an allegorical gown worn by Queen Elizabeth I (1533–1603) in a portrait.

49. "The Latin here, *deducti per quosdam consequentes gradus*, applies equally well to a logical argument 'deduced through certain successive steps' as to Dialectic's symbolic hairstyle." Translator's note, p. 107n.

the Greek schools. In her left hand she held a snake twined in immense coils; in her right hand a set of patterns carefully inscribed on wax tablets, which were adorned with the beauty of contrasting color, was held on the inside by a hidden hook; but since her left hand kept the crafty device of the snake hidden under her cloak, her right hand was offered to one and all. Then if anyone took one of those patterns, he was soon caught on the hook and dragged toward the poisonous coils of the hidden snake, which presently emerged and after first biting the man relentlessly with the venomous points of its sharp teeth then gripped him in its many coils and compelled him to the intended position.[50] If no one wanted to take any of the patterns, Dialectic confronted them with some questions; or secretly stirred the snake to creep up on them until its tight embrace strangled those who were caught and compelled them to accept the will of the interrogator.

[329] Dialectic herself was compact in body, dark in appearance, with thick bushy hair on her limbs, and she kept saying things that the majority could not understand. For she claimed that the universal affirmative was diametrically opposed to the particular negative, but it was possible for them both to be reversed by connecting ambiguous terms to univocal terms;[51] she claimed also that she alone discerned what was true from what was false, as if she spoke with assurance of divine inspiration. [330] She said that she had been brought up on an Egyptian crag and then had migrated to Attica to the school of Parmenides, and there, while the slanderous report was spread abroad that she was devoted to deceitful trickery, she had taken to herself the greatness of Socrates and Plato.

[331] This was the woman, well-versed in every deceptive argument and glorying in her many victories, whom [Mercury's] two-fold serpent, rising on his staff, tried to lick at, constantly darting its tongues, while [Athena's] Gorgon hissed with the joy of recognition. . . . [S]he was the most sharp-witted, and could not be scorned when she uttered her assertions. But [Athena] ordered Dialectic to hand over those items which she had brought to illustrate her sharpness and her deadly sure assertions, and told her to put on an appearance suitable for imparting her skill.

[333] Grammar was standing close by when the introduction was completed; but she was afraid to accept the coils and gaping mouth of the slippery serpent. Together with the enticing patterns and the rules fitted with the hook, they were entrusted to [Athena]. Thus Dialectic stood revealed as a genuine Athenian . . . by the beauty of her hair and especially because she was attended by a crowd in Greek dress, the chosen youth of Greece, who were filled with wonder at the woman's wisdom and intelligence. But, for assessing virtue as well as practicing it, Jupiter considered the levity of the Greeks inferior to the vigor of [the Romans], so he ordered her to unfold her field of knowledge in Latin eloquence. [334] Dialectic did not think she could express herself adequately in Latin;[52] but presently her confidence increased, the movements of her eyes were confined to a slight quivering, and, formidable as she had been even before she uttered a word, she began to speak as follows:

[335] "Unless amid the glories of the Latin tongue the learning and labor of my beloved and famous Varro had come to my aid, I could have been found to be a Greek by the test of Latin speech,

---

50. The metaphor portrays the experience of being induced to adopt some attractive propositions (the patterns), trapped by their hidden implications (the hook), and then slowly and painfully compelled to yield to the logical scrutiny of an interlocutor. The view that the deceptive and malevolent craftiness, represented by the hidden snake, was "unknown in all the Greek schools" reflects a deeply pejorative view of the philosophical schools in late antiquity. Compare the confirming testimony of Cicero in selection #4, Quintilian in selection #6, and Boethius in selection #9.

51. The meaning of this sentence is not clear, according to the translator. Perhaps Martianus is manipulating technical terms in logic to demonstrate the point of his previous sentence.

52. Observe the comparison of Greek and Roman characteristics, which persisted in the liberal arts tradition, as noted by Cicero in selection #4 and by Bathsua Makin in selection #30.

or else completely uncultivated or even quite barbarous. Indeed, after the golden flow of Plato and the brilliance of Aristotle it was [Varro's] labors which first enticed me into Latin speech and made it possible for me to express myself throughout the schools of [Italy]. [336] I shall therefore strive to obey my instructions and, without abandoning the Greek order of discussion, I shall not hesitate to express my propositions in [Latin]. First, I want you to realize that the toga-clad Romans have not been able to coin a name for me, and that I am called Dialectic just as in Athens: and whatever the other Arts propound is entirely under my authority. [337] Not even Grammar herself, whom you have just heard and approved, nor the lady renowned for the richness of her eloquence, nor the one who draws various diagrams on the ground with her rod, can unfold her subject without using my reasoning."[53] . . .

V. Rhetoric

[425] Meantime the trumpets sounded, their strident song pierced the sky and heaven reechoed with an unfamiliar din; the gods were frightened and confused, the host of heaven's minor inhabitants quaked. . . . [426] But while a great group of the earth-gods was disturbed by such thoughts, in strode a woman of the tallest stature and abounding self-confidence, a woman of outstanding beauty; she wore a helmet, and her head was wreathed with royal grandeur; in her hands the arms with which she used either to defend herself or to wound her enemies, shone with the brightness of lightning. The garment under her arms was covered by a robe wound about her shoulders in the Latin fashion; this robe was adorned with the light of all kinds of devices and showed the figures of them all, while she had a belt under her breast adorned with the rarest colors of jewels. [427] When she clashed her weapons on entering, you would say that the broken booming of thunder was rolling forth with the shattering clash of a lightning cloud; indeed it was thought that she could hurl thunderbolts like [Jupiter].[54] For like a queen with power over everything, she could drive any host of people where she wanted and draw them back from where she wanted; she could sway them to tears and whip them to a frenzy; and change the countenance and senses not only of cities but of armies in battle. She was said to have brought under her control, amongst the people of Romulus, the senate, the public platforms, and the law courts, and in Athens had at will swayed the legislative assembly, the schools, and the theaters, and had caused the utmost confusion throughout Greece.

[428] What countenance and voice she had as she spoke, what excellence and exaltation of speech! It was worth even the gods' effort to hear such genius of argument, so rich a wealth of diction, so vast a story of memory and recollection. What order in structure, what harmonious delivery, what movement of gesture, what profundity of concept! She was light in treating small topics, ready with middling topics, and with exalted topics a firebrand.[55] In discussion she made her whole audience attentive, in persuasion amenable, full of conflict in disagreements, full of pride in speeches of praise. But when she had, through the testimony of some public figure, proclaimed some matter of dispute, everything seemed to be in turbulence, confusion, and on fire.[56] This golden-voiced woman, pouring out some of the jewels of crowns and kingdoms, was followed by a mighty army of famous men, amongst whom the two [Demosthenes and Cicero] nearest her outshone the rest. These

---

53. The arts referred to in this sentence are, respectively, grammar, rhetoric, and geometry. The subsequent parts (344–354) draw heavily from the *Introduction* of Porphyry (c. 232–c. 304), broaching the initial epistemological problems of dialectical inquiry raised by Aristotle in his introductory books on logic.

54. Why are military metaphors found throughout the liberal arts tradition?

55. See selection #7 by Augustine (IV xvii 34).

56. "The diction echoes Cicero's translation of Aristophanes's description of Pericles." Translator's note, p. 157n.

two were of different nationalities and styles of dress, one wearing the Greek pallium, the other the Roman trabea. Each spoke a different language, though one professed to have studied Greek culture at Athens and was considered quick in the studies of the Greek schools and in the constant disputes and discussions of the Academy. Both were men from poor families, who rose to fame from humble beginnings. . . . [436] She then, looking at the whole assembly of gods, with some emotion began to speak. . . .

VI. Geometry

[580] Immediately there came into view a distinguished-looking lady, holding a geometer's rod in her right hand and a solid globe in her left. From her left shoulder a [shawl] was draped, on which were visible the magnitudes and orbits of the heavenly bodies, the dimensions, intersections, and outlines of the celestial circles, and even the shadow of the earth, reaching into the sky and giving a dark purplish hue to the golden orbs of the sun and the moon amidst the stars. [581] The [shawl] itself glistened with the sheen of the vernal sky; it was marked with many figures—to serve the purposes of her sister Astronomy as well—numbers of various kinds, gnomons of sundials, figures and designs showing intervals, weights, and measures, depicted in many colors. This tireless traveler was wearing walking shoes, to journey through the world, and she had worn the same shoes to shreds in traversing the entire globe. [582] She entered the senate of the gods. Though she could have told at once how many stadia and fathoms, down to the inch, she had measured in the distance between the earth and the celestial sphere, instead, moved by the majestic appearance of [Jupiter] and the heavenly company, she hastily made her way to the uncovered abacus board, glancing about at the adornment of the outer canopy and the palace studded with constellations. [583] Geometry came to a halt, struck with amazement at the glittering sky. . . .

[586] Geometry finally broke the spell of her rapt admiration of the glittering heavens and turned her eyes to regarding the gods about her, with a reserve becoming a dignified lady who enjoyed the respect of all and was considered mistress of the other arts which are known to the gods. A request was made that she begin disclosing the secrets of her knowledge, from the very beginning. As she brushed aside a lock of hair, her face shone with distinction and majesty. [587] She began drawing diagrams on the powdery surface of her abacus and spoke thus: "I see my Archimedes and the most learned Euclid among the philosophers present. I could call upon them to expound my doctrines to you at length, to ensure that every matter is expertly explained and no veil of obscurity is interposed. However, I deem it more appropriate, on this occasion which calls for rhetorical skill, to disclose these matters to you myself, as best I can, in the Latin tongue, something that rarely happens in this field. Those men, in fact, speak no Latin, and expound what I have taught them only in Greek.

[588] "First, I must explain my name, to counteract any impression of a grimy itinerant coming into this gilded senate chamber of the gods and soiling this gem-bedecked floor with dirt collected on earth. I am called Geometry because I have often traversed and measured out the earth, and I could offer calculations and proofs for its shape, size, position, regions, and dimensions.[57] There is no portion of the earth's surface that I could not describe from memory"[58] . . . .

---

57. Though often unreliable, Isidore of Seville states correctly in selection #11, "geometry has been named from 'earth' and from "]'measure.' For 'earth' is called ge in Greek, and 'measure' is *metron*" (III 10.)

58. Martianus proceeds to interpret geometry less as a mathematical art than as geography, and incorporates material from a popular travelogue rather than an informed account of geography. The interchanging of geography for geometry continues in the liberal arts tradition, as Bathsua Makin implies in selection #30.

VII. Arithmetic[59]

[753] Some numbers are perfect, some are superabundant, and some are deficient; the Greeks call them perfect, overperfect, and underperfect. Perfect numbers are those that are equal to the sum of their parts; superabundant, those that have more in their parts than in themselves; and deficient, those that have less in their parts than in themselves. For example, let us take six. It can be divided into units, two, or three, since six times one, three times two, or two times three makes six; thus its parts are 1, 2, and 3; let these parts be added together and the sum is 6. This number is equal to its parts, and this type of number derives its virtue from that fact; the other types are faulty, because of superabundance or deficiency, as, for example, the number 12. Twelve times one, six times two, four times three, three times four, or two times six makes 12. The parts are 1, 2, 3, 4, and 6, which, when added together, make 16. The number twelve is therefore superabundant. Now take the number 16; it is made of sixteen times one, two times eight, four times four, or eight times two, and these are the only factors of the number. Add the numbers together and you get only 15, less than the number from which they sprang. This number is deficient.

[754] Some numbers are plane, others are solid. The Greeks call a number plane which is the product of two numbers. That is to say, in the reckoning of measures, they consider that as much is contained by the carpenter's square [*norma*] as by the entire rectangle of which the carpenter's square is a part. Thus, those numbers are regarded as plane numbers that are arranged along two sides so that they form a right angle and present the appearance of a carpenter's square. For example, if one side is extended to a length of 4, another side to 3, the product of these two numbers is 12; and they call this a plane number.

According to the Greeks, solidity arises from three numbers. Let one side be four, another three; then four be added above.[60] They say that altitude is filled out by these numbers placed above the underlying carpenter's square, and that twenty-four is represented. There is no point in being obscure in this matter: it is very clear that a plane number comes from single numbers joined together in such a way that one is not above another; and that solidity is produced from numbers placed above other numbers. . . .

VIII. Astronomy[61]

IX. Harmony

[890] But the father of the gods had been advised by [Juno] to hasten the proceedings. Nevertheless, so as not to scrimp the wedding preparations or dispense with the performance of so erudite a lady, pleasant as it would be to speed the marriage, Jupiter refused to be rushed: he asked how many bridesmaids remained to be heard from. [891] [Apollo] suggested that Medicine and Architecture

---

59. This selection from the discourse by Arithmetic about her art lends a sense of the material that Martianus borrowed from standard, elementary textbooks of his day and that constituted the study of the liberal arts in the early middle ages.

60. This literal translation points to Martianus's "limited comprehension of the subject of solid numbers. He conceives of a solid number as a plane number multiplied by 2; or, represented geometrically, as two identical plane surfaces, one superimposed on the other, the altitude being two. . . . The figure that Martianus uses is called a 'brick' by Greek arithmeticians." Translator's note, p. 291n.

61. This chapter was the shortest and most popular book of Martianus's treatise, because the content presented the most informed account of its subject until the recovery of Greek learning in the 1200s. The Polish astronomer Nicholas Copernicus (1473–1543) subsequently credited Martianus for advancing the idea of the heliocentric orbits of the planets. *On the Revolutions of the Celestial Spheres*, bk. X, pt. 10.

were standing by, among those who had been prepared to perform. "But since these ladies are concerned with mortal subjects and their skill lies in mundane matters, and they have nothing in common with the celestial deities, it will not be inappropriate to disdain and reject them.[62] They will keep silent in the heavenly company and will be examined in detail later by [Philologia] herself. But it would be a grave offense to exclude from this company the one bridesmaid who is the particular darling of the heavens, whose performance is sought with joy and acclamation.[63]

[892] "But first of all I would like to inform you that the mother of the maiden has brought along [the seven prophetic arts], endowed with lavish gifts, to be added to the dowry; she has agreed to submit them to that test of knowledge. These young women are of the same number and are equally attractive, and in the impressiveness of their erudition few of the maidens standing by them are on a par with them. They have been instructed in the more mystic and holy secrets of the maiden. With what displeasure or with what delight or weakness on the part of the celestial senate these girls would be passed over, I leave it to you, in the strength and majesty of your judgment, O [Jupiter], to decide. . ."

[897] After [Apollo] had spoken thus, [Jupiter] ordered Harmony to appear, as it was suggested to him, the last of the learned handmaids that remained. . . . [900] It will be both a pleasure and a profit to listen to this maiden, rediscovered after so many generations and restored to the melic arts. But the other learned and reverend sisters, when another day has dawned, will be introduced and given a thorough examination.[64]

9. Boethius, *Consolation of Philosophy* (c. 524)

INTRODUCTION

Ancius Manlius Severinus Boethius (c. 480–525) was born into a prominent, wealthy family in Italy. Upon the death of his father, another patrician family adopted the boy and gave him the finest education available. Extraordinarily precocious, Boethius's accomplishments attracted the attention of influential individuals, including his kinsman Cassiodorus and Theodoric, king of the Ostrogoths. Having conquered Italy in about 490, Theodoric exercised autocratic control over his kingdom, but recognized the titular sovereignty of the Roman emperor who ruled the eastern half of the empire from Constantinople. This policy perpetuated the fiction of a single unified Empire, as well as governance through the longstanding Roman bureaucracy, replete with the traditional offices. Boethius rose rapidly through the administrative ranks and became Master of the King's Offices, assuming responsibility for the entire public bureaucracy as well as the palace officials.

Apart from his administrative career, Boethius made outstanding achievements as a scholar and became the most authoritative source of secular scholarship throughout the middle ages. In particular, he took upon himself the breathtaking task of translating, interpreting, and reconciling the works of Aristotle and Plato. Boethius died before proceeding very far on this immense project and finished translating only the first two of Aristotle's six treatises on logic, out of Aristotle's entire corpus. Yet,

---

62. This is the exclusion of medicine and architecture that Marcus Terentius Varro had included among the arts to be studied, as discussed in the introduction to Martianus.

63. Each planet was said to emit a particular note as it orbited the earth, and together they made a harmony.

64. "Melic" derives from the Greek *melos*, meaning poetry or song. The "reverend sisters" refers to the seven prophetic arts, whom Jupiter passes over.

those two introductory treatises became the sum total of Aristotle's works available to Western Europe until the middle of the twelfth century, and they remained the standard authority on logic until the other four of Aristotle's treatises, setting forth the deductive syllogism, reappeared in the final third of the twelfth century.[65]

Boethius also wrote or translated influential works on arithmetic, geometry, music, and possibly astronomy. In the introduction to his *Arithmetic*, he maintained that mathematics is the study of "abstract quantity" and coined the term *quadrivium* to describe the four mathematical arts serving as the "four roads" to philosophy.[66] In addition to producing the authoritative works on logic and mathematics for the next 700 years, Boethius wrote several influential treatises on theology, applying logical analysis to complex theological problems in order to demonstrate the truth of orthodoxy.

These scholarly accomplishments, no less than his successful career, inspired jealousy among others, and in about 423 he was charged with treason. The charge was apparently fabricated, but Boethius's integrity and personal devotion to Roman culture, combined with Theodoric's perception of a growing threat to his power from the eastern Roman Empire, may have led the aging autocrat to credit the charge against Boethius. During his imprisonment, Boethius wrote the work for which he is chiefly known today: *Consolation of Philosophy*. This is a "satire" in the same sense as *The Marriage* of Martianus Capella; it offers a "stew" of literary forms including prose, poetry, and dialogue.[67] In form, *The Marriage* is the most direct antecedent to the *Consolation*, although Martianus and Boethius are far apart intellectually. Boethius weaves Platonic and Aristotelian motifs and metaphors throughout his work in an attempt to show that love of wisdom, represented by lady Philosophy, leads human beings to discover and enjoy the supreme good, notwithstanding severe tribulations of life.

The *Consolation* did not receive a great deal of attention until the ninth century, when the first of many commentaries appeared. One of the early influential commentators, Remigius of Auxerre (c. 841–908), interpreted the feminine figure of Philosophy to represent education in the seven liberal arts, leading the student toward divine revelation. Though doubtful, this interpretations is not inappropriate for an author who contributed so much to the form and content of the medieval liberal arts and became the most authoritative source of secular scholarship in the middle ages. The tone of "nostalgic sadness"[68] conveyed by the *Consolation* is also appropriate, because Boethius was sentenced without a trial, cruelly tortured, and executed at about age forty-five.

---

65. These two introductory treatises of Aristotle's logic were often accompanied in the middle ages by an *Introduction*, written by Porphyry and translated by Boethius, broaching the epistemological problems of dialectical inquiry raised by Aristotle.

66. Boethius, *Arithmetic* I 1. Boethius's *Arithmetic* is a translation of the *Introduction to Arithmetic* by Nicomachus of Gerasa, and *quadrivium* (actually Boethius's term is *quadruvium*) is a translation of the Greek *tessares methodoi* (four ways to pursue study).

67. In Latin, *Satura*. "The Latin term means a dish of mixed ingredients, a stew; it became the name of a literary form invented by early Latin writers—a mixture of prose and verse on a miscellany of topics. This is the genre satire; one type of satire became purely verse (e.g., the satires of Horace, Persius, Juvenal); the other, Menippean satire, retained the mixture of prose and verse—this is what Martianus is writing. The caustic tone which is implied in the modern word 'satire' was not essential to the ancient genre, but was present in the writing of Lucilius and Juvenal, and from the latter was taken over into European satirical writing." William H. Stahl and Richard Johnson, *Martianus Capella and the Seven Liberal Arts*, 2 vols. (New York: Columbia University Press, 1977), v. 2, p. 4n.

68. Henry Chadwick, *Boethius: The Consolations of Music, Logic, Theology, and Philosophy* (Oxford: Clarendon Press, 1981), p. 128.

SELECTION[69]

Meter 1

Verses I made once glowing with content;
Tearful, alas, sad songs must I begin.
See how the Muses grieftorn bid me write,
And with unfeigned tears these elegies drench my face.
But them at least my fear that friends might tread my path
Companions still
Could not keep silent: they were once
My green youth's glory; now in my sad old age
They comfort me.
For age has come unlooked for, hastened by ills,
And anguish sternly adds its years to mine;
My head is white before its time, my skin hangs loose
About my tremulous frame; I am worn out.
Death, if he come
Not in the years of sweetness
But often called to those who want to end their misery
Is welcome. My cries he does not hear;
Cruel he will not close my weeping eyes.
While fortune favored me—
How wrong to count on swiftly-fading joys—
Such an hour of bitterness might have bowed my head.
Now that her clouded, cheating face is changed
My cursed life drags on its long, unwanted days.
Ah why, my friends,
Why did you boast so often of my happiness?
How faltering even then the step
Of one now fallen.

Prose 1[70]

While I was thinking these thoughts to myself in silence, and set my pen to record this tearful complaint, there seemed to stand above my head a woman. Her look filled me with awe; her burning eyes penetrated more deeply than those of ordinary men; her complexion was fresh with an ever-lively bloom, yet she seemed so ancient that none would think her of our time. It was difficult to say how tall she might be, for at one time she seemed to confine herself to the ordinary measure of man, and at another the crown of her head touched the heavens; and when she lifted her head higher yet, she penetrated the heavens themselves, and was lost to the sight of men.[71] Her dress was made of very fine,

---

69. Boethius, *Consolation of Philosophy*, tr. S. J. Tester in *Boethius, "Tractates," "De Consolatione Philosophiae,"* new edition (Cambridge. MA: Harvard University Press, 1973), bk. I, pp. 131–45. Reprinted by permission of the President and Fellows of Harvard College and the Trustees of the Loeb Classical Library. The *Consolation of Philosophy* has frequently been translated; this version has been selected for its preservation of the literary qualities of the original.

70. See in selection #28 Queen Elizabeth's translation of the opening lines of the following paragraph.

71. Boethius is sometimes considered the first scholastic philosopher due, in part, to the implication here and throughout the *Consolation* that philosophy leads to divine wisdom, or theology.

imperishable thread, of delicate workmanship: she herself wove it, as I learned later, for she told me.[72] Its form was shrouded by a kind of darkness of forgotten years, like a smoke-blackened family statue in the atrium. On its lower border was woven the Greek letter pi and on the upper theta, and between the two letters, steps were marked like a ladder, by which one might climb from the lower letter to the higher.[73] But violent hands had ripped this dress and torn away what bits they could.[74] In her right hand she carried a book, and in her left, a scepter.

Now when she saw the Muses of poetry standing by my bed, helping me to find words for my grief, she was disturbed for a moment, and then cried out with fiercely blazing eyes: "Who let these theatrical tarts in with this sick man?[75] Not only have they no cures for his pain, but with their sweet poison they make it worse. These are they who choke the rich harvest of the fruits of reason with the barren thorns of passion. They accustom a man's mind to his ills, not rid him of them. If your entice- ments were distracting merely an unlettered man, as they usually do, I should not take it so serious- ly—after all, it would do no harm to us in our task—but to distract this man, reared on a diet of Elea- tic and Academic thought![76] Get out, you Sirens, beguiling men straight to their destruction! Leave him to *my* Muses to care for and restore to health." Thus upbraided, that company of the Muses dejec- tedly hung their heads, confessing their shame by their blushes, and dismally left my room.[77] I myself, since my sight was so dimmed with tears that I could not clearly see who this woman was of such commanding authority, was struck dumb, my eyes cast down; and I went on waiting in silence to see what she would do next. Then she came closer and sat on the end of my bed, and seeing my face worn with weeping and cast down with sorrow, she bewailed my mind's confusion bitterly in these verses:[78]

Meter 2

Ah! How steep the seas that drown him!
His mind, all dulled, its own light fled,
Moves into outer dark, while noxious care

---

72. How might the metaphorical appearance of Philosophy—her age, her dimensions, the fabric of her dress, and other aspects—be interpreted? Boethius's image of Philosophy appears in the iconography of medieval cathe- drals throughout Europe.

73. The markings on the dress likely represent Aristotle's division of philosophy into practical philosophy, be- ginning with the Greek letter Pi, and theoretical philosophy, beginning with the Greek letter Theta. The Carolin- gian commentator Remigius of Auxerre (c. 841–908) interpreted these markings to represent the ascent from secular knowledge (pi) to divine knowledge (theta) via the steps of the seven liberal arts. This interpretation ap- pears in later iconography.

74. A reference to the sectarianism of the philosophical schools in late antiquity, during which time "true" phi- losophy was forgotten, as Boethius asserts above. See the similar, extended image in Prose 3 below.

75. Boethius may be drawing this scene from the opening chapters of *Proverbs* in which the female figure of "Wisdom" is represented as a woman shooing away harlots. Or Boethius may be recalling Plato, *Crito* 44a–b, in which Socrates, awaiting death in prison, dreams that a beautiful woman, clothed in white, came and called to him.

76. The Eleatics constituted a school of philosophy founded some time after 540 B.C. and most famously represented by Parmenides and his student Zeno of Elea. The Academics were the successors of Plato in the Academy at Athens.

77. How can this dismissal of the Muses of poetry be reconciled with Boethius's own use of poetry?

78. Boethius's purposes and technique of interweaving prose and poetry have stimulated a great deal of specula- tive commentary. Is Boethius following the example of Socrates, who, while waiting to be executed, reports that he was visited by his Muse who told him to write poetry, which he did? (Plato, *Phaedo* 60e–61b.)

Swollen by earthbound winds
Grows beyond measure.
    This man
Used once to wander free under open skies
The paths of the heavens;[79] used to gaze
On rosy sunlight, and on the constellations
Of the cold new moon,
And on each star that on its wandering ways
Turns through its changing circles—all such things
He mastered and bound by number and law.
Causes, moreover, he sought and knew:[80]
Why the winds howl and stir up the waves of the sea,
What breath turns the fixed stars' sphere,
Why the sun rises in the red east
And sinks beneath the Western waves,
What warms the spring's calm hours
So that the earth is lovely with flowers of roses,
And who makes fruitful autumn heavy, as the year fills,
With the full grapes, He sought and told
All Nature's secret causes.
But now he lies
His mind's light languishing,
Bowed with these heavy chains about his neck,
His eyes cast down beneath the weight of care,
Seeing nothing
But the dull, solid earth.

Prose 2

"But," she said, "now is the time for cure rather than complaint."[81] Then, gazing keenly and directly on me, she said: "Are you the same man who was once nourished with my milk, once fed on my diet, till you reached your full manhood? And did I not furnish you with such weapons as would now keep you steadfast and safe if you had not thrown them away? Do you recognize me? Why do you say nothing? Were you silent because you were ashamed or stupefied? I should like to think that you were ashamed, but I can see that you are quite stupefied. Seeing that I was not merely silent, but altogether speechless and dumb, she gently laid her hand on my breast and said: "He is in no real danger, but suffers only from lethargy, a sickness common to deluded minds. He has for a little forgotten his real self. He will soon recover—he did, after all, know me before—and to make this possible for him, let me for a little clear his eyes of the mist of mortal affairs that clouds them."[82] And so saying she gathered her dress into a fold and dried my eyes, flowing as they were with tears.

---

79. Following his curiosity, perhaps? Is this an image of free inquiry?

80. "Bound by number and law" is likely a reference to Platonic philosophy; "causes" to Aristotelian. Note that Boethius had written treatises on both mathematics and logic.

81. Compare the purpose and tone of the prose sections with those of the poetic sections.

82. The images of "forgotten his real self" and trying to see clearly are, again, Platonic metaphors.

Meter 3

Then was the night dispersed, and darkness left me;
My eyes grew strong again.
Just as when north-west winds pile up the weather
And rain-clouds fill the sky and the sun is hidden,
And before the stars come out
Night comes flooding down upon the world;
And then the north wind from the Thracian cavern
Sweeps away night and lets the daylight out
So that the sparkling sunlight
Suddenly flashes on our wondering eyes.[83]

Prose 3

Just so the clouds of misery were dispelled, and I drank in the clear light, recovering enough to recognize my healer's face. So, when I looked on her clearly and steadily, I saw the nurse who brought me up, whose house I had from my youth frequented, the lady Philosophy.[84] And I said: "Why have you come, Queen of all the virtues, why have you come down from your high seat in heaven to these wastes where I am banished? So that you too stand in the dock with me, falsely accused?"

"Should I desert you, my pupil?" she replied; "Should I not share your labor and help to bear your burden, which you bear because my name is hated? It could not be right that Philosophy should leave an innocent man companionless on the road. Surely I should then be afraid that I should be charged myself; I should shudder with horror at such an unheard-of thing! Do you think that this is the first time that Wisdom has been attacked and endangered by a wicked society? Did I not often of old also, before my Plato's time, have to battle in mighty struggle with arrogant stupidity? And in his day, was I not beside his teacher Socrates when he won the prize of a martyr's death? And after him the crowd of Epicureans and Stoics and the rest strove as far as they could to seize his legacy, carrying me off protesting and struggling, as if I were part of the booty, tearing my dress, which I wove with my own hands, and then went off with their torn-off shreds, thinking they possessed all of me. And because they seemed to be wearing certain bits of my dress, some were ignorantly accepted as my servants, and were abused by the delusions of the uneducated mob.[85]

But even if you knew nothing of Anaxagoras's flight from Athens, or Socrates's draught of hemlock, or Zeno's sufferings, all these being foreign events, surely you could have thought of Canius and Seneca and Soranus whose stories are neither ancient nor obscure?[86] The only cause of their deaths was that they were brought up in my ways, so that their behavior and pursuits were seen to be utterly different from those of wicked men. So it is no wonder if we are buffeted by storms blustering round

---

83. Perhaps a metaphorical description of intuitive insight.

84. In the ninth and tenth centuries, Boethius' figure of Philosophy becomes interpreted as Divine Wisdom or Christian truth.

85. This image comports with Cicero's complaint against the sectarianism of philosophy in his day and the image of the liberal art of logic portrayed by Martianus Capella.

86. Anaxagoras (c. 500–428 B.C.), Greek philosopher and scientist and teacher of Socrates, fled from Athens for fear of persecution in about 450 B.C. "Zeno of Elea is said to have died helping to rid his native city of a tyrant in the second half of the fifth century B.C.; Socrates was condemned to death in Athens in 399 B.C.; Canius, or better, Canus, Seneca [the Younger] and Soranus are quoted as types of the 'Stoic opposition' to the emperors; Canus died under Caligula in about A.D. 40, Seneca and Soranus under Nero in 65 and 66." Translator's note, pp. 142–3n.

us on the sea of this life, since we are especially bound to anger the wicked. Though their forces are large, yet we should hold them in contempt, for they are leaderless and are simply carried hither and thither at random in their crazed ignorance. If ever they range against us and press about us too strongly, Wisdom our captain withdraws her forces into her citadel, while our enemies busy themselves ransacking useless baggage. But we are safe from all their mad tumult and from our heights we can laugh at them as they carry off all those worthless things; we are protected by such a wall as may not be scaled by raging stupidity."

Christian Appropriation of the Codification

10. Cassiodorus, *Introduction to Divine and Human Letters* (c. 562)

INTRODUCTION

Senator Flavius Magnus Aurelius Cassiodorus (c. 485–c. 585) was born into a leading family of southern Italy[87] and rose through the civil service to succeed Boethius in 525 as Master of the King's Offices under the Ostrogoth King Theodoric and his successor, Athalaric (d. 534). While honing his skill in writing official papers and correspondence in formal, diplomatic Latin for these offices, Cassiodorus gradually turned his attention to religion and scholarship. In 554, before falling victim to the religious and political intrigue that brought down Boethius, Cassiodorus retired to his estate in southern Italy and founded two monasteries: one, an austere hermitage; the other, located on his estate and called Vivarium, in which monks devoted their time to copying, and thus preserving, manuscripts. In this way Cassiodorus inaugurated the tradition of literary monasticism, a Christian application of the Aristotelian idea, invoked by Augustine, that liberal education presupposes "leisure which is the privilege of old age or some fortunate circumstances."[88]

Cassiodorus's most important writing during retirement was entitled *Introduction to Divine and Human Letters*, which comprises two books. The first is devoted to the study of Christian writings, including those by the Church Fathers, in which Cassiodorus, while quoting Augustine's *On Christian Learning*, endorses the belief expressed by Ambrose and Augustine that pagan learning and, particularly, the liberal arts had Egyptian, Hebraic, and thus Christian origins.[89] The second book is presented as an extended footnote, summarizing the content and most important sources of the seven liberal arts and discussing their importance for an informed interpretation of sacred literature. Apparently intended as an encyclopedic primer and bibliographical guide for monks who lacked the elements of a classical education, this second book served as one of the most widely used textbooks of the liberal arts in schools throughout Western Europe during the middle ages.

Selection #10 from the second volume of *Divine and Human Letters* provides material from the Christianized account of the liberal arts that Cassiodorus compiled largely from the works of Boethius, Martianus Capella, and a few other secondary sources that were still available to him, even as the turmoil in Western Europe made these sources increasingly inaccessible. In subsequent centuries this second volume of Cassiodorus's work became a prominent Christian source from which

---

87. Scholars now believe "Senator" to be part of Cassiodorus's name and not to signify a position held.

88. Augustine, *On the Order of Things* II xvi 44. Compare Aristotle's selection #3.

89. Cassiodorus, *Introduction to Divine and Human Letters* I xxviii 1–4.

students in monastic, parish, and cathedral schools drew their understanding of the liberal arts. *Divine and Human Letters* thus became a textbook, whose distribution of material among the seven liberal arts in the standard Latin edition is: grammar, 4 pages; rhetoric, 12 pages; dialectic, 22 pages; arithmetic, 11 pages; music, 9 pages; geometry, 3 pages; and astronomy, 5 pages.[90]

Cassiodorus himself long enjoyed "leisure which is the privilege of old age or some fortunate circumstances," and died at the age of nearly 100 on his estate.

SELECTION[91]

Book II
Preface

[1] The preceding book, completed with the aid of the Lord, contains, as you have seen, the principles of instruction for divine readings. It is comprised of thirty-three chapters, a number acknowledged to correspond with the age of the Lord when he offered eternal life to a world laid low by sin and granted rewards without end to those who believed. It is now the time for us to present in seven additional chapters the text of the second book, on secular readings; this number, continuously repeated throughout the weeks as they succeed one another, is ever being extended to the very end of the world.

[2] One surely ought to know that the Sacred Scripture frequently expresses by means of this number whatever it desires to be understood as continuous and perpetual, as David, for example, says, "Seven times a day I have given praise to thee," [*Psalms* 119: 164] though he elsewhere vows, "I will bless the Lord at all times; his praise shall be always in my mouth," [*Psalms* 34: 1] and Solomon says, "Wisdom hath built herself a house, she hath hewn her out of seven pillars." [*Proverbs* 9: 1] In Exodus as well the Lord said to Moses, "Thou shalt make seven lamps, and shalt set them to give light over against it." [*Exodus* 25: 37] Revelation constantly mentions this number in various applications. And this number leads us to that eternity which can have no end; with justice, then, is it always used whenever perpetuity is indicated.

[3] Thus, the science of arithmetic is endowed with great praise, since God the Creator has arranged his dispensations by the use of number, weight, and measure; as Solomon says, "Thou hast ordered all things in measure, and number, and weight." [*Wisdom of Solomon* 11: 21] Thus God's creation is known to have been ordered in number, since our Lord says in the Gospel, "But the very hairs of your head are numbered." [*Matthew* 10: 30] And likewise God's creation has been ordered in measure, as our Lord bears witness in the Gospel: "and which of you by taking thought can add to his stature by one cubit?" [*Matthew* 6: 27] And likewise the prophet Isaiah says, "Who doth measure heaven with the span and hold the earth confined in his hand?" [*Isaiah* 40: 12] Again, God's creation is acknowledged to have been ordered in weight, as it is written in the Proverbs of Solomon, "And he poised the fountains of waters," and a little farther on, "When he balanced the foundations of the earth, I was with him." [*Proverbs* 8: 28, 29–30] For this reason God's extraordinary and magnificent works are necessarily confined to definite limits, so that just as we know that he has created all things we may in some measure learn to know the manner of their creation. And hence it is to be understood that the evil works of the devil are not ordered by weight or measure or number, since, whatever iniquity does, it is always opposed to justice, as the thirteenth psalm declares, saying, "Contrition and

90. Cassiodorus, *Institutiones*, ed. R. A. Mynors (Oxford: Clarendon, 1937), bk. 2.

91. Cassiodorus, *Introduction to Divine and Human Letters*, tr. Leslie W. Jones (New York: Columbia University Press, 1946), pp. 142–9, 180–1, 196–9. Reprinted by permission of Columbia University Press.

unhappiness in their ways: and the way of peace they have not known."[92] Isaiah also says, "They have abandoned the Lord of hosts and have walked along crooked paths." [*Isaiah* 59: 8] God is really wonderful and extremely wise in having distinguished every one of his creatures by a unique dispensation lest unseemly confusion take hold of some of them; Father Augustine has discussed this topic in most minute manner in the fourth book of his work *On Genesis Considered Word for Word.*

[4] Let us now enter upon the beginning of the second volume, and let us attend with some care, for it is crowded with etymologies and full of a discussion of definitions. In this book we must speak first of the art of grammar, which is manifestly the source and foundation of liberal letters. The word "book" (*liber*) comes from the word "free" (*líber*);[93] a book, in other words, is the bark of a tree, removed and freed—the bark on which the ancients used to write oracular responses before the invention of papyrus. In view of this, therefore, we are permitted to make short books or extended ones, since we are allowed to limit the size of books in accordance with their nature, just as the bark encloses both tiny shoots and vast trees. We ought, moreover, as [Marcus Terentius] Varro says, to understand that the elements of all arts came into existence because of some usefulness.

"Art" is so called because it limits (*artet*) and binds us with its rules; according to others this word is taken over from the Greek expression *apo tés aretés*, which means "from excellence," the term applied by well-spoken men to skill in every manner. Second, we must speak of the art of rhetoric, which is deemed very necessary and honorable because of the splendor and fullness of its eloquence, especially in civil questions. Third, we must speak of logic, which is called dialectic; according to the statements of secular teachers, this study separates the true from the false by means of very subtle and concise reasoning. Fourth, we must speak of mathematics, which embraces four sciences, [namely], arithmetic, geometry, music, and astronomy. In Latin we may call mathematics the theoretical study; though we might apply this term to all studies which teach one to speculate on abstract principles, nevertheless, by reason of its excellence this study has claimed the common word strictly for itself, just as when "the Poet" is mentioned, Homer is understood in Greek writers, and Vergil in Latin writers, and when one refers to "the Orator," Demosthenes is indicated in Greek writers and Cicero in Latin writers, although many poets and orators are shown to have used both languages. Mathematics is the science which considers abstract quantity; abstract quantity is that which we separate from matter or from other accidents by our intellect and treat by reasoning alone.[94]

[5] By stating the contents of the entire book in advance I have, as it were, given bail to secure the performance of my promise. Let us now, with the Lord's aid, give an account of the individual topics, as they have been promised, by means of their divisions and definitions, since learning is in a certain sense twofold in character, inasmuch as a clear description first carefully permeates the sense of sight and then, after having prepared the ears, penetrates the hearing. And, moreover, we shall not fail to reveal the authors, both Greek and Latin, whose explanations of the matters which we discuss have become famous, in order that those who desire to read zealously may more lucidly understand the words of the ancients after having first been introduced to them in abridged form.

i. On Grammar

[1] Grammar gets its name from the letters of the alphabet, as the derived character of the word itself shows.[95] Sixteen of these letters are said to have been invented by Cadmus, who handed them down to

---

92. *Psalms* 13: 3. "Not included in the Authorized Version." Translator's note, p. 143n.

93. Many of Cassiodorus's etymologies were borrowed by Isidore; and most, including this one, are incorrect.

94. These lines come from Boethius's *Arithmetic* I 1, as mentioned above.

95. See selection #8 by Martianus Capella (III 229).

the studious Greeks, who in turn supplied the rest by their liveliness of mind. On the positions and worth of the letters Helenus has written a subtle treatise in Greek and Priscian another in Latin.[96] Grammar is skill in the art of cultivated speech—skill acquired from famous writers of poetry and of prose; its function is the creation of faultless prose and verse; its end is to please through skill in finished speech and blameless writing. But although such authors of earlier times as Palaemon, Phocas, Probus, and Censorinus have written on the art of grammar with variety of method and have been highly esteemed in their own day,[97] nevertheless, for the good of all we intend to quote from Donatus, who is considered to be especially appropriate for boys and suitable for novices; we have left you his twofold treatise in order that a twofold explanation may make even clearer him who is already clear.[98] We have also discovered that St. Augustine has written a short course of instruction on the same topic for the simple brothers; and we have left you this work to read, lest anything seem to be lacking to the inexperienced who are being made ready for high achievement in this great study.

[2] In the second part of his work Donatus discusses the following topics: the spoken word, the letter, the syllable, feet, accentuation, punctuation and proper phrasing, the eight parts of speech (for the second time), figures of speech, etymologies, and orthography. . . .

[3] Let these words, which concern brief definitions alone, suffice. But let him who desires wider and fuller knowledge of these matters read both preface and body of the codex which I have had written on the art of grammar, in order that the careful reader may find the facts which he knows are considered to belong to the subject.[99] Let us now come to the divisions and definitions of the art of rhetoric; as its extensiveness and richness deserve, it has been amply treated by many illustrious writers.

ii. On Rhetoric

[1] Rhetoric is said to be derived *apo tou rhetoreuein*, ("from speaking in public") that is, from skill in making a set speech. The art of rhetoric, moreover, according to the teaching of professors of secular letters, is expertness in discourse on civil questions. The orator, then, is a good man skilled, as has just been said, in discoursing on civil questions.[100] The function of an orator is speaking suitably in order to persuade; his purpose is to persuade, by speaking on civil questions, to the extent permitted by the nature of things and persons. Let us now, therefore, take up a few matters briefly in order that we may understand the main points of almost the entire art and the excellence of the art from a description of several of its parts. According to Fortunatianus, a modern writer on rhetoric, civil

---

96. Cadmus was the legendary Greek founder of Thebes. The identity of Helenus is obscure.

97. The Latin grammarian Palaemon published his *Grammatical Art*, probably at Rome between A.D. 67 and 77. Phocas published his *Art of Names and Words* at Rome in the fifth century A.D. Probus was the foremost grammarian of the first century A.D., who flourished at Rome between A.D. 56 and 88. Translator's note, p. 146n. Censorinus was a Latin grammarian of the third century A.D.

98. Aelius Donatus, Roman grammarian of the mid-fourth century A.D., wrote a standard textbook in grammar, divided into the *Lesser Art* or *First Art* (addressing the eight parts of speech) for novices and the *Greater Art* or *Second Art* for more advanced students.

99. This reference supports the view in the introduction that Cassiodorus intended his work not as a textbook or encyclopedia, but as a kind of annotated bibliography.

100. Attributed to Cato the Elder, the standard, epigrammatic definition of the Ciceronian orator ("a good man, skilled in speaking") was quoted by Quintilian (*Education of the Orator* XII i 1), by Cassiodorus (II ii 1) in selection #10, and by Isidore (II 3) in selection #11, and is mentioned by Francesco Petrarca in selection #24.

questions are questions "which can fall within the range of common understanding, that is, questions which everyone can comprehend, since they concern what is fair and good."[101]

[2] Rhetoric has five parts: invention, arrangement, proper expression, memorization, delivery.[102] *Invention* is the devising of arguments which are true or which resemble true arguments to make a case appear credible. *Arrangement* is the excellent distribution in regular order of the arguments devised. *Proper expression* is the adaptation of suitable words to the arguments. *Memorization* is a lasting comprehension by the mind of the arguments and the language. *Delivery* is the harmonious adjustment of voice and gesture in keeping with the dignity of the arguments and the language. . . .

iv. On Arithmetic

[1] Writers of secular letters have meant to convey the idea that arithmetic is the first among the mathematical sciences, inasmuch as music and geometry and astronomy, which follow it, require it for explanation of their own potentialities. Music, for example, requires it because music deals, among other things, with the relationship between a simple number and its double; geometry, likewise requires it, because geometry deals with the triangle, the quadrangle, and the like; astronomy too requires it, because astronomy deals with the reckoning of the changing positions of the heavenly bodies; arithmetic, however, depends for its existence neither upon geometry nor upon astronomy. On that account arithmetic is recognized as being the origin and source of the others, and Pythagoras is known to have praised this science to such a degree as to state that all things were created by God on the basis of number and measure, saying that some things were fashioned in motion, and other things at rest, but that all things were fashioned in such a way that nothing had any substance beyond the substratum mentioned above; I believe that this explanation is correct, and I derive my belief in the origin of things, as many philosophers have done, from that prophetic statement which says that God ordered all things *in measure, and number, and weight.* [*Wisdom of Solomon* 11: 21]

[2] The present study, therefore, consists of separate quantity, which produces varieties of number that do not possess a common boundary. For 5 is not united to 10 by any common boundary; nor is 6 thus united to 4; nor 7 to 3. Our study is called arithmetic because it has numbers as its special province. Now a number is a quantity made up of units: for example, 3, 5, 10, 20, and so forth. The purpose of arithmetic is to teach us the nature of abstract number and its accidents; for example, evenness, oddness, and so forth. . . .[103]

v. On Music

[10] Most pleasant and useful, then, is the branch of learning which leads our understanding to heavenly things and soothes our ears with sweet harmony. Among Greek writers Alypius, Euclid, Ptolemy, and others have instructed us in it with excellent elementary treatises; among Latin writers Albinus, a man of distinction, has written a compendious work on this subject, which we recall having had in the library at Rome and having read carefully. If perchance this work has been destroyed by the barbarian assault, you still have Gaudentius; and if you read him punctiliously, he will open the entrance halls of this science to you. Apuleius of Madaura is also said to have written an elementary

101. This is quoted from the Latin rhetorician Fortunatianus, *Three Books on the Art of Rhetoric* I 1, written in the last half of the fourth century A.D. and modeled upon Quintilian's *Education of the Orator* with illustrations drawn from Cicero's works. Translator's note.

102. This is the classical five-fold division, and Cassiodorus draws the following account largely from Cicero, *On Discovery* I 9.

103. The following three paragraphs are derived directly from Boethius's *Arithmetic.*

treatise on this subject in Latin.[104] Father Augustine too has written a work in six books entitled *On Music*, in which he has pointed out that the human voice can by reason of its nature utter rhythmical sounds and melodious harmony in long and short syllables.[105] Censorinus too has discussed accents, which are most necessary to our voice, in subtle fashion, and he states that they have to do with musical science; I have left you a copy of his work among others. . . .

vi. On Geometry

[1] Geometry is rendered into Latin as the measuring of the earth, because, according to some, Egypt was at first divided among its own lords by means of the various forms of this science; and those who taught it used to be called measurers. But Varro, the greatest of Latin writers in practical knowledge, explains the origin of the name as follows: at first, when the existing boundaries were unsettled and conflicting, measuring of the earth brought the people the benefits of tranquility; thereafter, the circle of the entire year was divided by the number of the months and consequently the months themselves, so called because they measure the year, were established. But after these things were discovered, learned men, incited to learn about intangible objects, began to seek the distance between the moon and the earth, and between the sun itself and the moon, and the distance to the very top of the sky; he relates that the most skillful geometers arrived at these facts. He then gives an excellent account of the measuring of the entire earth; and it was for this reason that this science happened to be called geometry, a name which it has guarded for many generations. And consequently Censorinus has carefully described the size of the circumferences of heaven and earth in stades in the book which he has written and dedicated to Quintus Cerellius; and if anyone desires to examine this book, he will not read long before learning many secrets of the philosophers.[106]

[2] Geometry is the science of immovable magnitude and of figures. Geometry has the following divisions: plane figures, numerable magnitude, rational and irrational magnitude, and solid figures. *Plane figures* are those which possess length and breadth. A *numerable magnitude* is one which can be [expressed in numbers.] *Rational and irrational magnitudes* are, respectively, commensurable and incommensurable. *Solid figures* are those which possess length, breadth, and thickness.

[3] The science of geometry is treated in its entirety in these parts and divisions, and the multiplicity of the figures which exists in earthly and heavenly objects is comprehended in the above description. Among the Greeks Euclid, Apollonius, Archimedes,[107] and other excellent writers have been conspicuous for their books on this science; the work of one of these men, Euclid, has been translated into Latin by the previously mentioned Boethius, a man of distinction. If this work be read carefully, the matter which has been set forth in the divisions mentioned above will be distinctly and clearly understood. . . .

---

104. Alypius, was a Greek writer on music, probably from the third century A.D.; Albinus, Latin writer on music from the fourth century A.D.; Gaudentius, Greek writer on music from the first three centuries A.D. The translator notes: "The elementary treatise on music which bears the name of Euclid is really the work of a pupil of Aristoxenus [Greek theorist of music from the fourth century B.C.]. [Ptolemy], the Alexandrian geographer and astronomer of the second century A.D., wrote a theoretical work on harmony." (translator's note, p. 196n.) Lucius Apuleius, Latin author of the second century A.D., wrote the only Latin novel to survive to modern time.

105. Augustine wrote *On Music* as one of a series of treatises addressing each of the seven liberal arts. But the series was not completed and several of the treatises have been lost.

106. Censorinus was a Latin grammarian of the third century A.D. A "stade" measured about 200 yards. On Varro, see the introduction to selection #8 by Martianus Capella.

107. This Apollonius is likely Apollonius of Perga (c. 262–c. 190 B.C.), who was an important Greek geometer, like Euclid and Archimedes. It is certainly not Apollonius of Alexandria, Greco-Alexandrian grammarian of the second century A.D., or Apollonius of Rhodes (c. 295–215 B.C.), Greco-Alexandrian epic poet.

vii. On Astronomy

[1] Astronomy, accordingly, is rendered into Latin as "the law of the stars" (the literal meaning of the word[108]), inasmuch as the stars can neither remain fixed nor move in any way other than that in which they have been arranged by their Creator; except perchance when they are changed at the will of the Divinity on the occasion of some miracle, as Joshua is said to have obtained his request that the sun stand still upon Gibeon [*Joshua* 10: 12], and as a star announcing to the world the coming of the Lord for its salvation is said to have been shown to the three wise men [*Matthew* 2: 2]; and in the passion of the Lord Christ as well the sun was darkened for three hours [*Luke* 23: 44]; and so forth. These events are called miracles because they concern unexpected matters that deserve wonder. For, according to the astronomers the stars which are fixed in the sky are supported without motion; the planets, however, that is, "the wanderers," do move, though the boundaries of the courses which they traverse are fixed.

[2] Astronomy, then, as has already been stated, is the science which surveys the movements of heavenly bodies and all their forms and investigates the accustomed state of the stars in relation to themselves and to the earth.

11. Isidore of Seville, *Origins or Etymologies in Twenty Books* (c. 620s)

INTRODUCTION

Isidore of Seville (c. 560–636) was orphaned soon after his birth and educated in a monastery in Seville, Spain. In about 600 his brother, the bishop of Seville, died, and Isidore was elected to succeed him. During the subsequent decades, Isidore played a significant role in several national councils held by the Spanish Church, and led the most important one, convened at Toledo in 633, which declared toleration of the Jews and the union of church and state. While serving as an ecclesiastical leader, Isidore read and wrote prolifically and contributed to scholarship largely by compiling and transmitting the residue of classical learning that was preserved in his extensive library at Seville. His writings include manuals on Christian worship and morals, treatises on natural science and cosmology, a chronicle of the Goths, Vandals, and Sueves, to whom he proselytized, and a history of the world from the time of creation. He died in Seville in 636.

Selection #11 is drawn from his best known work, a 20-volume encyclopedia covering all branches of knowledge and employing a method of explaining his topics by accounting for their origins or etymology. This widely used and cited work survives in about one thousand manuscripts in libraries across Europe. Although many of Isidore's etymologies are fanciful and much of his encyclopedia is uncritical borrowing, chiefly from Augustine and Cassiodorus, he became the author most read during the next five centuries; and the first three books of his encyclopedia, describing the seven liberal arts, became the most frequently cited of his writings.[109] In these three books the distribution of text devoted to the separate, liberal arts in the standard Latin edition is: 62 pages to grammar in Book I, 42 pages to rhetoric and dialectic in Book II, and 37 pages to the four

108. In Greek, *aster* is star, *nomos* is law.

109. Jacques Fontaine, *Isidore de Seville et la culture classique dans l'Espagne wisigothique* (Paris: Études Augustiniennes, 1959), pp. 3–4, 13–5, 32–3.

mathematical disciplines in Book III.[110] These three books have not yet been entirely translated into English, and the following translation of his descriptions of each of the seven arts is published here for the first time.

SELECTION[111]

Book I: On Grammar

1. On Discipline [or Science] and Art. The word *disciplina* [discipline] comes from Latin, *discere* (learning). A discipline can also be called a "science," because *scire* [to know] gets its name from *discere*, since none of us is a knower unless he is a learner. The other half of *disciplina* gets its name from *plena* (full), because what is learned is something complete or total. The word *ars* gets its name on the grounds of consisting of the precepts and rules of "art," of course. Others say this word was derived by the Greeks from *areté* (virtue, excellence), which they have termed a science.

Plato and Aristotle have proposed the following difference between "art" and "discipline," saying that art resides in those things which are capable of being otherwise than as they are; but discipline is assuredly what addresses those things which cannot turn out otherwise than as they are. Thus, whenever something is the subject of disquisitions that are true, there will prove to be discipline; but whenever something verisimilar and subject to opinion is what is being treated, the term "art" will apply.

2. On the Seven Liberal Disciplines. The disciplines of the liberal arts are seven in number. The first is grammar; that is, competence in speaking. The second is rhetoric which is reckoned as necessary most of all in those inquiries proper to citizens, due to the glamour of extemporaneous eloquence. Third is dialectic (or "logic" by another name), which separates the true from the false by reasonings of the greatest subtlety. Fourth is arithmetic, which contains the causes and divisions of numbers. Fifth is music, which consists in songs and chants. Sixth is geometry, which embraces the measurements and dimensions of the earth. Seventh is astronomy, which contains the law of the stars. . . .[112]

4. On the Latin letters. The Italian maiden Carmentis first devised the Latin letters. She was called Carmentis because she sang songs [*carmina*] of things to come. By others [the Greeks] she was called Nicostrata.[113] The term "letters," in fact, may be used in a common or a liberal sense. Letters are common in the sense that many people use them commonly to write and read. They are liberal in the sense that those know them who compose books and know the principle of speaking and writing correctly. . . .

5. On Grammar. Grammar is the science of speaking correctly, and is both source and foundation of liberal letters.[114] Among the disciplines this one was discovered right after the alphabet, in order that those who had learned to spell might straightway learn by it the technique of speaking correctly. . . . The divisions within grammatical art are counted by some up to thirty; that is, the eight parts of speech, plus: articulate voice, letter, syllable, metric feet, accents, word location, punctuation, ortho-

---

110. Isidore, Bishop of Spain, *Etymologiarum sive Originum Libri XX*, ed. W. M. Lindsay (Oxford: Clarendon, 1911), bks. I–III.

111. Isidore of Seville, *Origins or Etymologies in Twenty Books*, bks. I–III, adapted from a new, unpublished translation by J. Albert Dragstedt.

112. These definitions of the mathematical arts are more Glauconic than Socratic, as seen in selection #1 by Plato.

113. Compare this rare reference to a learned female in the Christian encyclopedias to selection #12 by Christine de Pizan and selection #30 by Bathsua Makin.

114. This definition exemplifies Isidore's borrowing directly from Cassiodorus (II pref. 4) in selection #10.

graphy, analogy, etymology, glosses, difference, barbarisms, solecisms, mistakes, metaplasms, outlines, tropes, prose, meters, stories and histories. . . .[115]

Book II: On Rhetoric and Dialectic

1. On Rhetoric and its Name. Rhetoric is the science of speaking well in those inquiries proper to citizens, with the purpose of convincing people of just and good causes. Rhetoric is so called after the Greek work, *rhetorizein*, that is, from "abundance of speech." *Rhesis* is the word for "expression" in Greek, *rhetor* is the word for "orator." Rhetoric, moreover, is joined to the art of grammar. For it is in Grammar that we learn the science of speaking correctly; after all, it is in Rhetoric that we learn how to enunciate the things that we have learned.

2. On the Discoverers of the Art of Rhetoric. . . .

3. On the Word, *Orator*, and the Parts of Rhetoric. So the orator is a good man, skilled at speaking.[116] A man becomes good through nature, character and arts. A man becomes skilled at speaking through technical eloquence which consists of five parts: intention, arrangement, style, memory, and delivery;[117] and includes the purpose of the function which is to bring about persuasion. Skill at speaking, moreover, in itself consists in three parts: nature, doctrine, practice. Nature is in talent; doctrine, in science; practice, in assiduity. For these are technical expectations not only of an orator, but of each and every human being for him to accomplish anything. . . .

22. On Dialectic. Dialectic is the discipline ordered towards explicating the causes of things. It is a part of that philosophy which is called Logic; that is, the reasoning part capable of defining, inquiring and explicating.[118] For it teaches how truth and falsity are distinguished by distribution in many kinds of inquiries. Certain of the first philosophers applied it in their discussions; but they did not constitute it as an art to be acquired by practice. After them, Aristotle brought the argumentation characteristic of this doctrine within the scope of certain rules, and he named it Dialectic because, within its discussion is conducted concerning utterances as such. For an utterance is called *lekton*. So dialectic comes next after Rhetoric as a discipline, because in many instances both turn out to be involved in common.

23. On the Difference between the Art of Dialectic and that of Rhetoric. Varro, in Book 9 of his work on the disciplines, defined Dialectic and Rhetoric by means of the following likeness: "Dialectic and Rhetoric are like a man's hand being a formed fist and then a spread-out palm: the former contracting words; the latter distending."[119] Dialectic is certainly sharper when the task is to explicate matters. Rhetoric is more inventive when the task is teaching those things which it strives for. The

---

115. Most of the following thirty chapters follow the organization of the authoritative, grammatical handbook for advanced students, the *Greater Art* of Donatus.

116. Attributed to Cato the Elder, the standard, epigrammatic definition of the Ciceronian orator ("a good man, skilled in speaking") was quoted by Quintilian (*Education of the Orator* XII i 1), by Cassiodorus (II ii 1) in selection #10, and by Isidore (II 3) in selection #11, and is mentioned by Francesco Petrarca in selection #24.

117. This fivefold division of rhetoric had become conventional by the first century B.C., as stated by Cicero in *On Discovery* I 9. See selection #10 Cassiodorus (II ii 2).

118. While employing "Logic" here as a term for a division of philosophy comprising grammar, rhetoric, and dialectic, Isidore proceeds to treat dialectic as an art of formulating arguments that is subsidiary to rhetoric.

119. Though attributed to the encyclopedic work of Marcus Terentius Varro, the quotation was borrowed by Isidore from Cassiodorus (II ii 2). This metaphor comparing logic and rhetoric originated with Zeno of Elea, according to Cicero (*Orator* 32, 113) and Quintilian (*Education of the Orator* II xx 7). Consequently, the metaphor was 1100 years old by the time of Isidore, and would continue to be invoked in the liberal arts tradition for another thousand years. See Juana Inéz de la Cruz in selection #31.

former comes to schools on occasion; the latter is perpetually on its way into the forum. The former requires students of rare application; the latter frequently requires actual populations. Philosophers, moreover, before they get to the exposition of the *Introduction*[120] are wont to provide a definition of philosophy, in order to demonstrate more easily the properties that pertain to it.

24. On the Definition of Philosophy. Philosophy is the understanding of matters both human and divine joined to the study of the good life. It clearly consists of two things, science and opinion. There is science when something is perceived with a reasoning that is certain; but there is opinion when the thing still lurks in uncertainty and it isn't seen with any firm reasoning—as, for example whether the sun is just as large as it seems, or is larger than the whole earth; and likewise whether the moon is spherical, or concave; and whether the stars stick to the sky, or are carried through the air on a free course; and how large the heavens themselves are and what matter they are made of; whether they are quiet and immobile, or revolve with incredible speed; how thick is the earth, or on what foundations does it stay balanced and suspended. The very name "philosophy," moreover, means "love of wisdom" translated into Latin. For the Greeks call "love" *philo* and "wisdom" *sophia*. The appearance of philosophy is tripartite: the first is "natural" which is named "Physics" in Greek, treating of inquiry into nature. The second is "moral" which is called "Ethics" in Greek, dealing with character. The third is "Rational," which is named by the Greek term "logic," disputing of the way truth itself is sought in the causes of things or in character as it is relevant to life. So physics is concerned with inquiry into cause; Ethics, with the order of living; Logic, with the reason for understanding.[121] . . .

I can assure you that it is within these three classifications of philosophy that those speeches which are divine take their shape. For they are wont to have as their subject either nature, as in *Genesis* and *Ecclesiastes*; or morality, as in *Proverbs* and scattered through all the other books; or logic, on behalf of which our people claim theoretical philosophy for themselves, as in the *Song of Songs* and in the Gospels. Similarly, other learned men have defined philosophy in its name and parts as follows. . .

Book III: On Mathematics

Mathematics is said in Latin to be the doctrinal science which considers abstract quantity.[122] That quantity is abstract which separates it from matter or from other accidental properties like equal and unequal or from others of this sort, within our thinking alone. It has four kinds: Arithmetic, Music, Geometry and Astronomy. Arithmetic is the discipline ordered to countable quantity in itself. Music is the discipline which speaks of those numbers which are found in sounds. Geometry is the discipline ordered to size and shapes. Astronomy is the discipline which contemplates the orbits and figure of heavenly bodies as a whole, and the habits of the stars. We proceed to point out these disciplines at somewhat greater length so that their causes may be shown adequately.

1. On the Name of the Discipline of Arithmetic. Arithmetic is the discipline ordered to numbers. For the Greeks call number *arithmus*. And the authors of secular literature have wished that it be first among the mathematical disciplines for the reason that it needs no other discipline in order to exist.

---

120. This reference is to the *Introduction* to the epistemological problems of dialectical inquiry raised by Aristotle, which was written by Porphyry and translated, along with Aristotle's two introductory treatises to logic, by Boethius.

121. This division of philosophy into physics, ethics, and logic was attributed to Plato by Cicero (*Academica* I v 19–21) and Augustine (*City of God* VIII 4, XI 25). But it seems to be derived from the Stoics, who passed it successively to Cicero, Augustine, then here to Isidore, and later to Hugh of St. Victor, as appears in selection #15.

122. Isidore's treatment of mathematics follows closely the borrowing by Cassiodorus from Boethius, while also drawing material from Augustine.

Music, Geometry and Astronomy, however, which come next, need the aid of it, in order to be and subsist. . . .

10. On the Discoverers of Geometry and Its Name. The discipline of geometry is said first to have been come upon by Egyptians because, upon the overflowing of the Nile and the covering of all possessions by mud, the beginning was made in dividing the earth by lines and measures, and a name was given to that art. And that art proceeded next to the point where people measure the spaces of sea, heavens and sky, thanks to the acuity of wise men. For driven as they were by zeal, they began to seek the spaces of the heavens, after measuring the earth: at how great a distance is the moon from the earth? The sun from the moon? And by how great a measurement is it to the top of the heavens? And thus they distinguished the very spaces of the heavens and the circumference of the orb down to a number of stades which had some probability. But because this discipline began with the measuring out of earth, it has retained the name from its origin; thus, geometry has been named from "earth" and from "measure." For "earth" is called *ge* in Greek, and "measure" is *metron*. The art of this discipline contains within itself lines, intervals, magnitudes and figures; and within figures it contains dimensions and numbers.

15. On Music and Its Name.[123] Music is the skill consisting of modulating in sound and in song. . . . So no discipline can be complete without music, since nothing can be, without it. For the very world itself is said to have been composed by a certain harmony, and the very heavens are said to revolve at the modulating effected by harmony. . . .

24. On the Name Astronomy. Astronomy is the law of stars which pervades the courses of heavenly bodies and the shapes and regularities of stars [moving] around one another and around the earth, obeying a rationale which cannot be discerned. . . .

27. On the Differences between Astronomy and Astrology.[124] There is, however, some difference between astronomy and astrology. For astronomy contains the rotation of the heavens, and the risings, settings and movements of heavenly bodies and the reasons why this terminology is as it is. Astrology is actually partly natural and partly superstitious. It is natural as long as it is following out the courses of the sun and moon, or the definite stopping-points in time of the stars. But it is actually superstitious in that part done by the so-called "mathematicals," who do augury on the basis of stars and even correlate the twelve constellations of the heavens with individual organs of the soul or body, and attempt to predict the births and characters of human beings by the course of heavenly bodies.

---

123. Indicative of the transition from late antiquity to the middle ages, Isidore's discussion of music ignores the philosophical, mathematical tradition of Pythagoras and Plato, and addresses the ecclesiastical and sonorous interpretation found in Augustine.

124. Having interchanged the terms astronomy and astrology in the previous paragraphs, Isidore now distinguishes them.

Transformation of the Female Images

12. Christine de Pizan, *Book of the City of Ladies* (c. 1404)

INTRODUCTION

Christine de Pizan (1365–c. 1430) was born in Venice and raised in Paris, where her father served as court astrologer to the French king Charles V, a learned and progressive monarch known as "Charles the Wise." The stimulating atmosphere of this court provided Christine with the unusual opportunity to receive a sound education, which her father encouraged and her mother opposed.[125] In 1380 fifteen-year-old Christine wedded a twenty-four-year-old court notary and secretary. Their marriage was happy and produced three children; but in 1385 her father died in debt, and during an epidemic in 1389 her husband died followed by one of her children. Suddenly bereft of financial means or a husband, twenty-five-year-old Christine turned to writing to earn a living and became the first woman of letters in Europe to do so.

The range and quality of her writing are remarkable. She began by addressing the popular themes of courtly love and chivalry in lyric poems, short narratives, and didactic works, and quickly gained an audience and success. She was then named the official biographer of Charles V, and after 1400 began producing her mature works addressing the vicissitudes of fortune and *la querelle des femmes* ("the woman question"). This latter topic was prompted by Christine's desire to respond to the misogynist vein in Western letters and, in particular, to the cynical views about women expressed in *The Romance of the Rose*, an influential work of French literature composed in the thirteenth century. Christine became the chief correspondent in the associated literary debate called "The Quarrel of *The Romance of the Rose*" that was ignited, in part, by the appearance of *Concerning Famous Women* (c. 1359), a work composed by the prominent Italian writer and poet, Giovanni Boccaccio (1313–1375).

While recounting the lives of 104 women, Boccaccio's *Concerning Famous Women* "recognized that women can live and achieve glory just as men do. . . . Women can become great scholars, rulers, painters, and poets, if they put their minds to it. But this requires a greater effort on their part since Nature has not made them the equals of men. Nature has given them frail bodies and sluggish minds, and to achieve glory they must first overcome these handicaps. Many of them have done so, and therefore deserve greater praise than men, according to Boccaccio. . . . To lavish praise on a woman, Boccaccio can think of no better adjective than 'manly,' and his greatest condemnation of sluggish and insignificant men is to call them women."[126]

Responding to Boccaccio in *Book of the City of Ladies* (c. 1404), Christine did not explicitly criticize his backhanded praise of "exceptional" women, but revised many of his biographies in order to compose a history demonstrating the universality, rather than exceptionality, of accomplished women.[127] Beyond retouching the blemishes that Boccaccio included in many of his profiles, Christine expands the number of accomplished women with many Christians from the period after antiquity,[128] and introduces the metaphor of the city of women, signifying that women have founded

---

125. See *The Book of the City of Ladies* (II 36).

126. Guido A. Guarino, "Introduction," in *Concerning Famous Women by Giovanni Boccaccio*, tr. Guido A. Guarino (New Brunswick, NJ: Rutgers University Press, 1963), pp. ix, xxvi–xxvii.

127. For example, see 28 below. Even when quoting an example of Boccaccio's exceptionalism (29), Christine refrains from criticizing it.

128. Only five of Boccaccio's 104 profiles were of Christian women after about A.D. 400.

and built a tradition of their own. The metaphor also implies that women belong in public life and deserve education in the liberal arts, which prepare students for public roles.[129]

As a work of literature, *Book of the City of Ladies* incorporates a number of different motifs and perspectives. Christine's background as a learned woman of late fourteenth-century Venice implies the viewpoint of an early Italian Renaissance feminist.[130] But her residence in northern Europe contributes to the medieval technique of indirectly establishing her voice through a supernatural visitation. At the same time, the premodern seems to meet the postmodern in *Book of the City of Ladies* when Christine observes that, since historical writing is influenced by the biases and situation of the historians, the tradition must be reconstructed in order to give voice to those who have not been heard. In this endeavor, the female imagery of the liberal arts was readily at hand; and Christine employs it to ascribe to women the intellectual autonomy and creativity that she herself developed. Nevertheless, her final position was moderate from a modern perspective, for she never argued for social or political equality with men.

In her later years Christine turned to political topics, and in 1418 fled Paris during the bloody civil war. Retreating to a convent where her daughter was a nun, she continued writing until her death in about 1430.

SELECTION[131]

1. Here begins the book of the city of ladies, whose first chapter tells why and for what purpose this book was written.

[i] One day as I was sitting alone in my study surrounded by books on all kinds of subjects, devoting myself to literary studies, my usual habit, my mind dwelt at length on the weighty opinions of various authors whom I had studied for a long time. I looked up from my book, having decided to leave such subtle questions in peace and to relax by reading some light poetry. With this in mind, I searched for some small book.

By chance a strange volume came into my hands, not one of my own, but one which had been given to me along with some others. When I held it open and saw from its title page that it was by Mathéolus,[132] I smiled, for though I had never seen it before, I had often heard that like other books it discussed respect for women. . . . Because the subject seemed to me not very pleasant for people who do not enjoy lies, and of no use in developing virtue or manners, given its lack of integrity in diction and theme, and after browsing here and there and reading the end, I put it down in order to turn my attention to more elevated and useful study. But just the sight of this book, even though it was of no authority, made me wonder how it happened that so many different men—and learned men among them—have been and are so inclined to express both in speaking and in their treatises and writings so many wicked insults about women and their behavior. Not only one or two and not even just this Mathéolus (for this book had a bad name anyway and was intended as a satire) but, more generally,

---

129. Christine's urban metaphor of a sanctuary of public and intellectual life for women may be compared with "the republic of women" in Laura Cereta's letter of 1488 in selection #27.

130. See the introduction to Laura Cereta in selection #27.

131. Christine de Pizan, *Book of the City of Ladies*, Book I, drawn from the translation by Earl J. Richards (New York: Persea Books, 1982), pp. 3–6, 63–5, 70–1, 80–1. Reprinted by permission of Persea Books, Inc.

132. This book is generally believed to be *Book of Lamentations*, written by Mathéolus in the final third of the thirteenth century. This diatribe against women and marriage comprised 5,614 lines of Latin verse, and was translated into Old French in the final third of the fourteenth century by Jean le Fèvre who added his reply. Christine is likely responding to the appearance of the recent translation. Translator's note, p. 259n.

judging from the treatises of all philosophers and poets and from all orators—it would take too long to mention their names—it seems that they all speak from one and the same mouth. They all concur in one conclusion: that the behavior of women is inclined to and full of every vice. Thinking deeply about these matters, I began to examine my character and conduct as a natural woman[133] and, similarly, I considered other women whose company I frequently kept, princesses, great ladies, women of the middle and lower classes, who had graciously told me of their most private and intimate thoughts, hoping that I could judge impartially and in good conscience whether the testimony of so many notable men could be true. To the best of my knowledge, no matter how long I confronted or dissected the problem, I could not see or realize how their claims could be true when compared to the natural behavior and character of women. Yet I still argued vehemently against women, saying that it would be impossible that so many famous men—such solemn scholars, possessed of such deep and great understanding, so clear-sighted in all things, as it seemed—could have spoken falsely on so many occasions that I could hardly find a book on morals where, even before I had read it in its entirety, I did not find several chapters or certain sections attacking women, no matter who the author was.

This reason alone, in short, made me conclude that, although my intellect did not perceive my own great faults and, likewise, those of other women because of its simpleness and ignorance, it was however truly fitting that such was the case. And so I relied more on the judgment of others than on what I myself felt and knew. I was so transfixed in this line of thinking for such a long time that it seemed as if I were in a stupor. Like a gushing fountain, a series of authorities, whom I recalled one after another, came to mind, along with their opinions on this topic. And I finally decided that God formed a vile creature when He made woman, and I wondered how such a worthy artisan could have deigned to make such an abominable work which, from what they say, is the vessel as well as the refuge and abode of every evil and vice. As I was thinking this, a great unhappiness and sadness welled up in my heart, for I detested myself and the entire feminine sex, as though we were monstrosities in nature. And in my lament I spoke these words:

[ii] "Oh, God, how can this be? For unless I stray from my faith, I must never doubt that Your infinite wisdom and most perfect goodness ever created anything which was not good. Did You yourself not create woman in a very special way and since that time did You not give her all those inclinations which it pleased You for her to have? And how could it be that You could go wrong in anything? Yet look at all these accusations which have been judged, decided, and concluded against women. I do not know how to understand this repugnance. If it is so, fair Lord God, that in fact so many abominations abound in the female sex, for You yourself say that the testimony of two or three witnesses lends credence, why shall I not doubt that this is true? Alas, God, why did You not let me be born in the world as a man, so that all my inclinations would be to serve You better, and so that I would not stray in anything and would be as perfect as a man is said to be? But since Your kindness has not been extended to me, then forgive my negligence in Your service, most fair Lord God, and may it not displease You, for the servant who receives fewer gifts from his lord is less obliged in his service." I spoke these words to God in my lament and a great deal more for a very long time in sad

133. "If one chooses to view *Book of the City of Ladies* as Christine's ongoing commentary on the Quarrel of *The Romance of the Rose*, this phrase ["my character and conduct as a natural woman"] takes on a special significance: in the *Rose*, Nature, replying to Reason, presents extended attacks on the chastity of women. Christine turns the tables in *Book of the City of Ladies*. First, she presents a counterversion of Nature's portrayal of the 'natural' behavior of women, and second, she makes Reason—who came off so poorly in the *Rose*—her first guide and helper in constructing the City of Ladies." Translator's note, p. 259n.

reflection, and in my folly I considered myself most unfortunate because God had made me inhabit a female body in this world.[134]

2. Here Christine describes how three ladies [Reason, Rectitude, Justice] appeared to her and how the one who was in front spoke first and confronted her in her pain.

[i] So occupied with these painful thoughts, my head bowed in shame, my eyes filled with tears, leaning on the pommel of my chair's armrest, I suddenly saw a ray of light fall on my lap, as though it were the sun. I shuddered then, as if wakened from sleep, for I was sitting in a shadow where the sun should not have shone at that hour. And as I lifted my head to see where this light was coming from, I saw three crowned ladies standing before me, and the splendor of their bright faces shone on me and throughout the entire room. Now no one would ask whether I was surprised, for my doors were shut and they had still entered. Fearing that some phantom had come to tempt me and filled with great fright, I made the Sign of the Cross on my forehead.[135]

[ii] Then she who was the first of the three smiled and began to speak, "Dear daughter, do not be afraid, for we have not come here to harm or trouble you but to console you, for we have taken pity on your distress, and we have come to bring you out of the ignorance which so blinds your own intellect that you shun what you know for a certainty and believe what you do not know or see or recognize except by virtue of many strange opinions. You resemble the fool in the prank who was dressed in women's clothes while he slept; because those who were making fun of him repeatedly told him he was a woman, he believed their false testimony more readily than the certainty of his own identity. Fair daughter, have you lost all sense? Have you forgotten that when fine gold is tested in the furnace, it does not change or vary in strength but becomes purer the more it is hammered and handled in different ways? Do you know not that the best things are the most debated and the most discussed? . . ."

27. . . . [Christine questions Reason.]   "But please enlighten me again, whether it has ever pleased this God, who has bestowed so many favors on women, to honor the feminine sex with the privilege of the virtue of high understanding and great learning, and whether women ever have a clever enough mind for this. I wish very much to know this because men maintain that the mind of women can learn only a little."

She answered, "My daughter, since I told you before, you know quite well that the opposite of their opinion is true, and to show you this even more clearly, I will give you proof through examples. I tell you again—and don't doubt the contrary—if it were customary to send daughters to school like sons, and if they were then taught the natural sciences, they would learn as thoroughly and understand the subtleties of all the arts and sciences as well as sons.[136] And by chance there happen to be such women, for, as I touched on before, just as women have more delicate bodies than men, weaker and less able to perform many tasks, so do they have minds that are freer and sharper whenever they apply themselves."

---

134. Is Christine sincere or ironic in this introductory account of doubting the misogynist authors, finally accepting their acknowledged authority, and ultimately detesting herself?

135. The three ladies in Christine's vision portray the virtues of Reason, Rectitude, and Justice. This device of envisioning a supernatural visitation is typical of Christine's writings as well as medieval writings in which authors express themselves indirectly in order to speak on controversial topics that they lack the authority, or believe are too risky, to address.

136. This statement and the following elaboration echo in debates over women's access to the liberal arts in the late nineteenth century, as appear in the readings below from that period.

"My lady, what are you saying? With all due respect, could you dwell longer on this point, please. Certainly men would never admit this answer is true, unless it is explained more plainly, for they believe that one normally sees that men know more than women do."

She answered, "Do you know why women know less?"

"Not unless you tell me, my lady."

"Without the slightest doubt, it is because they are not involved in many different things, but stay at home, where it is enough for them to run the household, and there is nothing which so instructs a reasonable creature as the exercise and experience of many different things."

"My lady, since they have minds skilled in conceptualizing and learning, just like men, why don't women learn more?"

She replied, "Because, my daughter, the public does not require them to get involved in the affairs which men are commissioned to execute, just as I told you before. It is enough for women to perform the usual duties to which they are ordained. As for judging from experience, since one sees that women usually know less than men, that therefore their capacity for understanding is less, look at men who farm the flatlands or who live in the mountains. You will find that in many countries they seem completely savage because they are so simple-minded. All the same, there is no doubt that Nature provided them with the qualities of body and mind found in the wisest and most learned men. All of this stems from a failure to learn, though, just as I told you, among men and women some possess better minds than others. Let me tell you about women who have possessed great learning and profound understanding and treat the question of the similarity of women's minds to men's."

28. She begins to discuss several ladies who were enlightened with great learning,[137] and first speaks about the noble maiden Cornificia.[138] "Cornificia, the noble maiden, was sent to school by her parents along with her brother Cornificius when they were both children, thanks to deception and trickery.[139] This little girl so devoted herself to study and with such marvelous intelligence that she began to savor the sweet taste of knowledge acquired through study. Nor was it easy to take her away from this joy to which she more and more applied herself, neglecting all other feminine activities. She occupied herself with this for such a long period of time that she became a consummate poet, and she was not only extremely brilliant and expert in the learnedness and craft of poetry but also seemed to have been nourished with the very milk and teaching of perfect philosophy, for she wanted to hear and know about every branch of learning, which she then mastered so thoroughly that she surpassed her brother, who was also a very great poet, and excelled in every field of learning. Knowledge was not enough for her unless she could put her mind to work and her pen to paper in the compilation of several very famous books. These works, as well as her poems, were much prized during this time of St. Gregory[140] and he himself mentions them. The Italian, Boccaccio, who was a great poet, discusses

137. Under this heading, Christine addresses three female poets of antiquity: Cornificia, Proba, and Manto. Legends about each of them are recorded by Vergil, Dante, and Boccaccio.

138. The figures Cornificius and Cornificia that occasionally appear in medieval literature are difficult to identify positively. The best known Cornificius in Western letters was a Latin author who wrote a work on rhetoric in the first century B.C. and was mentioned as a detractor of Vergil in an apparent interpolation in Donatus's *Life of Vergil*. Boccaccio states that Cornificia and Cornificius were poets during the rule (31 B.C.–A.D. 14) of the Roman emperor Augustus. Boccaccio, *Concerning Famous Women*, LXXXIV, p. 188. See the reference to Cornificius in selection #16 by John of Salisbury, and the reference to Cornificia in selection #27 by Laura Cereta.

139. In a contemporaneous case of "deception and trickery," a young woman reportedly disguised herself as a young man in order to study the liberal arts at the University of Cracow, as related in selection #23. See also a similar incident in Juana Inéz de la Cruz, "The Poet's Reply" (1691) in selection #31.

140. Gregory the Great (c. 540–604), Roman monk and pope.

this fact in [*Concerning Famous Women*] and at the same time praises this woman: 'O most great honor for a woman who abandoned all feminine activities and applied and devoted her mind to the study of the great scholars!'

"As further proof of what I am telling you, Boccaccio also talks about the attitude of women who despise themselves and their own minds and who, as though they were born in the mountains totally ignorant off virtue and honor, turn disconsolate and say that they are good and useful only for embracing men and carrying and feeding children. God has given them such beautiful minds to apply themselves, if they want to, in any of the fields where glorious and excellent men are active; [and these arts and sciences] are neither more nor less accessible to them as compared to men if they wished to study them, and they can thereby acquire a lasting name, whose possession is fitting for most excellent men. My dear daughter, you can see how this author Boccaccio testifies to what I have told you and how he praises and approves learning in women."

29. Here she tells of Proba the Roman.[141] "The Roman woman, Proba, wife of Adelphus, was equally outstanding and was a Christian. She had such a noble mind and so loved and devoted herself to study that she mastered all seven liberal arts[142] and was an excellent poet and delved so deeply into the books of the poets, particularly Vergil's poems, that she knew them all by heart. After she had read these books and poems with profound insight and intelligence and had taken pains in her mind to understand them, it occurred to her that one could describe the Scriptures and the stories found in the Old and New Testament with pleasant verses filled with substance taken from these same works. . . ."

33. Christine asks Reason whether there was ever a woman who discovered hitherto unknown knowledge.

[i] I, Christine, concentrating on these explanations of Lady Reason, replied to her regarding this passage: "My lady, I realize that you are able to cite numerous and frequent cases of women learned in the sciences and the arts. But I would then ask you whether you know of any women who, through the strength of emotion and of subtlety of mind and comprehension, have themselves discovered any new arts and sciences which are necessary, good, and profitable, and which had hitherto not been discovered or known?[143] For it is not such a great feat of mastery to study and learn some field of knowledge already discovered by someone else as it is to discover by oneself some new and unknown thing."

She replied, "Rest assured, dear friend, that many noteworthy and great sciences and arts have been discovered through the understanding and subtlety of women, both in cognitive speculation, demonstrated in writing, and in the arts, manifested in manual works of labor. I will give you plenty of examples.

[ii] "First I will tell you of the noble Nicostrata whom the Italians call Carmentis. This lady was the daughter of a king of Arcadia, named Pallas. She has a marvelous mind, endowed by God with special gifts of knowledge: she was a great scholar in Greek literature and had such fair and wise

---

141. Commensurate with the effort to reconcile classical and Christian cultures in late Antiquity, the learned, upper-class, Roman woman Proba in about A.D. 360 wrote a Biblical history by weaving together verses drawn from Vergil. Compare the image of Proba in selection #27 by Laura Cereta.

142. Christine follows the introduction of Proba by Boccaccio, who also noted that "Whoever her teacher may have been, it can easily be seen that [Proba] excelled in the liberal arts" (*Concerning Famous Women*, XCV, p. 219). As appears in selections #15–21, the curriculum of "all seven liberal arts" had broken down by this point, even though such literary references and iconographical representations continued.

143. This question, posed in her own voice, may be the most original among Christine's innovative inquiries.

speech and venerable eloquence that the contemporary poets who wrote about her imagined she was beloved of the god Mercury. They claimed that a son whom she had with her husband, and who was in his time most learned, was in fact the offspring of this god. Because of certain changes which came about in the land where she lived, this lady left her country in a large boat for the land of Italy, and in her company were her son and a great many people who followed her; she arrived at the river Tiber. Landing there, she proceeded to climb a high hill which she named the Palentine [*sic*], after her father, where the city of Rome was later founded. There, this lady and her son and all those who had followed her built a fortress. After discovering that the men of that country were all savages, she wrote certain laws, enjoining them to live in accord with right and reason, following justice. She was the first to institute laws in that country which subsequently became so renowned and from which all the statutes of law derive. This lady knew through divine inspiration and the spirit of prophecy (in which he was remarkably distinguished, in addition to the other graces she possessed) how in time to come this land would be ennobled by excellence and famous over [the earth. . . .]"[144]

37. Concerning the great good accrued to the world through these women. "My lady, I greatly admire what I have heard you say, that so much good has come into the world by virtue of the understanding of women. These men usually say that women's knowledge is worthless. In fact when someone says something foolish, the widely voiced insult is that this is women's knowledge. In brief, the typical opinions and comments of men claim that women have been and are useful in the world only for bearing children and sewing."

She answered, "Now you can recognize the massive ingratitude of the men who say such things; they are like people who live off the goods of others without knowing their source and without thanking anyone. You can also clearly see how God, who does nothing without a reason, wished to show men that He does not despise the feminine sex nor their own, because it so pleased Him to place such great understanding in women's brains that they are intelligent enough not only to learn and retain the sciences but also to discover new sciences themselves, indeed sciences of such great utility and profit for the world that nothing has been more necessary. . . .

38. [iv] Then I said to her,[145] "Now, my lady, I indeed understand more than before why you spoke of the enormous ingratitude, not to say ignorance, of these men who malign women, for although it seems to me that the fact that the mother of every man is a woman is reason enough not to attack them, not to mention the other good deeds which one can clearly see that women do for men, truly, one can see here the many benefits afforded by women with the greatest generosity to men which they have accepted and continue to accept. Henceforth, let all writers be silent who speak badly of women, let all of them be silent—those who have attacked women and who still attack them in their books and poems, and all their accomplices and supporters too—let them lower their eyes, ashamed for having dared to speak so badly, in view of the truth which runs counter to their poems; this noble lady, Carmentis, through the profundity of her understanding taught them like a schoolmistress—nor can they deny it—the lesson thanks to which they consider themselves so lofty and honored, that is, she taught them the Latin alphabet!

[v] "But what did all the many nobles and knights say, who generally slander women with such false remarks? From now on let them keep their mouths shut and remember that the customs of

144. Christine may be drawing from Vergil's *Aeneid* (VIII 338–42) or from the selection by Isidore (I 4) in selection #11. See the reference to Carmentis, or Nicostrata, in selection #27 by Laura Cereta, as well as in Boccaccio, *Concerning Famous Women*, XXV, pp. 52–5.

145. Here is the resolution of the self-questioning and self-loathing that Christine posed at the outset.

bearing arms, of dividing armies into battalions, and of fighting in ordered ranks—a vocation upon which they so pride themselves and for which they consider themselves so great—came to them from a woman and were given to them by a woman. Would men who live on bread, or who live civil in cities following the order of law, or who cultivate the fields, have any good reason to slander and rebuff women so much, as many do, if they only thought of all the benefits? Certainly not, because thanks to women, that is, Minerva, Ceres, and Isis, so many beneficial things have come to men, through which they can lead honorable lives and from which they live and will live always. Ought not these things be considered?"

"Doubtless, my lady. It seems to me that neither in the teaching of Aristotle, which had been of great profit to human intelligence and which is so highly esteemed and with good reason, nor in that of all the other philosophers who have ever lived, could an equal benefit for the world be found as that which has been accrued and still accrues through the works accomplished by virtue of the knowledge possessed by these ladies."[146]

And she said to me, "They were not alone, but there are many others and I will tell you of them."

---

146. Is Christine's statement about the importance of these women to be understood as a literal assertion, a generalization about the overlooked contribution of all women collectively, or a somewhat ironic reversal of the "exceptionalism" presented by Boccaccio?

Section III

In the *modernus* University, 1100s–1500

Beginning in the late fifth and early sixth centuries, liberal education began a long period of decay due largely to the economic and political upheaval caused by repeated invasions and migrations throughout Western Europe. In the most Romanized areas, teaching in the seven liberal arts lingered on, but in the remote areas formal schooling was extinguished, and communities rapidly returned to clan life. The instability and impoverishment made impossible the leisure that writers from Aristotle to Augustine had said was a prerequisite for any kind of liberal education. Classical learning became more and more difficult to find; and most Greek writings were lost, including those of Plato[1] and Aristotle, except for two introductory treatises on logic.[2]

Nevertheless, the rudiments of the liberal arts continued to be taught in private tutorials in the homes of noble families; in parish and episcopal schools, though these flickered on and off; and above all, in monasteries such as the Vivarium of Cassiodorus or Monte Cassino of Benedict of Nursia. Being small, self-sufficient, and enclosed, monasteries were best suited to preserve liberal education during a period of political instability and social turmoil. The most significant attempt to reinvigorate and reestablish schools of liberal education occurred early in the ninth century when the Frankish king Charlemagne (c. 742–814) consolidated his empire in Western Europe. This Carolingian renaissance was led by such teachers and scholars as Alcuin (c. 730–804) of England and John "The Scot" Erigena (c. 810–c. 877), both of whom traveled across Europe to this center of learning.

But the Carolingian Empire gradually broke into several kingdoms after the death of Charlemagne, and the educational and cultural flowering shriveled along with the political sovereignty of the empire. By the end of the ninth century King Alfred the Great (849–899) of England was complaining in a letter to the bishops of his realm that no one could read Latin anymore, let alone scholarly books. The dissipation of learning worsened in the tenth century due to the destruction wrought by invaders from the north and east, and this period in Western Europe has traditionally been characterized as an epoch of "iron and lead."

The course of events began to change in the eleventh century. An economic revival prompted the beginnings of urbanization and the incorporation of cities and towns under charters. These develop-

---

1. Until Greek learning was reintroduced in the twelfth and thirteenth centuries via Middle Eastern sources, the only vestige of Plato's writing available in Western Europe was a part of Plato's *Timaeus* (greatly admired and translated into Latin in late antiquity) and an accompanying commentary written by Chalcidius, a Latin Neoplatonic scholar of the first half of the fourth century A.D. Additional knowledge of Plato was largely confined to a commentary on Cicero's *Dream of Scipio*, written by Macrobius, a Latin author who lived in North Africa in about A.D. 400. These commentaries were still authoritative in the late fourteenth century for leading humanist scholars, such as Francesco Petrarca, as seen in selection #24.

2. Aristotle wrote six treatises on logic. The two introductory treatises were translated into Latin by Boethius and were often read together with Porphyry's *Introduction*, also translated by Boethius. Due to their availability, these three translated treatises were widely known and studied, but did not include explanation of the deductive syllogism, which appeared in Aristotle's other four treatises.

ments contributed to the founding of several kinds of schools. Those in monasteries, such as Monte Cassino in Italy and Bec in Normandy, grew in stature and influence; some urban schools were begun, especially in northern Italy where the study of law was rekindled. But the new foundings consisted primarily of cathedral and parish schools, which greatly expanded in number between the 1050s and 1150s with the encouragement of the papacy and Church councils.

The increase in schooling was not merely quantitative, for intellectual activity and sophistication were enhanced as well. More and more masters and students gathered at schools and traveled among them, intensifying intellectual exchange. In the eleventh and early twelfth centuries, this activity reflected "literary-poetic as opposed to analytical philosophical culture of learning. That culture required a literature of examples, not texts that posed problems for solving or for rational penetration. Its dominant arts were grammar and rhetoric, not logic."[3] By the mid-twelfth century, however, there arose a powerful counter-movement subsequently dubbed "scholasticism," a name that would assume strongly negative connotations in later centuries. Here, however, it should be understood as a generic term for the "teaching of the schools" and, therefore, as a term intrinsically linked to the type of study promoted there. The scholastics employed a precise, dialectical method that systematized subject matter into genera and species by identifying and categorizing points of consistency and, when faced with a *contrarium*, searching for a *solutio* by making new *distinctiones* (categories) or citing an *exceptio*. Refined in the fields of theology and law, this scholastic method began to be taught in the liberal arts presupposed that traditional authorities "are different but not contradictory."[4]

This new type of liberal study was occasionally characterized as "modern" (*modernus*), a term that had been coined from the Latin *modo* ("now") in late Antiquity and long contrasted with *antiquus*. But in the course of the twelfth century, the tension between "moderns" and "ancients" became increasingly pronounced as the former term began to denote those who embraced the intellectual changes and new educational practices based upon dialectical method and the study of logic. As John of Salisbury says in the prologue to selection #16, "I have not been ashamed to cite moderns, whose opinions in many instances, I unhesitatingly prefer over those of the ancients." Revealed in the occasional phrase "subtlety of the moderns,"[5] there existed no small ambivalence toward the "moderns," ranging from admiration for their new learning to scorn for the pride and superficiality of those who neglected grammar and rhetoric or pursued dialectic merely in order to advance their reputation. The *modernus* schoolman is portrayed—in the worst light, some would say—in selection #14 by Peter Abelard, who apparently endorsed the scholastic proverb that "logic bites." The tension between "ancients" and "moderns" is specifically discussed by John of Salisbury below.

Hence, in the early 1100s reconsideration and reformation of liberal education were underway, as is shown by the selections from Peter Abelard and Hugh of St. Victor, each of whom died in the early 1140s. Indeed, the iconography of the seven liberal arts demonstrates that the arts described in the traditional literary sources were no longer understood or had been distorted by the mid-twelfth century.[6] The reconsideration and reformulation intensified in the second half of the twelfth century when new learning began to arrive from the Middle East.[7] This new learning included important discoveries

---

3. C. Stephen Jaeger, *The Envy of Angels: Cathedral Schools and Social Ideals in Medieval Europe, 950–1200* (Philadelphia: University of Pennsylvania Press, 1994), p. 128.

4. *diversi sunt sed non adversi.*

5. *subtilitas modernorum.*

6. See Philippe M. Verdier, "L'iconographie des arts libéraux dans l'art du moyen âge jusqu'à la fin du quinzième siècle" in *Arts libéraux et philosophie au Moyen Âge* (Montréal: Institut d'études médiévales, Université de Montréal, 1969), pp. 305–54.

7. See the discussion about Mehdi Nakosteen in the introduction to this documentary history.

in mathematics and optics from Islamic and Jewish scholars, but the understanding of liberal education was primarily influenced at this point by the recovery and translation of Greek philosophical learning. Through points of contact between Western Europeans and Middle Eastern culture—Syria, Constantinople, Sicily, Spain—this material arrived between the mid-twelfth and mid-thirteenth centuries; and the works of Aristotle were especially influential.

Between about 1160 and 1180 the remaining four treatises of Aristotle's logic, which Boethius had not translated and which included knowledge of the deductive syllogism, were recovered. The two introductory treatises translated by Boethius, which had stimulated the thinking of Abelard, Hugh, and their generation, were then labeled the "old logic"; and the four, more sophisticated treatises, including knowledge of the syllogism, were labeled the "new logic." This latter material was available to John of Salisbury at the school of Chartres, whose "modern" view on the role of logic on liberal education is included in selection #16. By the end of the twelfth century, Aristotle's natural and metaphysical philosophies had been recovered, followed by his *Politics, Ethics, Economics,* and *Rhetoric* in the first half of the thirteenth century. Taken together, these works stimulated a revolution in the conception and practice of liberal education, as is shown by the selections from Thomas Aquinas, which convey a sense of the teaching and curriculum of the liberal arts at the point when a "modern" consensus had emerged around its meaning in the middle of the thirteenth century.

The final development in this transformation of liberal education during the high middle ages concerned the nature of the educational institutions. Encouraged by the Third and Fourth Lateran Councils in 1179 and 1215, various cathedral, collegiate, and urban schools grew into universities, as seen in the following table. These institutions appeared when the "wandering masters" began to seek protection from the economic and political exploitation commonly practiced by inhabitants of the locale in which the various schools were located. The masters gained this protection by obtaining from the monarch or pope a charter incorporating them as a guild. These guilds assumed one of the standard legal names, *universitas*, which originally had no reference to the breadth of the curriculum or scholarship. The actual institution of teaching and learning was called the *studium*, or *studium generale* if it included faculties in the four primary fields of the time: arts, theology, medicine, and law. None of these terms should be pressed very hard, however, due to the diversity among the early universities and the decades involved in regularizing their practices. A sense of this diversity, as well as the practices themselves, is conveyed by the excerpts below from documents pertaining to the universities.

Amid this diversity, however, a consistent factor was the paradoxical exclusion of women from the new institution. As recounted in selection #23, women were not permitted to attend the universities, although some teaching of girls by women occurred in grammar schools adjunct to the universities, as seen in selection #22. Meanwhile, the paradox resided in the fact that the liberal arts were personified and honored as women and that St. Catherine was regarded as the patroness of the liberal arts and its faculty. By the end of the thirteenth century, liberal education had therefore become strikingly "modern," both in word and in concept. The selections in Section III portray the *modernus* scholastic, the *modernus* formulation of knowledge and the liberal arts, and the *modernus* institution of the university.[8]

---

8. The word "institution" (institutio) had long denoted "education" or "introduction," as appears in the Latin titles of Quintilian's *Institutio Oratoria* and Cassiodorus's *Institutiones Divinarum et Saecularum Litterarum*. When applied to education, the modern term "institution" thus conveys a double meaning in light of its history.

13. Founding of Universities, 1100s–1500[9]

Locality	late 1100s	1200s	1300s	1400s
Italy	Salerno Bologna Reggio	Vicenza 1204 Arezzo 1215 Padua 1222 Naples 1224*i* Vercelli 1228 Siena 1246 Rome (Curia) 1245*p* Piacenza 1248*p*	Rome (Urbis) 1303*p* Perugia 1308*p* Treviso 1318*i* Verona1339 Pisa1343*p* Florence1349*p* Pavia 1361*i* Lucca 1369 Ferrara 1391*p*	Turin 1404*p* Parma 1412 Catania 1444*p* Venice 1470 Genoa 1471
France		Paris c. 1200 Montpellier c. 1200 Orleans c. 1235 Angers c. 1250 Toulouse 1229,1233*p*	Avignon 1303*p* Cahors 1332*p* Grenoble 1339*p* Orange 1365*i*	Aix-en-Provence 1409*p* Dôle 1422*p* Poitiers 1431*p* Caen 1432*p* Bordeaux 1441*p* Valence 1452,1455*p* Nantes 1460*p* Bourges 1464*p*
Great Britain		Oxford c. 1200 Cambridge 1209		St.Andrews 1411*p* Glasgow 1451*p* Aberdeen 1494*p*
Spain, Portugal		Palencia 1208 Salamanca pre-1219 Seville 1254*r,p* Lisbon 1290*p* Coimbra 1290*p* Valladolid 1290	Lerida 1300*r* Perpignan 1350*p* Huesca 1354*r*	Gerona 1446 Barcelona 1450*p* Saragossa 1474*p* Palma 1483*r* Sïguenza 1489*p* Alcalá 1499*p* Valencia 1500*p*
Germany, Scandinavia, Eastern Europe, Low Countries			Prague 1347*p,i* Cracow 1364, 1397*p* Vienna 1365*p* Pècs 1367*p* Erfurt 1379 Heidelberg 1385*p* Cologne 1388*p* Buda 1389*p*	Würzburg 1402 Leipzig 1409*p* Rostock 1419*p* Louvain 1425*p* Trier 1454,1473*p* Greifswald 1428,1456*p* Freiburg-Breisgau 1455*p* Basel 1459*p* Ingolstadt 1459,1472*p* Poszony 1465*p* Mainz 1476*p* Tübingen c. 1476*p* Uppsala 1477*p* Copenhagen 1478*p*

i Founded by imperial bull   *p* Founded by papal bull   *r* Founded by royal charter

9. Compiled from Hastings Rashdall, *The Universities of Europe in the Middle Ages* (1895), 2nd ed., ed. F. M. Powicke and A. B. Emden, 3 vols. (Oxford: Clarendon Press, 1936), v. 1, p. xxiv; Jacques Verger, "Patterns," in *Universities in the Middle Ages*, ed. Hilde Symoens (New York: Cambridge University Press, 1992), pp. 62–5.

Schoolman

14. Peter Abelard, *The Story of My Misfortunes* (c. 1132)

INTRODUCTION

Born into a family of the minor nobility in Brittany, Peter Abelard (1079–1142) at an early age was offered the opportunity for formal education by his father, a soldier. The boy thus faced a choice that would become increasingly prevalent in the subsequent century: whether to pursue the vocation of a scholar or a soldier. By the time he was seventeen Abelard chose the former, while incorporating the spirit of the latter, for he became a "wandering scholar" devoted to studying the *trivium* and jousting through dialectic.

"Wandering scholars" denoted both the teaching masters and the students who perambulated Western Europe in the century before the founding of universities and congregated informally around cathedral and monastic schools, the most significant educational institutions of the eleventh and twelfth centuries. Arriving as a wandering scholar at Paris in about 1100, Abelard joined the prominent school of William of Champeaux (c. 1070–c. 1120) at the Cathedral of Notre Dame, and promptly made himself unwelcome by challenging his teacher. When Abelard's health broke down, he returned home, but six years later rejoined William's school, then located at the Abbey of St. Victor outside Paris, and engaged his master in a disputatious battle over one of the central intellectual questions of the day.

That question was prompted by renewed attention being given to Aristotle's two introductory treatises on logic, as well as the *Introduction* of Porphyry, all three of which Boethius had translated. In these introductory treatises arises the question of the nature of "universals," or abstract terms; and wandering scholars of the late eleventh and early twelfth century were divided between two basic positions. Some, including William, advocated the "realist" view that universals have independent existence apart from the individuals they comprise; others, including Abelard, maintained the "nominalist" position that universals are simply names for groups of individuals and have no existence in themselves. On this prominent issue, Abelard, the young, aggressive upstart, made a name for himself by forcing William, the well known teacher, to modify his position of strict realism.

Deciding next to study theology, Abelard went to Laon, where the most famous theological school of the time was headed by Anselm.[10] Again challenging a famous teacher, Abelard eclipsed Anselm in the analysis of Biblical texts and thereby advanced a relatively novel definition of "theology" as the carefully reasoned interpretation of closely read Biblical passages, rather than the validation of received doctrine by reference to the text. In the 1110s Abelard returned to Paris, bringing students from Laon with him, and became head of the cathedral school at Notre Dame and one of the most famous and provocative teachers in Europe.

While at the height of his powers, Abelard commenced to engage in intellectual and sexual transgressions that led to his self-destruction. Pride in his dialectical prowess led him further into theological investigation and steered him toward doctrinal reefs; meanwhile, he seduced his tutee Helöise (c. 1100–c. 1163), whose uncle had him castrated. In 1119 he retreated to an abbey in 1119, but two former pupils of Anselm of Laon convinced a Church council to charge him with heresy. In about 1136 he returned to a school in Paris, where John of Salisbury heard him lecture on dialectic,

---

10. This Anselm of Laon (c. 1040–1117) is not Anselm of Canterbury (c. 1033–c. 1109), who advanced the famous ontological proof deducing the existence of God from the existence of the human conception of a perfect being.

and his teaching enjoyed great success as always. But his adversaries continued to seek his downfall, and persuaded another Church council to charge him with heresy in 1140. Abelard appealed to the Pope and set out to Rome to plead his case, but collapsed on the way and died in 1142.

SELECTION[11]

Abelard's letter of consolation to a friend[12]

The experiences of others often serve to arouse or allay man's feelings better than words. And so to follow up the conversation in which I tried to console you at our meeting, I have decided to write you a letter of further encouragement based upon the experience of my own misfortunes so that when you compare your trials with mine you may consider them of little or no account and be stronger to endure them.

The place of his birth

To begin, then, I was born in a town called Le Pallet in Brittany near the border about eight miles, I would say, east of Nantes. I was lighthearted and had talent for letters, characteristics derived from my country and family. My father was a man who had acquired some literary knowledge before he donned the uniform of a soldier, and he retained such a liking for learning that he intended to procure for whatever sons he was to have a training in letters before their military service. And he carried out his purpose. As he loved me the more, being his first-born, so he saw to it that I was carefully instructed. The further I went in my studies and the more easily I made progress, the more I became attached to them and came to possess such a love of them that, giving up in favor of my brothers the pomp of military glory along with my right of inheritance and the other prerogatives of primogeniture, I renounced the field of Mars to be brought up at the knee of Minerva. Since I preferred the armor of logic to all the teaching of philosophy, I exchanged all other arms for it and chose the contests of disputation above the trophies of warfare.[13] And so, practicing logic I wandered about the various provinces wherever I heard that the pursuit of this art was vigorous and became thereby like the Peripatetics.

Master William's persecution of him

I finally reached Paris where this branch of learning was especially cultivated and enrolled under William of Champeaux, a man who at the time was an outstanding teacher in this branch both in reputation and in fact. I remained under him some little time; at first I was welcome but after a while he found me burdensome [because] I began to question some of his statements and quite often to argue against his position; sometimes I was apparently the winner in the discussions. Those of my fellow-students who were considered outstanding became the more deeply incensed at my conduct [because] they looked upon me as younger than they and as having spent less time at books. From this

---

11. Peter Abelard, *The Story of My Misfortunes*, tr. J. T. Muckle as *The Story of Abelard's Adversities*, rev. ed. (Toronto: Pontifical Institute of Medieval Studies, 1964), pp. 11–27. Reprinted by permission of the Pontifical Institute of Medieval Studies, Toronto. The traditional title, *Historia Calamitatum (The Story of My Misfortunes)*, is not original but was well known by the late 1300s.

12. The headings were added by another hand and are placed in brackets. The form of the letter was likely adopted as a rhetorical convention.

13. Abelard's choice between Mars and Minerva anticipates the cultural shift that would culminate in the founding of the universities in the 1200s, although he—and the university scholastic—may have combined, rather than chosen between, jousting and study.

my troubles began and have plagued me to this day; and the more widespread my fame has become, the more has the jealously of others been enkindled against me.

Finally it came about that, with a presumption of ability beyond my years, I formed the ambition, young as I was, to be at the head of a school and to get as a location what was then the renowned town of Melun which was also a royal seat. My above-mentioned master[14] sensed this, and in an attempt to have my school far removed from him, he slyly used every means in his power, before I withdrew from his school, to hinder the furtherance of my plans and to deprive me of the place I had now arranged for. But some men of influence were opposed to him, and relying on their help I accomplished my purpose, since his open antipathy gained for me the support of many.

With the establishment of this my first school, my reputation in dialectical skill began to spread so that the fame not only of my former fellow-students, but also of my master gradually lessened and went into eclipse. As a result, being more self-confident I transferred my school to Corbeil nearer Paris that I might prove a greater embarrassment and offer more frequent challenges to debate. But after the lapse of a comparatively short time, owing to the heavy strain of study, I fell sick and was forced to return home; and though absent [in Brittany] for several years, all those who were anxious for instruction in logic kept eagerly trying to seek me out.

After a few years had passed I was well recovered from my illness. My teacher William, archdeacon of Paris, had changed his state and entered the Order of Regular Clerics[15] for the purpose, it was said, of being considered more pious and thereby of gaining promotion to the rank of a major prelacy, as happened when he was made bishop of Châlons. But his taking the religious habit did not withdraw him from Paris or from his former philosophical pursuits. On the contrary, he immediately [resumed his public teaching], as formerly, right in the monastery to which he had gone for a life in religion.

At that time I returned to him to hear him lecturing on rhetoric. [In the course of our discussions], I forced him by clear proofs from reasoning to change, yes, to abandon his old stand on universals. For he held the position on the common existence of universals that the same thing exists wholly and essentially in all individuals of a class and that there is no distinction of essence in them but only variety through multiplicity of accidents. He subsequently so modified his position as to assert that the same thing exists in individuals, not essentially, but without differentiation. This problem of universals has always been a [debated] point among dialecticians and of such magnitude that even Porphyry when writing about universals in his *Introduction* did not venture to settle it but said "it is a very deep question." Once William had corrected, yes under compulsion, had abandoned his position, his lectures bogged down into such carelessness that they could scarcely be called lectures on logic at all, as though the whole art were confined to the problem of universals.

From then on my teaching gained such strength and prestige that those who formerly had somewhat vigorously championed the position of [William] and had most forcefully attacked mine now flocked to my school and even he who had taken over [William's] chair in the cathedral school of Paris offered his place to me that, along with the other students he might follow my lectures right where our common master had held sway. Within a few days after my taking over the chair of dialectics, envy began to eat the heart out of my master and anguish to seize him to a degree I can hardly express. His seething soul did not long endure the misery which had taken hold of him before he cunningly attempted to depose me. And because there was nothing [William] could do against me

---

14. "Master" refers to the teacher of a school.

15. The "regular" clergy refers to those who were governed by a *regula*, or rule, such as monks, in contrast to the "secular" or parish clergy, who were not.

personally, he set out by laying the basest charges to take the school away from him who had turned the chair over to me and to put another, one of my rivals, in that position. . . .

The disputes which followed the return of my master to the city between my students and him and his students and the outcome which fortune gave to my students and to me among them, facts have long since told you. But to speak with due moderation, let me boldly repeat those words of Ajax—"If you ask the result of this contest, I was not worsted by him"[16]—and if I should keep silence, the fact would cry out and tell the outcome. . . .

Abelard goes to Master Anselm at Laon

And so I enrolled under this old man whose great name rested on long practice rather than on ability or learning. If one in doubt about some point consulted him, one left him in greater doubt. He was a wonder in the minds of his listeners, but a nobody in the estimate of his questioners. He had a remarkable command of language, but it was despicable with respect to meaning and devoid of sense. While he kindled a fire, he filled his room with smoke but did not light it up. His tree appeared heavy with foliage to those viewing it from afar, but to those who came near and looked closely, it was found fruitless. And so when I went to this tree to gather fruit therefrom, I found that it was the fig tree which Our Lord cursed [*Matthew* 21: 18–19], or like the old oak to which Lucan likened Pompey, saying: "There he stood, the mere shadow of a great name, like an oak towering in a fruitful field."[17]

Realizing this, I did not delay long in the idleness of his shadow. I went to his lectures more and more irregularly, and for this the distinguished among his students were offended with me as despising a man of such renown; they secretly aroused him against me and by unfair suggestions brought him to become hostile towards me. One day after a session of *sentences*,[18] we students started joking with one another. One of them, trying me, asked what I, who had studied only philosophical works, thought of the lectures on the sacred books. I replied that they were very beneficial since we thereby learn the way of salvation, but that I was greatly astonished that [those who were educated could not understand the commentaries of the saints through their writings or glosses alone, without any form of teaching.]

Many who were there derided me and asked if I could and would attempt to show them how. I replied that, if they wished, I was ready to try. Then they were loud in their cries of derision and exclaimed: "All right, take some commentary on some unusual passage of scripture, and let us put your claim to the test." All agreed on a very obscure passage of the prophet Ezekiel. Taking the commentary, I straightway invited them to come to hear me on the next day. They started to give me unsolicited advice saying that I should not hasten to such a task, but, inexperienced as I was, I should take a longer time to establish and confirm my interpretation. I indignantly replied that it was not my custom to advance through practice but through talent, adding that either they were not to object to coming to hear me at the time of my own choosing or else I would break the bargain.

---

16. Ovid, *Metamorphoses* XIII 89, 90. In the correspondence about their separation, Abelard and Helöise frequently quote from Ovid, the Latin lyric poet of love.

17. Lucan, *Pharsalia* I 135–6. Lucan's epic recounts the civil war fought between Julius Caesar and Pompey.

18. "Anselm's teaching followed the traditional lines of study of the Scriptures (*lectio divina*), . . . with an exposition verse by verse from the teachings of the Fathers of the Church (*glossae*). Sentences (*sententiae*) were the deeper truths of Revelation to be arrived at after a study of the letter and sense of the text; these were stated by the teacher and then expounded and proved through citation from the Bible and the Fathers. Abelard's view was that [a philosopher] should be able to study the Scriptures alone with the aid of a commentary." Betty Radice, tr., *The Letters of Abelard and Helöise* (London: Penguin Books, 1974), p. 63n.

At my first lecture there were only a few, as all considered it ridiculous that I, utterly unlearned in sacred science, should attempt this so hastily. But those who did attend thought my lecture so good that they praised it highly and constrained me to comment on the text in the same vein as that in which I had lectured. When those who had not attended heard this, they vied with one another in getting in on my second and third lectures, and all alike were anxious to make a copy of the glosses which I had begun on the first day.[19]

Anselm persecutes Abelard

As a result, this old man, inspired by bitter envy and spurred on by the urgings of some against me, as I mentioned above, began to persecute me for my lectures in divinity with enmity no less than that of my master William for those in philosophy. There were then in the school of this aged man two students who appeared to excel, Alberic of Rheims and Lotulph the Lombard,[20] who were the more incensed against me as they thought highly of themselves. Moved especially by the suggestions of these two, as I afterwards learned, that old man arrogantly forbade me to continue in the place where he was teaching the work of interpretation which I had entered upon. He gave as an excuse that I might perhaps in that capacity write something erroneous, as I was unschooled in that branch, and the error would be imputed to him. When the students heard this, they became highly indignant at this open manifestation of envy and spite such as no one had ever experienced before. And the more open it was, the more it redounded to my credit, and by his persecution, he made me more esteemed.

Abelard at last enjoys renown in Paris

After a few days I returned to Paris and for some years enjoyed peaceful possession of the school of which, though long ago it had been yielded and turned over to me, I had been deprived.[21] As soon as I took over there, I was eager to finish the commentary on *Ezekiel* begun at Laon. My lectures proved so popular with my hearers that they considered I had acquired no less charm in lecturing in divinity than they had witnessed in philosophy. Through desire for lectures in both branches, my students increased greatly in number, and the financial gain and glory which accrued to me you know well from report. But success always puffs up fools, and worldly repose weakens the strength of one's mind and readily loosens its fiber through carnal allurement.

At a time when I considered that I was the one philosopher in the world and had nothing to fear from others, I, who up to that time had lived most chastely, began to relax the reins on my passions. And the more success I had in philosophy and sacred science, the more I withdrew from philosophers and divines through an unclean life. For it is well known that philosophers, not to speak of divines—I mean men attentive to the lessons of sacred scripture—were especially adorned with the virtue of chastity. And while I was laboring under my pride and lechery, God's grace provided a cure for each, though I willed it not, first for my lechery by depriving me of the organs by which I practiced it, then for my pride which my scholarship especially nursed in me in accordance with the saying of St. Paul:

---

19. In this way, Abelard advances the emerging conception of the study of theology as the critical, dialectical investigation of the meaning of the text, rather than the dogmatic illustration of received doctrine by reference to the text.

20. Alberic of Rheims and Lotulph were two of Abelard's chief opponents at the council that condemned him in 1120.

21. This was the school at Notre Dame, in which Abelard was established as master.

"Knowledge puffs up" [1 *Corinthians* 8: 1]. This was accomplished by humiliating me through the burning of the book which was my special glory.[22]

I would have you know correctly the story of each cure, just as it occurred, from the facts and not from hearsay. I had always detested unclean harlots and my constant attention to my books had kept me from frequent association with women of nobility and I knew little of society among women in the world. But perverse fortune, as the saying goes, by her blandishments found an easier way to cast me down from the height of my glory, or rather God in His goodness claimed me for Himself, a humbled man instead of one most proud and forgetful of the grace he had received.

How Abelard's love for Helöise brought about a fall
which afflicted both body and soul

There lived in Paris a maiden named Helöise, the niece of a canon named Fulbert, who from his deep love for her was eager to have her advanced in all literary pursuits possible. She was a lady of no mean appearance while in literary excellence she was the first. And as the gift of letters is rare among women, so it had gained favor for her and made her the most renowned woman in the whole kingdom. I considered all the qualities which usually inspire lovers and decided she was just the one for me to join in love.[23]

---

22. In the early 1120s the Council of Soissons burned his treatise, *On the Unity and Trinity of God*, addressing the same topic for which Abelard's first master Roscelin was charged with heresy.

23. See the warning of Juana Inéz de la Cruz in selection #31 about confiding young girls to older male tutors due to the failure to educate women in the liberal arts.

Reformulation of Knowledge and the Liberal Arts

15. Hugh of St. Victor, *Didascalicon* (c. 1127)

INTRODUCTION

Born into a noble family in Germany, Hugh of St. Victor (1096–c. 1141) was sent by his parents to a nearby Augustinian monastery to learn Latin and numbers, where, against the wishes of his parents, he elected to join the monks as a novice in order to pursue further learning. In about 1115 an army invaded the diocese, and Hugh fled to Paris and undertook vows at the Abbey of St. Victor, where he was placed in charge of teaching the liberal arts. Soon he became master of the school, which grew to be a chief rival and alternative to the nearby school of Peter Abelard.

Hugh's alternative lay primarily in his purpose of seeking to confirm, rather than to challenge or modify, orthodoxy by employing dialectical method. In line with Augustine, he viewed secular studies as intrinsically part of divine studies and as one step in a three-stage mystical ascent toward God. This ascent proceeded through a stage of "thought" in which God is seen in the nature of things, a stage of "meditation" in which God is seen in ourselves, and finally a stage of "contemplation" in which a direct vision of God is sought. This approach reveals the influence of Hugh's early education with Augustinians, which also shaped the *Didascalicon*.

Composed in the late 1120s, this work belonged to the genre of didascalic, or didactic, literature explaining and justifying the arts or disciplines that should be studied. In presenting his organization of knowledge, Hugh's *Didascalicon* incorporated the three predominant, competing epistemic arrangements. One was the traditional, tri-partite arrangement that had been passed from Cicero and Seneca to Augustine, to Isidore and then to Hugh. This divided philosophy into "physics" (natural philosophy), "ethics" (moral philosophy), and "logic" (including the three arts of grammar, rhetoric, and dialectic or logic), and incorporated a significant ambiguity in treating "logic" both as a genus and as a species. Another arrangement was Aristotelian and divided philosophy into "theoretical" sciences (including metaphysics, physics, and mathematics), "practical" or human sciences (such as politics, economics, ethics and, to a certain extent, rhetoric), and "productive" sciences (such as poetics and, in some respects, rhetoric).[24] Finally, there were the seven liberal arts, which served not only as a curricular organization, but also as the most influential, functioning epistemic arrangement. Out of these, Hugh attempted to generate a coherent organization of knowledge that was faithful to tradition and authority. Inevitably and ironically, the result was a wholly novel conception.

Although the *Didascalicon* was widely read and survives in nearly a hundred manuscripts in libraries across Europe, as well as in the iconography of the liberal arts, Hugh's conception did not have long lasting influence because an immense body of new knowledge flooded into Western Europe soon after his death, outmoding the prior medieval curricular arrangements. But Hugh did have lasting effect in exemplifying and legitimating the effort to reconceive the organization of knowledge and the liberal arts in the face of diverse conceptions. Thus, Thomas Aquinas quoted Hugh just at the point when Thomas declared obsolete the traditional formulation of the seven liberal arts, as seen below.

Hugh continued as master of the Abbey School for about thirteen years after completing the *Didascalicon* and died in about 1141.

---

24. Aristotle advances different versions of the organization of knowledge at various points in his writings, but this formulation is a fairly conventional interpretation of his view. See, for example, *Metaphysics* 1025b–1026a. The content of these Aristotelian sciences were not available to Hugh, but the categories and the formulation were known through the treatises of Aristotle and Porphyry that Boethius had translated.

SELECTION[25]

Book I
Chapter 11. Concerning the Origin of Logic.

Logic is so called from the Greek word *logos*, which has a double sense. For *logos* means either word or reason, and hence logic can be called either a linguistic or a rational science. Rational logic, which is called argumentative, contains dialectic and rhetoric. Linguistic logic stands as genus to grammar, dialectic, and rhetoric, thus containing argumentative logic as a subdivision.[26] It is linguistic logic that we put fourth after the theoretical, practical, and mechanical. It must not be supposed, however, that this science is called logical, that is, linguistic, because before its discovery there were no words, or as if men before its time did not have conversations with one another. For both spoken and written words existed previously, but the theory of spoken and written language was not yet reduced to an art; no rules for speaking or arguing correctly had yet been given. All sciences, indeed, were matters of use before they became matters of art.[27] But when men subsequently considered that use can be transformed into art, and what was previously vague and subject to caprice can be brought into order by definite rules and precepts, they began, we are told, to reduce to art the habits which had arisen partly by chance, partly by nature—correcting what was bad in use, supplying what was missing, eliminating what was superfluous, and furthermore prescribing definite rules and precepts for each usage.[28]

Such was the origin of all the arts;[29] scanning them all, we find this true. Before there was grammar, men both wrote and spoke; before there was dialectic, they distinguished the true from the false by reasoning; before there was rhetoric, they discoursed upon civil laws; before there was arithmetic, there was knowledge of counting; before there was an art of music, they sang; before there was geometry, they measured fields; before there was astronomy, they marked off periods of time from the courses of the stars. But then came the arts, which, though they took their rise in usage, nonetheless excel it.

This would be the place to set forth who were the inventors of the separate arts, when these persons flourished and where, and how the various disciplines made a start in their hands:[30] first, however, I wish to distinguish the individual arts from one another by dividing philosophy into its parts, so to say. I should therefore briefly recapitulate the things I have said thus far, so that the transition to what follows may more easily be made.

---

25. Jerome Taylor, tr., *The* Didascalicon *of Hugh of St. Victor, A Medieval Guide to the Arts* (1961; New York: Columbia University Press, 1991), pp. 59–73, 85–9. Reprinted by permission of Columbia University Press.

26. "Rational logic" or "argumentative logic" refers to the liberal art of logic. "Linguistic logic" apparently denotes one category of the Stoic division of philosophy into physics, ethics, and logic, which was borrowed successively by Cicero, Augustine, Isidore, and Hugh.

27. Hugh employs the terms "science" (*scientia*) and "art" (*ars*) interchangeably here, as was common, though he elsewhere distinguishes between the two terms. Inconsistency on this usage appears frequently in medieval writings on the liberal arts.

28. The translator (p. 195n) notes the similarity between this point and the view of Cicero appearing in *On the Orator* (I xlii 187–8): "Almost all things now comprehended in the arts were once scattered and disordered. So in music, ... in geometry, ... in astronomy, ... in grammar, all these things seemed unknown and without order. A certain art was therefore imposed on them from without ... to tie together the disconnected and fragmentary material and delimit it in some kind of rational order."

29. When Hugh turns to give examples, note that "all the arts" turns out to refer only to the seven liberal arts.

30. Hugh thus provides for the project that Christine de Pizan and Bathsua Makin undertake.

We have said that there are four branches of knowledge only, and that they contain all the rest: they are the theoretical, which strives for the contemplation of truth; the practical, which considers the regulation of morals; the mechanical, which supervises the occupations of this life; and the logical, which provides the knowledge necessary for correct speaking and clear argumentation. And so, here, we may not incongruously understand that number "four" belonging to the soul—that "four" which, for reverence of it, the ancients called to witness in their oaths, which we read: "By him who gave the quaternary number to our soul!"[31]

How these sciences are comprised under philosophy, and again what they themselves comprise we shall now show, briefly repeating first the definition of philosophy.

Book II
Chapter 1. Concerning the Distinguishing of the Arts.

"Philosophy is the love of that Wisdom which, wanting in nothing, is a living Mind and the sole primordial Idea or Pattern of things."[32] This definition pays special attention to the etymology of the word. For *philos* in Greek means love, and *sophia* means wisdom, so that from them "philosophy," that is, "love of wisdom," was coined. The words "which, wanting in nothing, is a living Mind and the sole primordial Idea or Pattern of things" signify the divine Wisdom, which is said to be wanting in nothing because it contains nothing inadequately, but in a single and simultaneous vision beholds all things past, present, and future. It is called "living Mind" because what has once existed in the divine Mind never is forgotten; and it is called "the primordial Idea or Pattern of things" because to its likeness all things have been formed. There are those who say that what the arts are concerned with remains forever the same.[33] This, then, is what the arts are concerned with, this is what they intend, namely, to restore within us the divine likeness, a likeness which to us is a form, but to God is his nature. The more we are conformed to the divine nature, the more do we possess Wisdom, for then there begins to shine forth again in us what has forever existed in the divine Idea or Pattern, coming and going in us but standing changeless in God.[34]

"Again, philosophy is the art of arts and the discipline of disciplines"[35]—that, namely toward which all arts and disciplines are oriented. Knowledge can be called an art "when it comprises the rules and precepts of an art"[36] as it does in the study of how to write; knowledge can be called a discipline when it is said to be "full"[37] as it is in the "instructional" science, or mathematics. Or, it is called art when it treats of matters that only resemble the true and are objects of opinion; and discip-

---

31. This verse is line 47 in the Pythagorean poem *Golden Song*, which was quoted by Porphyry, from whom it was taken by Macrobius in the late fourth century A.D. The sources of Hugh's quotations are drawn from the translator's notes.

32. Boethius, *Dialogues on Porphyry* I 3. See note at Isocrates, *Antidosis* 266, in Selection #2.

33. There is a strong Neo-Platonic influence here in Hugh's view that the arts restore us to unchanging archetypes.

34. "The arts intend restoration of the radical cognitive good lost to man through the fall—knowledge of his Creator, of himself, of things created with and for himself, and of things he is to make with these last." Translator's note, p. 196n.

35. Quoted from Cassiodorus, *Introduction to Divine and Human Letters* II iii 5, or Isidore, *Etymologies* II 9.

36. Isidore, *Etymologies* I 2.

37. Cassiodorus, *Introduction to Divine and Human Letters* II ii 17. Hugh changes the sense of Cassiodorus who writes "when it is said to be learned full[y]." Translator's note, p. 196n. Like the distinction between "art" and "science," Hugh cites but does not employ consistently this distinction between "art" and "discipline."

line when, by means of true arguments, it deals with matters unable to be other than they are. This last distinction between art and discipline is the one which Plato and Aristotle wished to establish.[38] Or, that can be called art which takes shape in some material medium and is brought out in it through manipulation of that material, as is the case in architecture; while that is called a discipline which takes shape in thought and is brought forth in it through reasoning alone, as is the case in logic.

"Philosophy, furthermore, is a meditating upon death, a pursuit of especial fitness for Christians, who, spurning the solicitations of this world, live subject to discipline in a manner resembling the life of their future home."[39] Yet again, philosophy is the discipline which investigates demonstratively the causes of all things, human and divine. Thus, the theory of all pursuits belongs to philosophy (their administration is not entirely philosophical), and therefore philosophy is said to include all things in some way.

Philosophy is divided into theoretical, practical, mechanical, and logical.[40] These four contain all knowledge. The theoretical may also be called speculative; the practical may be called active, likewise ethical, that is, moral, from the fact that morals consist in good action;[41] the mechanical may be called adulterate because it is concerned with the works of human labor; the logical may be called linguistic from its concern with words. The theoretical is divided into theology, mathematics, and physics—a division which Boethius makes in different terms, distinguishing the theoretical into the intellectible, the intelligible, and the natural, where the intellectible is equivalent to theology, the intelligible to mathematics, and the natural to physics. And the intellectible he defines as follows.[42]

Chapter 2. Concerning Theology.

"The intellectible is that which, ever enduring of itself, one and the same in its own divinity, is not ever apprehended by any of the senses, but by the mind and the intellect alone. Its study," [Boethius] says, "the Greeks call theology, and it consists of searching into the contemplation of God and the incorporeality of the soul and the consideration of true philosophy."[43] It was called theology as meaning discourse concerning the divine, for *theos* means God, and *logos* discourse or knowledge. It is theology, therefore, "when we discuss with deepest penetration some aspect either of the inexpressible nature of God or of spiritual creatures."[44]

Chapter 3. Concerning Mathematics.

The "instructional" science is called mathematics: *mathesis*, when the "t" is pronounced without the "h," means vanity, and it refers to the superstition of those who place the fates of men in the stars and

---

38. Adapted from Isidore, *Etymologies* I 3; Cassiodorus, *Introduction to Divine and Human Letters* II ii 17.

39. Quoted from Isidore, *Etymologies* II 9, or Cassiodorus, *Introduction to Divine and Human Letters* II iii 5.

40. Having stated a number of not easily reconcilable views, Hugh concludes with his own, seemingly unrelated to the formulations of philosophy that he states above.

41. Hugh seems to be justifying his conflation of Aristotle's category of practical philosophy (including ethics) with the Stoic category of moral philosophy, or ethics.

42. Drawn largely from Cassiodorus and Isidore, Hugh's discussion of Boethius's division of theoretical philosophy continues through II 17, while incorporating supplementary material on the liberal arts.

43. Boethius, *Dialogues on Porphyry* I 3. Employed in Aristotle's sense, the term "theology" refers to what was subsequently called "metaphysics," rather than reflection upon the nature of God or religious matters.

44. Quoted from Isidore, *Etymologies* II 13 and Cassiodorus, *Introduction to Divine and Human Letters* II iii 6.

who are therefore called "mathematicians"; but when the "t" is pronounced with the "h," the word refers to the "instructional" science.[45]

This, moreover, is the branch of theoretical knowledge "which considers abstract quantity. Now quantity is called abstract when, intellectually separating it from matter or from other accidents, we treat of it as equal, unequal, and the like, in our reasoning alone"[46]—a separation which it receives only in the domain of mathematics and not in nature. Boethius calls this branch of knowledge the *intelligible* and finds that "it itself includes the first or *intellectible* part in virtue of its own thought and understanding, directed as these are to the celestial works of supernal divinity and to whatever sublunary beings enjoy more blessed mind and purer substance, and, finally, to human souls. All of these things, though they once consisted of that primary intellectible substance, have since, by contact with bodies, degenerated from the level of intellectibles to that of intelligibles; as a result, they are less objects of understanding than active agents of it, and they find greater happiness by the purity of their understanding whenever they apply themselves to the study of things intellectible."[47] . . .

Chapter 6. Concerning the Quadrivium.[48]

Since, as we have said, the proper concern of mathematics is abstract quantity, it is necessary to seek the species of mathematics in the parts into which such quantity falls. Now abstract quantity is nothing other than form, visible in its linear dimension, impressed upon the mind, and rooted in the mind's imaginative part. It is of two kinds: the first is continuous quantity, like that of a tree or a stone, and is called *magnitude*; the second is discrete quantity, like that of a flock or of a people, and is called *multitude*. Further, in the latter some quantities stand wholly in themselves, for example, "three," "four," or any other whole number; others stand in relation to another quantity, as "double," "half," "once and a half," "once and a third," and the like. One type of magnitude, moreover, is *mobile*, like the heavenly spheres; another, *immobile*, like the earth. Now, multitude which stands in itself is the concern of arithmetic, while that which stands in relation to another multitude is the concern of music. Geometry holds forth knowledge of immobile magnitude, while astronomy claims knowledge of the mobile. Mathematics, therefore, is divided into arithmetic, music, geometry, and astronomy. . . .

Chapter 11. Concerning Arithmetic.[49]

Arithmetic has for its subject equal, or even, number and unequal, or odd, number. Equal number is of three kinds: equally equal, equally unequal, and unequally equal. Unequal number, too, has three varieties: the first consists of numbers which are prime and incomposite; the second consists of numbers which are secondary and composite; the third consists of numbers which, when considered in themselves, are secondary and composite, but which, when one compares them with other numbers [to find a common factor or denominator], are prime and incomposite.

---

45. "At the basis of the distinction are the Greek *máthésis*, knowledge, and *mataiótés*, vanity." Translator's note, p. 197n. The etymological link is fanciful, as are many of Hugh's etymologies.

46. These words are quoted from selection #10 by Cassiodorus (II pref. 4, or II iii 21). But the definition of mathematics in terms of abstract quantity is taken from Boethius, *Arithmetic* I 1, as noted in the introduction to Boethius above.

47. Boethius, *Dialogues on Porphyry* I 3.

48. This chapter has many verbal parallels with Boethius, *Arithmetic* I 1.

49. This chapter condenses the discussion in Boethius, *Arithmetic* I 3–17.

Chapter 12. Concerning Music.[50]

The varieties of music are three: that belonging to the universe, that belonging to man, and that which is instrumental. Of the music of the universe, some is characteristic of the elements, some of the planets, some of the seasons: of the elements in their mass, number, and volume; of the planets in their situation, motion, and nature; of the seasons in days (in the alternation of day and night), in months (in the waxing and waning of the moons), and in years (in the succession of spring, summer, autumn, and winter).

Of the music of man, some is characteristic of the body, some of the soul, and some of the bond between the two. It is characteristic of the body partly in the vegetative power by which it grows—a power belonging to all beings born to bodily life; partly in those fluids or humors through the mixture or complexion of which the human body subsists—a type of mixture belonging to all sensate beings; and partly in those activities (the foremost among them are the mechanical) which belong above all to rational beings and which are good if they do not become inordinate, so that avarice or appetite are not fostered by the very things intended to relieve our weakness. As Lucan says [in praise of Cato the Elder]:

> He feasted in conquering hunger;
> Any roof from storms served his hall;
> His dearest garb, the toga coarse,
> Civilian dress of the Roman.[51]

Music is characteristic of the soul partly in its virtues, like justice, piety, and temperance; and partly in its powers, like reason, wrath, and concupiscence. The music between the body and the soul is that natural friendship by which the soul is leagued to the body, not in physical bonds, but in certain sympathetic relationships for the purpose of imparting motion and sensation to the body. Because of this friendship, it is written, "No man hates his own flesh." [*Ephesians* 5: 29] This music consists in loving one's flesh, but one's spirit more; in cherishing one's body, but not in destroying one's virtue.

Instrumental music consists partly of striking, as upon tympans and strings; partly in blowing, as upon pipes or organs; and partly in giving voice, as in recitals and songs. "There are also three kinds of musicians: one that composes songs, another that plays instruments, and a third that judges instrumental performance and song."[52]

Chapter 13. Concerning Geometry.

Geometry has three parts: planimetry, altimetry, and cosmimetry. Planimetry measures the plane, that is, the long and the broad; and, by widening its object, it measures what is before and behind and to left and right. Altimetry measures the high, and; by widening its object, it measures what reaches above and stretches below: for height is predicated both of the sea in the sense of depth, and of a tree in the sense of tallness. *Cosmos* is the word for the universe, and from it comes the term "cosmimetry," or "universe-measurement." Cosmimetry measures things spherical, that is, globose and rotund, like a ball or an egg, and it is therefore called "cosmimetry" from the sphere of the universe, on account of the preeminence of this sphere—not that cosmimetry is concerned with the measurement of the universe alone, but that the universe-sphere excels all other spherical things.

---

50. This chapter is drawn from Boethius, *Music* I 2.

51. Lucan, *Pharsalia [The Civil War]* II 384–7.

52. Boethius, *Music* I 34.

Chapter 14. Concerning Astronomy.

What we have just said does not contradict our previous statement that geometry is occupied with immobile magnitude, astronomy with mobile: for what we have just said takes into account the original discovery of geometry, which led to its being called "earth measurement." We can also say that what geometry considers in the sphere of the universe—namely, the measure of the celestial regions and spheres—is immobile in that aspect which belongs to geometrical studies. For geometry is not concerned with movement but with space. What astronomy considers, however, is the *mobile*—the courses of the stars and the intervals of time and seasons. Thus, we shall say that without exception immobile magnitude is the subject of geometry, mobile of astronomy, because, although both busy themselves with the same thing, the one contemplates the static aspect of that thing, the other its moving aspect.

Chapter 15. Definition of the Quadrivium.

Arithmetic is therefore the science of numbers. Music is the distinguishing of sounds and the variance of voices. Or again, music or harmony is the concord of a number of dissimilar things blended into one. Geometry is the discipline treating immobile magnitude, and it is the contemplative delineation of forms, by which the limits of every object are shown. Putting it differently, geometry is "a fount of perceptions and a source of utterances."[53] Astronomy is the discipline which examines the spaces, movements, and circuits of the heavenly bodies at determined intervals. . . .

Chapter 16. Concerning Physics.

Physics searches out and considers the causes of things as found in their effects as derived from certain causes:

Whence the tremblings of the earth do rise, or from what cause the deep seas swell;

Whence grasses grow or beasts are moved with wayward wrath and will;

Whence every sort of verdant shrub, or rock, or creeping thing.[54]

The word *physis* means nature, and therefore Boethius places natural physics in the higher division of theoretical knowledge.[55] This science is also call physiology, that is, discourse on the natures of things, a term which refers to the same matter as physics.[56] Physics is sometimes taken broadly to mean the same as theoretical science, and, taking the word in this sense, some persons divide philosophy into three parts—into physics, ethics, and logic. In this division the mechanical sciences find no place, philosophy being restricted to physics, ethics, and logic alone. . . .[57]

---

53. This phrase was conventionally found in discussion of rhetoric and may have been misplaced here by Hugh. Translator's note, p. 203n.

54. Vergil, *Georgics* II 479ff.

55. Boethius, *Dialogues on Porphyry* II 3.

56. Hugh's usage of "physiology" is anomalous. "Natural philosophy" was customarily employed as a synonym for "physics."

57. This division of philosophy into physics, ethics, and logic was attributed to Plato by Cicero (*Academica* I v 19–21) and Augustine (*City of God* VIII 4, XI 25). But it seems to be derived from the Stoics, who passed it successively to Cicero, Augustine, and Isidore (*Etymologies* II 22, 24), from whom Hugh borrowed it.

Book III

Chapter 1. Concerning the Order and Method of Study and Discipline.

Philosophy is divided into the theoretical, the practical, the mechanical, and the logical. The *theoretical* is divided into theology, physics, and mathematics; mathematics is divided into arithmetic, music, geometry, and astronomy.[58] The *practical* is divided into solitary, private, and public. The *mechanical* is divided into fabric making, armament, commerce, agriculture, hunting, medicine, and theatrics. Logic is divided into grammar and argument: argument is divided into demonstration, probable argument, and sophistic: probable argument is divided into dialectic and rhetoric.

In this [arrangement] only the [divisions] of philosophy are contained; there are still other subdivisions of such parts, but those given may suffice for now. If you regard but the number of distinct sciences, you will find twenty-one; if you should wish to count each name mentioned in the scheme, you will find twenty-eight. We read that different persons were authors of these sciences. They originated the arts—some by beginning them, others by developing them, and others by performing them: and thus for the same art a number of authors are frequently cited. Of these I shall now list the names of a few. . . .

Chapter 3. Which Arts are Principally to be Read.

Out of all the sciences[59] above named, however, the ancients, in their studies, especially selected seven to be mastered by those who were to be educated. These seven they considered so to excel all the rest in usefulness that anyone who had been thoroughly schooled in them might afterward come to a knowledge of the others by his own inquiry and effort rather than by listening to a teacher. For these, one might say, constitute the best instruments, the best rudiments, by which the way is prepared for the mind's compete knowledge of philosophic truth.[60] Therefore they are called by the name tri*vium* and quadri*vium*, because by them, as by certain *ways* [*viae*], a quick mind enters into the secret places of wisdom.[61]

In those days, no one was thought worthy the name of master who was unable to claim knowledge of these seven. Pythagoras, too, is said to have maintained the following practice as a teacher: for seven years, according to the number of the seven liberal arts, no one of his pupils dared ask the reason behind statements made by him; instead, he was to give credence to the words of the master until he had heard him out, and then, having done this, he would be able to come at the reason of those things himself.[62] We read that some men studied these seven with such zeal that they had them completely in memory, so that whatever writings they subsequently took in hand or whatever questions they proposed for solution or proof, they did not thumb the pages of books to hunt for rules and reasons which the liberal arts might afford for the resolution of a doubtful matter, but at once had the particulars ready by heart. Hence, it is a fact that in that time there were so many learned men that they alone

---

58. This division of theoretical philosophy is derived from Aristotle.

59. Thus, Hugh uses the terms "art" and "science" interchangeably.

60. Given that the seven liberal arts are virtually the only sciences available among the many that Hugh has named, why is he devoting this time to schematizing the arts and sciences?

61. Quoted by Thomas Aquinas below in his *Disputation concerning ON THE TRINITY*, ques. V, art. 1, reply to objection 3.

62. For another account of Pythagoras's teaching method, see Aulus Gellius, *Attic Nights* I ix 1–7. Translator's note, p. 211n.

wrote more than we are able to read.[63] But the students of our day, whether from ignorance or from unwillingness, fail to hold to a fit method of study, and therefore we find many who study but few who are wise. Yet it seems to me that the student should take no less care not to expend his effort in useless studies than he should to avoid a lukewarm pursuit of good and useful ones. It is bad to pursue something good negligently; it is worse to expend many labors on an empty thing. But because not everyone is mature enough to know what is of advantage to him, I shall briefly indicate to the student which writings seem to me more useful than others, and then I shall add a few words on the method of study.

Chapter 4. Concerning the Two Kinds of Writings.

There are two kinds of writings. The first kind comprises what are properly called the arts; the second, those writings which are appendages of the arts. The arts are included in philosophy: they have, that is, some definite and established part of philosophy for their subject matter—as do grammar, dialectic, and others of this sort. The appendages of the arts, however, are only tangential to philosophy. What they treat is some extra-philosophical matter. Occasionally, it is true, they touch in a scattered and confused fashion upon some topics lifted out of the arts, or, if their narrative presentation is simple, they prepare the way for philosophy. Of this sort are all the songs of the poets—tragedies, comedies, satires, heroic verse and lyric, iambics, certain didactic poems, fables and histories,[64] and also the writings of those fellows whom today we commonly call "philosophers" and who are always taking some small matter and dragging it out through long verbal detours, obscuring a simple meaning in confused discourses—who, lumping even dissimilar things together, make, as it were, a single "picture" from a multitude of "colors" and forms. Keep in mind the two things I have distinguished for you—the arts and the appendages of the arts. . . .

It is in the seven liberal arts, however, that the foundation of all learning is to be found. Before all others these ought to be had at hand, because without them the philosophical discipline does not and cannot explain and define anything. These, indeed, so hang together and so depend upon one another in their ideas that if only one of the arts be lacking, all the rest cannot make a man into a philosopher.[65] Therefore, those persons seem to me to be in error who, not appreciating the coherence among the [seven liberal] arts, select certain of them for study, and, leaving the rest untouched, think they can become perfect in these alone.[66]

---

63. Having virtually acknowledged that most of the writings and knowledge about these arts and categories have been lost, why does Hugh not inquire about the existence of many of these lost writings and lost arts?

64. Hugh's views on excluding literature from grammar and the liberal arts were "flatly opposed to those of the school of Chartres . . . much given to elaborate commentary on poets, fables, and histories." Translator's note, p. 212n. Note the Boethian paradox that Hugh quotes below verses of Vergil in support of this view.

65. This medieval emphasis upon the necessity and uniformity of all the liberal arts for all students contrasts with the view in selection #25 from Pier Paolo Vergerio that individuals may choose what fits them from the range of liberal studies.

66. In these two paragraphs, Hugh virtually equates study of the seven liberal arts with philosophy in general. How is this judgment to be reconciled with the earlier division of philosophy that appears to belie this equating?

16. John of Salisbury, *Metalogicon* (1159)

INTRODUCTION

John of Salisbury (c. 1115–1180) was born in southern England into a family that could not provide for his education, but the local cleric noticed his intellectual promise and arranged for John to go to Paris to study in about 1136. Though he came into contact with several of the most prominent teachers of the day at Paris, John describes his master in the seven liberal arts as a "reliable lecturer, but somewhat dull when it comes to discussion." After completing his liberal education, John was ordained a priest and went to work in the papal court. In 1154 he became secretary to Theobald, Archbishop of Canterbury, and undertook frequent diplomatic missions across Europe, continuing to study and to write "only by dint of snatching [occasional] moments like a thief." In 1159 he completed and dedicated to Thomas Beckett, then chancellor to King Henry II, the *Metalogicon*, a synthetic term that John coined from Greek roots intending to mean "on behalf of" or "in defense of" logic, though *meta* generally meant "after," "beyond," "among," "with."[67]

Nevertheless, John's treatment of "logic" explicitly recognizes the two-fold ambiguity of the term then prevailing in the intellectual world; and this recognition makes the *Metalogicon* a signal document in the history of the liberal arts—and one very much complementary to the *Didascalicon* of Hugh of St. Victor. In Book I John defends a broad conception of "logic" incorporating all the arts pertaining to language and reason, namely the arts of the trivium,[68] as well as Cicero's and Martianus's theme of wedding eloquence to learning. In Book II John affirms the restricted conception of "logic" as the art of reasoning within the trivium. Then, within that restricted conception, John discusses in Book III the "old logic"[69] and, finally, in Book IV advocates the study of the "new logic,"[70] which had just been translated into Latin and was beginning to be studied again in Western Europe in the 1150s when John was writing. In this fashion, the *Metalogicon* addresses the twofold ambiguity of the term "logic" and incorporates the central intellectual tensions within the liberal arts of the mid-twelfth century.

Meanwhile, John also completed the foremost medieval treatise on statecraft: the *Policraticus*, or "statesman's book," which approved the assassination of tyrannical rulers and incurred the wrath of Henry II. Nevertheless, when Henry appointed Thomas Becket to succeed Theobald as archbishop in 1161, Beckett retained John as secretary. Shortly thereafter, Henry forced John into exile, and Beckett soon followed after defying Henry's wishes. The two expatriates reconciled with the king and returned to England, but the reconciliation was short-lived, and John witnessed the murder of Becket by Henry's soldiers in Canterbury cathedral on December 29, 1170. Six years later the pope named John of Salisbury to be bishop of Chartres, where he died in 1180.

---

67. *Metalogicon* bk. II pt. 10, bk. III prologue, bk. I prologue.

68. This broad conception stems from the division of philosophy into physics, ethics, and logic, which seems to be derived from the Stoics. It was attributed to Plato by Cicero (*Academica* I v 19–21) and Augustine (*City of God* VIII 4, XI 25). From Augustine, it was adopted by Isidore (*Etymologies* II 22, 24) and then John's contemporary Hugh of St. Victor, as seen in the reading above.

69. The "old logic" comprised Aristotle's two introductory treatises on logic and the *Introduction* of Porphyry, all three of which Boethius had translated.

70. The "new logic" comprised Aristotle's other four, more sophisticated treatises on logic, which included analysis of the syllogism. It seems that John had not really studied or understood this crowning addition to the liberal arts.

SELECTION[71]

My friends pressed me to compose[72] this work, even if I had practically to throw the words together.[73] For I had neither the leisure nor energy to enter into a subtle analysis of opinions, much less to polish my style. My regular duties have consumed all my time, save that required for eating and sleeping. By the commission of my lord, whom I cannot disappoint, the responsibility for the whole of Britain, as far as ecclesiastical matters are concerned, is on my shoulders.[74] Administrative concerns and the [time-consuming] trifles of court life have precluded study, and the interruptions of friends have used up practically all the time I had left. Consequently, I do not think I should be too harshly judged if any of my statements seem insufficiently considered. On the other hand, the credit for anything that I may say which seems more apt is to be referred to Him without Whom human weakness is powerless [*John* 5: 5.] I am by nature too dull to comprehend the subtleties of the ancients; I cannot rely on my memory to retain for long what I have learned; and my style betrays its own lack of polish. This treatise, which I have taken care to divide into four books for the reader's refreshment, is entitled *Metalogicon*. For, in it, I undertake to defend logic. . . .[75]

Book I
Chapter 1. The false accusation that has evoked this rejoinder to Cornificius.[76]

The malicious wrangler [to whom we have referred] has stirred up against one of the most extraordinary gifts of mother nature and grace, the embers of an outdated charge, long since discredited and dismissed as false and groundless by our ancestors. Barring no means in his effort to console himself for his own want of knowledge, he has contrived to improve his own reputation by making many others ignoramuses like himself. For inflated arrogance is marked by an overweening proclivity both to magnify its own good points, if it has any, and to belittle those of others, so that, measuring itself in comparison, it may count the shortcomings of others as signs of its own proficiency.

All who possess real insight agree that nature, the most loving mother and wise arranger of all that exists, has, among the various living creatures which she has brought forth, elevated man by privilege of reason, and distinguished him by the faculty of speech. She has thus effected, by her affectionate care and well-ordered plan, that, even though he is oppressed and handicapped by the burden of his earthly nature and the sluggishness of his physical body, man may still rise to higher things. [As if] borne aloft on wings of reason and speech, he is thus enabled, by this felicitous shortcut, to outstrip

---

71. Daniel D. McGarry, tr., *The* Metalogicon *of John of Salisbury, A Twelfth-Century Defense of the Verbal and Logical Arts of the Trivium* (Berkeley: University of California Press, 1955), pp. 3–16, 31–37, 212. Reprinted by permission of Mary Anne McGarry, trustee, on behalf of the estate of Daniel D. McGarry.

72. Literally, "dictated," which is often how medieval authors composed their works: dictating them to scribes.

73. The Latin editor indicates that this phrase may come from Quintilian, *Education of the Orator* X vii 12–13. If so, the phrase is likely taken from a secondary source.

74. The reference is to his responsibilities as secretary to Archbishop Theobald.

75. As seen in Chapter 10 below, John intends "logic" in its broader sense of all the arts of language and reason, namely the trivium.

76. "'Cornificius' is the *nom de plume* given by John to the adversary of 'logic,' the spokesman of those who advocated less attention to 'logical' studies (i.e. grammar, rhetoric, logic). Cornificius was a detractor of Vergil mentioned in an apparent interpolation in the *Life of Vergil* by Donatus. The real name of John's 'Cornificius' is uncertain." Translator's note, p. 11n. This detractor of Vergil is apparently the same Cornificius as the Latin author of a work on rhetoric in the first century B.C.

all other beings, and to attain the crown of true happiness. While grace fructifies [human] nature, reason looks after the observation and examination of facts, probes the secret depths of nature, and estimates all utility and worth. In the meantime, the love of good, inborn in all of us, seeks, as our natural appetite asserts itself, what alone or particularly seems best adapted to the attainment of happiness.

Since one cannot even imagine how any kind of happiness could exist entirely apart from mutual association and divorced from human society, whoever assails what contributes to establish and promote rightful order in [human society]—in a way the sole and unique fraternity among the children of nature—would seem to obstruct the way to beatitude for all. Having blocked the road to peace, [Cornificius] incites the forces of nature to concur for the destruction of the world. This is "To sow discord among brothers," "to supply arms" to those at peace, and last, but not least, to establish a new and "great chasm" between God and man.[77] The creative Trinity, the one true God, has so arranged the parts of the universe that each requires the help of the others, and they mutually compensate for their respective deficiencies, all things being, so to speak, "members one of another" [*Romans* 12: 5.] All things lack something when isolated, and are perfected on being united, since they mutually support one another. What is more reliable, helpful, and efficacious for the acquisition of happiness than virtue, which is practically the sole means grace has provided for the attainment of beatitude? Those who attain blessedness without meriting it by virtue, arrive at this state by being drawn thither, rather than by going there themselves.

I consequently wonder (though not sufficiently, as it is beyond me) what is the real aim of one who denies that eloquence should be studied; who asserts that it comes as a natural gift to one who is not mute, just as sight does to one who is not blind, and hearing to one who is not deaf; and who further maintains that although nature's gift is strengthened by exercise, nothing is to be gained by learning the art [of eloquence], or at least that the benefit accruing is not worth the effort that must be expended. Just as eloquence, unenlightened by reason, is rash and blind, so wisdom, without the power of expression, is feeble and maimed. Speechless wisdom may sometimes increase one's personal satisfaction, but it rarely and only slightly contributes to the welfare of human society. Reason, the mother, nurse, and guardian of knowledge, as well as of virtue, frequently conceives from speech, and by this same means bears more abundant and richer fruit. Reason would remain utterly barren, or at least would fail to yield a plenteous harvest, if the faculty of speech did not bring to light its feeble conceptions, and communicate the perceptions of the prudent exercise of the human mind. Indeed, it is this delightful and fruitful copulation of reason and speech which has given birth to so many outstanding cities, has made friends and allies of so many kingdoms, and has unified and knit together in bonds of love so many peoples.

Whoever tries to "thrust asunder what God has joined together" for the common good, should rightly be adjudged a public enemy [*Matthew* 19: 6.] One who would eliminate the teaching of eloquence from philosophical studies, begrudges Mercury his possession of Philology, and wrests from Philology's arms her beloved Mercury.[78] Although he may seem to attack eloquence alone, he undermines and uproots all liberal studies, assails the whole structure of philosophy, tears to shreds humanity's social contract, and destroys the means of brotherly charity and reciprocal interchange of services. Deprived of their gift of speech, men would degenerate to the condition of brute animals, and cities would seem like corrals for livestock, rather than communities composed of human beings united by a common bond for the purpose of living in society, serving one another, and cooperating as friends. If verbal intercommunication were withdrawn, what contract could be duly concluded, what

---

77. The quotations are respectively from *Proverbs* 6: 19; Vergil, *Aeneid* I 150; *Luke* 16: 26.

78. John here refers to the allegory of Martianus Capella and the Ciceronian theme of wedding eloquence and learning.

instruction could be given in faith and morals, and what agreement and mutual understanding could subsist among men?[79] It may thus be seen that our Cornificius, ignorant and malevolent foe of studies pertaining to eloquence, attacks not merely one, or even a few persons, but all civilization and political organization. . . .

Chapter 10. What "logic" means

Behold, the Cornificians disclose their objective, and advance to attack logic, although, of course, they are equally violent persecutors of all philosophical pursuits. They have to begin somewhere, and so they have singled out that branch of philosophy which is the most widely known and seems the most familiar to their heretical sect. First, bear with me while we define what logic is. Logic (in its broadest sense) is the science of verbal expression and [argumentative] reasoning.[80] Sometimes [the term] "logic" is used with more restricted extension, and limited to rules of [argumentative] reasoning. Whether logic teaches only the ways of reasoning, or embraces all rules relative to words, surely those who claim that it is useless are deluded. For either of these services may be proved by incontrovertible arguments, to be very necessary. The twofold meaning of logic stems from its Greek etymology, for in the latter language *logos* means both "word" and "reason."

For the present let us concede to logic its widest meaning, according to which it includes all instruction relative to words,[81] in which case it can never be convicted of futility. In this more general sense, there can be no doubt that all logic is both highly useful and necessary. If, as has been frequently observed (and as no one denies), the use of speech is so essential, the more concisely it is taught, the more useful and certainly the more reliable will be the teaching. It is foolish to delay a long time, with much sweat and worry, over something that could otherwise be easily and quickly expedited. This is a fault common among careless persons who have no sense of the value of time. To safeguard against this mistake, the arts of doing all things that we are to do should be taken up and cultivated. Our devotion to the arts should be augmented by the reflection that the latter stem from nature, the best of all mother, and attest their noble lineage by the facile and successful accomplishment of their objects. I would say, therefore, that the arts of doing things we are to do should be cultivated, with the exception of those [arts] whose purpose is evil, such as lot-reading and other mathematical methods of divination[82] that are reprobate. Arts such as the latter, which are wrong, should, by the decree of sound philosophers, be banished from human society. This matter, however, is discussed more at length in our *Policraticus*.

Chapter 11. The nature of art, the various kinds of innate abilities, and the fact that natural talents should be cultivated and developed by the arts.

Art is a system that reason has devised in order to expedite, by its own short cut, our ability to do things within our natural capabilities. Reason neither provides nor professes to provide the accomplishment of the impossible. Rather, it substitutes for the spendthrift and roundabout ways of nature a concise, direct method of doing things that are possible. It further begets (so to speak) a faculty of accomplishing what is difficult. Wherefore the Greeks also call it *methodon*, that is, so to speak, an effi-

---

79. Compare Isocrates's view (253–257) in selection #2.

80. This definition may come from the beginning of *Commentary on the Topics of Cicero* by Boethius.

81. Thus, while John explicitly recognizes the ambiguity of "logic" arising from its broad and restricted meanings, he is responding primarily to an attack upon the former commensurate with his defense of the wedding of eloquence and learning.

82. The editor and translator attribute this usage to John transliterating *matheseos*, "divinatory mathematics," from the Greek. But the reference may also come from selection #15 by Hugh of St. Victor (II 3).

cient plan, which avoids nature's wastefulness, and straightens out her circuitous wanderings, so that we may more correctly and easily accomplish what we are to do. However vigorous it may be, nature cannot attain the facility of an art unless it be trained. At the same time, nature is the mother of all arts, to which she has given reason as their nurse for their improvement and perfection.

Nature first evokes our natural capacity to perceive things, and then, as it were, deposits these perceptions in the secure treasury of our memory.[83] Reason then examines, with its careful study, those things which have been perceived, and which are to be, or have been, commended to memory's custody. After its scrutiny of their nature, reason pronounces true and accurate judgment concerning each of these (unless, perchance, it slips up in some regard). Nature has provided beforehand these three factors [innate ability, memory, and reason] as both the foundations and the instruments of all the arts. Naturally ability (according to Isidore) is "an immanent power infused into one's soul by nature."[84]

This description seems to mean that nature has endowed the soul with a certain force, which either constitutes or at least evokes the initial [and fundamental] activity of the soul in its investigations. Natural talent is said to be "immanent" inasmuch as it has need of nothing else as a prerequisite, but precedes and aids all subsequent [abilities]. In our acquisition of [scientific] knowledge, investigation is the first step, and comes before comprehension, analysis, and retention. Innate ability, although it proceeds from nature, is fostered by study and exercise. What is difficult when we first try it, becomes easier after assiduous practice, and once the rules for doing it are mastered, very easy, unless languor creeps in, through lapse of use or carelessness, and impedes our efficiency. This, in short, is how all the arts have originated: Nature, the first fundamental, begets the habit and practice of study, which proceeds to provide an art, and the latter, in turn, finally furnishes the faculty [reason] whereof we speak. Natural ability is accordingly effective. So, too, is exercise. And memory likewise, is effective, when employed by the two aforesaid. With the help of the foregoing, reason waxes strong, and produces the arts, which are proportionate to natural talents. . . .

Chapter 12. Why some arts are called "liberal."

While there are many sorts of arts, the first to proffer their services to the natural abilities of those who philosophize are the liberal arts. All of the latter are included in the courses of the Trivium and Quadrivium. The liberal arts are said to have become so efficacious among our ancestors, who studied them diligently, that they enabled them to comprehend everything they read, elevated their understanding to all things, and empowered them to cut through the knots of all problems possible of solution. Those to whom the system of the Trivium has disclosed the significance of all words, or the rules of the Quadrivium have unveiled the secrets of all nature,[85] do not need the help of a teacher in order to understand the meaning of books and to find the solutions of questions. They [the branches of learning included in the Trivium and Quadrivium] are called "arts" [either] because they delimit [*artant*] but rules and precepts; or from virtue, in Greek known as *ares*, which strengthens minds to apprehend the ways of wisdom; or from reason, called *arso* by the Greeks, which the arts nourish and

---

83. This image recalls Cicero, *On the Orator* I v 18.

84. Despite his attribution to Isidore (perhaps *Etymologies* X 122), John appears to draw his phrase from Hugh of St. Victor (III 8).

85. This view of the quadrivium comports with that of the Isocratean tradition in which the quadrivial arts are seen as funds of useful information, rather than as axiomatic mathematical sciences in the Platonic tradition.

cause to grow.[86] They are called "liberal," either because the ancients took care to have their children instructed in them;[87] or because their object is to effect man's liberation, so that, freed from cares, he may devote himself to wisdom. More often than not, they liberate us from cares incompatible with wisdom. They often even free us from worry about [material] necessities, so that the mind may have still greater liberty to apply itself to philosophy.

Chapter 13. Whence grammar gets its name.

Among all the liberal arts, the first is logic, and specifically that part of logic which gives initial instruction about words. As has already been explained, the word "logic" has a broad meaning, and is not restricted exclusively to the science of argumentative reasoning. [It includes] Grammar [which] is "the science of speaking and writing correctly—the starting point of all liberal studies."[88] Grammar is the cradle of all philosophy, and in a manner of speaking, the first nurse of the whole study of letters.[89] It takes all of us as tender babes, newly born from nature's bosom. It nurses us in our infancy, and guides our every forward step in philosophy. With motherly care, it fosters and protects the philosopher from the start to the finish [of his pursuits]. It is called 'grammar' from the basic elements of writing and speaking. . . .

Book IV
Chapter 6. The difficulty of the *Posterior Analytics*, and whence this difficulty proceeds.

The science of the *Posterior Analytics* is extremely subtle,[90] and one with which but few mentalities can make much headway. This fact is evidently due to several reasons. In the first place, the work discusses the art of demonstration, which is the most demanding of all forms of reasoning. Secondly, the aforesaid art has, by now, practically fallen into disuse.[91] At present demonstration is employed by practically no one except mathematicians, and even among the latter has come to be almost exclusively reserved to geometricians. The study of geometry is, however, not well known among us, although this science is perhaps in greater use in the region of Iberia and the confines of Africa. For the peoples

---

86. John's references to *artant* and *ares* appear to have a direct antecedent in Cassiodorus (II pref. 4) in selection #10. The reference to *arso* is mystifying, but may also stem from Cassiodorus's interpretation of Greek etymology.

87. John's reference to children, which can be found occasionally in modern historiography, follows by inferring from the fact that the liberal arts were studied by boys and adolescents and the fact that a secondary meaning of the Latin *liberi* is "children" (because the Latin *liber* means "free person" and *liberi* means "those who are free"), the conclusion that "liberal arts" originally meant "arts for children." This reasoning, however, has no historical basis.

88. Isidore, *Etymologies* I 5.

89. This broad definition, whereby "grammar" comprises the study of language and literature, comports with that in the oratorical branch of the liberal arts tradition.

90. Aristotle's *Posterior Analytics*, one of the four treatises of the "new logic," includes discussion of the syllogism, the culminating topic in the liberal arts of the medieval universities. See the reading by Thomas Aquinas below.

91. Aristotle's *Posterior Analytics* is not discussed in the encyclopedia of seven arts written by Thierry of Chartres (c. 1100–c. 1156), who became chancellor of the school of Chartres in 1141 and served until about 1150. Given that John is writing in the late 1150s, Aristotle's advanced treatises constituting the "new logic" first began to arrive and circulate in the interim. The following lines reveal John's awareness of the process of transmission of logic, mathematics, and other sciences from Middle Eastern sources into Western Europe, described by Mehdi Nakosteen in the introduction.

of Iberia and Africa employ geometry more than do any others; they use it as a tool in astronomy. The like is true of the Egyptians, as well as some of the peoples of Arabia.

The present book, which teaches demonstrative logic, is even more perplexing than the rest. This is partly a result of its complicated transposition of words and letters, as well as its out-moded examples, borrowed from various branches of study. Finally, though this is not the fault of the author, the book has been so mutilated by the bungling mistakes of scribes that it contains almost as many stumbling blocks as subjects. Indeed, we feel fortunate when we find that these stumbling blocks do not outnumber the book's chapters. Whence many assert that the latter has not been correctly rendered [into Latin] for us, and throw the blame for its difficulty upon the translator.

Chapter 7. Why Aristotle has come to be called "the philosopher" par excellence.

So highly was the science of demonstration esteemed by the Peripatetics that Aristotle, who also excelled practically all other philosophers in nearly every regard, established his right to the [otherwise] common name of "philosopher," as in a way his own special prerogative, by giving us this branch of knowledge [namely, demonstration]. For it was because of this, we are told, that Aristotle came to be called "the philosopher." If anyone does not believe me, let him at least heed Burgundio the Pizan, who is my source for this statement.[92] Since this science both dispels the shadows of ignorance, and illumines its possessor with the privilege of [foundational] knowledge, it has frequently served [as a lamp] to guide from darkness to light the school of the Academicians, with whom we [frankly] profess our agreement on questions that remain doubtful to a wise man. And just as, at the outset, Aristotle by forging a crucible [or method] for analysis [of arguments], made ready the judge, so here he now advances his client to the authoritative position of teacher. Which is in well-chosen order, since one who has creditably fulfilled the function of judge deserves to be elevated to the master's chair.

---

92. Burgundio the Pizan "was one of the chief translators of works from Greek to Latin in John's day. He held the office of judge at Pisa, and died in 1193." Translator's note, p. 213n.

Ordinary Lecture

17. Aristotle, *Posterior Analytics* (c. 350 B.C.)

INTRODUCTION

The following four selections (#17–21) belong to the late 1250s, a period when Thomas Aquinas (1225–1274) was teaching at the University of Paris. The selections convey a sense not only of his own teaching and ideas about liberal education, but also of the new program of liberal education that was being established at the leading university of the day, the University of Paris, and, by extension, at other aspiring universities in Western Europe, which looked to Paris as a model. Each document demonstrates both the pedagogical form and the curricular content of important aspects of this reformulation of liberal education that persevered for several centuries.

Born into a noble family in central Italy, Thomas was sent at age five to be educated by the Benedictine monks at the famed monastery of Monte Cassino, where his uncle had been abbot. In 1239 the emperor expelled the monks and fighting broke out between the papal and imperial armies, so Thomas went to the University of Naples, where he joined the Dominican Order in 1244. His family strongly opposed this decision, kidnapped him and brought him home. But his commitment to the Dominicans remained steadfast, and early in 1246 Thomas was allowed to rejoin the order at the University of Paris.

Over the next three years, he studied at Paris with the leading Dominican theologian, Albert the Great, who enlisted Thomas to found a college for the Dominicans at Cologne. According to tradition, it was there that Aquinas was nicknamed "the Dumb Ox" because "he was physically large and heavy...and also because he was reserved, silent, and therefore thought to be stupid. Tradition has it that, when Aquinas once performed well in the classroom, Albert observed: 'We call this lad a dumb ox, but I tell you the whole world is going to hear his bellowing!'"[93] Returning to Paris to complete his studies in theology, Thomas likely taught as a master in the liberal arts faculty during the mid-1250s.

In 1256 he earned the license to teach (*licentia docendi*) in the Paris faculty of theology and established his reputation as a leading theologian during the next three years, while lecturing amid the controversy over whether members of religious orders could teach or study at the university. In 1259 Thomas left Paris to teach in the college associated with the papal court, and returned to the university in 1268 to engage in controversies over the role of religious orders as well as over the doctrine of Ibn Rushd (1126–1198), the Spanish-Arabian philosopher and leading Islamic interpreter of Aristotle, known as Averroës in the West. Apart from those controversies, Aquinas attempted to reconcile systematically the new philosophical learning received over the prior century, particularly that of Aristotle, with the orthodox doctrine of Catholicism. Leaving Paris in 1272, Thomas again went to Naples to open a college for the Dominicans. In 1274 he was summoned by the Pope to participate in the Council at Lyons, but died on the way at the age of forty-nine.

Selection #17 is drawn from one of Aristotle's four advanced works on logic, which were collectively known as the "new logic" in the late twelfth century. This "new logic" included analysis of the deductive syllogism, regarded as the culminating and most demanding topic in the liberal arts at the scholastic universities. Studying the deductive syllogism was the penultimate hurdle to earning the "license to teach" (*licentia docendi*) and to being admitted to the guild of teaching masters. Becoming

---

93. Brian Davies, *The Thought of Thomas Aquinas* (Oxford: Clarendon, 1992), p. 5. See the comment of Juana Inéz de la Cruz on this point in Section V.

a "master of arts" in this way also informally qualified one to participate in the unofficial, public disputations about the newly received knowledge that was pouring into the universities and had become the focus of intellectual life there.

In pedagogical terms, this text presents the subject matter of an "ordinary lecture" within the liberal arts curriculum at the universities. Ordinary lectures were class meetings addressing the central texts of the liberal arts and were therefore scheduled at the primary times in the daily and weekly calendar of the university. They were offered on an established cycle, and it appears that students generally heard the cycle twice: once as a novice seeking to become a bachelor, and a second time as a bachelor seeking to become a master of arts.

The teaching master normally began the ordinary lecture by reading the assigned text, usually drawn from Aristotle's writings. Such reading (and rereading) was indispensable because, apart from universities where a large notary profession was established, as in Italy, most students did not own a copy of the assigned text. The numbers in brackets refer to the modern notation system for the Greek text of Aristotle's works and are inserted as cross references into the ensuing commentary of Thomas Aquinas.

SELECTION[94]

[71b8] We think that uncontingent [scientific] knowledge of a thing, rather than accidental knowledge in the sophistical mode, is present [b10] whenever we think that we cognize the cause of a thing and, in particular, the cause for that thing being unable to be other than it is. [b12] It is obvious, after all, that [scientific] knowing is such a thing as this, because this is the view both of those who do not know and of those who do: the former believe they know uncontingently [though they do not], whereas the latter actually do know in this way. [b14] In sum, a thing of which there is uncontingent [scientific] knowledge is unable to be otherwise than it is.[95]

[b16] We shall speak later of whatever other mode of knowing exists.[96] We are speaking now of knowing through demonstration. [b18] By "demonstration" I mean "syllogism of knowledge," and I say a syllogism is productive of knowledge just if we know [uncontingently] by grasping it. [b20] So if knowing is the sort of thing we have laid out, it is also necessary that demonstration be composed of *true*, *primary*, and *immediate premises*, and ones *better-recognized than*, *prior to*, and *causes of* the conclusion. [b22] For in this way, the premises will actually turn out to be proper to the thing being shown. [b23] There will be a syllogism even without these things to be sure; but there will not be a demonstration, for it will not make knowledge.

[b24] It is required that the premises be *true*, because there is no knowing of what is not (e.g., that the diagonal is commensurate with the side); [b27] and it is necessary that the premises be *primary* and *indemonstrable*, for otherwise one will require a demonstration of them in order to know them. Knowing is, after all, of demonstrable things of which there is demonstration, not contingently but unqualifiedly. [b29] Concerning the requirements that the premises be causes for, prior to, and better-recognized than, we say *causes for* because we know [scientifically] only when we know the causes for something; and they are *prior to* in as much as they are causes, and they enjoy a *priority in recognition* not simply in terms of their meaning but also by virtue of their factuality. [b34] But "prior

---

94. 71b8–72a8. Adapted from a new, unpublished translation by J. Albert Dragstedt.

95. Such unqualified scientific knowledge was the subject of "theoretical philosophy," in Aristotle's terms, while "practical philosophy" addressed human affairs. Since human affairs incorporate human volition and since human choice is idiosyncratic, the subject matter and findings of practical sciences can be other than what they are.

96. This is taken up in the following chapter.

to" and "better recognized than" are ambiguous, for it is not the same thing to be prior and better recognized in the nature of things and to be prior and better recognized by us. [72a1] I mean that those things which are nearer to sense perception are "prior to" and "better-recognized than" in relation to us, whereas the things unqualifiedly "prior to" and "better-recognized than" are furthest from sense. The most universal things are most distant from sense, while particulars are closest to sense, and these things stand in opposition to each other.

18. Thomas Aquinas, *Commentary on the POSTERIOR ANALYTICS* (c. 1259)

INTRODUCTION

After reading through the assigned text, the master commenced the next phases of the ordinary lecture: stating and elaborating the meaning in his own words, relating that meaning to other parts of the text, raising significant questions or contradictions appearing in the text, and finally addressing and resolving those questions or contradictions.[97] In selection #18, Thomas Aquinas undertakes this conventional practice in regard to the foregoing reading from Aristotle, as he probably did in the 1250s while teaching in the liberal arts faculty at the University of Paris. Like many masters, Thomas wrote down his lectures, possibly distributing them to his students. This set of lectures, pertaining to the culminating study of the liberal arts curriculum, was likely written during his theology professorship at Paris in the late 1250s, when he was doubtlessly delivering ordinary lectures on required theological texts.

SELECTION[98]

After the Philosopher[99] has shown the necessity of the demonstrative syllogism, he starts from this point to develop his discussion of the demonstrative syllogism itself. . . .[100]

Concerning the first point he poses five things. First [71b8], he discusses what sort of thing the [scientific] *knowing* is that he intends to define.

Concerning it one must know that we are said to know something *uncontingently* whenever we know that thing in itself. We are said to know something *relatively* whenever we know that thing in something else in which it exists, perhaps as a part does in a whole (just as, if we knew a house, we would be said to know a wall); or perhaps as an accident exists in a substrate (just as if we knew Coriscus, we would be said to know who approaches us); or perhaps as an effect exists in its cause (as has been remarked above, to the effect that we have prior knowledge of a conclusion within its principles), or perhaps in whatever is similar to this. And knowing relatively is this; namely, that we are said to know a thing which is implied in whatever manner in something that has become known through itself. So the Philosopher is

---

97. See "A Law Professor Introduces His Lectures at Bologna" in selection #21. Compare that medieval method—though outmoded by the advent of printing and, even more, by digital texts—with modern lecturing.

98. Lecture 4 (71b8–72a8). Adapted from a new, unpublished translation by J. Albert Dragstedt

99. The reliance upon and authority of Aristotle had become so well established by the late twelfth century that he was known simply as "the Philosopher." See selection #16 by John of Salisbury (IV 7).

100. In the following omitted part, Thomas begins his lecture by presenting a systematic outline of Aristotle's discussion leading up to the topic under consideration.

intending to define knowing uncontingently but not knowing relatively. The latter is the sophistical mode of knowing. For sophists employ the following type of argument: "I know Coriscus, Coriscus is approaching; therefore I know the person approaching."[101]

The second thing is determined in the passage [b10]. There he posits the definition of [scientific] knowing uncontingently. And concerning this matter one must consider that knowing something is recognizing that very thing in a complete manner, and by that we mean apprehending the thing's truth in a complete manner. For the principles of a thing's being and of a thing's truth are the same, as is clear from Aristotle's *Metaphysics* II. Therefore, someone who knows completely [and scientifically] must know the cause of the thing known. If, however, one knew only the cause, one would know the effect not in the way of knowing uncontingently, but only virtually, which is knowing relatively and accidentally, so to speak. Again, whoever knows uncontingently ought to understand the application of cause to effect. The fact is, knowledge is true and certain cognition of the thing. Moreover, whatever may exist otherwise than it is, may not be understood with certainty; so a further requirement is that what is known must be unable to be otherwise than it is. In sum, because knowledge is complete cognition he says, "Whenever we judge that we understand the cause"; and because this cognition is knowing uncontingently he adds: "the cause of that thing being unable to be other than it is." But because that cognition is certain, he adds, "And it is not a thing which just happens to allow of various dispositions."[102]

The third thing is determined in the passage [b12]. There [Aristotle] supports the definition by positing the fact that knowers and non-knowers (though thinking that they know, nevertheless) take their definition of knowing in the way that has been spoken of above. For non-knowers who think that they know have the opinion that they are in that state of understanding as has been spoken of, whereas those who know really are in that state. This is the straightforward expression of the definition. The definition, after all, is the account which the name signifies, as is stated in *Metaphysics* IV. The significance of the name must be taken from whatever those who use language in the commonly accepted way signify by that name. Thus, Aristotle says in *Topics* II that one must employ names as most people employ them.[103] If anyone considers the matter rightly, by this approach there is a clearer expression of what the name may signify than by the view that it directly signifies some particular thing. For knowing doesn't denote something concerning which a definition could be assigned in proper fashion, since it is a species of some genus, but it denotes knowing as such. Hence, he says even from the beginning [b8], "We think that knowing is," and he does not say, "Knowing is" something like this or like that.

Fourthly, [b14] he concludes a certain corollary from the definition posited; evidently, that knowledge which is held uncontingently must itself be necessary through being something to which it would not be otherwise than it is.

Fifthly [b16] he responds to the tacit question of whether there is any way of knowing [scientifically] other than the one aforementioned. He promises to speak about this later, for there is also a knowing through effect, as will be clear further on. There is even a knowing, in some manner, of indemonstrable principles as such of which there is no cause. But the proper and complete mode of knowing is the one aforementioned.

Next, he says in [b17] he is defining the demonstrative syllogism by comparison with its purpose which is knowing.

---

101. This sophism seems to result from the fact the second premise presupposes the conclusion.

102. [b11] Thomas's quotations from Latin translations of Aristotle sometimes vary from the English translation of Aristotle's Greek in selection #3.

103. Thomas invokes the authority—and affirms the coherence and consistency—of Aristotle's other works.

Concerning this matter he makes three points. First, he posits that knowing is the purpose of the demonstrative syllogism or its effect, since knowing seems to be nothing other than understanding the truth of some conclusion through a demonstration.

Second, he says in [b18] he defines demonstrative syllogism through a purpose of this kind: saying that a demonstration is a "knowing syllogism"; i.e., one bringing about that one knows.

Third, he explains why he spoke of a "knowing syllogism" (in the passage [b18–19]), saying that it is called a "knowing syllogism" because we know to the extent that we possess that syllogism, lest someone understand by "knowing syllogism" what a certain science employs.

Next, when he says in [b19], he is concluding from the remarks just made a definition of demonstrative syllogism based on its matter. Concerning this, he makes two points: first, he draws a conclusion; second, he makes it plain.

Concerning the first subject, he makes three points. First, [b20] he posits the consequence by which the definition of a material demonstration is concluded to from the earlier remarks, saying that if knowing signifies what we have mentioned, namely, to understand the cause for a thing etc., it is necessary that demonstrative science (i.e., what is acquired through demonstration) proceed from propositions which are *true*, *primary* and *immediate* (i.e., things that are not demonstrated by any mediating agent but are manifest through themselves: those propositions are called immediate to the extent that they lack a demonstrative mediator, and *primary* in their ordering towards other propositions which are proved through them.) Again, such demonstration is based on what is better-recognized than, prior to, and causative of the conclusion.

Second, in the passage [b22] he justifies excluding another element which seems to require being included: the fact that demonstration proceeds from principles which are proper to the subject matter. But he says that this circumstance is understood through those things which have been said already.[104] For if the premises of the demonstration are causes of the conclusion, it is necessary that they be principles proper to it, for it is appropriate that causes be proportionate to effects.

Third, in the passage [b23] he asserts the necessity of the consequence aforementioned, saying that although a syllogism does not require the aforementioned conditions to obtain in the premises from which it proceeds, nevertheless a demonstration does require them, for it would not make knowledge, otherwise.

Next, when he says [b24], he is clarifying the definition he has posited, clarifying as well what he had just spoken of; namely, that unless the aforementioned conditions were realized in the demonstration, it would not be able to make [scientific] knowledge.

So first he shows that a demonstration always proceeds from truths to the thing that makes knowledge since there is no knowing of what does not exist. For example, that the diagonal has common measurement, i.e., is commensurable with the side of the square (for quantities are said to be incommensurable which have no common measure able to be taken, and quantities of this sort are such as have no proportion one to another as there is of a number to a number;[105] and that is a circumstance which necessarily obtains between the diameter of a square and its side, as is clear from the tenth book of Euclid.)[106] A thing which is not true, moreover, is not: for to be and to be true are convertible terms. So whatever is known [scientifically] is constrained to be true, as well. Hence, the conclusion of a demonstration which produces scientific knowing must be true, and consequently its premises must be

104. Thomas raises a possible objection to Aristotle's analyses and then answers it.

105. That is, such a quantity is an irrational number because it cannot be expressed as the ratio of two whole integers.

106. This refers to Euclid's *Elements of Geometry*.

true as well, for it does not come about that something true is known from falsities, although conclusions can be drawn from them as he will show further on.

Second in the passage [b27], he shows that demonstration is from primary and immediate, or indemonstrable, principles. For it does not occur that someone has knowledge unless he has demonstration of those things of which there can be demonstration, and I mean unqualifiedly and not contingently. He says this because it is possible for someone to know some conclusion even if he does not have a demonstration of the premises, though they be demonstrable, since he would know the conclusion through other principles, and this would be contingent. . . .

Third, in the passage [b29], he proves that the premises of a demonstration are causes of the conclusion, since we know uncontingently whenever we understand the causes. And from this he draws the further conclusion that the causes are prior and better-known because each cause is naturally prior to and better-known than its effect.

It is necessary, however, that the cause of a demonstrative conclusion be better-known not only as regards the cognition of what it is, but also as regards the cognition that it is. For it does not suffice for demonstrating that a solar eclipse exists to know that this means the interposition of the moon; one also has to know that the moon is interposed between sun and earth. [b34] And since "prior" and 'better-known" are meant in two senses, that is in regard to us and according to the nature of things; he says that those things from which demonstration proceeds are prior and better-known uncontingently and according to nature, and not in regard to us.

[72a1] In order to explain this, he says that priors and better-knowns are uncontingently just those things which are remote from sense, being universals. Things prior and better-known in regard to us are those closest to sense, being singulars, which are opposite to universals (whether through the opposition of prior and posterior, or through the opposition of close and remote).

The contrary to this seems to be held in *Physics* I, where it is said that universals are prior in regard to us, and later according to nature.[107] But it must be said that [in the *Posterior Analytics*] he is speaking of the order of the singular to the universal unqualifiedly, whose order has to be taken according to the order of sensitive and intellective cognition in us. In us sensory cognition is prior to the intellective, since intellectual cognition in us proceeds from sense. Hence, the singular is prior and better-known in us than is the universal.

But *Physics* I does not address the order of universal to singular absolutely, but the order of the more universal to the less, as of animal to man, for example.[108] In this instance, regarding us the more universal has to be prior and more known. For in all generation, that which exists in potency is prior in time and later in nature, while that which is complete in act is prior in nature but posterior in time. Knowledge of a genus is potential, so to speak, in comparison with knowledge of a species in which all the essential aspects of the thing are known in actuality. Hence in the generation of our knowledge, understanding the more common is prior to understanding the less common.

Similarly, that book of the *Physics* states that the innate path in us is from things better-known [to the lesser-known]. So a demonstration is not made from things which are prior absolutely, but prior in regards to us.

But it must be said that here he is addressing the fact that what is sensory is better known in us than what it is in the intellect. There, however, he addresses the fact that what is better-known regarding us

---

107. Thomas here assumes the responsibility of refuting possible contradictions arising between the text under consideration and other works of Aristotle or other authorities.

108. Here follows the attempt to address and reconcile the potential contradiction that has been raised.

also exists in the intellect. Demonstrations, however, are not made from singulars which are in sense, but only from universals which are in the intellect.[109]

Or perhaps one should say that in each demonstration one has to proceed from things which are better-known in regards to us, but not from singulars; from universals, rather. For something cannot become known to us, unless through a thing which is more known to us. At times, however, that which is more known in regards to us is also more known uncontingently and according to the nature of things. This happens in mathematics, in which demonstrations are not made otherwise than from formal principles, owing to abstraction from matter. In such cases, demonstrations are made from things which are better-known unqualifiedly. Similarly, at times that which is better-known in regards to us is not better-known unqualifiedly, as happens in natural objects in which the essentials and capacities of things are hidden, due to the fact that they are in matter; but they become known to us through things which appear in an external way. Hence in such cases demonstrations are made for the most part through effects which are better-known in regards to us and not uncontingently. Now, however, he is not speaking of this mode of demonstrations but of the first mode.

---

109. The resolution of the potential contradiction rests on distinguishing between sensation and intellection, and between particular and universal.

Disputation

19. Thomas Aquinas, *Disputation concerning ON THE TRINITY* (c. 1259)

INTRODUCTION

In principle, the liberal arts course at medieval universities covered seven years; and toward the end of attending the second cycle of ordinary lectures, students began to prepare for their "determination." This was the culminating exercise in which a candidate to become a master of arts "determined," or decided, the outcome of a public disputation. The determination entailed not only rendering a decision, but also explaining why the arguments presented on one side of the question were stronger than the arguments presented on the other side. Students prepared for their determination by practicing various roles in mock disputations held before their masters and by attending the disputations between masters that occurred in all four faculties of the major universities: liberal arts, theology, law, and medicine.

Disputations, the signal intellectual events of the day, were highly formalized debates conducted according to specific rules and customs. As John of Salisbury relates, these rules and customs of disputing had begun to develop in the early 1100s and arose from a commitment to intelligent art rather than any kind of empty formalism.[110] Their purpose was to disaggregate the general question into the salient sub-questions and then to specify precisely the reasons and the responses advanced on each side of each sub-question. In this way, each point and argument was to be identified and rejoined through syllogistic reasoning, so that the substance of the issues would not be lost amid ambiguity, imprecision, or rhetorical devices. The disputation was thus a formal method of analysis intended to neutralize the power that Cicero attributed to rhetorical training: "our popular orator, even if he is mediocre and less than learned but practiced in speech, will trounce those philosophers merely through the power of that common mode of [rhetorical] practice."[111]

Due to its precision and balancing of viewpoints, the disputational form was esteemed by the scholastics, who employed it in their written analyses as well as in their verbal debates. The following example of that form is drawn from Thomas Aquinas's unfinished commentary on Boethius's treatise *On the Trinity*. The commentary was written in about 1259, near the end of Thomas's first term as a theology professor at the University of Paris. Although the work is a commentary and likely not a report of an actual debate, it does convey the disputational form adopted by the masters throughout the university. Here again, the substance deserves as much attention as the form because the work includes "the only extensive discussion of the sciences and scientific method written by Thomas."[112] Specifically addressing the liberal arts, Thomas's commentary reflects the effort among the scholastics in the mid-thirteenth century to reformulate the inherited epistemic and curricular framework in light of the century-long influx of new learning that had been received from Middle Eastern sources.

---

110. See selection #16 by John of Salisbury (I 11), as well as the continuing tradition of disputation expressed by Ignatius Loyola (para. 378) in selection #26.

111. Cicero, *On the Orator* III 79. See Cicero (III 76) in selection #4.

112. James A. Weisheipl, *Friar Thomas d'Aquino: His Life, Thought, and Works* (1974; Washington, DC: Catholic University of America Press, 1983), p. 134.

SELECTION[113]

Question V
The Division of Speculative Science

There are two questions here. The first concerns the division of speculative science which the text proposes,[114] the second the methods it attributes to the parts of speculative science. With regard to the first question there are four points of inquiry:

1. Is speculative science appropriately divided into these three parts: natural, mathematical, and divine?[115]
2. Does natural philosophy treat of what exists in motion and matter?
3. Does mathematics treat without motion and matter of what exists in matter?
4. Does divine science treat of what exists without matter and motion?

Article 1
Is Speculative Science Appropriately Divided Into These Three Parts: Natural, Mathematical, and Divine?

We proceed thus to the first article: It seems that speculative science is not appropriately divided into these three parts.[116]

Objection 1. For the parts of speculative science are those habits perfecting the contemplative part of the soul. But the Philosopher says in the *Ethics*[117] that the scientific part of the soul, which is its contemplative part, is perfected by three habits, namely, wisdom, science and understanding. Therefore these are the three divisions of speculative science, not those proposed in the text [of Boethius].

Objection 2. Again, Augustine says[118] that rational philosophy, or logic, is included under contemplative or speculative philosophy. Consequently, since no mention is made of it, it seems the division is inadequate.

Objection 3. Again, philosophy is commonly divided into seven liberal arts,[119] which include neither natural nor divine science, but only rational and mathematical science. Hence natural and divine should not be called parts of speculative science.

---

113. Thomas Aquinas, *The Division and Methods of the Sciences, Questions V and VI of his Commentary on the DE TRINITATE of Boethius*, tr. Armand Maurer, 4th rev. ed. (Toronto: Pontifical Institute of Medieval Studies, 1953), pp. 9–19. Reprinted by permission of the Pontifical Institute of Medieval Studies, Toronto.

114. Thomas is addressing the beginning of the second chapter of Boethius's *On the Trinity*. "Speculative science" might also be translated as "theoretical philosophy."

115. "Divine" science is the term employed to refer to the study that Aristotle called "theology" or "first philosophy" and was named "metaphysics" in about the first century B.C.

116. It was common for the disputant to begin by positing the view opposite to the one that was ultimately intended to be supported.

117. Aristotle, *Nicomachean Ethics* 1139a12ff, 1140b31ff, 1141a9ff. The references to Aristotle's works in this reading are drawn from the translator's notes.

118. Augustine, *City of God* VIII 4.

119. This statement reflects the actual situation, which had continued for another century following the similar statement by Hugh of St. Victor (III 4) in selection #15.

Objection 4. Again, medicine seems to be the most operative science, and yet it is said to contain a speculative part and a practical part. By the same token, therefore, all the other operative sciences have a speculative part. Consequently, even though it is a practical science, ethics or moral science should be mentioned in this division because of its speculative part.

Objection 5. Again, the science of medicine is a branch of physics,[120] and similarly certain other arts called "mechanical," like the science of agriculture, alchemy, and others of the same sort. Therefore, since these sciences are operative, it seems that natural science should not be included without qualification under speculative science.

Objection 6. Again, a whole should not be contradistinguished from its part. But divine science seems to be a whole in relation to physics and mathematics, since their subjects are parts of its subject. For the subject of divine science or first philosophy[121] is being; and changeable substance, which the natural scientist considers, as well as quantity, which the mathematician considers, are parts of being. This is clear in the *Metaphysics*.[122] Therefore, divine science should not be contradistinguished from natural science and mathematics.

Objection 7. Again, as it is said in the *On the Mind*, sciences are divided in the same manner as things.[123] But philosophy concerns being, for it is knowledge of being, as Dionysius says.[124] Now being is primarily divided with reference to potency and act, one and many, substance and accident. So it seems that the parts of philosophy ought to be distinguished by such divisions of being.

Objection 8. Again, there are many other divisions of beings studied by sciences more essential than the divisions into mobile and immobile and into abstract and inabstract: for example, the divisions into corporeal and incorporeal and into living and non-living, and the like. Therefore differences of this sort should be the basis for the division of the parts of philosophy rather than those mentioned here.

Objection 9. Again, that science on which others depend must be prior to them. Now all the other sciences depend on divine science because it is its business to prove their principles. Therefore Boethius should have placed divine science before the others.

Objection 10. Again, mathematics should be studied before natural science, for the young can easily learn mathematics, but only the more advanced natural science, as is said in the *Ethics*. This is why the ancients are said to have observed the following order in learning the sciences: first, logic; then mathematics before natural science; after that moral science; and finally the mature studied divine science.[125] Therefore, Boethius should have placed mathematics before natural science. And so it seems that this division is unsuitable.

---

120. The terms "physics," "natural philosophy," and "natural science" are generally interchangeable in this text and in medieval writings about the liberal arts.

121. Here again, Aristotle's term "first philosophy" is interchangeable with his term "theology," which Thomas and this translator render as "divine science" and which began to be called "metaphysics" in about the first century B.C.

122. Aristotle, *Metaphysics* 996b14–23, 1025b26–1026a16, 1061b4.

123. Aristotle, *On the Mind* 431b24.

124. Pseudo-Dionysius, *Letters* VII 2.

125. Aristotle, *Nicomachean Ethics* 1142a11–19. See selection #20 from Thomas's *Commentary on the NICOMACHEAN ETHICS*.

On the contrary,[126] the Philosopher proves the appropriateness of this division in the *Metaphysics*,[127] where he says, "There will be three philosophical and theoretical sciences: mathematics, physics and theology." Moreover, in the *Physics*[128] three methods of the sciences are proposed which indeed seem to belong to these three. Moreover, Ptolemy also uses this division in the beginning of his *Almagest*.[129]

Reply: The theoretical or speculative intellect is properly distinguished from the operative or practical intellect in this, that the speculative intellect has for its end the truth under consideration, while the practical intellect directs the truth under consideration to operation as to its own end. So the Philosopher says in *On the Mind* that they differ from each other with regard to their end.[130] And he says in the *Metaphysics*, "The end of speculative science is truth, while the end of practical science is action."[131] . . .

Now there are some objects of speculation which depend on matter with respect to their existence, for they can only exist in matter. And there is a distinction among these. Some depend on matter both with respect to their existence and their concept. This is the case with those whose definition contains sensible matter and which, therefore, cannot be understood without sensible matter; as, for instance, it is necessary to include flesh and bones in the definition of man. Physics or natural science studies things of this sort. There are some objects of speculation, however, which, although depending on matter with respect to existence, do not depend on it with respect to their concept, because sensible matter is not included in their definitions. This is the case with lines and numbers—the sort of things mathematics studies. There are still other objects of speculation which do not depend on matter with respect to their existence because they can exist without matter. This is true, whether they never exist in matter, e.g., God and the angels, or whether they exist in matter in some things and in others do not, e.g., substance, quality, being, potency, act, one and many, and the like. Theology or divine science (so called because God is the principal thing known in it) deals with all these. It is called by another name "metaphysics," that is to say, "[after physics]," because in the order of learning it comes after physics for us who must rise from sensible things to what is beyond the sensible. It is also called "first philosophy"[132] in so far as all the other sciences take their principles from it and so come after it.[133] It

---

126. Thomas now shifts to argue the opposite side of the case, beginning with citations of leading authorities and then undertaking a discursive reply.

127. Aristotle, *Metaphysics* 1026a18.

128. Aristotle, *Physics* 193b23ff, 194b14.

129. *Almagest* (I 1) is the Arabic title, adopted in the Latin West, of Ptolemy's *Syntaxis Mathematica*.

130. Aristotle, *On the Mind* 433a14.

131. Aristotle, *Metaphysics* 993b20.

132. "For a similar explanation of the three names of this science, see the "Foreword" to St. Thomas's *Commentary on the Metaphysics*. Divine science and theology are here used as synonymous with metaphysics. They are not the theology of Sacred Scripture, as Thomas explains below in ques. 5, art. 4. Aristotle himself calls this science [first] philosophy or theology. The name 'metaphysics' does not come from him, but from either Andronicus of Rhodes or some earlier editor of Aristotle's works in the first century B.C. who placed the treatises on [first] philosophy after the *Physics* and therefore called them the treatises after the *Physics*. It is also possible that the name was coined to signify that metaphysics goes beyond the order of physics." Translator's note, p. 8n.

133. "Of course the other sciences have their own proper principles, which can be known without an explicit knowledge of the principles of metaphysics. Hence, these sciences do not directly depend on metaphysics; they are autonomous in their own spheres. Yet the principles of metaphysics are the absolutely universal and primary principles. All the others can be resolved into them. It is in this sense that all the other sciences are said to take

is impossible, however, for some things to depend on matter with respect to their concept and not with respect to their existence, for the intellect by its very nature is immaterial. So there is no fourth kind of philosophy besides the ones mentioned.

Reply to objection 1.[134] In the *Ethics*,[135] the Philosopher considers the intellectual habits in so far as they are intellectual virtues. Now they are called virtues from the fact that they perfect the intellect in its operation; for virtue makes its possessor good and renders its work good. So he differentiates between virtues of this sort according as such speculative habits perfect the intellect in different ways. Now, in one way the speculative part of the soul is perfected by understanding, which is the habit of principles, through which some things become known of themselves. In another way it is perfected by a habit through which conclusions demonstrated from such principles are known, whether the demonstration proceeds from inferior causes, as in science, or from the highest causes, as in wisdom. But when sciences are differentiated in so far as they are habits, they must be distinguished according to their objects, that is, according to the things of which the sciences treat. And it is in this way that both here and in the *Metaphysics* speculative philosophy is distinguished into three parts.[136]

Reply to objection 2. As is evident in the beginning of the *Metaphysics*, the speculative sciences concern things the knowledge of which is sought for their own sake.[137] However, we do not seek to know the things studied by logic for themselves, but as a help to the other science. So logic is not included under speculative philosophy as a principal part but as something brought under speculative philosophy as furnishing speculative thought with its instruments, namely, syllogisms, definitions and the like, which we need in the speculative sciences. Thus, according to Boethius, logic is not so much a science as the instrument of science.

Reply to objection 3. The seven liberal arts do not adequately divide theoretical philosophy;[138] but, as Hugh of St. Victor says, seven arts are grouped together, leaving out certain other ones, because those who wanted to learn philosophy were first instructed in them. And the reason why they are divided into the trivium and quadrivium is "because by them, as by certain ways [*viae*], a quick mind enters" into the secrets of philosophy.[139] This is also in harmony with what the Philosopher says in the *Metaphysics*,[140] that we must investigate the method of scientific thinking before the sciences themselves. And the Commentator says in the same place[141] that before all the other sciences a person

---

their principles from metaphysics, and that this science is said to explain the principles of all the sciences." Translator's note, pp. 8n–9n.

134. Having replied discursively, Thomas now turns to respond to each point previously enumerated.

135. Aristotle, *Nicomachean Ethics* 1139b14ff.

136. Aristotle, *Metaphysics* 1026a18.

137. Aristotle, *Metaphysics* 981b21–982a17.

138. In this critical statement, Thomas explicitly declares that the seven liberal arts no longer serve as adequate epistemic (or curricular) categories.

139. See selection #15 from Hugh of St. Victor selection (III 3).

140. Aristotle, *Metaphysics* 995a12–14.

141. The Commentator is Ibn Rushd (1126–1198), Spanish-Arabian philosopher and prominent Islamic commentator on Aristotle, known in the west as Averroës. His authority was so great that he was known by this pseudonym. Thomas is citing from his *Commentary on Aristotle's* Metaphysics 995a.

should learn logic, which teaches the method of all the sciences; and the trivium belongs to the domain of logic. The Philosopher further says in the *Ethics* that the young can know mathematics, but not physics, which requires experience.[142] So we are given to understand that we should learn mathematics, to whose domain the quadrivium belongs, immediately after logic. And so these are as paths preparing the mind for the other philosophic disciplines.[143]

We may add, too, that these are called arts among the other sciences because they not only involve knowledge but a certain work which is directly a product of reason itself; for example, producing a composition, syllogism or discourse, numbering, measuring, composing melodies and reckoning the course of the stars. Other sciences, like divine and natural sciences, either do not involve a work produced, but only knowledge, and so we cannot call them arts, because, according to the *Metaphysics*, art is called "productive reason";[144] or they involve a material product, as in the case of medicine, alchemy and other sciences of this sort. These latter, then, cannot be called liberal arts because such actions belong to man on the side of his nature in which he is not free, namely, on the side of his body.[145] And although moral science is directed to action, still that action is not the act of science but rather of virtue, as is clear in the *Ethics*.[146] So we cannot call moral science an art; but rather in these actions virtue takes the place of art.[147] Thus, as Augustine says, the ancients defined virtue as the art of noble and well-ordered living.[148]

---

142. Aristotle, *Nicomachean Ethics* 1142a11–19. See selection #20 from Thomas's *Commentary on the* NICOMACHEAN ETHICS.

143. Hence, the seven liberal arts belong to, but do not comprehend, the course leading to the liberal arts degree.

144. Aristotle, *Metaphysics* 1025b22. "Aristotle defines art as a habit which is directed to making and which involves a true course of reasoning. (See *Nicomachean Ethics* 1140a10). Following Aristotle, Thomas defines it as an operative art accompanied by right reason." Translator's note, p. 11n.

145. Thomas elsewhere elaborates these characteristics of utility and physicality that are characteristic of "mechanical or servile arts, in distinction to the liberal arts, which, although they involve a work produced directly by reason itself, do not exist for the sake of that work, but rather are ordained to knowledge. St. Thomas says, 'Only those arts are called liberal which are ordained to knowledge. Those ordained to some utility to be achieved through action are called mechanical or servile.' (In *Commentary on Aristotle's Metaphysics* I, lect. 3, n. 59). 'Even in speculative matters there is something by way of work: e.g., the making of a syllogism or of a fitting speech, or the work of counting or measuring. Hence whatever habits are ordained to such works of the speculative reason are, by a kind of comparison, called arts indeed, but *liberal* arts in order to distinguish them from those arts that are ordained to works done by the body; for these arts are, in a fashion, servile, inasmuch as the body is in servile subjection to the soul, and man, as regards his soul, is free (*liber*). *Summa Theologica* I–II, 57, 3, reply to objection 3." Translator's note, p. 10n.

146. Aristotle, *Nicomachean Ethics* 1144b17–30.

147. Given that Thomas here attempts to "save" the definition of arts, without including ethics, where does "ethics" belong among the "liberal" and mechanical or servile arts posited above?

148. Augustine, *City of God* IV 21, XIX 1.

Extraordinary Lecture

20. Thomas Aquinas, *Commentary on the NICOMACHEAN ETHICS* (c. 1258)

INTRODUCTION

While ordinary lectures were the pedagogical staple and the determination was the culminating exercise, another exercise attended by the liberal arts students was the "extraordinary lecture." Scheduled around the ordinary lectures on afternoons or feast days, these exercises apparently followed the same format as the ordinary lectures except that they addressed texts on what were considered the less important topics, such as Aristotle's *Politics*, *Nicomachean Ethics*, and *Physics*. The secondary status is also apparent from the fact that bachelors, who had been through the entire course of lectures once, were sometimes enlisted to give the extraordinary lectures. The following excerpt from Thomas's *Commentary on the NICOMACHEAN ETHICS*, presents a glimpse of an extraordinary lecture.

The substance of the excerpt is also significant in that it addresses the relationship among certain disciplines that were beginning to be incorporated into liberal education. The scholastics had been struggling since Hugh of St. Victor in the early twelfth century to conceive a compelling organization of knowledge and, hence, the curriculum. The three primary formulations that Hugh had addressed were still circulating a century later in the mid-thirteenth century:

1. *Aristotelian*[149] (known via Boethius's translation of the "old logic")
   a. Theoretical Sciences, whose end is pure knowledge acquired through the most rigorous method and whose outcome is expressed in thoughts, words, and equations:
       theology (metaphysics)
       physics (natural philosophy)
       mathematics
       logic (as method)
   b. Practical Sciences, whose subject matter incorporates human volition, and whose truths are therefore contingent, and whose study results in action:
       politics
       economics
       ethics
       rhetoric (sometimes included under "productive")
       dialectic (as method)
   c. Productive Sciences, whose study results in a palpable product, especially a concrete artifact:
       poetics (fine arts)

2. *Stoic* (known via Augustine, Isidore of Seville, and Hugh of St. Victor)
   a. logic, meaning the trivium of grammar, rhetoric, dialectic
   b. ethics (moral philosophy)
   c. physics (natural philosophy)

3. *seven liberal arts* (known via traditional handbooks)

---

149. Aristotle advances different versions of the organization of knowledge at various points in his writings, and this formulation is a fairly conventional interpretation of his view.

    a. *trivium*: grammar, rhetoric, logic

    b. *quadrivium*: arithmetic, geometry, music, astronomy

In the opening decades of the thirteenth century, the creation of the university increased the need for a compelling curricular, if not epistemic, structure. Through a process of reflection and debate not entirely understood today, a *modernus* formulation of liberal disciplines gradually gained favor, a formulation that, though draped with the mantle of traditional authorities, was nevertheless a new creation drawing from each of the predominant, available schemas.[150] It is not known what role, if any, Thomas Aquinas played in this reformulation of the liberal arts; but in the following extraordinary lecture, Thomas elaborates the educational implications of a comment by Aristotle, and this elaboration conveys the reformulation and explains the way in which the inherited tradition was being reconceived.

SELECTION[151]

    1209. . . . . [Aristotle] raises a question about why a youth can become a mathematician but cannot become wise, i.e., a metaphysician or natural philosopher.[152] To this the Philosopher answers that the principles of mathematics are known by abstraction from sensible objects (whose understanding requires experience); for this reason little time is needed to grasp them. But the principles of nature, which are not separated from sensible objects are studied via experience. For this much time is needed.

    1210. As to wisdom, he adds that youths do not believe, i.e. grasp, although they mouth, things pertaining to wisdom or metaphysics. But the nature of mathematics is not obscure to them because mathematical proofs concern sensibly conceivable objects while things pertaining to wisdom are purely rational. Youths can easily understand whatever falls under imagination, but they do not grasp things exceeding sense and imagination; for their minds are not trained to such considerations both because of the shortness of their lives and the many physical changes they are undergoing.

    1211. Therefore, the proper order of education is that the young first be instructed in topics pertaining to logic, because logic teaches the method of the whole of philosophy. Next, they should be instructed in mathematics, which does not require experience and does not exceed the range of imagination. Third, in natural sciences, which, even though not exceeding sense and imagination, require experience. Fourth, in the moral sciences, which require experience and a soul free from passions, as was noted in the first book [of the *Nicomachean Ethics*.] Fifth, in the sapiential and metaphysical sciences, which exceed imagination and require a sharp mind.[153]

---

150. One of the best discussions of this reformulation is: James A. Weisheipl, "Classification of the Sciences in Medieval Thought," *Mediaeval Studies* 27 (1965): 51–90.

151. Thomas Aquinas, *Commentary on Aristotle's NICOMACHEAN ETHICS*, tr. C. I. Litzinger (1964; Notre Dame, IN: Dumb Ox Books, 1993), bk. VI, lect. 7, pp. 383–4. Reprinted by permission of Dumb Ox Books.

152. Aristotle, *Nicomachean Ethics* 1142a11–19.

153. Thomas's extraordinary lecture neatly sketches a fivefold educational sequence—logic, mathematics, natural philosophy, moral philosophy, metaphysics—that is rationalized on both epistemic and psychological grounds. This sequence formed the spine of the scholastic reformulation of liberal arts that became normative in subsequent centuries and was known as "the seven arts and three philosophies." Drawing three philosophical categories from the Aristotelian and Stoic frameworks, the scholastics posited a curriculum for the arts faculty comprising the seven traditional arts surmounted by natural, moral, and metaphysical philosophies. Indeed, if "logic" is understood in the Stoic sense as the trivium and if "mathematics" is taken to mean the quadrivium, then the seven arts and three philosophies are fully included in Thomas's extraordinary lecture.

Universitas

21. University Statutes and Documents

INTRODUCTION

Notwithstanding the rich program presented in "seven liberal arts and three philosophies," the scholastics in practice were interested primarily in deductive logic and metaphysics. The balance of the curriculum and even Aristotle's other writings were gradually sloughed away or preserved only in token form, as is revealed by the documentary record of the universities from the time of their genesis in the closing decade of the twelfth century.

During the late 1100s and throughout the 1200s some twenty-five institutions in Europe were chartered by a monarch or pope, thereby legally incorporating them as a guild or *universitas*. By the end of that century only about twenty were offering instruction and granting degrees. During the 1300s another two dozen were founded, and scores more were planned or chartered, but many failed or moved when funds did not materialize or political conditions changed. By the year 1500 the number of functioning universities approached seventy. Their proliferation is detailed on the table at the beginning of Section III. Most of these seventy new institutions left few written records about their curriculum during this period, but the following statutes and documents reveal telling aspects of their institutional life and their liberal arts education.

SELECTION[154]

Decree of the BishopS
Forbidding Certain Readings at Paris, 1210

Neither the books of Aristotle on natural philosophy nor their commentaries are to be read at Paris in public or secret, and this we forbid under penalty of excommunication. He in whose possession the writings of David of Dinant are found after the Nativity shall be considered a heretic.[155] As for the theological books written in French we order that they be handed over to the diocesan bishops, both *Credo in deum* and *Pater noster* in French except the lives of the saints, and this before the Purification, because [thereafter] he who shall be found with them shall be held a heretic.[156]

Papal Rules for the Studium of Paris, 1215

No one shall lecture in the arts at Paris before he is twenty-one years of age, and he shall have heard lectures for at least six years before he begins to lecture,[157] and he shall promise to lecture for at least

---

154. These records are drawn from Lynn Thorndike, ed. and tr., *University Records and Life in the Middle Ages* (New York: Columbia University Press, 1944), pp. 26–31, 52–5, 64–7, 102–5, 244–7, 296–7. Reprinted by permission of Columbia University Press.

155. This decree had condemned David of Dinant, an obscure figure, as a heretic.

156. The problem being addressed was that the Latin theological books were translated into the vernacular and made available to an unschooled audience.

157. Given the paucity of books, a prime responsibility of the masters was to lecture or "read" (*legere* or *praelegere*) to students the texts of the liberal arts course, as is described below. Here, "lecture" means more generally the activity, or teaching, of a master of arts. The minimum age of twenty-one and duration of six years of study

two years, unless a reasonable cause prevents, which he ought to prove publicly or before examiners.[158] He shall not be stained by any infamy, and when he is ready to lecture, he shall be examined according to the form which is contained in the writing of the lord bishop of Paris, where is contained the peace confirmed between the chancellor and scholars by judges delegated by the pope. . . .[159]

And they shall lecture on the books of Aristotle on dialectic old and new in the schools ordinarily and not *ad cursum*.[160] They shall also lecture on both Priscians ordinarily, or at least on one. They shall not lecture on feast days except on philosophers and rhetoric and the quadrivium and *Barbarismus* and ethics, if it please them, and the fourth book of the *Topics*.[161] They shall not lecture on the books of Aristotle on metaphysics and natural philosophy or on summaries of them or concerning the doctrine of master David of Dinant or the heretic Amaury or Mauritius of Spain.[162]

In the *principia* and meetings of the masters and in the responsions or oppositions[163] of the boys and youths there shall be no drinking. They may summon some friends or associates, but only a few. Donations of clothing or other things as has been customary, or more, we urge should be made, especially to the poor.[164]

None of the masters lecturing in arts shall have a cope except one round, black and reaching to the ankles, at least while it is new. Use of the pallium is permitted. No one shall wear with the round cope shoes that are ornamented or with elongated pointed toes. . . .[165]

---

were intended to halt the trend of students leaving the arts course as quickly as possible in order to enter the higher faculties.

158. New masters of arts provided much of the teaching in the arts faculty, because the more experienced and ambitious masters were inclined either to teach on their own (having been granted the *licentia docendi* when they completed the arts course) or, more likely, to proceed to one of the three graduate faculties to study theology, law, or medicine. This requirement that new masters of arts remain to teach for two years ensured the staffing for the arts faculty.

159. The office of the "chancellor" varied among the universities, but at Paris referred historically to the head of the cathedral school, who was appointed by the bishop, and then came to refer to the bishop's representative to the *studium*, who was delegated with authority to license the masters. The university of scholars and the chancellor were often in conflict because the former asserted its autonomy while relying on the protection of the pope, while the latter represented the interests of the bishop, who wished to maintain his authority over educational matters within his diocese. At Paris, this conflict escalated to the point that a truce had to be negotiated.

160. The point is that "the books of Aristotle on dialectic [logic] old and new" had to be included in the primary educational exercises of ordinary lectures. At Paris, "extraordinary" lectures were also known as "cursory" because they were given by a *cursor*: "a bachelor who was giving a lecture course for practice and would not go into the subject so deeply or at much length as a full-fledged doctor." Translator's note, p. 28n. Hence, a cursory treatment was more rapid and superficial.

161. The scheduling on feast days indicates the lesser status accorded to rhetoric, mathematics, ethics, and writings of certain philosophers other than Aristotle. The *Barbarismus* was an informal title assigned to one chapter of the conventional, medieval textbook on grammar, the *Greater Art* of Donatus. The *Topics* was one of Aristotle's four advanced treatises on logic, although at least part of it was written before his discovery of the syllogism.

162. Note the proscription in 1215 of certain writings of Aristotle.

163. The "responsions or oppositions" [*responsiones*] were an interrogatory exercise conducted either between a student and a master in private or in conjunction with a disputation, and in either case as part of the preparation for the determination. See the discussion of *repetitiones* in selection #26 from Ignatius Loyola.

164. It was customary for students to celebrate a successful determination through acts of revelry and charity.

165. A cope is a head covering; a pallium is a mantle or cloak.

Each master shall have jurisdiction over his scholar.[166]

No one shall occupy a classroom or house without asking the consent of the tenant, provided one has a chance to ask it.[167]

No one shall receive the licentiate from the chancellor or another for money given or promise made or other condition agreed upon.[168]

Also, the masters and scholars can make both between themselves and with other persons obligations and constitutions supported by faith or penalty or oath in these cases: namely, the murder or mutilation of a scholar or atrocious injury done a scholar, if justice should not be forthcoming, arranging the prices of lodgings, costume, burial, lectures and disputations, so, however, that the university be not thereby dissolved or destroyed.[169]

As to the status of the theologians, we decree that no one shall lecture at Paris before his thirty-fifth year and unless he has studied for eight years at least, and has heard the books faithfully and in classrooms, and has attended lectures in theology for five years before he gives lectures himself publicly. And none of these shall lecture before the third hour on days when masters lecture.[170]

No one shall be admitted at Paris to formal lectures or to preachings unless he shall be of approved life and science. No one shall be a scholar at Paris who has no definite master.[171]

Regulation Concerning Studies in the Order, Published in the General Chapter of the Friar Preachers at Paris, 1228[172]

The prior of the province or kingdoms, if he shall have brothers fitted for teaching who can be trained for it in short order, shall send them to study in a place where there is a university, and let not those to whom they are sent dare to employ them otherwise or send them back to their province unless they shall have been recalled.[173]

Since great care is to be taken concerning students, let them have some special brother without whose permission they shall not take notes or hear lectures and who shall correct those matters which require correction in their studies. And if he cannot control them, let him lay the matter before the prelate.

---

166. This provisions reinforced both the authority and the responsibility of the university guild.

167. For a long period, the universities owned no real property. Classrooms and lodging were rented by individual masters or students.

168. This provision ensures not only the educational integrity of the *studium* but also that the chancellor, being the officer of the bishop, does not gain undue influence over the *universitas*.

169. This provision confers upon the guild the right to collective bargaining about issues ranging from prices to criminal offenses by or against its members. When they did not get satisfaction through such collective bargaining, universities occasionally removed themselves to another city for a period of time.

170. The lectures of the masters of liberal arts were thus protected from competition with the theologians' lectures.

171. Even more than the provision noted above, this crucial point ensured the monopoly of the university guild and thus its responsibility for and authority over those studying and teaching within its locale. "Masterless" students were not permitted.

172. Friar Preachers was the conventional name for the Dominican Order, which had been founded only twelve years earlier.

173. Reporting directly to the pope, the monastic orders were perceived as interlopers both by bishops within their diocese and by universities, whose rules the friars would not obey. Consequently, their arrival often precipitated conflict within and about the *studium*.

They shall not study books of the Gentiles and philosophers, although they may inspect them briefly. They shall not learn secular sciences nor even the arts which are called liberal,[174] unless sometimes in certain cases the master of the Order or the general chapter shall wish to make a dispensation, but shall read only theological works whether they be youths or others. Moreover, we have decreed that each province shall provide for its brothers sent to the university at least three books of theology, and the brothers sent to the university shall study histories and sentences,[175] and text and glosses especially.

In the case of those studying thus the prelate shall issue a dispensation lest they be held back or impeded from study because of the offices or otherwise. And as shall seem good to the master of studies, an appropriate place shall be set aside, in which, after disputations or vespers or at other times when they are free, they may meet in his presence to propound doubts or questions. And while one is asking or propounding, the rest shall be silent, lest they impede the speaker. And if anyone gives offense by questioning or opposing or responding indecently or confusedly or loudly or basely, he shall straightway be rebuked by the presiding officer.

Let no one receive the doctorate unless he has attended lectures in theology for at least four years.

Rules for Determinations in Liberal Arts, 1252, Statutes of the Artists of the English Nation[176]

Concerning Bachelors of Arts who are to Determine During Lent. In the first place the proctor, touching the Bible, shall select two persons whom he believes qualified to choose examiners of those [bachelors in arts] determining, who, touching the Bible, shall swear that without hate or love of any person or any part of their nation, they will choose three masters, whom they know to be strict and qualified in examining faithfully, more intent on the promotion and advantage of the university, less susceptible to prayer or bribe. These three when chosen shall similarly swear on the Bible that they will faithfully examine and proceed with rigor of examination, licentiating the worthy and conducting themselves without hate of any person or group of their nation, also without envy or any rancor of mind or other sinister perturbation. Moreover, those who have insufficient standing in the examination and are unworthy to pass they shall fail, sparing no one, moved neither by prayer nor bribe nor fear nor love or any other occasion or indirect favor of persons.

The masters presenting candidates, moreover, and the bachelors themselves shall give personal security that they will make no entreaties on behalf of bachelors nor seek favor from the examiners or from the nation or from the university, either by themselves or through others, but will accept the simple statement of the examiners.

By the same token, if it happens that bachelors are failed, that they will not bring contumely or complaints or threats or other evils against the examiners, either by themselves or through others, because they ought to suppose that the examiners have acted according to their consciences and good faith for the honor of the university and the nation.

---

174. This sentence indicates that, at this point, the "arts which are called liberal" were no longer the sum total of the available "secular sciences," as they were for Hugh of St. Victor.

175. "Sentences" were statements of the truths of revelation set forth by the teaching master based upon long study of the letter and sense of the text of the Bible and traditional authorities.

176. In the course of the early thirteenth century at Paris, the university guild, headed by a rector, became divided into four groups, known as "nations," which roughly corresponded with different geographic areas in Europe and were each headed by a "proctor." Although the university remained a strong unit, each nation promulgated rules on certain issues, as seen here. These rules govern eligibility to "determine," as discussed under "disputation" above.

Moreover, a bachelor coming up for the licentiate in arts at Paris should be twenty years old or at least in his twentieth year, and of honorable life and laudable [behavior].[177]

He should not have a cope without a hood of the same cloth, nor a hood with knots. He should not wear a mitre on his head in the classrooms while he is determining. If he has the right to the tonsure, he may have the tonsure, nor may he or should he be blamed on this account.

Also before he is admitted to examination he shall give personal security that he has his own classroom of a master qualified to teach in it throughout Lent, and has his own master under whom he seeks the license of determining,[178] or a bachelor about to incept in arts[179] at the latest before Lent, in whose classroom he will determine.

Further, that he has attended lectures in arts for five years or four at least at Paris continuously or elsewhere in a university of arts.[180] Further, that he has heard the books of Aristotle on the Old Logic . . . at least twice in ordinary lectures and once cursorily, . . . the three first books of the *Topics* and the *Divisions* once in ordinary lectures or at least cursorily, the *Topics* of Aristotle and *Sophistical Refutations* twice in ordinary lectures and once at least cursorily or if not cursorily at least thrice in ordinary, the *Prior Analytics* once in ordinary lectures and once cursorily, or, if he is now attending, so that he has heard at least half before Lent and is to continue, the *Posterior Analytics* once in ordinary lectures completely.[181] Also that he shall have heard *Lesser Priscian* (books 17–18) and [Donatus] twice in ordinary lectures and at least once cursorily, *Greater Priscian* (books 1–16) once cursorily. Also he shall have heard Aristotle's *On the Mind* once or be hearing it as aforesaid.

Also he shall give satisfaction that he has diligently attended the disputations of masters in a recognized university for two years and for the same length of time has answered as required concerning sophisms in class. Also he shall promise that he will respond to questions for a full year from the beginning of one Lent to the beginning of the next.[182]

If, moreover, a bachelor shall be found sufficiently qualified in knowledge according to the examiners and shall not have completed the required number of years or books or lectures, the [English] nation reserves to itself the power to dispense with these, as shall seem expedient to it. And in such case only it shall be permissible for his master to petition the nation for him.[183]

Also if, after the exercise of cursory lectures has been made and finally completed, he shall have transgressed in the said exercise in any way, he shall in no case be admitted to the examination for determination. Nor similarly shall a master, whether now teaching or not, who, after the said exercise

---

177. Since 1215, the minimum age limit for the master of arts had thus officially dropped to age nineteen.

178. Another interdiction against "masterless" students.

179. The inception into the arts faculty was the act of formally being admitted into the university guild of the masters, with the privileges and obligations attendant thereto. The inception required permission of the members of the university, and was dependent upon, but distinct from, successful completion of the determination. Both the inception and determination were separate from licensing to teach, which was the responsibility of the chancellor. It is important to remember, however, that these practices and terms varied over time and location.

180. It was the custom in this early period for the universities to accord equal standing for studies and exercises completed at other universities.

181. The *Topics*, *Sophistical Refutations*, *Prior Analytics*, and *Posterior Analytics* constituted the "new logic" of Aristotle.

182. Among the prerequisites to determine, "responding" was an interrogatory exercise conducted either between a student and a master in private or in conjunction with a disputation and, in either case, as part of the preparation for the determination.

183. The pressure to lower or circumvent the minimum age requirements is evident here.

has been made as stated and finally confirmed by the masters, shall have transgressed in the said exercise, be accepted as presenting a bachelor, until full satisfaction shall have been made to the rector or proctors for the university by the master or the bachelor who has transgressed. . . .

Also, it shall be enjoined on him that all through Lent, and thereafter so long as he shall belong to the faculty of arts as student or teacher, he shall obey the mandate of rector and proctor in lawful and honorable matters.[184] Also he shall not give drinks except on the first day he begins to determine and the last, unless this is done by the permission of the rector or the proctor of his nation, who can give him a dispensation in this regard as shall seem expedient to them, considering nevertheless the many factors about the determiners which are here involved.

Also, the examiners shall diligently collect from the bachelors the money to be paid to the university and nation and faithfully keep what is collected, and at the summons of the rector and proctors of the four nations deposit it at the day set in the common chest of the university of artists.[185] Also the money received for the nation they shall deposit in the common chest before the Sunday after Ash Wednesday. Also none of the said examiners can by himself, without his associates deputed with him for determinations, license anyone or presume alone to examine.

Also, in addition to the aforesaid, after the candidates shall have been licensed, let them be present every Friday at the Vespers of the blessed Virgin and at mass the Saturday following, until Palm Sunday, under the penalty by which masters are bound. . . .

Rules of the University of Paris
for the Liberal Arts Course, 1255

Let all know that we, all and each, masters of arts by our common assent, no one contradicting, because of the new and incalculable peril which threatens in our faculty—some masters hurrying to finish their lectures sooner than the length and difficulty of the texts permits,[186] for which reason both masters in lecturing and scholars in hearing make less progress—worrying over the ruin of our faculty and wishing to provide for our status, have decreed and ordained for the common utility and the reparation of our university to the honor of God and the church universal that all and single masters of our faculty in the future shall be required to finish the texts which they shall have begun on the feast of St. Remy [October 1] at the times below noted, not before.

The Old Logic, namely the book of Porphyry [and those] . . . of Boethius, except the fourth, on the feast of the Annunciation of the blessed Virgin [March 25] or the last day for lectures preceding. *Lesser Priscian* and *Greater*, *Topics* and *Sophistical Refutations*, *Prior* and *Posterior Analytics* they must finish in the said or equal time.[187] The *Ethics* through four books in twelve weeks, if they are read with another text, if [by itself], not with another, in half that time. Three short texts [on grammar] . . . if read together and nothing else with them, in six weeks. Aristotle's *Physics*, *Metaphysics*, and *On Animals* on the feast of St. John the Baptist [June 24]; *Concerning Heaven and Earth*, first book of *Meteorology* with the fourth, on Ascension day [in May]; *On the Mind*, if read with the books on nature, on the feast of the Ascension, if with the logical texts, on the feast of the Annunciation of the

---

184. This oath of obedience ensures the authority and security of the guild.

185. The "common chest" contained all the property of the university, including the treasury and the seal of the guild.

186. Like the strictures establishing a minimum age for completing the liberal arts course, this attempt to prohibit rushing through the lectures stems from the fact that, already in the mid-thirteenth century, both students and masters were becoming eager to move rapidly through the liberal arts and on to the graduate faculties.

187. These four texts beyond *Lesser* and *Greater Priscian* are the Aristotelian treatises constituting the "new logic." In this paragraph, Thorndike's translation of the titles has been modified.

blessed Virgin; *On Coming to Be* on the feast of the Chair of St. Peter [February 24]; *On Causes* in seven weeks; *On Sensation* in six weeks; *On Sleep* in five weeks; *On Plants* in five weeks; *On Memory* in two weeks; *On Breath* in two weeks; *On Life and Death* in one week. Moreover, if masters begin to read the said books at another time than the feast of St. Remy, they shall allow as much time for lecturing on them as is indicated above. Moreover, each of the said texts, if read by itself, not with another text, can be finished in half the time of lecturing above. It will not be permitted anyone to finish the said texts in less time, but anyone may take more time. Moreover, if anyone reads some portion of a text, so that he does not wish, or is unable, to complete the whole of it, he shall read that portion in a corresponding amount of time.

If a bachelor shall incept before the feast of St. Denis [October 9], he may end his lectures with those resuming on the feast of the blessed Remy. Those who begin after the feast of St. Denis shall finish their texts by as much later as they began later than others. Each in good faith shall according to his estimate portion out his text proportionally to the time allowed for his lectures. Further, no one shall be allowed to give more than two ordinary lectures nor to make them extraordinary, nor to give them except at the ordinary hour and in ordinary wise.

Moreover, from the feast of St. John the Baptist till the feast of St. Remy each shall arrange his lectures as shall seem most convenient for himself and his auditors. Also no one shall presume to give more than two cursory lectures on any day when lectures are held, nor more than three on a day when there are not regular lectures, nor to begin any course until he has finished the preceding course, unless he shall have been detained by serious illness over fifteen days or shall have been out of town for good reason more than fifteen days, or if the scholars do not want to hear him further. Also, no one shall be permitted to deliver any lectures on the days of the apostles and evangelists or on the three days immediately following Christmas, Easter, and Pentecost, or after the third hour on the eve of those three days. These things, moreover, we have decreed and ordained to be observed inviolate. Let no one, therefore, infringe this page of our ordinance or rashly go against it. But should anyone presume to attempt this, let him know that he will incur the wrath of the whole university and suspension of lectures for a year. In testimony and support of which thing we have decreed that the present letter be sealed with the seals of the four nations by their consent.[188]

A Law Professor Introduces His Lectures at Bologna[189]

If you please, I will begin the [text] on the eighth day or thereabouts after the feast of St. Michael [September 29] and I will finish it entire with all ordinary and extraordinary [lectures], Providence permitting, in the middle of August or thereabouts. . . . The extraordinary lectures used not to be given by the doctors.[190] And so all scholars including the unskilled and novices will be able to make good progress with me, for they will hear their text as a whole, nor will anything be left out, as was once done in this region, indeed was the usual practice. For I shall teach [not only] the unskilled and novices but also the advanced students. The unskilled will be able to make satisfactory progress in [putting]

---

188. The seal was the most important possession of the university or nation, for it effected the corporate authority of the guild. The act of being chartered gave the corporate group legal standing, authorizing it to possess and employ a seal.

189. This document gives an unusually precise report of the procedure of teaching in medieval universities. The law professor is Odofredus, who wrote the classic text on the founding of Bologna, the leading university in the study of law, where he taught in the mid-thirteenth century. Compare the account of lecturing by Ignatius Loyola (para. 374) in selection #26 and by Charles Eliot in selection #40.

190. Extraordinary lectures were often given by bachelors of the subject in question, commensurate with the marginal status of these lectures.

the case and exposition of the letter; the advanced students can become more erudite in the subtleties of questions and contrarieties. I shall also read all the glosses, which was not done before my time. . . .

For it is my purpose to teach you faithfully and in a kindly manner, in which instruction the following order has customarily been observed by the ancient and modern doctors and particularly by my master, which method I shall retain.[191] First, I shall give you the summaries of each title before I come to the text. Second, I shall put forth well and distinctly and in the best terms I can the purport of each law. Third, I shall read the text in order to correct it. Fourth, I shall briefly restate the meaning. Fifth, I shall solve conflicts, adding general matters (which are commonly called *brocardica*) and subtle and useful distinctions and questions with the solutions, so far as divine Providence shall assist me. And if any law is deserving of a review by reason of its fame or difficulty, I shall reserve it for an afternoon review.

Prohibition on Private Teaching at Paris, 1276

The university of masters and scholars at Paris as a perpetual reminder . . . decree and likewise ordain that no master or bachelor, of whatever faculty he be, shall henceforth agree to lecture in private places on texts because of the many dangers which may result therefrom, but in common places where all can gather and give a faithful report of what is taught there, excepting only grammatical and logical texts in which there can be no presumption.[192] Moreover, these things we decree and ordain to be observed inviolably according to the tenor of the privileges granted by the apostolic see to the masters and scholars or Paris. Moreover, if anyone shall presume to act against this statute or ordinance, let him know that he will incur deprivation of the society of masters and scholars.

Requirements of Those Incepting in Arts at Paris, c. 1280

These are the articles which bachelors about to incept in arts are required to swear to, when they come before the rector pledging faith in person.[193] First, it should be said to them: You are to deliver ordinary lectures in the round cope or in the pallium. You will dispute at the hour set and you will discuss your questions for forty days continuously after you have incepted. You are to carry on for fifteen days in the said costume. You shall not have shoes with pointed toes or ornaments or openings, nor are you to wear a surcoat slashed on the sides, nor shall you have a mitre on your head so long as you lecture or dispute in the round cope. You will attend the meetings, obey the commands of the rector and proctor in things lawful and honorable.

You shall not permit dances to go on before your house nor anything unseemly to occur at your opening lecture under penalty of degradation from being a master. You shall not reveal the secrets of the university. . . .

You will promise to incept under the master under whom you were licentiated, or with his consent under another, so that you have adequately sought his consent or would gladly have done so if you could, and so that you intend no guile or fraud towards your master under whom you gained the licentiate with respect to your inception. Also, you will observe the order or ordinance as to the method of giving ordinary lectures and of disputing.

---

191. The "ancient method" of "commenting on the text and noting important glosses" is mentioned below in "Statutes for all Faculties of the University of Paris" of 1366.

192. Grammar and logic are here presumed to constitute neutral method, whereas a century earlier the "new logic"—and later "speculative grammar"—presented an ideological challenge.

193. Like "chancellor," the office of the "rector" varied from university to university, although it most often meant, as at Paris, the head of the university, or guild, of masters or students. Thus, the inception of new members into the guild occurred before the rector at Paris.

Also, you will stand with the secular masters and defend their status, statutes, and privileges all your lifetime, to whatever position you may come. Also, you will admit to examination no member of any religious order whatever, namely for the licentiate or decree, nor will you attend his inception or determination.[194]

Also, so long as you shall teach in arts, you will dispute no purely theological question, for example, concerning the Trinity and incarnation.[195] And if you chance to discuss any question which has to do with the faith and philosophy, you will settle it in favor of the faith and answer the arguments contrary to the faith as it shall seem to you they should be answered.

Also, you shall swear without any fraud that you have fulfilled the requirements in arts at Paris according to the custom hitherto observed, or in some university where there are at least twelve teachers.[196] Also, that you will observe the ordinance recently passed as to the method of announcing general meetings to the dean of the canon law faculty and the dean of the medical faculty. Also, you shall swear that, if you shall have known that a nation is going to rise against a nation or a province against a province or a person against a person, you will reveal it to the nation against which there is to be made an insurrection of a person or province. . . .

Also, you shall swear to, and to the best of your ability, obtain freedom of the university from debt. . . . Also, you shall swear that you are not less than twenty-one years of age. Also, you shall swear that you have heard lectures for six years in arts. Also, you shall swear that you will lecture for two years continuously unless a reasonable excuse shall occur. Also, you shall swear to defend the particular liberties of the faculty and the honorable customs of the faculty and the privileges of the whole university, to whatever position you may come.

Statutes for All Faculties of the University of Paris, June 5, 1366[197]

First, concerning the faculty of theology we decree by the said authority that all incepting and from the moment they begin to lecture on the *Sentences*,[198] even cursors in the said university, shall parade

---

194. It is telling that this contrast between "secular masters" and "religious orders" follows the strictures intended to maintain discipline and promote loyalty among masters of the university. Members of monastic orders, such as Dominicans or Franciscans, were called "regular clergy" because they lived by a rule (*regula*). In order to study or teach at the *studium*, masters who were not members of religious orders were required to swear to enter the priesthood and become "secular clergy," who did not live by a rule. These "secular masters" generally did not fulfill their vow to become priests. The secular masters belonged to the *universitas*, but the members of the monastic orders refused to join the university and follow its rules, believing that they owed allegiance only to the pope, who authorized and oversaw the orders. The secular masters in the university considered the monks interlopers who were allowed to circumvent the discipline required of all other masters due to the monks' special relationship with the papacy. As a result, the relations between the regular orders and secular masters were quite hostile at this time.

195. Why this restriction on the masters of liberal arts?

196. This provision indicates, on the one hand, that students and masters transferred rather easily among universities. On the other hand, the minimum standard of "twelve teachers" indicates that a restriction upon the ease of transfer was beginning to appear.

197. Note that all four faculties of the *studium generale* are discussed here: theology, law, medicine, and liberal arts, "which is, as it were, the foundation of the others," as stated below.

198. These statutes were issued by representatives of the pope, and the *Sentences* was the orthodox, foundational theological text of the time, which compiled opinions of earlier prominent theologians and was written by Peter Lombard, whose fame made him known simply as "the Master of the Sentences," as in selection #26 from Ignatius Loyola (para. 466).

through town in costume befitting their state, degree, and the honor of the said faculty, visiting in particular classes, churches and sermons. . . .

Also, that students may be promoted to honors in the said faculty not by leaps and bounds but according to merit, we have decreed that cursors[199] in theology conduct their courses in order, commenting on the text and noting important glosses according to the ancient method approved in the said university.[200]

Also, that no cursor of the Bible presume to cover more than one chapter of the book which he is reading in a single lecture except those giving ordinary biblical lectures.

Also, that no one be admitted to giving courses in theology unless he has reached his twenty-fifth year.

Also, that every cursor in theology in the time between his first course and the *Sentences* be required to respond in theology at least once, unless he shall have been lawfully excused by will of the chancellor and said faculty.

Also, that scholars who are just beginning to study theology for the first four years shall bring or have brought the *Bible* to classes of the *Bible* teacher, in order that they shall hear lectures on the *Bible* diligently.[201]

Also, that scholars just beginning to hear the *Sentences* shall for the first four years bring or have brought copies of the same to classes of the bachelor from whom they hear the *Sentences* in order that they may follow the text attentively. . . .

Also that lecturers on the *Sentences* do not treat logical or philosophical matters and question, except so far as the text of the *Sentences* requires or the solutions of arguments demand, but they shall raise and treat theological questions, speculative or moral, bearing on the Distinctions of the *Sentences*.

Also, that lecturers on the *Sentences* read the text of the same in order and expound it for the utility of their hearers.

Also, that no one lecturing on the *Sentences* shall read his question or *principium* from a manuscript. However, by this we do not forbid a bachelor to carry to the lecturer's desk some memorandum from which he can, if need be, recall to memory difficult points touching his questions or arguments and authorities bearing on the question and its exposition.

Also, we decree that no master or bachelor who lectures on the *Sentences* shall communicate his lectures directly or indirectly to the booksellers until his lectures have been examined by the chancellor and masters of the said faculty.

Also, that no one can become a licentiate in theology or incept to lecture on the *Sentences* or any course in theology under any master absent from Paris, unless that master is recognized as giving instruction by the faculty, nor shall the bedell of the absent master receive anything in any way from those incepting.[202]

Also, we ordain that those bachelors who have lectured on the *Sentences*, if they wish to obtain the master's degree, shall be required to remain in the university for the time accustomed to elapse between the lecturing and master's degree, in order that their science, character and life may be tested more certainly.

---

199. See the note above on *cursor*.

200. See "A Law Professor Introduces His Lectures at Bologna" in selection #21.

201. This provision, like those below concerning the *Sentences* and booksellers, demonstrates that by the mid-fourteenth century a cottage industry of scribes and notaries had arisen around the major universities.

202. The bedell was an assistant of the master and university.

Moreover, concerning the reformation of the faculty of *Decreta*[203] we decree by the aforesaid authority that no dispensation be granted anyone as to the books and lectures which according to the ordinance of the apostolic see and statutes of the faculty should have been heard and read before admission to the licentiate.

Moreover, concerning the faculty of medicine we decree that the medical students hear their books, complete their lectures, frequent disputations, as is contained in the statues of the faculty of medicine, all dispensation to the contrary being forbidden.

Moreover, concerning the faculty of arts, which is, as it were, the foundation of the others, we decree that those determining and about to receive the licentiate be required to wear their copes or cassocks to classes when they go to hear their lectures and at sermons . . . that the faculty may be honored in them and their degree recognized.

Also, that the said scholars hearing their lectures in the said faculty sit on the ground before their masters, not on seats or benches raised above the ground, as was the custom when the studies of the faculty [of arts] were more flourishing,[204] so that occasion of pride may be removed from the young.

Also, we decree by the said authority that scholars, before they are admitted to determining in arts, be properly trained in grammar and have heard [the books of Alexander of Villedieu and Evrard of Bethune], provided the said books are read in the schools or other places where they have learned grammar.[205] Also, that they have heard the entire [*Old Logic*], the book of *Topics* or at least four books of it, and the *Sophistical Refutations*, *Prior* and *Posterior Analytics* completely; also *On the Mind* in whole or part.

Also, that no one be admitted to determining in arts unless he has studied at Paris for two years at least, all dispensation being prohibited.

Also, that no one be admitted to the licentiate in the said faculty either in the examination of the Blessed Mary or in that of St. Geneviève,[206] unless in addition to the aforesaid books he has heard at Paris or in another university the *Physics*, *On Coming to Be*, *Concerning Heaven and Earth*, *Short Treatises on Natural Topics*, namely the books *On Sensation*, *On Sleep*, *On Memory*, *On the Length and Shortness of Life*, the *Metaphysics* or that he will hear it and that he has heard other mathematical works.

Also, that no one henceforth shall be admitted to the degree of master in arts unless he has heard the said books, also the moral works, especially most of the *Ethics*, and the *Meteorology*, at least the three first books, all dispensation being prohibited.

Also, that no one be admitted to the licentiate in any examination of the said faculty, unless he has attended disputations of masters of the same faculty for a year or the greater part of a year at the time of great Ordinary and unless he has responded in two disputations in the presence of masters, concerning which he shall be required to inform the chancellor in whose examination he seeks to obtain the licentiate by notes from the disputing masters.

Also, that in the tests of the examination of St. Geneviève there be present four masters of the four nations with the chancellor or vice-chancellor, who have sworn in the presence of the faculty that

---

203. This refers to the faculty of canon law.

204. Here is explicit acknowledgment that by the middle of the fourteenth century the arts course had shriveled, as indicated below, to a review of grammar and the works of Aristotle, primarily those on logic.

205. These metrical grammatical textbooks written by Alexander and Evrard displaced textbooks of Donatus and Priscian in the early 1200s.

206. "The licentiate could be obtained either from the chancellor of Notre Dame or the chancellor of St. Geneviève." Translator's note, p. 246n.

they will examine faithfully, admitting the deserving and rejecting the unworthy, just as there are four masters sworn and chosen by the chancellor of blessed Mary as examiners. . . .

Also, that bachelors in arts may read cursorily such books as they wish pertaining to the same faculty,[207] as they did of old, notwithstanding a statute of the same faculty made to the contrary, by which it is forbidden that any bachelor lecture on a text cursorily at that hour at which any master lecturers on that book cursorily. . . .

Texts Required for the A.B. Degree at the University of Erfurt, 1420[208]

1. the shorter edition of Donatus
2. the second part of the *Doctrinale* of Alexander of Villedieu
3. the *Supposition of Terms* of Thomas Maulivelt
4. the treatise of Confusions and *Sinkathegreumata* of the same
5. his treatise of Ampliations
6. his treatise of Restrictions
7. his treatise of Appellations
8. his treatise of Alienations, also his treatise of Remotions
9. his treatise of Consequences, otherwise that of John Sutton of England . . .
10. the treatise of Richard Biligam *On the Proofs of Propositions* . . .
11. the treatise of Obligations of Hollandrinus and of Insolubles of the same Hollandrinus . . .
12. the *Introduction* of Porphyry[209]
13. the *Categories* of Aristotle
14. the *On Interpretation* of Aristotle
15. the books of *Prior Analytics* of Aristotle[210]
16. the books of *Posterior Analytics* of Aristotle
17. the books of *Sophistical Refutations* of Aristotle
18. the books of *Physics* of Aristotle
19. the books *On the Mind* of Aristotle. . . .
20. also of the treatise of the *Material Sphere* of John of Sacrobosco

---

207. In the sentence "read" means "lecture upon."

208. The presentation of this document has been adapted from Thorndike's arrangement. The liberal arts at Erfurt comprised almost entirely dialectic, including seventeen texts in logic (3–17) compared to two in grammar (1–2), and one each in physics (18), psychology (19), and, possibly, astronomy (20). Compare the contemporary curricular recommendations for "humanistic studies" by Pier Paolo Vergerio in selection #25.

209. Items 12-14 constitute the "Old Logic."

210. Items 15-17 plus Aristotle's *Topics* constitute the "New Logic."

Women on the Margin

22. *Rules for Men and Women Teaching in Grammar Schools* (c. 1357)

SELECTION[211]

Each master or mistress[212] is held to these points by oath.
1. That he will exercise faithfully the office of teaching boys, diligently instructing them in letters, good morals and good examples.
2. That they show honor and reverence to the cantor and observe his regulations faithfully to the best of their ability, to whatever state they may come.
3. That in matters pertaining to the regulation of classes they will show obedience to the same cantor.
4. That no master shall keep boys allocated to another without his permission but rather be content with what he has.
5. No one shall remove by his own or other agency boys who have a contract with another.
6. No one shall defame another by detraction but he may report him to the cantor.
7. No one shall farm his classes out or have a partner but he may have a submonitor.
8. No one shall keep a submonitor who was with another master except in the three intermediate grades.
9. No proctor of any court shall teach school.
10. The same for any chaplain.
11. No submonitor shall hold a school near his master except in the three intermediate grades.
12. No master shall keep a woman of ill fame.
13. Each shall maintain peace with his fellows, and discord that arises as to schools shall be settled by the cantor under penalty of deprivation of one's school.
14. No one shall hail another before anyone except the cantor for a case concerning the schools under the aforesaid penalty.[213]
15. No one shall take a school from another source in any parish, supposing that another person than the cantor actually offers it to him.
16. Everyone should attend vespers on the eve of St. Nicholas, on the day itself mass and at vespers the vigils for the dead, and on the morrow mass.
17. Every master or mistress shall keep within his allotted bounds, not exceeding in number or sex of pupils or even in quality of books.
18. Everyone shall turn in his permit at the end of the year, namely, on the nativity of St. John or when school is dismissed.
19. The cantor means to assign no one classes except until the nativity of St. John and unless he takes oath and has a permit.

---

211. These regulations apply to the environs of the University of Paris. Grammar schools taught Latin to students who wished to enter the university. This statute is also drawn from Thorndike, ed. and tr., *University Records and Life in the Middle Ages.*

212. Although the patron saint of the medieval faculty of arts was St. Catherine, women were not permitted to enroll as students, and this is one of the few references in university statutes indicating that women were teaching or studying in the environs of universities.

213. Members of the guild ought not to appeal to outside authorities or courts. Why was the young woman in selection #23 brought before a civilian judge?

20. If anyone has too many pupils, the cantor will keep the fees above the number allowed.
21. No one shall leave town except on a holiday unless by permission of the cantor and unless he leaves a satisfactory submonitor and that with the cantor's permission.
22. All masters and mistresses should attend the funerals of masters and mistresses.
23. A woman should teach only girls.[214]
24. No one shall teach books of grammar unless he is a good and sufficient grammarian.
25. If anyone knows of anyone teaching boys without a license, he shall report it.
26. They shall swear that they have given or promised nothing to obtain classes and that in the future they will give or promise nothing.
27. Similarly to procure schools for any master they will take nothing from anyone or make any agreement.
28. Also, if you happen to hire a vice-master, you will present him to the cantor within eight days and before you have made any arrangement with the vice-master, and if the cantor is away, you will similarly present him to the proctor, in which case you will go to him whom the proctor shall name to you, and you shall not receive the vice-master except at the pleasure of the cantor.
29. Also, you shall not take a vice-master except by consent of the cantor or in his absence of his proctor or one deputed by him.[215]

23. A Female Student at the University of Cracow (c. 1464)

INTRODUCTION

Martin of Leibitz (c. 1400–1464) was born early in the 1400s, and little is known positively about his family or childhood except that he lived in Cracow at some point and studied at the university, which is the setting for the following story about a female student there. He was apparently an adolescent when the incident occurred and may already been a student, since the university of Cracow, being relatively young and remote, would have lost mature students, even bachelors of arts, to more prominent and established universities, thus necessitating the recruitment of younger students. Moreover, in the fourteenth and fifteenth centuries students customarily entered the liberal arts course in universities at age fourteen or fifteen. In any case, Martin matriculated in 1420 at the University of Vienna as a member of the Hungarian "nation," or formal sub-group, within the guild of masters and scholars. Shortly after his arrival at the university, he recalls that he witnessed the execution of the Jews of the community living in Vienna.

Eventually Martin became abbot of the *Schottenstift* run by the Benedictine monks in Vienna. A *stift* was a house or residence supported by a foundation, or endowment, in which visitors from a particular area could reside safely and conveniently in a distant land by virtue of the supervision and the support provided. The endowed residence that Martin oversaw was reserved for Scots (*Schotten*),

---

214. This gender restriction applies to the teachers but not to the students; men could teach both sexes. Coeducational grammar schools existed in the early 1400s and likely provided the preparation for the anonymous young woman who appears to have studied at the University of Cracow in the early 1400s, as described below.

215. A subsequent document in the university statutes of Paris "gives the names of forty-one men and twenty-one women teaching grammar schools in Paris who appeared before the cantor on May 6, 1380, and testified that they had already taken the required oaths to the above articles." Translator's note, pp. 240–1n.

although this designation, like that of "Hungarian" above, should not be interpreted as referring strictly or even closely to the present geographic boundaries of these countries. The practice of endowing residences for foreign students was well established by this time at the older universities, and was beginning to stimulate the founding of residential colleges, a widespread development in the universities during the fifteenth and sixteenth centuries. However, Cracow and Vienna, both of which were opened some 175 years after the University of Paris, were just beginning to receive such patronage.[216] Martin of Leibitz died in 1464, after recounting in his "autobiography" the following story from his youth of an unnamed young woman who attempted to study at the University of Cracow.

SELECTION[217]

> *Youth*: Tell me about some unusual event that occurred in Cracow if you know one.
>
> *[Martin of Liebitz]*: When I was there, a young woman who claimed to be a virgin attended the university for two years in male dress, and came close to the baccalaureate in arts. She lived in a student hostel, behaved properly toward others, did not frequent the baths, and attended the lectures diligently. In Magna Polonia[218] she had had a teacher [*pater scholasticus*], under whom she had studied with other children. When her parents died, she came into an inheritance and, after dressing in male clothing, she went to the university.
>
> *Youth*: How was she discovered? And what happened to her thereafter?
>
> *[Martin of Liebitz]*: Upon seeing her walk through the city, a soldier in the house of a burgher named Kaltherbrig said to his companions: "If that person walking about in the guise of a student is not a girl, I will pay you so much. If she is, you will pay me." They agreed. Later, as she approached the entrance of the house, the soldier called her as if to talk to her, and he set her on a table before his companions. Once she was undressed, it became clear what she was. She was taken before the judge. When asked why she had disguised her sex, she answered: "For the love of learning." The head of her hostel was questioned under oath, and her colleagues as well. They could find nothing improper to say about her. She chose to be taken to the convent, where she was made Mistress [*Magistra*] and Abbess over all the others. And I think she still lives there, for I recently heard news about her from someone who stayed in Cracow. . . .

Since the theme of female transvestism has a long tradition in patristic and medieval literature, this short story sounds like another variation on a familiar topos. One need only read the lives of St. Margaret (St. Pelagia) and St. Hildegund, for example, or skim Caesarius of Heisterbach's *Dialogue*

---

216. The University of Vienna was founded by papal bull in 1364. Although the University of Cracow was opened in 1365, it was not authorized by papal bull until 1397.

217. The translation and commentary in selection #23 are reprinted by permission of the University of Chicago Press from Michael H. Shank, "A Female University Student in Late Medieval Kráków" *Signs* 12 (1987): 373–80. The Anglicization in the selection has been converted to "Cracow."

218. "This designation covers present-day northwest Poland, bounded by East and West Prussia, Silesia, Brandenburg, and the Pilica and Bug rivers." Shank, p. 374n.

on Miracles to be convinced that the theme was well known. . . . Alerted by this insight, it becomes possible to see both how much of the story the narrator devotes to the crisis, and how extensively he has oriented it to males. All of the other protagonists are male—the *pater scholasticus*, the soldier and his companions, the head of the hostel, the fellow students, and the judge. In contrast to these men, the woman protagonist utters only two words. Whereas her successful disguise and her academic career for two years required much activity (mentioned in the preamble), the student's attitude in the body of the story is largely passive, as are the verbs used to recount it: she was undressed, taken to the judge, and so on. The very elements that the narrator identifies as the locus of the crisis betray a male outlook. The discovery of the student's identity casually glosses over the distressing features of the event, both in the short term (her humiliation) and in the long term (the end of her academic aspirations).

Although "male" in outlook and form, the account is nevertheless far from hostile. The narrator portrays the student as unimpeachable in character. She behaves properly and studies diligently. In this context, even her avoidance of the public baths is given a moral connotation, presumably because of the promiscuity associated with them, even though this behavior was a necessary prerequisite for the success of her disguise. Indeed her subsequent elevation to the head of a convent not only brings the story to a proper conclusion but also places it in a positive light.

Informative though they are, these structural and archetypal considerations ultimately avoid the obvious historical questions. How ought one to evaluate the narrator's claim to be recounting an event? What is the connection, if any, between this narrative and the transvestite motif in earlier saints' lives? Rephrased in the blunt language of a child, is this a true story?

The narrator's intentions are certainly not in doubt. The reader is to understand that the story takes place in historical time. Martin claims that the incident occurred during his youth and that the chief protagonist is still alive, as he has recently heard. . . . The strongest case for the historicity of the narrative rests on the allusion to the "house of a burgher named Kaltherbrig." . . . The matriculation registers of Cracow list a *dominus Keldeherberg* among the benefactors of the university. He is probably identical to the "Petrus Kaldherberg" whose name appears in town and university records between 1392 and 1421. A prominent merchant and citizen of Cracow, he served on the town council and was frequently involved in real-estate transactions. A document of August 13, 1400, even mentions him in connection with the purchase of a house for the university. This item suggests a plausible explanation not only for Martin's recollection of the name (which presumably remained associated with the building after the owner gave it to the university), but also for the student's presence in the neighborhood. The surprisingly thorough corroboration of this passing allusion to Kaldherberg's name gives the account a credibility that is difficult to impugn. Under these circumstances there is little reason to distrust Martin's story or his claim to have heard news about the abbess from a recent traveler.[219]

If the event is rooted in historical rather than imaginary time, it ought in principle to be datable. Although the chronological limits of the story are difficult to determine with precision, the narrative and its protagonists offer clues to date it within twenty years. The upper limit is 1420, the date of Martin's matriculation at the University of Vienna, where he witnessed the destruction of the Jewish community the following year. The lower limit is not so tidy. The oldest matriculation lists for Cracow mention neither Martin of Leibitz, nor Martin of Zips (as he is known), nor an incident involving a female student. The dialogue implies, however, that the event took place during the author's adolescence. Since Martin of Leibitz died in 1464, the early years of the fifteenth century suggest themselves as an approximate date. Before its revival in 1400, the University of Cracow was

---

219. The case for historicity is bolstered by the references to the same strategy by Christine de Pizan (I 28) in selection #12 and Juana Inéz de la Cruz in selection #31.

not a significant institution. It is unlikely that student hostels [*bursae*] existed in Cracow prior to this date. Since 1400 is also the year of Kaldherberg's gift to the university, a likely chronological frame for the event extends from 1400 to 1420, which is consistent with the meager biographical data available for both Kaldherberg and Martin of Leibitz.

Unfortunately the student herself remains shrouded in mystery. The reference to her *pater scholasticus* and her successful matriculation at the university suggest that she had first attended a coeducational grammar school,[220] where she had met the prerequisites for study in a faculty of arts. Her social origins are difficult to determine with certainty. The fact that her parents sent her to grammar school does suggest roots in the burgher class rather than the peasantry (where academic prospects for a girl would have been bleak) or the nobility (where tutoring or the convent were the norm). Thanks to her inheritance, she was in a position to support herself. Her irrepressible enthusiasm for learning pervades her brief but very moving answer to the judge (presumably a civilian authority since, as a fraudulent member of the university, she could scarcely appeal to scholarly immunity from civil prosecution).[221]

The ecclesiastical authorities acquiesced both to the former student's wish to join a convent and her subsequent elevation to the leadership of that institution. Hence they evidently did not think that her action placed a permanent blemish on her character but in the end recognized it as an achievement. In any case, it is unlikely that the student immediately assumed a position of responsibility at the convent. Her youth, compounded by her lack of experience with monasticism, would have made her a most improbable abbess, especially since the office was usually filled by election. Thus far, the convent that she eventually administered remains unidentified, and the student-turned-abbess is still anonymous. Some day, it is hoped, her name will transpire from the ongoing research on the religious orders of medieval Cracow.

---

220. Shank maintains that "coeducation was not unusual during this period" (p. 379n.)

221. Such immunity was a benefit that the masters and students had sought and won during their efforts to form incorporated guilds in the late twelfth century, as indicated by selection #21 of "University Statutes and Documents."

Section IV

The Humanist and Collegiate Traditions, 1350–1600

In the early 1300s about twenty universities were offering instruction and granting degrees in Europe, and the number of functioning universities approached seventy by the year 1500. Meanwhile, the study of logic and scholastic method—expressed in technical language, refined through disputation, and practiced particularly in the crowning philosophy of metaphysics—crowded out more and more of the longstanding liberal arts. Due to this scholastic influence as well as to the concomitant desire of students to advance to the graduate faculties as rapidly as possible, the course of study became narrower and shorter.

Against this "modern" devotion to employing a putatively neutral and rational method and pursuing advanced inquiry, a number of scholars in fourteenth- and fifteenth-century Italy (where mercantile and urban life was most developed) proposed and disseminated a different ideal of culture and, thus, of liberal education. These scholars focused their studies upon the literary and artistic heritage of the ancient world and lamented its neglect by the schoolmen in the universities, as seen in selections #24 and #25 by Francesco Petrarca and Pier Paolo Vergerio below.[1] These scholars also declared that classical letters were relevant to contemporary concerns, and thus envisioned a renaissance, or rebirth, of ancient culture. The ideal of this Renaissance movement was expressed by the term *humanitas*, or "humanism,"[2] which meant a combination of cultural refinement and virtuous citizenship or statesmanship.

Being concerned with the formation of a person, humanism necessarily addressed the content and methods of education, which the humanists denoted as *studia humanitatis*, or "humanistic studies." These included primarily the study of classical writings in Greek and, especially, in Latin drawn from the fields of grammar, poetry, history, ethics, and rhetoric.[3] Rhetoric was, in fact, the culminating study in humanist education "because oratory (the art rhetoric teaches) is the basis of all civilized discourse. This is Cicero's position, as it is Quintilian's. It is not that of late medieval education. . . . [The humanist] aligns his educational approach squarely with the Roman orators, and breaks decisively with scholastic training in . . . the formal language-game of the disputation. The ability to perform outstandingly in 'declamation' shows that the student has absorbed his *moral* as well as his intellec-

---

1. A contemporaneous contrast between the humanistic studies and the scholastic curriculum may be seen by comparing Vergerio's selection #25 written in 1370 with the curricular requirements in selection #21 from the universities of Paris in 1366 and Erfurt in 1420. The interweaving of these two branches appears in the selection #26 by Ignatius Loyola.

2. The English term "humanism" was coined in the nineteenth century, when such neologisms as "individualism" and "agnosticism" were also coined.

3. The English adjectives "humanist" and "humanistic" are employed inconsistently by scholars. The latter is used in the phrase "humanistic studies" in this documentary history.

tual lessons, has acquired a set of values as well as a set of argument techniques. It marks a man out as having 'leadership quality.'"[4]

The imitation of classical authors in these fields was thus believed to inculcate "humanism," the cultural ideal comprising the artistic and literary standards of elegant style and the guidelines of virtuous life defined according to the mores of the political, social, and economic elite of the Renaissance period. Plato was the classical author consulted most often when metaphysical or technical philosophical issues could not be avoided. Seneca the Younger was preferred in ethics, though not his epigrammatic style of writing. Quintilian, whose *Education of the Orator* was recovered from a monastic library in 1416, was the pedagogical touchstone. Above all, Cicero—nearly an Apostle, as Petrarca states below—served as an authority in all fields, but especially rhetoric. It is noteworthy that Petrarca wrote the following essay praising Cicero even before the recovery of the full text of *On the Orator* in 1422 that further elevated Cicero's authority.

Humanist scholars often claimed to form "men of affairs" and served as diplomats and advisors, while writing treatises offering guidance to kings and princes on how to manage the growing power of states. Given this, the humanistic liberal education was rarely offered to women. Yet, Renaissance humanists wrote in opposition to their exclusion, and the development of printing allowed women to circulate their writing without depending on the sponsorship of male patrons. In addition, the acceptance of vernacular language as a medium of learning meant that women did not need a thorough Latin education to participate in learned discourse. Nevertheless, only a few women received education, even in fifteenth- and sixteenth-century Italy, in which about one in eight women were literate, and the majority of these came from the upper and middle classes and studied the vernacular curriculum. About two percent of all women pursued humanistic studies and generally did so either with male tutors in the home or as visiting residents in a female monastery.[5] These two patterns are revealed below in selection #27 by Laura Cereta.

The resistance to liberally educating women stemmed directly from the public function of this education. Since women should not become statesmen, diplomats, civil servants, lawyers, or clergymen, they should not pursue liberal education, the reasoning went. The facts that Queen Elizabeth I (1548–1550) received such training and that Christine de Pizan and Laura Cereta associated their arguments for liberally educating women with a "city" or "republic" of women demonstrate that liberal education was viewed as preparation for a public role.

Meanwhile, the Protestant secession from the Catholic church ignited religious warfare on many fronts. This complicated sectarian conflict and its relationship to the Renaissance have been analyzed in a complex body of scholarship that is no less tortuous than the literature analyzing the nature of the Renaissance itself (or even whether there was one.) But what is clear is that the emphasis upon educa-

---

4. Anthony Grafton and Lisa Jardine, *From Humanism to the Humanities: Education and the Liberal Arts in Fifteenth- and Sixteenth-Century Europe* (Cambridge, MA: Harvard University Press, 1986), p. 131. Grafton and Jardine were specifically addressing Dutchman Rudolph Agricola (1443–1485), the progenitor of humanist education in northern Europe.

5. Paul Grendler, *Schooling in Renaissance Italy: Literacy and Learning, 1300–1600* (Baltimore: Johns Hopkins University Press, 1989), pp. 46–8, 93–6. By comparison, Grendler estimates that about one third of boys in Renaissance Italy were literate, and about one-third of those attended Latin school, where they pursued humanistic studies from ages 10 to 16. The rest attended to vernacular studies (pp. 45–8). In sum, "practically all sons of nobles and wealthy merchants, and sons of professionals such as lawyers, physicians, notaries, high civil servants, university professors, and pre-university teachers, attended school, usually a Latin School. Many boys from the next rank of society, master craftsmen and major shopkeepers, also attended school. Lower on the social ladder were petty artisans and shopkeepers and employees in large industries; some of their sons received schooling." Grendler, p. 102.

tion stemming from the humanists' concern for personal formation was heightened by the interest of religious partisans in controlling education.[6]

The institutional expression of this interest appeared in the development of pre-university education and in the founding of colleges throughout Europe. In some cases these colleges were established at universities and served merely as safe residences for foreign students; in other cases such colleges also assumed the function of teaching informally the humanistic studies that were excluded from the formal university curriculum;[7] and in other cases, where no university existed, colleges were founded as independent institutions offering bachelor's and even master's degrees in liberal arts. In all three cases, colleges sometimes assumed the additional role of offering education preparatory for the liberal arts course.

The proliferation of colleges and their diverse roles are reflected in selection #26, drawn from the *Constitutions* of the Society of Jesus. That selection also demonstrates the conflation of the scholastic curriculum and humanistic studies that came to constitute liberal education in most Protestant and Catholic colleges. Whether in the Spanish of Ignatius Loyola or the Latin of his translators, the terms "arts" or "liberal arts" referred to this conflation. In the Jesuit scheme, the lower or bachelor level incorporated the "humanistic letters" or "humanistic studies" of grammar, poetry, history, and rhetoric, while the higher or master's level, which was sometimes called the "faculty of philosophy," addressed logic, some mathematics, and natural, moral, and metaphysical philosophies. Of course, the emphasis on and ordering among the various fields of study—as well as the classical authorities—varied according to the religious allegiances and orientation of the particular college or university. Metaphysics often disappeared altogether. Nevertheless, "a curriculum revolution"[8] had occurred in liberal education as a result of the rebirth of classical letters. The following selections convey the nature of that revolution in its various dimensions.

---

6. See Erika Rummel, *The Humanist-Scholastic Debate in the Renaissance and Reformation* (Cambridge, MA: Harvard University Press, 1998).

7. The assumption of the teaching function due to dissatisfaction with the curriculum or pedagogy of the local university is noted in selection #21 by Ignatius Loyola (preamble).

8. Grendler, *Schooling in Renaissance*, p. 405.

Humanist Tradition of Liberal Education

24. Francesco Petrarca, *On His Own Ignorance and That of Many Others* (1370)

INTRODUCTION

Soon after his birth in Arezzo, Italy, Francesco Petrarca (1304–1374) and his family itinerated northward as his father, a notary and lawyer, searched for work. In 1311 they arrived at Avignon in southern France, which served as the seat of the papal court from 1309 to 1378.[9] In 1320 Petrarca was sent to study law at Bologna, the center of legal education in Europe, and remained there until 1326 when his father died. Returning to Avignon, he took minor ecclesiastical orders, allowing him to receive the income and privileges of church benefices without attendant obligations. In 1333 an acquaintance in Paris gave him a copy of the *Confessions* of Augustine, who came to provide the inspiration and model for his ultimate goal of reconciling classical learning and Christianity. By this time Petrarca had studied classical literature and Latin intensively, and in 1340 received invitations from both Paris and Rome to become poet laureate. He accepted the latter, and in 1341 was crowned on the Roman Capitol, placing his wreath on the tomb of St. Peter to signify his desire to unite classical literature and Christianity along the lines that Augustine set forth in *On Christian Learning*.

In the 1340s, between frequent diplomatic missions, Petrarca spent long periods in meditative retreat and despaired of reconciling his behavior with his moral and spiritual aspirations. Seeking to escape the plague, he made his way to Venice in about 1361 and took up residence as the most renowned humanist scholar in Europe. In 1366, however, four men from the Venetian social elite declared that Petrarca was a virtuous man but a poor scholar. Though pronounced at a private social gathering, this declaration received much attention in the cultured circles to which Petrarca belonged. In reply, he wrote a long essay examining the proper relationships both among virtue, learning, and Christian faith and among different traditions of learning. This reply set forth the intellectual background for the transformation of the liberal arts during the fourteenth and fifteenth centuries.

In responding, Petrarca was particularly mindful that the four men claimed to belong to the most up-to-date philosophical movement of their time, which partly explained their *hubris*. That claim and Petrarca's response relied on a significant distinction between the Aristotelianism in northern Europe, especially at Paris, and the version south of the Alps. In the north Aristotle was taught and studied primarily for his logic and metaphysics within the faculties of liberal arts or theology. In either faculty, the reconciliation of Aristotle with Christian doctrine was paramount, and this involved considerable revising of the interpretation of Aristotle made by Ibn Rushd, who was generally regarded as the authoritative guide to the study of Aristotle.[10] Italian universities were little concerned with the study of theology, and their approach to Aristotle was naturalistic and scientific, involving far less revision of Ibn Rushd. This Italian version of Aristotelianism has become known as Latin Averroëism or Arabian Aristotelianism, and those who learned it in the Italian universities regarded themselves as adopting the most progressive approach to the most sophisticated intellectual authority of the day.

The pride of these four *au courant* gentlemen, whom Petrarca addresses below, offended his Augustinian piety, and the offense was worsened by the spiritual danger that Petrarca identified in Latin Averroëism. These Venetian gentlemen and their teachers espoused the supremacy of natural

---

9. The following draws upon the "Introduction" in *The Renaissance Philosophy of Man*, ed. Ernst Cassirer, Paul O. Kristeller, and John H. Randall, Jr. (Chicago: University of Chicago Press, 1948).

10. See selection #19 from Thomas Aquinas, *Disputation concerning ON THE TRINITY*.

reason, the unity of all human minds in a separate single Intellect, the immortality of this impersonal unity rather than the individual soul, and the denial of creation. Such propositions led to religious skepticism, which Petrarca abhorred. His criticism of Aristotelianism, then, relies on a distinction not only between the Greek philosopher and his disciples, but also between the northern Christianized view of Aristotle and the secular and naturalistic interpretation in the south. Most fundamentally, Petrarca was reacting against the pride stimulated by human learning, particularly natural philosophy; selection #24 thus echoes the Augustinian synthesis of Latin letters, Platonic wisdom, and Christian doctrine.

In line with his customary practice of continually revising his writings over several years, Petrarca did not publish this treatise until 1370. Soon thereafter, Petrarca suffered a stroke, and the resulting decline in his capacities confined him to writing for the next few years. While reading Vergil one night in 1374 he died and was found in the morning with his head resting on the text.

SELECTION[11]

Let them certainly be philosophers and Aristotelians, though they are neither, but let them be both: I do not envy them these brilliant names of which they boast, and even that wrongly. In return they ought not to envy me the humble and true name of Christian and Catholic. But why do I ask for this? I know they are willing to comply with this demand quite spontaneously and will do what I ask. Such things they do not envy us; they spurn them as simple and contemptible, inadequate for their genius and unworthy of it. We accept in humble faith the secrets of nature and the mysteries of God, which are higher still; they attempt to seize them in haughty arrogance. They do not manage to reach them, not even to approach them; but in their insanity they believe that they have reached them and strike heaven with their fists. They feel just as if they had it in their grip, satisfied with their own opinion and rejoicing in their error. They are not held back from their insanity—I will not say by the impossibility of such an attempt, as is expressed in the words of the Apostle to the Romans: "Who has known the mind of the Lord, or who has been His counselor?" [*Romans* 11: 34] Not even by the ecclesiastical and heavenly counsel: "Seek not what is above thee and search not out things above thy strength; the things that God hath commanded to thee, think thereupon always and be not inquisitive in His many works; for it is not necessary for thee to behold what is hidden." [*Ecclesiastes* 3: 22] Of all this I will not speak: indiscriminately they despise whatever they know has been said from Heaven—yea, let me say, what is actually true—whatever has been said from a Catholic point of view. However, there is at least a witty word not ineptly said by Democritus: "No one looks at what is before his feet," he said; "it is the regions of the sky they scrutinize."[12] And there are very clever remarks Cicero made to ridicule frivolous disputants who are heedlessly arguing and arguing about nothing, "as if they just came from the council of the gods"[13] and had seen with their eyes what was going on there. . . .

But let us return to Aristotle. His brilliance has stunned many bleary and weak eyes and made many a man fall into the ditches of error. I know, Aristotle has declared himself for the rule of one, as Homer had done before him. For Homer says thus, as far as it has been translated for us into our

---

11. Francesco Petrarca, *On His Own Ignorance and That of Many Others*, tr. Hans Nachod, in *The Renaissance Philosophy of Man*, ed. Ernst Cassirer, Paul O. Kristeller, and John H. Randall, Jr. (Chicago: University of Chicago Press, 1948), pp. 76–80, 85, 101–15. Reprinted by permission of the University of Chicago Press.

12. Democritus (c. 460–c. 370 B.C.), a Greek philosopher, first posited the thoroughly mechanistic view that the universe was composed of atoms. This line is actually derived, via Cicero, from the drama *Iphigenia* by Ennius (239–169 B.C.), who was regarded as the first Latin poet. Compare the remark by Isocrates (268) in selection #2.

13. Cicero, *Nature of the Gods* I viii 18. See, too, Cicero (III 61–64) in selection #4.

prose: "Multidominion is not good; let one be the lord, one the supreme commander";[14] and Aristotle says: "Plurality of rule is not good; let therefore one be the ruler."[15] Homer meant human rulership, Aristotle divine dominion; Homer was speaking of the principate of the Greeks, the other of that of all men; Homer made Agamemnon the Atride king and ruler,[16] Aristotle God—so far had the dazzling brightness of truth brought light to his mind. He did not know who this king is, I believe, nor did he know how great He is. He discussed the most trifling things with so much curiosity and did not see this one and greatest of things, which many illiterate people have seen, not by another light, but because it shed a very different illumination. If these friends of mine do not see that this is the case, I see that they are altogether blind and bereft of eyesight; and I should not hesitate to believe that it must be visible to all who have sound eyes, just as it can be seen that the emerald is green, the snow white, and the raven black.

Our Aristotelians will bear my audacity in a more balanced mood when I say that this is not merely my opinion of a single man, though I mention him alone. However ignorant I am, I do read, and I thought I understood something, before these people discovered my ignorance. I say, I do read; but in my more flourishing years I read even more assiduously. I still read the works of poets and philosophers, particularly those of Cicero, with whose genius and style I have been particularly delighted since my early youth. I find much eloquence in them and the greatest elegance and power of words. What he says regarding the gods themselves, on whose nature he has published books under this title, and religion in general, sounds to me all the more like an empty fable the more eloquently it is presented.[17] I thank God in silence that He gave me sluggish and moderate gifts and a mind that does not saunter wantonly and "does not seek things above itself" [*Ecclesiastes* 3: 22], not curious in scrutinizing what is difficult to investigate and pestiferous when discovered. I am grateful that I love Christ all the more and become all the firmer in the faith in Him, the more I hear sneering at His faith. My experience has been like that of one who has been rather lukewarm in his love for his father and hears people now raise their voice against him. Then the love which seemed to be lulled to sleep flames up immediately; and this must necessarily happen if the son is a true and genuine son. Often, I call Christ Himself to witness, blasphemies uttered by heretics have turned me from a Christian into a most ardent Christian. For while the ancient pagans may tell many fables about their gods, they do not, at any rate, blaspheme; they have no notion of the true God; they have not heard of Christ's name—and faith results from hearing. The voices of the Apostles were heard all over the earth, and their words spread unto the end of the world; but, when their words and doctrines were resounding all over the globe, these men were already dead and buried. Thus they are to be pitied rather than culpable. Then envious soil had obstructed their ears, through which they might have drunk in the saving faith.

Of all the writings of Cicero, those from which I often received, the most powerful inspiration are the three books which as I said before, he entitled *Nature of the Gods*. There the great genius speaks of the gods and often ridicules and despises them—not too seriously, it is true. It may be that he was afraid of capital punishment, which even the Apostles feared, before the Holy Ghost came to them.[18]

---

14. Homer, *Iliad* II 204. "Translating the Homeric word *polykoiranie*, Petrarca's Greek interpreter, Leontius Pilatus, used a Latin word of his own invention: *multidominium*." Translator's note, p. 77n.

15. Aristotle, *Metaphysics* 1076a4. "Though Petrarca does not mention it here, he knew that this line . . . is but another translation of the Homeric hexameter." Translator's note, p. 77n.

16. Agamemnon, legendary Greek hero, led the Greek army against Troy in the Trojan War (c. 1200 B.C.), as described in the *Iliad* of Homer.

17. Petrarca refers to Cicero's *Nature of the Gods*, quoted above and below, which "was one of the main sources for his knowledge of Greek philosophy." Translator's note, p. 79n.

18. See Cicero, *Nature of the Gods* I xxii 60–xxiii 63; *John* 20: 19–23.

He ridicules them with very effective jokes, of which he has always so many at hand, to make it clear to everyone who understands how he feels with regard to what he has undertaken to discuss. When I read these passages, I often have compassion for his fate and grieve in silent sorrow that this man did not know the true God. He died only a few years before the birth of Christ. Death had closed his eyes when, alas, the end of the error-stricken night and darkness, the first rise of truth, the dawn of true light and the sun of justice were so near. In the countless books he wrote, Cicero, indeed, often falls short and speaks of "gods," engulfed by the torrent of vulgar error, as I said before; but at least he ridicules them, and even in his youth, when he wrote his book *On Discovery*, he said that "those who have devoted their energies to philosophy do not believe there are gods."[19] Now it is a fact that it is true and supreme philosophy to know God, not "the gods"—always provided that such knowledge is accompanied by piety and faithful worship.

When the same Cicero in his later years, in the books he wrote about the Gods—not about God— gains control of himself, how is he lifted up by the wings of genius! At times you would think you were hearing not a pagan philosopher but an Apostle. . . .

You might be astonished, if you did not know me, that I can hardly tear myself away from Cicero, so much am I fascinated by this genius. . . .

But let me now at last, though late enough, return to where I started.[20] For I have been driven off my course by the chain of related subjects. In this whole field Aristotle must be most carefully avoided, not because he committed more errors, but because he has more authority and more followers.

Forced by truth or by shame, they will perhaps confess that Aristotle did not see enough of divine and eternal things, since they are far removed from pure intellect. However, they will contend that he did foresee whatever is human and temporal. Thus we come back to what Macrobius says when he is disputing against this philosopher either jokingly or in earnest. "It seems to me that there was nothing this great man could not know."[21] Just the opposite seems to me true. I would not admit that any man had knowledge of all things through human study.[22] This is why I am torn to pieces; and though envy has another root, this is what is claimed to be the reason: I do not adore Aristotle.

But I have another whom to adore. He does not promise me empty and frivolous conjectures of deceitful things which are of use for nothing and not supported by any foundation. He promises me the knowledge of Himself. When He grants this to me, it will appear superfluous to busy myself with other things that are created by Him—one will see that it is easy to grasp them and, consequently, ridiculous to investigate them. It is He in whom I can trust, whom I must adore; it is He whom my judges ought to worship piously. If they did, they would know that philosophers have told many lies—those I mean who are philosophers by name, for true philosophers are wont to say nothing but what is true. However, to their number Aristotle does not belong, nor even Plato, of whom our Latin philosophers have said that "he came nearer to truth than any one of the entire set of ancient philosophers."[23]

---

19. Cicero, *On Discovery* I xxix 46.

20. Petrarca turns from considering human learning in general to address the relationship between Aristotle and his scholastic followers and between Aristotle and Plato.

21. Macrobius, *Commentary on [Cicero's] Dream Of Scipio* II xv 18. A Latin author who lived in North Africa in about 400 A.D., Macrobius is earnestly accusing Aristotle of being disingenuous in criticizing Plato.

22. See Augustine (book II) in selection #7.

23. Augustine, *City of God* VIII 9.

These friends of ours, I have already said, are so captivated by their love of the mere name "Aristotle" that they call it a sacrilege to pronounce any opinion that differs from his on any matter. From this position they derive their crucial argument for my ignorance, namely, that I said something of virtue—I do not know what—otherwise than he did and did not say it in a sufficiently Aristotelian manner. It is very possible that I said something not merely different but even contradictory. I should not necessarily have said it badly, for I am "not bound to swear to the words of any master," as Horace says of himself.[24] It is possible, too, that I said the same thing he said, though in other words, and that these friends of mine who judge of everything without understanding everything, had the impression that I said something else. The majority of the ignorant lot clings to words, as the shipwrecked do to a wooden plank, and believe that a matter cannot be better said and cannot be phrased otherwise: so great is the destitution of their intellect or of their speech, by which conceptions are expressed. I must confess, I have not too much delight in that man's style, as we have it; though I have learned from Greek witnesses and from Cicero's authority, long before I was condemned by the verdict of ignorance, that it is sweet and rich and ornate in his own tongue.[25] It is due either to the rudeness or to the envious disposition of his interpreters that his style has come down to us so harsh and shabby. It cannot fully please our ears and does not stick to our memory. For this reason it is occasionally more agreeable for the hearer and more convenient for the speaker to express Aristotle's mind not in the words he used but in one's own.

Moreover, I do not dissemble what I have said very often to friends and must now write down here. I am well aware of the great danger threatening my fame and of the great new charge of ignorance brought against me. Nevertheless, I will write it down and will not fear the judgment of men: Let all hear me who are Aristotelians anywhere. You know how easily they will spit at the lonely stranger, this tiny little booklet; they are a lot prone to insult. But for this the little book may take care itself. Let it look for a linen cloth to wipe itself clean; I shall be content if they do not spit at me. Let all the Aristotelians hear, I say, and since Greece is deaf to our tongue, let all those hear whom all Italy harbors and France and contentious Paris with its noisy Straw Lane.[26]

I have read all Aristotle's moral books if I am not mistaken. Some of them I have also heard commented on. I seemed to understand something of them before this huge ignorance was detected. Sometimes I have perhaps become more learned through them when I went home, but not better, not so good as I ought to be; and I often complained to myself, occasionally to others too, that by no facts was the promise fulfilled which the philosopher makes at the beginning of the first book of his *Ethics*, namely, that "we learn this part of philosophy not with the purpose of gaining knowledge but of becoming better."[27] I see virtue, and all that is peculiar to vice as well as to virtue, egregiously defined and distinguished by him and treated with penetrating insight. When I learn all this, I know a little bit more than I knew before, but mind and will remain the same as they were, and I myself remain the same. It is one thing to know, another to love; one thing to understand, another to will. He teaches what virtue is, I do not deny that; but his lesson lacks the words that sting and set afire and urge toward love of virtue and hatred of vice or, at any rate, does not have enough of such power. He who

24. Horace, *Letters* I i 14.

25. See Petrarca's opening discussion.

26. The University of Paris was located on the "Street of Straw," referring to the fact that students spread straw on the floor of the rented rooms in which the scholastic masters conducted classes.

27. Aristotle, *Nicomachean Ethics* 1094b23–1095a61.

looks for that will find it in our Latin writers, especially in Cicero and Seneca, and, what may be astonishing to hear, in Horace, a poet somewhat rough in style but most pleasing in his maxims.[28]

However, what is the use of knowing what virtue is if it is not loved when known? What is the use of knowing sin if it is not abhorred when it is known? If the will is bad, it can, by God, drive the lazy wavering mind toward the worse side, when the rigidity of virtue and the alluring ease of vice become apparent. Nor ought we to be astonished. Aristotle was a man who ridiculed Socrates, the father of this kind of philosophy, calling him—to use his own words—"a peddler in morals, and despised him," if we believe Cicero, "though Socrates despised him no less."[29] No wonder that he is slow in rousing the mind and lifting it up to virtue. However, everyone who has become thoroughly familiar with our Latin authors knows that they stamp and drive deep into the heart the sharpest and most ardent stings of speech, by which the lazy are startled, the ailing are kindled, and the sleepy aroused, the sick healed, and the prostrate raised, and those who stick to the ground lifted up to the highest thoughts and to honest desire. Then earthly things become vile; the aspect of vice stirs up an enormous hatred of vicious life; virtue and "the shape, and as it were, the face of honesty," are beheld by the inmost eye "and inspire miraculous love" of wisdom and of themselves, "as Plato says."[30] I know but too well that all this cannot be achieved outside the doctrine of Christ and without His help: no one can become wise and good who has not drunk a large draught—not from the fabulous spring of Pegasus in the folds of Mount Parnassus[31]—but from the true and unique source which has its origin in heaven, the source of the water that springs up in eternal life. Those who drink from it no longer thirst. However, much is achieved also by the authors of whom I have just spoken. They are a great help to those who are making their way to this goal. . . .

Since this is the case, it is perhaps not reprehensible, as my judges think, to trust our own philosophers, although they are not Greek, particularly in matters of virtue.[32] If following them, and perhaps my own judgment too, I said something, even if Aristotle has said it otherwise or said something different, I hope not to lose my good reputation before fairer judges. Well known is the Aristotelian habit, as it is expressed by Chalcidius in Plato's *Timaeus*: "In a manner peculiar to him he picks out from a complete and perfect dogma what appears to him to be right and neglects the rest in disdainful lack of interest."[33] I may therefore have said that he disdained to treat or neglected some matters or perhaps did not think of them. I may really have said so; it is not incompatible with human nature, though, if we follow our friends, that it does not agree with the fame of the great man—provided I

---

28. "Petrarca mentions Horace together with the two moral philosophers, because the Roman poet was admired much more for the sound moral advice [of] his satirical sermons . . . than for the artistic quality of his poetry." Translator's note, p. 104n.

29. Petrarca quotes Aristotle *Metaphysics* I vi 987b from Cicero's *On Duty* I i 4, and mistakenly construes Aristotle as ridiculing Socrates. One reason for the mistake is that Petrarca's copy of the Ciceronian text erroneously read "Socrates" instead of "Isocrates." A second reason is that the Latin rendering in the mid-thirteenth-century "old translation" of Aristotle could easily mislead the reader into thinking that Aristotle was engaging in ridicule. Translator's note, p. 104n.

30. Cicero, *On Duty* I v 14.

31. The reference is from an account in *Metamorphoses* V 250–267, in which Ovid conflates myths about the winged horse Pegasus and Mount Parnassus in Greece, considered sacred to Apollo and the Muses.

32. Petrarca repeats the longstanding view that "for assessing virtue as well as practicing it, . . . the levity of the Greeks [is] inferior to the vigor of" the Romans, as Martianus Capella (IV 333) states in selection #8.

33. *Commentary on Plato's Timaeus* XI 250, by Chalcidius, a Latin Neoplatonic scholar of the first half of the fourth century A.D. Chalcidius's commentary and Macrobius's *Commentary on [Cicero's] Dream Of Scipio* were the most important sources about Plato in western Europe during the middle ages.

said something of the kind—for I do not remember well what it was, and these men assail me with accusations that are not all too sincere and not definite enough and make use of suspicions and murmured hints instead. Is this, then, a sufficient reason for plunging me so deep into the floods of ignorance and charging me with every error, because I was mistaken on one single point—on a point on which I was perhaps not even wrong while they were? Must I be condemned as always in error and knowing nothing whatever?

Here someone might say: What does all this mean? Do you snarl at Aristotle too? At Aristotle not in the least but on behalf of the truth which I love though I do not know it. I snarl at the stupid Aristotelians, who day by day in every single word they speak do not cease to hammer into the heads of others Aristotle whom they know by name only. He himself, I suppose, and their audience will at last become sick and tired of it. For recklessly these people distort his words into a wrong sense, even those which are right. Nobody loves and respects illustrious men more than I. To genuine philosophers and particularly to true theologians I apply what Ovid says: "Whenever poets were present, I believed gods were there in person."[34] I would not say all this of Aristotle if I did not know him to be a very great man. He was a very great man, I know, but, as I have said, he was human. I know that much can be learned from his books, but I am convinced that outside of them much can be learned also; and I do not doubt that some men knew a great deal before Aristotle wrote, before he studied, before he was born. I will mention only Homer, Hesiod, Pythagoras, Anaxagoras, Democritus, Diogenes, Solon, and Socrates, and the prince of philosophy, Plato.

And who, they will say, has assigned this principate to Plato? I answer not I, but truth, as is said—that truth which he saw and to which he came nearer than all the others, though he did not comprehend it. Moreover, there are many authorities who assign this highest rank to him: first of all Cicero and Vergil—who does not mention his name, it is true, but was a follower of his—then Pliny and Plotinus, Apuleius and Macrobius, Porphyry, and Censorinus, Josephus,[35] and among our Christian authors Ambrose, Augustine, and Jerome, and many others still. This could easily be proved if it were not known to everybody.

And who has not assigned this principate to him except the crazy and clamorous set of Scholastics? That Averroës prefers Aristotle to all others comes from the fact that he undertook to comment upon his works and made them, as it were, his own property. These works deserve much praise, but the man who praises them is suspect. For it comes back to the old adage: "Every tradesman praises his own merchandise." There are people who do not dare to write anything of their own. Eager to write, they become interpreters of the works of others. Like those who have no notion of architecture, they make it their profession to whitewash walls. They attempt to obtain the praise they cannot hope to acquire by themselves, not even with the help of others, unless they praise above everyone else those authors and their books—the objects of their efforts—in an excited and at the same time immoderate tone and always with great exaggeration. There are a great many people who comment upon the works of others—or, should I say, devastate them—especially nowadays. More than any other work the *Book of Sentences* would bear witness to such devastation in a clear and complaining voice if it could speak: it has been the victim of thousands of such craftsmen.[36] And was there ever a commenta-

---

34. Ovid, *Tristia* IV x 42.

35. Plotinus (c. A.D. 250s), leading Neo-Platonic philosopher; Lucius Apuleius (c. A.D. 100s), author of the only Latin novel to survive to modern time; Censorinus (c. A.D. 200s), Latin grammarian; Josephus (A.D. 37–c. 97), Jewish historian and soldier.

36. The *Book of Sentences*, the foundational theological text of the Catholic Church at this time, was written by Petrarca's countryman Peter Lombard (1100–c. 1160), who became bishop of Paris. Many "craftsmen," or later theologians, including Thomas Aquinas, wrote commentaries on the *Sentences*.

tor who did not praise the work he had adopted as though it were his own, or even more profusely than he would have extolled his own, since it is a token of refined manners to praise the work of another, while it betrays vanity and haughtiness to praise one's own product? . . .

Having reached this point under the impulse of whatever kind of inspiration it may be, I shall at last try to find my way out as well as I can. I shall say what I remember having answered often enough to great men who asked me. If the question is raised, "Who was the greater and more brilliant man, Plato or Aristotle?" my ignorance is not so great—though my friends attribute to me so much of it—that I should dare to pronounce a hasty judgment. We ought to keep our judgment under control and ponder it scrupulously even in matters of minor importance. Moreover, it does not slip from my memory how often a great dispute has broken out among learned men about learned men, for instance, about Cicero and Demosthenes, or the same Cicero and Virgil, about Virgil and Homer, or Sallust and Thucydides, finally about Plato and his schoolfellow Xenophon, and many others.[37] In all these cases an inquiry is difficult to make and an appraisal would be questionable. Who will then sit in court and pass a judgment in the case Plato versus Aristotle? However, if the question is asked, "Which of the two is more praised?" I would state without hesitation that in my opinion the difference between them is like that between two persons of whom one is praised by princes and nobles, the other by the entire mass of common people. Plato is praised by the greater men, Aristotle by the bigger crowd; and both deserve to be praised by great men as well as by many, even by all men. Both have come as far in natural and human matters as one can advance with the aid of mortal genius and study. In divine matters Plato and the Platonists rose higher, though none of them could reach the goal he aimed at. But, as I have said, Plato came nearer to it. No Christian and particularly no faithful reader of Augustine's books will hesitate to confirm this, nor do the Greeks deny it, however ignorant of letters they are in our time; in the footsteps of their forebears they call Plato "divine" and Aristotle "demonious."

On the other hand, I know quite well how strongly Aristotle has the habit of disputing against Plato in his books. Let him look to it, how honestly he does so and how remote from suspicion of envy he is. It is true that in some passage he asserts that "Plato is his friend, but truth his better friend still,"[38] but at the same time he ought to take to himself particularly the saying: "it is easy to quarrel with a dead man."[39] Moreover, many very great men took up the defense of Plato after his death, especially on account of his Ideas, against which this eminently passionate disputant exerted every nerve of his genius so powerfully. Best known and very effective is the defense made by Augustine.[40] I should believe that a pious reader will agree with him no less than with Aristotle or Plato. . . .

---

37. Much as Petrarca portrays Cicero, Christian scholars often described Vergil as a proto-Christian due, for example, to his prophesying in *Eclogue* IV the coming of a boy who will pacify the world. Christians, therefore, created the convention of spelling his name as "Virgil" in order to bring to mind the Virgin Mary.

38. "For Aristotle's disapproval of Plato's theory of ideas the most conclusive passages are found in *Metaphysics* (I, X, XIII, XIV). It is in one of the many other passages in which Aristotle is attempting to justify his different point of view, that he recalls the advice of Socrates in Plato's *Phaedo* (91c), not to care too much for his person but rather for truth, and continues: 'Being philosophers, we must undo what is nearest to us [*sic*], that we may save the truth. If both are our friends, it is our duty to prefer truth.' (*Nicomachean Ethics* 1096a16). The pregnant wording of the sentence as we read it in Petrarca's text here has become common property as early as the fourteenth century, though it is generally said that it cannot be traced back before the Renaissance period." Translator's note, p. 111n.

39. Quotation is from *Natural History*, pref. 31, an encyclopedic treatise on the natural world, written by Pliny the Elder (c. A.D. 23–79).

40. Augustine, *On Various Questions* LXXXIII 46.

Much too vagrantly am I rambling along at the heels of my ignorance, much too much am I indulging my mind and my pen. It is time to return. These and similar reasons brought me before the friendly and nevertheless unfair court of my friends—a strange combination of attributes! As far as I understand, none has so much weight as the fact that, though I am a sinner, I certainly am a Christian. It is true, I might well hear the reproach once, launched at Jerome, as he himself reports: "Thou liest, thou art a Ciceronian. For where thy treasure is, there is thy heart also."[41] Then I shall answer: My incorruptible treasure and the superior part of my soul is with Christ; but, because of the frailties and burdens of mortal life, which are not only difficult to bear but difficult merely to enumerate, I cannot, I confess, lift up, however ardently I should wish, the inferior parts of my soul, in which the irascible and concupiscible appetites are located, and cannot make them cease to cling to earth. I call upon Christ as witness and invoke Him: He alone knows how often I have tried again and again, sadly and indignantly and with the greatest effort, to drag them up from the ground and how much I suffer because I have not succeeded. Christ will perhaps have compassion on me and lend me a helping hand in the sound attempt of my frail soul, which is weighed down and depressed by the mass of its sins.

In the meantime I do not deny that I am given to vain and injurious cares. But among these I do not count Cicero. I know that he has never done me harm; often has he brought me benefit. Nobody will be astonished to hear this from me, when he hears Augustine assert that he has had a similar experience. I remember discussing this a little while ago and even more explicitly. Therefore, I shall now be content with this simple statement: I do not deny that I am delighted with Cicero's genius and eloquence, seeing that even Jerome—to omit countless others—was so fascinated by him that he could not free his own style from that of Cicero, not even under the pressure of the terrible vision and of the insults of Rufinus. It always retained a Ciceronian flavor. He feels this himself, and in one place he apologizes for it.[42]

Cicero, read with a pious and modest attitude, did no harm to him or to anybody else at any time. He was profitable to everybody, so far as eloquence is concerned, to many others as regards living. This is especially true in Augustine's case, as I have already said. Augustine filled his pockets and his lap with the gold and silver of the Egyptians when he was about to depart from Egypt.[43] Destined to be the great fighter for the Church, the great champion of Faith, he girded his loins with the weapons of the enemy, long before he went into battle. When such weapons are in question, especially when eloquence is concerned, I confess, I admire Cicero as much or even more than all whoever wrote a line in any nation. However, much as I admire him, I do not imitate him. I rather try to do the contrary, since I do not want to be too much of an imitator of anybody and am afraid of becoming what I do not approve in others.

If to admire Cicero means to be a Ciceronian, I am a Ciceronian. I admire him so much that I wonder at people who do not admire him.[44] This may appear a new confession of my ignorance, but this is how I feel, such is my amazement. However, when we come to think or speak of religion, that

41. Jerome, *Letters* VI xxii 30. See the discussion Jerome in the introduction to Section II.

42. Jerome, *Apology to Rufinus* I 30–31.

43. Petrarca adapts this metaphor from Augustine (II xl 60) in selection #7. Cassiodorus employed the metaphor in *Introduction to Divine and Human Letters* I xxviii 4.

44. "It would be difficult to think of any other figure of Western cultural history who has suffered the eclipse of reputation that Cicero has undergone. To the humanists, he was the quintessential model for and of the Renaissance man. In our time, he is generally considered . . . derivative as a thinker and pretentious as a man of letters." Harold C. Gotoff, *Cicero's Elegant Style: An Analysis of the Pro Archia [Poeta]* (Urbana: University of Illinois Press, 1979), p. 3. Is Petrarca misguided, or are we?

is, of supreme truth and true happiness, and of eternal salvation, then I am certainly not a Ciceronian, or a Platonist, but a Christian.

25. Pier Paolo Vergerio, *On Noble Character and Liberal Studies of Youth* (c. 1402)

INTRODUCTION

In about the same year that Francesco Petrarca published the treatise above, Pier Paolo Vergerio (c. 1370–1444) was born near Trieste, Italy. Very little is known about his early life, but by age twenty-five Vergerio had studied the liberal arts, medicine, and law at the universities of Padua, Bologna, and Florence. In the latter city he was tutored by Manuel Chrysoloras (1350–1415) who had traveled there from Constantinople to become the foremost teacher of classical Greek in Western Europe. Meanwhile, Vergerio taught logic at the universities of Bologna and Florence. Leaving the region in about 1398 Vergerio itinerated among several cities, avoiding either the plague or local wars.

In about 1402 he wrote *On Noble Character and Liberal Studies of Youth*, which became "the most frequently copied and reprinted Renaissance pedagogical treatise" for the next century and a half.[45] Vergerio's treatise recommends a set of liberal studies that he inferred from the conception of revived classical learning, especially languages and learning, that Petrarca had advanced and authorized.[46] In this way Vergerio shaped the definition of "humanistic studies" in the Renaissance. Given that the treatise was composed during the emergence of this new or "reborn" approach to liberal education, it is not surprising that Vergerio interwove these loosely conventionalized "humanistic studies" with other, inherited curricula. The four Greek subjects that already seemed outmoded to Plato and Aristotle,[47] the seven liberal arts, even the three professional studies of the medieval university make their appearance along with the "humanistic studies." Moreover, Vergerio's interweaving was unsystematic and unorthodox in its reinterpretation of certain aspects of the traditional program. Hence, "this celebration of traditional subjects along with the appeal for the *studia humanitatis* underlined the transitional and mixed nature of Vergerio's treatise."[48] Nevertheless, the subjects can be sorted into the following groups, though Vergerio adopts a different order of presentation:

> *studia humanitatis*
>> history (first)
>> moral philosophy or ethics (second)
>> eloquence or rhetoric (third)
>> poetry (eighth)

> Greek tradition via Aristotle

---

45. Paul Grendler, *Schooling in Renaissance Italy: Literacy and Learning, 1300–1600* (Baltimore: Johns Hopkins University Press, 1989), p. 118.

46. Vergerio later wrote a biography of Petrarca.

47. See Plato (521d–522b) in selection #1 and Aristotle (1337b23–35) in selection #2.

48. Grendler, *Schooling in Renaissance Italy*, pp. 118–9. This eclectic character has led scholars to suggest "Vergerio wrote for anyone who might give their son an extended liberal arts education." Michael Katchmer, *Pier Paolo Vergerio and the Paulus a Latin Comedy* (New York: Peter Lang, 1998), p. 26.

letters (fourth)
gymnastics (fifth)
music (sixth)
[drawing omitted]

Seven Arts (rhetoric included above)
  disputation or dialectic (seventh)
  music (ninth)
  arithmetic (tenth)
  geometry (eleventh)
  astronomy (twelfth)

Three Philosophies
  natural philosophy (thirteenth)
  (moral philosophy included above)
  "metaphysics" (sixteenth)

Three Professional Disciplines
  medicine (fourteenth)
  law (fifteenth)
  theology, understood in Aristotle's sense of "divine science" or "metaphysics," rather than
    scholastic theology

Vergerio addressed *On Noble Character and Liberal Studies of Youth* to Ubertinus of Carrara, whose grandfather and father had served as ruling lords of Padua. Likely a student of Vergerio's, Ubertinus was merely thirteen years old at the time, and died by poison a few years after the treatise appeared. In 1405 or 1406 Vergerio left Padua for Rome where he became secretary to successive Roman popes during the Great Schism in the papacy. When a church council ended the schism in 1417, Vergerio moved back toward his homeland and assumed a minor role in the court of King Sigismund of Hungary.[49] Very little is recorded about Vergerio's final twenty-six years; one report indicates that he became senile before his death in 1444.

As rapidly and brightly as the influence of Vergerio's treatise shone forth, it flickered and died out by the end of the sixteenth century. After 1700 no Latin edition was published again until that of Gnesotto in 1914; the first translation was published in 1878 only in Italian; the first translation in English appeared in 1897.[50] The latter, occasionally republished, is actually a loose and expurgated paraphrase rather than a translation; hence, selection #25, newly translated by J. Albert Dragstedt, has some claim to be the first English rendering.[51]

---

49. Sigismund (1368–1437) was King of Hungary (1387–1437) and of Germany (1410–37) and Holy Roman Emperor (1433–1437).

50. William H. Woodward, tr., "The Treatise *De Ingenuis Moribus* by Petrius Paulus Vergerius," in *Vittorino da Feltre and Other Humanist Educators: Essays and Versions* (Cambridge: Cambridge University Press, 1897), pp. 94n1, 96–118.

51. In the critical Latin edition the treatise is divided into a preface of six printed pages, including notes; a first part addressing the nature and nurturance of noble character of eleven pages; and a second part addressing "liberal studies" of thirty-four printed pages. The second half of the second part, addressing physical exercises and recreation, is omitted from this selection.

SELECTION[52]

Preface to Ubertinus of Carrara

Parents cannot provide any surer resources or more steadfast protections for life for their sons than if they have them instructed in honorable arts and liberal disciplines. If they have been endowed with these, they are found to elevate and render illustrious both the name of their clan even if obscure, and the father even if humble. For it is permitted by the laws to each and every man to change his name, provided this be done without fraud; and no one is prevented from transferring his place of residence whenever he likes. But surely, unless someone should have been instructed in good arts from adolescence, or if he should prove to have been infected with perverse arts, he would not easily hope to be able in later years either to throw aside the latter, or straightaway provide himself with the former. Therefore, the foundations of a good life must be laid in youth; and the spirit must be formed with a view to virtue while it is tender and facile at admitting an impression of whatever sort. As that impression will be, so will it be preserved in the remainder of life.[53] Truly, though it behooves everyone (parents, above all) to take seriously the education of their children (then such sons as seem worthy of good parents), it is nevertheless especially fitting that those who are of elevated rank, none of whose words or deeds can escape detection, be so instructed in the principal arts that they be held worthy of the fortune and dignity that they hold. For it is fair that those who want the best of everything should offer up the best of themselves. Nor is there any more secure or stable legitimation of rule than if those who rule be judged by all the most worthy of all to rule. . . .

Second Part: On Liberal Studies

We call studies liberal therefore, which are worthy of a free man:[54] those by which virtue and wisdom are either exercised or sought after, and by which the body or the mind is disposed in the direction of all the best things, from which honor and glory are usually sought, being the first rewards after virtue which are offered to the wise. For just as money and pleasure are established as the goal of illiberal capacities, so virtue and glory are for the free-born. Thus, it is necessary to aim for them from first infancy and to try for wisdom with all zeal:[55] if none of the private arts (even of those less demanding of acuity) could be mastered by anyone without applying himself to it from early years, what will we judge regarding wisdom which consists of so many great things, and in whose art the precepts and reasons of the entirety of life are contained?[56] . . .

Although two of the studies and liberal arts of men have especial affinity to the cultivation of virtue and preparation of glory—the discipline of arms and the discipline of letters—and you are allowed

---

52. Pier Paolo Vergerio, *On Noble Character and Liberal Studies of Youth*, adapted from a new, unpublished translation by J. Albert Dragstedt of *De ingenuis moribus at liberalibus studiis adulescentiae*, ed. Attilio Gnesotto, in *Atti e memorie della R. Accademia di scienze lettre ed arti di Padova* 34 (1917): 95–154. Translations from Gnesotto's notes are made by Bruce Kimball.

53. Vergerio draws here from *On Anger* (II xviii 2) by Seneca the Younger and *Moralia* (I 3f) by Plutarch.

54. The original sense of this quotation is found in selection #5 by Seneca (2). Note the shift from the scholastic approach of asking whether the students are worthy of the subjects to asking whether the subjects are worthy of human nature. Is epistemology or human nature the appropriate standard for liberal studies?

55. Quintilian, *Education of the Orator* I i 15–19.

56. This point seems to presuppose Cicero's view that education for oratory must be comprehensive due to its public and, therefore, virtuous nature. This Ciceronian presupposition would explain Vergerio's otherwise anomalous phrase "private arts." See Cicero (III 54–55) in selection #4.

through parental indulgence to pursue the military art alone,[57] which is a virtual property of your family, you nevertheless have embraced both with such tenacious industry and zeal that you can compete with elders in both sources of praise, leaving your contemporaries far behind. So you do well not to neglect military discipline in which your ancestors have always excelled, and you have set about adding to this glory of your family a new source of praise in letters.[58] For you show no eagerness to imitate that crowd of folk numerous in our days who shudder at a reputation for learning as a disgrace, nor do you applaud the view of Licinius, a Roman emperor of old, who used to call literature a virus and public plague.[59] But all the more do you applaud the remark of that famous man who said that republics would be happy either if lovers of wisdom ruled them or if their rulers happened to have a zeal for wisdom.[60]

Granted, literary training removes neither mental debility nor a malignant character, to the point that just as it helps greatly those who are born to virtue and wisdom so it amounts to evidence revealing folly or a means for realizing an even more pernicious disposition to injustice. Thus, Claudius (to stay with Roman emperors) was quite learned, and Nero, his step-son and successor as emperor, was among the best educated; but the former was of remarkable folly and the latter contaminated with ferocity and crime of all kinds.[61] Nero once said, with a pretense of clemency, that he wished he was ignorant of literature, because that would have to be his wish if he could not be clement on any other basis than as ignorant of literature.[62] If he had been able to eject literature completely out of himself (and he was no proper dwelling place for it), my view is that he would have done it as quickly and gladly as he cast off that clemency which he simulated for a time, lest there be any place left in himself for any virtue or good art. The true opposite of this was Jacobus of Carrara, your great grandfather: a prudent man and a magnanimous prince. He was not, to be sure, very learned himself; but he cultivated the learned to an admirable extent, because he judged (as much as a modest man might be permitted the judgment) that the one thing lacking to his fortune was that he was not learned. So one may well have such wishes in old age, but it is difficult to realize them unless we have prepared ourselves for learning through zeal and effort from the beginning of life. The sources of solace, which could delight an honorable old age, must be prepared in youth, for those studies which are laborious to the time of youth will provide enjoyable leisure in old age.

These studies also provide important assistance whenever we need a remedy for languid torpor or solace for frenzied occupations. For there are two kinds of liberal ways of life: one which is totally composed of leisure and contemplation, and a second which consists in activity and affairs.[63] It is clear to

---

57. "In 1392 Vergerio had solemnly and energetically recommended to Francisco [Ubertinus's father] that he protect and promote equally letters and military studies." Gnesotto, p. 116n1.

58. Vergerio's formulation recalls the conjoining of the traditions of knighthood and learning expressed by Peter Abelard in selection #14. When this conjunction of the humanist model of letters and the notion of courtesy derived from the medieval tradition of knighthood was adumbrated with Christian piety, there emerged the ideal of Christian gentility, which became the archetype of a liberally educated person that was subsequently transmitted to Britain and the American colonies.

59. Licinius (250–325) became Emperor in the eastern half of the Roman empire in 308.

60. The original source is Plato, *Republic* 473c–d; the direct source for Vergerio is Cicero, *Letters to his Brother Quintus* I i 29.

61. Claudius lived from 10 B.C. to A.D. 54; Nero from A.D. 37 to 68 See the introduction to Seneca in selection #5.

62. Seneca, *On Clemency* II i 2.

63. Perhaps Vergerio's "two kinds" correspond to Aristotle's and Cicero's views of liberal education.

everyone just how necessary the knowledge and use of books is in the former case; how useful they are even in the latter can readily be discerned from the following consideration.

Those who apply their mind to the conduct of affairs (regardless of how important) can become more prudent by reading the precepts and the examples found in letters. Whether they are managing the republic or are occupied in wars abroad or in their own or their friends' affairs at home, there is no other means able more pleasantly to provide recreation from their fatigue. Since times and hours befall us when we must leave such occupations alone (given that we are often kept from politics against our will, wars are not always being waged, and one day or another some cause keeps us at home and behooves us to keep to ourselves), for such an occasion, whenever we can accomplish nothing outside our walls, reading and books will come to our rescue, unless we are willing to subside into sleep or rot away in inertia or imitate the custom of the Emperor Domitian who, in secret, used to pursue flies with an iron stylus at various times. He was a son of Vespasian and the younger brother of Titus, but was by no means the equal of either of them.[64] In fact, he was considered much the most horrible of all as Titus was the most gracious of all, whom the history books have called the most beloved of the human race. Hence, the memory of the latter is as celebrated as the memory of the latter is execrated.

Posterity, you see, makes an independent judgment of human affairs and ways of life, and neither fears to denounce the impious nor begrudges the meritorious their praises. In this matter, as we see, a great prerogative is offered princes (or I might more properly speak of a necessity) to conduct affairs well, if they should have a regard for the judgment of men in posterity and the eternity of reputation. In the case of more humbly placed citizens, great force and virtue are required to emerge into the light, and their sins are hidden by the obscurity of their lot. But in the case of princes and grandees, probity, even if is just average, is held to be signal and distinguished, whether because it is rare among the fortunate and therefore held more an object of admiration, or because it is better profiled against the splendor of fortune. But malfeasance, however secret, can neither escape notice, nor long be kept unremarked once it is known. For the very ones who are ministers to pleasures or allies in crime and aware of what was done are the first to report and condemn. For example, it was one of the servants of that very same Domitian who noted his dementia by a clever joke. Once asked whether anyone was inside with Domitian, he answered, "Not even a fly," as if he had killed them all with his stylus! This version of bird catching could perhaps meet with an indulgent pardon despite its unseemliness, if only it were clear what he had been accustomed to accomplish through his lonely winters, or that he had not shown himself worthy of greater hatred for his foul deeds than of mockery for his disgraceful pursuits. The circumstance that Scipio used to refer to about himself, that he was never less alone than when at leisure, or less at leisure than when he seemed alone,[65] cannot easily befall just anyone, but only great spirits or those endowed with excellent virtue. Nevertheless, that man seems in no way lesser to me who is able to conserve his solitude right within a crowd and in opposition to it; and his quiet, within affairs. That is written of Cato the younger who frequently read books right in the senate house while the senate was gathering. Hence, it is no wonder that he kept enunciating the healthiest policies for the country both for the short term and for all time.

Even if no other fruit were gathered from studying letters (numerous and extensive as that fruit is), it ought to seem sufficient that, while reading, we are distracted from the greatest part of those matters which we would not be able to think of without shame or remember without annoyance. Whatever there is offensive either in ourselves or our fortune, we are easily alleviated in this way because learning begets wondrous pleasures in the minds of men, and produces the most luscious fruits in time, if the seed

64. Vergerio draws here from Suetonius, *Domitian* 3, in *Lives of the Caesars*. The Roman emperor Vespasian lived from A.D. 9 to 79; Emperor Titus from A.D. 39 to 81; Emperor Domitian from A.D. 51 to 96.

65. Cicero, *On Duty* III i 1.

falls into a good mind suitable for such culture.[66] Therefore, whenever we are alone, free of all kinds of care, what can we do better than to collect books in which everything is either very pleasant to learn or very effective for a good and holy way of life?[67] For letters have the greatest relevance to other concerns, and are monuments necessary to preserve the memory of the past: that in which the deeds of men, unexpected turns of events, unusual natural occurrences, and reflections about all these things at the times are contained.

Memories, you see, and what is passed down from hand to hand, gradually slip away and scarcely survive one generation of men. But what has been well entrusted to books remains perpetually, unless a picture, perhaps, or marble inscriptions, or metal statuary can provide some such thing. Of course, those things do not indicate particular eras or actions, but only express an external character and are somewhat inspecific. What is handed down in literature not only does these other things, but also both records conversations and portrays the thinking of men. If it has been promulgated in a number of copies, it cannot easily pass away, provided that such speech is dignified with style, for what is written without dignity is not given credibility and cannot long subsist. What way of life, therefore, can be more pleasant or, at least, more commodious than to be reading always, or writing, or to learn of antiquities recently discovered, to speak as men of the present with those of the past, and thus to render all time, both past and future, our own? Oh, what a wonderful furniture books are! (I say this on my own.) Oh, happy family (as Cicero rightly calls them[68])—a frugal one and one that will do you favors! It doesn't tease, it doesn't nag, is not greedy or voracious or contumacious. Books speak or keep silent when bidden. Always at hand for every use, books say nothing but what you wish and to the extent you wish.[69] So I judge that they must be considered a second memory, since our own memory is not capacious enough for all, retains only a few, and scarcely suffices for particulars. Surely letters and books are the definite memory of things and a public library of all the knowable.

We ought to make sure that we hand on uncorrupted to posterity the ones we have received from our forebears even if we are perhaps unable to beget anything ourselves. In this respect we have a just complaint to direct at the centuries closest to us, perhaps.[70] One may feel a sense of indignation, though it does no good, at the fact that they have allowed so many distinguished works of illustrious authors to be lost. Of some, it is only the names, though decorated with the highest praises, that have gotten through to us; of others, part of the literary exercises of other and certain fragments of works. Whence it happens that we miss having their works due to the prestige of their reputation and name, and we resent the fact that the rest of their works have perished, basing our judgments on the excellence and value of those things still extant, although we have them so badly emended in most respects (even excerpted and mutilated) that it would almost have been better that nothing of them had come down to us. Not the least part of this loss, great as it is, is the fact that many of our own affairs, being of Italy and most worthy of our awareness, are largely hidden from us, the knowledge having perished along with the books and monuments that record them. Thus, it is that we know the deeds of the barbarians but are ignorant of most of our own, because we exact our knowledge of Latin history as well from Greek authors. A great

---

66. Vergerio emphasizes the pleasure of learning, which comports with his view that individuals must choose studies that suit, or gratify, their own nature.

67. Vergerio may have been thinking of Quintilian, *Education of the Orator* II xviii 3.

68. See Cicero, *Letters to Octavius* IX 1.

69. Consistent with the autonomy accorded to individuals to choose their studies, it seems that the knowledge in a library depends upon the wish of the reader.

70. Vergerio gently expresses the humanists' criticism of the period that they named the "Middle Ages" or "Dark Ages," extending between classical antiquity and their own resuscitation of classical culture.

many things written up in a cursory way or totally unknown are expounded by them, although that very tradition of Greek oratory, once so familiar as to be a household concern for our ancestors, has almost perished among them,[71] and is nearly extinct among us, except for a few who have presently applied themselves during these very times to summon it from the grave into the light of day.[72]

The loss of the study of history is thus more serious the more knowledge of it is useful and pleasant.[73] The studies of history and of moral philosophy are suited to those with liberal minds and to those involved in public affairs and human community. All the other liberal arts, you see, are called so because they befit free men, but philosophy is really liberal because the study of it makes us free.[74] In the latter we find teachings of what it is appropriate to follow or to avoid, whereas in the former we find examples. In the latter the appropriate duties of all men are discovered; in the former, what was done or said at each occasion. To these a third liberal study must be added (if I am not mistaken); that is, eloquence, which is a part of political science.[75] If it is through philosophy, after all, that we can come to a correct sense of things (and that is in all matters the very first consideration), we must yet grant that it is through eloquence that we can speak with gravity and abundance, and it is through historical studies that we are assisted in both categories. For if we judge old men as more prudent and enjoy listening to them because, through their long life, they have both experienced by themselves and heard broadly from others, what ought our judgment to be of historical writings that have in their memory deeds worthy of being known for many centuries and that can produce some illuminating example relevant to each event? The answer is that the greatest man with the simply excellent endowment possesses the capacity to speak at the highest level and the eagerness to act at the highest level.

There were, moreover, four studies which the Greeks used to teach their children: letters, gymnastics, music and drawing,[76] which some call "sketching." Drawing is not currently pursued as a liberal art except, perhaps, insofar as it regards writing (which is itself both sketching and designing), while the rest of the art belongs to painters. This was, moreover, as Aristotle says, not just useful but a business such as to be reckoned honorable among them: for it assisted in the purchases of vases, paintings and statues (in which Greece took its highest pleasure), and in preventing any easy deception in price.[77] It also made a great contribution to apprehending the beauty and charm of nature and art, which is judged and discussed by the great.

The study of letters[78] always provides a large benefit for each way of life and each class of men, but above all for those who study it in order to learn, to form the habit of that state of mind, and to revive the memory of times gone by. Before all other matters, if we wish to make progress in education, we must

---

71. Cicero, *Pro Archia* III 5.

72. Vergerio now begins his specification of liberal studies. What are the four curricular schemes that he conflates below?

73. Out of the four subjects in the loosely conventionalized "humanistic studies," three (history, moral philosophy, and eloquence) are discussed in this paragraph. The fourth, poetry, is incorporated below. Compare Ignatius Loyola (para. 448) in selection #26.

74. See Seneca (2) in selection #5.

75. This apparently refers to Aristotle's inclusion of the art of rhetoric under political science within the study of the human sciences. Vergerio's direct source is Quintilian, *Education of the Orator* II xv 33, who cites Cicero, *On Discovery* I v 6.

76. See Aristotle (1337b23–28) in selection #3.

77. Aristotle, *Politics* 1338a1–5.

78. Vergerio begins addressing the three trivial arts of grammar, dialectic, and rhetoric.

aim to attain the level of discourse which befits such progress, and must make sure that we do not falter shamefully in lesser topics while we are pursuing greater ones.[79] In another study most closely associated with this, a method of disputation must be developed for seeking, by straightforward argumentation, the truth or falsity in each and every matter. That method, since it is the science of learning and discipline of science, readily opens the path to all kinds of education.

Now rhetoric is the third among the rational disciplines,[80] through which that eloquence which comes by art is sought,[81] which we have also put down as third among the eminent parts of politics. But although in former times it used to be given great attention in the studies of noble men, it has grown almost obsolete at present. It has been utterly ejected from trials, wherein argument proceeds not through continuous oratory but in dialectical fashion, with laws adduced in the case by one side and the other. In forensic argument of the past, Roman youth attained great glory either by convicting the guilty or defending the innocent. Likewise, in the deliberative category,[82] there is no space left as far as princes and masters of affairs are concerned, since they want a position introduced into council in a few unadorned words and reasons; and those who can speak copiously even without art are held to be distinguished. There remains the "demonstrative" [or epideictic] category, which is scarcely ever applied with method though its use has never been abandoned. In making speeches, almost everybody makes use of those arts which are hostile to the art of speaking well. Since that is so, he who wishes to be well-instructed must work very hard to be able to speak in all kinds of cases in an eloquent and copious fashion on the basis of art.

Following closely is poetry, whose study seems more oriented towards pleasure although it can contribute much to life and oratory.[83]

The art of music was greatly honored among the Greeks of old[84] (for it, too, delights the listener) and no one was thought to be liberally educated unless he knew song and lyre. Hence, Socrates both learned it as an old man and had well-born youth trained in these things, not as an incitement to sensuality but in order to moderate the motions of the soul by rule and method. For, just as not every voice but only one sounding good produces a melodious sound, so not all the movements of the soul, but only those consistent with reason, contribute to the genuine harmony of life. Since the employment of modulation greatly helps in the recreation of the mind and assuaging of the passions, the knowledge of music is worthy of a man of liberal mind. By its method, we theorize concerning the various natures and powers of sounds: how consonances and dissonances happen to ensue from the proportional relationships one to another.

---

79. Vergerio elsewhere clarifies this elliptical phrasing by referring to "grammar, the primordial pedagogical science." Gnesotto, p. 123n3.

80. See Hugh of St. Victor (I 2) in selection #15.

81. Quintilian, *Education of the Orator* II xvii 2.

82. Aristotle had famously described the longstanding threefold categories in rhetoric: deliberative, concerning recommendations for personal or public policy in the future; forensic, arguing judgments about past events; and epideictic, providing an observer's statement on a certain situation or event, such as a eulogy or testimonial. (*Rhetoric* 1358a30–b5.) Vergerio is incorporating Quintilian's adaptation of this categorization. *Education of the Orator* II xxi 23.

83. Vergerio apparently takes a passing remark of Aristotle (*Rhetoric* 1371b1–5) out of context in order to provide an opportunity for inserting the study of poetry here. This insertion demonstrates his effort to interweave the various curricular schemes available to him.

84. Vergerio now turns to the four mathematical arts.

Similar is the study of numbers called arithmetic, and the study of magnitudes called geometry, in which the various species of numbers and magnitudes are constituted and many properties are proved to hold in these areas, in accordance with the various relations of equals or unequals and similarly of lines, planes, or bodies. This very charming kind of study contains the highest level of precision, but that treating of motions, magnitudes and distances of stars is also beautiful in the highest degree. It summons us forth from these shadows and thick air, leading our eyes and minds on to that higher luminous mansion arrayed with so many luminaries.[85] It is a pleasant task for one gazing upward to distinguish the constellations of fixed stars, to track the wandering stars in their places with their names along with their conjunctions, and likewise to foresee and predict the eclipses of sun and moon.

Natural philosophy[86] is congruent and conforming with the human mind: the intellectual faculty by which we come to know the principles and features of animate and inanimate objects and the causes and effects of the motions and changes of the things bounded by heaven and earth. We are in fact able to ascribe causes to things which typically seem miraculous to the common people. Understanding regarding anything is pleasant, but especially regarding those physical impressions from the air and earth. Certain kinds of knowledge derived from them contain modes of inquiry which are equally beautiful: for example, perspective and mechanics.[87]

Having proceeded so far in my speech, I shall touch upon the remaining disciplines as well.[88] Medicine is beautiful to know, and adapted to the preservation of bodily health, but it allows of an employment which is liberal only to a minimal degree. Law is useful in both public and private realms and is held everywhere in great honor, and it is just as clearly derived from moral philosophy as medicine is from natural. Though it is honorable to offer interpretations to an audience or to express one's legal judgment to those engaged in a dispute, it lacks decorum for those litigating cases to sell their efforts for a price or a contract. The science of the most exalted causes and of the things most removed from our senses, which we attain to only by our intelligence, is divine.[89]

Thus, we have counted up about all the principal disciplines, but not because an individual must have command of all in order to be or to be considered learned. Each discipline by itself can completely occupy a person. In addition, two guidelines should be followed: one should seek moderate, not

---

85. The belief that leading intellectuals were gathered together in paradise extended back to late antiquity. See selection #8 by Martianus Capella (II 211), as well as Dante's *Paradise* bks. 10–12.

86. Like the transitions above to poetry and to mathematical arts, this abrupt transition to one of the medieval three philosophies indicates that Vergerio feels compelled to interweave all the studies conventionally taught by the faculties of arts in the universities.

87. It is telling that Vergerio employs these two examples. A scholastic and Christianized view of mechanics was challenged and overturned in the fourteenth century, and important developments in perspective were made in the first few decades of the fifteenth century.

88. In another abrupt transition, Vergerio turns to address the three higher and professional disciplines of the university by way of the link between natural philosophy and medicine.

89. Having discussed medicine and law, it would be appropriate for Vergerio to address next the third professional discipline of theology, and he does introduce the potential synonym "divine science." But he employs that term in the Aristotelian sense of metaphysics. (See the discussion of these terms in Hugh of St. Victor, *Didascalicon* II 2, and Thomas Aquinas, *The Division and Methods of the Sciences*, ques. V, art. 1, preface to reply to objection 1.) This usage suggests a reluctance to recommend the study of theology, and allows Vergerio to complete his treatment of the medieval three philosophies—moral, natural, and metaphysical—having considered them in three different places: the first in connection with the "humanistic studies" and the last in the place of theology among the three professional disciplines within the university.

excessive learning;[90] and one should study those arts to which one is most suited.[91] Granted, all the disciplines are so related that none at all could be grasped to a distinguished degree, if the others are totally unknown.[92]

Collegiate Movement and Catholic Appropriation of "Humanistic Studies"

26. Ignatius Loyola, *Constitutions of the Society of Jesus* (1594)

INTRODUCTION

Born into a noble wealthy family in a Basque province located between modern France and Spain, Ignatius of Loyola (1491–1556) spent his youth preparing for a position among the military and diplomatic elite in the realms of Navarre and Castile. At the age of thirty, while fighting the French at Pamplona, he was severely injured, and during a long period of convalescence, he read extensively in the biographies of saints, who were portrayed as combining the chivalrous tradition of knighthood with complete devotion to God. Inspired by their example, Loyola in 1522 was converted to an intensely spiritual life and resolved to do penance for his sins by embracing evangelical poverty.[93]

Leaving his home and renouncing the comforts and ambitions of his past, Loyola spent the ensuing year engaged in spiritual exercises and physical debasement, and made a pilgrimage to Jerusalem. But the ecclesiastical authorities were unreceptive to his evangelism, and he decided that he needed a liberal and theological education in order to pursue his mission. Though far beyond the age when most men would have completed the liberal arts, he attempted to study at universities in Spain over the next four years, but was repeatedly arrested and charged with heresy due to his unorthodox behavior and the fact that he had attracted a small band of followers. He therefore moved to the University of Paris in 1528, but again came under the suspicion of church authorities for the same reasons. Nevertheless, he completed his studies and was graduated a Master of Arts in 1534. Ordained as priests, he and a small informal group of followers traveled to Venice and Rome while continuing their private study, prayer, and penance over the next five years.

Deciding to organize formally, the group received papal authorization to establish the Society of Jesus in 1540, and Loyola was elected general, and entrusted with the responsibility of elaborating the brief provisions of the papal bull of 1540 into a code of statutes for the Society. This became his chief work by 1546, and the resulting *Constitutions* were provisionally completed in Spanish by 1551, when Loyola became severely ill. After his death in 1556, his followers continued revising and produced the summative Spanish edition of 1594. Among the ten parts of the *Constitutions*, Part IV shaped the

---

90. Compare the admonitions of Aristotle (1337b3–23) in selection #3 and Seneca (36) in selection #5.

91. In contrast to the medieval affirmation of the indispensability of all the liberal arts and the implicit uniformity of liberal education, expressed by Hugh of St. Victor (III 4) in selection #15, Vergerio maintains that not all the liberal arts are necessary for an education and that individuals should choose the studies most suited to their mind and character. Compare the views of Charles Eliot in selections #40 and #47 and Robert Hutchins in selection #58.

92. Gnesotto cites Cicero, *Pro Archia* I 2; but see Hugh of St. Victor (III 4) in selection #15 on the same point.

93. This introduction and the ensuing notes draw upon John W. O'Malley, *The First Jesuits* (Cambridge, MA: Harvard University Press, 1993).

policy of all Jesuit colleges and became the foundation for all educational documents subsequently issued by the Jesuits, including the better known *Ratio Studiorum* ("Plan of Studies"), which detailed procedures in the colleges and was issued in 1599.

Meanwhile, the Society came to regard itself as a teaching order, and when Loyola died in 1556, 33 colleges had been opened. By the time of their centennial in 1640, the Jesuits had established 521 colleges, 49 seminaries, and 280 residences and missions. In 1750, at the peak of its expansion before it began to be suppressed, the Society had founded 669 colleges, whose students in some cases included only candidates for the order, in other cases only "extern" students, and sometimes a combination.

The phenomenal growth of the Jesuit institutions stemmed from several factors. Their organization and methods both inside and outside the classroom were unusually systematic and disciplined, while they balanced that rigor by moderating certain pedagogical strictures of the day through the introduction of regular vacation periods and the reduction of daily class time to 5–6 hours. Further, the student population in Jesuit colleges became dominated by sons of the ruling elites, though this occurred only after the Jesuits became so successful at their original mission of educating and elevating the lower classes that they were criticized by the elites for fomenting social unrest by filling the lower classes with unwarranted aspirations.

Above all, the Jesuits succeeded because they introduced the new "humanistic studies" into the liberal arts of their colleges. It was the Society of Jesus that led Catholic educators in melding humanistic studies with the traditional scholastic program. The Jesuits' teaching of Greek and Latin letters was unsurpassed, and they did this without following Petrarca's advice to lay down Aristotle. The resulting program of liberal education, appearing in selection #26, ultimately consisted of a lower course of 3–4 years study in the "humane letters" (consisting of Greek and Latin grammar, poetry, history, and rhetoric) and an upper course of about 3 years in logic and natural, moral, and metaphysical philosophy along with some mathematics.

The humanistic and scholastic strains are clearly apparent in this program, whose overriding purpose was the training of Christian gentlemen, notwithstanding the fact that a four-year course in theology was envisioned after the upper course. That overriding purpose is demonstrated by the gentlemanly subjects available to students of Jesuit colleges, such as "The Knightly Exercises" in dancing and fencing.[94] Such exercises, ironically enough, seem more reminiscent of the Ignatius before the battle at Pamplona than the spiritual and ascetic leader afterward. Nevertheless, Loyola's disciplined commitment to education, serving as a means to spiritual and ecclesiastical advancement, continued to animate the Society of Jesus for centuries after his death in 1556.

---

94. See "Letter from the Rector of the College of Savoy known as 'of the Nobles,'" appended to Aldo Scaglione, *The Liberal Arts and the Jesuit College System* (Philadelphia: John Benjamin's Publishing, 1986), pp. 175–6.

SELECTION[95]

Part IV
The instruction of those who are retained in the Society, in learning and in other means of helping their fellowmen

[Preamble] . . . [308] The aim and end of this Society is, by traveling through the various regions of the world at the order of the supreme vicar of Christ our Lord or of the superior of the Society itself, to preach, hear confessions, and use all the other means it can with the grace of God to help souls. Consequently it has seemed necessary to us, or at least highly expedient, that those who will enter the Society should be persons of good life and sufficient learning for the aforementioned work. But in comparison with others, those who are both good and learned are few; and even among these few, most of them already seek rest from their previous labors. As a result, the increase of the Society from such men of letters who are both good and learned is, we find, something very difficult to achieve, because of the great labors and the great abnegation of oneself which are required in the Society.

Therefore all of us, desiring to preserve and develop the Society for greater glory and service to God our Lord have thought it wise to proceed by another path. That is, our procedure will be to admit young men who because of their good habits of life and ability give hope that they will become both virtuous and learned in order to labor in the vineyard of Christ our Lord.[96] We shall likewise accept colleges under the conditions stated in the apostolic bull, whether these colleges are within universities or outside of them; and, if they are within universities, whether these universities are governed by the Society or not.[97] For we are convinced in our Lord that in this manner greater service will be given to His Divine Majesty, because those who will be employed in that service will be multiplied in number and aided to make progress in learning and virtues.

Consequently, we shall treat first of what pertains to the colleges and then of what concerns the universities. With regard to the colleges, we shall discuss first what pertains to the founders [in Chapter 1]; second, what pertains to the colleges founded in regard to their material or temporal aspects [Chapter 2]; third, what pertains to the [students] who will study in them, in regard to their admission [Chapter 3], preservation [Chapter 4], progress in learning [Chapters 5, 6, 7] and in other means of helping their fellowmen [Chapter 8], and their removal from study [Chapter 9]; fourth, what pertains to the government of colleges [Chapter 10]. . . .

---

95. Ignatius Loyola, *The Constitutions of the Society of Jesus*, tr. George E. Ganss (St. Louis, MO: Institute of Jesuit Sources, 1970), pt. IV, pp. 171–4, 187–98, 213–23. Reprinted by permission of The Institute of Jesuit Sources, St. Louis, MO.

96. "In a typical case, a boy might receive his elementary education from tutors at the ages of 5 through 9, then enter a Jesuit university and study languages from 10 through 13, arts from 14 through 16, and theology from 17 through 21." Translator's note, p. 214n5.

97. As provided in the papal bull of 1540, these colleges were originally intended to be only residences, without any educational functions, for novitiates planning to join the Society and attending a nearby university. "They were established at Paris in 1540, Coimbra, Padua, and Louvain in 1542, Cologne and Valencia in 1544, and elsewhere. However, the university lectures were often found to be unsatisfactory and without organized sequence, e.g. at Padua. Consequently, lectures were gradually introduced into some of these Jesuit colleges. The practice of educating extern students, lay or clerical, in addition to Jesuits arose later, in 1543 in India and in 1546 in Gandía, Spain." Translator's note, p. 173n5. This gradual assumption of an educational function by the Jesuit colleges exemplifies the general pattern of development in colleges in Western Europe during the sixteenth and seventeenth centuries.

Chapter 5 The subjects which the [students] of the Society should study

[351] 1. Since the end of the learning which is acquired in this Society is with God's favor to help the souls of its own members and those of their fellowmen, it is by this norm that the decision will be made, both in general and in the case of individual persons, as to what branches ours ought to learn, and how far they ought to advance in them. And since, generally speaking, help is derived from the humane letters of different languages, logic, natural and moral philosophy, metaphysics,[98] scholastic and positive theology,[99] and Sacred Scripture, these are the branches which those who are sent to the colleges should study. They will devote themselves with greater diligence to the parts which are more helpful for the end mentioned above, with circumstances of times, places, persons, and other such factors taken into account, according to what seems expedient in our Lord to him who holds the principal charge.[100]

[352] In addition to grammar, rhetoric is understood to be under the classification of humane letters. [353] If these should not be enough time in the colleges to read the councils, decrees, holy doctors, and other moral subjects, each one could, with the approval of his superiors, read these privately after his departure from studies, especially if he is well grounded in the scholastic doctrine. [354] According to the age, ability, inclination, and basic knowledge which a particular person has, or in accordance with the common good which is hoped for, he could be applied to all these branches or to one or several of them. For one who cannot distinguish himself in all of them ought to try to do so in the case of some one of them.[101]

[355] 2. In detail, what some or other [students] ought to study will likewise be left to the discretion of the superiors. But when someone has aptitude, the better the foundation he lays in the aforementioned branches, the better will it be. . . .

[357] 3. The rector will consider and decide by means of a suitable examination how much time should be given to one branch, and when the [students] should pass on to another.

[358] 4. The doctrine which they ought to follow in each branch should be that which is safer and more approved, as also the authors who teach it. The rectors will take care of this, by conforming themselves to what is decided in the Society as a whole for the greater glory of God. . . .

---

98. The striking juxtaposition of the term "humane letters" with the categories of the scholastic curriculum reflects the novelty of their incorporation into one program of liberal education. The boundary between the two hemispheres was nevertheless maintained inasmuch as moral philosophy, or ethics, was drawn from "Aristotle, rather than Cicero and Seneca who were so much favored by the humanists." George E. Ganss, *St. Ignatius's Idea of a Jesuit University* (Milwaukee, WI: Marquette University Press, 1954), p. 297. See para. 470 below.

99. "By positive theology the student seeks to possess the data of revelation more accurately, through study, e.g. of biblical history, the Fathers, definitions and decrees of councils, canon law, archaeology, and other organs of tradition. By scholastic or speculative theology, he seeks deeper insight into the revelation itself, especially through the methods used by the medieval schoolmen." Translator's note, p. 188n5.

100. The Jesuits generally treated the study of humane letters and Christian doctrine as the lower faculty in their colleges; a higher faculty completed the liberal arts by addressing logic, mathematics, and natural, moral, and metaphysical philosophies.

101. The principle of accommodating curricular and pedagogical strictures to the local situation and to the individual contributed greatly to extending the influence of the Jesuits. This accommodation to the individual reflects the humanists' view, as seen in selection #25 from Pier Paolo Vergerio.

Chapter 6 Means by which the Scholastics will progress
toward learning the aforementioned branches well

[360] 1. In order to make great progress in these branches, the [students] should strive first of all to keep their souls pure and their intention in studying right, by seeking in their studies nothing except the glory of God and the good of souls. Moreover, they should frequently beg in prayer for grace to make progress in learning for the sake of this end.

[361] 2. Furthermore, they should keep their resolution firm to be thoroughly genuine and earnest students, by persuading themselves that while they are in the colleges they cannot do anything more pleasing to God our Lord than to study with the intention mentioned above; likewise, that even if they never have occasion to employ the matter studied, their very labor in studying, taken up as it ought to be because of charity and obedience, is itself work highly meritorious in the sight of the Divine and Supreme Majesty.[102]

[362] 3. The impediments which distract from study should also be removed, both those arising from devotions and mortifications which are too numerous or without proper order and also those springing from their cares and exterior occupations whether in duties inside the house or outside it in conversations, confessions, and other activities with one's fellowmen, as far as it is possible in our Lord to excuse oneself from them. . . .

[366] 4. An order should be observed in pursuing the branches of knowledge. The [students] should acquire a good foundation in Latin before they attend lectures on the [liberal] arts;[103] and in the arts before they pass on to scholastic theology; and in it before they study positive theology. Scripture may be studied either concomitantly or later on.

[367] 5. The languages too in which Scripture was written or into which it was translated may be studied either previously or later on,[104] according to what seems best to the superior in accordance with the various cases and the diversity of the persons. This too will remain within his discretion. But if the languages are learned, among the ends which are pursued one should be to defend the version which the Church holds as approved. . . .

[369] 6. All those who are studying should attend the lectures of the [university] professors whom the rector will designate for them. It is desirable that these professors should be learned, diligent, and assiduous; and that, whether they be members of the Society or from outside it, they should be eager to further the progress of the students, both during the lectures and in the academic exercises.[105] [370] If another procedure is expedient for someone, the superior will consider the matter with prudence and he may grant a dispensation. What has been said about [university] lectures does not exclude private lectures within the college or outside it when these may be necessary or profitable. [371] No member of the Society will give lectures publicly without the approbation and permission of the provincial superior, except in the lower classes or for a time because of some necessity. . . .

---

102. Note the commitment to study regardless of apparent utility.

103. Loyola generally used the term *las artes* in Spanish for "liberal arts." "On at least three occasions, he added the adjective to form the term 'liberal arts.'" Occasionally, the Jesuit translators subsequently rendered *las artes* into "liberal arts" in Latin. Ganss, *St. Ignatius's Idea of a Jesuit University*, p. 57.

104. This attention to Biblical languages is also evidence of humanist influence.

105. The educational organization and practices of Spain, France, the Low Countries, and Italy often lacked order. Students, not arranged in classes according to age or ability, often studied higher branches before acquiring a foundation in the lower ones. Exercises or repetitions to supplement the lectures were rare. But the colleges of the University of Paris required an orderly sequence and much self-activity of the students; and Loyola adopted that as his model.

[372] 7. There should be a general library in the colleges, if possible, and those who in the judgment of the rector ought to have a key should have one.[106] Furthermore, the individuals should have the books which are necessary for them. [373] However, they ought not to write annotations in these books; and he who has charge of the books should keep an account of them.

[374] 8. The [students] should be regular in going to the lectures, diligent in preparing for them beforehand, in repeating them afterwards, in asking about points they do not understand, and in noting down what may be useful to assist the memory later on. . . .[107]

[376] The superiors should consider whether it will be helpful for those just beginning their studies in the lower classes to have paper notebooks in order to write down the lectures, and note above and in the margin whatever seems useful. Those who are more advanced in the humanities and the other faculties would carry with them paper to jot down what they hear or anything which strikes them as noteworthy. Later on they should rewrite in the paper notebooks, with better arrangement and order, what they desire to keep for the future.[108]

[377] 9. The rector of the college should also take care to see how all, the teachers as well as the students, are fulfilling their duty in our Lord.

[378] 10. Because of the utility there is in the practice of disputation,[109] especially for those who are studying arts and scholastic theology, the [students] should participate in the disputations or ordinary circles of the schools which they attend, even though these schools are not those of the Society itself; and they should endeavor to distinguish themselves both by their learning and by their modesty. Within the college too, after dinner on Sunday or some other day of the week (unless a special reason impedes the exercise), it is good to have someone from each class of the students of arts and theology, whom the rector will designate, defend some theses. During the preceding afternoon these theses will be posted in writing on the door of the schools, that those who wish may come to dispute or to listen. After these defendants have briefly proved their theses, those from within and without the house who wish to object may do so. Someone will preside to direct the disputants, to sum up the doctrine about the subject under discussion and to make it clear for the benefit of those listening, and to give the signal to stop to those who are disputing, meanwhile distributing the time in such a way that there will be room for the disputations of all of [the students]. . . .[110]

[380] 12. Those who are studying humanities should also have their fixed times to discuss and debate about the matters of their branch in the presence of someone who directs them. After dinner on one Sunday or other designated day they too will defend theses; and on another they will exercise themselves in writing compositions in prose or in verse, whether that is done impromptu to show their facility, or whether they bring a composition previously written and read it publicly there.[111] In the

---

106. Libraries at this time were small. For example, that of Queen's College, Oxford, contained 199 volumes in 1472. Due to their scarcity and great value, the books did not circulate and were often chained to the reading tables.

107. Loyola's emphasis on lecturing, repeating, and memorizing reflects the practices of the medieval and Renaissance universities. See "A Law Professor Introduces His Lectures at Bologna" in selection #21 and Charles Eliot's selection #40.

108. This procedure amounts to "commonplacing," as mentioned in selection #29 about Harvard College in 1642.

109. See the discussion about disputation in selection #19 of Thomas Aquinas, *Disputation concerning ON THE TRINITY.*

110. See the discussion of "determining" in selections #17–19 of Thomas Aquinas and selection #21 concerning "Rules for Determinations in Liberal Arts, 1252."

111. Here is glimpsed a third kind of pedagogy: the declamation of the humanists.

first case the subject to write about is given at the place of the exercise, and in the latter case it is given earlier.

[381] 13. All, and especially the students of the humanities, should ordinarily speak Latin,[112] and commit to memory what was indicated by their teachers, and bestow much practice upon the style in their compositions, and have someone to correct them.[113] Moreover, some with the approval of the rector may read privately some authors besides those on whom they have lectures. After dinner on some day of each week, one of the more advanced students should deliver a Latin or Greek oration about some subject likely to edify those within and without the college and to encourage them to greater perfection in our Lord. . . .[114]

[383] That the students may be helped more, it would be wise to place together some of equal ability who with holy rivalry may spur one another on. . . . It will also aid them if they are reminded, upon their arrival at the houses, that after their studies they will have to be examined in all the branches which they have learned.

[384] 14. Moreover, especially those studying the arts and theology, but also the rest, ought to have their own private and undisturbed study, that they may better and more profoundly understand the matters treated. [385] In this private study (if the rector thinks it good), they could read some commentary. While they are still attending lectures in a group, there should be one, and that carefully chosen. The students could also write down what seems likely to be more useful to them.

[386] 15. Just as it is necessary to restrain those who are running too rapidly, so is it proper to stimulate, urge on, and encourage those for whom this is necessary. . . .[115] If it is seen that someone is wasting his time in the college because either he does not care to advance or cannot, it is better to remove him from it and to let someone else enter in his place who will make better progress for the end sought, the service of God. [387] If someone should be unfit to study but fit for other ministries, he could be employed within the colleges or houses of the Society in something judged proper. But if he entered to become a [student] and should be unfit for both study and the other ministries, he may be dismissed. However, it will be good for the rector, after considering the case, to inform the provincial or general and to follow his order.

[388] 16. When the subject matter of one faculty has been completed, it will be good to review it, by reading, with the rector's approval, one or more authors than the one used the first time, and by making, also with his approval, a compendium of what pertains to that branch. This compendium can be briefer and more accurately digested than the first notes which the [student] composed while he did not yet have the understanding of the matter which he has after his courses have been completed. . .[116]

[390] 17. At the times designated for them they should prepare themselves for the public acts of examinations and replies. Those who after careful examination are found to deserve their degrees may

---

112. Latin, the standard language of the academy and the church, was required in all grammar schools, colleges, and universities. Compare the requirements of Latin in selection #29 about Harvard College in 1642 and selection #32 about Yale College in the 1700s.

113. "Ignatius saw Ciceronian style . . . as an important means of reaching some people, 'especially in these times' [para. 447] of the Renaissance." Translator's note, p. 196n16.

114. Loyola may have had preaching in mind here. In any case, this exercise resembles the standard and culminating humanist, pedagogical exercise of declamation: a written or spoken theme in which the student wove abundant and appropriate allusions to classical literature, while addressing a given topic.

115. In contrast to the recommendations of the humanists, the Jesuits' students move generally at a uniform pace through a uniform curriculum.

116. Compare the M.A. thesis at Puritan Harvard College in selection #29.

receive them. But to avoid every appearance of ambition or inordinate desires, they should not take special places. Rather, they should place themselves in a group independently of rank, even though indications of rank are customarily given in the university where they are studying.[117] Moreover, they should not make expenditures inappropriate for poor men when they take their degrees, which should be received without detriment to humility, for the sole purpose of being better able to help one's fellowmen for glory to God.

[391] 18. The superior should consider whether it is advisable for those who have finished their studies to lecture in private or in public for their own progress or for that of others. He should make provision according to what seems more expedient in our Lord. . . .

Chapter 12 The branches to be taught
in the universities of the Society[118]

[446] 1. Since the end of the Society and of its studies is to aid our fellowmen to the knowledge and love of God and to the salvation of their souls; and since the branch of theology is the means most suitable to this end, in the universities of the Society the principal emphasis ought to be put upon it. Thus diligent treatment by highly capable professors should be given to what pertains to scholastic doctrine and Sacred Scripture, and also to the part of positive theology which is conducive to the aforementioned end, without entering into the part of the canons which is directed toward trials in court.

[447] 2. Moreover, since both the learning of theology and the use of it require (especially in these times[119]) knowledge of humane letters and of the Latin, Greek, and Hebrew languages, there should be capable professors of these languages, and that in sufficient number. Furthermore, there may also be teachers of other languages such as Chaldaic, Arabic, and Indian, where these are necessary or useful for the end stated, with attention given to the diversities of place and reasons which may move us to teach them.

[448] Under the heading of humane letters is understood, in addition to grammar, what pertains to rhetoric, poetry, and history.[120]

[449] When a plan is being worked out in some college or university to prepare persons to go among the Moors or Turks, Arabic or Chaldaic would be expedient; and Indian would be proper for those about to go among the Indians; and the same holds true for similar reasons in regard to other languages which could have greater utility in other regions.[121]

[450] 3. Likewise, since the arts or natural sciences dispose the intellectual powers for theology, and are useful for the perfect understanding and use of it, and also by their own nature help toward the

---

117. See also para. 478. How can this practice of ignoring academic rank or honor be reconciled with that of promoting "holy rivalry" (para. 383) or with Vergerio's recommendation of "competition for praise and approval devoid of hatred" in selection #25?

118. A Jesuit university generally included the higher or philosophical, faculty of the liberal arts, as described in the note to para. 351 above, as well as a faculty of theology. The lower faculty of languages and humane letters might also be included or left to neighboring colleges.

119. This phrase refers to the Renaissance period of humanistic learning.

120. This clarifying definition comports closely with what the Renaissance humanists conventionally understood as "humanistic studies," while it is also consistent with the broader definition of "grammar" employed in the Ciceronian tradition of liberal education.

121. This provision demonstrates the relative flexibility and liberality of the Jesuits' program, contributing to their success in settling new colleges.

same ends, they should be treated with fitting diligence and by learned professors. In all this the honor and glory of God our Lord should be sincerely sought.

[451] Logic, physics, metaphysics, and moral philosophy should be treated, and also mathematics in the measure appropriate to secure the end which is being sought. To teach how to read and write would also be a work of charity if the Society had enough members to be able to attend to everything. But because of the lack of members these elementary branches are not ordinarily taught.

[452] 4. The study of medicine and laws, being more remote from our Institute, will not be treated in the universities of the Society, or at least the Society will not undertake this teaching through its own members.[122]

Chapter 13 The method and order of treating
the aforementioned branches

[453] 1. To give such treatment of both the lower branches and also of theology, there should be a suitable arrangement and order both for the morning and the afternoon.

[454] 2. And although the order and hours which are spent in these studies may vary according to the regions and seasons, there should be such conformity that in every region [what is done should be judged] most conducive to greater progress in learning.

[455] Concerning the hours of the lectures, their order, and their method, and concerning the exercises both in compositions, which ought to be corrected by the teachers, and in disputations within all the faculties, and in delivering orations and reading verses in public—all this will be treated in detail in a separate treatise, approved by the general. This present constitution refers the reader to it, which the remark that it ought to be adapted to places, times, and persons, even though it would be desirable to reach that order as far as this is possible.[123]

[456] 3. Furthermore, there should be not only lectures which are delivered in public but also different masters according to the capacity and number of the students. These masters should take an interest in the progress of each one of their students, require them to give an account of their lessons, and make them hold repetitions. They should also make those who are studying humane letters gain practice by ordinarily speaking Latin, and by composing in a good style and delivering well what they have composed. They should make them, and much more those studying the higher branches, engage in disputations often. Days and hours should be designated for this; and in these disputations the students should debate not only with the members of their own class, but those who are somewhat lower down should dispute about matters they understand with students who are more advanced, and conversely those who are more advanced should debate with those lower down by coming down to subjects which these latter are studying. The professors too ought to hold disputations with one another, always preserving the proper modesty and having someone preside to stop the debate and give the doctrinal solution. . . .[124]

[460] 4. Likewise, it will always be the function of the rector to see to it himself or through the chancellor[125] that the newcomers are examined and placed in those classes and with those teachers

---

122. A flagship medieval university, the *studium generale*, comprised a faculty of liberal arts surmounted by three graduate faculties of theology, law, and medicine.

123. This paragraph authorized the writing a "plan of studies" (*Ratio studiorum*), which the Society adopted in 1599.

124. See the discussion of "determining" in selections #17–19 of Thomas Aquinas and selection #21 concerning "Rules for Determinations in Liberal Arts, 1252."

125. Here and below the chancellor is regarded as the subordinate of the rector. Compare the relationship posited between the two offices in selection #21 of "University Statutes and Documents."

that are suitable for them. . . . According to the difference of abilities, ages, and other circumstances that must be considered, it will be the rector's function to investigate how far each student should progress into these branches and how long he should apply himself to them, although it is better for those who have the age and ability to advance and distinguish themselves in all these areas for the glory of God our Lord. . . .

[462] 5. Just as steady application is necessary in the work of studying, so also is some relaxation. The proper amount and the times of this relaxation will be left to the prudent consideration of the rector to determine, according to the circumstances of persons and places. . . .

Chapter 14 The books which should be expounded

[464] 1. In general, as was stated in the treatise of the colleges,[126] in each faculty those books will be lectured on which are found to contain more solid and safe doctrine; and those which are suspect, or whose authors are suspect, will not be taken up. But in each university these should be individually designated. In theology there should be lectures on the Old and New Testaments and on the scholastic doctrine of St. Thomas; and in positive theology those authors should be selected who are more suitable for our end.

[465] Even though the book is without suspicion of bad doctrine, when its author is suspect it is not expedient that it be lectured on. For through the book affection is acquired for the author; and some part of the credence given to him in what he says well could be given to him later in what he says unsoundly. Furthermore, it rarely occurs that some poison is not mixed into what comes forth from a heart full of it.[127]

[466] The [*Book of Sentences*] will also be lectured on. But if in time it seems that the students will draw more help from another author, as would be the case through the writing of some compendium or book of scholastic theology that seems better adapted to these times of ours, it will be permitted to make this book the subject of the lectures, after much weighing of counsel and examination of the matter by the persons deemed fit in the whole Society and with the superior general's approval. . . [128]

[468] 2. In regard to the books of humane letters in Latin or Greek, in the universities as well as in the colleges, lecturing to the adolescents on any book which contains matters harmful to good habits of conduct should be avoided, as far as possible, unless the books are previously expurgated of the objectionable matters and words. [469] If some books, such as Terence, cannot be expurgated at all, it is better that they should not be lectured on, in order that the nature of the contents may not injure the purity of the minds.[129]

[470] 3. In logic, natural and moral philosophy, and metaphysics, the doctrine of Aristotle should be followed, as also in the other liberal arts. In regard to the commentaries, both on these authors and

---

126. See para. 358.

127. Thus, after reading Desiderius Erasmus's *Education of a Christian Prince* (1516) at Barcelona, Loyola always held Erasmus in suspicion, likely because Erasmus advocated a monarchy limited by law, and a papacy limited by secular authority.

128. Paras. 464 and 466 indicate a significant shift in the assigned texts in theology. The aphoristic *Book of Sentences*, written by Peter Lombard (1100–c. 1160), served as the authoritative, foundational text in Catholic theology until the late 1500s. Early in the sixteenth century, the University of Paris began to assign the theological treatises of Thomas Aquinas, and Loyola came under this influence when he studied theology at Paris in 1534. Hence, the early Jesuits promoted the study of Aquinas.

129. By contrast, some humanist scholars, such as Erasmus, recommended the plays of Terence with their realistic, earthy humor.

on those treating humanities, a selection should be made. Those which the students ought to see should be designated, and also those which the masters ought to follow by preference in the doctrine they teach.

Chapter 15 The terms and degrees

[471] 1. In the study of humane letters and the languages a definite period of time for their completion cannot be established, because of the difference in abilities and knowledge of those who attend the lectures. . . . [472] In the case of beginners of good ability, an effort should be made to discern whether a semester in each of the four lower classes would be enough, and two semesters in the highest class spent in studying rhetoric and the languages. But a definite rule cannot be given.

[473] 2. In the arts, it will be necessary to arrange the terms in which the natural sciences are to be lectured upon. It seems that less than three years would be insufficient for them. Another half year will remain for the student to review, perform his academic acts, and take the degree of master in the case of those who are to receive degrees. In this way the whole curriculum enabling a student to become a master of arts will last three years and a half.[130] Each year with the help of God one such cycle of treatises will begin and another will come to its end. . . .

[478] 4. In the matter of the degrees, both of master of arts and of doctor of theology, three things should be observed. First, no one, whether a member of the Society or an extern, should be promoted to a degree unless he has been carefully and publicly examined by persons deputed for this office, which they should perform well, and unless he has been found fit to lecture in that faculty. Second, the door to ambition should be closed by giving no fixed places to those who receive degrees; rather, they should "anticipate one another with honor" [*Romans* 12: 10], without observing any distinction which arises from places. Third, just as the Society teaches altogether gratis, so should it confer the degrees completely free, and only a very small expenditure, even though it is voluntary, should be allowed to the extern students, that the custom may not come to have the force of law and that excess in this matter may not creep in with time. The rector should also take care not to permit any of the teachers or other members of the Society to accept money or gifts, either for themselves of for the college, from any person for anything he has done to help him. For according to our Institute, our reward should be only Christ our Lord, who is "our reward exceedingly great" [*Genesis* 15: 1].

[479] If it appears, for sufficiently weighty reasons, that someone ought not to be examined publicly, with the permission of the general or provincial that may be done which the rector judges will be for the greater glory of God our Lord.

[480] Thus, banquets should not be permitted, nor other celebrations which are costly and not useful for our end. Neither should there be any conferring of college caps or gloves or any other object.

---

130. It is presupposed here that the six semesters or three years devoted to humane letters, stipulated in para. 472, will result in the bachelor of arts degree.

Humanist Liberal Education of Women Outside of Colleges and Universities

27. Laura Cereta, Letters (1486, 1488)

INTRODUCTION

Laura Cereta (1469–1499) was born into an urban, upper-class family in Brescia, Italy. She endured several maladies as a child, and her relationship with her mother was apparently full of tension and conflict. Cereta's father, like that of Christine de Pizan and Bathsua Makin and the grandfather of Juana Inéz de la Cruz., supported his daughter's desire to study and arranged for her education. In fifteenth- and sixteenth-century Italy the small minority of women who pursued the "humanistic studies" of the liberal arts did so either with tutors in the home or as visiting residents in a female monastery. Laura's father, an attorney and magistrate, adopted the latter course by sending the seven-year-old girl to a local convent, where she apparently studied with the prioress, who encouraged her to draw during her nightly periods of insomnia.

Within two years Laura returned home, but her father "soon sent me back to my instructoress in liberal studies," she states below, "since I had already begun to be bored with childish pursuits and he feared that at my age I might slip into indolent habits and grow dull from the free time I would have." At age eleven she returned home to take care of her five younger siblings, continuing her studies as much as possible and assuming the role of her father's secretary during her early teens when war broke out with the city of Ferrara. At age fifteen in about 1484, Cereta married a merchant from Venice, who died within eighteen months, probably of the plague. Distraught, the sixteen-year-old widow appears to have turned her attention toward lamentation and spiritual matters.

Continuing her studies during the subsequent decade, she corresponded with a number of prominent, learned men and women throughout Italy, and may have met regularly with a group of such scholars and given readings of her work. Meanwhile, Cereta's writing shifted away from Ciceronian Latinity toward the more compact style found in later Latin writers. Earlier humanists, including Francesco Petrarca and Pier Paolo Vergerio, had opposed such a shift, as had Quintilian in his time; but the trend was common among humanists in the late fifteenth century. When she died at the age of thirty in 1499, Cereta's writings amounted to eighty-two letters plus a dialogue.

Selection #27 includes two of those letters. The first, an autobiographical letter written in 1486, describes some of the circumstances that allowed and curtailed the liberal education of upper-class women in Renaissance Italy. Learned Italian women in the century preceding Cereta came from the ruling class and did not distinguish themselves from their families or its interests. Cereta belongs to the second generation of women humanists who "came typically from the urban, citizen classes rather than the nobility or the courts" and "were the first female writers in Italy to mobilize their talents to advance their own interests rather than those of their families."[131] This first letter is addressed to a friend and nun, Nazaria Olympica.

Cereta's second letter of 1488 examines the longstanding dispute over learned women, which recalls Giovanni Boccaccio's *Concerning Famous Women* (c. 1359) and Christine de Pizan's *Book of the City of Ladies* (c. 1404). While borrowing from the former work, Cereta appears not to have known the latter, a fact demonstrating the isolation experienced by these early feminist scholars.

---

131. Diana Robin, "Translator's Introduction," in Cereta, *Collected Letters of a Renaissance Feminist*, p. 7.

SELECTION[132]

It is well established from our family records that I was born in the fourth month before the coming of the seventieth year in the century one thousand four-hundred of our Savior. Our laurel tree, which shaded with its bold branches a polished and burgeoning garden, had grown shriveled and dry in the wake of the icy frost that followed a brutal storm. I myself kept the name with which this tree was endowed. And thus, the whole house rang constantly with this sweet appellation, and I, who was carried around alternately in each of their arms, became for my adoring parents their most precious source of delight, for parents usually favor their firstborn child. . . .

As a sickly infant I often fell prey to dangerous intestinal worms. But afterwards I developed into a little girl who was charming and delicate. I was a playful, spirited child and I wandered everywhere freely, though I suffered from blistering sores on my skin of various sorts. Recently, the extraction of several teeth has given me back my energy. Since then, divine providence has taken it upon herself to look after my otherwise excellent health.

But in order to move quickly beyond the trivia of the ensuing years, I shall begin with events that followed the first seven years of my life. For what can that tender age bequeath to history except precocious babble? During this period, as soon as I had scarcely learned for the first time to use the letters of the alphabet to form syllables, I was entrusted to a woman highly esteemed both for her counsel and sanctity, whose learning, habits, and discipline I, who was to be educated, intently absorbed.[133]

She kept me constantly at her side in the inner chambers of the convent, the doors to which were opened and shut with a hundred locks. She was the first to teach me to find a passage through my nights of insomnia by using an embroidery needle to draw pictures. My hand, obedient enough after a brief period of time, committed the rudiments of my new learning to thread and fabric. There was in fact no embroidery stitch so elegant or difficult that I could not master it, once I discerned its fine points through delicate and gentle probings.[134] In this way a mind quite helpless and quite deficient in knowledge was able to raise itself up, once it was inspired, to those gentle breezes of hope.

With rough and trembling hands I designed, ornamented, and embroidered a tunic for the nursling baby Christchild, which was to be as precious as pearls. For trembling necklaces hung around his face with gleaming brilliance, from which hairlike threads of silver flowed down, which were surrounded by violet rosebuds on a bed of verdant grass. And little scales of many colors stood stiff with thread of gold, sewn under a knotty bough twisted and tawny with thorns, and these alone adorned the curving orb. One purple thread was braided into the weave of the fabric, but embossings, equal in size and divided by fissures and embroidered dots, embellished the many-colored threads and cloths of the decorative bands. But on the left shoulder of the tunic, a translucently burning gem cast its rays toward the embroidered likeness of a flashing star.

Once I had completed this work of art, which was like an empty simulacrum of my sleepless nights, I withdrew my idle hands from the pomp and vanity of such work. The next year, which pre-

---

132. Laura Cereta, "A Narrative of Her Life [letter to Nazaria Olympica]," and "In Defense of a Liberal Education for Women [letter to Bibolo Semproni]," in Laura Cereta, *Collected Letters of a Renaissance Feminist*, ed. and tr., Diana Robin (Chicago: University of Chicago Press, 1997), pp. 23–9, 74–80. Reprinted by permission of the University of Chicago Press.

133. "While her biographers have emphasized her father's role in her intellectual formation, Cereta herself indicates that her first and subsequent teachers . . . were intellectual women." Translator's note, p. 25n15.

134. "Cereta makes the point here that the way she masters intricacies of advanced needlework is stereotypically 'feminine': her . . . adjectives, *tenuis* and *mollis* are conventionally linked not only with the feminine but the effeminate in Latin literature." Translator's note, p. 26n18.

pared me for the more tranquil work of contemplation, removed me from all things secular. After this, insofar as I could, imbued both with the fear of God and humility and kindliness toward everyone, I blamelessly devoted myself to obedience and I was always ready—like a little sparrow trained to come to one's hand—to go to the aid of those who called me.[135] In more private places I prostrated myself as I prayed that I might sacrifice my innocent heart. This was the root of a change of heart, and from this the seeds of hope soon sprouted—because of which I shall eventually sleep in the bosom of God, the king and redeemer of men, in the company of Christ, the fruit of the law redeemed.

Within a full two-year period from the time I had entered the convent, my father called for my return home and I departed, to everyone's sorrow. As soon as I crossed my father's threshold, my mother greeted me, clasping me to her in an [overly constricting] embrace. Feeling joy for herself yet pity for me, she began to comfort me, following me wherever I went as though she did not know how to satisfy herself in her delight at my homecoming.

My father, however, the more purposeful figure in the family in his role as our governor and, above all, a man of temperate counsel, soon sent me back to my instructoress in liberal studies, since I had already begun to be bored with childish pursuits and he feared that at my age I might slip into indolent habits and grow dull from the free time I would have. With all the vigor of my genius depending on her, my teacher, I immersed myself night and day, blinking back my fatigue, in long vigils of study. Then in my eleventh year, after I had entered into this dry diet, I was removed from the discipline of the rod, for by this time I had already digested all the necessary elements in the obligatory paradigms of grammar.

At home, as though starving for knowledge, I diligently studied the eloquence of the tragic stage and the polish of Tully insofar as I was able.[136] But when scarcely a year had gone by, I assumed the responsibility for almost all of the household duties myself. Thus it was my lot to grow old when I was not far from childhood. Even so, I attended lectures on mathematics during the days I had free from toil, and I did not neglect those profitable occasions when, unable to sleep, I devoured the mellifluous-voiced prophets of the Old Testament and figures from the New Testament, too. Even then, when I was only a girl, I saw my father occupy three external magistracies, happy in my studies and full of the pleasure of peace and tranquility.

Then, when the third lustrum[137] of my life was scarcely over, my lot destined me to be—oh sadness—the wife of a merchant whose fate wrapped him with her severe threads within the space of twelve months in a mournful end. Alas, dark day. Oh, heart struck with sorrow and pain deep within, how tearful has this wound been and how wretched has it been for me. Really, under how high a tower of troubles I lie, abandoned and overwhelmed by the burden of a widowhood that grows more bitter each day, has been said enough and more than enough times. One person has said it one way and another differently. . . .

I myself used to enjoy these studies; now because I imitate the first cause, I consider of lesser importance secondary causes, because of their instability. Owing to this, I would prefer to be ignorant rather than to know what the fates have in store for me. In any case, among those who believe in Christ, fate—once linked to the causes of things—now has no meaning. For God is one and the same

135. The image of the sparrow is drawn from the *Songs* (2, 3) of the Roman poet Catullus (c. 84–c. 54 B.C.), who likens himself to his lover's pet bird. Elsewhere in her letters, the sparrow becomes "an important Ceretan metaphor for the self-destructive and inappropriate obedience of women." Translator's note, p. 25n20.

136. According to the translator, "the tragic stage" refers to the tragedies of Seneca the Younger, popular in the Renaissance (p. 27n25). See selection #5

137. A lustrum is a period of five years, derived from a traditional, Roman rite of purification.

everlasting and omnipotent being, who moves and rules us in harmony with the arching vault of heaven. . . .

§ § §

Your complaints are hurting my ears, for you say publicly and quite openly that you are not only surprised but pained that I am said to show this extraordinary intellect of the sort one would have thought nature would give to the most learned of men—as if you had reached the conclusion, on the facts of the case, that a similar girl had seldom been seen among the peoples of the world. You are wrong on both counts, Semproni, and now that you've abandoned the truth, you are going to spread information abroad that is clearly false.[138]

I think you should be deeply pained—no, you should actually be blushing—you who are no longer now a man full of animus but instead a stone animated by the scorn you have for the studies that make us wise, while you grow weak with the sickness of debilitating leisure. And thus in your case, it is not nature that goes astray but the mind, for which the path from the appearance of virtue to villainy is a fairly easy one. In this manner, you appear to be flattering a susceptible young girl because of the glory that has accrued to her—my—name. But the snare of flattery is seductive, for you who have always set traps for the sex that has been revered all throughout history have been ensnared yourself. And duped by your own madness, you are trying, by running back and forth, to trample me underfoot and smash me to the ground with your fists. Sly mockery is concealed here, and it is typical of the lowborn, plebeian mind to think that one can blind Medusa with a few drops of olive oil.[139] You would have done better to have crept up on a mole than a wolf, since the former, being shrouded in darkness, would see nothing clearly, while the latter's eyes radiate light in the dark.

In case you don't know, the philosopher sees with her mind; she furnishes paths with a window of reason through which she can ascend to a state of awareness. For Providence, the knower of the future, conquers marauding evil, trampling it with feet that have eyes. I would remain silent, believe me, if you, with your long-standing hostile and envious attitude towards me, had learned to attack me alone; after all, a ray of Phoebus's can't be shamed by being surrounded by mud.[140] But I am angry and my disgust overflows. Why should the condition of our sex be shamed by your little attacks? Because of this, a mind thirsting for revenge is set afire; because of this, a sleeping pen is wakened for

---

138. This second letter is "a typical example of humanist invective," which Cereta "characterizes her adversary, Bibolo, and other detractors as alternatively insane, bestial, plebeian, ignorant, and drunk."Robin, "Translator's Introduction," p. 74. Bibolo might be translated "tippler," so "Cereta's correspondent might be either a real acquaintance whom she is addressing with a comical nickname . . . or a fictional creation and vehicle for her polemic." Translator's note, p. 74n35.

139. Interpreting Boccaccio as derogating the accomplishments of women, the translator states, "Boccaccio downplays as a mere fiction of the poets [Medusa's] famous ability to turn men into stone." (Translator's note, p. 75n36.) Yet, Boccaccio notes, Medusa's "eyes had such great and pleasant force that if she looked kindly at someone, he remained almost motionless and beside himself. . . . These deeds inspired the stories of the poets where we read that the Gorgon Medusa often changed into stone men who gazed upon her." Giovanni Boccaccio, *Concerning Famous Women*, tr. Guido A. Guarino (New Brunswick, NJ: Rutgers University Press, 1963), XX, p. 43.

140. Phoebus, meaning "brilliant" or "shining" in Greek, was another name for Apollo, Greek god of light, arts, muses, medicine, and prophecy, as seen in Martianus Capella (II 210, 218) in selection #8.

insomniac writing.[141] Because of this, red-hot anger lays bare a heart and mind long muzzled by silence.

My cause itself is worthy: I am impelled to show what great glory that noble lineage which I carry in my own breast has won for virtue and literature—a lineage that knowledge, the bearer of honors, has exalted in every age. For the possession of this lineage is legitimate and sure, and it has come all the way down to me from the perpetual continuance of a more enduring race.[142]

We have read that the breast of Ethiopian Sabba, imbued with divinity, solved the prophetic riddles of the Egyptian king Solomon.[143] The first writers believed that Amalthea, a woman erudite in the knowledge of the future, sang responses near the banks that surround the Avernus, not far from Baiae. She, who as a Sybil was worthy of the gods of this lineage, sold books full of oracles to Priscus Tarquinius. Thus the Babylonian prophetess Eriphila, looking into the future with her divine mind far removed, described the fall and the ashes of Troy, the fortunes of the Roman empire, and the mysteries of Christ, who would later be born. Nicostrata, too, the mother of Evander and very learned in prophecy as well as literature, attained such genius that she was the first to show the alphabet to the first Latins in sixteen figures. The enduring fame of Inachan Isis will flourish, for she alone of the Argive goddesses revealed to the Egyptians her own alphabet for reading.[144] But Zenobia, an Egyptian woman of noble erudition, became so learned not only in Egyptian but also in Latin and Greek literature that she wrote the histories of barbarian and foreign peoples.[145]

Shall we attribute illiteracy to Theban Manto, the prophesying daughter of Tiresias, and to Pyromantia, too, who was full of those Chaldaean arts when she spoke with the shades of the dead and foretold events in the future through the movements of flames, the flight of birds, and livers and entrails of animals?[146] Where did all the great wisdom of Tritonian Pallas come from, which enabled her to educate so many Athenians in the arts, if it was not that she succeeded in unraveling the mysteries of the scriptures of Apollo, the physician, to the delight of everyone?[147] Those little Greek women

141. Cereta's letters frequently refer "to her lucubration, her necessity for night writing, which she calls her *vigiliae*, her night watches." Translator's note, p. 75n38.

142. "*Generositas* (noble lineage, lineage, birth, nobility of stock) is the key image in Cereta's letter, the term suggests the notion of a noble race of learned women from which she, Laura, is descended. . . . Cereta expresses the notion of women as a collectivity, as a race, breed, or generation 'more enduring' than that of males." Translator's note, p. 76n39–40.

143. The translator states that, according to Boccaccio, "Saba has a royal lineage and great wealth but she is not a seer." (p. 76n41.) Yet, Boccaccio states that "we do know that [Saba] had so much knowledge that it seemed miraculous." Boccaccio, *Concerning Famous Women*, XLI, p. 93.

144. The portraits in this paragraph are drawn faithfully from Boccaccio. Nicostrata, or Carmentis, is discussed by Isidore of Seville (I 4) in selection #11 and Christine de Pizan (I 33 ii) in selection #12.

145. Zenobia (d. c. 272), ruler of Palmyra in central Syria, was known for her intelligence and military leadership. "Boccaccio says Zenobia was believed to have written summaries of certain ancient histories. Cereta carries Boccaccio a step further by asserting that Zenobia was so erudite that she herself wrote histories." Translator's note, pp. 76–7n46. Boccaccio, *Concerning Famous Women*, XCVIII, pp. 226–230.

146. Cereta seems to be distinguishing two figures from the description of Manto in Boccaccio, *Concerning Famous Women*, XXVIII, pp. 60–1. Boccaccio apparently combined the accounts of Manto from Vergil and Dante, as noted by Christine de Pizan in *Book of the City of Ladies* I 31. Tiresias, a blind soothsayer, appears in many legends in Greek mythology.

147. In order to show that Pallas, or Athena, was literate, Cereta sacrifices Boccaccio's affirmation that Athena invented the arts herself. Boccaccio, *Concerning Famous Women*, VI, pp. 14–5. Christine de Pizan makes Athena's originality the central theme of her account in *Book of the City of Ladies* I 34.

Phyliasia and Lasthenia were wonderful sources of light in the world of letters and they filled me with new life because they ridiculed the students of Plato, who frequently tied themselves in knots over the snare-filled sophistries of their arguments.[148]

Lesbian Sappho serenaded the stony heart of her lover with tearful poems, sounds I might have thought came from Orpheus's lyre[149] or the plectrum of Phoebus. Soon the Greek tongue of Leontium, full of the Muses, emerged, and she, who had made herself agreeable with the liveliness of her writing, dared to make a bitter attack on the divine words of Theophrastus.[150] Nor would I omit here Proba, noted both for her exceptional tongue and her knowledge; for she wove together and composed histories of the *Old Testament* with fragments from Homer and Vergil.[151]

The majesty of the Roman state deemed worthy a little Greek woman, Semiramis, for she spoke her mind about the laws in a court of law and about kings in the senate.[152] Pregnant with virtue, Rome bore Sempronia, who, forceful in her eloquent poetry, spoke in public assemblies and filled the minds of her audiences with persuasive orations.[153] Hortensia, the daughter of Hortensius, and also an orator, was celebrated at a public meeting with equal elegance. Her grace of speech was so great that she persuaded the triumvirs, albeit with the tears of a loyal mother, to absolve the women of Rome from having to pay the debt levied against them.[154] Add also Cornificia, the sister of the poet Cornificius, whose devotion to literature bore such fruit that she was said to have been nurtured on the milk of the Castalian Muses and who wrote epigrams in which every phrase was graced with Heliconian flowers. I will not mention here Cicero's daughter Tullia or Terentia or Cornelia, Roman women who reached

---

148. Cereta's reference here is somewhat obscure. Diogenes Laertius, Greek author of the third century A.D., recorded that two of Plato's students were women: Lastheneia of Mantinea and Axiothea of Phlius. *Lives of Eminent Philosophers* III 46.

149. Sappho wrote influential lyric poetry in the late sixth century B.C. A portrait of Sappho appeared in Christine de Pizan, *Book of the City of Ladies* I 30, and in Boccaccio, *Concerning Famous Women*, XLV, pp. 99–100.

150. Leontium, a female philosopher of the fourth century B.C., wrote in defense of her teacher Epicurus and challenged Theophrastus, head of the Lyceum. She is also invoked by Christine de Pizan, *Book of the City of Ladies* I 30.

151. The learned Roman woman Proba in about A.D. 360 is said to have constructed a Biblical history drawn entirely from verses of Vergil. According to the translator, Boccaccio's "emphasis is on Proba's exceptionality in comparison to most other women, whom he dismisses as idle and pleasure-seeking." (p. 77n52). Cereta does virtually the same thing in discussing her own exceptionality below, while Boccaccio also observes, in describing Proba, that most men are ignorant. *Concerning Famous Women*, XCV, pp. 219–220. Compare the portrait of Proba by Christine de Pizan (I 29) in selection #12.

152. Semiramis's "sexual relationships and her incest with her son with which she is associated in most accounts of her life are suppressed in Cereta." Translator's note, p. 77n53. Cf. Boccaccio, *Concerning Famous Women*, II, pp. 4–7.

153. Boccaccio portrays two different Sempronias, both of which are Roman, although he refers to one as "the Roman Sempronia." Following Sallust, Boccaccio portrays the latter Sempronia as a learned poet and magnificent orator, but lascivious and immoral. Following the Roman poet Ovid, he describes the other Sempronia as steadfastly virtuous. *Concerning Famous Women*, LXXIV, LXXVII, pp. 166–7, 173–5. Cereta seems to combine the positive aspects of these two portraits into one figure.

154. Hortensia, daughter of a great orator, is reported to have made this speech in A.D. 42. Cf. Boccaccio, *Concerning Famous Women*, LXXXIII, p. 185.

the pinnacle of fame for their learning; and accompanying them in the shimmering light of silence will be Nicolosa of Bologna, Isotta of Verona, and Cassandra of Venice.[155]

All history is full of such examples. My point is that your mouth has grown foul because you keep it sealed so that no arguments can come out of it that might enable you to admit that nature imparts one freedom to all human beings equally—to learn.[156] But the question of my exceptionality remains. And here choice alone, since it is the arbiter of character, is the distinguishing factor. For some women worry about the styling of their hair, the elegance of their clothes, and the pearls and other jewelry they wear on their fingers. Others love to say cute little things, to hide their feelings behind a mask of tranquility, to indulge in dancing, and lead pet dogs around on a leash. For all I care, other women can long for parties with carefully appointed tables, for the peace of mind of sleep, or they can yearn to deface with paint the pretty face they see reflected in their mirrors. But those women for whom the quest for the good represents a higher value restrain their young spirits and ponder better plans. They harden their bodies with sobriety and toil, they control their tongues, they carefully monitor what they hear, they ready their minds for all-night vigils, and they rouse their minds for the contemplation of probity in the case of harmful literature. For knowledge is not given as a gift but by study. For a mind free, keen, and unyielding in the face of hard work always rises to the good, and the desire for learning grows in depth and breadth.[157]

So be it therefore. May we women, then, not be endowed by God the grantor with any giftedness or rare talent through any sanctity of our own. Nature has granted to all enough of her bounty; she opens to all the gates of choice, and through these gates, reason sends legates to the will, for it is through reason that these legates can transmit their desires. I shall make a bold summary of the matter. Yours is the authority, ours is the inborn ability. But instead of manly strength, we women are naturally endowed with cunning; instead of a sense of security, we are suspicious. Down deep we women are content with our lot.[158] But you, enraged and maddened by the anger of the dog from whom you flee, are like someone who has been frightened by the attack of a pack of wolves. The victor does not look for the fugitive; nor does she who desires a cease-fire with the enemy conceal herself. Nor does she set up camp with courage and arms when the conditions are hopeless. Nor does it give the strong any pleasure to pursue one who is already fleeing.

Look, do you tremble from fear alone of my name? I am savage neither in mind nor hand. What it is you fear? You run away and hide in vain, for the traps that await you around every corner have been more cunningly set. Is it thus that you, a deserter, leave this city and our sight? Is it thus that, regretful of what you have done, you rely on flight as the first road to safety for yourself? May your shame then stay with you. My goodness towards men isn't always rewarded, and you may imagine in your disdain for women that I alone marvel at the felicitousness of having talent—I, who in the light

---

155. Tullia, daughter of Cicero, and Terentia, wife of Cicero, lived in the first century B.C. and were relatively well educated but not renowned for their learning. Cereta balances references to the ancient women with learned, Italian feminists of her own time, including Isotta Nogarola (1418–1466) and Cassandra Fedele (1465–1558).

156. "The idea that both women and men were born with a right to an education was a radical statement for any fifteenth-century thinker." Translator's note, p. 78n58.

157. Why is Cereta justified in asserting and explaining her own exceptionality, while, in the view of the translator, Sempronia (and Boccaccio) are not?

158. "Yours is the authority, ours is the inborn ability" is "one of Cereta's key feminist aphorisms. It suggests that the greatest source of tension between the sexes lies in the unjustifiable power differential: though men are born with the [physical] power to rule, women have superior intellectual gifts." Translator's note, p. 79n61. Does this assessment fit Cereta's words here?

of the well-deserved fame of other women, am indeed only the smallest little mouse. Therefore when you hide your envy under a bogus example, you clothe yourself with defensive words in vain.

For truth which is dear to God always emerges when falsehoods are overthrown. That road is twisted where you walk under the black gaze of an envious mind—far from human beings, from duties, and from God. Who will be surprised, do you think, Bibolo, if the lacerated and wounded heart of a girl who is filled with indignation bitterly rears itself up against your sarcasm and satire from this day on, now that your trifling arrogance has wounded her with bitter injuries? Do not think, most despicable of men, that I might believe I have fallen out of favor with Jove.[159] I am a scholar and a pupil who has been lulled to sleep by the meager fire of a mind too humble. I have been too much burned, and my injured mind has accumulated too much passion; for tormenting itself with the defending of our sex, my mind sighs, conscious of its obligation. For all things—those deeply rooted inside us as well as those outside us—are being laid at the door of our sex.

In addition, I, who have always held virtue in high esteem and considered private things as secondary in importance, shall wear down and exhaust my pen writing against those men who are garrulous and puffed up with false pride. I shall not fail to obstruct tenaciously their treacherous snares. And I shall strive in a war of vengeance against the notorious abuse of those who fill everything with noise, since armed with such abuse, certain insane and infamous men bark and bare their teeth in vicious wrath at the republic of women,[160] so worthy of veneration. January 13, 1488.

---

159. Jove, or Jupiter, was the lord and father of the Roman pantheon.

160. Cereta's novel metaphor "republic of women" is doubtlessly adapted from the well known, humanistic image of a "republic of letters." Translator's note, p. 80n62. This metaphor recalls Christine de Pizan's term "city of ladies" in her selection signifying that women have founded and built an intellectual tradition of their own. Both metaphors also imply that women belong in public life, the exclusion from which was the fundamental justification for the exclusion of women from the liberal arts, which prepared students for public roles.

28. Roger Ascham, Letters on Tutoring Queen Elizabeth I (1548–1550)

INTRODUCTION

Arguing on behalf of liberally educating women, Bathsua Makin observes in selection #30: "I thought of Queen Elizabeth first, but purposely mention her last as the crown of all. How learned she was, the world can testify. It was usual for her to discourse with foreign agents in their own languages. Mr. Ascham, her tutor, used to say she read more Greek in a day then many of the doctors of her time did Latin in a week." Queen Elizabeth thus became the exemplar for those advocating liberal education for women in early modern England. Elizabeth's accomplishment derived from the typical arrangement of studying with a male humanist tutor. Roger Ascham occupied this position, and his letters describe the personal and professional intricacies involved, all of which were magnified due to Elizabeth's station and family.[161]

Ascham (1515–1568) was born near York, England, and entered St. John's College at Cambridge University in 1530. Ascham followed the traditional pattern of earning the B.A. after four years and the M.A. after another three years in 1537. His father advised him to enter into some honorable profession, but the son "chose to neglect this advice, and to plunge into the uncertainties of a political and literary life,"[162] as did many Renaissance humanists. To begin, Ascham accepted an appointment as a reader in Greek at the University, and soon sought to augment his meager salary by writing a treatise on archery that was published in 1545. Incorporating classical learning, addressing military training, and being the first book on archery in English, the work impressed King Henry VIII, who granted him a modest but adequate annuity. Ascham's prospects further improved when his teacher and friend, John Cheke (1514–1557), went to court to tutor Prince Edward, and Ascham's protégé William Grindal (d. 1548) followed Cheke and became tutor to Princess Elizabeth in 1544.

Elizabeth (1533–1603) was the daughter of King Henry VIII and Ann Boleyn, Henry's second wife. Desiring a male heir for the throne, Henry was deeply disappointed at the birth of Elizabeth, his second daughter, and had Ann charged with adultery and treason and beheaded before Elizabeth was three years old. Despite these tragic events and the disfavor shown her, Elizabeth displayed remarkable seriousness and intellectual gifts at an early age and persevered through Henry's successive marriages. By the time her father died in 1547 and her half-brother assumed the thrown as King Edward VI (1537–1553), Elizabeth had earned a reputation for her accomplishments in studying classical and vernacular languages and classical writings in the humanistic subjects. In 1548 her tutor Grindal died suddenly, and with the help of Cheke, Ascham was named to the position. Ascham "for nearly two years instructed the Princess with great diligence. But at the end of 1549 he abruptly left the Court, offended, as he tells us, by the impertinence of some of the servants. . . . [H]e would probably have felt the effects of his imprudence to his death, if he had not taken extraordinary pains to reinstate himself in Elizabeth's favor."[163] Aspects of these events and his tutoring of Elizabeth are reported in selection #28 drawn from his letters.

In 1553 King Edward died, and the longstanding political intrigue prompted by Edward's sickliness and minority status deepened into a series of political upheavals. Lady Jane Grey, a Protestant and great granddaughter of King Henry VII, was enthroned for a few days and then

---

161. Compare the estimates of Elizabeth's literary accomplishments in T. W. Baldwin, *William Shakspere's Small Latine and Lesse Greeke* 2 vols. (Urbana: University of Illinois Press, 1944), v. 1, p. 284; Leah S. Marcus et al., eds., *Elizabeth I: Collected Works* (Chicago: University of Chicago Press, 2000).

162. Giles, *The Whole Works of Roger Ascham*, v. 1, p. xxviii.

163. Giles, *The Whole Works of Roger Ascham*, v. 1, pp. xlviii–xlix.

deposed by supporters of Catholic Queen Mary I (1516–1558). Mary, being the daughter of the first wife of Henry VIII, was the elder half-sister of Elizabeth and had been treated even worse than Elizabeth. Mary had survived due primarily to the protection and support provided by her cousin, Emperor Charles V. Through all these developments, Ascham was fortunate in not falling out of favor in court and maintaining his position as Latin secretary.[164]

Upon Mary's death by illness in 1558, Elizabeth ascended the throne and confirmed Ascham in his position as Latin secretary in 1559. Over the next decade Elizabeth employed him to write official correspondence and read classical authors with her. During this period, Ascham composed his best known work: *The Schoolmaster*, an English treatise on teaching and learning that was published soon after his death in 1568. Queen Elizabeth meanwhile established her reputation as a learned and sagacious monarch who gave her name to an admirable period of political stability and cultural flowering that lasted until her death in 1603.

SELECTION[165]

Roger Ascham to John Cheke, recommending Ascham's protégé, William Grindal, for the position of tutor to Elizabeth at the royal court (September 1544).
In proportion to the pleasure which I always felt, when we were together, from your prudence in putting a stop to our squabbling [among the faculty at Cambridge] and encouraging us in the pursuit of learning, the more bitterly do I feel the necessity, by the change which has followed your leaving, of writing to you this present letter in which I have to express my grief at our losing the benefit of your counsel, rather than the common joy arising from the fruits of that counsel which when you were here we did not all equally follow. For things are now brought to such a pass that I know not what good can any longer be expected from that consensus of good men for the advancement of letters, which checked the turbulence and intolerance of some among us and which, although much supported by the goodness of the cause, was nevertheless kept up in great measure by your prudent management. Thus some have tried mightily to prevent me, to whom they owe anything they have accomplished, from ever again looking forward to your support from which I may bring honor to my friends, who are also yours, or ever support myself in my present humble lot.

For lately, if I may tell you the whole matter, when we were selecting the readers, I wished much to help my friend Grindal (on account of his poverty) and to that end sought to make use of, not every means in my power, but only such means as I thought you would approve of. I told my plan to M[adew], B[ill], and others of that stamp,[166] only one or two days before the thing was to be settled, when suddenly F., and your friend B., either by a perfidious plan of their own or prompted by H . . . ,

---

164. "Ascham's services in this office were in demand and were useful to the government for three reasons: first, he was noted for his excellent Latin style; second, he had a reputation for his excellent penmanship, which was regular, legible, and beautiful; and third, he knew the virtue of silence. . . . During the reign of Mary . . . of his immediate friends, Cheke was imprisoned and humiliated, by being forced to a public recantation, [another] was burned at the stake, and Lady Jane Grey was beheaded. Curiously enough, no mention can be found of these friends in letters written at this time; it is easy to believe that he carefully destroyed any mention of them so as to escape possible danger himself." Maurice A. Hatch, "The Latin Letters of Roger Ascham and John Sturm" (M.A. Thesis, University of Kansas, 1936), xix–xx.

165. The letters in this selection are adapted from J. A. Giles, tr., *The Whole Works of Roger Ascham*, 3 vols. (London: John Russell Smith, 1864), v. 1, pp. xli–xliii, lv–lvi, lvi–lvii, lix–lxii.

166. The translator construes this "M" as the University Vice-Chancellor Madew, but it also might be Nicholas Medcalfe, the Master of St. John's College. "B" apparently refers to William Bill, a contemporary and learned friend of Cheke and Ascham at St. John's College.

upset all the authority which we had so long possessed. Although they might have achieved the very same result through us, they counted [us] . . .as nothing and declared openly they were able and willing without our help to name anyone they pleased.[167] If this is to be approved, or even tolerated, the prudent and moderate men who can look out on all sides to protect their own interests, and the others, who are open to ridicule, and their friends, who are endangered by supporting their cause, are no better than fools. I at that time despised those noisy fellows due to my interest in gaining my object and protecting my friend Grindal, and I am now glad that I stuck so closely to the point. If out of this storm any evil hereafter befall the College, which has hitherto been under your guidance, you, whose love and approbation I wish always to possess, will clearly be able to understand all about it.

But you will say perhaps that I take offense from a slight cause.[168] Is it a slight cause that our president and seniors have had their authority despised and limited? Could I see all my hopes shattered, when I had the best opportunity of defending my friends and of wounding those who bore me malice? when neither my kindness in showing leniency nor my power of hurting was of the least avail in checking their hatred? I knew for certain that my friend Grindal, next to you and S . . . , was second to none in Greek and so poor that he had neither heart for study nor a sufficiency to live on, and that he was so attached to me that all our interests are in common. Could I then forgive his being separated forever from the learning in which he excelled, the studies to which he was elevated, and me his most familiar friend? In short, if he were to overlook all the offenses and wounds which have been aimed at our friendship and at myself, yet I cannot put up with faithlessness, backbiting, boasting, and intolerance, which, instead of being allayed, has been aggravated by the shameful affair that has just happened among us. . . . I hope it may be brought to pass by your prudent admonition, that the authority of Madew, which we ought to obey, may no longer be counted for nothing, that the seniors may have due respect paid to them, and that all insolent boasting may be checked. . . .

And now a few words about myself privately. My lord of York, as you know, is dying, to the great detriment of my fortunes.[169] But that is the least evil. I am looking out for another master to take the place of L . . . : I should like nothing better than that the good bishop of Westminster should succeed him. Give me over, if you will, to any one you please or keep me yourself; nothing could be better. If you can think of anything hereafter, favor me with the slightest notice thereof.

As I was sealing my letter, Madew and Bill came to me about sending Grindal to you [at court]. I felt a pang at the recollection of our close friendship, but was overjoyed for his sake. . . . I commend him to you as a man of mark, and promise that you shall find him diligent and respectful, zealous in learning and love of you, silent, faithful, temperate, and honest, and in every way devoted and well fitted for your service. . . . Farewell.

Roger Ascham to Elizabeth offering consolation upon the death of her tutor, William Grindal (January 1548).
I can easily estimate, most illustrious lady, your grief at the death of our friend Grindal,[170] from the great love and respect which he always used to feel towards you; and I should fear that reminding you

---

167. Those advocating humanistic liberal education were not above the typical faculty disputes over whose protégé would be supported by the minor teaching appointments in the college.

168. Perhaps this anticipates what will happen to Ascham as Elizabeth's tutor.

169. This evidently refers to Ascham's longtime patron.

170. Ascham later wrote to the Protestant educational reformer John Sturm that he "left the Court plunged in deeper sorrow at his [Grindal's] death than any one, I think, who has died there for many years, and caused me greater grief than I felt at the death of both my parents, who died the same day and almost the same hour, after they had lived together in the greatest harmony forty-seven years." Letter 117 (Jan. 1551) in Giles, *The Whole*

of it would increase rather than assuage your sorrow, if I did not clearly understand your great prudence, strengthened by the counsels of Mistress Catherine Astley and the precepts of my dear Grindal himself. This leads me to see that your own reflections and your own prudence will remove the bitterness from that grief which time alone heals in the minds of fools. If you expect consolation from this mournful letter, written by one who has enough to do to console himself, the best comfort, in my judgment, will be to bring to maturity that excellent learning of which you have had the seeds laid by Grindal. To this end, you must not hope, now that your own Grindal is dead, to get a better tutor in his place than is that other Grindal, who comes as near to him in sweetness and gentleness of manners as he does in name and in kindred.[171]

From the close friendship which I had for so many years with Grindal, I never hoped to reap more benefit than your goodwill which by his means you have shown towards me. Nor do I ask for anything so much in my daily payers, as that your former favor may continue in the judgment that Grindal so long held about me, and not be swayed by the judgment of any one else; for, although I have lost him, I do not wish to lose the benefit of his good opinion.[172] I will do my best to make my diligence in serving you match the hopes that I have formed from your goodness, so that all my zeal, loyalty, and obedience may fulfill all your wishes and redound to your honor and dignity. I shall think it my greatest happiness, if the time ever comes when my services can be of use to you. May the Lord Jesus ever have you in his keeping.

Roger Ascham to John Cheke (February 1548), expressing hopes of securing the appointment as Elizabeth's tutor.

That illustrious lady is thinking of having me in the place of Grindal. . . . I was with the illustrious lady during these last days: she signified to me this preference, and I did not try to make any bargain for my own advantage but at once declared that I was ready to obey her orders. She told me how the Queen and the Lord Admiral were favoring G . . . ; and I advised her to comply with their choice.[173] I praised G . . . to her and exhorted her, as much as I could, to follow their judgment in such a matter. I prayed her not to think of any good to be got for me, but to let nothing stand in the way of bringing to perfection that singular learning of which Grindal had sown the seeds.

It cannot be believed, most accomplished sir, what a knowledge of the Latin and Greek tongues she will attain, if she goes on as she has begun under Grindal. We are at least agreed in one point, she got out of her good will to me and I out of loyalty and respect for her, that she ought to have the best teacher that could be got. I can say nothing about myself; but I hope, although I am foolish and in fact nobody in almost everything, yet that I can be of use to her in teaching her Greek and Latin and in performing the duties of her secretary.

Works of Roger Ascham, v. 1, p. xlviiin. Ascham went on to ask if Sturm would insert a reference in an edition of his letters giving Grindal credit for laying the foundations for Queen Elizabeth's attainments in Greek and Latin.

171. This other Grindal may be Edmund Grindal, later Archbishop of Canterbury, who was at Cambridge University at this time, as was a third Grindal named James. Translator's note, p. lvn. Catherine Astley, the wife of John Astley (d. 1595), attended upon the Queen in her household.

172. This explicit statement of the instrumental value of personal relationships, inserted into this letter of consolation over the death of his protégé, seems to confirm the warning of Ascham's father about directing his career.

173. The Queen here is the sixth and last wife of Henry VIII, Catherine Parr, who married the Lord High Admiral, Thomas Seymour, almost immediately after Henry's death in 1547. They were promoting a different candidate to become Elizabeth's tutor. In 1549, shortly after Catherine's death, Seymour was beheaded for treasonously plotting to marry Elizabeth and become king.

When the Lady Elizabeth comes to London, she will talk over this matter with the Queen and the Lord Admiral; and I think they will not settle anything without consulting you. As for me, I trust all my labor, studies, and course of life to your prudence, which I will ever try to follow. May the Lord Jesus have you in his keeping.

Roger Ascham to John Sturm (April 1550), recalling his tutoring of Elizabeth.[174]
There are here at Cambridge many eminent men, among whom is most conspicuous my friend Walter Haddon, now vice-chancellor of this University.[175] He seems worthy to be compared with [John Cheke and Thomas Smith[176]], rather than to be reckoned among us. I do not know what all the Oxford men are about, but some months ago at Court, I fell in with a man from that University who, by his preference for Lucian, Plutarch, Herodian, Seneca, Aulus Gellius, and Apuleius, seemed to bring both of those tongues down to their latest and most debased age.[177] Our illustrious King Edward surpasses all men, as well as his own years and everyone's expectation, in talent, industry, perseverance, and learning. I do not speak from hearsay, but happily have seen it with my own eyes. His mind has become the dwelling-place of a whole troop of virtues. France will, I have no doubt, find out the superior learning of the Duke of Suffolk,[178] and the rest of that noble company of young men who have set out this very day with the king to visit France.

There are many honorable ladies now who surpass Thomas More's daughters in all kinds of learning; but among all of them the brightest star is my illustrious Lady Elizabeth, the king's sister; so that I have no difficulty in finding subject for writing in her praise, but only in setting bounds to what I could write. I will write nothing however which I have not myself witnessed. She had me for her tutor in Greek and Latin two years; but now I am released from the Court and restored to my old literary leisure [at Cambridge], where by her beneficence I hold an honest place in University. It is difficult to say whether the gifts of nature or of fortune are most to be admired in that illustrious lady. What Aristotle describes as excellence is wholly apparent in her—beauty, stature, prudence, and industry.

She has just passed her sixteenth birthday, and shows such dignity and gentleness as are wonderful at her age and in her rank. Her study of true religion and learning is most energetic. Her mind has no womanly weakness, her perseverance is equal to that of a man, and her memory retains as long and

---

174. Adapted from Giles, *The Whole Works of Roger Ascham*, v. 1, pp. lxii–lxiv; and from Hatch, "The Latin Letters of Roger Ascham and John Sturm," pp. 12–7.

175. Walter Haddon (1516–1572) attended King's College, Cambridge University, in the 1530s and studied civil law, earning a rare doctorate.

176. Thomas Smith (1513–1577) earned degrees at the universities of Cambridge and Padua before becoming Professor of Greek and Vice-Chancellor at Cambridge. In his famous work on the constitution and government of England, he wrote the often quoted statement from the liberal arts tradition: "Whosoever studieth the laws of the realm, who studieth in the universities, who professeth liberal sciences, and to be short, who can live idly and without manual labor . . . he shall be called master, the title of which men give to . . . gentlemen, and shall be taken for a gentleman." Thomas Smith, *De Republica Anglorum*, ed. L. Alston (Cambridge: Cambridge University Press, 1906), pp. 39–40.

177. Herodian is apparently a reference to Herodes (fl. 200s B.C.), a Greek poet who often portrayed vulgar situations; Aulus Gellius (c. A.D. 130–c. 180) Roman lawyer, wrote a compendium of quotations and stories; Lucius Apuleius, Latin author of the second century A.D., wrote the only Latin novel to survive to modern time.

178. Henry Brandon (1535–1551) was tutored by John Cheke along with Prince Edward, as described in the introduction above. The early death of both Brandon and Edward "made a remarkable impression on the world." Hatch, "The Latin Letters of Roger Ascham and John Sturm," p. 154.

as much as anyone I know.[179] She speaks French and Italian as well as English: she has often talked to me readily and well in Latin and moderately so in Greek. When she writes Greek and Latin, nothing is more beautiful than her hand-writing.[180] She is as much delighted with music as she is skillful in the art. In adornment she is elegant rather than showy, and by her contempt of gold and headdresses, she reminds one of Hippolyta rather than of Phaedra.[181]

She read with me almost all of Cicero and a great part of Livy, for she drew all her knowledge of Latin from these two authors. She used to give the morning to the Greek Testament, and afternoons to select orations of Isocrates and the tragedies of Sophocles. For I thought that from those sources she might gain purity of style, and her mind derive instruction that would be of value to her to meet every contingency of life. To these I add Saint Cyprian, *The Commonplaces* of Melanchthon, and other similar works of this kind, as best suited, after the Holy Scriptures, to teach her the foundations of religion, together with elegant language and sound doctrine.[182] Whatever she reads she at once perceives any word that has a doubtful or curious meaning. She cannot endure those foolish imitators of Erasmus, who have tied up the Latin tongue in those wretched fetters of proverbs.[183] She likes a style that grows out of the subject; chaste because it is suitable, and beautiful because it is clear. She very much admires modest metaphors, and comparisons of contraries well put together and contrasting felicitously with one another. Her ears are so well practiced in discriminating all these things, and her judgment is so good, that in all Greek, Latin, and English composition, there is nothing so loose on the one hand or so concise on the other, which she does not immediately attend to, and either reject with disgust or receive with pleasure, as the case may be.

I am not inventing anything, my dear Sturm; it is all true: but I only seek to give you an outline of her excellence, and while doing so, I have been pleased to recall to my mind the dear memory of my most illustrious lady. . . .

Roger Ascham to John Cheke (1550), explaining why Ascham left the Court and position as Elizabeth's tutor.

I have always heartily thanked God, and shall do so all my life, for having been allowed by His especial goodwill to spend so large a part of my life at the University of Cambridge, and more particularly, that I should find there such a good friend and such a learned teacher as you. For whatever aids I there obtained, whether moderately bestowed by fortune for the wants of life, or the still more moderate aids of learning for the improvement of my mind, all have originated from your singular and abundant love towards me, and from those sources of learning which for so many years you happily and constantly opened for me by your superior intellect, supplying me thereby both precept, example, and advice.

---

179. How may this thoroughly exceptionalist view of Elizabeth be reconciled with Ascham's acknowledgment above that the number of learned women is increasing?

180. Elizabeth is known among modern scholars for the beautiful handwriting of her youth, in contrast to that of many of her contemporaries.

181. The virtuous Amazonian warrior Hyppolyta bore a son, Hyppolytus, of the Greek mythical hero Theseus, who later married Phaedra, who then tried to seduce her stepson Hyppolytus, as dramatized in the *Hyppolytus* of Euripides.

182. Protestant Reformer and prominent humanist educator Philipp Melanchthon (1497–1560) wrote *Commonplaces of Theological Matters* (1521), the first systematic theology presented by a reformer. Cyprian (c. 200–258) was a teacher of rhetoric and bishop of Carthage.

183. In 1508 Desiderius Erasmus (c. 1466–1536) had published *Adages*, a vast collection of proverbs drawn from classical authors that established his reputation as the leading humanist scholar in northern Europe.

And in proportion as I have found greater pleasure from the frequent recollection, day and night, of that most pleasant life which I enjoyed at College in your company; and from the remembrance of those discourses which we carried on apart in your room, wherein you declared your particular interest in me and led me to place my hopes in you; as well as, lastly, of all your past kindness, which, both at College and at Court, has been abundantly bestowed on me, so now is my present desolation the harder to bear in this late shipwreck which I have suffered, overcome by court violence and wrongs. Though the blame is rather to be laid on my bad fortune than on any fault of my own, certain men have, at a time so unlucky for me, made great endeavors to put an end to your kindness towards me. But wronged as I have been on all sides, I have been chiefly sustained by the fact that by no means could it be so painful to me to be accused to you, through hatred and by false statements, as it would be agreeable to be defended by the silent testimony of your judgment in my behalf: which indeed I easily understood from your words to me the last time I was at Court. I have never yet been led, nor shall I ever be, to fear more from any new calumny of my enemies than to place a firm reliance on your old friendship.

And now this would seem a fit place for me to explain the whole affair of my life at Court and why I left it; and this, indeed, I would willingly do, except that the matter can be more easily explained to you by word of mouth, than by a short letter. Moreover, I do not wish any trust to be placed in my pleading my own cause about matters relating to myself, unless the most weighty testimony of most worthy men has attested to my innocence in all my words and deeds. It is enough that I can bring forward R. and S., an upright man, on behalf of a just cause, to oppose the unjust censures of triflers. But him, the participator in my thoughts and sharer of my fortunes, I bring not forward. But C. and W. have long been known to you as men of mark, and they will neither speak falsely, nor refuse to speak the truth in this matter. If by their testimony all those injuries (with which the storm at Court overwhelmed me), cannot be proved to have sprung from that very source whence I ought rather to have enjoyed the fruits of my occupation than have labored under any fear of offense, then I shall easily put up with the loss of your kindness towards me, from which the whole course of my former life has flowed and a bright hope still shines forth of help on many occasions to occur.

But if you shall discover [anything other than] that I have been injured, without any fault of my mine, not by my most illustrious mistress, but by her steward, I beg of you not to let any letters of men or circumstances prevent you from regarding with that same goodwill and defending your old friend Ascham. And this I wish so much the more because I have never valued your love more than your approbation; and I will labor with all care, diligence, and respect that this may always be so. But now, in this my abject and humble condition, nothing can more excite my hopes than if, next to the king's majesty and my most illustrious mistress (whose favor I should part with most unwillingly), my earnest fidelity and service which you have already sometimes commended may be still of some account and value in your eyes. You will surely not blame this desire of mine, since it arises from nothing else but a certain induction and tendency of a mind for so many years devoted to you.

The other things that I had to write to you about, either concerning settling my life comfortably at the University, or passing two years in studies abroad, to the accomplishment of which I promise myself a little assistance and favor from you, I will shortly explain to you in another letter or, more to the purpose, by word of mouth. . . .

Roger Ascham to John Sturm (1662) assessing Elizabeth's Learning.
But the glory she derives from herself, and the adornments of talent and learning that she possesses, I have described to you in another letter. I will now only state in addition, that neither at Court, nor in the universities, nor among our heads of church or state, are there four of our countrymen who understand Greek better than the Queen herself. When she is reading Demosthenes or Aeschines, I am very

much astonished at seeing her so ably to understand,[184] I do not mean, the force of the words, the structure of the sentences, and the propriety of the language, the ornaments of the oratory, and the harmonious and elegant bearing of the whole discourse; but also, what is of more importance, the feeling and spirit of the speaker, the struggle of the whole debate, the decrees and inclinations of the people, the manners and institutions of every state, and all other matters of this kind.

All her own subjects, and very many foreigners, are witnesses to her proficiency in other languages. I was one day present when she replied at the same time to three ambassadors, the Imperial, French, and Swedish, in three languages: Italian to one, French to the other, Latin to the third; easily, without hesitation, clearly, and without being confused, to the various subjects thrown out, as is usual in their discourse.

§ § §

Modern authorities have been skeptical of Ascham's praise for the Queen's proficiency in classical languages. Evaluating Elizabeth's translations from Boethius in 1593 and from Plutarch and Horace in 1598, one scholar concludes, "In exactitude of translation the three works appear to me to slide down in a descending scale in the order in which they appear, Boethius being indifferent, Plutarch bad, and Horace worse, being in many cases absolutely unintelligible, probably because this was the most difficult of the three. . . . The 'Queen's English' appears to our modern ideas most defective, and her orthography to have been untrammeled by any rules whatsoever." [185]

The reader may wish to compare selection #9 with the opening lines of Queen Elizabeth's rendering of Boethius, *Consolation of Philosophy*, Prose 1:

> While of al this alone in silence I bethought me, and tearesful complaint in stiles office ment, over my hed to stand a woman did apeare of stately face, with flaming yees, of insight above the comun worth of men; of fresche coulor and unwon strength, thogh yet so old she wer, that of our age she seemed not be one; her stature suche as skarse could be desernd. For sume while she skanted her to the comen stature of men, straight she semed with croune of hed the heavens to strike, and lifting up the same hiar, the heavens them selves she enterd, begiling the sight of lokars on. Her eyes they wer of smalist thrides, parfaict for fine workmanship and lasting substance, as, after by her selfe I knewe, was by her handes al wrogt. Whose forme, as to smoky imagis is wont, a certain dimnis of dispised antiquitie overwhelmed. Of thes wides in the loweste skirtz Pi, in the upper side a Theta, was reade, al woven. [186]

---

184. Aeschines (c. 390–c. 314 B.C.) and Demosthenes (c. 384–322 B.C.) were Athenian orators.

185. Caroline Pemberton, *Queen Elizabeth's Englishings* (London: Early English Text Society, 1899), pp. x–xii.

186. Quoted from Pemberton, *Queen Elizabeth's Englishings*, pp. 2–3.

Section V

Humanist, Scholastic, and Sectarian Strains in the Colonial College

In addressing the seventeenth century, this documentary history begins to focus upon the United States and its antecedent colonies. As in Europe, the Protestant sects vied for control of the colleges, because they provided liberal arts education for the clergy and thereby defined religious orthodoxy. As appears in the selections about the colonial colleges that eventually became Harvard, Yale, and Princeton Universities, the religious controversies and battles for institutional control ramified into the curriculum and teaching of the liberal arts. These disputes influenced, for example, the study of natural and moral philosophy and Biblical languages, as well as the response to the pedagogy of the French Protestant Peter Ramus, mentioned below in regard to Harvard College.

Notwithstanding the influence of those sectarian disputes, the content and nature of liberal arts at the colonial colleges largely conformed to the European accommodation between the scholastic *artes liberales* and the *studia humanitatis* that had emerged over the course of the fifteenth and sixteenth centuries. Only in the second half of the eighteenth century did the formal curriculum begin to evidence "modern" influences, as manifested at Princeton in selection #33. Prior to that, the most significant modification in liberal education introduced by the colonial colleges in the future United States was their form of governance.

These colleges represented both a culmination and a transformation of the colleges, halls, and houses, which had begun to appear in the thirteenth century. Lacking authority to grant degrees, these earlier institutions originated as safe domiciles for young students living far from their homeland and for certain groups, particularly the religious orders, seeking to limit the university's authority over their students. This latter motivation became more pronounced in the late fifteenth and sixteenth centuries when the number of colleges, halls, and houses grew enormously, led by those of the Society of Jesus. These extramural domiciles circumvented the authority of the medieval and Renaissance universities in two ways.

On the one hand, some colleges nurtured a different understanding of liberal education by offering informal study in humanistic texts and subjects that were excluded from the statutory liberal arts of universities. On the other hand, most colleges had an extramural form of governance, because they were founded and overseen by groups or individuals outside of the faculties of teaching masters of the universities. Governed by outsiders, the colleges became more responsive to the public and the religious purposes advanced by the non-resident trustees, sometimes called "visitors" in England. These non-resident trustees were usually clergymen or men of affairs concerned about "the education or form of bringing up the child of a gentleman who is to have authority in the public weal," as famously described by Thomas Elyot in 1531.[1] In the American colonies, this collegiate form of governance employing external "governours" was coupled with the power to grant degrees and became the normative model of organization, as seen below in the formation of Harvard College. This organizational

---

1. Thomas Elyot, *The Boke Named "The Governour"* (1531), ed. Henry H. S. Croft, 2 vols. (1883; New York: Burt Franklin, 1967), bk. 1, ch. 4.

model thus became the most significant modification in liberal education introduced by the colonial colleges.

The nine colonial colleges were consequently shaped by both sectarian and public purposes, and this arrangement resulted in the general pattern that these colleges were founded one to a colony in conjunction with the established or predominant Protestant sect in the colony. This general correlation among colony, sect, and college avoided competition for public funds and reduced sectarian bickering to some extent, at least within the college itself. Hence, in Massachusetts the Puritans, who became Congregationalists, founded Harvard College (1636); in Virginia the Anglicans established the College of William and Mary (1693); in Connecticut the Congregationalists, who leaned toward Presbyterianism, founded Yale College (1701). New Jersey was a partial exception, in as much as the dominant Presbyterians split their efforts between Princeton University (1746), founded as the College of New Jersey by English and Scottish Presbyterians, and Queen's College (1766), later Rutgers University, founded by Dutch Reformed Presbyterians. Both of these groups shared virtually the same doctrine and the two colleges nearly merged in 1793. In New York City the Anglicans fought off the Presbyterians to maintain tenuous control over King's College, later Columbia University, in the early years after its founding in 1754. In pluralistic Pennsylvania, an alliance of Presbyterians and Anglicans dominated the future University of Pennsylvania from its chartering in 1755. In anomalous Rhode Island the Baptists founded the future Brown University (1765); and in the northern colony of New Hampshire the Congregationalists established Dartmouth College (1769). Notwithstanding this cooperative pattern among colony, sect, and college, these foundings were rarely harmonious and, particularly after the mid-1700s, were often fraught with disputes among religious parties and between the colonial government and clerical leaders.

Amid these debates, the college founders in the American colonies agreed without question that women were unsuited for liberal education, despite vociferous arguments to the contrary, such as those expressed contemporaneously by Bathsua Makin in England and Juana Inéz de la Cruz in Mexico. While these arguments often defended women's capabilities, this exclusion rested on the fact that liberal education prepared students for public leadership and professional opportunities that were barred to women.

29. Harvard College, *New England's First Fruits* (1643)

INTRODUCTION

Between 1620 and 1646 a relatively large number of Puritans who had studied at Oxford and Cambridge universities emigrated to New England. This group comprised about thirty Oxonians and one hundred Cantabridgians, and from these came the founders and early governors of the first college in the American English colonies. Because of the Puritan character of Cambridge and because of the predominance of its alumni, the New England Puritans looked to the colleges of Cambridge for a model when they sought "to advance learning and perpetuate it to posterity."

That effort formally commenced in 1636 when "a schoale or college" was established by legislative act of the Great and General Court of the Massachusetts Bay Colony. This act of foundation was technically illegal because the colony was a chartered corporation, which, under English law, did not have authority to charter another corporation, such as a college. But it was precisely to escape such restrictions on their efforts to form a godly commonwealth that these Puritans had emigrated to Massachusetts, so the unlawful college was opened for instruction in 1638. This was the same year that a thirty-year-old alumnus of Cambridge and émigré to Massachusetts died, leaving half of his considerable estate and his library to the fledging college. Very little is known of John Harvard or the actual dispensation of the gift, but it is certain that in 1639 the grateful General Court voted to name the institution "Harvard College."

After an inauspicious start under a tyrannical and scurrilous master who was soon dismissed, the college Overseers sought another head and were reportedly refused by Jan Amos Komenský (1592–1670), the famous Moravian educator and bishop and an acquaintance of Bathsua Makin, author of the reading below. The Overseers then settled on Henry Dunster (1609–1659), who had graduated with a B.A. in 1631 and an M.A. in 1634 from Magdalene College, Cambridge University. Beginning in 1640 Dunster served as lone professor and first president of the college until his ouster in 1654 for adopting anti-pedobaptismal principles. Dunster was greatly respected for his knowledge of Middle Eastern languages, which explains the surprising appearance of Hebrew, Aramaic, and Syriac in the early Harvard curriculum.

That curriculum is described in selection #29, drawn from the 26-page pamphlet, *New England's First Fruits*, published in London in 1643. The pamphlet was produced in order to aid a delegation of Puritan ministers sent by Massachusetts in 1641 to solicit support from English sympathizers for the Puritan colony across the Atlantic.[2] Because it was thought that potential supporters would be particularly interested (and reassured) to learn about the founding of a college, Harvard was described in the second part of the pamphlet, which thus became the first publication in the development effort that would ultimately produce the largest university endowment in the world.

This account is the most detailed statement available of the Harvard curriculum during the seventeenth century; and virtually all the subjects listed in the pamphlet are confirmed by other data, indicating that the description is largely reliable, notwithstanding the promotional purpose of the pamphlet. In terms of pedagogy, subjects, and organization, this course of liberal education interwove the scholastic and humanist traditions that the Englishmen had carried across the Atlantic Ocean. In its traditional conception, the scholastic program comprised the "seven liberal arts" (the three verbal arts of grammar, rhetoric, and logic, and the four mathematical arts of arithmetic, geometry, astronomy, and music) and the "three philosophies" (natural, moral, and metaphysical), which were

---

2. This introduction draws upon Samuel E. Morison, *The Founding of Harvard College* (Cambridge, MA: Harvard University Press, 1935).

taught by lectures, recitations, and disputations. This program required four years of study to become a bachelor of arts and three years to become a master of arts. The humanist program, though never codified as formally as the scholastic, comprised the studies of grammar and literature, poetry, history, ethics, and rhetoric, which were taught largely by recitations and declamations. Nearly all of these elements appear below along with attention to the study of scripture that was demanded by the Puritans' religious convictions.

SELECTION[3]

II. In respect of the college,
and the proceedings of learning therein.

1. After God had carried us safe to New England and we had builded our houses, provided necessaries for our livelihood, reared convenient places for God's worship, and settled the civil government, one of the next things we longed for and looked after was to advance learning and perpetuate it to posterity, dreading to leave an illiterate ministry to the churches when our present ministers shall lie in the dust.[4] And as we were thinking and consulting how to effect this great work, it pleased God to stir up the heart of one Mr. *Harvard* (a godly gentleman and a lover of learning there living among us[5]) to give the one half of his estate (it being in all about 1,700 pounds) towards the erecting of a college, and all his library. After him, another gave 300 pounds; others after them cast in more, and the public hand of the state added the rest. The college was, by common consent, appointed to be at Cambridge (a place very pleasant and accommodate) and is called (according to the name of the first founder) Harvard College.

The edifice is very fair and comely within and without, having in it a spacious hall (where they daily meet at commons, lectures, exercises); and a large library with some books to it, the gifts of diverse of our friends; chambers and studies also fitted for and possessed by the students; and all other rooms of office necessary and convenient, with all the needful offices thereto belonging. And by the side of the college [is] a fair grammar school for the training up of young scholars and fitting them for academical learning,[6] that [when] they are judged ripe they may be received into the college of this school. . . . Over the College is Master Dunster placed as president, a learned conscionable and industrious man, who has so trained up his pupils in the tongues and arts and so seasoned them with the principles of divinity and Christianity, that we have to our great comfort (and, in truth, beyond our hopes) beheld their progress in learning and godliness in this also. The former of these has appeared in their public declamations in Latin and Greek, and disputations logical and philosophical, which they have become [accustomed] to make and uphold (besides their ordinary exercises in the college hall) upon set days, constantly once every month, in the audience of the magistrates, ministers, and other scholars, for the probation of their growth in learning.[7] The latter has been manifested in sundry

---

3. *New England's First Fruits With Divers Other Special Matters Concerning That Country* (London, 1643; New York: J. Sabin, 1865), sect. 2: "In respect of the College and the proceedings of Learning therein."

4. Scholars have debated how long—and how strongly—Harvard maintained this primary purpose of educating ministers. Of the 431 graduates from Harvard College during the seventeenth century, 54 percent pursued a career in the ministry, 7 percent in medicine, 3 percent in law, and the rest in a variety of other fields.

5. In this description of John Harvard are merged the three traditions of Christianity, gentility, and learning that had been coalescing for the previous three centuries.

6. In contrast to modern usage, the "grammar school" sat at the apex of the schools below the university.

7. The word order has been modified to facilitate the reading of this sentence. The two pedagogies associated with the two educational traditions—declamations with Renaissance humanism and disputations with scholastic-

of them by the savory breathings of their Spirits in their godly conversation, in so much that we are confident, if these early blossoms may be cherished and warmed with the influence of the friends of learning and lovers of this pious work, they will by the help of God come to happy maturity in a short time.

Over the college are twelve overseers chosen by the General Court,[8] six of them are of the magistrates, the other six of the ministers, who are to promote the best good of it and (having a power of influence into all persons in it) are to see that everyone be diligent and proficient in his proper place.[9]

2. Rules and precepts
that are observed in the college.

i. When any scholar is able to understand Tully,[10] or such like classical Latin author *ex tempore*, and make and speak true Latin in verse and prose [without any assistance],[11] and decline perfectly the paradigms of nouns and verbs in the Greek tongue, let him then and not before be capable of admission into the college.

ii. Let every student be plainly instructed and earnestly pressed to consider well [that] the main end of his life and studies is "to know God and Jesus Christ which is eternal life" (*John* 17: 3). . . .

iii. Everyone shall so exercise himself in reading the Scriptures twice a day, that he shall be ready to give such an account of his proficiency therein, both in theoretical observations of the language and logic and in practical and spiritual truths, as his Tutor[12] shall require according to his ability, seeing "the entrance of the word gives light, it gives understanding to the simple" (*Psalms* 119: 130). . . .

v. That they studiously redeem the time, observe the general hours appointed for all the students, and the special hours for their own classes, and then diligently attend the lectures without any disturbance by word or gesture. And if in anything they doubt, they shall inquire, as of their fellows, so (in case of *non satisfaction*) modestly of their Tutors.

vi. None shall, under any pretense whatever, frequent the company and society of such men as lead an unfit and dissolute life. Nor shall any, without his Tutor's leave or (in his absence) the call of parents or guardians, go abroad to other towns.

vii. Every scholar shall be present in his Tutor's chamber at the seventh hour in the morning, immediately after the sound of the bell, at his opening of his scripture and prayer. So also at the fifth hour at night, and then give account of his own private reading as aforesaid (in particular the third)

---

ism—are incorporated here as are, below, the studies derived from each of those traditions. Note that these are the *public* exercises, whereas the pedagogy predominantly employed in the daily classroom exercises is the recitation. These methods are noted in selection #32 from the Yale College statutes.

8. The General Court was the colonial legislature. Both this legislative authority and the public appropriation for the college indicate that, like the other colonial colleges, Harvard was originally organized more along the lines of what we now conceive as a public institution, rather than a private one.

9. The establishment of an external board of visitors or trustees constituted of men of affairs was a different governance structure than that of the historical *universitas*, which was overseen by the chosen leaders of this academic guild.

10. The conventional nickname given to Marcus Tullius Cicero.

11. By the 1640s, the usage of and facility in Latin was rapidly eroding; and the requirement to speak only Latin disappears at Yale between 1748 and 1774, as seen in selection #32 from the Yale College statutes.

12. Tutors were recent graduates of the college who stayed on to act as teaching assistants and, as indicated here, to oversee the academic progress and personal conduct of the students.

and constantly attend lectures in the Hall at the hours appointed. But if any (without necessary impediment) shall absent himself from prayer or lectures, he shall be liable to admonition, if he offend above once a week.

viii. If any scholar shall be found to transgress any of the laws of God or of the school, after twice admonition, he shall be liable, if not *adultus*, to correction; if adultus, his name shall be given up to the Overseers of the college that he may be admonished at the public monthly Act.[13]

3. The times and order of their studies,
unless experience shall show cause to alter.[14]

The second and third day of the week,[15] read lectures, as follows.[16] [Morning.] To the first year at eight of the clock in the morning: Logic the first three quarters, Physics the last quarter. To the second year, at the ninth hour: Ethics and Politics, at convenient distances of time. To the third year at the tenth: Arithmetic and Geometry, the three first quarters, Astronomy the last.[17] Afternoon. The first year disputes at the second hour. The second year at the third hour. The third year at the fourth everyone in his Art.[18]

The fourth day reads Greek. [Morning.] To the first year Etymology, Syntax at the eighth hour. To the second at the ninth hour: Prosody[19] and Dialectics. Afternoon. The first year at second hour practice the precepts of Grammar in such authors as have variety of words. The second year at third hour practice in Poetry . . .[20] The third year perfect their theory before noon, and exercise Style, Composition, Imitation, Epitome, both in prose and verse, afternoon.

The fifth day reads Hebrew and the eastern tongues. [Morning.] Grammar to the first year hour the eighth. To the second Chaldee[21] at the ninth hour. To the third Syriack at the tenth hour.

---

13. "Correction" denotes corporal punishment. The age of becoming *adultus* was customarily eighteen. Most of the students at this time were younger.

14. Dunster was apparently trying to follow the methods recommended by the French Protestant educator Peter Ramus (1515–1572), who insisted that one subject be studied each day. "During the first hour, the teacher should lecture on the topic of the day, giving underlying principles and essential explanations, but little or no dictation. During the next two hours the scholars individually work over the subject-matter of the lecture. At the fourth hour the class recite to the teacher, in order to make certain that they understand the lecture—a survival of the medieval repetition. During the last two hours the students discuss and dispute, in order to practice and apply independently what they have learned." Samuel E. Morison, *Harvard College in the Seventeenth Century*, 2 parts (Cambridge, MA: Harvard University Press, 1936), pt. 1, p. 140. The times of these various sessions are staggered by hour and class because the one professor, Dunster, delivered or supervised them all.

15. The first day of the week was Sunday.

16. These lectures followed generally the medieval pattern described in selection #21. Compare the lectures at Dartmouth College in the 1850s in selection #38.

17. The remnants of the quadrivium appear here for one hour in the final year.

18. Although the pamphlet indicates that the bachelor's course was completed in three years, this anomalous term was converted to the customary four-year term within a decade.

19. Prosody refers to poetical meter or versification.

20. This subject consisted of Biblical books in verse.

21. "Chaldee" is now identified as Aramaic, which was the language of the books of *Ezra* and *Daniel* in Henry Dunster's personal copy of the *Bible*.

Afternoon. The first year practice in the *Bible* at the second hour. The second in *Ezra* and *Daniel* at the third hour. The third at the fourth hour in Trost's *New Testament*.[22]

The sixth [day] reads Rhetoric to all at the eighth hour. Declamations at the ninth. So ordered that every scholar may declaim once a month. The rest of the day [is left to the study of rhetoric.]

The seventh day reads divinity catechetical at the eighth hour, common places at the ninth hour.[23] Afternoon. The first [year] reads history in the winter. The nature of plants in the summer. The sum of every lecture shall be examined, before the new lecture be read.

Every scholar, that on proof is found able to read the original of the Old and New Testament into the Latin tongue, and to resolve them logically, with all being of Godly life and conversation, and at any public act has the approbation of the Overseers and Master of the College, is fit to be dignified with his [B.A.] degree.

Every scholar that gives up in writing a system or synopsis[24] or sum of logic, natural and moral philosophy, arithmetic, geometry, and astronomy, and is ready to defend his theses or positions, withal skilled in the originals as above said and of Godly life and conversation, and so approved by the Overseers and master of the college, at any public act is fit to be dignified with his [M.A.] degree.[25]

4. The manner of the late commencement expressed in a letter
sent over from the governor and diverse of the ministers . . .

The students of the first class that have been these four years [1638–1642] trained up in university-learning (for their ripening in the knowledge of the tongues and arts) and are approved for their manner (as they have kept their public acts in former years, ourselves being present at them) have lately kept two solemn acts for their commencement, when the Governor, Magistrates, and the Ministers from all parts, with all sorts of scholars and others in great numbers, were present and did hear their exercises (which were Latin and Greek orations and declamations; and Hebrew analysis, grammatical, logical and rhetorical of the *Psalms*; and their answers and disputations in logical, ethical, physical and metaphysical questions) and so were found worthy of the first degree, commonly called bachelor, "according to the practices of the Universities in England"[26]: being first presented by the president to the Magistrates [and] Ministers; and by him, upon their approbation, solemnly

---

22. This was a Syriac version of the New testament published by Martin Trost (1588–1636), a professor in German universities.

23. Compare the description of "commonplacing" by Ignatius Loyola (para. 376) in selection #26.

24. Comprising some thirty pages, such a "system" or "synopsis" set forth a logical outline of an academic discipline or a branch of philosophy, usually following Peter Ramus's model presenting a succession of dichotomies branching out like a decision tree. Compare Ignatius Loyola (para. 388) in selection #26.

25. Whereas the requirements for the B.A. prescribe a Puritanized version of the humanistic studies, the requirements for the M.A. reflect the scholastic, philosophical side of the liberal education, and comport closely with Ignatius Loyola (paras. 351, 451) in selection #26. However, this second half of the liberal arts course had, by this time, been reduced to writing a thirty-page "system." By the beginning of the eighteenth century this requirement was further reduced to merely the passage of time and the M.A. was granted "in course," as seen in the catalog of Dartmouth College in selection #38.

26. *pro more academiarum in Anglia*. It had long been customary for European universities of the same rank to credit each other's degrees, and this phrase indicates the desire of Massachusetts' Puritans that Oxford and Cambridge would credit and legitimate the degrees of Harvard, particularly given the illegality of the college's foundation.

admitted unto the same degree, and a book of arts delivered into each of their hands and power given them to read lectures in the hall upon any of the arts,[27] when they shall be thereunto called, and a liberty of studying in the library.

All things in the college are at present, like to proceed even as we can wish, may it but please the Lord to go on with his blessing in Christ and stir up the hearts of his faithful and able servants in our own native country and here (as he has graciously begun) to advance this honorable and most hopeful work. The beginnings whereof and progress hitherto (generally) do fill our hearts with comfort and raise them up to much more expectation of the Lord's goodness for hereafter, for the good of prosperity, and the churches of Christ Jesus.

Boston in New England, September the 26, 1642. Your very loving friends, etc.

A copy of the questions given and maintained by the commencers
in their public acts, printed in Cambridge in New England,
and reprinted here verbatim as follows.[28]

To the . . . faithful inspectors of Harvard College of New Cambridge, and to other magistrates and vigilant Elders of the Churches of that colony, it is these philological and philosophical theses, which, with God leading, under the presidency of Henry Dunster, these young men, initiated into the liberal arts, will attempt publicly and manfully to fight for, and dedicate and consecrate for the sake of honor and observance. . . .[29]

Philological Theses[30]

Grammatical

The knowledge of languages is very useful.

Letters do not express as much as the vocal organs project.

Hebrew is the mother of languages.

The Latin language is the most eloquent.

Rhetorical

Rhetoric differs from logic at the level of species.

In elocution ornament is less important than perspicuity; abundance is less important than ornament.

It is proper for an orator to conceal art.

Logical

Universals do not exist outside the intellect.

All arguments are relative.

That cause expressing necessary preconditions [*sine qua non*] is a unique cause distinct from the four general [Aristotelian] causes remaining.

---

27. This provision is in keeping with the original policy of the European universities that admittance to the degree and, therefore, the guild of masters of arts entitled one to the "license to teach" in the *studium*.

28. The balance of this reading is adapted from a new translation of the Latin by J. Albert Dragstedt. The categories of the following theses recall the traditional subjects of liberal education, which roughly correlate with the subjects studied in the bachelor's program above.

29. These words seem to echo the chivalric tradition that informed selection #14 by Peter Abelard. The early Harvard students, who were generally born in England, graduated at an older age than those in later classes, who were generally born in the colonies.

30. The meaning of the adjective *philologica* has now become narrower than *Philologia* in selection #8 by Martianus Capella. Only a few of the Latin theses are translated here.

The cause and its effect exist simultaneously.
The precepts of art ought to be particular to each, absolute, and universal in the primary sense.

Philosophical Theses
  Ethical
    Practical philosophy is the goal of erudition.
    Action is higher than the habit of virtue.
    The will is subject to moral virtue.
    The will is formally free.
    Modesty is the highest ornament for a youth.
  Physical
    The subject of Physics is the natural, moveable body.
    Secondary matter cannot exist without a form.
    The form is accident.
    What is perceived violently destroys the sensing organ.
  Metaphysical
    Each thing is good.
    Every created thing is composite.
    Whatever is eternal is also without measure.
    The metaphysical good does not admit of gradations.[31]

31. Is it true that "the theory underlying [Harvard's] program of 1642 was directly or indirectly derived from St. Augustine's *On Christian Learning*?" Arthur O. Norton, *Harvard Text-Books and Reference Books of the Seventeenth Century* (Boston: Colonial Society of Massachusetts, 1935), p. 8n.

30. Bathsua Makin, *Essay to Revive the Ancient Education of Gentlewomen* (1673)

INTRODUCTION

Bathsua Makin (c. 1600—c. 1675), "the first Englishwoman to recommend a systematic program of advanced education for females,"[32] was the daughter of Henry Reginald, a middle-class schoolmaster who lived on the outskirts of London. In about 1600 his wife gave birth to a daughter who was christened Bathsua, an abbreviated form of Bathsheba. As in the case of Christine de Pizan and Laura Cereta, "the father was an especially important figure" in his daughter's life.[33] Doubtlessly encouraged by the example of Queen Elizabeth I, described in selection #28, Henry Reginald gave Bathsua an unusually thorough education and affinity for letters.

Bathsua excelled as a student and, commencing at about age 15, as a teacher in her father's school. Famously accomplished in languages, Bathsua published her first work at the age of sixteen: a sixteen-page booklet of poems and epigraphs written in English, French, Latin, Greek, and Hebrew, praising King James I and his relatives. This work "repeatedly emphasizes the author's virginity, with the implication that a married woman should have no time for such endeavors."[34] However conservative her views in this writing, Bathsua adopted the unorthodox pedagogical practices that her father gathered from prominent Protestant reformers of education, who established the Dissenting Academies that later influenced the founders of Princeton University. These practices included avoiding rote drilling in the grammar of classical languages, teaching modern languages and applied subjects, incorporating experience as a medium of instruction, and expanding access to education.

In 1622 Bathsua Reginald married Richard Makin, a servant in the household of King James I. Over the next twenty years, she gave birth to eight children, while managing the family's household and expanding her network of ties to learned men and women throughout Europe. In 1640 this network helped to arrange her appointment as tutor to the youngest daughter of King Charles I (1600–1649). But her bright future darkened when her husband was defrauded by a court official, leaving the family impoverished. Frequent appeals to King Charles I went unheeded. By the 1650s Bathsua and several of her small children were living without her husband in a run-down house in London. In order to make ends meet, Bathsua continued teaching, tutoring, and drawing on her network of learned acquaintances.

In about 1670 Makin and Mark Lewis, a schoolmaster and author of textbooks, opened a school for boys and girls. The seventy-year-old Makin and much younger Lewis offered "all things ordinarily taught [gentlewomen] in other schools . . . dancing, music, singing, writing, keeping accounts," as well as the liberal arts and sciences, normally reserved for boys. In order to publicize their project, Makin published an advertising pamphlet that makes the case for educating women liberally. Her audience included the prominent Protestant reformers in education to whom the leaders of the colonial colleges attended. For example, in about 1650 she had the opportunity to meet the well-known Czech educational reformer, Jan Amos Komenský (1592–1670), shortly after he was offered

---

32. Moira Ferguson, "Bathsua Pell Makin (1608?–1675?)," in *First Feminists, British Women Writers, 1578–1799*, ed. Moira Ferguson (Bloomington: Indiana University Press, 1985), p. 128. Until recently, Makin had been identified as the sister of John Pell, a prominent seventeenth-century mathematician, and of Thomas Pell, a soldier who emigrated to the American colony of Connecticut.

33. Frances Teague, *Bathsua Makin: Woman of Learning* (Lewisburg, PA: Bucknell University Press, 1998), p. 27. Material for this biography is drawn from this source.

34. Teague, *Bathsua Makin*, p. 42.

the presidency of Harvard College. Komenský subsequently influenced the textbooks written by Mark Lewis, the co-founder of Makin's coeducational school.

Due to Makin's frequently deferential tone and expressed acquiescence to the subordinate station and role of women, feminist scholars of the late twentieth century generally interpreted Makin's essay as "overcautious"[35] and "proto-feminist," being compromised by "ritual invocations of masculine superiority"[36] and "shifting away from and back into the dominant ideology."[37] In this way, Makin may be employing both wisdom and subtle irony in order to argue her case as effectively as possible in a public forum of the time. By this view, what distinguishes Makin from other advocates of educating women is not docility, but that she was promoting an institution for the public. Whatever the judgment about Makin's feminism, she was incontestably the most profound advocate for the higher education of women during her time.

Following the publication of her essay, Makin's life becomes obscure. Nothing is known about the fate of her school, how long she taught, or when or where she died.

SELECTION[38]

Your great question is whether to breed up women in arts and tongues is not a mere new device, never before practiced in the world. This you doubt the more because women are of low parts and not capable of improvement by this education. If they could be improved, you doubt whether it would benefit them. If it would benefit them, you enquire where such education may be had, or whether they must go to school with boys? to be made twice more impudent than learned?[39] At last you muster up a legion of objections. I shall speak distinctly to your questions, and then answer your objections.

Women have formerly been educated
in arts and tongues.

Little is recorded concerning the manner how women were educated formerly. You can expect my proof to be only topical and by circumstances.[40] It does appear out of sacred writ that women were

---

35. Teague, *Bathsua Makin*, p. 93. Teague presents a balanced assessment of these views in pp. 93–9..

36. Mitzi Myers, "Domesticating Minerva: Bathsua Makin's 'Curious' Argument for Women's Education," *Studies in Eighteenth-Century Culture* 14 (1985): 174, 175.

37. Catherine Sharrock, "De-ciphering Women and De-scribing Authority: The Writings of Mary Astell," pp. 109–124, in *Women, Writing, and History 1640–1740*, ed. Isobel Grundy and Susan Wiseman (Athens: University of Georgia Press, 1992), p. 121.

38. Bathsua Reginald Makin, *An Essay to Revive the Ancient Education of Gentlewomen, in Religion, Manners, Arts and Tongues with an Answer to the Objections against this Way of Education* (London: J.D. to be sold by Thomas Parkhurst, 1673), pp. 8–42. Makin's essay adopts the form of a reply to a letter stating the conventional arguments against giving women any advanced or academic education.

39. Note Makin's systematic organization, which is carried through the essay. These four questions are addressed successively—the last in an excised postscript advertising Makin's school. Compare the literary conventions and flourishes of Juana Inéz de la Cruz in selection #31.

40. Some feminist scholars in the late twentieth century have dismissed Bathsua's ensuing historical account of learned women as "a primitive variety of women's history" [Myers, "Domesticating Minerva," p. 185] or "forced and . . . based on inferences" indicating "the tenuous nature of her historical proof" [Jean R. Brink, "Bathsua Makin: Scholar and Educator of the Seventeenth Century," *International Journal of Women's Studies* (1978): 421] because "it simply lists and makes no attempt to analyze the quality of its exemplars, many of whom are

employed in most of the great transactions that happened in the world, even in reference to religion. Miriam seems to be next to Moses and Aaron; she was a great poet and philosopher, for both learning and religion were generally in former times wrapped up in verse [*Exodus* 15: 20–1.] The women met David singing triumphant songs, composed (it's likely by themselves) a great specimen of liberal education [1 *Samuel* 18: 6–7.] Deborah, the deliverer of Israel, was without all doubt a learned woman, that understood the law [*Judges* 5: 2–31]. . . . In the New Testament we find Anna a prophetess [*Luke* 2: 36–8.] Paul (*Romans* 16: 1) commends unto them Phoebe, who was not only a servant of Christ but a [deaconess] of the church at Cenchreae. He tells us Tryphaena, Tryphosa and Persis labored much in the Lord (*Romans* 16: 12.) Priscilla instructed Apollos [*Acts* 18: 25–6]. . . .

We may infer from the stories of the Muses that this way of education was very ancient. All conclude the heroes were men, famous in their generation, therefore canonized after their deaths. We may, with like reason, conclude Minerva and the nine Muses were women famous for learning while they lived and therefore thus adored when dead.[41] There is no question the Greeks and Romans, when most flourishing, did thus educate their daughters, [because] so many among them were famous for learning . . .[42] There was a contest between twenty Grecian and twenty Roman ladies, which were most excellent in learning. The Roman dames were the best orators: but the Grecian ladies the best philosophers.[43] This plainly shows they both were instructed in all kind of good literature.

Women educated in arts and tongues
have been eminent in them.

I should be too tedious if I should commemorate all upon record that have been smatterers in learning. I shall only mention some few ladies that have been equal to most men.[44]

It is reported of Zenobia, queen of Palmeria, that she was not only excellent herself in arts and arms, but learning in her (like light in the sun) influenced her whole people, only famous in her days.[45] Olympia Fulvia Maurata, tutress to the Empress of Germany, understood French, Latin, Dutch; she was so good a Grecian that she read public lectures in that language. She was also reputed to be

---

inadequately described. The catalog is put together from other catalogs rather than from primary research into the women it names." Teague, *Bathsua Makin*, p. 96.

41. By making this analogy to men's history, Makin bolsters Christine de Pizan's argument in selection #12, that myth has a foundation in historical truth.

42. Nine lines of passing references to twenty-three learned women from the Old Testament, the New Testament, classical antiquity, and early Christian history are omitted.

43. Having given examples of educated women, Makin concludes with an example recalling the longstanding distinction between two traditions of liberal education and between the preferences of Greek and Roman culture for those traditions. See Cicero (III 69) in selection #4 and Martiánus Cappella (IV 334–335) in selection #8.

44. Again, Makin's tone and stated claim are deferential and modest.

45. Zenobia (d. c. 272), ruler of Palmyra in central Syria, was known for her intelligence and military leadership. Portrayals of Zenobia appear also in selection #12 by Christine de Pizan, in selection #27 by Laura Cereta, and in Giovanni Boccaccio, *Concerning Famous Women*, tr. Guido A. Guarino (New Brunswick, NJ: Rutgers University Press, 1963), XCVIII, pp. 226–30.

well skilled in divinity.[46] The Lady Jane Grey excelled Maurata in this; she understood the Hebrew also. . . .[47]

I thought of Queen Elizabeth first, but purposely mention her last as the crown of all. How learned she was, the world can testifie. It was usual for her to discourse with foreign agents in their own languages. Mr. Ascham, her tutor, used to say she read more Greek in a day then many of the doctors of her time did Latin in a week.[48] You see some women have been good proficients in most kinds of learning. I shall now show you how they have been excellent in some particular parts of it, as the tongues, oratory, philosophy, divinity, and lastly poetry. . . .

Care ought to be taken by us to educate women in learning.[49]

That I may be more distinct in what I intend, I shall distinguish of women. Women are of two sorts: RICH (of good natural parts), POOR (of low parts)[50]

I do not mean that it is necessary to the essence, to the subsistence, or to the salvation of women to be thus educated. Those that are mean in the world have not an opportunity for this education. Those that are of low parts, though they have opportunity, cannot reach this: "Minerva cannot be made out of wood."[51] My meaning is, persons that God has blessed with the things of this world, that have competent natural parts, ought to be educated in knowledge. That is, it is much better they should spend the time of their youth to be competently instructed in those things usually taught to gentlewoman at schools, and the overplus of their time to be spent in gaining arts and tongues and useful knowledge, rather than to trifle away so many precious minutes merely to polish their hands and feet, to curl their Locks, to dress and trim their bodies, and in the meantime to neglect their souls and not at all, or very little, to endeavor to know God, Jesus Christ, themselves, and the things of nature, arts and tongues subservient to these. I do not deny but women ought to be brought up to a comely and decent carriage, to their needle, to neatness, to understand all those things that do particularly belong to their sex. But when these things are competently cared for and where there are endowments of nature and leisure, then higher things ought to be endeavored after.[52]

Merely to teach gentlewomen to frisk and dance, to paint their faces, to curl their hair, to put on a [scarf], to wear gay clothes is not truly to adorn but to adulterate their bodies, yea (what is worse) to defile their souls. This (like Circe's cup) turns them to beasts. While their belly is their God, they become swine; while lust, they become goats; and while pride is their God, they become very devils.[53]

Doubtless this under-breeding of woman began among heathen and barbarous people; it continues with the Indians, where they make their women mere slaves and wear them out in drudgery.[54] It is

---

46. Olympia Fulvia Maurata [or Morata] (1526–1555) excelled in her classical education received as the daughter of a tutor in the court of Ferrara. Converting to Protestantism like her father, she married a young German physician and died in Heidelberg, leaving few writings.

47. See the discussion of Lady Grey in selection #28 about Queen Elizabeth.

48. See selection #28 about Queen Elizabeth.

49. Makin now turns to her second purpose: demonstrating the value of liberally educating women.

50. In Makin's view, what is the relationship between social class and natural ability?

51. The source of Makin's Latin epigram has not been identified; the metaphor likely refers to the statue of Athena, or Minerva, standing in the Parthenon in Athens.

52. Compare Bathsua's view on "endowments of nature and leisure" to Aristotle's in selection #3.

53. Homer, *Odyssey* X 140–270.

54. Makin likely draws this view from travelers' popular accounts about India.

practiced among degenerate and apostate Christians upon the same score and now is a part of their religion. It would therefore be a piece of reformation to correct it, and it would notably countermine them who fight against us, as Satan against Adam, by seducing our women, who then easily seduce their husbands.[55]

Had God intended women only as a finer sort of cattle, he would not have made them reasonable. Brutes a few degrees higher than mandrils or monkeys (which the Indians use to do many offices) might have better fitted some men's lust, pride, and pleasure; especially those that desire to keep them ignorant to be tyrannized over.

God intended woman as a help-meet to man in his constant conversation and in the concerns of his family and estate when he should most need, in sickness, weakness, absence, death, etc. While we neglect to fit them for these things, we renounce God's blessing [that] he has appointed women for, are ungrateful to him, cruel to them, and injurious to ourselves. I remember a discourse in Erasmus between an Abbot and a learned woman.[56] She gives many good reasons why women should be learned: that they might know God, their savior, understand his sacred word, and admire him in his wonderful works; that they might also better administer their household affairs among a multitude of servants, who would have more reverence towards them because they were above [the servants] in understanding. Further, she found a great content in reading good authors at spare times. He gives her one answer to all this: *that women would never be kept in subjection if they were learned*, as he found by experience among his monks. Of all things in the world he hated nothing so much as a learned monk, who would always be contradicting his superior from the decretals out of Peter and Paul. He cared not if all his monks were turned into swine, so long as they would be obedient and not disturb him in his pleasures.

Doubtless if that generation of sots (who deny more polite learning to women) would speak out they would tell you: If women should be permitted arts, they would be wiser than [men] (a thing not to be endured) [and] they would never be such tame fools and very slaves as now [men] make them. Therefore, it is a wicked mischievous thing to revive the ancient custom of educating them. Seeing nature produces women of such excellent parts that they do often equalize, sometimes excel men in what ever they attempt, what reason can be given why they should not be improved? . . .[57]

If any desire distinctly to know, what they should be instructed in?

I answer: I cannot tell where to begin to admit women nor from what part of learning to exclude them in regard of their capacities. The whole encyclopedia of learning may be useful some way or other to them.[58] Respect indeed is to be had to the nature and dignity of each art and science, as they are more or less subservient to religion, and may be useful to them in their station. I would not deny them the knowledge of grammar and rhetoric because they dispose to speak handsomely. Logic must be allowed because it is the key to all sciences. Physic, especially, visibles as herbs, plants, shrubs, drugs, etc., must be studied because this will exceedingly please themselves and fit them to be helpful to others. The tongues ought to be studied, especially the Greek and Hebrew; these will enable to the

---

55. Makin invokes the spirit of religious conflict between Protestants and Catholics and between Puritans and the "established" Church of England.

56. Desiderius Erasmus, "The Abbot and the Learned Lady" (1524).

57. What prompts Makin here to adopt a more radical tone and view?

58. This liberality in curriculum demonstrates the influence of the Protestant Dissenters, whose academies inspired American colonial colleges, such as Princeton, to broaden the curriculum in the late eighteenth century.

better understanding of the scriptures. The mathematics, more especially geography,[59] will be useful; this puts life into history. Music, painting, poetry, etc., are a great ornament and pleasure.

Some things that are more practical are not so material because public employments in the field and courts are usually denied to women. Yet some [women] have not been inferior to many men even in these things also[60]. . . . In these late times, there are several instances of women, when their husbands were serving their king and country, defended their houses and did all things as soldiers, with prudence and valor, like men. They appeared before committees and pleaded their own causes with good success.[61]

This kind of education will be very useful to women.

1. The profit will be to themselves. In general they will be able to understand, read, write, and speak their mother-tongue, which they cannot well do without this. They will have something to exercise their thoughts about, which are busy and active. Their quality ties them at home; if learning be their companion, delight and pleasure will be their attendants, for there is no pleasure greater, nor more suitable to an ingenious mind, than what is found in knowledge. It is the first fruits of heaven and a glimpse of that glory we afterwards expect. There is in all an innate desire of knowing, and the satisfying this is the greatest pleasure. Men are very cruel that give them leave to look at a distance, only to know they do not know; to make any thus to tantalize, is a great torment.[62]

This will be a hedge against heresies. Men are furnished with arts and tongues for this purpose, that they may stop the mouths of their adversaries. And women ought to be learned, that they may stop their ears against seducers. It cannot be imagined so many persons of quality would be so easily carried aside with every wind of doctrine, had they been furnished with these defensive arms. I mean, had they been instructed in the plain rules of artificial reasoning, so as to distinguish a true and forcible argument from a vain and captious fallacy. . . .

More particularly, persons of higher quality, for want of this education, have nothing to employ themselves in and are forced to cards, dice, plays, and frothy romances merely to drive away the time; whereas knowledge in arts and tongues would pleasantly employ them and upon occasion benefit others. Seneca, endeavoring to comfort his mother Helvia in her affliction when he was under banishment, suggests to her that she had been liberally brought up and might now have an opportunity to be farther improved and might comfort herself in the study of philosophy[63]. . . .

---

59. The continued interchanging of geography for geometry reflects the treatment by Martianus Capella (VI 588) in selection #8.

60. While seeming to acquiesce to women's exclusion from public employment, Makin then implicitly challenges the exclusion by presenting counterexamples.

61. See selection #35 by Emma Willard.

62. The pleasure, or happiness, to be enjoyed from learning is discussed, or represented, by Aristotle in selection #3, Martianus Capella in selection #8, and Pier Paolo Vergerio in selection #25.

63. See selection #5 by Seneca the Younger, who wrote to Helvia, "I would lead you to the place for all those fleeing misfortune: to liberal studies. These will heal your wounds and remove all your sadness. To these you should now attend, even if you had never done so previously, although you did not learn them thoroughly and became acquainted with the liberal arts only so far as my father's traditional reservations permitted." Kimball's translation of "Dialogue to Helvia, His Mother, On Consolation" in *Twelve Books of Dialogues*, ed. L. D. Reynolds (Oxford: Clarendon Press, 1977), sect. XII, pt. 17.

More particularly, women are unmarried, married, widows.[64] As for unmarried persons who are able to subsist without [employment], they have a fairer opportunity than men, if they continue long in that estate, to improve the principles they have sucked in and to ripen the seeds of learning which have been sown in their minds in their tender years. Besides, this will be an honest and profitable diversion to possess their minds to keep out worse thoughts. Maids that cannot subsist without [employment] may, as servants, choose their places to attend upon honorable persons, or to be employed in nurseries [and], by their conversation, to teach tongues to children while carried in arms who, perhaps when they find their own feet, will not abide the tedium of a school. The famous Lord Montagu was thus improved to the amazement of all, which made him ever after hate all pedantic education.[65] Julius Caesar also received such a tincture while he was in the nursery, [so] that he was the reviver of the purity of the Latin tongue in his days.

Married persons, by virtue of this education, may be very useful to their husbands in their trades, as the women are in Holland, and to their children by timely instructing them before they are fit to be sent to school, as was the case of Caesar and the Lord Montagu.

I need not show how any persons thus brought up, if they happen to be widows, will be able to understand and manage their own affairs.

2. Women thus educated will be beneficial to their relations. . . . How many families have been ruined by this one thing, the bad education of women? Because the men find no satisfactory converse or entertainment at home, out of mere weariness they seek abroad; hence they neglect their business, spend their estates, destroy their bodies, and oftentimes damn their souls. . . . Many learned men, having married wives of excellent parts, have themselves instructed them in all kinds of learning, the more to fit them for their converse and to endear them and their society to them and to make them admired by others. The woman is the glory of the man. We joy in our children when eminent and in our wives when excellent, either in body or mind. . . .

3. Women thus instructed will be beneficial to the nation. Look into all history. Those nations ever were, now are, and always shall be, the worst of nations, where women are most undervalued, as in Russia, Ethiopia, and all the barbarous nations of the world. One great reason why our neighbors the Dutch have thrived to admiration is the great care they take in the education of their women, from whence they are to be accounted more virtuous and, to be sure, more useful than any women in the world. We cannot expect otherwise to prevail against the ignorance, atheism, prophaneness, superstition, idolatry, lust that reigns in the nation, than by a prudent, sober, pious, virtuous education of our daughters. Their learning would stir up our sons, whom God and nature hath made superior, to a just emulation.

Had we a sufficient number of females thus instructed to furnish the nurseries of the noble families, their children might be improved in the knowledge of the learned tongues before they were aware. I mention this a third time because it is of such moment and concern. . . .

Before I mention the objections, I shall state the propositions I have endeavored to prove. That which I intend is this: that persons of competent natural parts, indifferently inclined and disposed to learn-

64. "Makin continues her categorization of women, showing that education will benefit every woman, no matter what her personal situation is. She starts with the standard early modern categories; each woman was either a maid, wife or widow." Teague, *Bathsua Makin*, p. 133.

65. This likely refers to Makin's contemporary the English admiral Edward Montagu, first Earl of Sandwich, (1625–1672).

ing, whom God has blessed with estates [and who] are not encumbered in the world but have liberty and opportunity in their childhood and, afterwards, being competently instructed in all things now useful that concern them as women,[66] may and ought to be improved in more polite learning, in religion, arts, and the knowledge of things, in tongues also as subservient to these, rather than to spend the over-plus time of their youth in making points for bravery, in dressing and trimming themselves like Bartholomew-babies, in painting and dancing, in making flowers of colored straw, and in building Houses of stained paper, and such like vanities.[67]

Objection. Nobody means gentlewomen should be thus educated in matters of mere vanity, but in practicing their needle, in knowing and doing those things that concern good housewifery, which is women's particular qualification. Answer. I know not what may be meant, but I see what is generally done. In most schools for educating this sex, little more is proposed by the undertakers or expected by the parents. As far as I can observe, the less any thing of solidity is taught, the more such places are frequented. I do acknowledge, in the state of the question, that women should be accomplished in all those things that concern them as women. My meaning is [that] the over-plus time maybe employed in polishing their minds with the knowledge of such things as may be honorable, pleasant and profitable to them and their relations afterwards. . . .

Objection: If we bring up our daughters to learning, no persons will adventure to marry them. Answer: 1. Many men, silly enough, (God knows) think themselves wise, and will not [hesitate] to marry a wise woman. 2. As some Husbands, debauched themselves, desire their wives should be chaste and their children virtuous, so some men, sensible of their own want (caused by their parents neglect) will choose a learned woman in whom they may glory and by whose prudence their defect may be supplied. 3. Learned men, to be sure, will choose such the rather because they are suitable. Some men marrying wives of good natural parts, have improved themselves in arts and tongues, the more to fit them for their converse. 4. Many women have formerly been preferred for this very thing. . . .

Objection: It is against custom to educate gentlewomen thus. Answer: Bad customs ought to be broken, or else many good things would never come into use. I have shown this is a heathenish custom, or a worse, continued amongst us upon very bad grounds. . . .

Objection: Women are of ill natures and will abuse their education. They will be proud and not obey their husbands: they will be pragmatic and boast of their parts and improvements. The ill nature that is in them will become more wicked, the more wit you furnish them with. Answer: This is the killing objection, and every thick-skulled fellow that babbles this out thinks no Billingsgate woman[68] can answer it. I shall take the objection in pieces. 1. "They will abuse learning." So do men. He is egregiously simple that argues against the use of a necessary or very convenient thing from the abuse of it. By this argument, no men should be liberally brought up, strong drinks should never be used any more in the world, and a hundred such like things. 2. "They are of ill natures." This is an impudent calumny—as if the whole of the sex of women, or the greatest part of them, had that malice infused

---

66. Note Makin's cautious qualifications.

67. "Making points for bravery" means "making lace to decorate their dresses and make them 'brave' or fine." "Bartholomew babies were dolls sold at the annual St. Bartholomew's fair in London." "Stained paper" is colored paper. Teague, *Bathsua Makin*, p. 164n51.

68. "A woman using coarse and [vulgar] language, like one of the woman vendors in Billingsgate market." Teague, *Bathsua Makin*, p. 164n56.

into their very natures and constitutions that they are ordinarily made worse by that education that makes men generally better: "Faithful study of the liberal arts Softens one's manner and makes it be not arrogant"[69]. . . .

Objection: The end of learning is public business, which women are not capable of. They must not speak in the church, and it is more proper for men to act in the commonwealth than they. Answer: They may not speak in church, but they may inquire of their husbands at home.[70] It is private instruction I plead for, not public employment.[71] Yet there is no such contradiction in the terms: Miriam and Deborah were extraordinarily called forth by God, as well as Aaron and Barak. Sometimes women may have occasions for public business, as widows and wives when their husbands are absent, but especially persons born to government. The Salique law has not prevailed all the world over,[72] and good reason too, for women upon thrones have been as glorious in their governance as many men, as I have showed before. . . .

Objection: Women do not desire learning. Answer: Neither do many boys, as schools are now ordered, yet I suppose you do not intend to lay fallow all children, that will not bring forth fruit of themselves, to forebear to instruct those which at present do not thank you for it. But I have said there is in all an innate desire of knowing, in women as well as men. If the ways to the temple of [Athena] be so tedious and intricate that they confound or tire her servants, or if you dress up learning in such an ugly and monstrous shape that you afright children, I have nothing to say to such, but that they should reform their schools or else all will think they have no desire [that] any, either male or female, should be instructed.[73]

Objection: Women are of low parts. Answer: So are many men. We plead only for those which have competent parts. To be sure, some women are as capable of learning and have attained to as great height in it as most men. Witness those examples before produced. . . .

If all I have said may conveniently be done, I expect many will deride this design. I am contented, let them abound in their own sense and have wives as silly as themselves desire, over whom they may tyrannize. I hope I shall by this discourse persuade some parents to be more careful for the future of the breeding of their daughters. . . . I hope some of these considerations will at least move some of this abused sex to set a right value upon themselves according to the dignity of their creation, that they might, with an honest pride and magnanimity, scorn to be bowed down and made to stoop to such follies and vanities, trifles and nothings, so far below them, and unproportionable to their noble souls, nothing inferior to those of men and equally precious to God in Christ, in whom there is neither male nor female.

---

69. Translation, from the Latin of Ovid, in Teague, *Bathsua Makin*, p. 164n57.

70. 1 *Timothy* 2: 12–5; 1 *Corinthians* 14: 34–5.

71. Makin once again concedes the subordinate status and role of women and then gradually eviscerates the concession in the ensuing discussion. On women speaking and acting in public, see selection #35 by Emma Willard.

72. Salique law, a sixth-century code prohibiting women from inheriting a throne or ruling a nation, is the subject of a long speech in William Shakespeare's *The Life of King Henry V* (I ii 35–100), written in 1599.

73. Makin's critique of the convention of all-male liberal education is matched by her critique of standard school practices.

31. Juana Inéz de la Cruz, "The Poet's Reply" (1691)

INTRODUCTION

Juana Inéz de la Cruz (c.1648-1695) was born in a small village not far from Mexico City. Little is known about her father, who soon left the family and is scarcely mentioned in her writings. Being sensitive about her uncertain paternity, she used her mother's family name, Ramírez, until adulthood. Her mother inadvertently provided an early opportunity to learn to read, and this strengthened Juana's profound inclination for study, which, she says below, was almost beyond her power to control. Following this impulse, Juana schemed to pursue a liberal education at the university in Mexico City, but her mother blocked the plan. Nevertheless, Juana's desire for learning was advanced by her mother's father, a cultured man who had a large library library in which she read extensively.[74] But when her grandfather died, she was sent away at about age twelve to live with relatives in Mexico City. The period between this event and her entrance to a convent at about age 20 is passed over in the autobiographical section of "The Poet's Reply" below. Yet, this period was decisive in her intellectual and personal development.

While living as a ward with her wealthy relatives, Juana gained entrance into the highest social circles in Mexico and acquired a reputation for precocious erudition. At the age of seventeen, she went to live in the court of the viceroy, serving as lady-in-waiting to the vicereine, and began to write Baroque verse on courtly themes: poems honoring court and city figures, love poems, satires. In about 1669 she entered a convent with the encouragement of her confessor, a Jesuit theologian and censor for the Inquisition, who arranged for a wealthy patron to pay the expensive dowry of 3,000 pesos and the heavy cost of the ceremony of profession.

Although she could not leave the convent, life there was not austere. The nuns lived "private," rather than communal lives, occupying separate cells, which were sold or rented. These "cells" often had two stories and included a sitting room, sleeping quarters, kitchen, and bathroom; and the nuns were generally accompanied by maids or attendants confided to their supervision. In addition, the convent belonged to the Hieronymite order, which followed the academic tradition established by its patron saint Jerome, who had served as the intellectual and spiritual advisor for a number of sophisticated Christian women in the late fourth century.[75] Juana was elected to the offices of archivist and keeper of the library, which prospered under her guidance and acquired collections of musical and scientific instruments, jewels, and rare objects.

Meanwhile, Sister Juana's influence and stature in the secular world continued to grow. She was widely praised for her talents in music, embroidery, liberal learning, and writing. Above all, she was renowned for her poetry, which adopted the baroque style of the Spanish Golden Age. In fact, "Sister Juana's versification is one of the most elegant and refined in Spanish. Few poets in our language equal her, and those who surpass her can be counted on the fingers of one hand."[76] She continued to

---

74. Note that a father or grandfather played an important role in providing liberal education for Christine de Pizan, Laura Cereta, and Bathsua Makin, and Juana. Similarly, in "a survey of Vassar [College] alumnae from the classes of 1865 through 1900. . .fathers were mentioned five times more frequently than mothers as sources of inspiration for college attendance." Lynn D. Gordon, *Gender and Higher Education in the Progressive Era* (New Haven: Yale University Press, 1990), p. 20.

75. Jerome (c. 347–c. 420) was a Christian scholar and editor. See the discussion of Jerome in the introduction to Section II.

76. Octavio Paz, *Sor Juana or, The Traps of Faith*, translated by Margaret Sayers Peden (Cambridge: Harvard University Press, 1988), p. 159.

exchange gifts, favors, and correspondence with the vicereine and others in court, and she received royal and ecclesiastical commissions to compose carols, plays, and poems. Cultural, political, and ecclesiastical leaders of Mexico came to visit her in the convent. One of these was Manuel Fernández de Santa Cruz, who arrived in Mexico in 1673 to assume the bishopric of Puebla, the diocese second in power and prestige to that of the archbishop of Mexico. Sister Juana and the Bishop of Puebla became good friends. Nevertheless, a number of clerics began to disapprove of Sister Juana extending her learning and reputation. Despite his earlier contrary assurances, Juana's confessor publicly urged her to stop studying and sell her library. More serious and politically complicated was the disapproval of Francisco Aguiar y Seijas, Archbishop of Mexico,[77] which led to her writing "The Poet's Reply," excerpted in the selection below.

In 1650, when Juana was only an infant, an eminent Portuguese Jesuit and good friend of Archbishop Seijas had delivered a sermon in which he challenged the opinions of Augustine, Aquinas, and other saints as to which of Christ's gifts to humanity was the greatest. Archbishop Seijas arranged for the sermon to be republished in 1685, and, after Juana criticized the sermon in a discussion in her convent with some friends, she was asked to write down her critique. Without her knowledge or permission, the Bishop of Puebla, her friend, published Juana's critique in 1690 under the laudatory title of *Athenagoric Letter*, meaning "worthy of Athena," the Greek goddess of wisdom. The Bishop prefaced Juana's critique with his own letter written under the pseudonym "Sister Filotea [Lover of God] de Santa Cruz." This prefatory letter lavished praise on Sister Juana for her learning, but also remonstrated her for criticizing a prominent prelate and warned that educating herself, studying theology in particular, and writing poetry were unbecoming of a woman and a nun.

The Bishop's actions may be variously interpreted in light of the complexity of ecclesiastical politics and the situation of women religious. He and Juana may have collaborated in order to provide her with a public forum in which to discuss these issues and respond to her critics without having to address powerful clerical leaders directly.[78] Or he may have sincerely been repeating the public warnings that Juana had already heard, or he may have been trying to gain favor with his superior, the Archbishop, by betraying Juana and sacrificing her friendship to his own ends. However, because the Bishop had originally been named Archbishop until officials in Madrid intervened on behalf of Aguiar y Seijas, because an attack upon the republished sermon amounted to an attack upon the Archbishop, because the feminist source of the attack and the pseudonymous praise of Juana would infuriate the misogynist Archbishop, and, finally, because it was well known that the Bishop of Puebla had written the preface attributed to Sister Filotea, it seems likely that the Bishop acted on his own and published the *Athenagoric Letter* at Juana's expense, in order to make a public humiliating criticism of his superior under the pretext of scolding the critic. Moreover, the Bishop was shielded from the consequences of this publication both by his position and by the countervailing remonstrance of Sister Juana in the preface.

Whatever the circumstances behind the publication of the *Athenagoric Letter*, Juana responded with her most famous work, "The Poet's Reply" in 1691. This "is a unique document in the history of Hispanic literature, in which there are few confessions relating to the life of the mind, its illusions and disillusions. . . . It is also, and first of all, . . . a defense of secular letters." But Juana "realized that she

---

77. A compulsively strict and misogynistic prelate, Archbishop Aquiar y Seijas scourged himself, slept on a vermin-infested mattress, and prohibited women from coming into his sight. He is said to have ordered stones from his courtyard destroyed after a cleaning woman stepped across them. The Archbishop openly condemned Juana's writings, particularly her sonnets, love poems, and a ballad written at the request of the Queen of Spain and dedicated to a popular bullfighter. Translator's introduction.

78. This indirect approach resembles the vision of Christine de Pizan in her selection (I 1) in Section III.

was being attacked above all for being a woman, and thus her defense was immediately transformed into a defense of the female sex."[79] In contrast to the formal organization adopted by Bathsua Makin and Emma Willard in their selections, Juana employs irony, hyperbole, and other literary devices to make her argument.

"The Poet's Reply" first describes Juana's intense "natural impulse" to study "that I shall be less ignorant," as she states below. Hence, she presents "a compelling treatment of and support for the liberal arts," ranging from the most erudite to the most practical.[80] The second theme is Juana's response to the doctrine "Let women keep silent in church, for it is not permitted for them to speak" [1 *Corinthians* 14: 34.] She defends the rights of women to cultivate their intellect and to study all branches of knowledge, including the liberal arts and the crowning discipline of theology. The third theme is "her explanation of her obedience to the religious state of life, to the Church, and to God. Despite her courageous opposition, Juana remains "an obedient daughter of the Church, fearful of . . . causing a scandal."[81]

This final theme, though less pronounced in "The Poet's Reply," predominated during the rest of Juana's life, even as the *Athenagoric Letter* and "The Poet's Reply" were under furious attack in Mexico and in Spain. Both her friend, the Bishop of Puebla, and her Jesuit confessor deserted her and would not communicate with her. In 1693 Sister Juana bowed to the pressure of her censors, signed a confession in her own blood, and sent her entire collection of texts, scientific equipment, and musical instruments to Archbishop Aquiar y Seijas for his disposition. She then devoted herself to ministering to others, and began to engage in painful mortification of her flesh. She died in the following year while nursing her sister nuns during a plague in Mexico City.

SELECTION[82]

My Most Illustrious Lady, Sister Filotea, Not my will, my poor health, nor my justified fear have delayed for so many days my response to your letter.[83] How long might it not have been, if from the start my clumsy pen had not stumbled upon two obstacles? The first obstacle, (and for me the most severe) is not knowing how to respond to your very learned, prudent, saintly and most loving letter. If I recall that when St. Thomas, the Angel of the Schools, was asked about his silence with Albert the Great, his mentor, he answered that he was silent because he knew nothing to say which would be worthy of Albert,[84] then with how much better reason would I be silent, not like St. Thomas, out of humility, but because in reality I could know nothing worthy of you.

The second obstacle rests in not knowing how to thank you appropriately for the unexpected favor of giving my writings to the press without my knowledge: such a favor without measure that it surpasses my most ambitious hopes and wildest dreams. Not even as a reasonable being could it fill my greatest thoughts, and having an end of such magnitude that not only does it stretch the limits of approval, but it also exceeds my capacity for gratitude, as much for its greatness as for its unexpected-

79. Paz, *Sor Juana*, pp. 414-415.

80. Translator's introduction.

81. Translator's introduction.

82. Juana Inéz de la Cruz, "The Poet's Reply to the Very Illustrious Sister Filotea de La Cruz," (1691) adapted from a new, unpublished translation by Frances M. Sweeney. Section breaks have been added.

83. The Preface to the *Athenagoric Letter*.

84. See the introduction to Thomas Aquinas in Section IV.

ness, which is what Quintilian said: "The less glory the hopes produce, the better are the benefits."[85] And such, that it makes speechless the rewarded. . . .

I

Moses, because he was a stammerer, did not find himself worthy to speak with Pharaoh. Later, seeing himself so favored by God, he became infused with such courage that not only did he speak to God Himself, but also dared to ask Him an impossible favor: "Show me your face." [*Exodus* 33: 13] Likewise, My Lady, those two obstacles stated at the beginning no longer appear so, in view of how much you have favored me. Because whoever published my letter without my consent, whoever entitled it, whoever paid its publishing costs, whoever honored it so much (it being so unworthy both in itself and in its author), what will this person not do? What will she not pardon? What will she leave undone? What will she leave unpardoned?

And so, on the assumption that I speak with the safe conduct of your favor, and under the security of your benevolence, and that, like another Esther, you have given me the point of the golden scepter of your goodness to kiss as a symbol of granting me free license to speak and to propose my own ideas in your venerable presence [*Esther* 5: 2], I say that I receive in my soul your most holy admonition not to apply my study to the Sacred Books, and that although it comes only under the guise of suggestion, for me it will have substance of precept. As no small consolation, it seems that even before your pastoral advice, my obedience foresaw your guidance, as may be inferred from the subject and proofs of the *Athenagoric Letter* itself.[86] I know well that your prudent advice does not pertain solely to the Letter, but to all that you must have seen regarding human affairs about which I have written. Thus, everything I have said serves no other purpose than to make amends with this Letter for the lack of ability you must have inferred (with great reason) in my other writings.

Speaking to you more openly, I confess with the candor owed to you and with the truth and clarity that is always natural and customary for me, that my not having written much about sacred matters is not for lack of desire nor for lack of diligence, but rather for a surplus of fear and reverence owed to those Sacred Scriptures, for whose understanding I know myself so incapable and for whose handling I am so unworthy. . . .

There was no similar difficulty with my writing on secular subjects, because it is not the Holy Office[87] that punishes acts of heresy against art, but rather the intelligent, with laughter, and the critics, with censure. For this censure: "Just or unjust, there is no reason to fear"[88] does not stop one from attending mass and receiving communion, and thus gives me little or no concern. And, according to that same opinion of those who slander my writing,[89] I am under no obligation to learn nor do I have

---

85. Quintilian, *Institutio Oratoria*, III vii 13. "The Poet's Reply" includes many Latin phrases from scriptural and classical sources, as well as common expressions of the day. These are indicated by quotation marks and identified, where possible. The Latin employed by Juana often differs from that of modern critical editions; some of the quotations may come secondarily from the anthology, *Selections of Latin Poets* published in 1590 by Octavio della Mirandola, of which Juana's signed copy was discovered in a bookstore in 1930. Paz, *Sor Juana*, p. 78.

86. Juana had not written much about religious matters, and so was already obeying the admonition before it was given.

87. The "Holy Office" refers to the Spanish Inquisition, which exercised great control over all literatures even into the eighteenth century, both in the Americas and in Spain. Translator's note.

88. By this expression, Juana compares the censure upon her to that issued by the Inquisition.

89. Juana refers here to her critics, the defenders of Vieyra and other Church officials who censored her writings. Juana ironically presents herself as naive, obedient and uneducated (just as her critics would like her to be) in the

any aptitude for study; thus, if I err, there is no fault nor any discredit. There is no fault because I have no obligation; there is no discredit because I have no aptitude and "nobody is obliged to attempt the impossible."[90]

And, honestly, I have never written unless I felt pressured and forced, and then only to please others, not only without complacency but rather with outright repugnance. Never have I judged myself as possessing a great ability for letters or the genius required of one who writes; this is my ordinary answer to those who urge me, and even more so if it involves a sacred subject: what aptitude have I, what educational preparation, what familiarity with the subjects, and what qualifications, except four simple bachelor degrees?[91] Leave this for those who understand such matters, because I want no noise with the Holy Office, for I am ignorant and I shudder of creating any illsounding proposition or distorting any genuine intelligence of some sector. I do not study in order to write, and much less in order to teach (which would be a presumptuous arrogance in me). I study only to see if through studying I shall be less ignorant. This is my answer and my conviction.

For me, writing has never been a voluntary action, but a foreign force, and I could truthfully say: "You have driven me to it." [2 *Corinthians* 12: 11] What is true and I will not deny (first, because it is well known to all, and second, because although it may hurt me, God has done me the mercy of granting me a great love for truth) is that since the first light of reason struck me, my inclination for letters was so vehement and powerful that neither other pressures (and I have had many) nor my own reflections (of which I have had no little amount) have been sufficient to stop this natural impulse which God has implanted in me. His Majesty knows why and for what purpose; and He knows I have prayed to Him that He dim this light of my desire for understanding, and leave only what is enough to maintain His law. According to some, anything more is too much in a woman, and there are even those who say it is harmful.

His Majesty knows also that not obtaining this halt to my desire, I have attempted to bury my inclination with my religious title, and sacrifice it only to Him alone who gave it to me; and for no other reason did I enter the religious life, even though the exercises and company of a community were repressive to the freedom and quiet required by my inclination to study. Later, while in this community, God knows (and the other who knows it is the only one on earth who should know it) all that I attempted in order to hide my name (and that he did not permit me to do so, saying it was a temptation of the devil; and, yes, it would be[92]). If I could pay back some of what I owe you, My Lady, I think I would repay you only by telling you this that has never left my mouth except to one for whom it should. But I want you to know that, having freed wide-open to you the gates of my heart and made evident its most closely guarded secrets, what I owe to your venerable personage and excessive favors does not slip from my trust nor my memory.

To continue this story of my inclination, about which I want you to know everything, I was not yet three when my mother sent an older sister of mine to learn to read at [school] and partly out of affection, partly out of mischief, I followed her. When I saw that they were giving her a lesson, I became so inflamed with a desire to learn to read that I told the teacher, whom I thought I was deceiving, that my mother wanted me to have a lesson. She did not believe it, since it was unbelievable, but in order to humor my acting she gave me the lesson. I kept going and she kept teaching me, but it was

---

course of a measured defense, extensively citing scientific, classical and biblical references that reveal her to be the opposite of their wishes. Translator's note.

90. This Latin proverb (*ad impossibilia nemo tenetur*) was incorporated into the Roman civil law.

91. No explanation for this reference to "four simple bachelor's degrees" has been found.

92. The parenthetical statements are references to and covert allegations against Juana's confessor.

no longer in fun, since the experience had shown her otherwise. I learned to read in such a short time that I already knew how before my mother found out, because the teacher had kept it from her in order to surprise her and to receive a reward for her services, and I kept quiet about it, thinking they would spank me for doing it without their permission. The one who taught me is still living (may God preserve her) and is witness to what I say.

I remember that in those days, though my appetite was ordinary for my age, I abstained from eating cheese because I had heard that it made one stupid, and my desire to learn was stronger than my will to eat, even though this urge is so powerful in children. Later, when I was six or seven and already knew how to read and write, along with all the skills of housework and sewing that women learn,[93] I found out there was a university in Mexico City with schools where the sciences were studied, and as soon as I heard this I started to hound my mother with insistent and incessant pleas that, having me dress as a boy, she send me to Mexico to live with relatives in a house she owned, so I could study and attend the university.[94] She refused, and rightly so. I still found a way to further my desire by reading the vast variety of books belonging to my grandfather, despite the punishments or scoldings. When I did go to Mexico City, they were astonished, not so much at my genius as much as at the memory and knowledge I had at an age when I should barely have had time to learn how to speak.

I began to study Latin, in which I believe I took less than twenty lessons. I was so assiduous that, even though the natural adornment of hair is very important for women, especially in the flower of youth, I would cut off four to six finger widths of mine after measuring its original length. I made a rule for myself that if my hair grew back that far without my knowing such and such, which I had set out to learn while the hair grew, I was to cut it again as a punishment for my ignorance. It turned out that the hair grew back and I had not learned what I had proposed to learn, because the hair grew quickly and I learned slowly. As a result, I cut off the hair in punishment for my head's ignorance, for it did not seem right that a head so bare in knowledge be dressed by hair, since knowledge is a more desirable ornament.

I became a nun because, although I knew the religious life had many things that were repulsive to my nature (I mean the accessories rather than the fundamental aspects), nevertheless, owing to my complete disinclination to marriage, it was the least unreasonable and the most suitable life I could choose, anxious as I was to secure my salvation, to whose consideration (as the most important end) all my petty whims ceded and were subjected. These whims included wanting to live alone and not wanting any obligatory maternal occupation, which would obstruct the freedom of my study, or the noise of a community about me which might upset the complete silence required by my books.[95] This [pettiness] made me vacillate a bit in my decision, until some learned people showed me that hesitation was temptation. Thus I conquered it by divine grace and embraced the life which I now so undeservingly have. I thought I was fleeing myself when I entered the convent but (wretch that I am!) I brought myself along, as well as my worst enemy: this inclination to study. I cannot determine whether Heaven gave it to me as reward or punishment, for instead of dying down or choking amidst the great amount of activity which religion requires, my inclination to study exploded like gunpowder and I was living proof of the saying: "privation is cause for appetite."

---

93. Like Bathsua Reginald Makin in selection #30 and Emma Willard in selection #35, Juana is careful to note that arts "that women learn" were not sacrificed for academic education.

94. It is noteworthy that Christine de Pizan in selection #12 Martin of Liebitz in selection #23 also refer to girls disguising themselves as boys in order to study in schools.

95. Scholars have debated Juana's reasons for entering the convent.

I returned (poorly said, for I never ceased); I continued, then, with the studious pursuit (which for me was a respite in all the time remaining after my religious requirements) of reading and more reading, of study and more study, without other teachers than the books themselves. Easily one might see how difficult it is to learn with teachers who have no soul, and thus lack the live voice and explanation of real masters. I suffered all this work most enjoyably, out of my sheer love of learning. Oh, if only it were for love of God, which was more proper, then how much more merit might it have had! At least I tried to elevate it to Him as much as I could, and to direct it to service of Him, because the end to which I aspired was to study theology. It seemed to me a wretched inability, being Catholic, not to know by natural means all that one can understand in this life of the divine mysteries; and [it seems] that in my ecclesiastical status as a nun and not secular, I should take a profession of letters; and also that, as a child of St. Jerome and of St. Paula,[96] it would be degenerate for a daughter of such learned parents to be an idiot. I proposed this for myself and it appeared appropriate, unless it was--and this is the most probable--merely a means to flatter and applaud my own inclination, construing the pleasure derived from it as an obligation itself.

II

With this I continued, directing always, as I have said, the path of my study to the heights of sacred theology. To reach this goal I believed it propitious to ascend by the steps of the sciences and liberal arts, because how will one understand the style of the queen of a science without even knowing that of her maids?[97]

How without logic would I learn the general and particular methods in which the Sacred Scripture is written?[98]

How without rhetoric could I understand Scripture's figures, types, and expressions?

How without physics the many natural questions regarding the nature of sacrificial animals, which symbolize so many of these things already stated (and the many more that exist)?

How could I understand if the curing of Saul, upon hearing the sound of David's harp, was due to the natural virtue and power of the music or a supernatural ability that God instilled in David?

How, without arithmetic, could one understand the many computations of years, days, months, hours, weeks, like those mysterious seventy weeks of Daniel, and other computations for whose intelligence it is necessary to know the nature, concordance, and properties of numbers?

How without geometry could one measure the Holy Arc of the Testament and the Sacred City of Jerusalem, whose mysterious measures make a cube with all its dimensions, and create that marvelously proportional distribution of all its parts?

How without architecture could one view the great Temple of Solomon, of which God Himself was the artist who gave the layout and the plan and the wise King served merely as the foreman who executed it? For in it there was no base without a mystery, no column without a symbol, no cornice without allusion, no architrave without significance. Likewise, to this were added the other parts, without the least edge being only for the service and complement of art and not symbolizing important ideas.

---

96. Widowed in her early 30s, Paula and her daughter followed Jerome to Bethlehem in the late fourth century, where they established two monasteries, one for men and one for women. Out of these foundations arose the Hieronymite order of nuns to which Juana belonged and for which Jerome served as the patron saint.

97. These words might be echoes of the central metaphors of Boethius and Martianus Capella, from their selections in Section III, suffusing the liberal arts tradition.

98. Compare Juana's rationale in this account of the liberal arts--logic, rhetoric, physics, music, arithmetic, geometry, astronomy, architecture, history, law--with that of Augustine in selection #7.

How without the great knowledge of rules and elements which constitute history, is it possible to understand the historical books and those recapitulations, which many times include a narration that postpones what in fact happened previously?

How without full knowledge of both codes of law is it possible to understand legal books? How without great erudition, could one know many things about worldly history mentioned in the Sacred Scripture-- the many customs of Gentiles, the many rites, the many means of communication? How without knowing rules and lessons of the Holy Fathers is it possible to understand the obscure expression of the prophets?

Without being very skillful in music, how is it possible to understand those musical proportions, and all their beauty, which exist in so many places, especially in the petitions Abraham made to God for [Sodom and Gomorra], asking Him if He would pardon these Cities if He found fifty just citizens, and this number lowered to forty-five, that is sesquinone, and is as the distance between the musical note "mi" to "re"; the number lowered again from here to forty, that is sesquioctave, and is as "re" to "mi"; from here to thirty, that is sesquitierce, and is the diatessaron; from here down to twenty, that is the sesquialter or the diapente; from here down to ten, that is the duple or diapason; and went no further, as there are not any more harmonic proportions.[99] Did not the musical terms derive from that occurrence with Abraham? Well, how can one understand this without studying music?

Similarly, as God tells Job, "Will you be able to unite the brilliant stars of the Pleiades or can you stop the shout of Orion? Are you he who compares his time to Lucifer or he who guides the Vesper over the sons of the earth?" [*Job* 38: 31-32] These terms, without awareness of astronomy, would be impossible to understand.

And it is not only these noble sciences, for neither is there any mechanical art that goes unmentioned in studying the Book that encompasses all books and the science that includes all sciences, for whose understanding all the arts serve.

And after all other disciplines are mastered (which is clearly not easy, nor perhaps possible), God expects another deed which is greater than all the aforementioned: continuous prayer and purity in life, in order to beg for that purging of spirit and illumination of mind which are imperative for knowing such exalted matters. If this is lacking, nothing else matters. The Church says this about the Angelic Doctor St. Thomas: "In the difficult places of Sacred Scripture, he joined fasting to prayer. And to Brother Reginald, his companion, he used to say that for all that he knew, he owed not so much to study and work, as to what he had received in as a gift from God."[100]

III

Well, how could I, so far removed from virtue and learning, have the strength for writing? Thus, in order to have some basic principles, I continuously studied a variety of subjects, having an inclination not for any particular subject but for all subjects in general.[101] For this reason, if I have studied one more intently than others, it was not by choice but chance, the result of having stumbled on some books more easily than others. Thus fate, not free will, has made the selection.

---

99. Believing that all fields of study are interconnected units and foundations for the study of theology, Juana finds a correlation between the descending numbers in Abraham's petitions to God before the destruction of Sodom and Gomorra (*Genesis* 28: 24-32) and the measures of Pythagorean music found in Pietro Cerone, *Music and Master* (Naples, 1613). Translator's note.

100. *Roman Breviary*, Office of the Feast of St. Thomas Aquinas, March 7, Lesson 5. Translator's note.

101. Compare the following analysis and defense of general education and rebuttal to the advantages of academic concentration with those in selections #53 and #54.

Since I did not have any particular subject to motivate me, nor a time limit that required I study one thing to attain a degree, I would study diverse things at the same time or drop some to start up others. It was good that through this random approach I did observe a natural order, because some I called study and others diversion, and with the latter I took a break from the former. As a consequence I have studied many things, but I know nothing, because one always hinders another. I say this referring only to those subjects with a manual element obviously, for it is clear that while the pen moves the compass must rest, and while the harp plays the organ is quiet, and so forth. Because much physical practice is necessary to acquire a habit or skill, never can one who divides time into doing many exercises gain perfection in any.[102]

But, referring to those subjects in the formal and speculative realms, the opposite occurs. How I would like to persuade everyone that, from my experience, not only do diverse subjects *not* interfere with each other, but they help each other--one sheds light on another and offers a new approach to understanding it, through variations and hidden connections! It was for this universal chain, created with the wisdom of their Author, that they were connected together in such a manner that all subjects correspond and are united with remarkable consistency and order. This is the chain that the ancients believed had spewed out of the mouth of Jupiter and that strung and linked together all things. Reverend Father Athanasius Kircher treats this in the curious book, *On Magnetism.*[103] All things proceed from God, who is at one time the center and the circumference from where all created lines start and stop.[104]

For myself, I can attest that what I do not understand in an author of one discipline, I tend to understand in an author of another discipline, which seems very clear. Indeed, to explain themselves, authors use metaphorical examples from other arts, as when logicians say that the mean is to the end as a measuring rod is between two distant bodies, in order to determine if they are equal or not. The logician's sentence walks a straight line on the shortest road, while that of the rhetorician forms a curve, taking the longest route, but the two end up at the same point. Similarly, they say that expositors are like an open hand and the scholastics are like a closed fist.[105] Thus, my having studied diverse subjects is not an excuse, nor do I give it as such, for these all help develop each other. Not having mastered and used them is due to my ineptitude and faulty understanding, and no fault of the diversity.

---

102. Compare Juana's approach to study during leisure with that of Aristotle in selection #3.

103. Athanasius Kircher (c.1601-1680) was a prominent German, Jesuit mathematician, physicist, and archaeologist. The metaphor of the chain of Jupiter comes from Macrobius, the north African, Latin scholar who lived c.400 A.D.

104. The metaphor of God being both center and circumference was Juana's "favorite maxim." Paz, *Sor Juana,* p. 420. The metaphor was proposed by Nicholas of Cusa (c.1401-1464), a German humanist, scientist and Church cardinal who discussed the Chain of Jupiter in *Of Learned Ignorance* (1440).

105. See the note regarding the origins of this comparison between logic and rhetoric in selection #11 (II 23) by Isidore of Seville, from whom Juana likely borrowed the famous metaphor. The two-thousand-year-old metaphor was prominent in Juana's time. "Over and over again in logical and rhetorical treatises of the English Renaissance, logic is compared to the closed fist and rhetoric to the open hand . . . to explain the preoccupation of logic with the tight discourses of the philosopher, and the preoccupation of rhetoric with the more open discourses of [the] orator and popularizer. The fact that this metaphor gives both arts the same flesh and blood, the same defensive and offensive function, and the same skeletal structure, is merely an indication of the conviction of Renaissance learning that logic and rhetoric are the two great arts of communication, and that the complete theory of communication is largely identified . . . with both." Wilbur Samuel Howell, *Logic and Rhetoric in England, 1500-1700* (Princeton: Princeton University Press, 1956), p. 4. Does Juana's usage conform to this interpretation?

What might in fact serve as an excuse for me is the extreme work it has been, not only lacking a teacher, but also fellow students with whom to confer and practice the studied material. My only teacher was a mute book, my only classmate a senseless inkwell. Instead of explanations and exercises, I have had a great many interruptions, not only those of my religious obligations (these clearly are a useful and appropriate use of time) but also those that are distractions inherent to living in a community.

For example, I might be reading and in the next cell they are in the mood for playing instruments and singing. Or when I am studying and two maids having a squabble come to me to settle their argument. Or when I am writing and a friend comes to visit me, thereby doing me a bad deed with a good will--whereupon it is proper not only to welcome the interruption, but also to be grateful for the injury. This happens constantly, since the time I have for study is likewise the free time for the whole community, and so the other sisters come to interrupt me. Only those who have experienced community life can know how true this is and only the strength of my vocation helps me handle it good-naturedly--that and the great love between me and my beloved sisters. Since love is union, there are no differences too extreme for it. . . .

Among other blessings, I owe God for a very soft and affable disposition for which the sisters love me very much (and kindheartedly disregard my faults) and greatly enjoy my company. Knowing this and moved by the great love I hold for them (their love for me being a greater feat), I also enjoy their company thoroughly. Thus, I used to join them whenever we had free time, to console them and to enjoy myself with their conversation. I realized that in these moments I neglected my studies, and I made a resolution not to enter another room unless obedience and charity obliged me to do so. Without such a harsh brake, love might easily break any other restriction based on will alone. Knowing my weakness, I would impose this sentence for fifteen days or a month, then give myself a day or two of respite before renewing the restriction. The day off served not so much as a rest (not studying has never been "rest" for me) it was more so as not to repay the undeserved love which my dear sisters felt for me by being harsh, reclusive or ungrateful.

And so, the strength of my inclination is clearly visible. Blessed be God that He willed this inclination towards study rather than a different vice, one that for me might be insuperable. It can also be easily inferred just how much my poor studies have had to sail against the current (or, better said, have shipwrecked).

There is still the need to explain the most arduous of the obstacles I have had, for those related until now have been about my own daily requirements and random interruptions; indirectly they too are obstacles. They do not, however, explain the outright interruptions: those that have directly tried to interfere and prohibit my study. Who would doubt that, seeing such widespread praise for my work, I have sailed with anything but favorable winds across a shining sea, powered by the clapping palms of general acclaim? The Lord knows it has hardly been like this, for among the blossoms of that same acclaim have stirred and risen such stinging asps of emulation and persecution that I could not count them. The most harmful and hurtful are not those who have pursued me with open hatred and malevolence, but those that while loving me and wishing me well (and perhaps deserving much favor with God for their good intention) have mortified and tormented me more than the others, with the statement: "This study is not suitable to the sacred ignorance to which you belong: you could be lost, you could disappear amidst the very heights you attain through your perception and sharpness of mind."[106] What it has cost me to resist this! This rare species of martyrdom, in which I am the martyr and the executioner.

---

106. Juana refers to the warnings of her Jesuit confessor and other prelates that she cease studying theology.

With respect to my ability for writing verse, which for me is doubly unlucky, even when it is sacred verse, which nightmares has it never caused me?[107] Better said, which has it never stopped causing me? Sometimes, My Lady, I stop to wonder why a person who stands out--or one whom God singles out, as He alone is the one who really can--why is this person received like a common enemy? Is it because it seems to some that he usurps the applause *they* deserve, or because he belittles the admiration to which they aspire, and so they persecute him?

That politically barbarous law of Athens, by which he who stood out because of his deeds and virtue was exiled so that his feats would not threaten the common public freedom, still endures and still can be observed in our times, although for a different motive from that of the Athenians. There is another rationale, however, that is no less efficient, though less well-founded, for it seems to be a maxim of that impious Macchiavelli: hate the one who stands out because by standing out he discredits others.[108] So it was believed then and is today.

If not so, then what was the cause of that rabid hatred the Pharisees held against Christ, they having so many reasons to feel the opposite?. . .My sainted mother, my mother Theresa, says that once she beheld the beauty of Christ she was freed from any inclination toward other creatures, because everything she saw was ugly compared to that beauty.[109] How did the opposite effect result with men? Being coarse and vile, they might not have had the knowledge nor could they estimate His perfections, but even as interested beings, did not His other qualities and usefulness in ability to do so many good works move them, such as healing the sick, resuscitating the dead, or curing the possessed? How could they not love Him? Oh, God, it is precisely for that goodness itself that they did not love Him, for this reason they abhorred Him! They confessed this themselves!. . .[110]

I confess that I, too, find myself far removed from the fundamentals of wisdom and have wanted to pursue it, though "at a distance." But all of this has brought me closer to the flames of persecution, the crucible of torture, and it has reached such an extreme that they have come to prohibit my study.

Once, they achieved their end through a very innocent and saintly prelate who thought that my study could be a matter for the Inquisition and thus mandated that I not study.[111] I obeyed (for some three months--the duration of the order) by not handling a book, but as for not studying at all, since it does not fall under my power to quit, I could not do it. And although I did not study books, I studied all the things God has created, and these served me well as letters, just as the great universal machination became my book. I saw nothing without reflecting on it; I heard nothing without giving it a consideration, even those things most common and base. There is no thing existing, no matter how small, to which "God made me" does not apply. Likewise, there is nothing that cannot stir one's wonder, when it is considered as it deserves.

As I was saying, then, I watched and admired all things, in such a manner that even from the people with whom I was speaking, and from what they would say, thousands of thoughts were igniting inside me. From where could such a variety of minds and personalities emanate, if all were from one species? What subtleties and idiosyncrasies in character must have caused them? Whenever I saw a figure, I used to calculate the proportion of its lines, measure it with understanding and refigure it

---

107. Like Bathsua Reginald Makin and, perhaps, Christine de Pizan, Juana seems to regard poetry here and below as the crowning study among the liberal arts.

108. See Niccolò Machiavelli, *The Prince* XIX.

109. St. Theresa of Ávila (1515-1582) established a reformed branch of the Carmelite Order of nuns and helped to lead the Catholic Reformation. In 1970 she became the first woman named a Doctor of the Church.

110. Four pages of examples of men's rejection of Christ are here omitted.

111. This ironic description refers to Juana's Jesuit confessor.

along different lines. Sometimes I would pace the floor of our sleeping room--a very large room--and observe how, since the lines of its two sides were parallel and its roof one straight level, one's vision could make its lines appear to curve into each other, and the roof would seem shorter from a distance. From this I inferred that visual lines run straight but not parallel, and seemingly create a pyramidal figure. Then I debated if this were the reason our ancestors doubted the world was round. Because, although it may appear so, it might just be an optical illusion, creating concavities where there might be none. . . .

How much I could tell you, My Lady, of the secrets of Nature I have discovered even while cooking! That an egg holds together and fries well in butter or oil, but crumbles in syrup. That, in order to preserve sugar as liquid, it suffices to pour into it only a drop or so of water that had held the juice of a quince or some other tart fruit. That the yolk and white of the same egg are themselves so contrary, that in some dishes in which eggs serve for sugar, either the yolk or the white may be used alone, but not together. I should not tire you with such frivolities, but I only relate these accounts to give you an idea of my natural inclination towards study, and I think it must surely make you laugh. But, My Lady, what *can* we women know after all, except the philosophies of cooking? Lupercio Leonardo rightly remarked that one can perfectly well philosophize *and* prepare dinner.[112] I tend to believe, seeing these little things, that if Aristotle had cooked, he would have written much more.

Continuing with my manner of reflection, I declare that this habit is so constant in me I do not need books. On one occasion in which, because of some grave stomach illness, the doctors prohibited my study, I refrained a few days, but then I proposed to them that it was less harmful to allow me to study, because my reflections were so strong and so vehement that they consumed more energy in a quarter of an hour than the study with books did in four days. So the doctors reluctantly conceded to allow me to read.

My Lady, not even in sleep did this continued movement of my mind relax itself. In fact, in sleep it tends to work more freely and unobstructed, combining with major clarity and simplicity whatever it had remembered of the day's activity, then even debating it and writing verse (of which I could make you a very good catalog). There are some ideas and delicate matters that I have resolved in sleep better than while awake, which I will omit as not to bore you. Let everything I have said suffice for your own keen judgment and advanced aptitude to empathize and understand fully my natural disposition, from its inception to the current means and state of my study.

Even if these qualities, My Lady, were merits, (as I so see them celebrated in men), they would not have been so in me, because I work out of necessity. If they are wrong, neither do I think I carry the blame, because of that same necessity. Nevertheless, with everything, I live so unsure of myself that not in this nor in anything do I trust my judgment, and so I defer the decision to your sovereign talent, submitting myself then to whatever sentence, without offering contradiction nor reluctance. After all, this has not been more than a simple narration of my inclination to study.[113]

IV

I confess also that, though truth such as this requires no substantiation, the many cases I have read both in divine and human letters have helped me incessantly. . . .[114]

---

112. The source of this remark is not the seventeenth-century poet Lupercio Leonardo, but his brother, Bartholomew Leonardo of Argensola in *First Satire* (c.1625). Translator's note. Works of both poets were included in Juana's library.

113. Is Juana arguing fundamentally about the natural inclinations of women?

114. Like Christine de Pizan, Laura Cereta, and Bathsua Makin, Juana presents a history of learned women (here omitted) in order to justify women's access to learning in her day.

The venerable Dr. Arce (worthy professor of Scripture by his virtue and education), raises this question in his *On the Study of the Bible*: "Is it legitimate for women to apply themselves to study of the Holy Bible and to interpret it?"[115] And to defend his argument against it, he uses many quotations from saints, especially one of the Apostle: "Let women keep silent in church, for it is not permitted for them to speak." [1 *Corinthians* 14: 34].[116] He then incorporates other phrases, and from the same apostle, Paul, his letter to Titus: "The elder women, themselves, by their blessed conduct, must be teachers of the good." [*Titus* 2: 3] With these interpretations of the Holy Fathers, and also by his own opinion, Dr. Arce resolves that lecturing publicly in the classroom and preaching from the pulpit is wrong for women, but studying, writing, and teaching privately is not only permissible, but also most advantageous and useful. Of course, it is clear that this is not meant for all women, but only for those to whom God has granted a unique virtue and prudence, and who are very mature and erudite, with the talent and qualifications necessary for such a sacred undertaking.

This resolve is so appropriate that it should apply not only to women who are believed to be so inept, but also to men who are considered wise only by virtue of their classification as men. For both these types of men and women the interpretation of Sacred Scripture must be prohibited, because they are not very learned or virtuous and do not possess open and well-conditioned minds.[117] The absence of such a restriction, I think, has created many sects and been the root of many heresies, because there are many who study in order to become ignorant, especially those of arrogant, unquiet, and controlling natures who favor innovations with the Law (when the Law usually opposes them). . . .

Learning caused them harm, even though education is the best nourishment and the very life of the soul. The better the nourishment for an insanely infirm and feverous stomach, the more arid, putrid and poisonous will be the humors it produces--likewise with these ill-inclined people: the more they study the more they will generate consistently worse opinions. The very study meant to nourish their understanding will obstruct them, because they study much and assimilate very little, without any proportion between their work and the limited capacity of their understanding. About this, the Apostle Paul notes: "Well, in virtue of the favor given us, I warn each of you not to think more highly of himself than he ought. Let him measure himself with the measure of faith that God has apportioned to him." [*Romans* 12: 3] And, actually, the Apostle spoke not to women, but to men, so it is that this idea of "silence" applies not just to women, but to all who are not very able. If I wanted to know as much or more than Aristotle or St. Augustine but did not have their aptitude, respectively, then even if I were to study more than the two put together, I would never reach my goal. In fact, I would most likely weaken and befuddle my existing knowledge because of its entire disproportion to the objective.

If only all of us--and I the first since I am ignorant--would take measure of our talents before beginning to study, or even worse, writing with ambitious envy to equal or exceed another, how much less enthusiasm would we then have! And how many errors could we avoid! How many mixed up notions floating about would be grounded. And I put my own right up front, for if I considered it, as I should have, I would not even be writing this. However, I protest that I only write this to obey you, My Lady, and I write with such reluctance that you owe me more for my having taken up the pen in spite of my fear, than you would if I sent you perfect works. But, it is appropriate that this reply goes

---

115. Juana quotes from *On the Study of the Bible* by Juan Díaz de Arce, a Mexican theologian and university professor (d. 1653).

116. Juana here begins an interpretation of scripture, continuing through this section, that demonstrates her willingness to dispute with church authorities.

117. "Sister Juana is writing for a small group and knows that none of her barbs will pass unnoticed. . . .[She] is a true intellectual pugilist. Fortunately, she never abandons either good manners or irony." Paz, *Sor Juana*, p. 390.

to you for correction: erase it, destroy it, and reprove me for it. I will appreciate your criticism more than all the vain applause others might give me: "The just will correct me and will scold me with compassion, but the oil of the sinner will not anoint my head." [*Psalms* 140: 3]

Returning to our Arce, he brings as confirmation of his beliefs those words of my father, St. Jerome (to Laeta, on the education of her daughter), when he says: "Let her tongue, however, be initiated into the sweetness of the psalms. Let the very names out of which she is beginning to form phrases be not random ones but chosen on purpose. For example, those of the Prophets and the Apostles, and let the whole succession of Patriarchs beginning with Adam be taken from Matthew and Luke, so that, while otherwise engaged, she may be made ready for future tasks of memorization. Have her bring you a daily quote culled from the flowers of Scripture."[118]. . .The "Have her bring you" of my great Father makes it understood that the teacher of the daughter is to be Laeta, her very mother.

Oh, how much damage in our republic might have been avoided if the elderly women were as learned as Laeta and if they knew how to teach as St. Paul and my father St. Jerome mandate! As it stands, due to a dearth of women scholars and because of the incredible state of carelessness in which women have been left, if some fathers wish to educate their daughters more than the ordinary amount, the need for and the lack of elderly wise women forces the fathers to hire male mentors to instruct the girls how to read, write, and calculate, to play instruments and to have other abilities. No little harm arises, as realized each day in pitiful examples of ill-formed unions; from the close contact and constant communication over time, what was thought impossible happens rather easily.[119] Therefore, many fathers would rather leave their daughters barbarous and uncultured than to expose them to such a notorious danger as is the familiarity with men. All of this would be avoided if there were elderly women scholars, as St. Paul wished,[120] and the education were being passed down the generations along with knowledge of housework and other customs.

After all, what would be the bother if an older woman, learned in letters, holy conversation and customs were to have the responsibility of educating maidens? These maidens, then, would suffer neither for lack of doctrine nor for having it supplied to them through such risky mediums as are male masters. Even when there was no other risk than the indecency of a strange man sitting aside a bashful young lady (who blushes even when her father looks her in the face) and treating her with domestic familiarity and classroom courtesy, the embarrassment at the contact with men and the conversations between them suffices to stop the arrangement. Nor do I see how this system of having men teach women might exist without danger, unless it occurred in the severe tribunal of a confessional or in the formality of the pulpit, or via the remote knowledge of books, but not with the close contact inherent to tutoring. Everyone knows this is true, but in spite of it the tutoring is permitted, only because there are no elderly women who are learned. Hence it is a grave danger not to have them.

This fact should be considered by those who, armed with the idea, "Women should be silent in church," blaspheme the notion that women should learn and teach, as if it were not the Apostle himself who said, "be good teachers." Besides which the actual account of that prohibition was an historical one relayed by Eusebius, that in the early Church women had begun to teach doctrine to each other in the temples and their voices interfered with the apostles when they preached, so they were asked to be quiet. This is true today, that when the preacher speaks, no one prays aloud.

------

118. Juana is paraphrasing from Jerome's Letter 107 "To Laeta, on the education of her daughter." See Jerome, *Select Letters*, tr. F. A. Wright (Cambridge: Harvard University Press, 1933), pp. 345, 347. Laeta was a late fourth-century disciple of Jerome and mother of Paula, founder of the Hieronymite order of nuns.

119. See selection #14 by Abelard.

120. This likely refers to *Titus* 2: 3.

There is no doubt that a well-rounded education requires knowledge of history, customs, ceremonies, proverbs and even the manners of speaking in the time in which these all were recorded, in order to grasp the reference and allusion of certain citations in Scripture. For example, "Rend your heart and not your garments." [*Joel* 2: 13] Is this not an allusion to the ceremony performed by the Hebrews, of rending their clothes as a sign of pain, as the evil pontiff did when he said that Christ had blasphemed? And are not many passages of the Apostle describing aid for widows also reflections of the customs of those times? With respect to that passage regarding the strong wife--"Your husband will be prominent at the gates of the city" [*Proverbs* 31: 23]--does it not allude to the custom that the judges' tribunals were located at the gates of the city?. . .

All of this requires more education than what some think, these who as mere students of grammar--or its equivalent study with only four compendiums of logic--purport to interpret Sacred Scripture and grasp on to the aforementioned "Women in church be silent," without knowing how it should be understood. And they cite from another place in the Bible, "Women should learn in silence" [1 *Timothy* 2: 11], when actually this quote favors women more than opposes them, since it mandates that they learn. Obviously silence is necessary while doing so. It is also written: "Listen, Israel, and keep silent" [*Job* 33: 31], where men and women collectively are addressed and all are told to be quiet, because it makes sense that whomever listens and learns should pay attention and be quiet.

If none of this is so, then I would like for these interpreters and expounders of St. Paul to explain to me how *they* understand the quote, "Women in church be silent." They have to interpret it either in a literal manner, referring concretely to pulpits and clerics' chairs, or in a formal manner, referring to the universality of the faithful, which is the entire Church itself. If they interpret it in the first fashion, (which I believe is the true sense of the phrase, since we know that in effect women are not permitted to lecture or preach publicly in church), then why do they reprimand those who study privately? If they interpret it in the second sense, and they want the Apostle's prohibition to be taken transcendentally, that not even in secret are women allowed to write or study, then how do we view the fact that the Church has permitted women to write, including Gertrude, Theresa,[121] Bridget,[122] the nun of Agreda,[123] and many other women?. . .

So, now, I do not presume to teach--for me that would be too great a presumption--and writing requires more talent than I possess, and much greater thought. As St. Cyprian says: "That which we write requires careful consideration."[124] My only desire is to study so I will be less ignorant, for according to St. Augustine some things are learned in order to do something, as a means, and others are learned merely to know them, as an end itself.[125] So what has been my crime, especially since I have not even done that which *is* legitimate for women, teaching women through my writings, because I

---

121. St. Gertrude (1256-1303) was a German Benedictine nun who became famous for her writings on the Bible, though she once halted her study after receiving an admonishing vision from Christ. Theresa is mentioned above.

122. This Bridget is probably St. Bridget of Sweden (c.1300-1373), a noble woman who became a nun and founded the Order of the Most Holy Savior and whose description of her mystical visions was widely read. Another possibility is the Irish St. Bridget (c.453-c.523), who founded a prominent monastery at Kildare.

123. The nun of Agreda was María de Jesús (1602-1665), a celebrated Augustinian nun, from the convent of Agreda, Spain, who was an advisor and confidant of King Philip IV (1605-1665) and wrote a text on mysticism which Juana doubtlessly knew. Translator's note.

124. This Latin quotation (*gravi consideratione indigent, quae scribimus*) from St. Cyprian (c.200-258), bishop of Carthage, has not been located.

125. A number of different places in the writings of Augustine could serve as Juana's reference for this point. The reconciliation of classical learning and Christian truth in *On Christian Learning* rests fundamentally on the distinction that the former serves as a vehicle to advance the latter, the knowledge of God, which is its own end.

know I have no aptitude for it, and following the advice of Quintilian: "Each learns who not only takes advice from others, but who follows his own instinct."[126]

If the crime rests with my *Athenagoric Letter*, was that more than simply relating my views with all the propriety I owe to our Holy Mother Church? If she, with her most holy authority, does not prohibit me, why should others prohibit me? Holding an opinion contrary to Vieyra was daring on my part, but was it not more daring for him, in his role as a priest, to have taken one that opposed the three Holy Fathers of the Church?[127]. . .If [the *Athenagoric Letter*] is heretical, as the Censor says, why does he not denounce it? With that he would be avenged and I would be content, because I most esteem, as I should, the label of Catholic and that of being an obedient daughter of my Holy Mother Church, much more than I appreciate any acclaim as a scholar. If he believes the letter has no [literary merit]--and saying that would be most appropriate--let him laugh, even if it be a snicker; I do not ask him to applaud me, since, as I was free to dissent from Vieyra, so is anyone to dissent from my views. . . .

V

Well, if I focus now on my much censored facility for writing verse, which in me is so natural that I even have to force myself to keep this letter from becoming poetry, and I might cite that: "Whatever I set out to say comes out in verse."[128] Seeing such condemnation and censure of poetry, I have judiciously searched for some sign of harm verse might hold, but I have found none. Instead I find that verses are applauded by the mouths of Sibyls and sanctified in the pens of the prophets, especially by King David, about whom that great expositor and beloved father of mine says, explaining the metrical measure: "In the manner of Horace and Pindar, now the lines appear iambic, then they resound in Alcaic verse, then in Sapphic, and then in half-feet."[129]

Most of the sacred books are in meter, like the *Canticle of Moses*. Regarding those of Job, St. Isidore, in his *Etymologies,* says they are in heroic verse.[130] Solomon wrote verse in the *Song of Songs,* as did Jeremiah in *Lamentations*. Thus says Cassiodorus: "Every poetic expression has its origin in Sacred Scripture"[131]. . . .

If the evil of poetry rests in the idea of women writing the verses, it has already been noted how many have done so praiseworthily. What is wrong, then, in my doing so? I confess of course my baseness and vileness, but I doubt that even a couplet of mine has been judged as indecent. Besides, I have never written of my own volition, but at the requests and pleas of others. In fact, the only thing I remember writing for my own pleasure is a little paper entitled *The Dream*.

That *[Athenagoric] Letter* which you, My Lady, honored so much, I wrote with more reluctance than anything, firstly, because it dealt with holy matters, about which (as I have said) I have great te-

---

126. Quintilian, *Institutio Oratoria* IX iv 7.

127. Antonio de Vieyra (1608-1697) was the eminent Portuguese Jesuit who gave the sermon in 1650 that his good friend, Archbishop Seijas, republished in 1685. Juana alludes to the unjust irony that her presumption in addressing theological issues is vastly overshadowed by Vieyra's arrogance in correcting saints, such as Augustine and Aquinas.

128. Ovid, *Letters [poems] from the Black Sea* IV 10. Translator's note. Compare Juana's impulse to versify and to study with the association made by Christine de Pizan (I 28) in selection #12.

129. Jerome, Preface to Book 2 of Eusebius, *Chronicle.* Translator's note.

130. Isidore of Seville, *Etymologies* I 39.

131. The point, if not the quotation, may be found in Cassiodorus, *Introduction to Divine and Human Readings* I 27-28.

merity and reverence and, secondly, because it seemed as though I wanted to contradict them, which I have a natural aversion to doing. I think that if I could have foreseen the lucky destiny to which the letter was born--like another Moses, I cast it unexposed to the waters of the Nile of silence, where a princess such as yourself found and cherished it[132]--I do think, I repeat, that had I known the outcome, I would have drowned it first with the same hands into which it was born, fearful that the clumsy mistakes of my ignorance would show up in the light of your knowledge. From whence the greatness of your mercy is known, for your will is applauding precisely what your supreme intelligence must be wishing to reject.

Since its fate has already cast the letter upon your doorstep, however, such a foundling and orphan that even its name you gave it, it bothers me that, besides other deformities, it carries also the defects of having been written hastily. And it was written thusly because of the poor health I continually have, the extra duties my religious obedience places upon me, and because, lacking anyone to help me write it out, everything had to come from my own hand.[133] Also, since it was written against my will and I only wanted to keep my word to one whom I could not disobey, I did not set a lengthy schedule for completion. I left out entire considerations and many proofs that occurred to me, in order not to write more.

Had I known, however, that the letter was to be published, I would not have omitted these, even if just to satisfy some anonymous objections that have been provoked and to which I could have responded. I would not be so disobedient as to place these indecent objections before the pureness of your eyes. It is enough that I offend your sight with my own ignorance, without exposing other audacities. But, if these, by themselves, should fly to you in some way (they are so weightless they most likely shall) you will mandate what I must do, for, unless it interferes with your orders, I will never take up the pen to defend myself, for it seems unnecessary for me to respond to one who, through concealing himself, already acknowledges his error. . . . If the style of this letter, my venerable Lady, has not been such as you deserve, I beg your pardon for the household familiarity or for the lack of reverence I perhaps have shown, since in treating you as a veiled nun, a sister of mine, I have forgotten the eminence of your most illustrious person. Had I seen you unveiled, this would not have happened.[134]

Hold me in your favor, so that I might also receive divine favor, and may the Lord grant you many blessings and keep you, as I pray and hope He will. From this convent of our Father St. Jerome in Mexico City, this first day of March of the year sixteen hundred ninety-one, your most favored daughter kisses your hands, Juana Inéz de la Cruz.

---

132. See *Exodus* 2: 1-10.

133. The previously cited male scholars, writers, and ecclesiastical leaders generally dictated their words to secretaries, who wrote them down. Juana did not have this luxury.

134. Juana finally reveals that she knows the identity of the pseudonymous Sister Filotea de la Cruz, namely, the Bishop of Puebla.

32. Yale College, "Concerning Scholastic Exercises" ([1748], 1774)

INTRODUCTION

In the summer of 1701 ten Connecticut clergymen, including nine Harvard graduates, proposed to found a second college in New England.[135] The distance from Cambridge prompted this proposal, though less geographical than theological, for the Congregational-Presbyterian clergy in Connecticut and New Haven were worried about a "latitudinarian" or liberal drift among the faculty and Overseers of Harvard. In autumn the Connecticut General Assembly authorized the founding of a "Collegiate School"; and the ministers, in solemn gathering, subsequently affirmed that "the Liberall and Relligious Education of Suitable Youth is, under the blessing of God, a chief and most probable expedient" and declared "that there shal, and hereby is Erected and formed a Collegiate School, Wherein shal be taught the Liberal Arts, and Languages." These ten clerical trustees also established rules of governance, set out a curriculum, and named the first rector, Rev. Abraham Pierson.

The arrangement was for Rector Pierson to hold classes in his home and continue serving his parish as a way to augment the meager income from the college. But the remote and isolated location of the town, the unsuitable living arrangements for students, and the insufficient financial support, made the college untenable by 1706, when Rector Pierson died. The college was then divided among different towns and locations, and continued in a fragmented state for a decade until student dissatisfaction prompted the trustees to obtain an appropriation from the General Assembly for erecting a building. Competition among various towns then delayed the choice of a permanent site, so "it was not until the summer of 1719 that the college had, for the first time, a resident rector, a building, and an entire student body in one location,"[136] namely New Haven, Connecticut.

Despite these problems over the first two decades, the enrollment had risen to about ten students in each of four classes. By the 1740s and the period reflected in the reading below, the total number of students had climbed to between eighty and one hundred. In the 1750s the enrollment rapidly rose to about 170 and then declined in the 1760s and early 1770s to a range of 100–130.[137]

Over this latter period of fluctuating enrollment, the curriculum and teaching did not change dramatically, as is shown by the fact that the 1774 laws of Yale College, from which the following reading is drawn, merely translate into English the Latin laws of 1748 with one substantive change. The tenth statute prescribing that students speak only in Latin was dropped, demonstrating the decreasing use of Latin in academic and intellectual culture.[138] In its place, the tenth statute in the 1774 laws proscribed marriage among students, a proscription necessitated by the increasing age of entering students. This new statute also indicates Yale's struggle, amid the changing circumstances of the 1760s and 1770s, to provide a "Liberall and Relligious Education" without compromising its commitment to Reformed Orthodoxy and to nurturing godliness in its students.

Among Yale's graduates, 39 percent pursued a career in theology, 10 percent in medicine, 10 percent in law, 8 percent in commerce, and 8 percent in teaching, among the classes between 1702

---

135. Yale was the third colonial college, the College of William and Mary having been founded by Anglicans in Virginia in 1693. A fire consumed William and Mary and all its records in 1705, and it was rebuilt in 1723, but then closed again in 1781.

136. Quotations are from Richard Warch, *School of the Prophets: Yale College, 1701–1740* (New Haven, CT: Yale University Press, 1973), pp. 33, 95.

137. Pierson, *A Yale Book of Numbers*, Table A11.

138. Pierson, *A Yale Book of Numbers*, 211n.

and 1776. By the latter date, "the existence of two New England cultures" was apparent. "Yale Ministers dominated the towns in all but eastern Connecticut and had made significant inroads into Massachusetts along the Connecticut River Valley. By 1800 Yale had sent pastors throughout all of Connecticut and most of western Massachusetts and had reduced Harvard's sphere of theological [and educational] influence to the seacoast."[139]

SELECTION[140]

Concerning Scholastic Exercises

1. Every student shall diligently apply himself to his studies in his chamber, as well as attend constantly upon all public exercises appointed by the President or his Tutor; and no Student shall walk abroad, or be absent from his chamber without liberty, except half an hour after breakfast, and an hour and half after dinner, and from prayers at night to nine o'clock, upon penalty of two pence, or more, to six pence, at the discretion of the President or Tutors.

2. Both before and after noon, and after nine o'clock, the tutors in their turn shall daily visit all the chambers of the students, to observe whether they be there and at their Studies; and shall punish all those that shall be absent without liberty or necessity.

3. The President and each of the Tutors, according to the best of their discretion, shall teach and instruct his own class in the three learned languages,[141] and the liberal arts and sciences. In the first year the students are principally to learn the languages and arithmetic; and through the two next following years they are required to pursue the study of the languages in some measure. The second year they recite logic, rhetoric, geometry and geography; the third the other branches of the mathematics, natural philosophy and astronomy; in the fourth metaphysics, ethics, history and civil policy.

The respective classes shall recite the usual books, and in the accustomed manner,[142] or such other books, and in such manner as the President, with the advice of the Tutors, shall appoint; but every Saturday shall be devoted chiefly to the study of divinity.[143] And each class through the whole time of their pupilage shall recite either the assembly's catechism, the confession of faith received and approved by the Churches of this colony,[144] Wollebius, Ames's *Medulla*, or some other system of divinity approved of by the President and Fellows.[145]

---

139. Warch, *School of the Prophets*, pp. 307–8.

140. Yale College, "Concerning Scholastic Exercises" [1748], drawn from The Laws of Yale College (1774), reprinted in George W. Pierson, *A Yale Book of Numbers: Historical Statistics of the College and University, 1701–1976* (New Haven, CT: Yale University, 1983), pp. 209–11. Reprinted by permission of Yale University.

141. That is, Hebrew, Greek, and Latin.

142. The "accustomed manner" is discussed in selection #37 from the Yale Report of 1828 and Charles Eliot's selection #40.

143. "The amount of time spent on the study of divinity was shrinking. In the 1726 college laws Friday afternoon and Saturday had been devoted to it. By 1745 only Saturday was used. [Subsequently] even that amount would be lessened." Brooks M. Kelley, *Yale: A History* (New Haven: Yale University Press, 1974), p. 80.

144. These two options refer to the Westminster Catechism and its modification by a convention of Connecticut divines in 1708.

145. Johann Wollebius (1586–c. 1630) was a Swiss theologian who published his *Compendium Theologiae Christianae* in 1611. It was translated as *The Abridgement of Christian Divinity* in 1650 and added to the Yale

On Tuesdays and Fridays every undergraduate in his turn, about six at a time, shall declaim in the English, Latin, Greek or Hebrew Tongue, and in no other, without special liberty from the President, and shall presently after deliver up his declamation to his Tutor, fairly written, with his name subscribed. The two senior classes shall dispute twice a week in the chapel;[146] and if any undergraduate shall be absent from recitation or disputation without liberty, he may be fined two pence, and if from declaiming six pence.[147]

4. If any student shall very frequently neglect the public exercises aforesaid or perform them very slightly, or if he be frequently absent from public prayers, or from his chamber in studying time, or spend the main of his time in sloth and idleness; he shall be punished by fine, admonition, the having some extraordinary exercises appointed him, or by dismission from college, as the nature and degree of the crime shall require.[148]

5. The senior sophisters shall attend recitation and the other public exercises until the twentieth day of July, yearly; nor may they depart from college before they have completed their theses, and the other necessary preparations for the public commencement, nor then without the President's liberty.

6. About the twentieth of July (on a day appointed by the President) the senior sophisters shall appear in the chapel, to be examined by the President, Fellows, Tutors, or any other gentlemen of liberal education, touching their knowledge and proficiency in the learned languages, the liberal arts and sciences, and other qualifications requisite for receiving a bachelor's degree.

7. All resident Masters and Bachelors are required to attend prayers, lectures, and all other exercises of divine worship in the chapel, under penalty of being deprived the privilege of the library.[149]

8. All resident Bachelors shall dispute in the hall before the President every week, or otherwise, according to the President's direction, upon penalty of four pence for absence without sufficient reason.

---

curriculum in the early 1710s. William Ames (1576–1633) was a leading English Puritan theologian, who wrote most of his works while exiled in Leyden. His *Medulla Theologiae* (1620) was translated as *The Marrow of Sacred Divinity* and included in the Yale curriculum from the beginning.

146. "Up to about 1750 this exercise had always been in Latin in the syllogistic form, but [President Thomas] Clap then introduced forensic disputation in English along with the old method." Kelley, *Yale*, p. 81. See the contemporaneous distinction between these two kinds of disputations at Princeton in selection #33.

147. The humanistic declamation and the scholastic disputation are thus incorporated as supplements to the recitation, as seen in selection #29 concerning Harvard College in 1642.

148. Note, in the third and fourth statutes, the absence of corporal punishment, which was stipulated at Harvard College in selection #29.

149. The library contained the works of John Locke, Isaac Newton, the Philosophical Transactions of the Royal Society, many philosophical and theological works, and some belles lettres. "In 1718, after the school had finally settled in New Haven, the trustees prohibited anyone except themselves from using the library without the rector's consent. In 1723 this rule was relaxed to allow seniors and graduates-in-residence to borrow books on their own. . . . In 1727 the library laws were relaxed further so that any undergraduate could take out one book for one month." Warch, *School of the Prophets*, pp. 240–1.

9. The President shall order the resident Bachelors and undergraduates to make analysis, or perform any other scholastic exercises in the chapel, for the improvement and tryal of their skill and learning, as he shall judge proper.

10. Whereas the marriage state is very incongruous with the state of pupilage in this college, it is ordered, that if any undergraduate shall contract matrimony, he shall be dismissed from college.[150]

---

150. During the eighteenth century, the average age of Yale's entering students was seventeen, while about a quarter were fifteen or sixteen, substantial numbers only thirteen or fourteen, and a few even eleven or twelve. There were also a number of men in their twenties. Over this period, the age of the students gradually became more homogeneous, with the modal age becoming older, necessitating this statute. Pierson, *A Yale Book of Numbers*, p. 106.

33. College of New Jersey, *An Account* (1764)

INTRODUCTION

The nine colleges in the American colonies were founded in a pattern reflecting both public and religious purposes: each colony built one college in conjunction with its established or predominant Protestant sect. This pattern was set by the three earliest colleges: Harvard (1636) founded in Massachusetts by Puritans, who became Congregationalists; the College of William and Mary (1693) founded by Anglicans in Virginia; and Yale (1701) founded in Connecticut by Congregationalists, who leaned toward Presbyterianism.[151]

Although this monopolistic pattern served to conserve resources and, to some extent, lessen sectarian bickering within the colleges, the institutions were not long insulated from the religious ferment around them. Disputants on all sides of the sectarian controversies were acutely aware that control of the colleges meant control of the clergy filling the pulpits. Consequently, when an evangelical revival stormed through the colonies in the 1730s and 1740s, the religious influence on the founding of colleges became even more pronounced, particularly on the College of New Jersey, chartered in 1746 and renamed Princeton University in 1896.

The early stirrings of this "Great Awakening" were prompted by the warmly enthusiastic preaching of individuals such as the Dutch Reformed pastor Theodore Jacob Freylinghuysen (1691–1748) in the Raritan Valley of New Jersey and Jonathan Edwards (1703–1758) in the Connecticut River Valley in Massachusetts and Connecticut. By informing Calvinist theology with the insights of the British empiricist philosophers, Edwards became the most significant theologian in the American colonies and was ultimately called to the presidency of Princeton shortly before his death. Meanwhile, an evangelical Presbyterian graduate of the University of Edinburgh, William Tennent (1673–1745), had emigrated to the colonies in 1718 and been called to a Presbyterian parish in Neshimany, Pennsylvania, in 1726. There he founded his "Log College" which educated several of the most prominent itinerating revivalists of the Great Awakening.

By the time that the Methodist George Whitefield (1714–1770) extended the revival throughout the colonies during his tour from 1739 to 1741, two significant developments had occurred. On the one hand, the Congregational and Presbyterian religious establishments in most colonies had split into a camp of evangelicals, generally termed "New Lights" or "New Side," and a camp suspicious of the emotionalism and affronts to clerical authority prompted by the revival, generally termed "Old Lights" or "Old Side." On the other hand, Tennent's evangelical "Log College" experienced great success and came under threat from the Old Lights, prompting the New Lights to try to found a recognized, degree-granting, evangelical college that could serve as an alternative to Harvard and Yale, which they regarded as moribund and "unconverted." In 1746 the evangelicals succeeded when they received a charter to erect a college "for the Education of Youth in the Learned Languages and in the Liberal Arts and Sciences."[152]

In 1747 the New Side college opened for instruction, and the early presidents emulated the academies founded by Dissenters from the established Anglican Church in England and thus "became

---

151. New Jersey was the exception in that it had two colleges, though both were Presbyterian and nearly merged in 1793. One was Queen's College, now Rutgers University, founded as a Dutch Reformed institution. The other was Princeton discussed here.

152. Quoted from Thomas J. Wertenbaker, *Princeton, 1746–1896* (Princeton, NJ: Princeton University Press, 1946), p. 397.

channels for the latest intellectual and pedagogical currents of the time."[153] Within fourteen years, the college had moved to the town of Princeton, erected a building, grown to nearly one hundred students, and gone through four presidents. In 1761 Samuel Finley was elected the fifth president. An Irishman by birth, Finley came to the American colonies as a young man in 1734, and may have studied at William Tennent's Log College. Beginning in 1744 he served a Presbyterian church on the Maryland-Pennsylvania border for the next seventeen years, while conducting a prominent academy modeled on the Dissenting Academies of England. His graduates included two signers of the U.S. Declaration of Independence, at least three state governors, and some of the most important early medical educators in America.

Under Finley's administration, the College in 1764 issued *An Account of the College of New-Jersey*, providing the first comprehensive and official statement about the curriculum of the college since its founding. As portrayed in this *Account*, the College of New Jersey represents a medial stage between the traditional curriculum of Harvard and Yale and the radical departures of the Dissenting Academies in England. In basic outline, the Princeton four-year plan reflected the influence of the New England colleges, where three of the first five presidents had studied. However, the more pragmatic interest of the Dissenting educators appeared through courses in mathematics and sciences, the study of history, and the system of oratorical practice.[154]

SELECTION[155]

The importance of liberal education of youth, both to church and state, and the necessity of public schools and colleges for that end, is now so universally acknowledged, as to render an enlargement upon it unnecessary, by way of introduction to the following account. The main design of this publication is to acquaint the world with the rise, progress, and present state of the College of New Jersey. . . .

As to the branches of literature taught here, they are the same with those which are made parts of education in the European colleges, save only such as may be occasioned by the infancy of this institution. The students are divided into four distinct classes, which are called the *Freshman*, the *Sophomore*, the *Junior*, and the *Senior*. In each of these, they continue one year; giving and receiving, in their turns, those tokens of respect and subjection which belong to their standings in order to preserve a due subordination. The *Freshman* year is spent in the Latin and Greek languages, particularly in reading *Horace, Cicero's Orations*, the *Greek Testament, Lucian's Dialogues*, and *Xenophon's Cyropaedia*.

In *Sophomore* year, they still prosecute the study of their languages, particularly *Homer, Longinus*,[156] etc.; and enter upon the sciences, geography, rhetoric, logic, and the mathematics. They con-

153. Douglas Sloan, ed., *The Great Awakening and American Education: A Documentary History* (New York: Teachers College Press, 1973), p. 128.

154. Darrell L. Guder, "The History of Belles Lettres at Princeton" (Unpublished Ph.D. diss., University of Hamburg, 1965), pp. 120–34.

155. *An Account of the College of New-Jersey. In which are described the methods of government, modes of instruction, manner and expenses of living in the same, etc.* (Woodbridge, NJ: James Parker, 1764), pp. 5, 23–34.

156. "Longinus" is the name given by early modern writers to an ancient Greek literary critic, whose chief work was first published in 1554 and translated in 1674. Since that time, Longinus's work, though unmentioned by any ancient writer, "has probably been the most influential single work of criticism in modern times." Moses Hadas, *Ancilla to Classical Reading* (New York: Columbia University Press, 1954), p. 86. It is also possible that this

tinue their mathematical studies throughout the *Junior* year, and also pass through a course of natural and moral philosophy, metaphysics, chronology, etc. and the greater number, especially such as are educating for the service of the church, are initiated into the Hebrew. As to this so unhappily unpopular language, no constraint is laid upon the youth to the study of it. But it is to be wished, it may soon be more universally esteemed a useful and important acquisition, as we are told it already is among the politest *literati* in *Europe*. It opens an inexhaustible fund of criticism, both to the divine and the poet. But the reader is referred to Mr. Addison, *Spectator* (v. 6, no. 5), where are displayed the superior beauties of the sacred poesy.[157]

To return, the Senior year is entirely employed in reviews and composition. They now revise the most improving parts of the Latin and Greek classics, part of the Hebrew Bible, and all the arts and sciences.[158] The weekly course of disputation is continued, which was also carried on through the preceding year. They discuss two or three theses in a week; some in the syllogistic and others in the forensic manner, alternately;[159] the forensic being always performed in the English tongue. A series of questions is also prepared on the principal subjects of natural and revealed religion. These are delivered publicly on Sundays before a promiscuous congregation, as well as the college, in order to habituate them early to face an assembly, as also for other important and religious ends to which they are found conducive. There is likewise a monthly oration-day when harangues, or orations of their own composition, are pronounced before a mixed auditory. All those compositions before mentioned are critically examined with respect to the language, orthography, pointing, capitalizing, with the other minutiae, as well as more material properties of accurate writing.

Besides these exercises in writing and speaking, most of which are proper to the Senior class, on every Monday three—and on the other evenings of the week, excepting Saturdays and Sundays, two—out of each of the three inferior classes, in rotation, pronounce declamations of their own composing on the stage. These too are previously examined and corrected, and occasion taken from them early to form a taste for good writing. The same classes also—in rotation three on Tuesday evenings and two on the other evenings, with the exceptions just mentioned—pronounce in like manner such select pieces from *Cicero, Demosthenes, Livy,* and other ancient authors and from *Shakespeare, Milton, Addison,* and such illustrious moderns,[160] as are best adapted to display the various passions and exemplify the graces of utterance and gesture. A good address and agreeable elocution are accomplishments so ingratiating and so necessary to render a public speaker especially popular and, consequently, useful that they are esteemed here as considerable parts of education, in the cultivation of which no little pains are employed.[161]

---

refers to "Longolius," Christopher de Longeuil (1490–1522), a Belgian scholar and one of the most noted Latinists of the sixteenth century, who edited and commented on the works of Cicero and Quintilian.

157. Note the citation of this contemporaneous, vernacular authority. Writing in the *Spectator*, Englishman Joseph Addison (1672–1719) became famous as an essayist in Britain and America during the eighteenth century.

158. Such senior-year revising, or reviewing, harked back to the practice in the liberal arts faculty at the medieval universities and was abandoned over the next century.

159. See the third statute in selection #32 of Yale College statutes.

160. Note the explicit contrast between ancient and modern authors, which had been the subject of intense controversy in England beginning in the 1690s and was named "The Battle of the Books" in 1710 by the English essayist Jonathan Swift.

161. In sum, the Freshman Year included Latin and Greek Languages and Literature; Sophomore Year: Latin and Greek Languages and Literature, Sciences, Geography, Rhetoric, Logic, Mathematics; Junior Year: Mathematics, Natural and Moral Philosophy, Metaphysics, Chronology, Hebrew; Senior Year: Review, Composition, and Crit-

The classics are taught for the first three years in nearer the usual method of grammar schools,[162] than in the last. The students then revise them, principally as examples of fine composition. They first give a more literal translation of a paragraph, afterwards the sense in a paraphrase of their own, and then criticize upon the beauties of the author, in which work they are assisted by the president. No authors are read more particularly with this view, than Homer, Horace, and especially Longinus—

Whose own example strengthens all his laws,
And is himself the great sublime he draws.[163]

Each class recites twice a day, and have always free access to their teachers to solve any difficulties that may occur.

The bell rings for morning prayer at six o'clock, when the Senior class read off a chapter from the original into English. The president then proposes a few critical questions upon it, which, after their concise answers, he illustrates more at large.

The times of relaxation from study are about one hour in the morning, two at noon, and three in the evening: and in these are included the public meals. Evening prayer is always introduced with psalmody; and care is taken to improve the youth in the art of sacred music.

The usual method of instruction in the sciences is this—the pupils frequently and deliberately read over such a portion of the author they are studying on a particular science, as it is judged they can be able thoroughly to impress upon their memories. When they attend their recitations, the tutor proposes questions on every particular they have been reading. After they have given in their turns such answers as show their general acquaintance with the subjects, he explains it more at large, allows them to propose any difficulties, and takes pains to discover whether his explications be fully comprehended.[164] [These are] advantages which are seldom attainable in the usual method of teaching by lecture.[165]

In the instruction of the youth, care is taken to cherish a spirit of liberty and free inquiry, and not only to permit, but even to encourage their right of private judgment, without presuming to dictate with an air of infallibility, or demanding an implicit assent to the decisions of the preceptor.[166]

The Senior, Junior, and (towards the conclusion of their year) the Sophomore classes, are allowed the free use of the college library, that they may make excursions beyond the limits of their stated studies into the unbounded and variegated fields of knowledge; and, especially, to assist them in preparing their disputations and other compositions. . . .[167]

---

icism. The Junior and Senior classes conducted weekly disputations, both in Latin and in English. The Seniors engaged in extra theological studies. The lower three classes engaged in weekly declamations both in Latin and in English.

162. This likely refers to recitation and repetition in contrast to criticism and revision.

163. The source of this quotation has not been identified.

164. This account of recitation, however idealistic, does appear more interlocutory and "Socratic," than was the conventional practice of asking students merely to repeat what they had been "able thoroughly to impress upon their memories."

165. "Lecture" is evidently meant in the longstanding sense of *lectio*, or "reading," to students what they should know or memorize.

166. This declaration, whether or not observed, indicates both the influence of Enlightenment thinking by 1764 and a vast attitudinal change from Harvard and Yale in previous decades.

167. This provision also indicates a remarkable new attitude and institutional policy.

On the third Wednesday in August annually, the Senior class are examined by the trustees, the college officers, and other gentleman of learning then present, throughout all the branches of literature they have been here taught. And if approved, as worthy of academical honors, the president assigns them the parts, they are respectively to perform at the anniversary commencement, the general proceedings of which are so publicly known, as to supersede all necessity of description. They are then graduated Bachelors of Arts. After an interval of three years, they are usually admitted to the master's degree. . . .[168]

As to admission into the several classes, these are the regulations—Candidates for admission into the lowest or freshman class, must be capable of composing grammatical Latin, translating Vergil, Cicero's *Orations*, and the four evangelists in Greek, and, by a late order, must understand the principal rules of vulgar arithmetic. . . .

Besides these examinations for admission into the respective classes, and the last examination of the Senior class, previous to their obtaining the first collegiate honors, the three inferior classes at the end of every year are examined in such of the classics, arts and sciences, as they have studied, in order for admission into the next. And such as are found unqualified, are not allowed to rise in the usual course. These, in like manner as the last examination of the Senior class, are attended by the president and tutors in conjunction with any other gentleman of liberal education who choose to be present.

---

168. Compare the granting of the M.A. described in selection #29 about Harvard College in 1642 and selection #38 about Dartmouth College in 1851.

Section VI

Intellectual and Social Challenges to the College, 1790s–1850s

In 1765 Joseph Priestley observed in "An Essay on a Course of Liberal Education for Civil and Active Life" that "young gentleman themselves so frequently hear the learning which is taught in schools and universities ridiculed."[1] Over the subsequent decades, as that essay was republished and eventually appeared in an American edition in 1803, such ridicule became particularly vociferous in the American colonies and intensified after the founding of the United States, with its sense of being set apart and pioneering a "new order of the ages."

The intellectual and cultural shifts prompting that ridicule are exemplified by the life and writing of Joseph Priestley, a leading figure of the British Enlightenment. Born in England, Priestley became a freethinking clergyman who left the Calvinism of his youth to become a Unitarian; a political theorist who wrote in support of the French Revolution; and an important scientist who discovered oxygen, nitrogen, and ammonia. Priestley's theology and politics incited fierce opposition that drove him in 1794 to emigrate to the United States and settle near Philadelphia, where he was offered, but declined, a chair in chemistry at the University of Pennsylvania. By that point, Priestley's theological, political, scientific, and personal pilgrimage seemed to increase the urgency of his warning from three decades earlier that "a proper course of studies is not provided for gentlemen who are designed to fill the principal stations of *active life*. . . . We have hardly any medium between an education for the counting-house . . . and a method of institution in the abstract sciences: so that we have nothing liberal that is worth the attention of *gentlemen*, whose views neither of these two opposite plans may suit."[2]

Tacitly agreeing with Priestley—perhaps even stimulated by his words or arrival—the American Philosophical Society, based in Philadelphia, announced in 1795 an essay contest for writings describing "the best system of liberal education and literary instruction, adapted to the genius of the government of the United States; comprehending also a plan for instituting and conducting public schools in this country, on principles of the most extensive utility." Of the two winning essays, the one written by Samuel H. Smith appears in selection #34 and embraces the three themes of civic engagement, scientific study, and "most extensive utility" that undergirded Priestley's call for "some new articles of academical instruction, such as have a nearer and more evident connexion with the business of active life, and which may therefore bid fairer to engage the attention, and rouse the thinking powers of young gentlemen of an active genius."[3] Smith's essay thus gave expression to the growing demand in the United States that liberal education should incorporate the useful study of sciences, of modern languages, and of social and political subjects appropriate for citizens of a republic. This education would be "liberal" not only in its open-mindedness, but also in its diffusion to all, wrote Smith.

---

1. Joseph Priestley, "An Essay on a Course of Liberal Education for Civil and Active Life," prefixed to *Lectures on History and General Policy*, ed. J. T. Rutt (London: Printed for Thomas Tegg, 1826), p. 5.

2. Priestley, "An Essay on a Course of Liberal Education," p. 1. "Institution" here means education, as noted in the introduction to Section III. "Abstract sciences" likely refers to philosophy and theology.

3. Priestley, "An Essay on a Course of Liberal Education," p. 7.

Or, almost all. Smith added, "It follows that the great object of a liberal plan of education should be the *almost universal* diffusion of knowledge." What he meant by this qualification eventually became clear: "Two subjects connected with a general system of education, viz. female instruction and that which has been called ornamental, have been avoided. Both of these certainly involve very important considerations. But in the existing diversity of opinion respecting the nature and extent of the first, such coincidence and agreement as to produce a system must absolutely be despaired of. It is sufficient, perhaps, for the present that the improvement of women is marked by a rapid progress and that a prospect opens equal to their most ambitious desires."[4]

It is unlikely that accomplished women of letters, such as Margaret Bayard, agreed with the sufficiency of this mere "prospect" (although Margaret consented to marry Smith). Certainly, Emma Hart Willard disagreed, as can be seen in selection #35. In the words of an early twentieth-century biographer, Willard "revolutionized the ideas of the civilized world on the subject of women's education, a movement which has culminated in the founding of grand colleges exclusively for women and in the admission of women to older colleges on equal terms with men. For it is not too much to say that Wellesley and Vassar and their sister institutions on either side of the Atlantic are the fair fruitage, in time, of those seminal ideas so ably set forth in Mrs. Willard's *Plan of Female Education*."[5]

This "fair fruitage" of seminaries and colleges for women ripened amid a bumper crop of colleges planted during the first half of the nineteenth century, as portrayed in selection #35. The historical interpretation of this college-founding movement is a matter of some controversy, but an incontrovertible point is that the increasing number of colleges heightened the significance of the debate over the purposes and content of liberal education. The views of Priestley and Smith did not easily carry the day. In 1828 the Yale president and faculty issued a famous report, appearing in selection #37, in which they rebutted a proposal "to leave out of said course the study of the *dead languages*, substituting other studies therefor."[6] Even as it quoted Cicero in rebuttal, however, the Yale Report also employed the language of Francis Bacon, the philosophical champion of the new empirical sciences. Thus, Yale, like all colleges, could not and did not remain immune to the calls for change.

By the 1850s, colleges were routinely responding to these calls by instituting parallel courses of study, as seen in selection #38 drawn from the 1852–53 catalog of Dartmouth College, which offered a fairly typical B.A. track as well as a new B.S. course. An alternative institutional strategy to the parallel course of study was the introduction of electivism, so that the students themselves could make the choice among the new and traditional studies crowding into the curriculum. Although the latter approach eventually became the most noteworthy innovation in nineteenth-century liberal education, the former was the most successful in the antebellum era.[7] The strategy of instituting parallel courses of study was successful due, in part, to the fact that diverse populations could more easily be incorpo-

4. Samuel H. Smith, *Remarks on Education: Illustrating the Close Connection Between Virtue and Wisdom. To Which is Annexed a System of Liberal Education* (Philadelphia: John Ormrod, 1798), pp. 37, 77–8. Emphasis added.

5. Ezra Brainerd, "Mrs. Emma Willard's Life and Work in Middlebury," in George G. Bush, *History of Education in Vermont United States Bureau of Education Circular of Information*, no. 4 (Washington, DC: GPO, 1900), pp. 130–1.

6. *Reports on the Course of Instruction in Yale College* (New Haven, CT: Hezekiah Howe, 1828), p. 3.

7. A detailed look at the financial, political, and intellectual conflicts over electivism in the antebellum period is presented in the retrospective account of Harvard's "long transition from a uniform required curriculum to a regulated freedom of choice in studies," 1825–1867. Charles W. Eliot, *Annual Report of the President and Treasurer of Harvard College 1883–84* (Cambridge, MA: Harvard University Press, 1885), pp. 7–24. Quotation is from p. 24.

rated into one institution. For example, young men without a classical preparation could be accommodated, as at Dartmouth. In addition, parallel courses facilitated the radical step of enrolling women, as seen at Alfred University in selection #39. The conventional meaning of the liberal arts degree, the B.A., was thus challenged, on the one hand, by new kinds of knowledge thought to be worthy of study and, on the other, by new kinds of students whose background and goals did not fit the traditional norm, in part because they were circusmscribed by the mores of the day. By the 1850s liberal arts colleges increasingly faced the choice of whether to accommodate the liberal arts degree to either of these imperatives or both.

Revolutionary Influences on the Colleges

34. Samuel H. Smith, *A System of Liberal Education* (1798)

INTRODUCTION

Samuel Harrison Smith (1772–1845) was born in Philadelphia, the son of Jonathan Bayard Smith, a 1760 graduate of the College of New Jersey, a merchant in Philadelphia, and a member of the Continental Congress. His mother was Susannah Bayard, daughter of a prominent Maryland family, whose name Samuel's father incorporated into his own upon marriage. Being precocious and devoted to literary pursuits, Samuel attended school, entered the University of Pennsylvania as a young boy, and graduated in 1787 at the age of fifteen.

During the 1780s and 1790s newspapers and magazines were proliferating faster and being read by a greater cross section of the population in the new United States of America than anywhere else in the world. Building on the legacy of Benjamin Franklin, Philadelphia was the heart of this journalistic industry, and Samuel Smith founded his own newspaper there in 1796. This endeavor established not only the course of his career but also his political affiliation, for his newspaper aligned itself with Thomas Jefferson and Smith remained a staunch supporter and, eventually, friend of Jefferson for the rest of his life. Meanwhile, in 1795 the American Philosophical Society announced its contest for essays describing "the best system of liberal education and literary instruction, adapted to the genius of the government of the United States." This contest, "characteristic of the society's expansive concern with institutions and social supports, was one of several authorized in 1795 at a meeting which also recorded interest in ship pumps, vegetable dyes, the longevity of peach trees, and domestic heating."[8] Only seven essays were submitted in the contest, and the prize was shared between two of the authors, one of whom was 25-year-old Samuel Smith. Although the competition was not severe and the distinction shared, Smith attracted the attention of Jefferson, who urged him to come to Washington after Jefferson's election to the presidency in 1800.

The themes of Smith's essay must have been pleasing to Jefferson, a chief architect of the new republic and the consummate American scion of the European Enlightenment. On the one hand, Smith invokes the virtuous commitment that each citizen owes to the corporate community and state, the *res publica*. This commitment was the ideological cornerstone of the early republic. On the other hand, Smith identifies the pursuit of happiness as the goal of life and maintains that great progress has been

---

8. Quotations are from Frederick Rudolph, "Introduction," in *Essays on Education in the Early Republic*, ed. Rudolph (Cambridge, MA: Harvard University Press, 1965), p. xv.

and will continue to be achieved through the advance of knowledge and the virtuous application of that knowledge to socially and technologically useful purposes. This viewpoint was heavily influenced by the eighteenth-century intellectual movement known as the Enlightenment, which enshrined reason and freedom (characteristically conjoined as "freethinking"[9]) as the leading attributes of humanity and civilization. The Enlightenment influence on Smith may, in fact, reflect the writing on liberal education by Joseph Priestley, discussed in the introduction above. Despite the prominence of Priestley's reputation and the timing of his arrival in Philadelphia in 1794 shortly before Smith wrote his essay, there is no direct evidence linking Samuel Smith to Priestley. But an intriguing similarity exists between points in Smith's essay and Priestley's twenty-five-page "An Essay on a Course of Liberal Education for Civil and Active Life."[10] If Smith did not draw from Priestley's essay, then the similarity demonstrates the remarkable consonance among the ideas of leading Enlightenment figures about liberal education. Certain points of similarity are observed in the notes to the following reading.

In 1800 Smith moved to Washington with President-elect Jefferson and married his brilliant second cousin Margaret Bayard, who published stories for magazines and two novels. In 1804 the Smiths bought a country estate, now part of the campus of the Catholic University of America, and became important figures in the Washington social and political circles. Due to ill health he sold his newspaper in 1810 and held various public posts until his death in Washington at the age of seventy-three.

SELECTION[11]

The two great objects of a correct education are to make men virtuous and wise. The terms virtuous and wise do not seem susceptible to absolute definition. Accordingly, as applied to different persons and varying circumstances, they present different aspects, though it be possible, nay probable, that the elements or first principles of each, however modified by endless combination, are the same.[12] This hypothesis derives some confirmation from the great affinity of one virtue to another and the close alliance between the several departments of science and literature.

Without attempting precise definition, it may be sufficiently correct so far as it regards the objects of this essay, to style VIRTUE that active exertion of our faculties which in the highest degree pro-

9. Joseph Priestley was heavily influenced by the writings of an early and notorious advocate of the movement, Anthony Collins, who authored: *A Discourse of Free-Thinking Occasion'd by the Rise and Growth of a Sect call'd Free-thinkers* (London, 1713).

10. Priestley's quotations in the notes that follow are drawn from an 1826 edition: Joseph Priestley, "An Essay on a Course of Liberal Education for Civil and Active Life," prefixed to *Lectures on History and General Policy*, ed. J. T. Rutt (London: Printed for Thomas Tegg, 1826), pp. 1–25. This essay is not as well known as Priestley's *Miscellaneous Observations Relating to Education, more especially as it respects the Conduct of the Mind*, which has been interpreted as presenting his views on liberal education. But the fact that he originally published these two essays together indicates that *Miscellaneous Observations* was not intended to address liberal education, which it does not mention. *Miscellaneous Observations*, 2nd ed. (Birmingham, United Kingdom: M. Swinney, 1788), p. xv.

11. Samuel H. Smith, *Remarks on Education: Illustrating the Close Connection Between Virtue and Wisdom. To Which is Annexed a System of Liberal Education* (Philadelphia: John Ormrod, 1798), pp. 10–20, 36–53, 81–6.

12. Seneca the Younger discusses the relationship between virtue, wisdom, and learning in selection #5, as does Pier Paolo Vergerio in selection #25 and James McCosh in selection #48.

motes our own happiness[13] and that of our fellow men;[14] and WISDOM, that intelligent principle which improves our faculties, affords them the means of useful exertion, and determines the objects on which they are exercised.[15]

While wisdom and virtue have united, time immemorial, to panegyrise each other in reference to the general good they produce in the world, two questions of great importance have remained undecided, viz.

I. Whether wisdom and virtue are in any degree necessarily connected; and, if they are, whether universally or partially.

II. Whether wisdom, in its greatest practical extension, would, if universally diffused, produce the greatest portion of general happiness.[16]

It will be acknowledged that these points deserve a patient discussion, as their decision will determine the definite objects of education and as it is absolutely necessary that man should know the *objects* he desires to accomplish before he can apply, with the prospect of a successful result, the *means* adapted to secure them.

I. The first inquiry is, "Whether wisdom and virtue are, in any degree, necessarily connected; and if they are, whether universally or partially."

It has been the opinion of some distinguished philosophers that virtue and instinct are the same and that a wise providence has not left the direction of the moral principle under the capricious and feeble influence of reason, while others have contended that although man be by nature ignorant and entirely destitute of moral principle, yet that he possesses faculties capable of high improvement, if not of perfection itself. Both these systems, notwithstanding their numerous votaries, are probably founded in error. . . . Nature is neither so liberal nor education so omnipotent as the rival systems affirm; that man is indebted to both; that certain passions are born with him which he cannot exterminate but may control; that a varied capacity is imparted to him which by education he can weaken or improve; but that still the traces of nature are visible in his thoughts and actions; and that her voice never ceases to be heard amidst all the refinements of art. . . .

We cannot, therefore, err in assuming it is a fact that virtue and wisdom are in some degree necessarily connected, that the crude wisdom which nature bestows is unequal to the production and government of virtue such as man in his pursuit of happiness discovers it to be his interest to practice, and that to insure this desirable object it is necessary that the original faculties of the mind should be vigorously exercised, extended, and strengthened.

It still remains to be considered whether wisdom and virtue are partially or universally connected. . . . From a review of history, it will appear that just in proportion to the cultivation of science and the arts has the happiness of man advanced in the nation which cultivated them. . . .[17] Hence the origin of

---

13. Compare this eudaemonistic definition of virtue, derived from Greek philosophical influences prevalent in the eighteenth-century Enlightenment, with the relationship between virtue and the liberal arts posited in Christian writings, as well as the eudaemonistic rationale of Emma Willard (II) in selection #35.

14. This potentially significant qualification on the eudaemonistic definition echoes views in Joseph Priestley's *Essay on the First Principles of Government* (1769), which English philosopher and political economist Jeremy Bentham (1748–1832) credited with inspiring his famous utilitarian principle and phrase: "the greatest good for the greatest number."

15. What does Smith mean by "wisdom" throughout this essay?

16. What precisely is the relationship between happiness and virtue posited by Smith?

17. In the liberal arts tradition has the view previously been advanced that "just in proportion to the cultivation of science and the arts has the happiness of man been advanced"?

new and permanent regards, the parents of a thousand new virtues! From what source do these proceed, but from the development of reason, suggesting to man the improvement of his situation? This improvement seems susceptible of endless extension.[18] Hence the conclusion that reason in alliance with virtue admits of progression without termination and that the purity of the last is best secured by the strength of the first.

We proceed to consider, II. Whether wisdom itself, in its greatest extension, would if universally diffused, produce the greatest portion of general happiness.[19]

The affirmative side of this question will be illustrated by considering: that the diffusion of knowledge actually produces some virtues, which without it would have no existence, and that it strengthens and extends all such virtues as are generally deemed to have, in a limited degree, an existence independent of uncommon attachments. And that, the exercise of these virtues is the only certain means of securing real happiness. The virtues, which are the exclusive and appropriate offspring of an enlightened understanding, are those which are disconnected with any particular time, person, or place. Existing without reference to these, a spirit of universal philanthropy is inspired that views the whole world as a single family and transfers to it the feelings of regard which are indulged towards the most amiable of our acquaintance. This sentiment, free from the alloy of personal consideration or national attachment, lifts the mind to an elevation infinitely superior to the sensation of individual regard, superior to the ardent feelings of patriotism, and rivals, in a measure, the enjoyment of the sublime ideas we connect with the apprehension of the divine mind. . . .[20]

The diffusion of knowledge, co-extensive with that of virtue, would seem to apply with close precision to a republican system of education,[21] because:

1. An enlightened nation is always most tenacious of its rights.
2. It is not the interest of such a society to perpetuate error, as it undoubtedly is the interest of many societies differently organized.
3. In a republic the sources of happiness are open to all without injuring any.
4. If happiness be made at all to depend on the improvement of the mind and the collision of mind with mind, the happiness of an individual will greatly depend upon the general diffusion of knowledge and a capacity to think and speak correctly.

---

18. Compare the views of Werner Jaeger and Paul Kristeller in the Introduction to Smith's optimistic vision of an "endless extension" of social and human improvement.

19. Priestley had anticipated that extending "the fund of knowledge" will extend "the present happier state of affairs" to "a more perfect and improved state of society" Priestley, "An Essay on a Course of Liberal Education," pp. 1–2.

20. In the omitted pages, Smith cites John Locke on behalf of the view that "all kinds of knowledge are intimately allied and that the perfection of one department of science depends as much on the advancement of other departments as it does on the accurate development of its own peculiar principles. An exclusive devotedness of the mind to one branch of knowledge, instead of enlarging, will impair it. Instead of furnishing it with truth, it will burden it with error" (pp. 23–4).

21. In a footnote to the American edition (1803) of "An Essay on a Course of Liberal Education," Priestley observed, "What is said in this essay . . . is much more applicable to Americans, as every individual has much more influence in public measures. In fact, the greatest attention is actually given to them by almost all persons in the United States. It is therefore the more necessary that they be well instructed in the true principles of government and general policy, that they may be better qualified to give their votes on public occasions with real judgment, and without prejudice, to which members of free states are peculiarly liable" Priestley, "An Essay on a Course of Liberal Education," p. 25n.

5. Under a republic, duly constructed, man feels as strong a bias to improvement as under a despotism he feels an impulse to ignorance and depression.

We have now reached the goal of the preceding speculations. . . . that human happiness depends upon the possession of virtue and wisdom, that virtue cannot be too highly cultivated, that it is only secure when allied with knowledge, and of consequence that knowledge itself cannot possibly be too extensively diffused. It follows that the great object of a liberal plan of education should be the almost universal diffusion of knowledge.[22]

But as knowledge is infinite and its complete attainment requires more time than man has at his command, it becomes interesting to assign:

I. The time fit to be devoted to education,

II. The objects proper to be accomplished, and

III. The manner of accomplishing them.

I. *The time fit to be devoted to education.* Previously to any prospect of success, one principle must prevail. Society must establish the right to educate, and acknowledge the duty of having educated, all children. A circumstance so momentously important must not be left to the negligence of individuals. It is believed that this principle is recognized in almost all our state constitutions. If so, the exercise of it would not be contested. Indeed, whether at present acknowledged or not, it would produce such beneficial effects, as well in reference to the parent as the child, that a general acquiescence might be relied on.[23]

Having contemplated in reference to man an abatement of two hours of labor, the next object of inquiry is what time should be devoted to the education of youth. It should unquestionably be much larger, as during this period the mind is unimproved, as impressions of the greatest strength are rapidly made, and as the future bias of the mind entirely depends upon the improvement of these impressions. The period, however, should have its limits. Study should never be continued after it becomes oppressive. The preceptor should be as cautious in using every means necessary to prevent disgust as he ought to be zealous in exciting a thirst of knowledge. Without aiming at rigid precision, in considering the claims of labor and study, we shall not, perhaps, materially err in assigning four hours each day to education.

II. *The objects proper to be accomplished.* Let us, then, with mental inflexibility, believe that though all men will never be philosophers, yet all men may be enlightened, and that folly, unless arising from physical origin, may be banished from the society of men.[24]

The ideas already expressed, and those which succeed, must be understood as applicable to a system of general education. They only prescribe what it is necessary every man should know. They do

---

22. This terminology circulated widely and was given prominence by "A Bill for the More General Diffusion of Knowledge," drafted by Thomas Jefferson in 1779 for the Virginia Legislature.

23. In a note, Smith translates a sentence ("It is proper to remind parents that their children belong to the state and that in their education they ought to conform to the rules which it prescribes") from a speech, published in 1796, by Jean Jacques Regis de Cambaceres (1753–1824), French statesman and legal expert who helped to draft the Napoleonic Code.

24. In a note, Smith quotes Francis Bacon (1561–1626), English statesman and philosopher of science, who published the *Advancement of Learning* in 1605. See *The Works of Francis Bacon*, ed. James Spedding at al., 7 vols. (London: Longman, Green, 1857–1859), v. 1, p. 417.

not attempt to limit his acquisitions. Wealth and genius will always possess great advantages. It will be their prerogatives, if properly directed, to carry improvement to its highest eminences.

In forming a system of liberal education, it is necessary to avoid ideas of too general a character as well as those which involve too minute a specification. Considerable latitude must be allowed for the different degrees of natural capacity and the varying shades of temper and bias. It seems, therefore, fit to lay down principles which possess properties common to every mind and which will, of course, in their application, admit of few, if any, exceptions.

[II.A.] The first great object of a liberal system of education[25] should be the admission into the young mind of such ideas only as are either absolutely true or in the highest degree probable; and the cautious exclusion of all error. . . .

Whether we consider man's existence as terminated by the grave or view him, as he doubtless is, the heir of a future life, we must consider his happiness as altogether dependent on the observance of certain moral principles. The universality with which these have been received may be considered as the test of their truth. These principles are few and simple. As the mind expands they should be explained. They require no other aid than clear illustration. The unperverted understanding acknowledges their truth, as it were, by intuition.[26] Let then those truths in which all men agree be firmly impressed, let those which are probable be inculcated with caution, and let doubt always hang over those respecting which the good and the wise disagree. Above all things let the infant mind be protected from conviction without proof.[27]

But it will be said that in almost all the departments of a general plan of education, the perusal of approved books must be chiefly relied on. The indispensable economy of arrangements which are to pervade a whole society will prohibit the employment of preceptors of either great or original talents. It will therefore be fit that the preceptor, instead of inculcating his own immature ideas, should be guided by prescribed works. It is asked where performances explaining and enforcing plain and undeniable truths and avoiding prejudices or falsehoods are to be found. Such productions are acknowledged to be rare. It is also granted that this difficulty presents one of the most serious obstacles to successful education. But it is not insurmountable. It is attempted to be removed, as will appear hereafter, by offering large rewards for books of this nature and by inciting the learned by other inducements to embark in so noble a service.[28] At present we must be satisfied in giving the preference to those works which abound most with truth and are the most exempt from error.

The elements of education, viz. reading and writing, are so obviously necessary that it is useless to do more than enumerate them.

Of nearly equal importance are the first principles of mathematics, as at present almost universally taught.

A tolerably correct idea of geography would seem, in a republic especially, to involve great advantages. The interest of the mercantile part of the community is closely connected with correct geo-

---

25. This phrase, like the "liberal plan of education" in selection #34 by Samuel Smith, relies on the conventional, eighteenth-century English usage of "liberal" to mean "generous, capacious." Smith's interchanging of these phrases with "a system of liberal education," as he does in these two paragraphs, indicates a transformation in the meaning of "liberal education" along the lines expressed by Joseph Priestley: "to enlarge the minds of young men and give them liberal views of many important subjects." Priestley, *Lectures on History and General Policy*, p. iii.

26. Does this statement contradict Smith's denial of instinctual virtue above?

27. Compare Smith's appeal to intuition just above.

28. Joseph Priestley states (pp. vii–ix) that he wrote his *Lectures on History and General Policy* in order to perform this service.

graphical knowledge. Many important departments of science include an accurate knowledge of it. But the most important consideration is that which contemplates the United States as either allied in friendship or arrayed in hostility with the other nations of the earth. In both which cases, it becomes the duty of the citizen to have just ideas of the position, size, and strength of nations, that he may as much as possible, confide in his own judgment in forming an opinion of our foreign relations, instead of yielding his mind to a dangerous credulity. A most interesting part of geography relates to a knowledge of our own country. Correct information on this subject will always conduce to strengthen the bands of friendship and to dissipate the misrepresentations of party prejudice.[29]

The cultivation of natural philosophy, particularly so far as it relates to agriculture and manufactures, has been heretofore almost entirely neglected. The benefits, however, which it would produce are great, both as they regard the happiness of the individual and as they regard national wealth. Many of the labors of the farmer and the mechanic, so far from forbidding reflection, invite it.[30] Thus the constant development of new beauties in nature and the almost as constant production of new wonders in art extort admiration from the most ignorant and even impress their minds with considerable delight. And yet how little do they know of the energies of nature or art? Lost in the contemplation of effects, the tribute of a grateful mind finds vent in simple wonder.

If we reverse the scene and behold the farmer enlightened by the knowledge of chemistry, how wide a field of reflection and pleasure, as well as profit, would acknowledge his empire? The ingenuity of the mechanic would not long remain passive. Repeated efforts at improvement would often prove successful and be the source of new and rapid wealth. At any rate, in all these cases, whether prospered with the expected success or not, an adequate compensation would be conferred on the mind thus employed whose thoughts generally bring with them their own reward.

The circumscribed advantages, attending geographical knowledge, will be greatly enlarged by a liberal acquaintance with history.[31] In proportion as this branch of education shall be cultivated, men will see the mighty influence of moral principle, as well on the private individuals of a community as on those who are called to preside over its public concerns. It will be distinctly seen that ambition has generally risen on a destruction of every sentiment of virtue and that it much oftener merits execration than applause. . . . In short the mirror which history presents will manifest to man what it is probable he will become, should he surrender himself up to those selfish pursuits, which centering in his own fame alone have enabled him without horror to wade through the blood and tears of millions. . . .

[II B.] The second leading object of education should be to inspire the mind with a strong disposition to improvement.

It is acknowledged that science is still in its infancy. The combination of ideas is infinite. As this combination advances, the circle of knowledge is enlarged and of course the sphere of happiness extended. At present science is only cultivated by a few recluse students, too apt to mingle the illusions

---

29. Note this Republican justification for the study of geography.

30. Smith apparently proposes to address agricultural, mechanical, and mercantile topics in liberal education, which Priestley did not, a distinction likely arising from the different backgrounds of the young American born in Benjamin Franklin's Philadelphia and the mature, British immigrant. Cf. Priestley, "An Essay on a Course of Liberal Education," pp. 1–2.

31. Explaining the reason for preparing his textbook *Lectures on History and General Policy*, Joseph Priestley wrote, "I found that the far greater part of the students were young gentlemen designed for civil and active life, whereas the course of study, as in all other places of liberal education, was almost entirely adapted to the learned professions; and it occurred to me that, beside the lectures which they had been used to attend, other courses might be introduced, which would bring them acquainted with such branches of knowledge as would be of more immediate use to them when they should come into life." (pp. vii–viii.)

of imagination with the results of indistinct observation. Hence the reproach that theory and practice oppose each other. But no sooner shall a whole nation be tributary to science than it will dawn with new luster. To adopt a physical illustration, its rays may be expected to meet with little absorption from ignorance but to be reflected with additional luster from every object they strike. The most splendid discoveries have not been made by philosophers of profound erudition and abstracted reflection but by men of moderate attainments and correct observation.[32] They have proceeded from steady and patient observation. . . .[33]

[II C.] This progressive improvement would be promoted, in the third place, by inspiring youth with a taste for and an attachment to science, so firm that it should be almost impossible to eradicate it in the subsequent periods of life. For this purpose studies which address themselves to the heart, as well as those which require strong mental attention, should invite the exercise of their thoughts. Rewards should be liberally bestowed, as well those which furnish the means of moderate pleasure as those which confer distinction. Coercion should be seldom if ever applied.

[II D.] But this great object would be assisted more than by any other consideration by—rendering, in the fourth place, knowledge as highly practical as possible. This idea has been already noticed. But it merits a more extensive discussion. Next to the first object it claims the greatest notice.

All science ought to derive its rank from its utility.[34] The real good which it actually does, or is capable of doing, is the only genuine criterion of its value. Man may indulge himself in sublime reveries, but the world will forever remain uninterested in them. It is only when he applies the powers of his mind to objects of general use that he becomes their benefactor; until he does this he is neither entitled to their gratitude or applause.

He is the best friend of man who makes discoveries involving effects which benefit mankind the most extensively. Moral truths are therefore of importance but little short of infinite. For they apply to numbers which almost evade enumeration and to time which loses itself in eternity. These truths, all agree, are not to be sought in the cloister.[35] They are only acquired by uniting the calm and patient reflection of retirement with the bold and penetrating observation of active life.

In physics the happiness of mankind is in the highest degree increased by discoveries and improvements connected with agriculture and manufactures.[36] These two occupations employ nine-tenths of most communities and a much larger proportion of others. Does it not then become an interesting inquiry whether it be not expedient in infancy and youth to communicate to the mind the lead-

---

32. Are these sentiments of anti-intellectualism entailed by Smith's other views?

33. Here and in his above definition of "philosophy" as "but another word for experience," Smith seems to embrace wholeheartedly the empiricism associated with Francis Bacon and John Locke, both of whom he quotes and cites in his notes.

34. Such statements, enshrining utility and, elsewhere, castigating "idle curiousity," have led to the judgment that, among early republican writers, "the bitterest attack on philosophy was made by Samuel Harrison Smith" in this essay. Eva T. H. Brann, *Paradoxes of Education in a Republic* (Chicago: University of Chicago Press, 1979), p. 94.

35. Throughout the essay, Smith makes derogatory references to monastic or "scholastic" practices and influences. Such pejorative references were common in subsequent decades, as noted by Noah Porter in the introduction to selection #38.

36. Priestley regretted "that a proper course of studies is not provided for gentlemen who are designed to fill the principal stations of *active life*." Priestley, "An Essay on a Course of Liberal Education," pp. 1–2. But Priestley did not endorse Smith's very American concern for useful mundane issues in agriculture and mechanics. Jeremiah Day addresses the latter concern in selection #37.

ing principles of nature and art in these departments of labor, not only by a theoretical exposition of them but also by their practical development. . . .

[II E.] The fifth object should be the inspiring youth with an ardent love for mankind. To accomplish this end, the preceptor should cautiously avoid instilling into the mind of his pupil a mean idea of human nature. The pages of the moralist by debasing man have aided that degeneracy which they deprecate. We should not even convey a suspicion of the honesty of him whom we wish to be virtuous. Those who have led the public mind, so far from attending to this maxim, have almost universally portrayed the heart and conduct of man as infinitely depraved, and we have often beheld the gloomy spectacle of a misanthropic infant. If we examine the tendency of the unperverted principles of nature, we must acknowledge their hostility to that suspicion and jealousy which have proceeded from the force of education. . . .

III. *The manner of accomplishing the objects of education.* . . .
Let us contemplate the effects of a just system:
    1. on the individual citizen;
    2. on the United States;
    3. on the world.[37]

1. *The citizen*, enlightened, will be a free man in its truest sense. He will know his rights, and he will understand the rights of others; discerning the connection of his interest with the preservation of these rights, he will as firmly support those of his fellow men as his own. Too well informed to be misled, too virtuous to be corrupted, we shall behold man consistent and inflexible. Not at one moment the child of patriotism, and at another the slave of despotism, we shall see him in principle forever the same. Immutable in his character, inflexible in his honesty, he will feel the dignity of his nature and cheerfully obey the claims of duty. He will look upon danger without dismay, so he will feel within himself the power of averting or the faculty of disarming it. . . .

2. *Viewing the effects of such a system on the United States*, the first result would be the giving perpetuity to those political principles so closely connected with our present happiness. In addition to these might be expected numerous improvements in our political economy. By these means government without oppression and protection without danger will exist in their necessary strength. . . . Possessed of every source of happiness under the guardianship of all necessary power, she would soon become a model for the nations of the earth. This leads in the third place to,

3. *The consideration of the effects of such a system on the world.*[38] Nation is influenced as powerfully by nation as one individual is influenced by another. Hence no sooner shall any one nation demonstrate by practical illustration the goodness of her political institutions than other nations will imperceptibly introduce corresponding features into their systems. No truth is more certain than that man will be happy if he can. He only wants a complete conviction of the means to pursue them with energy and success. This conviction the United States may be destined to flash on the world.

Independent of this necessary effect, other effects will be produced. Many of the most enlightened of our citizens will traverse the globe with the spirit of philosophical research. They will carry with

---

37. On the debate about political "effects" of the liberal arts colleges in this early republican era, see David W. Robson *Educating Republicans: The College in the Era of the American Revolution, 1750–1800* (Westport, CT: Greenwood Press, 1985), chs. 5–6.

38. The optimistic rationalism of the Enlightenment, the virtuous Republicanism, and the exceptionalism of the United States converge in this closing part III.

them valuable information and an ardent enthusiasm to diffuse it. Its diffusion will be the era of reform wherever it goes.

But more important, still, will be the example of the most powerful nation on earth, if that example exhibit dignity, humility, and intelligence. Scarcely a century can elapse before the population of America will be equal and her power superior to that of Europe. Should the principles be then established, which have been contemplated, and the connection be demonstrated between human happiness and the peaceable enjoyment of industry and the indulgence of reflection, we may expect to see America too enlightened and virtuous to spread the horrors of war over the face of any country and too magnanimous and powerful to suffer its existence where she can prevent it. Let us, then, with rapture anticipate the era when the triumph of peace and the prevalence of virtue shall be rendered secure by the diffusion of useful knowledge.

35. Emma Willard, *A Plan for Improving Female Education* (1819)

INTRODUCTION

Emma Hart (1787–1870) was born the sixteenth of seventeen children in a farming family in Berlin, Connecticut. Being descended from learned New England clergymen, both her father and mother valued education, so Emma progressed beyond elementary school and attended the town grammar school for two years. This was unusual because, although most New England towns were providing free elementary education for girls, grammar school led to college, which women could not attend. The many newly founded "female academies" were offering only unacademic, "ornamental" studies. At age seventeen Emma began teaching in a nearby district school and earned a sterling reputation as a schoolmistress, leading to her appointment as head of the female academy in Middlebury, Vermont, in 1807. Two years later she resigned to marry John Willard, a well-to-do and publicly involved physician, twenty-eight-years-older than she.

To that point, Emma Willard had not expressed any unorthodox views on education in general or women's education in particular. But while energetically performing domestic duties, she began reading her husband's medical books during his frequent periods away and then took up a copy of Euclid's *Elements of Geometry* belonging to her nephew who was attending college. Beset initially by self-doubt similar to that of Christine de Pizan described in selection #12, Willard "thinks she understands [Euclid]; but the general belief in the incapacity of 'the female mind' for mathematics causes misgivings, until she submits herself to her nephew for examination, and he pronounces her learning correct."[39] This encounter with Euclid in her late twenties stimulated a personal, intellectual awakening and the full realization that the intellectual capacity of women is no less than that of men. She then proceeded to study works in natural philosophy, ethics, and epistemology.

Soon thereafter Dr. Willard fell into debt, and in 1814 Emma opened a boarding school in their home in order to help financially. Her new school at first taught only the "ornamental" studies, such as drawing and penmanship, that were normally offered to girls. But gradually she began to expand and deepen the curriculum with liberal studies reserved for young men, such as mathematics, history,

39. Ezra Brainerd, "Mrs. Emma Willard's Life and Work in Middlebury," in George G. Bush, *History of Education in Vermont, United States Bureau of Education Circular of Information*, no. 4 (Washington, DC: GPO, 1900), p. 133. Compare Mary Fairfax Somerville's encounter with Euclid in selection #45. In selection #1 Plato suggests (526b–c) that the difficult study of mathematics is the best starting point for liberal education, as further implied in Socrates's dialogue with the slave boy in Plato's *Meno*.

and languages. This expansion was prompted by her own intellectual development through her private reading, while the contrast between the studies in her academy and those reserved for young men at neighboring Middlebury College "made me bitterly feel the disparity in educational facilities between the two sexes."[40] Willard's appreciation of this disparity and of institutional finances led her to realize that a female academy could not afford to innovate educationally if it was dependent on tuition revenue and satisfying the conventional preferences of young women or their parents. Hence, she decided to draw up a proposal to establish a publicly supported seminary offering more demanding education to women.

The writing of *A Plan for Improving Female Education* occupied her nearly three years and entailed seven revisions eliminating three-quarters of the original material. "No one knew of my writing it, except my husband, until a year after it was completed," she later recalled, "for I knew that I should be regarded as a visionary, almost to insanity, should I utter the expectations . . . that . . . influential men would carry my project before some legislature, for the sake of obtaining a good school."[41] Consciously avoiding such terms as "college" and "liberal education,"[42] Willard nevertheless "called for a liberal arts curriculum incorporating some essentials from men's colleges."[43] In an often repeated phrase, a later president of Middlebury College called the *Plan* "the Magna Carta of the rights of woman in matters of education."[44]

In 1818 the *Plan* became public when Willard's friends arranged for her to send it to DeWitt Clinton, then governor of New York. His positive response prompted Willard and her husband to move to Albany in order to petition the state legislature to adopt the proposal and appropriate monies. But the state legislature repeatedly voted it down, so Willard published the *Plan* at her own expense in 1819 and sent copies to prominent persons around the country. Presidents James Monroe, Thomas Jefferson, and John Adams, among others, wrote approvingly to her; and the tract was circulated in Europe. Despite such positive responses, "the opposition was vocal, declaring that book learning would not help women knit stockings or make puddings, and one indignant farmer entered his protest with 'They'll be educating the cows next.'"[45]

Given this response, Willard assented to overtures from citizens in Troy, New York, to establish a female seminary. From 1821 to 1838 Willard headed the Troy Female Seminary, which grew into one of the most famous female academies in the United States and Europe. Apart from the advanced curriculum, Willard also instituted a pedagogy relying less on memorization and more on visual aids and problem-solving than was conventional at the time. While leading the Academy, she co-authored

---

40. Quoted from Henry Fowler, "Educational Services of Mrs. Emma Willard," *The American Journal of Education* 6 (Mar 1859): 133.

41. Quoted from Fowler, "Educational Services of Mrs. Emma Willard," p. 134.

42. Willard employs the word "seminary," derived from *seminarium* in Latin, originally denoting a nursery for young trees or "seedlings" and, subsequently, a school. This generic meaning was common in Willard's time, and still appeared in Daniel C. Gilman, "Is It Worthwhile to Uphold Any Longer the Idea of Liberal Education?" *Educational Review* 3 (1892): 105–119. By that point, however, "seminary" primarily denoted schools for training clergy. Hence, Edward H. Clarke considered the generic usage "odd" in selection #42.

43. Barbara Miller Solomon, *In the Company of Educated Women: A History of Women and Higher Education in America* (New Haven, CT: Yale University Press, 1985), p. 18.

44. Ezra Brainerd, "Mrs. Emma Willard's Life," p. 136. Ezra Brainerd (1844–1924) wrote this account in the late 1880s while serving as president of Middlebury College.

45. Quotations are from Alma Lutz, *Emma Willard: Pioneer Educator of American Women* (Boston: Beacon Press, 1964), pp. 28, 33.

a geography textbook employing these principles, which became one of the most popular geography texts in the country. In 1838 she retired from Troy seminary at age fifty-one and joined various campaigns on behalf of improving education. Upon her death in 1870 at the age of eighty-three, the New York state legislature joined newspapers and educational journals throughout the country in recognizing her pioneering efforts to advance education for women.

SELECTION[46]

The object of this Address is to convince the public that a reform with respect to female education is necessary, that it cannot be effected by individual exertion, but that it requires the aid of the legislature; and further, by showing the justice, the policy, and the magnanimity of such an undertaking, to persuade that body to endow a seminary for females as the commencement of such reformation.

The idea of a college for males will naturally be associated with that of a seminary instituted and endowed by the public, and the absurdity of sending ladies to college may, at first thought, strike every one to whom this subject shall be proposed. I therefore hasten to observe that the seminary here recommended will be as different from those appropriated to the other sex, as the female character and duties are from the male.[47] The business of the husbandman is not to waste his endeavors in seeking to make his orchard attain the strength and majesty of his forest, but to rear each to the perfection of its nature. . . .

If the improvement of the American female character, and that alone, could be effected by public liberality employed in giving better means of instruction, such improvement of one half of society (and that half which barbarous and despotic nations have ever degraded) would of itself be an object worthy of the most liberal government on earth. But if the female character be raised, it must inevitably raise that of the other sex, and thus does the plan proposed offer as the object of legislative bounty to elevate the whole character of the community.

As evidence that this statement does not exaggerate the female influence in society, our sex need but be considered in the single relation of mothers.[48] In this character, we have the charge of the whole mass of individuals who are to compose the succeeding generation, during that period of youth when the pliant mind takes any direction to which it is steadily guided by a forming hand. How important a power is given by this charge! Yet, little do too many of my sex know how either to appreciate or improve it. Unprovided with the means of acquiring that knowledge (which flows liberally to the other sex) [and] having our time of education devoted to frivolous acquirements, how should we understand the nature of the mind, so as to be aware of the importance of those early impressions which we make upon the minds of our children? Or how should we be able to form enlarged and correct views either of the character to which we ought to mold them, or of the means most proper to form them aright?

Considered in this point of view, were the interests of male education alone to be consulted, that of females becomes of sufficient importance to engage the public attention. . . . In the arrangement of my remarks, I shall pursue the following order.[49]

46. Emma Willard, *A Plan for Improving Female Education*, 2nd ed. (Middlebury, VT: J. W. Copeland, 1819), pp. 3–8, 17–43, 46–60.

47. This difference apparently contributed to Willard's choice of the term "seminary," rather than "college."

48. Compare the argument of Bathsua Makin on this point.

49. The attention to arrangement is significant. Like Bathsua Makin, Willard seems intent on "proving that the female mind could evolve a thesis, logical and clear, worthy of a legal mind. Compared with Mary Wollstonecraft's [1759–1797] passionate appeal for education, social equity, and independence of women in her *Vindica-*

I. Treat of the defects of the present mode of female education and their causes.

II. Consider the principles by which education should be regulated.

III. Sketch a plan of a female seminary.

IV. Show the benefits which society would receive from such seminaries.

I. Defects in the present mode of female education, and their causes. Civilized nations have long since been convinced that education as it respects males will not, like trade, regulate itself;[50] and hence, they have made it a prime object to provide that sex with everything requisite to facilitate their progress in learning.[51] But female education has been left to the mercy of private adventurers; and the consequence has been to our sex the same as it would have been to the other, had legislatures left their accommodations and means of instruction to chance also.

Education cannot prosper in any community unless, from the ordinary motives which actuate the human mind, the best and most cultivated talents of that community can be brought into exercise in that way. Male education flourishes because, from the guardian care of legislatures, the presidencies and professorships of our colleges are some of the highest objects to which the eye of ambition is directed. Not so with female institutions. Preceptresses of these are dependent on their pupils for support, and are consequently liable to become the victims of their caprice. . . .[52]

Thus the writer has endeavored to point out the defects of the present mode of female education chiefly in order to show that the great cause of these defects consists in a state of things in which legislatures,[53] undervaluing the importance of women in society, neglect to provide for their education and suffer it to become the sport of adventurers for fortune, who may be both ignorant and vicious.[54]

II. Of the principles by which education should be regulated. To contemplate the principles which should regulate systems of instruction and consider how little those principles have been regarded in educating our sex, will show the defects of female education in a still stronger point of light and will also afford a standard by which any plan for its improvement may be measured.

Education should seek to bring its subjects to the perfection of their moral, intellectual and physical nature in order that they may be of the greatest possible use to themselves and others or, to use a different expression, that they may be the means of the greatest possible happiness of which they are

---

tion of the Rights of Women [1792], [Willard's *Plan*] reads like a lawyer's brief. It is the work of a woman who, in a scientific spirit, had tested the ability of her sex and was now presenting her case." Alma Lutz, *Emma Willard: Pioneer Educator*, pp. 29–30. Compare the literary conventions and flourishes of Juana Inéz de la Cruz in selection #31.

50. Perhaps this comment reflects the influence of Adam Smith's *Wealth of Nations* (1776).

51. Compare the opening line of Aristotle's selection #3.

52. In 1833 Catharine Beecher (1880–1878), another pioneer of higher education for women, observed, "The decline of Hartford Seminary after I left was the necessary result of want of endowment. . . . Had [it] been endowed with only half the funds bestowed on our poorest colleges for young men . . . most of my best teachers would have remained." Quoted in Willystine Goodsell, ed., *Pioneers of Women's Education in the United States* (New York: McGraw-Hill, 1931), pp. 11–2.

53. In the omitted three pages of text, Willard describes seven defects of the current boarding schools that "furnish the best [available] mode of education provided for females."

54. Willard's warnings against the deleterious effects of leaving education to private entrepreneurs reflects "the grasping personal ambition and private profiteering" that pervaded the 1820s. Jack C. Lane, "The Yale Report of 1828 and Liberal Education: A Neorepublican Manifesto," *History of Education Quarterly* 27 (1987): 329.

capable, both as to what they enjoy and what they communicate.[55] Those youth have the surest chance of enjoying and communicating happiness who are best qualified, both by internal dispositions and external habits, to perform with readiness those duties which their future life will most probably give them occasion to practice. Studies and employments should, therefore, be selected from one or both of the following considerations: either because they are peculiarly fitted to improve the faculties or because they are such as the pupil will most probably have occasion to practice in future life.

These are the principles on which systems of male education are founded, but female education has not yet been systematized. Chance and confusion reign here. . . .

Not only has there been a want of system concerning female education, but much of what has been done has proceeded upon mistaken principles. One of these is that, without a regard to the different periods of life proportionate to their importance, the education of females has been too exclusively directed to fit them for displaying to advantage the charms of youth and beauty. Though it may be proper to adorn this period of life, yet it is incomparably more important to prepare for the serious duties of maturer years. Though well to decorate the blossom, it is far better to prepare for the harvest. In the vegetable creation nature seems but to sport when she embellishes the flower, while all her serious cares are directed to perfect the fruit.

Another error is that it has been made the first object in educating our sex to prepare them to please the other. But reason and religion teach that we too are primary existences [and] that it is for us to move in the orbit of our duty around the Holy Centre of perfection, the companions, not the satellites of men; else, instead of shedding around us an influence that may help to keep [men] in their proper course, we must accompany them in their wildest deviations.

I would not be understood to insinuate that we are not, in particular situations, to yield obedience to the other sex.[56] Submission and obedience belong to every being in the universe except the great Master of the whole. Nor is it a degrading peculiarity to our sex to be under human authority. Whenever one class of human beings derive from another the benefits of support and protection, they must pay its equivalent, obedience. Thus, while we receive these benefits from our parents, we are all, without distinction of sex, under their authority; when we receive them from the government of our country, we must obey our rulers; and when our sex take the obligations of marriage and receive protection and support from the other, it is reasonable that we too should yield obedience. Yet is neither the child, nor the subject, nor the wife under human authority, but in subservience to the divine. Our highest responsibility is to God and our highest interest is to please him; therefore, to secure this interest should our education be directed.

Neither would I be understood to mean that our sex should not seek to make themselves agreeable to the other. The error complained of is that the taste of men, whatever it might happen to be, has been made a standard for the formation of the female character. In whatever we do, it is of the utmost importance that the rule by which we work be perfect. For if otherwise, what is it but to err upon principle? A system of education which leads one class of human beings to consider the approbation of another as their highest object teaches that the rule of their conduct should be the will of beings, imperfect and erring like themselves, rather than the will of God, which is the only standard of perfection. . . .

But should the conclusion be almost admitted that our sex too are the legitimate children of the legislature and that it is their duty to afford us a share of their paternal bounty, the phantom of a col-

---

55. Do these two expressions really convey the same purpose? If not, to which is Willard most faithful? Why does she treat them as interchangeable? Compare the treatment of this eudaemonistic purpose by Samuel Smith and by Aristotle.

56. As Bathsua Makin wrote in the dedication to her treatise: "To ask too much is the way to be denied all."

lege-learned lady would be ready to rise up and destroy every good resolution which the admission of this truth would naturally produce in our favor. To show that it is not a masculine education which is here recommended and to afford a definite view of the manner in which a female institution might possess the respectability, permanency, and uniformity of operation of those appropriated to males—and yet differ from them, so as to be adapted to that difference of character and duties to which the softer sex should be formed—is the object of the following imperfect.

III. Sketch of a female seminary. From considering the deficiencies in boarding schools, much may be learned with regard to what would be needed for the prosperity and usefulness of a public seminary for females.

[A.] There would be needed a building with commodious rooms for lodging and recitation [and] apartments for the reception of apparatus and for the accommodation of the domestic department.

[B.] A library, containing books on the various subjects in which the pupils were to receive instruction, musical instruments, some good paintings to form the taste and serve as models for the execution of those who were to be instructed in that art, maps, globes, and a small collection of philosophical apparatus.

[C.] A judicious board of trust, competent and desirous to promote its interests would in a female, as in a male, literary institution be the corner stone of its prosperity. On this board it would depend to provide

[D.] Suitable instruction. This article may be subdivided under four heads.[57]
   1. Religious and Moral.
   2. Literary.
   3. Domestic.
   4. Ornamental.

1. Religious and Moral. A regular attention to religious duties would, of course, be required of the pupils by the laws of the institution. The trustees would be careful to appoint no instructors who would not teach religion and morality both by their example and by leading the minds of the pupils to perceive that these constitute the true end of all education. It would be desirable that the young ladies should spend a part of their Sabbaths in hearing discourses relative to the peculiar duties of their sex. The evidences of Christianity and moral philosophy would constitute a part of their studies.[58]

2. Literary Instruction. To make an exact enumeration of the branches of literature which might be taught would be impossible, unless the time of the pupils' continuance at the seminary and the requisites for entrance were previously fixed. Such an enumeration would be tedious, nor do I conceive that it would be at all promotive of my object. The difficulty complained of is not that we are at a loss what sciences we ought to learn, but that we have not proper advantages to learn any. Many writers

57. Given that Willard organizes the *Plan* with great care, why does she choose this order and apportion the attention to these subjects in the following fashion?

58. In the first half of the nineteenth century, "Evidences of Christianity" was a standard topic or course, as appears in the catalog of Dartmouth College below. This summative, senior-year course was normally taught by the president who tried to show how all the studies harmonized into a coherent view of the world that was ultimately explained by or consistent with Christianity. Many colleges continued this practice for decades. John Dewey recalled that when attending the University of Vermont in the late 1870s he took such a course, which "was regarded as a kind of intellectual coping to the structure erected in earlier years, or, at least, as an insertion of the key-stone of the arch." John Dewey, "From Absolutism to Experimentalism," in *Contemporary American Philosophy, Personal Statements*, eds. George P. Adams and William P. Montague (New York: Macmillan, 1930), v. 2, p. 13.

have given us excellent advice with regard to what we should be taught, but no legislature has provided us the means of instruction. Not, however, to pass lightly over this fundamental part of education, I will mention one or two of the less obvious branches of science which, I conceive, should engage the youthful attention of my sex.

It is highly important that females should be conversant with those studies which will lead them to understand the operations of the human mind. The chief use to which the philosophy of the mind can be applied, is to regulate education by its rules. The ductile mind of the child is intrusted to the mother, and she ought to have every possible assistance in acquiring a knowledge of this noble material, on which it is her business to operate, that she may best understand how to mold it to its most excellent form.[59]

Natural philosophy has not often been taught to our sex.[60] Yet why should we be kept in ignorance of the great machinery of nature and left to the vulgar notion that nothing is curious but what deviates from her common course? If mothers were acquainted with this science, they would communicate very many of its principles to their children in early youth. . . . A knowledge of natural philosophy is calculated to heighten the moral taste by bringing to view the majesty and beauty of order and design and to enliven piety by enabling the mind more clearly to perceive, throughout the manifold works of God, that wisdom in which he hath made them all. . . .

3. Domestic Instruction should be considered important in a female seminary. It is the duty of our sex to regulate the internal concerns of every family; and unless they be properly qualified to discharge this duty, whatever may be their literary or ornamental attainments, they cannot be expected to make either good wives, good mothers, or good mistresses of families. And if they are none of these, they must be bad members of society, for it is by promoting or destroying the comfort and prosperity of their own families that females serve or injure the community.[61] To superintend the domestic department, there should be a respectable lady, experienced in the best methods of housewifery and acquainted with propriety of dress and manners. Under her tuition the pupils ought to be placed for a certain length of time every morning. . . .

In the present state of things, it is not to be expected that any material improvements in housewifery should be made. There being no uniformity of method prevailing among different housewives; of course, the communications from one to another are not much more likely to improve the art, than a communication between two mechanics of different trades would be to improve each in his respective occupation. But should a system of principles be philosophically arranged and taught, both in theory and by practice, to a large number of females whose minds were expanded and strengthened by a course of literary instruction, those among them of an investigating turn would, when they commenced housekeepers, consider their domestic operations as a series of experiments, which either proved or refuted the system previously taught. They would then converse together like those who practice a common art and improve each other by their observations and experiments, and they would

---

59. Willard's appreciation of the study of psychology and its implications for education were unusually progressive, and led the well known Scottish phrenologist George Combe (1788–1858) to publish Willard's *Plan* in his *Phrenological Journal*.

60. "Natural philosophy" here refers to natural science.

61. Willard here explicitly endorses what historians have called the early nineteenth-century "cult of domesticity" or ideology of "separate spheres," whereby men dominated the public world of politics and commerce, and the private sphere of the household was confided to women. See the introduction to the selections from the *Liberal Education of Women* in Section VII.

also be capable of improving the system by detecting its errors and by making additions of new principles and better modes of practice.[62]

4. The Ornamental branches which I should recommend for a female seminary are drawing and painting, elegant penmanship, music, and the grace of motion. Needle-work is not here mentioned. The best style of useful needle-work should either be taught in the domestic department or made a qualification for entrance, and I consider that useful which may contribute to the decoration of a lady's person or the convenience and neatness of her family. But the use of the needle for other purposes than these, as it affords little to assist in the formation of the character, I should regard as a waste of time.   The grace of motion must be learnt chiefly from instruction in dancing. . . .

[E.] There would be needed for a female, as well as for a male, seminary a system of laws and regulations so arranged that both the instructors and pupils would know their duty, and thus the whole business [would] move with regularity and uniformity. . . .

The direct rewards or honors used to stimulate the ambition of students in colleges are, first, the certificate or diploma which each receives who passes successfully through the term allotted to his collegiate studies and, secondly, the appointments to perform certain parts in public exhibitions, which are bestowed by the faculty as rewards for superior scholarship. The first of these modes is admissible into a female seminary; the second is not, as public speaking forms no part of female education.[63]

The want of this mode might, however, be supplied by examinations judiciously conducted . . . .[64]

Perhaps the term allotted for the routine of study at the seminary might be three years. The pupils probably would not be fitted to enter until about the age of fourteen. Whether they attended to all or any of the ornamental branches should be left optional with the parents or guardians. Those who were to be instructed in them should be entered for a longer term, but if this was a subject of previous calculation, no confusion would arise from it. . . .

IV. Benefits of female seminaries. Let us now proceed to inquire, what benefits would result from the establishment of female seminaries. They would constitute a grade of public education superior to any yet known in the history of our sex; and through them, the lower grades of female instruction might be controlled. The influence of public seminaries over these would operate in two ways; first, by requiring certain qualifications for entrance; and secondly, by furnishing instructresses, initiated in their modes of teaching and imbued with their maxims. Female seminaries might be expected to have important and happy effects on common schools in general; and in the manner of operating on these,

---

62. Drawing on the eighteenth-century faith in the improvement of life through the advance of reason, Willard's conception of scientifically improving housewifery is analogous to efforts at improving husbandry that was being promoted by organizations such as the American Philosophical Society, as described in selection #34 by Samuel Smith.

63. This curricular exclusion is tantamount to conceding women's exclusion from any public role, because training in public speaking was regarded chiefly as preparation for public life, as noted in selection #30 by Bathsua Makin.

64. Compare the discussions of academic honors, ambition, and competition by Ignatius Loyola (paras. 383, 390, 478) in selection #26, by Pier Paolo Vergerio in selection #25, by Charles Eliot in selection #40, by William R. Harper in selection #49, and by Frank Aydelotte in selection #60.

would probably place the business of teaching children in hands now nearly useless to society; and take it from those whose services the state wants in many other ways.[65]

That nature designed for our sex the care of children, she has made manifest by mental, as well as physical, indications. She has given us, in a greater degree than men, the gentle arts of insinuation to soften their minds and fit them to receive impressions; a greater quickness of invention to vary modes of teaching to different dispositions;[66] and more patience to make repeated efforts. There are many females of ability to whom the business of instructing children is highly acceptable and who would devote all their faculties to their occupation. They would have no higher pecuniary object to engage their attention, and their reputation as instructors they would consider as important; whereas, whenever able and enterprising men engage in this business, they consider it merely as a temporary employment to further some other object, to the attainment of which their best thoughts and calculations are all directed.[67] If then women were properly fitted by instruction, they would be likely to teach children better than the other sex; they could afford to do it cheaper; and those men who would otherwise be engaged in this employment might be at liberty to add to the wealth of the nation by any of those thousand occupations from which women are necessarily debarred.[68]

But the females who taught children would have been themselves instructed either immediately or indirectly by the seminaries. Hence, through these, the government might exercise an intimate and most beneficial control over common schools. Any one who has turned his attention to this subject must be aware that there is great room for improvement in these, both as to the modes of teaching and the things taught. And what method could be devised so likely to effect this improvement as to prepare by instruction a class of individuals whose interest, leisure, and natural talents would combine to make them pursue it with ardor? Such a class of individuals would be raised up by female seminaries. And therefore they would be likely to have highly important and happy effects on common schools.[69]

It is believed that such institutions would tend to prolong or perpetuate our excellent government.
. . .

The inquiry to which these remarks have conducted us is this: . . .
    1. Females, by having their understandings cultivated [and] their reasoning powers developed and strengthened, may be expected to act more from the dictates of reason and less from those of fashion and caprice.

---

65. At this time, the great majority of schoolteachers were men. Willard's ensuing argument that women are naturally suited for teaching became prominent in subsequent decades; and was perhaps expressed most powerfully by Catherine Beecher in her "Address on the Evils Suffered by American Children and American Women" in 1846. By the beginning of the twentieth century, women predominated in schoolteaching, which was the leading option among the "female professions," including librarianship, social work, nursing, and journalism.

66. Note Willard's example in this regard, as described in the introduction.

67. Male college graduates often taught school "temporarily," while waiting to establish themselves in one of the three "liberal professions": ministry, law, or medicine.

68. Compare the role envisioned for women in the public sphere and its influence upon the liberal education proposed for women, as presented by Christine de Pizan in selection #12, Laura Cereta in selection #27, and Bathsua Makin in selection #30.

69. These comments anticipate Willard's work in the common school movement after she left the Troy Female Seminary.

2. With minds thus strengthened they would be taught systems of morality, enforced by the sanctions of religion; and they might be expected to acquire juster and more enlarged views of their duty, and stronger and higher motives to its performance.

3. This plan of education offers all that can be done to preserve female youth from a contempt of useful labour. The pupils would become accustomed to it in conjunction with the high objects of literature and the elegant pursuits of the fine arts; and it is to be hoped that both from habit and association, they might in future life regard it as respectable. To this it may be added that if housewifery could be raised to a regular art and taught upon philosophical principles, it would become a higher and more interesting occupation; and ladies of fortune, like wealthy agriculturalists, might find that to regulate their business was an agreeable employment.

4. The pupils might be expected to acquire a taste for moral and intellectual pleasures, which would buoy them above a passion for show and parade and which would make them seek to gratify the natural love of superiority, by endeavoring to excel others in intrinsic merit, rather than in the extrinsic frivolities of dress, furniture, and equipage.

5. By being enlightened in moral philosophy and in that which teaches the operations of the mind, females would be enabled to perceive the nature and extent of that influence which they possess over their children, and the obligation which this lays them under to watch the formation of their characters with unceasing vigilance, to become their instructors, to devise plans for their improvement, to weed out the vices from their minds, and to implant and foster the virtues. . . .

Where is that wise and heroic country, which has considered that our rights are sacred though we cannot defend them? That though a weaker, we are an essential part of the body politic, whose corruption or improvement must affect the whole? And which, having thus considered, has sought to give us by education that rank in the scale of being, to which our importance entitles us? History shows not that country. It shows many whose legislatures have sought to improve their various vegetable productions and their breeds of useful brutes, but none whose public councils have made it an object of their deliberations to improve the character of their women.[70]

---

70. Recall the business of the 1795 meeting of the American Philosophical Society, described in the introduction to Samuel H. Smith.

36. Liberal Arts Colleges Opened for Instruction, 1600-1820

In the late 1700s and early 1800s, while Joseph Priestley, Samuel H. Smith, Emma Willard and others were calling for more practical, republican, and enlightened or scientific liberal education, as well as for opening liberal education to women, new liberal arts colleges were springing up to join the nine colonial colleges. The precise number and even the existence of certain colleges in the early nineteenth century are indeterminate because some were founded in name only, others merely chartered, and still others that began to offer instruction closed soon thereafter. The following table includes colleges and universities that were chartered to grant degrees by 1820,[71] and lists the institutions by the year in which they opened for collegiate instruction, which is a more salient, if elusive, criterion than the date of chartering. Institutions that never opened for instruction are listed by the date of their charter. Some of the institutions opened earlier as academies that did not grant bachelor degrees.

Current Name	Year Opened	Location as of 1820
1. Harvard University	1638	Cambridge, MA
2. College of William and Mary	1694	Williamsburg, VA
3. Yale University	1702	New Haven, CT
4. Princeton University	1747	Princeton, NJ
5. Columbia University	1754	New York, NY
6. University of Pennsylvania	1755	Philadelphia, PA
7. Brown University	1765	Providence, RI
8. Dartmouth College	1769	Hanover, NH
9. Rutgers, The State University	1771	New Brunswick, NJ
10. Washington and Lee University	1782	Lexington, VA
11. Hampden-Sydney College	1783	Hampden-Sydney, VA
12. Dickinson College	1784	Carlisle, PA
13. Mount Sion College	1785	Winnsborough, SC
14. College of Cambridge (SC)	1785	Never opened for instruction.
15. Franklin and Marshall College	1787	Lancaster, PA
16. Transylvania University	1789	Lexington, KY
17. St. John's College	1789	Annapolis, MD
18. College of Charleston	1789	Charleston, SC
19. Williams College	1793	Williamstown, MA
20. Cokesbury College (MD)	1794	No longer operating in 1820.
21. University of North Carolina	1795	Chapel Hill, NC
22. Union University	1795	Schenectady, NY
23. Washington College Academy	1795	Limestown, TN
24. College of Beaufort (SC)	1795	Never opened for instruction.
25. Alexandria College (SC)	1797	Never opened for instruction.
26. University of Vermont	1799	Burlington, VT

71. The table draws upon Jurgen Herbst, *From Crisis to Crisis: American College Government, 1636–1819* (Cambridge, MA: Harvard University Press, 1982), pp. 244–53; James W. Fonseca and Alice C. Andrews, *The Atlas of American Higher Education* (New York: New York University Press, 1993), pp. 20–1; Martin Gilbert, *American History Atlas* (New York: Macmillan, 1968), p. 15; Kenneth T. Jackson, ed., *Atlas of American History*, rev. ed. (New York: Charles Scribner's sons, 1978), p. 76.

27. Middlebury College	1800	Middlebury, VT
28. University of Georgia	1801	Athens, GA
29. Bowdoin College	1802	Brunswick, ME
30. Jefferson College	1802	Washington, PA
31. Baltimore College[72]	1804	Baltimore, MD
32. Tusculum College	1805	Greenville, TN
33. University of South Carolina	1805	Columbia, SC
34. St. Mary's University	1805	Baltimore, MD
35. University of Orleans and College of New Orleans (LA)	1805	Never opened for instruction; abolished in the 1820s.
36. Washington College	1806	Washington, PA
37. George Peabody College	1806	Nashville, TN
38 University of Maryland[73]	1807	Baltimore, MD
39. Ohio University	1808	Athens, OH
40. Hamilton College	1812	Clinton, NY
41. Georgetown University	1812	Washington, DC
42. Allegheny College	1817	Meadville, PA
43. Miami University	1818	Oxford, OH
44. Asbury College	1818	Baltimore, MD
45. Colby College	1818	Waterville, ME
46. University of Virginia	1819	Charlottesville, VA. Opened in 1825.
47. University of Cincinnati	1819	Cincinnati, OH
48. Worthington College[74]	1819	Worthington, OH
49. University of Pittsburgh	1819	Pittsburgh, PA
50. University of Tennessee	1820	Knoxville, TN
51. Centre College	1820	Danville, KY

In the antebellum decades following 1820, the number of liberal arts colleges became even more indeterminate due to the explosive proliferation in college-founding. This explosion was widely attributed to an American impulse that Noah Porter, president of Yale College from 1871 to 1886, later derided as "college enthusiasm,"[75] referring to the effort of small municipalities to aggrandize

---

72. Merged with the University of Maryland in 1830.

73. The College of Medicine opened in 1807; the university granted its first B.A. in 1859.

74. Chartered in 1819, Worthington College was founded upon Worthington Academy and may have immediately enrolled college students. According to the Ohio Historical Society, Salmon P. Chase, future governor of Ohio and Chief Justice of the Supreme Court of the United States, studied at the college from 1820 to 1822. However, since Chase (1808–1873) was very young and later received the B.A. from Dartmouth College, his attendance implies that Worthington was not yet offering collegiate instruction.

75. See Noah Porter, "College Enthusiasm," in *The American Colleges and the American Public* (New Haven, CT: Charles C. Chatfield, 1870), pp. 9–38. Already in 1828 Yale President Jeremiah Day observed in selection #37: "There must be, in the union, as many colleges, at least, as states. Nor would we complain of this arrangement as inexpedient provided that starvation is not the consequence of patronage so minutely divided. We anticipate no disastrous results from the multiplication of colleges, if they can only be adequately endowed. We are not without apprehensions, however, that a feeble and stinted growth of our national literature will be the consequence of the very scanty supply of means to most of our public seminaries."

themselves and of religious denominations to extend their influence by founding colleges (not unlike the forces spawning the medieval universities.) Porter's derision stemmed from the judgment that the United States was founding more colleges than the population was able to sustain and that, as a result, many of the new foundations were financially and intellectually weak, if not moribund. In 1932, an often-cited study by Donald G. Tewksbury seemed to confirm this judgment with its finding that in sixteen states, outside of New England, 516 colleges were founded before the Civil War and 412, or 81 percent, closed.[76] The judgment was then codified when Richard Hofstadter famously labeled the first half of the nineteenth century as "the Great Retrogression" of the American college.[77] According to this traditional view maintained for nearly a century, the antebellum colleges were being enthusiastically founded at the same time that they were financially strapped, intellectually backward, and thoroughly unpopular with their students.

Beginning in the 1970s there emerged a revisionist interpretation that is still being refined today.[78] The revised interpretation contends that the antebellum colleges were more effective in elevating the general educational level and in graduating successful professionals, more popular with students, and less susceptible to failure than the traditional view gave them credit for. While providing much new research and a salutary reevaluation of the traditional view judgment, this revisionist interpretation of the liberal arts colleges in the first half of the nineteenth century tended to sidestep the heart of the criticism of Porter, Hofstadter and others, whose primary complaint was that the antebellum colleges did not maintain high academic standards.

Their agreement on the *decline* in standards did not mean, however, that Porter and Hofstadter concurred in the nature of those standards. For Porter, the decline reflected a dilution in "the study of the classics" induced by "a limited class of *educational reformers*, whose stock in trade consists of a scanty outfit of a few facts imperfectly conceived and incorrectly recited, in respect of the modes of education pursued in the middle ages. It is the profession or trade of these men to assail the colleges of this country as medieval, cloistered, scholastic, and monkish."[79] For Hofstadter, the decline stemmed rather from the fact that "the standard college curriculum was the program of classical-mathematical studies inherited from Renaissance education," which had remained largely insulated from new studies due to "the pervasive national reaction from the Enlightenment."[80] These different standards by which to evaluate the liberal arts curriculum in general and intellectual rigor in particular are mirrored in the various interpretations of the most extensively debated, institutional report on a liberal arts curriculum in United States history, issued by Yale College.

---

76. Donald G. Tewksbury, *The Founding of American Colleges and Universities Before the Civil War* . . . (New York: Teachers College, Columbia University, 1932), p. 28.

77. Richard Hofstadter and Walter P. Metzger, *The Development of Academic Freedom in the United States* (New York: Columbia University Press, 1955), pp. 209–22.

78. See, for example, Roger L. Geiger, ed. *The American College in the Nineteenth Century* (Baltimore: Johns Hopkins University Press, 2000).

79. Porter, "College Enthusiasm," p. 29. See the references to monastic practices in selection #34 by Samuel H. Smith.

80. Hofstadter and Metzger, *The Development of Academic Freedom in the United States*, pp. 226, 209.

Institutional Responses

37. Jeremiah Day, "Course of Instruction in Yale College" (1828)

INTRODUCTION

In the fall of 1827 a senior senator in the Connecticut legislature, who served ex officio on the governing board of Yale College, proposed that the college consider "so altering the regular course of instruction . . . as to leave out . . . the *dead languages*, substituting other studies therefor."[81] At that point, Yale's four-year course was almost entirely prescribed and was dominated by recitations in Greek and Latin literature. During the first three years, recitations were also held in mathematics, English grammar and rhetoric, geography, history, and astronomy; during the fourth year, additional recitations were conducted in political economy, moral philosophy, and "natural theology."[82]

Aside from the senator's political influence, a number of factors caused the Yale governing board to give the proposal serious consideration. Demands that liberal arts colleges make their studies more practical, republican, and "modern" had been heard for several decades, as indicated by the foregoing readings. The dissatisfaction with the classical course evidently contributed to a student uprising at Yale in 1825, shortly after the faculty extended the required study of Greek and Latin into the senior year, from which it had previously been eliminated. Student dissatisfaction, in turn, may have worried the governing board because Yale was facing financial problems in the 1820s, even though its enrollment of some 300 undergraduates was among the largest in the country.

In view of the vociferous criticism of the classical studies, the student dissatisfaction, and the prospect of declining tuition, the board appointed a committee to study the senator's proposal, comprising Governor Gideon Tomlinson, President Jeremiah Day, the Connecticut senator, and two clergymen. The committee's investigation produced three documents. The first, written by President Day, assayed and justified the curriculum in general. The second, by the professor of classical languages, James L. Kingsley, echoed Day's justification and then defended specifically the teaching of the "dead languages." Kingsley argued from convention that, if Yale granted the liberal arts degree for completion of a course lacking classical subjects, "it would be to declare *that* to be a liberal education, which the world will not acknowledge to deserve the name. . . . A liberal education, whatever course the college should adopt, would without doubt continue to be, what it long has been."[83] The third, written by Governor Tomlinson on behalf of the committee, endorsed Day's and Kingley's views. Combined together, these three documents became known as the "Yale Report," and were published both independently and in the *American Journal of Science and Arts*, the leading scientific journal in the United States at this time.[84]

---

81. *Reports on the Course of Instruction in Yale College*, p. 3.

82. "Course of Instruction 1822–23" and "Course of Instruction 1823–43" in George W. Pierson, *A Yale Book of Numbers: Historical Statistics of the College and University, 1701–1976* (New Haven, CT: Yale University, 1983), pp. 214–6. The characteristic, antebellum subject of natural theology was devoted to demonstrating that the prevalent theories and successive discoveries of natural science were concordant with Christian doctrine. Note its appearance below in the catalog of Dartmouth College.

83. *Reports on the Course of Instruction in Yale College*, p. 41.

84. *American Journal of Science and Arts* was founded and edited by Yale Professor Benjamin Silliman, who wrote in an understated epilogue: "The following papers relate to an important subject, respecting which there is at present some diversity of opinion." "Original Papers in Relation to a Course of Liberal Education," *American Journal of Science and Arts* 15 (Jan. 1829): 297.

Kingsley was surely disingenuous in asserting that Yale's example could have little effect on the norm of liberal education. But no member of the committee or the Yale governing board anticipated the great influence of the Report. By 1829 Yale had "the largest enrollment, the widest geographical distribution, and the largest living alumni roll of any of the American colleges."[85] These graduates extended Yale's influence by itinerating westward and founding many colleges, such as Illinois College and Beloit College. In 1840 Yale graduates served as president of at least thirty-six of the seventy-five colleges offering instruction in the United States.

Historians have long interpreted the Yale Report as conservative: defending the amalgam of humanistic and scholastic studies that had been inherited from the colonial college and opposing calls for introducing practical, republican, and "modern" studies into liberal education. Against this longstanding view establishing "Yale's reputation for extreme educational conservatism," there has arisen a revisionist interpretation asserting that the Yale Report was "comprehensive, open-minded and liberal" and "did not differ in any of its essentials from the views held by most of America's foremost champions of university reform at the time."[86] Overlooked amid this continuing historiographical debate is the fact that, in presenting the key argument of the Report, Jeremiah Day drew directly upon Cicero's *On the Orator*, as discussed in the notes below. Reading the Yale Report is thus a matter of subtle interpretation, and the most quoted and influential part is that of Jeremiah Day, written on behalf of the faculty.

Born the son of Congregational minister in Connecticut, Day (1773–1867) was tutored by David Hale, the brother of the revolutionary war hero Nathan, and entered Yale College in 1789. From that point until about 1803, he suffered from tuberculosis, which periodically interrupted his studies, schoolteaching, and preaching. Nevertheless, he graduated in 1795 and in 1803 assumed the professorship of mathematics and natural philosophy at Yale. In 1817 Day was appointed president of Yale and served for twenty-nine years in this office, while acquiring a reputation for extreme caution and reserve. Whether these qualities predominate in Day's part of Yale Report is much debated and must be decided in light of context of liberal education at the time.

SELECTION[87]

We are decidedly of the opinion that our present plan of education admits of improvement. We are aware that the system is imperfect, and we cherish the hope that some of its defects may ere long be remedied. We believe that changes may, from time to time, be made with advantage to meet the varying demands of the community, to accommodate the course of instruction to the rapid advance of the country in population, refinement, and opulence. We have no doubt that important improvements may be suggested by attentive observation of the literary institutions in Europe and by the earnest spirit of inquiry which is now so prevalent on the subject of education.

The guardians of the college appear to have ever acted upon the principle that it ought not to be stationary, but continually advancing. Some alteration has accordingly been proposed almost every

85. Frederick Rudolph, *Curriculum: A History of the American Undergraduate Course of Study Since 1636* (San Francisco: Jossey-Bass, 1977), p. 65.

86. Quotations are, respectively, from Brooks Mather Kelley, *Yale: A History* (New Haven, CT: Yale University Press, 1974), p. 175; Stanley M. Guralnick, *Science and the Antebellum American College* (Philadelphia: American Philosophical Society, 1975), p. 30; Douglas Sloan, "Harmony, Chaos, and Consensus: The American College Curriculum," *Teachers College Record* 73 (1971): 243.

87. Jeremiah Day, "Course of Instruction in Yale College," in *Reports on the Course of Instruction in Yale College* (New Haven, CT: Hezekiah Howe, 1828), pp. 5–30.

year from its first establishment. It is with no small surprise, therefore, we occasionally hear the suggestion that our system is unalterable; that colleges were originally planned in the days of monkish ignorance; and that "by being immovably moored to the same station, they serve only to measure the rapid current of improvement which is passing by them."[88]

How opposite to all this is the real state of facts in this and the other seminaries in the United States. Nothing is more common than to hear those who revisit the college, after a few years absence, express their surprise at the changes which have been made since they were graduated. Not only the course of studies and the modes of instruction have been greatly varied; but whole sciences have, for the first time, been introduced: chemistry, mineralogy, geology, political economy, etc. By raising the qualifications for admission, the standard of attainment has been elevated. Alterations so extensive and frequent satisfactorily prove that, if those who are entrusted with the superintendence of the institution still firmly adhere to some of its original features, it is from a higher principle than a blind opposition to salutary reform. Improvements, we trust, will continue to be made as rapidly as they can be without hazarding the loss of what has been already attained.[89]

But perhaps the time has come when we ought to pause and inquire whether it will be sufficient to make *gradual* changes as heretofore; and whether the whole system is not rather to be broken up and a better one substituted in its stead. From different quarters, we have heard the suggestion that our colleges must be *new-modelled*, that they are not adapted to the spirit and wants of the age; that they will soon be deserted unless they are better accommodated to the business character of the nation.[90] As this point may have an important bearing upon the question immediately before the committee, we would ask their indulgence while we attempt to explain, at some length, the nature and object of the present plan of education at the college. . . .

What then is the appropriate object of a college? It is not necessary here to determine what it is which, in every case, entitles an institution to the *name* of a college. But if we have not greatly misapprehended the design of the patrons and guardians of this college, its object is to *lay the foundation of a superior education*; and this is to be done at a period of life when a substitute must be provided for *parental superintendence*. The groundwork of a thorough education must be broad and deep and solid. For a partial or superficial education, the support may be of looser materials and more hastily laid.

The two great points to be gained in intellectual culture are the *discipline* and the *furniture* of the mind, expanding its powers and storing it with knowledge.[91] The former of these is, perhaps, the more

---

88. This unidentified quotation likely comes from the Connecticut state senator who challenged Yale's curriculum.

89. The conciliatory language and progressive goals expressed in Day's prologue provide support for the revisionist interpretation of the Yale Report. The traditional interpretation attended, rather, to what Day subsequently affirmed as unalterable in the curriculum.

90. A longstanding interpretation maintains that the Yale Report was reacting against and opposing the materialism and "business character of the nation." Ralph H. Gabriel, *Religion and Learning at Yale* (New Haven, CT: Yale University Press, 1958), pp. 103–4. Others maintain that the Yale Report aimed at reshaping the classical curriculum "to fit the present and future needs of an expanding entrepreneurial society" in Jacksonian America. By this latter view, the Yale Report created a new justification for classical liberal education, consistent with the "grasping personal ambition and private profiteering" that were becoming accepted in social life by the 1820s. Jack C. Lane, "The Yale Report of 1828 and Liberal Education: A Neorepublican Manifesto," *History of Education Quarterly* 27 (1987): 336–7, 329.

91. These words are the most famous and often quoted lines from the Report, and convey the popular nineteenth-century theory of mental discipline: that learning in a certain subject trains faculties of the mind to learn in other areas. Day's wording suggests his reliance on the Common Sense philosophy of Scottish philosopher Thomas Reid (1710–1796), who had countered empiricist skepticism by arguing that inherent faculties of the mind exist

important of the two.[92] A commanding object, therefore, in a collegiate course should be to call into daily and vigorous exercise the faculties of the student. Those branches of study should be prescribed, and those modes of instruction adopted, which are best calculated to teach the art of fixing the attention; directing the train of thought; analyzing a subject proposed for investigation; following, with accurate discrimination, the course of argument; balancing nicely the evidence presented to the judgment; awakening, elevating, and controlling the imagination; arranging with skill the treasures which memory gathers; arousing and guiding the powers of genius. All this is not to be effected by a light and hasty course of study: by reading a few books, hearing a few lectures, and spending some months at a literary institution. The habits of thinking are to be formed by long, continued and close application. The mines of science must be penetrated far below the surface before they will disclose their treasures. If a dexterous performance of the manual operations in many of the mechanical arts requires an apprenticeship with diligent attention for years, much more does the training of the powers of the mind demand vigorous and steady and systematic effort.

In laying the foundation of a thorough education, it is necessary that *all* the important mental faculties be brought into exercise. It is not sufficient that one or two be cultivated while others are neglected. A costly edifice ought not to be left to rest upon a single pillar. When certain mental endowments receive a much higher culture than others, there is a distortion in the intellectual character. The mind never attains its full perfection unless its various powers are so trained as to give them the fair proportions which nature designed. If the student exercises his reasoning powers only, he will be deficient in imagination and taste, in fervid and impressive eloquence. If he confines his attention to demonstrative evidence, he will be unfitted to decide correctly in cases of probability. If he relies principally on his memory his powers of invention will be impaired by disuse. In the course of instruction in this college, it has been an object to maintain such a proportion between the different branches of literature and science as to form in the student a proper *balance* of character.[93]

From the pure mathematics, he learns the art of demonstrative reasoning. In attending to the physical sciences, he becomes familiar with facts, with the process of induction, and the varieties of probable evidence.[94] In ancient literature he finds some of the most finished models of taste. By English reading, he learns the powers of the language in which he is to speak and write. By logic and mental

---

and yield certain essential truths with which everyone agrees. "Such original and natural judgments are, therefore, a part of that furniture which Nature hath given to the human understanding. . . . They make up what is called *the common sense of mankind*." Thomas Reid, "Inquiry into the Human Mind on the Principles of Common Sense," in *The Works of Thomas Reid*, ed. William Hamilton (Edinburgh, UK: MacLachlan and Stewart, 1858), ch. 7, sec. 4, p. 209.

92. According to a refinement of the revisionist view, Day's argument for mental discipline constitutes the key accommodation to the social mores of Jacksonian America. By justifying classical studies on the grounds of disciplining mental faculties, the Yale Report supplants the rationale of inculcating public virtue with an intellectualized justification "intended to prepare the individual for personal success." In this way, the Report is said to shift the rationale for liberal education from advancing virtue to strengthening the intellect, and from promoting the polity to enhancing the (pecuniary) prospects of the individual. Lane, "The Yale Report of 1828," p. 335.

93. Day has been arguing for balancing mental faculties. Why does he shift to "character" in the last line? Some have said that the Yale Report was "reaffirming the classics not only as foundational but as a concrete means for inculcating moral character without resorting to any denominational or sectarian interpretation of piety." Paul H. Mattingly, "The Political Culture of America's Antebellum Colleges," *History of Higher Education Annual* 17 (1997): 87.

94. Given the prominent influence—even upon theology—of Francis Bacon's understanding of science in the first half of the nineteenth century, Day's references to induction and probable evidence seem intended to show that Yale's approach to physical science is up to date.

philosophy, he is taught the art of thinking; by rhetoric and oratory, the art of speaking. By frequent exercise on written composition, he acquires copiousness and accuracy of expression. By extemporaneous discussion, he becomes prompt and fluent and animated. It is a point of high importance that eloquence and solid learning should go together, that he who has accumulated the richest treasures of thought should possess the highest powers of oratory. To what purpose has a man become deeply learned, if he has no faculty of communicating his knowledge? And of what use is a display of rhetorical elegance from one who knows little or nothing which is worth communicating? "For volubility is hollow and laughable without the understanding of many things"—Cicero.[95] Our course, therefore, aims at a union of science with literature, of solid attainment with skill in the art of persuasion.

No one feature in a system of intellectual education is of greater moment than such an arrangement of duties and motives, as will most effectually throw the student upon the *resources of his own mind*. Without this, the whole apparatus of libraries and instruments and specimens and lectures and teachers, will be insufficient to secure distinguished excellence. The scholar must form himself by his own exertions. The advantages furnished by a residence at a college can do little more than stimulate and aid his personal efforts. The *inventive* powers are especially to be called into vigorous exercise. However abundant may be the acquisitions of the student, if he has no talent at forming new combinations of thought, he will be dull and inefficient. The sublimest efforts of genius consist in the creations of the imagination, the discoveries of the intellect, the conquests by which the dominions of science are extended. But the culture of the inventive faculties is not the only object of a liberal education. The most gifted understanding cannot greatly enlarge the amount of science to which the wisdom of ages has contributed. If it were possible for a youth to have his faculties in the highest state of cultivation, without any of the knowledge which is derived from others, he would be but poorly fitted for the business of life. To the discipline of the mind, therefore, is to be added instruction. The analytic method must be combined with the synthetic. Analysis is most efficacious in directing the powers of invention; but it is far too slow in its progress to teach, within a moderate space of time, the circle of sciences.

In our arrangements for the communication of knowledge as well as in intellectual discipline, such branches are to be taught as will produce a proper symmetry and balance of character. We doubt whether the powers of the mind can be developed in their fairest proportions by studying languages alone, or mathematics alone, or natural or political science alone. As the bodily frame is brought to its highest perfection not by one simple and uniform motion but by a variety of exercises, so the mental faculties are expanded and invigorated and adapted to each other by familiarity with different departments of science. . . .[96]

Having now stated what we understand to be the proper *object* of an education at this college, viz. to lay a solid *foundation* in literature and science; we would ask permission to add a few observations on the *means* which are employed to effect this object.

---

95. This quotation is from Cicero, *On the Orator* I 17, and these two paragraphs, in which Day introduces and explains his famous doctrine of mental discipline, appear to echo phrasing from the opening parts of the first book of *On the Orator*. For example, Day seems to draw the image of "the treasures which memory gathers" from *On the Orator* I v 18, as did John of Salisbury (I 11) in selection #16. By drawing on Cicero, while interweaving contemporary intellectual themes, such as induction and probable evidence, Day is explicitly invoking tradition and accommodating modernity.

96. The two, omitted paragraphs assert that "the *kind* of government which ought to be maintained in our colleges . . . should approach as near to the character of parental control as the circumstances of the case will admit."

In giving the course of instruction, it is intended that a due proportion be observed between *lectures* and the exercises which are familiarly termed *recitations*—that is, examinations in a textbook.[97] The great advantage of lectures is that, while they call forth the highest efforts of the lecturer and accelerate his advance to professional eminence, they give that light and spirit to the subject which awaken the interest and ardor of the student.[98] They may place before him the principles of science in the attractive dress of living eloquence. Where instruments are to be explained, experiments performed or specimens exhibited, they are the appropriate mode of communication. But we are far from believing that *all* the purposes of instruction can be best answered by lectures alone. They do not always bring upon the student a pressing and definite responsibility. He may repose upon his seat and yield a passive hearing to the lecturer without ever calling into exercise the active powers of his own mind. This defect we endeavor to remedy, in part, by frequent examinations, on the subjects of the lectures.

Still it is important that the student should have opportunities of retiring by himself and giving a more commanding direction to his thoughts than when listening to oral instruction. To secure his steady and earnest efforts is the great object of the daily examinations or recitations. In these exercises, a textbook is commonly the guide. A particular portion of this is assigned for each meeting. In this way only, can the responsibility be made sufficiently definite. If it be distributed among several books upon the same subject, the diversity of statement in these will furnish the student with an apology for want of exactness in his answers. Besides, we know of no method which will more effectually bewilder and confound the learner on his first entrance upon a new science, than to refer him to half a dozen different authors to be read at the same time. He will be in danger of learning nothing effectually. When he comes to be engaged in the study of his profession, he may find his way through the maze and firmly establish his own opinions by taking days or weeks for the examination of each separate point. Text-books are, therefore, not as necessary in this advanced stage of education as in the course at college, where the time allotted to each branch is rarely more than sufficient for the learner to become familiar with its elementary principles. These [principles], with a few exceptions, are not new and controverted points, but such as have been long settled; and they are exhibited to the best advantage in the consistent and peculiar manner of some eminent writer.

Opportunity is given, however, to our classes for a full investigation and discussion of particular subjects in the written and extemporaneous *disputes*, which constitute an important part of our course of exercises.[99] So far as the student has time to extend his inquiries beyond the limits of his textbook, first faithfully studied, his instructor may aid him greatly by referring to the various authors who have treated of the more important points in the lessons, and by introducing corrections, illustrations and comments of his own. In this way, no small portion of our daily exercises become informal and extemporaneous lectures. But the business of explaining and commenting is carried to an extreme whenever it supersedes the necessity of effort on the part of the learner. If we mistake not, some portion of the popularity of very copious oral instruction is to be set to the account of the student's satisfaction in escaping from the demand for mental exertion. . . .[100]

---

97. These "examinations" refer to oral reciting in class of memorized passages from the textbook. The standard pedagogies of the nineteenth-century American colleges—disputations, declamations, recitations—are discussed by Charles Eliot in selection #40.

98. Day expresses the conventional nineteenth-century view that the lecture required greater effort by the professor and greater sophistication and engagement on the part of the student.

99. Having discussed the "modern" pedagogy of lecture, in comparison to recitation, Day turns to the scholastic pedagogical inheritance of disputation.

100. Compare Day's implicit assumption that students wish to "escape" mental exertion with the views of Charles Eliot in selections #40 and #47.

We deem it to be indispensable to a proper adjustment of our collegiate system that there should be in it both professors and tutors. There is wanted, on the one hand, the experience of those who have been long resident at the institution and, on the other, the fresh and minute information of those who, having more recently mingled with the students, have a distinct recollection of their peculiar feelings, prejudices, and habits of thinking.

At the head of each great division of science, it is necessary that there should be a professor to superintend the department, to arrange the plan of instruction, to regulate the mode of conducting it, and to teach the more important and difficult parts of the subject. But students in a college, who have just entered on the first elements of science, are not principally occupied with the more abstruse and disputable points. Their attention ought not to be solely or mainly directed to the latest discoveries. They have first to learn the principles which have been [studied] in a course of investigation through successive ages, and have now become simplified and settled. Before arriving at regions hitherto un-explored, they must pass over the intervening cultivated ground. The professor at the head of a de-partment may, therefore, be greatly aided in some parts of the course of instruction by those who are not as deeply versed as himself in all the intricacies of the science. Indeed, we doubt whether elemen-tary principles are always taught to the best advantage by those whose researches have carried them so far beyond these simpler truths that they come back to them with reluctance and distaste. Would Sir Isaac Newton have excelled all others of his day in teaching the common rules of arithmetic?[101] Young men have often the most ardor in communicating familiar principles and in removing those lighter difficulties of the pupil, which, not long since, were found lying across their own path. . . .[102]

Each professor is accountable for the judicious arrangement of his own department and for the success with which it is conducted, so far as this depends on his personal efforts and talents. Each tutor is responsible, to a certain extent, for the progress and correct deportment of his division. But responsibility is little felt when held as common stock among numbers, without a distinct appropria-tion to individuals. By a due proportion of professors and tutors, we may unite the advantages of ex-perience with ardor and activity; of profound investigation with minute attention to elementary prin-ciples; of personal attachment and individual responsibility, with such an adjustment of the different parts of the system as will give unity and symmetry to the whole.

The collegiate course of study, of which we have now given a summary view, we hope may be carefully distinguished from several *other* objects and plans, with which it has been too often been con-founded. It is far from embracing *everything* which the student will ever have occasion to learn. The object is not to *finish* his education, but to lay the foundation and to advance as far in rearing the super-structure as the short period of his residence here will admit. If he acquires here a thorough knowledge of the principles of science, he may then in a great measure educate himself. He has, at least, been taught *how* to learn. . . .

The course of instruction which is given to the undergraduates in the college is not designed to include *professional* studies. Our object is not to teach that which is peculiar to any one of the profes-sions, but to lay the foundation which is common to them all. There are separate schools for medicine, law, and theology connected with the college, as well as in various parts of the country, which are open for the reception of all who are prepared to enter the appropriate studies of their several profes-sion. With these, the academical course is not intended to interfere.

---

101. In curricular debates over the role of natural science, it was common to invoke the name of Isaac Newton on behalf of one's views, as the Yale Report does repeatedly.

102. Does Day's rationale for tutors justify the heavy reliance upon teaching fellows in undergraduate instruction at current universities?

But why, it may be asked, should a student waste his time upon studies which have no immediate connection with his future profession? Will chemistry enable him to plead at the bar, or conic sections qualify him for preaching, or astronomy aid him in the practice of physic? Why should not his attention be confined to the subject, which is to occupy the labors of his life? In answer to this it may be observed that there is no science which does not contribute its aid to professional skill. "Everything throws light upon everything." The great object of collegiate education, preparatory to the study of a profession, is to give that expansion and balance of the mental powers, those liberal and comprehensive views, and those fine proportions of character which are not to be found in him whose ideas are always confined to one particular channel.[103]

When a man has entered upon the practice of his profession, the energies of his mind must be given principally to its appropriate duties. But if his thoughts never range on other subjects, if he never looks abroad on the ample domains of literature and science, there will be a narrowness in his habits of thinking, a peculiarity of character, which will be sure to mark him as a man of limited views and attainments. . . . Professional studies are designedly excluded from the course of instruction at college to leave room for those literary and scientific acquisitions which, if not commenced there, will in most cases never be made. They will not grow up spontaneously amid the bustle of business. . . .

As our course of instruction is not intended to complete an education in theological, medical, or legal science; neither does it include all the minute details of *mercantile, mechanical,* or *agricultural* concerns. These can never be effectually learned except in the very circumstances in which they are to be practiced. The young merchant must be trained in the counting room, the mechanic in the workshop, the farmer in the field. But we have on our premises no experimental farm or retail shop, no cotton or iron manufactory, no hatter's or silversmith's or coach-maker's establishment.[104] For what purpose, then, it will be asked, are young men who are destined to these occupations ever sent to a college? They should not be sent, as we think, with an expectation of *finishing* their education at the college; but with a view of laying a thorough foundation in the principles of science, preparatory to the study of the practical arts. As everything cannot be learned in four years, either theory or practice must be, in a measure at least, postponed to a future opportunity. But if the scientific theory of the arts is *ever* to be acquired, it is unquestionably first in order of time. The cornerstone must be laid before the superstructure is erected. If suitable arrangements were made, the details of mercantile, mechanical, and agricultural education might be taught at the college to *resident graduates*. Practical skill would then be grounded upon scientific information.

The question may be asked, What is a young man fitted for, when he takes his degree? Does he come forth from the college qualified for business? We answer, no—if he stops here. His education is begun, but not completed. Is the college to be reproached for not accomplishing that which it has never undertaken to perform? Do we complain of the mason who has laid the foundation of a house that he has done nothing of purpose, that he has not finished the building, that the product of his labor is not habitable, and that, therefore, there is nothing practical in what he has done? Do we say of the planter who has raised a crop of cotton that he has done nothing practical, because he has not given to his product the form of wearing apparel?

In education, as well as in morals, we often hear the suggestion that principles are of no consequence, provided the practice is right. Why waste on theories the time which is wanted for acquiring practical arts? We are aware that some operations may be performed by those who have little or no

---

103. In Day's view, what distinguishes the nature of professional studies from that of liberal studies? Are these distinctions the same as Aristotle sets forth in selection #3?

104. Compare Day's views on the role of practice in education for "*mercantile, mechanical,* or *agricultural* concerns" with the relationship between theory and practice in scientific education, discussed just below.

knowledge of the principles on which they depend. . . . But the labors of such a one are confined to the narrow path marked out to him by others. He needs the constant superintendence of men of more enlarged and scientific information. If he ventures beyond his prescribed rule, he works at random with no established principles to guide him. By long continued practice, he may have gained a good degree of manual dexterity. But the arranging of plans of business, the new combinations of mechanical processes, the discoveries and improvements in the arts must generally come from minds more highly and systematically cultivated. . . .

We are far from believing that theory *alone* should be taught in a college. It cannot be effectually taught except in connection with practical illustrations. These are necessary in exciting an interest in theoretical instructions, and especially important in showing the application of principles. It is our aim therefore, while engaged in scientific investigations, to blend with them as far as possible practical illustrations and experiments. Of what use are all the sublime discoveries which have immortalized the names of Newton, Archimedes, and others; if the principles which they have unfolded are never to be taught to those who can reduce them to practice? Why do we bestow such exalted encomiums on inventive genius, if the results of original investigations are to be confined to a few scientific men, and not diffused among those who are engaged in the active duties of life? To bring down the principles of science to their practical application by the laboring classes, is the office of men of superior education. It is the separation of theory and practice, which has brought reproach upon both. Their union alone can elevate them to their true dignity and value. The man of science is often disposed to assume an air of superiority when he looks upon the narrow and partial views of the mere artisan. The latter in return laughs at the practical blunders of the former. The defects in the education of both classes would be remedied by giving them a knowledge of scientific principles preparatory to practice.[105]

We are aware that a thorough education is not within the reach of all. Many, for want of time and pecuniary resources, must be content with a partial course. A defective education is better than none. If a youth can afford to devote only two or three years to a scientific and professional education, it will be proper for him to make a selection of a few of the most important branches and give his attention exclusively to these. But this is an imperfection arising from the necessity of the case. A partial course of study must inevitably give a partial education.

This we are well convinced is far preferable to a *superficial* education. Of all the plans of instruction which have been offered to the public, that is the most preposterous which proposes to teach almost everything in a short time. In this way, nothing is effectually taught. The pupil is hurried over the surface so rapidly that scarce a trace of his steps remains when he has finished his course. What he has learned, or thinks he has learned, is just sufficient to inflate his vanity, to expose him to public observation, and to draw on him the ridicule of men of sound judgment and science. A partial education is often expedient; a superficial one, never.[106] Whatever a young man undertakes to learn, however little it may be, he ought to learn it so effectually that it may be of some practical use to him. If there is any way in which everything worth knowing may be taught in four years, we are free to acknowledge that we are not in possession of the secret.

But why, it is asked, should *all* the students in a college be required to tread in the *same steps*? Why should not each one be allowed to select those branches of study which are most to his taste, which are best adapted to his particular talents and which are most nearly connected with his intended profession? To this we answer that our prescribed course contains those subjects only which ought to

105. Does Day give a satisfactory account of the relationship between theory and practice in scientific education within the liberal arts?

106. What precisely is the difference between a partial and a superficial education?

be understood, as we think, by everyone who aims at a thorough education. They are not the peculiarities of any profession of art. These are to be learned in the professional and practical schools. But the principles of science are the common foundation of all high intellectual attainments.[107]

As in our primary schools, reading, writing, and arithmetic are taught to all, however different their prospects, so in a college all should be instructed in those branches of knowledge which no one destined to the higher walks of life to be ignorant. What subject which is now studied here, could be set aside, without evidently marring the system? Not to speak particularly in this place of the ancient languages,[108] who that aims at a well proportioned and superior education will remain ignorant of the elements of the various branches of the mathematics, or of history and antiquities, or of rhetoric and oratory, or natural philosophy, or astronomy, or chemistry, or mineralogy, or geology, or political economy, or mental and moral philosophy?

It is sometimes thought that a student ought not to be urged to the study of that for which he has *no taste or capacity*. But how is he to know whether he has a taste or capacity for a science before he has even entered upon its *elementary* truths. If he is really destitute of talent sufficient for these common departments of education, he is destined for some narrow sphere of action. But we are well persuaded that our students are not so deficient in intellectual powers as they sometimes profess to be, though they are easily made to believe that they have no capacity for the study of that which they are told is almost wholly useless.

When a class have become familiar with the common elements of the several sciences, then is the proper time for them to *divide off* their favorite studies. They can then make their choice from actual trial. This is now done here, to some extent, in our junior year. The division might be commenced at an earlier period and extended farther, provided the qualifications for admission into the college were brought to a higher standard.

If the view which we have thus far taken of the subject is correct, it will be seen that the object of the system of instruction at this college is not to give a partial education consisting of a few branches only, nor, on the other hand, to give a *superficial* education containing a smattering of almost every thing; nor to finish the details of either a professional or practical education; but to *commence* a *thorough* course, and to carry it as far as the time of residence here will allow. It is intended to occupy, to the best advantage, the four years immediately preceding the study of a profession or of the operations which are peculiar to the higher mercantile, manufacturing, or agricultural establishments. . . .[109]

Our institution is not modelled exactly after the pattern of *European* universities. Difference of circumstances has rendered a different arrangement expedient. It has been the policy of most monarchical governments to concentrate the advantages of a superior education in a few privileged places. In England, for instance, each of the ancient universities of Oxford and Cambridge is not so much a single institution as a large number of distinct, though contiguous colleges. But in this country, our republican habits and feelings will never allow a monopoly of literature in any one place. There must be, in the union, as many colleges, at least, as states.[110] Nor would we complain of this arrangement as inexpedient provided that starvation is not the consequence of patronage so minutely divided. We an-

---

107. See the debate between Charles Eliot and James McCosh in selections #47 and #48 over whether students should be allowed to elect their studies.

108. This issue was left to Professor James L. Kingsley to address in Part 2 of the faculty report.

109. In the omitted paragraphs, Day observes that the advanced age of students in professional schools means that "a much greater proportion of *lectures* is admissible. . . . The age of the student and the prospect of soon entering on professional practice will commonly be sufficient to secure his assiduous application without the coercive influence of laws and penalties" found in recitations.

110. This had been the pattern in the colonies, as noted in the introduction to Section V.

ticipate no disastrous results from the multiplication of colleges, if they can only be adequately endowed. We are not without apprehensions, however, that a feeble and stinted growth of our national literature will be the consequence of the very scanty supply of means to most of our public seminaries.[111]

The universities on the continent of Europe, especially in Germany, have of late gained the notice and respect of men of information in this country.[112] They are upon a broad and liberal scale, affording very great facilities for a finished education. But we doubt whether they are models to be copied in every feature by our American colleges. We hope, at least, that this college may be spared the mortification of a ludicrous attempt to imitate them, while it is unprovided with the resources necessary to execute the purpose. The only institution in this country, which, so far as we know, has started upon the plan of the European universities, required an expenditure, before commencing operations, of more than three hundred thousand dollars, a sum far greater than Yale College has received in a century and a quarter, from the bounty of individuals and the state together. . . .[113]

We are sensible there is great imperfection in the *execution* of the purpose to give a thorough course of instruction. The observations which we have made on this subject relate rather to what we would *wish* to see effected, than to what we profess to have actually accomplished. Numerous and formidable difficulties are to be perpetually encountered. One of the principal of these is the call, which is so frequently made upon us, to admit students into the college with *defective preparation*. Parents are little aware to what embarrassments and injury they are subjecting their sons by urging them forward to a situation for which they are not property qualified. Of those who are barely admitted, one and another is, from time to time, dropped off from the class. Here and there one, after making his way with much perplexity and mortification through the four years, just obtains a degree at last, which is nearly all the benefits he derives from his residence here. Whereas, if he had come to us well prepared, he might have held a respectable rank in his class and acquired a substantial education.

Another serious difficulty with which we have to contend, is the impression made on the minds of a portion of our students, from one quarter and another, that the study of any thing for which they have not an instinctive relish or which requires vigorous and continued effort or which is not immediately connected with their intended professional pursuits, is of no practical utility. They, of course, remain ignorant of that which they think not worth the learning. We are concerned to find that not only students, but their parents also, seem frequently more solicitous for the *name* of an education than the substance. . . .

Our duty to our country demands of us an effort to provide the means of a thorough education. There is, perhaps, no nation whose interests would be more deeply affected by a substitution of superficial for solid learning. The universal diffusion of the common branches of knowledge renders it necessary that those who aspire to literary eminence should ascend to very elevated ground. They must take their position on a summit which towers above the height of surrounding ranges of hills. In the

---

111. See the introduction to Section VI and to selection #36 on Colleges Opened for Instruction, 1600–1820.

112. By 1828 a steady stream of young American scholars had begun to travel to Europe, particularly Germany, in order to study; and they returned often touting what they proclaimed to be a new model of higher education, enshrining the "freedom to teach" and "freedom to study" whatever one wished. The extent to which the German universities actually provided a model for nineteenth-century reformers of American higher education is much debated.

113. This is apparently a reference to the University of Virginia, which had opened in 1824–1825 following largely the plan set forth by Thomas Jefferson, James Madison, and their fellow commissioners in 1818. By 1831 the curricular innovations at Virginia had been radically scaled back, just as they had been at other reforming American colleges.

midst of so enlightened a population, can he be distinguished whose education has scarcely given him more enlarged views than he might acquire by conversation in stages and steam boats or the reading of newspapers and a volume or two of elegant extracts?[114]

The unexampled multiplication of schools and academies in this country requires that colleges should aim at a high standard of literary excellence. The conviction is almost universal that the former, as well as the latter, admit of great improvements. But who are to make these improvements and give character and tone to our systems of instruction, if there are few men of thorough education in the country? He who is to arrange an extensive scheme of measures ought himself to stand on an eminence from which he can command a view of the whole field of operation. Superficial learning in our higher seminaries will inevitably extend its influence to the inferior schools. If the fountains are shallow and turbid, the streams cannot be abundant and pure. Schools and colleges are not *rival* institutions. The success of each is essential to the prosperity of the other.

Our republican form of government renders it highly important that great numbers should enjoy the advantage of a thorough education.[115] On the Eastern continent, the *few* who are destined to particular departments in political life may be educated for the purpose, while the mass of the people are left in comparative ignorance. But in this country where offices are accessible to all who are qualified for them, superior intellectual attainments ought not to be confined to any description of persons. *Merchants, manufacturers*, and *farmers*, as well as professional gentlemen, take their places in our public councils. A thorough education ought therefore to be extended to all these classes. It is not sufficient that they be men of sound judgment who can decide correctly and give a silent vote on great national questions. Their influence upon the minds of others is needed, an influence to be produced by extent of knowledge and the force of eloquence. Ought the speaking in our deliberative assemblies to be confined to a single profession? If it is knowledge, which gives us the command of physical agents and instruments, much more is it that which enables us to control the combinations of moral and political machinery. . . .

The active, enterprising character of our population renders it highly important that this bustle and energy should be directed by sound intelligence, the result of deep thought and early discipline. . . . Light and moderate learning is but poorly fitted to direct the energies of a nation so widely extended, so intelligent, so powerful in resources, so rapidly advancing in population, strength, and opulence. Where a free government gives full liberty to the human intellect to expand and operate, education should be proportionably liberal and ample. When even our mountains and rivers and lakes are upon a scale which seems to denote that we are destined to be a great and mighty nation, shall our literature be feeble and scanty and superficial?

---

114. Compare the American glorification of non-academic knowledge: "I have tried, by going into the minutiae of the science of [steam boat] piloting, to carry the reader step by step to a comprehension of what the science consists of; and at the same time I have tried to show him that it is a very curious and wonderful science." Mark Twain's *Life on the Mississippi* (New York: James R. Osgood, 1883), ch. 14.

115. Like Samuel Smith and Emma Willard, Day repeatedly links liberal education, citizenship, and the American polity.

38. *Catalog of Dartmouth College for the Academical Year 1852–53*

INTRODUCTION

In 1769 Dartmouth College became the last of the nine colleges founded before the Revolutionary War, and its remote location in New Hampshire seemed to portend a marginal existence. But this location proved auspicious both because it provided a haven during the Revolutionary War when Dartmouth was the only college to continue graduating students without interruption, and because it sheltered Dartmouth from competition with the more established institutions to the south. This college therefore became predominant in northern New England from which it drew most of its students, who were generally of modest means. By the 1850s Dartmouth had quietly grown into one of the largest colleges in the country. In September 1852, when the enrollment of most colleges in the United States was less than 100, a total of 294 total students were attending Dartmouth, including 225 in the "academical" liberal arts course.[116] Beyond location, another advantage was Dartmouth's fidelity to Congregationalism, which still held sway in New Hampshire and throughout New England.

In contrast, Brown University, founded in Rhode Island in 1765, had a similar pedigree; but its proximity to Harvard and Yale, the two most influential colleges of the time, and its heterodox Baptist tradition weakened Brown's appeal to students. Another distinction lay in Brown's reputation for favoring educational reform under the energetic and far-sighted leadership of Francis Wayland (1796–1865), a Baptist minister who served as President from 1827 to 1855 and issued a call for change in his renowned *Thoughts on the Present Collegiate System in the United States*.[117] But the call went unheeded, and after working zealously to reverse declining enrollments and revenues at Brown, Wayland announced his retirement in 1849, due partly to fatigue and partly to disappointment. The Brown trustees pleaded with him to continue, and he agreed upon the condition that they would endorse his plan for adding new subjects on an equivalent standing with the old, increasing the student body and faculty, and introducing an elective system, among other changes.[118]

This reform at Brown University was "the most sweeping and fundamental revision of the college curriculum to be attempted before the Civil War."[119] Yet, it failed to attract students, as Yale President Noah Porter smugly observed in 1870: "The new system was hailed by its advocates with great enthusiasm and . . . the speedy downfall of the old scholastic system was confidently predicted. But these predictions were not fulfilled. On the contrary, the words which Dr. Wayland had written in 1842 . . . were signally realized at his own university: 'The colleges . . . which have obeyed the suggestions of the public, have failed to find themselves sustained by the public.'"[120]

116. Contemporaneously, the total enrollment at Yale was 604, including 447 students in the liberal arts course, and the figures at Harvard were 626 and 304, respectively.

117. Francis Wayland, *Thoughts on the Present Collegiate System in the United States* (Boston: Gould, Kendall, and Lincoln, 1842).

118. Francis Wayland, "Report to the Corporation of Brown University, On Changes in the System of Collegiate Education, read March 28, 1850" (Providence, RI: Brown University, 1850).

119. Douglas Sloan, "Harmony, Chaos, and Consensus: The American College Curriculum," *Teachers College Record* 73 (1971): 247. "Wayland was not wholly at odds with the [Yale] Report. Like it, he stressed the moral ends of education, favored strict paternalistic supervision of youthful students, and accepted the current faculty psychology and its corollary, mental discipline. It was on the question of what subjects were conducive to mental discipline, however, that Wayland decisively parted company with the Report." (Sloan, p. 248.)

120. Noah Porter, *The American Colleges and the American Public* (New Haven, CT: Charles C. Chatfield, 1870), pp. 14, 15. Does Wayland's quotation express a truism about the American college curriculum?

While Brown was jerking to and fro under one of the most prescient nineteenth-century college reformers, Dartmouth was heeling closely to the longstanding, liberal arts course of study, while making certain concessions to modern studies. As seen in the following reading selected from the 1852–53 course catalog, Dartmouth modified the inherited, scholastic-humanist liberal arts by incorporating some practical, scientific studies as well as modern languages and social studies. Yet, careful inspection reveals how these modifications were, in some respects, isolated and marginalized so as not to compromise the traditional curriculum. What resulted was a liberal education that was comfortably conventional but also presented a "modern" appearance.

The primary modern characteristic was the establishment of the Chandler Scientific School within the college, after Abiel Chandler of New Hampshire bequeathed $50,000 for the endowment of a scientific school in 1851. The previous year Harvard had opened its Lawrence Scientific School as the first such college-based school in the country, which awarded Harvard's first Bachelor of Science degree in 1851. The scientific-school innovation was rapidly adopted elsewhere, and Chandler's gift put Dartmouth near the front of the movement.[121] Even this signal innovation, however, demonstrates the resistance to reforming the liberal arts course in the 1850s, because the Dartmouth trustees, in accepting the Chandler gift with its unorthodox purpose, stipulated that the scientific school would be "an experiment" leaving the liberal arts course "untouched . . . as a foundation for the learned professions."[122]

Dartmouth therefore established a separate Bachelor of Science degree to be conferred upon students passing through the three-year course in the Chandler School, which was explicitly regarded as extra-liberal education. This introduction of a "parallel course" was becoming the typical strategy of preserving the sanctity of the liberal arts course, while incorporating unconventional subjects. Wesleyan introduced the B.S. degree in 1838, and Brown introduced the B.Phil. in 1850. Together with the B.Litt., these became the degrees most commonly awarded for completion of a course in which modern languages, literatures, and sciences replaced the study of Greek and Latin.[123] Until the end of the nineteenth century, the great majority American colleges reserved the B.A. degree to signify completion of a curriculum including some amount of study of Greek and Latin.[124]

By 1880 the Chandler faculty was promoting the B.S. course as "liberal education on a scientific basis." Even at that point, however, the Dartmouth President wrote to an applicant for admission to the Chandler B.S. course "that he had better take the classical course and that if he could not do that, he had better not go to Dartmouth."[125] Hence, the B.S. degree remained a poor cousin to the B.A. for decades after the appearance of the following catalog, which conveys a fairly typical, if modestly progressive, course of liberal education at one of the largest colleges in the nation near the middle of the nineteenth century.

---

121. The pressure upon the defenders of the classical course is shown by the fact that Yale President Noah Porter, while dismissing Francis Wayland's reforms as injudicious pandering, backdated the foundation of scientific schools at Harvard and Yale as far as possible in order, doubtlessly, to show how early these colleges were accommodating practical, scientific studies. Porter, *The American Colleges and the American Public*, p. 16.

122. Quoted in Marilyn Tobias, *Old Dartmouth of Trial: The Transformation of the Academic Community in Nineteenth Century America* (New York: New York University Press, 1982), p. 109.

123. By 1850 it appears that nearly a third of the students in sixteen Baptist colleges were enrolled in such "parallel courses." David B. Potts, *Baptist Colleges in the Development of American Society, 1812–1861* (New York: Garland, 1988), p. 323.

124. See James McCosh's defense of the Greek and Latin requirement in selection #48.

125. Quotations are from Tobias, *Old Dartmouth of Trial*, pp. 45, 148.

SELECTION[126]

Admission. All candidates for admission must present satisfactory testimonials of good moral character; and, if from other colleges, of unexceptionable standing. Candidates for the freshman class are examined in the following books:[127]

    Greek. Xenophon's *Anabasis*; Homer's *Iliad*, four books; Greek grammar, including prosody.[128]

    Latin. The whole of Virgil; Cicero's *Select Orations*; Sallust; Andrews and Stoddard's *Latin Grammar*, including prosody. Writing Latin.[129]

    Mathematics. Arithmetic; Chase's *Algebra* through equations of the first degree.[130]

    English. English grammar; ancient and modern geography.[131]

Candidates for advanced standing, *in addition to the above studies*, are examined in the studies that have been pursued by the class which they propose to enter or in others equivalent to them. The times for examination are the Tuesday after Commencement and the close of the vacation immediately following. . . .

Note. It is very important that the candidates for admission should be thoroughly prepared, particularly in elementary knowledge. The deficiency of many in Greek, Latin, and English grammar, in prosody, Latin composition, arithmetic, and geography makes it necessary to require especial attention to these branches of the preparatory course.[132]

---

126. *Catalog of the Officers and Students of Dartmouth College for the Academical Year 1852–53* (Hanover, NH: Dartmouth College, 1852).

127. Each college stipulated certain books upon which applicants for admission were examined. Although the same books appeared in many of the stipulations, the particularity of each college's requirements naturally reduced the number of colleges to which a young person could apply. In addition, the requirement that the applicant travel to the college and be personally examined by a faculty member also restricted the number and location of colleges to which one might apply. In practice, young persons generally aimed at one college and prepared themselves for that admissions examination. This was often the alma mater of the applicant's tutor, grammar master, or clergyman, who could exercise some influence over the faculty's admission examiner, particularly if the college wished to be fed more students by that tutor or teacher.

128. Certain Greek Readers were "accepted as an equivalent to these requisitions in Greek," indicating a modest step toward both flexibility and standardization in admissions.

129. *A Grammar of the Latin Language, for the Use of Schools and Colleges* was composed by Ethan Allen Andrews (1787–1858) and Solomon Stoddard (1800–1847), whose names (drawn from an American Revolutionary War hero and a prominent seventeenth-century Massachusetts clergyman respectively) indicate the early nineteenth-century shift from European to American textbooks. Prosody refers to poetical meter or versification.

130. Stephen Chase (1813–1851), *A Treatise on Algebra, for the Use of Schools and Colleges* (New York, 1849). Admissions requirements in mathematics became widespread in the first quarter of the nineteenth century.

131. Such additional requirements in non-classical languages and subjects began to appear in the second quarter of the nineteenth century.

132. The mutual consultation among colleges is shown by the fact that the Yale College catalog of 1850–1851 includes a note in this same location with highly similar language.

Course of Study

Freshman Year

    Fall Term
        Greek. Homer, *Iliad*, Bks. 16, 17, 18; Crosby's *Greek Grammar*.[133]
        Latin. Livy, Bks. 21, 22; Arnold's Latin Prose Composition.[134]
        Mathematics. Chase's *Algebra*, ch. 13, and Loomis's *Geometry*, three books.[135]

    Winter Term[136]
        Physics. Somerville's *Physical Geography*.[137]
        The Italian Language.

    Spring Term
        Greek. Grammar continued; Homer, *Iliad*, Bks. 19, 20, 21; Coleridge's *Introduction to the Greek Classic Poets*.[138]
        Latin. Ovid, *Metamorphoses*, Bks. 1, 2, and 3; Arnold's *Latin Prose Composition*; Horace, *Odes*; Bojeson's *Manual of Greek and Roman Antiquities*.[139]
        Mathematics. Loomis's *Geometry* completed.
        Rhetoric. Themes or declamations once a week.[140]

    Summer Term
        Greek. Felton's *Selections from the Greek historians*; grammar continued.[141]
        Latin. Horace, *Odes*; Arnold's *Latin Prose Composition*.
        Mathematics. Loomis's *Plane Trigonometry*; mensuration; and linear calculation.
        Rhetoric. Themes and declamations.

---

133. Alpheus Crosby (1810–1874), *A Grammar of the Greek Language, for the Use of Schools and Colleges* (c. 1850).

134. Thomas K. Arnold (1800–1853), *A Practical Introduction to Latin Prose Composition* (1846). This is not Thomas Arnold (1795–1842), the British evangelical educator and historian, but an English textbook author who published an analogous text for Greek, which Dartmouth also prescribed.

135. In the mid-nineteenth century Elias Loomis (1811–1889) was one of the leading mathematicians and astronomers in the United States, who taught at several colleges, and amassed a fortune from his textbooks.

136. Why were winter course offerings few and marginal?

137. In 1848 Mary Fairfax Somerville (1780–1872) published *Physical Geography*, which went through seven editions and became her most popular book. See the introduction to selection #45.

138. Henry N. Coleridge (1798–1843), *Introduction to the Study of the Greek Classic Poets, designed principally for the Use of Young Persons at School and College* (London, 1846).

139. Ernest F. C. Bojeson (1840–1865), *A Manual of Grecian [sic] and Roman Antiquities*, translated into English.

140. These are English exercises, whose stipulation demonstrates the pedagogical norm of recitations.

141. Cornelius C. Felton (1807–1862) was an American classical scholar at Harvard who served as professor of Greek (1832–1860) and president (1860–1862).

Sophomore Year

Fall Term
Greek. Felton's *Selections*; grammar continued.
Latin. Horace, *Satires*, *Epistles*, and *Art of Poetry*; Arnold's *Latin Prose Composition*; Keightley's *History of Greece*.[142]
Mathematics. Loomis's *Surveying and Leveling*, with the use of the instruments and practice in the field; navigation; drawing of plans and maps; spherical trigonometry; Loomis's *Analytical Geometry* to section 6.[143]
Rhetoric. Campbell's *Rhetoric*; themes and declamations.[144]

Winter Term
Physics. Somerville's *Physical Geography*.
The Italian Language.

Spring Term
Greek. Aeschylus, *Prometheus*; grammar continued.
Latin. Tacitus, *Germania* and *Agricola*; Arnold continued.
Mathematics. Loomis's *Analytical Geometry* completed; Chase's *Algebra* completed.
Rhetoric. Themes and declamations; Russell's *American Elocutionist*.[145]
Philosophy. Paley's *Natural Theology*.[146]

Summer Term
Greek. Sophocles, *Ajax*; Arnold's *Greek Prose Composition*.
Latin. Tacitus, *Histories*; Schmitz, *History of Rome*.[147]
Mathematics. Loomis, *Differential and Integral Calculus*.[148]
Rhetoric. Themes and declamations.

---

142. Thomas Keightley (1789–1872), *The History of Greece* (American ed., 1839).

143. The nature and range of these subjects, as well as the "practice in the field," were highly unusual and demonstrate Dartmouth's progressive inclination in this area, reflected in the foundation of the Chandler Scientific School.

144. *The Philosophy of Rhetoric* (New York, 1841) was written by George Campbell (1719–1796), professor of Aberdeen University in Scotland.

145. *The American Elocutionist* (1844) was written by William Russell (1798–1873), a Scottish schoolmaster who emigrated to Georgia and ultimately to New England, where he founded a number of schools and normal schools, as well as the *American Journal of Education* in 1826.

146. The study of philosophy appears here for the first time, and was devoted to the reading of modern Protestant theologians. The works read under the study of Greek and Latin texts are histories, poetry, and drama, to this point. William Paley (1743–1805) was a prominent, latitudinarian, Anglican theologian. His *View of the Evidences of Christianity [in human history]* (1794), mentioned below, became renowned; his complementary *Natural Theology, or Evidences of the Existence and Attributes of the Deity collected from the Appearances of Nature* (1802), pref., argues for "the necessity, in each particular case, of an intelligent designing mind for the contriving and determining of the forms which organized bodies bear."

147. Leonhard Schmitz (1807–1899), *A History of Rome from the Earliest Times to . . . A.D. 192* (1847).

148. To require this level of mathematics in the sophomore year was advanced at the time.

Junior Year

Fall Term
Greek. Demosthenes, *On the Crown*; Arnold Continued; Bojeson's *Manual of Greek and Roman Antiquities.*
Latin. Cicero, *On Duty.*
Philosophy. Whately's *Logic.*[149]
Physics. Olmsted's *Natural Philosophy*, with lectures.[150]
Rhetoric. Themes and declamations.

Winter Term
History. Stephen's *Lectures on the History of France.*[151]
Philosophy. McCosh, *Method of the Divine Government.*[152]

Spring Term
Greek. Plato, *Gorgias*; Arnold continued.
Latin. Juvenal.
Physics. Olmsted's *Philosophy and Astronomy*, with lectures; Dana's *Mineralogy* with lectures.[153]
Philosophy. Paley's *Evidences of Christianity.*[154]
Rhetoric. Whately's *Rhetoric*; themes and declamations.

Summer Term
Greek. Plato, *Gorgias* continued.
Latin. Terence, *Andria.*
Physics. Olmsted's *Astronomy*, with lectures.
Rhetoric. Themes and declamations; lectures on rhetoric and criticism.
Original declamations before the college during the year.

------

149. Richard Whately (1787–1863), Anglican archbishop of Dublin, wrote *Elements of Logic* (1826) and *Elements of Rhetoric* (1828), both of which became standard textbooks.

150. After teaching briefly at the University of North Carolina, Denison Olmsted (1791–1859) was appointed to the professorship of mathematics and natural philosophy at Yale, where he was succeeded by Elias Loomis, mentioned above.

151. James Stephen, *Lectures on the History of France* (London, 1851).

152. *The Method of the Divine Government, Physical and Moral* (Edinburgh, 1850), was the first book written by James McCosh and went through a second edition and at least nine printings in Britain and the United States by 1868, when McCosh began his twenty-year tenure as president of Princeton. See selection #48.

153. This might refer to either of two celebrated books: *System of Mineralogy* (1837) or *Manual of Mineralogy* (1848), written by Yale professor James D. Dana (1813–1895). Note the reference to lectures, which normally denoted empirical demonstrations, to supplement recitations of the textbook.

154. In the first half of the nineteenth century, "Evidences of Christianity" was a standard topic or course that is prescribed by Emma Willard, for example. This summative course was normally taught by the president who tried to show how all the studies harmonized into a coherent view of the world that was consistent with Christianity. The standard text was this book by William Paley, described above.

Senior Year

Fall Term
  Philosophy. Stewart's *Elements of the Philosophy of the Mind*; Say's *Political Economy*; *The Federalist*.[155]
  Rhetoric. Schlegel's *Dramatic Art and Literature*;[156] themes and declamations; lectures on the English language and literature.
  Anatomy and Physiology. Lectures.[157]

Winter Term
  History. Stephen's *Lectures on the History of France*.
  Philosophy. McCosh's *Method of the Divine Government*.

Spring Term
  Philosophy. Edwards *On the Will*; Wayland's *Moral Philosophy*.[158]
  Physics. Silliman's *Chemistry*,[159] with lectures.

Summer Term
  Philosophy. Butler's *Analogy*[160]

---

155. Influenced by Thomas Reid, discussed above in regard to the Yale Report, Scottish philosopher Dugald Stewart (1753–1828) became a leading exponent of the "common sense" school of philosophy. *Elements of the Philosophy of the Human Mind* (1792, 1814, 1827) was often reprinted. Before his death, the French economist Jean Baptiste Say (1767–1832) published five French editions of *A Treatise on Political Economy, or, the Production, Distribution, and Consumption of Wealth* (New American edition, 1848). Included among the "American classics" by Robert M. Hutchins in selection #58 and by St. John's College in selection #65, *The Federalist* was a series of eighty-five political essays written in the late 1780s by Alexander Hamilton, John Jay, and James Madison.

156. August W. von Schlegel (1767–1845), a leading scholar in the German Romantic movement, originally delivered *Lectures on Dramatic Art and Literature* (1846) in German in 1801.

157. This highly unusual course is apparently explained by the desire or the need to employ the faculty of Dartmouth's medical school, the fourth oldest in the country, founded in 1797.

158. The college president normally taught moral philosophy in the spring term of the senior year and tried to show that the various subjects fit together into one coherent system that was consistent with, if not made comprehensible by, Christianity. As time passed, new studies and findings made this conceptual and curricular project more difficult. Dartmouth prescribed *The Elements of Moral Science* (1835) by President Francis Wayland of Brown University; and the famous *A Strict and Careful Inquiry into . . . Freedom of the Will* (1754) by Jonathan Edwards.

159. This might refer to *Elements of Chemistry* (1830) by Benjamin Silliman (1779–1864), who graduated from Yale, studied for the law, and, with little expertise on the topic, was appointed Professor of Chemistry and Natural History at Yale in 1802 and continued in this position until 1853. More likely, it refers to *First Principles of Chemistry for Colleges and Schools* (1847), written by his son Benjamin Silliman (1816–1885), who graduated from Yale and assumed his father's professorship upon the latter's retirement in 1853.

160. In his famous *The Analogy of Religion, Natural and Revealed, to the Constitution and Course of Nature* (1736), Anglican Bishop Joseph Butler (1692–1752), chaplain to Caroline, wife of King George II, attacked the theological movement of deism, which gave more authority to reason and natural law than to revelation. In an appendix, he also rejected the hedonist principle that self-interest is the basis of all morality.

Physics. Lyell, *Elements of Geology*, with Lectures.[161]
History. Guizot's *History of Civilization*.[162]
Rhetoric. Themes and Forensic discussions.
Original declamations before the college during the senior year.

Biblical exercise is attended by all classes on Monday morning. Occasional lectures are delivered by the president to the senior class on subjects relating to the studies of the year. Courses of lectures are also delivered during the year on natural philosophy and astronomy, to the juniors; on chemistry and geology to the seniors and on mineralogy to the juniors; on rhetoric and belles lettres to the seniors and juniors; on history to the sophomores; on theology and moral philosophy; and anatomy and physiology to the seniors.[163]

Examinations. There are two public examinations of the several classes, the one at the close of the fall term and the other immediately before commencement. Each examination is conducted in the presence and under the direction of a committee of gentlemen of education, invited by the faculty to attend for that purpose. The committee are expected, at the close of the examination, to express their judgment upon the merits of each student and to recommend that he be advanced or degraded, as in their opinion he may deserve.

Libraries. There are three libraries accessible to the students beside the medical library and the library of the Northern Academy of Arts and Sciences. An annual appropriation is made for the increase of the college library. The libraries of the two literary societies are increased by annual donations from the members of each.[164] The number of books in the different libraries connected with the college is . . . 23,400. The Library contains, besides bound volumes, a large number of newspapers and pamphlets, carefully arranged.

Apparatus and Cabinet[165] In addition to the usual apparatus for illustrating the several branches of physical science, the college is furnished with the best instruments now used in practical surveying and engineering. The large telescope recently purchased is mounted in a temporary building, until means can be provided for the erection of a permanent observatory. The instrument was manufactured at Munich by Merz and Mahler and is like the refractors of the Cambridge and Cincinnati Observato-

161. *Elements of Geology* (2nd American ed., 1851) by the eminent Scottish geologist Charles Lyell (1797–1875) was originally published in 1838.

162. During the 1820s, François Guizot (1787–1874), French politician and historian, wrote several multivolume works with this short title.

163. This sentence has been shortened. "Belles lettres" was the term employed at this time to refer to literature in the vernacular language.

164. Outside the formal curriculum, literary societies, or lyceums, constituted an important part of students' education in nineteenth-century colleges. Usually comprising students of the same sectarian, ethnic, geographic, or socio-economic backgrounds, these student-run societies sponsored lectures by outside speakers and student debates on significant topics of the day.

165. During the first half of the nineteenth century, it became increasingly common for colleges to purchase and advertise "apparatus and cabinet" in order to indicate their attention to scientific and practical subjects, although these accouterments were rarely employed in the classroom or were sometimes even reserved for use by the faculty. Dartmouth was unusual in its provision for scientific apparatus, purchased from Europe and used by students and people in the community.

ries. . . . The Hall Cabinet, presented by the late Professor Frederick Hall, contains a large collection of specimens of rocks, minerals and fossils, both American and foreign, sufficient for extensive illustration in mineralogy and geology. The instruction in geology is aided by a series of well-executed drawings on a large scale. The chemical laboratory is amply furnished with apparatus and chemicals for the illustration of the lectures in that department.

Funds for the Assistance of Indigent Students. Indigent students belonging to New Hampshire are assisted, in respect to tuition, by funds delivered from the income of certain lands granted by the state. Students preparing for the ministry receive appropriations from funds given for their particular benefit. These several funds now yield an income of about 700 dollars, which is distributed according to the necessities of students in sums ranging from 12 to 30 dollars.

Resident Graduates. Graduates of this or other colleges desirous of pursuing their studies are allowed, as Resident Graduates, to attend the public lectures of the college and to use the library and scientific collections, subject to such rules as the faculty may establish.

Degree of Master of Arts. The degree of Master of Arts is conferred, in course, on every Bachelor of three years' standing, on the payment of the usual fee.[166] Graduates of longer standing may have the Master's degree upon the same condition. The fee is five dollars, payable in advance. Application should be made to the President or the Treasurer as early as the day before Commencement.

Expenses for the Academic Year.[167] Tuition $36.00. Room rent from $6.00 to 12.00. Board, from $1.20 to 2.00 per week for 39 weeks. Wood, lights, and washing 9.00 to 14.00. [Total] 97.80 to 140.00. Library according to the use of it. Room-rent, wood, and lights are estimated on the supposition that two students occupy a chamber. Other incidental expenses, such as books and stationery, furniture, expenses in societies, class taxes, traveling expenses, etc., vary according to circumstances and the character of the habits of the individual. Payment of the college bills is required in advance, at the beginning of each term.

College Calendar.

1852

    August 27 Fall term begins—Friday morning.

    November 22–25 Fall examinations.

    November 25 Fall term ends—Thursday night.

    Vacation of seven weeks. Students whose circumstances render it necessary for them to take schools in the winter are permitted to be absent fourteen weeks from the close of fall term.[168]

---

166. "In course" meant that the M.A. was granted without requiring any formal academic work, the standard practice in the United States and Britain. One of Francis Wayland's radical proposals was to require academic work for the M.A. Wayland, *Thoughts on the Present Collegiate System*, p. 111.

167. In general during the second quarter of the nineteenth century, unskilled workers earned annually between $200 and $400; skilled artisans, craftsmen, and mechanics between $400 and $800; the merchant class, comprising perhaps a fifth of the workforce, between $800 and $5,000. Male schoolteachers earned between $400 and $600; female teachers half that amount; male professors at the most established colleges earned about $800 to $1,000. Overall, the average income for non-farm employees in 1860 was $363.

168. This explains why few and marginal subjects were taught during winter term. Being of modest means and from northern New England, most of Dartmouth's students taught school for three months in the winter and at-

1853

    January 14 Winter term begins—Friday morning.

    March 4 Spring term begins—Friday morning.

    May 12 Spring term ends—Thursday night.

    Vacation of two weeks.

    May 27 Summer term begins—Friday morning.

    July 18–23 Summer examination.

    July 28 Commencement—Last Thursday in July.

    Vacation of four weeks.

    August 25 Examination for admission to college—Thursday.

    August 26 Fall term begins—Friday morning.

Chandler Scientific School

This department of instruction was established by a resolution of the Trustees, in acceptance of the sum of *fifty thousand dollars*, bequeathed to them, in trust, by Abiel Chandler, Esq. . . ."to carefully and prudently invest or fund the principal sum, and faithfully apply and appropriate the income and interest thereof for the establishment and support of a permanent department or school of instruction in the college in the practical and useful arts of life, comprised chiefly in the branches of mechanics and civil engineering, the invention and manufacture of machinery, carpentry, masonry, architecture, and drawing, the investigation of the properties and uses of the materials employed in the arts, the modern languages, and English literature, together with book-keeping, and such other branches of knowledge as may best qualify young persons for the duties and employments of active life."[169]

Admission. All candidates for admission must present satisfactory testimonials of good moral character; be fourteen years of age; and, for admission to the [first] year, be examined in reading, spelling, penmanship, English grammar and parsing; arithmetic; and geography; and, for advanced standing, in the studies which the class have pursued in addition, or a full and satisfactory equivalent. The school is open to a limited number of indigent and worthy students for gratuitous instruction.

Tuition. In all cases payable in advance at the beginning of each term. For the junior department, $5.00 a term or per year, $20.00. Senior Department, $10.00 a term, or per year, $30.00. Including all necessary incidental expenses.

[*Degree of Bachelor of Science.*] None are admitted for less than two terms. Those completing the regular course on three years will be entitled to the degree of Bachelor of Science on passing a satisfactory examination. For a less term the student will be entitled to a certificate of his standing and proficiency.

---

tended college in spring and summer when schoolchildren were working the farms. In the 1860s and 1870s, as the socio-economic level of the Dartmouth student body increased, the Trustees gradually discouraged and restricted students' schoolkeeping by reducing the long vacation winter vacation and forcing students to make up work missed during the winter term. Marilyn Tobias, *Old Dartmouth of Trial*, p. 116.

169. Compare the level of the entrance requirements and of the curriculum in the same subjects for the B.A. degree and B.S. degree.

Course of Study

Juniors

Fall Term. Chase's *Algebra* to ch. 5; English grammar; Somerville's *Physical Geography*; Linear drawing.

Winter Term. Loomis's *Geometry*, Bks. 1 and 2; History and Constitution of the United States; Elements of Physiology and Hygiene; Elocution.

Spring Term. Loomis's *Geometry*, Bks. 3 and 4; Bookkeeping and penmanship; English composition; French.

Summer Term. Bookkeeping and penmanship; Loomis's *Problems in Geometry*, Bk. 5; Elementary graphics and use of mathematical instruments; Elements of Botany; French.

Seniors, First Year.

Fall Term. Chase's *Algebra*, ch. 13; Loomis's *Geometry*, finished; Graphics; Composition and elocution; Modern languages.

Spring Term. General chemistry; Mineralogy and geology; Loomis's *Conic Sections*; Modern Languages; Moral Philosophy.

Summer Term. Geology; History; Loomis's *Plane Trigonometry*; Mensuration and linear calculation; A French Work on Practical Science, in the Original.

Seniors, Second Year

Fall Term. Mechanics, text book and lectures; Chemistry of the arts and agriculture and practical chemistry; Loomis's *Surveying*; drawing of plans and sections; and field work; Civil engineering; English literature.

Spring Term. Descriptive geometry; Mechanics; Electricity, magnetism, and optics, with lectures; Use of the barometer; Civil engineering and field work; Modern languages.

Summer Term. Shades, shadows, and perspective; Application of mechanics and physics; Mathematical geography and astronomy, theory, and practice; Practical geology; Modern languages.

Resident Graduates. Will be instructed in the following advanced subjects, through an additional course of one or two years: analytical chemistry, mining geology, analytical geometry and calculus, analytical and celestial mechanics, application of mechanics to carpentry and masonry continued, mechanical agents, geodesy, practical astronomy. The arts of design with reference to their application to the useful arts.

Lectures. Lectures will be given by the professors, in addition to the above, during the different years of the course, on morals, Evidences of Christianity, political economy, didactics, history, English, and general literature. Also, the students of the Chandler School may attend any of the College lectures that do not interfere with the regular exercises of their own department; and the lectures of the School are open, on the same conditions, to the College students.

39. *Catalog of Alfred University for the year ending June 30, 1858*

INTRODUCTION

In 1847 female students in the liberal arts course at coeducational Oberlin College were not permitted to read their graduation essays in public, a policy based upon the prevailing view that women's role was private and public activities by women were unseemly.[170] One such student, Lucy Stone, commenced her career as a social reformer by refusing to write her graduation essay unless permitted to deliver it.[171] Annoyed by Stone's protest and the resulting controversy, Oberlin Professor James H. Fairchild asked Oberlin student, 24-year-old Jonathan Allen, who had graduated from coeducational Alfred Academy, "How do they get along with that question at Alfred?" Allen replied, "The most natural way in the world. If a young woman is capable of writing a paper, she ought to be able to read it."[172]

Founded in the hills of western New York in 1836 as a coeducational school sponsored by the Seventh Day Baptists, Alfred was incorporated as an academy in 1843 and dedicated to teacher education. In 1857 Alfred Academy received a charter from the state to found Alfred University and then established a number of parallel courses of study leading to a bachelor's degree. In this way, Alfred joined the small group of pre-Civil War coeducational colleges, including Oberlin College in Ohio (founded 1833), Knox College in Illinois (1837), Genesee College in New York (1849), Antioch College in Ohio in (1853), and St. Lawrence University (1856) in New York. All of these colleges wrestled with the triangular relationship among men, women, and the liberal arts course.

At those other institutions, coeducation was somewhat "unnatural." Oberlin and Antioch discouraged women from engaging in public roles. Knox separated female and male students in the classroom and did not permit women into its college courses until 1870. Coeducation at St. Lawrence was adopted by the college's local managers largely out of expediency to bolster enrollment, because the founder, who lived in Massachusetts, opposed not only coeducation but all higher education for women. At Genesee College, as at most early coeducational schools, women were always a small minority of the student body, making little impact on the school. The few women at Genesee did not share classes with men, and there were no women on the faculty. Among coeducational institutions, Alfred University was distinctive.

Several factors made an egalitarian environment for women seem "natural" at Alfred University when virtually all colleges considered it "unnatural." Alfred's egalitarian ethos had deep roots in the Seventh Day Baptist denomination, while the reform spirit pervading the upstate New York led Alfred to place emphasis on vocational roles aiding evangelism. In other coeducational colleges this meant preparing women for the dependent role of minister's wife, as at Oberlin. But, although the Seventh Day Baptists charged Alfred in 1857 to train clergy, the college commenced offering theological education only in 1864 and only modestly at that point. Due to the subsidiary role of theological educa-

---

170. On women speaking and acting in public, see Bathsua Makin's selection #30, Emma Willard's selection #35, and Juana Inéz de la Cruz's selection #31.

171. Lucy Stone (1818-1893) paid her way through Oberlin with earnings from several years of teaching. She began lecturing for an anti-slavery society after graduation and became one of the best-known social reformers in the nineteenth-century. See the biographical introduction to the address by James H. Fairchild (and his comment about Lucy Stone) in the selection from *The Liberal Education of Women* (1873) in Section VIII.

172. Jonathan Allan (1823-1892) graduated from Alfred Academy in 1844, taught school for three years, and then matriculated at Oberlin College in 1847. He served as a teacher at Alfred from 1849 and president from 1865 until 1892.

tion and the relative absence of clergy, Alfred focused upon offering parallel courses leading to different bachelor's degrees in order to prepare women for the independent vocation of teaching, which was held in high regard by Seventh Day Baptists.

The Enlightenment philosophy of natural rights also contributed to the egalitarian ethos at Alfred because the first Women's Rights Convention was held in nearby Seneca Falls, New York, in 1848, and the convention's *Declaration of Sentiments and Resolutions* invoked the natural rights tradition while echoing the U.S. *Declaration of Independence*. Finally, the agrarian economy and family structure of western New York supported egalitarianism. As an economically accessible institution located in a rural area outside of New England, Alfred offered social mobility to local young people and particularly to young women.[173] In addition, the marital partnerships common in the farm lives of its students and the marriages of its presidents for fifty years presented a positive model for coeducation.[174]

Consequently, Alfred from its beginning supported women, who attended in large numbers, found respected intellectual models on the faculty, and learned not subservience, but independence. Women's public speaking was considered natural because they were on the faculty in large numbers and many alumnae worked after marriage.[175] Even late in the nineteenth century, as coeducation became the leading mode of higher education and then suffered a severe reaction when fears of "feminization" arose at many institutions, Alfred University's faculty and students persisted in their support of coeducation.

This environment nourished the equal rights beliefs of Abigail and Jonathan Allen, she a member of the faculty from 1846 until her death in 1902, he a faculty member from 1849 and president from 1867 until his death in 1892. Abigail (Maxson) Allen explicitly rejected the prevailing gender ideology of separate education for the separate spheres of men and women, expressing her confidence that coeducation was natural: Alfred "has no more thought of changing than parents, who find in their families boys and girls, would think of organizing two households to train them," she said in 1874. In these words, she identified the connection between the public dispute over coeducation and the fundamental debate over women's nature and capabilities.

Much research on the nineteenth-century debate over higher education for women has focused on the elite women's colleges founded after the Civil War rather than the more numerous and earlier coeducational colleges, and many studies dismiss coeducation as demeaning to women or inferior to single-sex education. Historian Barbara Solomon asserts, "consistently, one generalization holds: coeducational schools made plain . . . that society attached greater importance to men's achievements" and "it was in the separate female academy that . . . the values of women's liberal education pre-

---

173. Between 1848 and 1861 about 85 percent of the Alfred students came from the two surrounding counties. Other students came from Seventh-Day Baptist communities in Rhode Island, New Jersey, and Wisconsin. A few were referred by missionaries, including two African-American women and at least two Native American women in the early 1850s. Kathryn M. Kerns, "Farmers' Daughters: The Education of Women at Alfred Academy and University before the Civil War," *History of Higher Education Annual* (1986): 18-19.

174. Having studied at reformist Union College and become head of the Alfred school in 1839 and then the first president of Alfred University in 1857, William C. Kenyon (1812-1867) married Elvira E. Kenyon (d. 1863) and then Ida F. Sallan, who were the first two female students in the liberal arts course in 1857 and who both taught on the faculty.

175. At Alfred, professorial rank was granted to all faculty who held college degrees, and women's salaries were comparable to those of men with the same training. Between 1836 and 1866, 18 men and 11 women were ranked as 'Professors,' while 25 men and 15 women were listed in the catalogs as 'Teachers.' Although women generally taught such subjects as music, painting, and modern languages, some taught Latin, mathematics, and natural sciences. In contrast, Oberlin first appointed women to the faculty in the 1880s, Cornell in 1897, and St. Lawrence in 1902.

vailed."[176] Likewise, Jill Ker Conway maintains that coeducational colleges offered only "compensatory education" for women and considered women "only from the point of view of the services they might provide for men." Not until women's colleges were established, in Conway's view, did women receive intellectual training that was not "derivative."[177] These generalizations rely on scholarship emphasizing the conservative aspects of a few well-known coeducational institutions.

Until recently, institutional histories treated coeducation superficially, praising the admission of women as an advance and rarely examining the actual campus environment in depth. Revisionist historians now suggest that any progressivism associated with the earliest co-educational colleges was heavily tempered by conservative values. The revisionists have asserted that the first coeducational colleges--notably Oberlin and Antioch--were conservative ventures, perpetuating traditional roles of subservience and subordination for women, restricting their public speaking, and discouraging professional aspirations. They argue that these coeducational institutions did not depart radically from contemporary norms; rather, college founders' conceptions of women's education lay well within the separate spheres ideology, assigning women a private, domestic role, subordinate to men's public responsibilities.

After the Civil War, coeducation spread from the small colleges to the new land grant universities.[178] There were numerous confrontations and idiosyncratic resolutions in the 1870s and 1880s when the new universities dealt with women's demands and powerful opposition to those demands. Many of these institutions initially resisted demands for coeducation, as Michigan and Cornell did, or ambivalently admitted women then separated them, as Wisconsin did. While proponents of coeducation viewed women's admission as a victory, admission did not guarantee equitable or even respectful treatment. When women were admitted to the University of Missouri in 1870, they were marched to class in a group. In addition to administrative resistance, student culture was hostile to women in some institutions.

Thus, in assessing the early history of coeducation, both traditional and revisionist historians have typically focused on the conservative model and on resistance to educating men and women together. The history of Alfred University suggests that there was some diversity among early coeducational colleges and their approaches to women's education. The conservative model was not universal, for at Alfred University cooperative gender roles in an ethically and economically homogenous farming community joined with belief in the natural rights of women to create an atypically egalitarian model of higher education. In the hill country of western New York, Alfred University nourished and supported its women to an unusual degree, with less dispute and resistance, before and after the Civil War, than at many other institutions. At Alfred it was "natural" for young women and men to wish for liberal education, "natural" for women and men to be educated together, "natural" for women to speak publicly, and ultimately "natural" for women to seek suffrage, as Abigail Maxson Allen and her husband, Jonathan Allen, advocated.[179]

This selection offers a detailed look at the formal structure that allowed and, in some respects, inhibited that natural approach.

---

176. Barbara Miller Solomon, *In the Company of Educated Women: A History of Women and Higher Education in America* (New Haven: Yale University Press, 1985), pp. xix, 15.

177. Jill Ker Conway, "Perspectives on the History of Women's Education in the United States," *History of Education Quarterly* 14 (1974): 6, 8. Conway was the president of Smith College from 1975 to 1985.

178. See Geraldine Jonçich Clifford, ed. *Lone Voyagers: Academic Women in Coeducational Universities, 1870-1937* (New York: Feminist Press, 1989).

179. This introduction draws upon Susan Rumsey Strong, "The Most Natural Way in the World": Coeducation at Nineteenth-Century Alfred University," (Ph.D. diss., University of Rochester, 1995), pp. 1-10, 193-4, 210-216.

SELECTION[180]

Organization of the Academy and University. A university charter was granted March, 1857, locating a college with university privileges in connection with Alfred Academy. By this arrangement the two institutions become as far as possible united. A large and permanent board of trustees have charge of the various departments, ranging through both the academy and university, securing thereby an efficiency and thoroughness unattainable by any other arrangement.[181]

Departments.[182] The general departments of the institution are two--a Male Department and a Female Department. Ladies and Gentlemen are provided with separate buildings, and are under special care and separate supervision but recite together as far as practicable. There are also established as subdivisions of the general departments, the following special departments:[183]

I. English Department.

II. Department of Pure Mathematics.

III. Department of Modern Languages.[184]

IV. Department of Ancient Languages.   It will be the aim, by means of thorough training, to enable the student both to read and write Greek and Latin [and Hebrew] with facility, and thus to render the study of these languages an important means of increasing the knowledge and mental power of the learner. . . .

V. Department of General and Agricultural Chemistry.   It is the design to impart, in this department, a practical knowledge of the science of chemistry, together with its application to agriculture and the arts.

---

180. *Catalog of Alfred University and Alfred Academy for the year ending June 30, 1858* (Alfred, NY: Alfred University, 1858), pp. 23-36. I am grateful to Susan Rumsey Strong for leading me to this source.

181. Colleges incorporating an academy generally enrolled most of their students in the preparatory department. This catalog reports (pp. 7-22) that Alfred's total enrollment of 478 during 1857-58 included 218 students (118 men, 100 women) in the "preparatory teachers' course" and 104 (78 men, 31 women) students in the "preparatory college course." When Antioch opened in 1853, 200 students enrolled in the preparatory department; six (four men, two women) in the college course. See the financial and curricular criticism of these academy-cum-colleges, made by William R. Harper in selection #49.

182. "While Alfred University's charter authorized 'separate departments or courses of study for males and females; both departments possessing equal privileges and powers,' such separation was barely detectable in practice. Women were not barred from enrolling in the classical or scientific course or from public speaking, and shared all classes with men." Strong, "Most Natural Way," p. 206. This published distinction was apparently made for public relations.

183. These "special departments" are simply the subjects (with their subtopics and textbooks) taught within the courses of study that are listed below. In substantive terms, the "special departments" reveal the incursion of modern subjects into a reformist institution such as Alfred; in organizational terms, they anticipate the departmentalization of the university that accompanied the proliferation of subjects and disciplines over the next half century. The prescribed texts listed under each "department" are omitted.

184. Numbering French, Italian, and, significantly, German.

VI. Department of Natural Philosophy and Astronomy. This course occupies one year and comprises mechanics, hydrostatics, pneumatics, acoustics, optics, and astronomy, both descriptive and mathematical. In addition to the daily recitations, the student is directed by lectures, illustrations, and experiments[185] in reducing *principles to practice* in their application to the useful arts.

VII. Department of Natural History. . . . The above course is designed to develop the laws which pervade and govern the three great kingdoms of nature. Especial attention will be given to the laws of hygiene as applied to the human constitution, as well as to its relations and analogies to the lower orders of animals and to vegetables. The apparatus for the demonstration and illustration of the sciences is very ample and will be found quite sufficient for a thorough course of illustrative experiments[186] in anatomy, physiology, mechanics, hydrostatics, pneumatics, electricity, magnetism, electromagnetism, optics, astronomy, and chemistry.

VIII. Metaphysical and Historical Department.

Music Painting and Penciling. Vocal music is pursued as a regular study, the same as any other branch of education. Those desiring to take instrumental music, drawing, or painting in its various forms, will find at this institution ample facilities and competent instructors.

Teachers' Department. It is one of the prime objects of this institution to fit young ladies and gentlemen for the profession of teaching. In carrying out this object, a course of study has been adopted with especial reference to the wants of teachers. In order for a teacher to enjoy the benefits of the State provisions or to be recommended by the authorities of the institution, he must attend one full course of lectures upon the subject of teaching and manifest the qualities of a successful teacher.[187] No individual will receive a recommendation from the authorities of this institution, who is not deemed competent to fulfill all of the specifications of his recommendation.

Courses of Instruction.[188] The courses of instruction embrace every department of science and literature usually taught in the best academies and colleges of this country. It is intended that ample advantages shall be furnished to both ladies and gentlemen for obtaining a useful and finished education. Four courses of study have been established, viz.: the English or Teachers', the Scientific, the Ladies', and the Classical.[189]

---

185. Note the pedagogical variation from recitation, as discussed in selection #40.

186. In keeping with the use of such apparatus in most nineteenth-century colleges, the purpose of experiments is to illustrate and demonstrate established laws.

187. The predominant interest in preparing to become teachers in combination with this minimal requirement for the recommendation for a teaching license explains, in part, why 90 percent of male or female Alfred students never graduated.

188. "All students on entering college are required to decide which course they desire to pursue, and no exchange from one course to another will be allowed, except by special permission of the faculty. Studies of the teachers' course cannot be exchanged with those of any other course." *Catalog*, p. 32n.

189. In addition to these four parallel courses, Alfred employed a category called the "college course," comprising the scientific, ladies' and classical courses of study, as suggested by point 5 below. Thus, the catalog (pp. 11-

1. The English or teachers' course is arranged for those who, while not intending to complete either of the longer courses, yet are desirous of preparing for teachers or for efficient laborers and influential members of society. An individual in order to enter upon the studies for this course, must have made good proficiency in the elementary studies of a common school education.

2. The scientific course is designed for those desiring a thorough education with reference to future scientific pursuits.

3. The ladies' course is arranged to meet the growing demand for a higher standard of female education. It is intended to harmoniously blend thorough intellectual discipline with the cultivation of a refined and elegant taste, high moral principles, and pure religious sentiments.

4. The Classical course is designed for those seeking thorough education with reference to the learned professions.[190]

5. Candidates for admission to either of the three last named courses must pass a satisfactory examination in the following studies--Greek being elective for the Ladies course--arithmetic; English grammar; geography; Latin: [grammar], prose composition, Caesar, Cicero's *Select Orations*, and Virgil, six books; Greek: [grammar], prose composition, [Xenophon's] *Anabasis* three books; American history; algebra.

6. Those students who having sustained a good moral character and completed either of the above courses, will be admitted to a degree, after having passed a satisfactory examination.

The degree of [Bachelor of Philosophy] will be conferred on those who complete the English or teachers' course, and the degree of [Bachelor of Arts] on those who complete either of the other courses.[191] The diploma for the scientific course to be in French.[192] Those who shall pursue, for three

---

22) listed the degree candidates during 1857-58 as 138 students (59 men, 79 women) in the teachers' course and 18 students (16 men, 2 women) in the college course, without any further breakdown.

190. It was not unusual for the classical course to have very small enrollments at colleges likeAlfred. At Oberlin in 1850, only 69 of 500 students were enrolled in the classical course; in 1860, 199 of 1311. At Alfred, less than 18 out of 478 students were enrolled in the classical course in 1857-58. "Of the 108 degrees awarded at Alfred University between 1859 (when the first collegiate degree was granted) and 1865, 69 were for the teachers' course (of which 40 went to women), 7 were for the classical, 13 for the scientific course, and 19 were for the ladies' course (including the women who followed the classical course.)" Kerns, "Farmers' Daughters," p. 16. Thus, within the college course, 20 men and 19 women earned degrees.

191. That is, the ladies, the scientific, or the classical course. Although Oberlin awarded women the bachelor of arts degree (while giving only diplomas for completing the Ladies' course) and Genesee awarded women the same degree as men in the four-year classical course or the three-year scientific course, the use of the term "bachelor" for women was generally considered odd. Wheaton College used the degree "sister of arts"; Waco College used "maid of arts." At its first collegiate graduation in 1859, Alfred originated the "laureate of arts" degree for women completing the classical, scientific, or ladies' course. Women completing the teachers' course were awarded the "laureate of philosophy" or L.B. St. Lawrence University awarded the Laureate of Arts to its women from 1865 to 1869; the term was then dropped in favor of bachelor of arts. The L.A. was discontinued by Alfred after 24 years at the request of the female students. Strong, "Most Natural Way," pp. 205-206.

years after graduation, literary or scientific or professional studies and who shall, in the interval, have sustained a good moral character, shall be entitled to the Master's Degree in their respective courses.[193]

English or Teachers' Course.[194]

First Year
    English grammar
    Arithmetic
    Algebra
    Geography, Reading, and Penmanship
    Etymology or vocal music
    Book-keeping or penciling
Second Year
    Physiology
    Algebra
    Geometry, five books
    Latin [grammar], Caesar
    American History
    Natural Philosophy
Third Year
    Chemistry
    Solid geometry, trigonometry, and conic sections
    [English] Rhetoric
    Astronomy
    Ancient history
    Modern history, or Teaching
    Intellectual philosophy[195]
    Surveying, or Cicero
Fourth Year
    Didactics
    Logic
    Moral philosophy
    Science of government,[196] or Virgil
    Ecclesiastical history

192. This point underscores the anomaly of awarding the A.B. for completing the scientific course.

193. Alfred subsequently awarded women the degree of mistress of arts instead of master of arts.

194. The breakdown of the listed courses into individual terms has been omitted from the description of the following four courses. The catalog (pp. 7-21) listed the enrollments during 1857-58 as 59 men and 79 women in the teachers' course and 118 men and 100 women in the "preparatory [academy-level] teachers' course."

195. This subject was termed "mental philosophy" in prior readings and "philosophy of mind," or psychology, in the twentieth century. Alfred prescribed the newly published work by the Congregational minister and professor of mental and moral philosophy at Amherst College Joseph Haven (1816-1874): *Mental Philosophy, including the Intellect, Sensibilities and Will* (Boston, 1857).

196. Virtually all colleges employed a textbook expounding the principles of the republican government of the United States, as did Alfred, which prescribed Andrew W. Young (1802-1877) *Introduction to the Science of Government*, whose twenty-third printing was issued in nearby Buffalo, New York, in 1853.

Physical geography, music, or painting
Kames' *Elements of Criticism*[197]
Geology
Evidences of Christianity
In the above course students can take Greek or one of the modern languages instead of Latin.

Scientific Course.

Freshman Year
    Algebra
    French
    Physiology
    Astronomy (descriptive)
    Geometry, five books
    Botany
Sophomore Year
    Geometry and trigonometry
    German or zoology
    Physical geography
    Natural philosophy
    German or Botany
    Surveying
Junior Year
    Chemistry
    Calculus
    [English] rhetoric
    Anglo-Saxon (optional)
    Mathematical astronomy
    Ancient history
    Modern history
    Geology
    Intellectual philosophy
    Analytical chemistry (optional)
    Civil Engineering (optional)
Senior Year
    Logic
    Moral philosophy
    Mathematical philosophy
    Science of government and political economy (optional)[198]
    Analytical chemistry (optional)
    Natural theology
    Ecclesiastical history, or Meteorology and Mineralogy
    Constitutional law

---

197. Henry H. Kames (1696-1782), Scottish lord and jurist, wrote the *Elements of Criticism* (3 vols. completed in 1762), famous for its naturalistic approach to aesthetics.

198. Alfred prescribed the *Elements of Political Economy* (Boston, 1837, 1846) by Francis Wayland, president of Brown University.

Kames' *Elements of Criticism*
Evidences of Christianity[199]
Geology, or History of literature and of philosophy

Ladies' Course.[200]

Protomathian Year[201]
  Algebra
  French[202]
  Physiology
  Astronomy (descriptive)
  Geometry (five books)
  Botany
Sophomore Year
  Geometry and Trigonometry
  German
  Music, Italian, or Anglo-Saxon
  Music, Italian, or Anglo-Saxon
  Music, Italian, or Anglo-Saxon
  Natural philosophy
Junior Year
  Chemistry
  Rhetoric
  Painting, or Critical reading of Young's *Night Thoughts*[203]
  Painting, or Critical reading of [John] Milton
  Ancient history
  Modern history
  Geology
  Intellectual philosophy

---

199. In the first half of the nineteenth century, "Evidences of Christianity" was a standard course that is prescribed by Emma Willard and Dartmouth College above. This summative, senior-year course was normally taught by the president who tried to show how all the studies harmonized into a coherent view of the world that was ultimately explained by or, at least, consistent with Christianity. The standard text was that of William Paley (1743-1805) as noted in the Dartmouth catalog.

200. At Oberlin and Genesee the ladies' course was not treated as a "college course," and graduates received a diploma rather than a degree; but women were allowed to enroll in the classical course and were awarded the bachelor of arts degree. At Alfred, the ladies course was treated as a "college course" with the option of studying any subject offered at the institution, and graduates were awarded the laureate of arts degree; but women could not earn the B.A. degree, and in subsequent catalogs women were listed only in the ladies' course regardless of whether they were pursuing the scientific course or classical course.

201. This is a nineteenth-century version of "freshperson" in as much as "first-year women were called 'protomathian,' then 'novian,' to avoid calling them freshmen." Strong, "Most Natural Way," p. 208.

202. About half of the women enrolled in the college course exercised the right noted in the catalog: "Students in the scientific or ladies' course can take the ancient or some other modern language instead of the ones laid down in these courses."

203. The English poet Edward Young (1683-1765) wrote *Night Thoughts*, a popular, ten-thousand-line, blank verse poem about death.

Senior Year
    Logic
    Moral philosophy
    Mathematical philosophy
    Science of government and political economy
    Natural theology
    Ecclesiastical history, or Meteorology and Mineralogy
    Constitutional law
    Kames' *Elements of Criticism*
    Evidences of Christianity
    History of literature and of philosophy

Classical Course.

Freshman Year
    Livy
    Homer's *Iliad*
    Algebra
    Cicero, *On Old Age* and *On Friendship*
    Xenophon, *Memorabilia*
    Geometry, five books
    Physiology
Sophomore Year
    Horace
    Herodotus
    Geometry and Trigonometry and Conic Sections
    Thucydides
    Cicero, *Tusculan Disputations*
    Euripides, *Electra* and Aeschylus, *Prometheus Bound*
    Natural Philosophy (Mathematical)
    Surveying and Botany (optional)
Junior Year
    Cicero, *On the Orator*
    Plato, *Gorgias*
    [English] rhetoric
    Chemistry
    Tacitus, *Histories*
    Demosthenes, *On the Crown*
    Seneca
    Astronomy (mathematical)
    Ancient history
    Intellectual philosophy
    Modern history
Senior year
    Logic
    Moral Philosophy
    Science of government and political economy
    Hebrew (optional)
    Natural theology

Constitutional law
Geology
Kames' *Elements of Criticism*
Evidences of Christianity
History of literature and philosophy.[204]

Miscellaneous Information.

Location. The seminary is located at Alfred, Allegany County, New York, two miles from the Alfred Depot, on the line of the New York & Erie Railroad. The location is retired and healthy--in a rural district, surrounded by romantic and delightful scenery. Few spots are so well adapted to the quiet and successful pursuit of science and literature, as the village of Alfred.

Moral and Religious Influence. The morals of the village and surrounding community are of the highest order. A people of more stern integrity and of more industriousness and unobtrusive habits can seldom be found. Students are not exposed here to many of the ordinary allurements to vice and dissipation. The members of the Board of Instruction belong to different religious denominations and adopt an enlightened religious policy.

Room and Board. The buildings for the accommodation of the school and boardinghall are under the supervision of several of the professors and their families. By this arrangement for boarding and rooming, students are placed under the immediate care of those who watch over their morals, their manners and their health with parental solicitude. Parents and guardians may be assured that good board will always be furnished and that all reasonable attention will be given to the comfort and convenience of boarders. Each room for the accommodation of students is designed for two individuals and is furnished with stove, bed, and bedding, two chairs, table, and pail. Any additional furniture required students provide for themselves. There is also a large and commodious building, used exclusively for chapel, recitation and society rooms.

Library. The institution library consists of a choice selection of histories, biographies, Greek and Latin classics, mathematical and scientific works, and standard English literature. Additions are made to it yearly.

Summary of Regulations.

Things Required.
1. Registry of name at the office before reciting in any class.
2. Payment or security of bills in advance.
3. Punctuality in attending all regular academic exercises.
4. Strict observance of study hours.
5. Regularity in rising and retiring at given signals.
6. Strict observance of one's own Sabbath.[205]
7. Strict observance of temporary prudential rules.
8. Information, if asked, concerning delinquencies or misconduct of others.
9. Free access of any teacher to the rooms of students.
10. Habits of good order and propriety at all times and places.

---

204. In this regard, compare the senior years in the scientific, ladies' and classical courses.

205. Consistent with the "enlightened religious policy" promised above, this stricture is quite liberal for a community defined by its own observance of the Sabbath.

Things Prohibited.
1. Unpermitted association of ladies and gentlemen.
2. Visiting on one's Sabbath or during study hours.
3. The use of tobacco; the use of intoxicating drinks.
4. Games of chance; profane or obscene language.
5. To change or drop a study without permission.
6. Leaving school or village without permission.
7. Absence from examination.
8. The use of gunpowder in any form about the premises.
9. Driving nails, screws, or tacks, etc. into walls or ceilings without permission.
10. Lounging on beds or disorder in study rooms.

Regular Academic Exercises. The regular exercises, at which all the students will be required to attend, unless specially excused, are: Chapel exercises each day during the term; recitations from two to four, five days each week, from Monday morning until Friday evening [sic]; regular exercises in compositions and declamations; spelling, reading, and writing; literary, scientific, and moral lectures by the faculty; and public worship each week, either on Saturday or Sunday, according as the students may be in the habit of keeping the sabbath, either on the seventh or first day of the week.

Government. The government of the students will be in the hands of the faculty, and will be strictly and steadily exercised and, at the same time, strictly parental. The object of our academic government being to secure the greatest possible amount of physical, intellectual, and moral good to the students themselves. No unwarrantable means will be made use of to enforce the observance of the Regulations; yet our constant endeavors will be to make the means resorted to as effective as human means may be.   Parents who place their children in this institution and all students who are sufficiently old to understand the necessity of order can not be too well assured that the foregoing regulations form the most essential part of the contract between them and us; and that whatever student wantonly violates them and shows himself incorrigibly determined on pursuing his waywardness will be expelled from the privileges of the institution, and will not be permitted to re-enter it again, without special proof of reformation. Nor will an expelled student have any deduction made from full term charges.

Societies. The Alleganian, the Orophilian Lyceum, the Ladies' Literary Society, and Phi Mu Society and the Religious Union are the *permanently* organized societies of the institution. They are managed with ability and are important aids to those who are desirous of becoming good writers, speakers, or efficient laborers in the intellectual, moral or religious world. . .[206]

---

206. In the important literary societies where much of the social life and intellectual self-culture occurred, women at Alfred participated in the debates and addressed all the topics, except commerce.

Expenses Per Term.[207]

All bills must be arranged in advance. An addition of 10 percent will be added where payment is deferred till the close of the term.

Board by the term of 14 weeks	26.00
Room rent	2.00
Washing	2.00
Fuel, Spring and Fall terms	1.50
Fuel, winter term	3.00
Providing wood for boarders and care of Gentlemen's rooms	1.00
Library and incidentals	1.00
Tuition, per year	20-30.00

Extras.

Analytical chemistry	10.00
Music on the Piano forte	10.00
Oil painting	10.00
Drawing	3.00
Cultivation of the voice	5.00

1. All bills must be paid in advance or satisfactorily arranged.
2. An increase of ten percent will always be made where payment is not made until the close of the term.
3. In cases of absence, no deduction will be made on tuition bills as arranged, except in cases of absence from sickness, and then not more than one-half of the full bill; and no deduction on board bill except in cases of sickness or leaving to teach.

The Institution and the Public. The trustees of the institution, in presenting their twenty-second annual catalog to the public, would return their acknowledgment for the marked favor and liberal patronage received from its numerous friends and patrons. Their highest ambition and only object have been to found a seminary of unsurpassed excellence--a seminary that shall bless the Church and the world. They have appreciated the necessity of laying the foundation of intellectual and moral attainments and discipline upon a broad and permanent basis; and they have provided in a liberal manner the appliances and facilities for securing these objects. They labor to send forth young men and women so educated as eminently to qualify them for the realities and responsibilities of active life.

---

207. As noted in selection #38, Dartmouth College, which also drew from an agrarian population of modest means, was nevertheless more expensive than Alfred. Similarly, Emma Willard's Troy Female Seminary was more than twice as expensive Alfred University. These differences were partly due to the more modest backgrounds of those in the Baptist denominations, to the smaller sources of charitable support for younger, "frontier" colleges such as Alfred, and to the fact that many families were willing to pay more to educate a son than a daughter. A study of the female students at Alfred found that none came from wealthy families and nearly three-quarters came from middle-income farming families. Kerns, "Farmers' Daughters," pp. 20-22.

Section VII

Struggle between the University and the College, 1860s–1900s

During the final third of the nineteenth century, the university arose and displaced the liberal arts college as the polestar of American higher education. This shift was prompted by the 1862 Morrill Act establishing land grant universities,[1] by the founding of new universities such as Cornell University in 1868 and Johns Hopkins in 1876, and by the reformation of existing institutions, such as Harvard, commencing in 1869, and the University of Michigan, beginning in 1871. These universities instituted many innovations, including lectures, seminars, election of courses, departments, laboratories, opportunities for research and academic honor, and abolition of required chapel and recitations.[2] University leaders regarded the shift as natural and inevitable. "The university idea . . . has taken root, great things are to be expected," maintained the president of the University of Chicago in 1900, "with this tendency the small college must battle. . . . The laws of institutional life are very similar to those of individual life, and in the development of institutions we may confidently believe in 'the survival of the fittest.'"[3]

The shift becomes apparent when the late nineteenth-century situation is compared with the most noteworthy antebellum call for "university education," issued by Henry P. Tappan in 1851. A graduate of Union College, where he was exposed to heterodox education, Tappan (1805–1881) was ordained into the Congregational ministry, achieved some renown for his writings on ethics and theology, and taught at the University of the City of New York (later New York University). In 1851 he published *University Education*, which praised Francis Wayland's "Report to the Corporation of Brown University" and, more especially, the Prussian system of education that had been designed by Victor Cousin in 1832:

> In Protestant Germany, what an advance has been made! In no part of the world has University education been so enlarged, and made so liberal and thorough. The Universities of Protestant Germany stand forth as model institutions. . . . The Educational System of Germany, and particularly of Prussia, is certainly a very noble one. We cannot well be extravagant in its praise. Thorough in all its parts, consistent with itself, and vigorously sustained, it furnishes every department of life with educated men, and keeps up at the universities themselves, in every branch of knowledge, a supply of erudite and elegant scholars and authors for the benefit and glory of their country and the good of mankind.[4]

---

1. The Morrill Land Grant Act of 1862 gave federal lands to the separate states to be sold for the purpose of supporting universities offering technical, mechanical, and agricultural education in each state.

2. See the magisterial interpretation of these developments in Laurence Veysey, *The Emergence of the American University* (Chicago: University of Chicago Press, 1965).

3. William R. Harper, "The Situation of the Small College" (1900), in *The Trend in Higher Education in America* (Chicago: University of Chicago Press, 1905), pp. 369–70, 375.

4. Henry P. Tappan, *University Education* (New York: George P. Putnam, 1851), pp. 39, 45. Victor Cousin (1792–1867) was an eclectic French philosopher.

Having been influenced by Cousin in his other writings, Tappan's admiration for the German educational system was unsurprising, as was his approval of the plan for the University of Michigan.

That university was founded in 1837, and the authors of the Michigan state constitution drew from Cousin's 1832 report on Prussian education a model both for the university's governance and for its role within the state educational system. However, "lacking any distinctive idea of what the curriculum ought to be, the university copied the traditional classical pattern. The faculty even adopted the language of the 1828 Yale Report." When Henry Tappan was installed as the first permanent president in 1852, his actual borrowing from the Prussian model was also selective. "Independent learning based on lectures and reading, rather than recitation tested by regular examinations; pursuing the latest knowledge, rather than imbibing traditional learning; concentrating on a few chosen fields, rather than following a standard and rigid curriculum—in all these respects Tappan's program borrowed heavily and self-consciously from the German universities of his day. Yet Tappan did not borrow the elements that loom so large in the received history of German influence and the rise of graduate education. He shied away from narrow specialization, avoiding even the German pattern of examination in one major subject and two minors. He ignored the German Ph.D. degree . . . and apparently never mentioned the seminar, already the symbol of erudition in Germany."[5] Nevertheless, by the time of his resignation in 1863, Tappan had anticipated the course of university education in the United States.

Notwithstanding his emulation of the Prussian universities, Tappan, like the early Michigan faculty, gave his allegiance to Yale when it came to considering liberal education. In *University Education* he made a cardinal distinction: "We have spoken of the German universities as model institutions. Their excellence consists in . . . [that] they are purely universities, without any admixture of collegial tuition. . . . Collegial tuition in the German universities does not exist, because wholly unnecessary, the student being fully prepared at the Gymnasium before he is permitted to enter the university."[6] Having distinguished the university from liberal education, Tappan then "reaffirmed the basic ideas of the Yale Report" for the latter.[7] After apparently paraphrasing Jeremiah Day, Tappan observed, "The course at the Gymnasium embraces a very thorough study of the Latin and Greek languages, a knowledge of the mathematics below the differential and integral calculus, general history, and one or two languages besides the German, and Hebrew if the student design for the study of theology."[8]

In accordance with this view, Tappan finessed the reformation of the liberal arts by establishing a parallel course in the Department of Literature, Science and the Arts, in which modern languages, sciences, and additional mathematics displaced Greek and Latin. Tappan's approach persevered for decades, as demonstrated by the founding in 1889 of Catholic University and Clark University as purely graduate institutions, eschewing liberal education. The perseverance of Tappan's strategy warns against equating the reform of liberal education with the emergence of universities in the late nineteenth century, while it is nevertheless true that the university movement gave further impetus to

---

5. Quotations are from James Turner and Paul Bernard, "The Prussian Road to University? German Models and the University of Michigan, 1837–c. 1895," *Rackham Reports, University of Michigan* (1988–89): 13, 17.

6. Tappan, *University Education*, pp. 43, 44.

7. Douglas Sloan, "Harmony, Chaos, and Consensus: The American College Curriculum," *Teachers College Record* 73 (1971): 245.

8. Tappan, *University Education*, p. 44. Tappan occasionally seems to paraphrase Jeremiah Day when, for example, the former wrote, "The conditions of human life may forever limit a thorough education to the few" (p. 14), and the latter wrote, "a thorough education is not within the reach of all." *Reports on the Course of Instruction in Yale College* (New Haven, CT: Hezekiah Howe, 1828), p. 18.

the antecedent challenges to the regnant liberal education. As a result, liberal education was transformed over the final third of the nineteenth century.

After the decades-long siege by "parallel courses," the bastion of classical studies was overrun, and new subjects displaced them in the vaunted B.A. course. "The idea of liberal education, as it was held in American colleges prior to 1862, no longer commands the unqualified respect of thoughtful men," maintained the president of Johns Hopkins University in 1892.[9] In particular, "thoughtful men" had lost confidence in the idea that a unified body of truth could be conveyed to students,[10] a shift demonstrated by the emergence of the elective system, which ceded to students "a regulated freedom in choice of studies" in the words of Harvard President Charles W. Eliot.[11]

The selections in Section VII address the debates about the conceptions of knowledge and human nature that underlay the broad shift in liberal education. These readings also address the controversies concerning the liberal arts college, which, by the 1900s, was being kicked about like "the pedagogical football of university presidents."[12] Above all, controversy surrounded colleges enrolling marginalized populations amid the transformation of liberal education at leading universities, which served primarily white Protestant males. Fighting for their legitimacy, these colleges took refuge "in the conserving power of safe imitation" amid the innovations advanced by the university leaders.[13] The complex debate about liberal education at these colleges, as well as at the universities, is related in the following selections.

9. Daniel C. Gilman, "Is It Worthwhile to Uphold Any Longer the Idea of Liberal Education?" *Educational Review* 3 (1892): 109.

10. See Julie A. Reuben, *The Making of the Modern University: Intellectual Transformation and the Marginalization of Morality* (Chicago: University of Chicago Press, 1996).

11. Charles W. Eliot, *Annual Report of the President and Treasurer of Harvard College 1883–1884* (Cambridge, MA: Harvard University Press, 1885), p. 24.

12. William T. Foster, *Administration of the Curriculum* (Boston: Houghton Mifflin, 1911), p. 160. This metaphor suggested other changes in the extra-curriculum, as mentioned in selection #48 by James McCosh.

13. Mabel L. Robinson, *The Curriculum of the Woman's College*, Bulletin no. 6, U.S. Bureau of Education (Washington, DC: GPO, 1918), p. 108.

40. Charles W. Eliot, "Many New Methods of Giving Instruction" (1880)

INTRODUCTION

Charles W. Eliot (1834–1926) was born into socially and politically prominent families in Boston. His father was a Harvard graduate who served as mayor of Boston and in the U.S. Congress; his mother's father was a well known merchant who also became mayor of Boston. In 1849, after attending Boston Latin School, Charles entered Harvard College at the age of fifteen and graduated in 1853. Harvard's course of study at the time was fairly conventional, and "almost wholly required," as Eliot observes in selection #40. Nevertheless, he took advantage of an unusual opportunity to do field work in chemistry and mineralogy with some professors, and in 1854 was made tutor in mathematics. Four years later, he was appointed to the newly created rank of assistant professor in mathematics and chemistry.

Though only in his mid-twenties, Eliot filled a crucial role on the faculty due to his skill at administration, which made him "virtually assistant to the president," as well as acting dean of Lawrence Scientific School.[14] He was thus the inside candidate when a chair in chemistry became vacant in 1863. However, the prominent zoologist and professor Louis Agassiz used his influence to secure the appointment for his friend, Wolcott Gibbs (1822–1908), who was teaching in New York and had, in fact, greater promise of contributing significant new research in chemistry. Eliot was offered a full professorship, but at a salary two-thirds of what a normal professor would earn, the balance of which he was expected to make through income from laboratory fees.[15] This reversal was made more difficult by the fact that Eliot's father was bankrupted in the Panic of 1857, and Charles lost the prospect of a large inheritance. Stung by the rejection and meager offer, Eliot resigned and traveled in Europe for two years studying chemistry and the educational institutions. Returning home in 1865, he accepted a professorship of chemistry at the Massachusetts Institute of Technology, and in 1869 published a long, two-part article on "The New Education: Its Organization" in the *Atlantic Monthly*, which attracted widespread attention. Meanwhile, a committee established by the Board of Overseers was assessing the state of affairs at Harvard and recommended extensive reforms that fit Eliot's vision. That vision plus Eliot's administrative acumen secured the thirty-five-year-old Eliot election to the presidency of Harvard in 1869.

For the next forty years, Eliot presided over Harvard, transforming the college, along with its conception of liberal education, into the leading university in the nation. Eliot began this transformation by replacing the paternalistic approach to the presidency with an efficient system of management. As he stated in his inaugural address, "The President of the University is primarily an executive officer . . . The principle of divided and subordinate responsibilities, which rules in government bureaus, in manufactories, and all great companies, which makes a modern army a possibility, must be applied to the University."[16] This new model did not endear him to old-time college presidents such as Martin B. Anderson of the University of Rochester, who observed that Eliot "never teaches the students and has not the least formative control over their minds or characters. He is really a sort of general manager with duties analogous to those of a superintendent or

14. Hugh Hawkins, *Between Harvard and America: The Educational Leadership of Charles W. Eliot* (New York: Oxford University Press, 1972), p. 16.

15. Edward Lurie, *Louis Agassiz: A Life in Science* (Chicago: University of Chicago Press, 1960), pp. 329–30.

16. Charles W. Eliot, "Inaugural Address as President of Harvard College," *Educational Reform: Essays and Addresses* (New York: Century, 1908), p. 34.

president of a railroad."[17] Those, like Anderson, who favored a personalized administration and faculty found Eliot cold and aloof, and some even considered him "to be an enemy of the college." Nor did the researchers and scientists on the faculty warm to Eliot. Ironically, they feared "that he was a 'College' rather than a 'University' man" because he did not value original research as much as teaching.[18]

But Eliot succeeded, advancing many reforms beyond administrative reorganization. Having written an original and successful textbook of inorganic chemistry that discouraged memorization and presented specific examples for each theory and definition, Eliot supported "new methods of giving instruction" at Harvard, as indicated in selection #40 drawn from his tenth annual report. In addition, Eliot welcomed into the Harvard curriculum "the various new subjects which were pressing for admittance," as he states below; and he championed free election among those subjects.

Eliot's efforts were by no means limited to liberal education. He was largely responsible for upgrading the Harvard professional schools by advancing the requirement of a bachelor's degree for admission to degree candidacy, the tiered curriculum, the establishment of minimum academic standards for continuation in a degree program, and the professorial career track for faculty members. Meanwhile, Eliot also turned his attention to strengthening and standardizing secondary education, particularly with an eye to facilitating the transition from school to university. By the time of his retirement in 1909, Eliot's forty-year tenure, prominence of position, record of accomplishments, and irrepressible character had made him one of the leading educational spokesmen in the country. He died at his summer home in Northeast Harbor, Maine, at the age of ninety-two.

SELECTION[19]

Many new methods of giving instruction, of awakening interest (or enforcing attention) on the part of the students, and of testing their progress have been tried in the various departments of the university during the past ten years. . . .[20] The inventive activity of the instructors has undoubtedly been stimulated by the gradual abolition throughout the university of all disciplinary methods of enforcing the attendance of the students at lectures and recitations.[21] The student now goes to the lecture-room because he is interested in the work done here; or because it is easier to accomplish the prescribed work of the course with the daily help of the instructor than in any other way; or because he finds attendance indispensable if he would pass the stated examinations; or, finally, because he is urged to attend by his friends, his parents, or the officers of the university on the ground that attendance is both an advantage to him and a duty. . . . It follows that in all departments the instructors have felt prompted anew to make their exercises interesting, profitable, and indeed indispensable, to their students.

17. Quoted in Arthur J. May, *A History of the University of Rochester, 1850–1962*, ed. Lawrence E. Klein (Rochester, NY: University of Rochester, 1977), p. 101.

18. Quotations are from Hawkins, *Between Harvard and America*, pp. 116, 47. A further irony in this regard is that Eliot's "pro-university" effort to raise the academic standards of professional schools by requiring a bachelor's degree for admission strengthened the position of liberal arts colleges (p. 202).

19. Charles W. Eliot, *Annual Report of the President and Treasurer of Harvard College 1879–1880* (Cambridge, MA: Harvard University Press, 1880), pp. 12–9.

20. In his inaugural address of 1869, Eliot had emphasized the importance of teaching, addressing this first in his list of topics: "The actual problem to be solved is not what to teach, but how to teach it. . . . In every department of learning the University would search out by trial and reflection the best methods of instruction." "Inaugural Address," p. 3.

21. James McCosh discusses the abolition of these disciplinary methods below.

Within the same period, a thorough system of stated written examinations, as tests of the students' attainments and progress, has been elaborated and applied throughout the university.[22] As well-conducted periodical examinations lead students to work hard during the examination periods, and to relax their exertions when no such crisis is imminent, the instructors, recognizing this inevitable tendency and feeling the importance of keeping the students up to their daily work,[23] have been diligent in devising means to enforce the regular performance of the work which they give out from day to day.[24] Again, the elective system, which prevails in the college and to some degree in the Law School and Medical School, has also a tendency to make every instructor desirous of adopting the most interesting and effective method of teaching his subject, lest, in the multitude of courses open to the students' choices, his subject should be neglected.[25]

For these various reasons, many modifications of the simple recitation and the simple lecture of former times have been lately introduced. The main objections to the recitation, at which the students simply recite a lesson previously set in a book, are, that good scholars who have learned the lesson well and could recite it readily, get little or no instruction from the exercise, and that the teacher examines rather than teaches. The objections to the simple lecture are that the hearers are too often listless and at best completely passive, and that there is no opportunity of meeting their difficulties or enforcing the instruction given. The recitation, considered as an opportunity of examining a student to see whether he has learned the lesson of the day and to give him a mark of merit or demerit, has well-nigh disappeared from the university.[26]

[Recitation] has become for the teacher an opportunity to give conversational instruction by asking questions, addressed either to an individual or to the class, with a view to correct misapprehensions and to bring out the main points of the subject clear of the details, by explaining the author in hand, or by contravening, reinforcing, or illustrating his statements: for the student it has become an opportunity to ask questions, to receive, either in a critical or in a docile spirit, the explanations and opinions of the instructor; to review the lesson or re-examine the subject of the day; and to test occasionally his own power of translating, of stating a proposition, a case, an argument, or a demonstration, of narrating a series of events, or of describing a plant, an animal, a disease, a building, a person, or an institution. For teacher and students alike the recitation gives opportunity for personal acquaintance and a somewhat intimate intercourse. In many recitations (so-called, perhaps, because a text or treatise affords a basis for the instruction) the teacher does the greater part of the work. . . .

If, in the recitation as it now exists, there is something of the lecture, on the other hand in the lecture there is, ordinarily, a large admixture of the Socratic method.[27] The lecturer does not read or

---

22. Tutor Eliot and a fellow tutor had substituted written examinations for oral examinations during recitations at Harvard in the 1850s; therefore, it was natural that he should see them "elaborated and applied throughout the university" as president. The educational reformer Horace Mann (1796–1859) had introduced written exams in Boston Latin School in 1845. Since Eliot graduated from Boston Latin School in 1849, it is likely that Eliot was adopting Mann's innovation.

23. Compare the rationale of Jeremiah Day in selection #37 for "the daily examinations or recitation."

24. Sandwiched between two affirmations of teachers' accountability to students' choices is this recognition of teachers' obligations "to enforce the regular performance of the work."

25. Should teaching methods be determined by the market of students' preferences?

26. Oral recitations had served as the primary means of grading students' work until written examinations were instituted.

27. First discussed in American colleges in the mid-1700s, references to "Socratic method" of teaching begin to proliferate during the late nineteenth century, correlated with the rise of the university in the United States. Regarding the nineteenth-century phenomenon in British universities, see Sheldon Rothblatt, *Tradition and Change*

speak continuously himself, but frequently interrupts his exposition to address a question to an individual or to the class or to invite the class to ask questions and suggest difficulties. In subjects which deal with chains of reasoning—like mathematics, logic, and law—the skillful lecturer may draw from the class by successive questions the whole process of a long argument, getting a step from each student called upon. By asking a sudden question and subsequently indicating the person who is to answer it, he may keep a large class upon the alert.[28] There are but few courses of lectures in which the students are obliged to rely exclusively on the lectures; in most of the courses in which the instructor, either from necessity or choice, has adopted the lecture method, the students are advised to use a book, or books, for parallel reading, or are required to read specified selections from a variety of books. . . .

The practice of referring a large class of students to a considerable number of different books or serials not owned by the students, but to be found in one of the libraries of the university, presents grave inconvenience. The number of accessible copies of some of the books being probably but small, a large part of the class may not get seasonable access to the designated reading; moreover, the books themselves are sure to be destroyed in a few years by excessive use upon a number of pages perhaps inconsiderable in proportion to the whole bulk of the volumes. This difficulty presents itself most frequently in the courses upon history, natural history, and law. But in the Law School some of the professors have overcome it by printing collections of the important cases on the subjects of their several courses with the addition of summaries or elaborate indices. It is a good indirect effect of this method that it facilitates the study of original sources and thereby tends to emancipate the student from treatises and other second-hand authorities.[29] That this method may prove to be capable of advantageous application in other departments of instruction is much to be wished.

Both in recitations and lectures the practice of taking notes prevails; but various devices are employed by instructors and students to lighten the labor of note-taking. Some professors place upon the blackboard before the exercise begins the references, titles, tables, or diagrams which they wish the students to copy; others distribute to the class all such matter in manuscript, reproduced in sufficient quantities by some of the cheap copying processes and others issue a printed syllabus of their course more or less detailed.[30] One professor gives his students beforehand full notes of all his lectures; and another instructor has lately authorized an advanced student to prepare elaborate notes of his lectures and distribute them in excellent printed form to such of the class as are willing to pay a moderate price for them. These various devices save the time which would otherwise be spent in dictating references, quotations, and abstracts during the lecture itself, and they also prevent in a measure the students' attention from being given to the mechanical operation of rapid writing instead of to the subject-matter of the lecture.

---

in English Liberal Education: An Essay in History and Culture (London: Faber and Faber, 1976), pp. 178–80. Compare Eliot's image of an elentic Socrates with that in selection #1 by Plato.

28. A portrayal of this teaching method at Harvard is reconstructed from student and faculty notes of the 1870s and 1880s may be found in Bruce A. Kimball, *"Warn Students that I Entertain Heretical Opinions, Which They Are Not to Take as Law*: The Inception of Case Method Teaching in the Classrooms of the Early C. C. Langdell, 1870–1883," *Law and History Review* 17 (1999): 57–140.

29. Eliot's argument on behalf of casebooks was advanced originally by Christopher C. Langdell, dean of Harvard Law School from 1870 to 1895, in *A Selection of Cases on the Law of Contracts . . . Prepared for Use as a Text-Book in Harvard Law School* (Boston: Little, Brown, 1871), preface. Langdell introduced case method teaching and published the first legal casebooks for this purpose.

30. All three examples—blackboard, cheap copying processes, and more efficient printing techniques—indicate changes in teaching practice facilitated by nineteenth-century advances in educational technology.

For the purpose of testing the daily or weekly progress of the student, and his faithfulness in keeping up with the work of each of his courses, various processes are used in addition to the oral questioning which makes part of the regular exercises. In the languages, there are several tests of easy application from which there is no escape;[31] such are translation at sight, writing the foreign language at dictation, and rendering dictated English into the foreign language; in the mathematics, problems connected with the subject in hand may always be given to any and all students; in history, philosophy, and political economy, an essay may be periodically demanded upon some special point, or limited topic, within the student's capacity and not beyond the range of his reading; in clinical medicine, an actual case can always be given to a student to study and report upon; in all the scientific courses, and in some others, each student can be required to give before the class, from time to time, a short lecture upon a suitable subject previously assigned to him; and in the laboratory courses, like those in chemistry, mineralogy, botany, biology, histology, physiology, and zoölogy, actual analyses, determinations, or dissections are sure tests of the student's skill and knowledge. . . .

That the recitation method and the lecture method have each some peculiar advantage is to be inferred, both from the long use of the two methods separately and from the present endeavors to combine the two in a single exercise. This exercise, the resultant of the two diverging methods, may perhaps be best described by a word already used in the Theological and Medical Schools and in the graduate department, but not as yet in the other departments—the word "conference," signifying a meeting for the serious consideration and discussion under the guidance and criticism of a teacher, of a text, topic, or treatise previously studied. While this form of university exercise more and more prevails, there are still many occasions for the use of the pure lecture method: as, for example, in imparting information which is inaccessible to the students in print (perhaps because the material is original, or because the sources of information are in a language unknown to them, or because the instructor prefers a novel order of topics or develops his successive subjects in proportions unlike those of any accessible treatise or textbook) in giving rapid and elegant translations from other languages into English, and in summing up long descriptions, narratives, or expositions.

The illustrated lecture, though in an abbreviated form, is an essential part of most laboratory courses of instruction; for the students must be shown how to use their tools, to handle specimens, to keep notes, and to observe with accuracy and system. In many courses in natural science, including medicine, a short, descriptive lecture is given at the opening of each laboratory exercise; but in other courses the descriptive lecture is given after, not before, the students have made, under the personal supervision of the instructor, their experiments, observations, or dissections upon the subject or object in hand. Some teachers of science think that students should be told, before they look at a natural object, normal or morbid, what they ought to see; others think that they should first try to see for themselves and then be told what they ought to have seen.[32] The two methods are good, each for its own end: the first is the quickest way to fix in the memory natural appearances as useful facts; the second to acquire strong powers of observation. The first is of great use in teaching medicine; the latter in training naturalists.

---

31. Is Eliot inconsistent in justifying new instructional methods, at some points, by presuming intrinsic motivation on the part of students; and, at other points, by suggesting that "students" will try to "escape" their work?

32. Over the next four decades, the latter approach was increasingly promoted and termed "inductive teaching," while the former was sometimes called "deductive teaching." See the textbook *An Inductive Greek Method* (New York: American Book, 1888) by William R. Harper and William E. Water.

Debate over "The Liberal Education of Women"

INTRODUCTION

Before the Civil War, women seeking higher education had to choose primarily among normal schools, academies, and seminaries. Many of these educational institutions were at the secondary or even elementary level. Notwithstanding the collegiate standard pursued by Troy Female Seminary, founded in 1821 under Emma Willard, as described in selection #35, only a few coeducational colleges existed.[33] The opening of Vassar College in 1865 as a full-fledged college granting the B.A. only to women was therefore a milestone and initiated a significant period of growth in collegiate education for women. Between 1870 and 1890 the number of women attending higher education increased more than sixfold to 68,400, with 70 percent (39,500) in coeducational institutions and 30 percent (16,800) in single-sex institutions, including 21 percent (12,100) enrolled in private women's colleges.[34]

This increasing access of women to liberal education was, however, circumscribed by the ideology of "separate spheres" or "cult of true womanhood," which predominated during the nineteenth century and comprised three basic tenets.[35] Biological differences were said to cause certain behavioral differences between the genders. Women were believed to be naturally submissive, nurturant, and emotional; men were said to be aggressive, competitive, and intellectual. Second, social life was sharply divided into two supposedly equal spheres: the domestic world of tranquility and familial care, and the public world of economic and political competition. This division was sharpened by industrialization which not only forced the worker to leave home to earn income via wages, but also obviated many alternative, domestic industries. Finally, the biological, behavioral, and social differences were said to be causally linked. Men, by their nature, dominated the competitive public arena; women were naturally suited to "govern" the domestic sphere. Despite the putative equality, women were deprived of authority and autonomy, whether politically, economically, or occupationally.

Nineteenth-century discussion about "the problem of woman's sphere, to use the modern phrase"[36] particularly addressed liberal education, because college was a route through which women might rise to significant positions in professional and public arenas. Hence, "protests came from

---

33. The prominent antebellum coeducational colleges included: Oberlin College in Ohio (founded 1833), Knox College in Illinois (1837), Lawrence College in Wisconsin (1847), Genesee College in New York (1849), Antioch College in Ohio in (1853), and Alfred University (1857) in New York. The number of women enrolled in the B.A. course at each of these institutions was usually less than ten. See selection #39 on Alfred University.

34. Compare the figures in Mabel Newcomer, *A Century of Higher Education for American Women* (New York: Harper, 1959), p. 49. Two decades later, in 1910, 76 percent of female undergraduates attended coeducational institutions and 24 percent single-sex institutions. At that point, the percentage in single-sex, private colleges had dropped to 15 percent; but this group no longer represented nearly all of the female B.A. candidates, since the liberal arts course in many universities had become coeducational.

35. The signal article, analyzing magazines, sermons, novels, cookbooks, diaries, and other writings in the antebellum period, is: Barbara Welter, "The Cult of True Womanhood, 1820–1860," *American Quarterly* 18 (1966): 151–74.

36. Edward H. Clarke, *Sex in Education; or, A Fair Chance for the Girls* (1873; Boston: James R. Osgood, 1874), p. 12.

doctors, clergy, and writers already uneasy about the expansion of women's public roles."[37] The ideology of separate spheres therefore shaped the debate about "the liberal education of women," which intensified in the late 1860s and early 1870s as the women's college movement and the push for coeducation began to make headway. In fact, so many articles and speeches had been issued by 1873 that Professor James Orton of Vassar College edited and published a collection of them.

Born in 1830 in Seneca Falls, New York, James B. Orton (1830–1876) attended Williams College and graduated at the belated age of 25, having enjoyed the unusual opportunity to participate in scientific explorations to Nova Scotia and Newfoundland. Intending to follow the vocation of his father, he studied divinity at Andover (Massachusetts) Theological Seminary, graduated in 1858, and assumed a pastorate. In 1866 he switched careers, successively becoming an instructor in natural history at the University of Rochester in New York, making a scientific exploration to equatorial South America, and in 1869 accepting a professorship in natural history at Vassar College.

Soon after arriving, Orton wrote an article about Vassar that argued strongly on behalf of liberal education for women, but also demonstrated the conservatism of Vassar, which embraced the Yale curriculum and "the old military path of 'drill and review'" in teaching.[38] In light of their obligation "to demonstrate the propriety of women's higher education to a dubious public," women's colleges could not afford to risk curricular or pedagogical innovations, such as those advanced by Charles W. Eliot at Harvard. Partly for the same reason, these colleges maintained the strict, religious, and moral oversight of the antebellum ladies' seminaries.[39]

Orton's writing and editing about the liberal education of women was a sidelight to his academic specialty. In 1873 he made a second expedition to equatorial South America, collecting animal and plant specimens for museums of natural history in the United States. In 1876 he published *Comparative Zoology: Structural and Systematic* and undertook a third expedition to South America, during which he drowned attempting to cross Lake Titicaca in Peru. Orton's death extinguished a consummate advocate for women's education, whose theological training, scientific expertise, and Vassar experience prepared him well for compiling the 40 essays and speeches in *The Liberal Education of Women*.[40] The following selections from that work present a range of viewpoints on the nature and organization of liberal education of women, and their relationship to the underlying separate-spheres ideology.

37. Lynn D. Gordon, *Gender and Higher Education in the Progressive Era* (New Haven, CT: Yale University Press, 1990), pp. 16–7.

38. Quotations are from James B. Orton, "Vassar College" (1871), republished in *The Liberal Education of Women: The Demand and the Method, Current Thoughts in England and America*, ed. James Orton (New York: A. S. Barnes, 1873), pp. 273–7, 281, 284.

39. Gordon, *Gender and Higher Education*, p. 29. Beginning in the 1880s the students at leading women's colleges, such as Wellesley and Mount Holyoke, successfully rebelled against this oversight, but curricular and pedagogical conservatism persevered longer, as evident in selection #52 by William T. Foster.

40. James B. Orton, ed., *The Liberal Education of Women: The Demand and the Method, Current Thoughts in England and America* (New York: A. S. Barnes, 1873).

41. "The Question of Health" (1872)

INTRODUCTION

What may be termed the conservative position in Orton's collection subscribed to the doctrine of "separate spheres." Proponents inferred from the differences between men and women in both nature and social roles that their education should also be different. Not only was liberal education therefore inappropriate for women, it was also physically harmful because it "expands the intellect at the expense of reproductive vitality" and "an undue proportion [of vital energy] is drawn to the brain," thereby competing with "the maternal draft upon her energies" and exhausting the female B.A. candidate, as stated in the following reading.

Orton drew this article from an anonymous editorial appearing in *College Courant* in September 1872. The anonymous author was apparently responding to James Freeman Clarke (1810–1888), the prominent Unitarian minister, social critic, and Harvard Professor of Natural Religion and Christian Doctrine, who advocated admitting women to the university.[41]

SELECTION[42]

Possibly Nature and Providence are at fault in expecting of woman a distinct and significant function in the economy of human life—a function which means more to the vigor and happiness of the race than any place within the reach of man. But here is the fact of motherhood, and until sons bear children we trust that a little physiological knowledge will enter into the grounds of even individual reports on co-education. For our part we are convinced that too much has been done already in forcing girls through courses of hard study, and that any further steps in that direction will necessitate hospitals and asylums alongside of colleges for women. The training provided for girls in our common schools even, largely incapacitates them for the duties and the joys of their natural future, and that without raising either their character or their intelligence materially above what these would have been with simpler training; if indeed moral and mental health are not decidedly lowered by the physical depression induced by hard study. And in our great schools of learning, the admission of women . . . must similarly mean a virtual abdication of their best functions; and that [must be] without reason, either in any service to be rendered by it or in any happiness to be found in it, but through a mistake full of unreason and fruitful of sorrow.[43]

It already appears, to an alarming extent, that this is the tendency, although by far the greater portion of these sad fruits of error will be reaped chiefly after some years by the next generation. We have always found that inquiries, directed particularly to this point, revealed a terrible skeleton in the colleges which receive women or which attempt to give girls the severe training to which boys are subjected. Dr. Clarke does not seem to have made inquiries in this direction, nor to have taken note of the decisive facts which meet the critical observer wherever he turns. And if he should now make these inquiries, he would probably content himself with answers which entirely leave out of sight the mischief to motherhood and to women's usefulness and happiness, which is done without any immediate overthrow of health—the mischief of a brain overtaxed and weakened, instead of stored with the happy vigor which is needed to make motherhood effective and blessed.

---

41. See James Freeman Clarke, "Co-education at Harvard," in *The Liberal Education of Women*, pp. 231–7.

42. Orton, *The Liberal Education of Women*, pp. 85–7.

43. The wording of this sentence has been rearranged.

It is an astonishing circumstance that neither the profound suggestions of the Christian religion nor the imperative intimations of modern science, should have led Dr. Clarke to reflect that the mother and child are to be first considered in this matter of women's training, and that on no account can the case of daughters be made the same as that of sons. He must be incompetent moreover for social and psychological observation who does not detect, in much of the demand of women for the chance allotted to men, a sad twist of womanly thought away from the best instincts of womanhood, and sometimes a perversity and almost an insanity of demoralized sensibilities, the cure of which is not in masculine opportunity, but in wise return to womanly tasks, however simple.[44]

Exceptional women, arrived at years of full discretion and fully conscious of what life is and what their own irrepressible aspirations are, may wisely make their womanhood undertake some of the offices of manhood; and from such women the race may undoubtedly expect a peculiar and a significant service, the fruit of a special sacrifice. But to ask young women, and young girls, who are not yet conscious what life is and are not wise with regard to their way through the world, to forget their distinct office in life and to undertake [what] sons are expected to undertake is one of those mistakes which bring woe greater than any fruit of crime, because they blast expectation in its source, and lay upon innocent and noble endeavor the course of comprehensive defeat. Rather would we send our women, who can counsel and can execute, to devise ways of undoing much that has been already done in what is called "the education of women," and of proving a real education of *women* as distinct in its aims and methods as woman's part in life is distinct.[45]

Woman's physical qualifications as mother are of paramount importance; and whatever seriously conflicts with the efficacy of this function is full of evil and should not be voluntarily put in force. If we adopt a system of education which expands the intellect at the expense of the reproductive vitality, there is a serious wrong in that education. The supply of vital energy from its natural source—the assimilation of food—has, as we have already said, its limits, and, if an undue proportion is carried to the brain, the physical will suffer. This is true of man as well as of woman, but still more true of her than of him, because the maternal draft upon her energies is more imperious than any draft which nature makes upon his. An education for woman which is to be derived mainly through sedentary and bookish habits, to the detriment of vital expansion, cannot be too emphatically reprobated.[46]

---

44. How does this sentence attempt to reconcile the supposed contradiction that liberal education violates women's nature and happiness but that women want liberal education?

45. What is it that exceptional women who "can counsel and execute" should "devise ways of undoing?"

46. The final paragraph was added as a note to the text.

42. Edward H. Clarke, *Sex in Education* (1873)

INTRODUCTION

Thirteen months after the foregoing reading appeared in the *College Courant* and shortly after Orton published his collection, a different, unrelated Dr. Clarke addressed the liberal education of women. Orton could not have reprinted this treatise, but an excerpt is included here because Edward H. Clarke's *Sex in Education; or, A Fair Chance for the Girls* exemplified the conservative argument found in Orton's collection and ignited a firestorm of debate over the next two decades. Orton was therefore prescient in including this viewpoint and responses to it.

Edward H. Clarke (1820–1877), the son of a Congregational minister from Massachusetts, became a prominent physician, a fellow of the American Academy of Arts and Sciences, and a professor of Harvard Medical School in 1855, when faculty were paid directly out of tuition. Between 1870 and 1872, President Charles W. Eliot and the Harvard Corporation advanced a plan to upgrade the Medical School academically, and Dr. Clarke, who had maintained his practice on the side and taught clinical topics, joined other senior members of the faculty in opposing the progressive plan. When the plan was approved, Clarke resigned in 1872 to focus on his clinical practice.[47]

In the following year, Clarke published *Sex in Education; or, A Fair Chance for the Girls*, in which he addressed the much-debated question of the appropriate education for young women. He maintained that "women who choose to do so can master the humanities and the mathematics, encounter the labor of the law and the pulpit, endure the hardness of physic and the conflicts of politics;" but "it is not true that she can do all this, and retain uninjured health and a future secure from neuralgia, uterine disease, hysteria, and other derangements of the nervous system." The reason is that the "perfect development of their organization," is to bear children and that women can not endure the physiological strain of both this function and the higher learning.[48] The first edition of his treatise sold out in a week, and fifteen more followed by 1890, as the work prompted enormous controversy.[49]

As seen in prior selections, the central points of Edward Clarke's argument had been made many times before. What distinguished his work was the claim to infer his conclusion "from physiology, not from ethics or metaphysics." Claiming to avoid "abstract principles of right and wrong" and appealing "to Agassiz and Huxley, not to Kant or Calvin, to Church or Pope," Clarke presented his view in the language of medicine and evolutionary biology, including case records of his patients.[50] Writing with the authority of a Harvard Medical School professor, Clarke thus imparted scientific legitimacy to the ideology of separate (educational) spheres that predominated in the nineteenth century. The controversy stimulated by Clarke subsided within twenty years as the evidence contradicted his thesis

---

47. Thomas F. Harrington, *The Harvard Medical School: A History, Narrative and Documentary*, ed. James G. Mumford, 3 vols. (New York: Lewis, 1905), v. 3, p. 1051.

48. Clarke, *Sex in Education*, pp. 18, 17, 19.

49. Both Clarke's *Sex in Education* and Orton's *The Liberal Education of Women* were among the twenty-two books studied by the trustees of Johns Hopkins University during the two years of planning for the university's opening in 1876.

50. Compare the data of James H. Fairchild's below to that presented by Clarke, who claimed to be empirical and scientific. Data such as Fairchild's overturned Clarke's argument by 1890. See the appeal to "observation and experiment" by Lydia Ernestine Becker in selection #46.

and B.A.s thrived. Clarke died in 1877, after completing his final work, a study of hallucinations and illusions.[51]

SELECTION[52]

Clinical observation confirms the teachings of physiology. The sick chamber, not the schoolroom; the physician's private consultation, not the committee's public examination; the hospital, not the college, the workshop, or the parlor—disclose the sad results which modern social customs, modern education, and modern ways of labor, have entailed on women. Examples of them may be found in every walk of life. On the luxurious couches of Beacon Street; in the palaces of Fifth Avenue; among the classes of our private, common, and normal schools; among the female graduates of our colleges; behind the counters of Washington Street and Broadway; in our factories, workshops, and homes—may be found numberless pale, weak, neuralgic, dyspeptic, hysterical, menorrhagic, dysmenorrhoeic girls and women, that are living illustrations of the truth of this brief monograph.[53]

It is not asserted here that improper methods of study and a disregard of the reproductive apparatus and its functions, during the educational life of girls, are the sole causes of female diseases; neither is it asserted that all the female graduates of our schools and colleges are pathological specimens. But it is asserted that the number of these graduates who have been permanently disabled to a greater or less degree by these causes is so great as to excite the gravest alarm and to demand the serious attention of the community. If these causes should continue for the next half-century, and increase in the same ratio as they have for the last fifty years, it requires no prophet to foretell that the wives who are to be mothers in our republic must be drawn from transatlantic homes. . . .

It has already been stated that the excretory organs, by constantly eliminating from the system its effete and used material, the measure and source of its force, keep the machine in clean, healthy, and working order, and that the reproductive apparatus of woman uses the blood as one of its agents of elimination. Kept within natural limits, this elimination is a source of strength, a perpetual fountain of health, a constant renewal of life. Beyond these limits it is a hemorrhage that, by draining away the life, becomes a source of weakness and a perpetual fountain of disease.

The following case illustrates one of the ways in which our present school methods of reaching girls generate a menorrhagia and its consequent evils. Miss A—, a healthy, bright, intelligent girl, entered a female school, an institution that is commonly but oddly called a *seminary* for girls,[54] in the State of New York, at the age of fifteen. She was then sufficiently well developed and had a good color; all the functions appeared to act normally, and the catamenia were fairly established. She was ambitious as well as capable, and aimed to be among the first in the school. . . . She went to school regularly every week and every day of the school year, just as boys do. She paid no more attention to the periodical tides of her organization than her companions; and that was none at all. She recited standing at all times, or at least whenever a standing recitation was the order of the hour. She soon found,

---

51. Edward H. Clarke, *Visions: A Study of False Sight* (Boston: Houghton, Osgood, 1878).

52. Edward H. Clarke, *Sex in Education; or, A Fair Chance for the Girls* (1873; Boston: James R. Osgood, 1874), pp. 61–72.

53. Dysmenorrhea is difficult, painful menstruation; menorrhagia is excessive menstrual flow, which Clarke claimed to be the primary mechanism whereby study weakens women physically.

54. *Seminarium* in Latin originally denoted a nursery for young trees or "seedlings" and, subsequently, a school for young students. By the late nineteenth century, the term "seminary" referred primarily to schools for training clergy; hence, Clarke considers the term odd, though Daniel C. Gilman used the term generically in "Is It Worthwhile to Uphold Any Longer the Idea of Liberal Education?" *Educational Review* 3 (1892): 105–119.

and this history is taken from her own lips, that for a few days during every fourth week, the effort of reciting produced an extraordinary physical result. The attendant anxiety and excitement relaxed the sluices of the system that were already physiologically open, and determined a hemorrhage as the concomitant of a recitation. Subjected to the inflexible rules of the school, unwilling to seek advice from any one, almost ashamed of her own physique, she ingeniously protected herself against exposure and went on intellectually leading her companions and physically defying nature.

At the end of a year, she went home with a gratifying report from her teachers, and pale cheeks and a variety of aches. Her parents were pleased and perhaps a little anxious. She is a good scholar, said her father, somewhat overworked possibly; and so he gave her a trip among the mountains, and a week or two at the seashore. After her vacation she returned to school, and repeated the previous year's experience—constant, sustained work, recitation and study for all days alike, a hemorrhage once a month that would make the stroke oar of the University crew falter, and a brilliant scholar. Before the expiration of the second year, nature began to exert her authority. The paleness of Miss A's complexion increased. An unaccountable and uncontrollable twitching of a rhythmical sort got into the muscles of her face, and made her hands go and feet jump. She was sent home, and her physician called, who at once diagnosticated chorea (St. Vitus's dance),[55] and said she had studied too hard, and wisely prescribed no study and a long vacation.

Her parents took her to Europe. A year of the sea and the Alps, of England and the Continent, the Rhine and Italy, worked like a charm. The sluiceways were controlled, the blood saved, and color and health returned.

She came back seemingly well, and at the age of eighteen went to her old school once more. . . . The labor and regimen of the school soon brought on the old menorrhagic trouble in the old way, with the addition of occasional faintings to emphasize Nature's warnings. She persisted in getting her education, however, and graduated at nineteen, the first scholar, and an invalid.

Again her parents were gratified and anxious. She is overworked, said they, and wondered why girls break down so. To insure her recovery, a second and longer travel was undertaken. . . . She returned to America better than she went away, and married at the age of twenty-two. Soon after that time she consulted the writer on account of prolonged dyspepsia, neuralgia, and dysmenorrhagia, which had replaced menorrhagia. Then I learned the long history of her education and of her efforts to study just as boys do. Her attention had never been called before to the danger she had incurred while at school. She is now what is called getting better, but has the delicacy and weaknesses of American women, and, so far, is without children.

It is not difficult, in this case, either to discern the cause of the trouble, or to trace its influence through the varying phases of disease from Miss A's school-days, to her matronly life. She was well, and would have been called robust up to her first critical period. She then had two tasks imposed upon her at once, both of which required for their perfect accomplishment a few years of time and a large share of vital force: one was the education of the brain, the other of the reproductive system. . . .[56] Ambitious, earnest, and conscientious, she obeyed the visible power and authority of the school, and disobeyed, or rather ignorantly sought to evade, the invisible power and authority of her organization. She put her will into the education of her brain, and withdrew it from elsewhere. The system does not do two things well at the same time. One or the other suffers from neglect, when the attempt is made. Miss A made her brain and muscles work actively, and diverted blood and force to them when her organization demanded active work, with blood and force for evolution in another region.

---

55. A nervous disease causing involuntary contractions of the muscles.

56. Conservation of "vital energy" or "vital force" is a key principle here and in the reading above.

At first the schoolmaster seemed to be successful. He not only made his pupil's brain manipulate Latin, chemistry, philosophy, geography, grammar, arithmetic, music, French, German, and the whole extraordinary catalog of an American young lady's school curriculum, with acrobatic skill; but he made her do this irrespective of the periodical tides of her organism, and made her perform her intellectual and muscular calisthenics, obliging her to stand, walk, and recite at the seasons of highest tide. . . . Fortunately graduation soon occurred, and unintermitted, sustained labor was no longer enforced. The menorrhagia ceased, but persistent dysmenorrhea now indicates the neuralgic friction of an imperfectly developed reproductive apparatus. Doubtless the evil of her education will infect her whole life.

43. "The Sexes in College" (1870)

INTRODUCTION

The moderate view in Orton's collection appeared in articles conceding that the same, or virtually the same, liberal arts curriculum could be pursued by both men and women. But this moderate view endorsed separate educational spheres fearing that moral transgressions would ensue from mixing young men and women together. This fear primarily concerned the females due to the longstanding double standard of morality. "Many a boy . . . stumbles and recovers himself; but a girl cannot retrace a false step as her brother can. For her, once to fall is ruin," as stated below. Hence, coeducation was opposed; separate but equal education was approved. This moderate view appears in the following article that James Orton drew from *The Nation*. Appearing originally in March 1870, the anonymous article was likely written by William F. Allen, who, after receiving the B.A. from Harvard in 1851, became Professor of Greek and Latin at Antioch College in Ohio and then Professor of Ancient Languages and History at the University of Wisconsin from 1867 until his death in 1889.

SELECTION[57]

The admission of women to our colleges and universities is, if not the most important educational problem yet to be solved, at least the most pressing and the most clamorous for an immediate solution. It hangs closely together with the question of female suffrage, and indeed may almost be said to depend upon that; for, if women are once admitted to vote, there will be little likelihood of their being long excluded from college classes, and if, on the other hand, the suffrage is still denied them, it will be largely on grounds which will be equally weighty against the reform in question.[58] Still the separation of the sexes in education has nothing to do with any alleged inferiority of the one to the other—hardly, indeed with any difference in "sphere"; for all agree as to giving women as good an education as men, and an identical one if they desire it. And in those institutions which are designed to comple-

---

57. Orton, *The Liberal Education of Women*, pp. 187–91, 191.

58. Compare this view of the relationship between liberal education and political participation of women with that implied by Christine de Pizan's "city of ladies" in selection #12, by Laura Cereta's "republic of women" in selection #27, and by Emma Willard's *Plan* in selection #35.

ment college education, such as the university courses at Cambridge,[59] no objection is made to the admission of ladies, and no mischief can result.

The subject of coeducation in colleges and universities must be regarded from two points of view—that of the character and demeanor of the students, and that of their intellectual training. In the [university] courses just spoken of, intellectual considerations are the only ones, as the students are supposed to be old enough and mature enough to look after themselves. The lecturers have no responsibility but to give their best; it is for the hearer to determine whether it meets his or her wants. But the college has higher aims than mere intellectual training—to turn out well developed men, in both intellect and character; and it is the essential feature of a college that it assumes the responsibility of the student's entire development. Any college, therefore, before making so radical a change as that proposed must satisfy itself that it is ready to assume this added responsibility; that it feels prepared to turn out as good members of society, men and women, as it could men alone or women alone. The assumption that it is "natural" or "right" in itself has nothing to do with it; the sole question is as to the results,[60] and that not merely or mainly in securing, good discipline and good lessons, but in producing manly men and womanly women, fitted to do the work of life in their generation. President Eliot, for the faculty of Harvard College, frankly says that [the faculty] are not prepared to assume this responsibility; and, so long as this is the case, the question of duty is settled for them.[61]

The colleges are distinguished from those institutions of higher culture which are able to make a certain provision for women, by the fundamental fact that they take the young man at the most critical period of his youth, and retain the entire control of him for a period long enough to form his character, and give his mind the training he needs in order to prepare him for the work of life. This is what the American colleges undertake to do, and, with all their defects, they may claim a fair degree of success; the college graduates as a class are not unworthy of the pains and expense that have been bestowed upon them. . . .

The normal schools lack the essential features of the colleges. They are not established to make men and women, but schoolteachers; the students are, on the average, not far from the age of the higher college classes, but they go to the school with the definite purpose of fitting themselves for a special work, not with the vague desire of being disciplined into manhood. The school authorities, to be sure, have their rules, and maintain more or less supervision over the demeanor of the students; but this discipline is wholly subsidiary professional training [and] not itself an end. And as to the high schools, they are simply the last and highest grade of our mixed common schools, touching upon the lower edge of the college course, as the normal schools do upon the upper.

---

59. In 1869–1870 Harvard began to offer "University Courses of Instruction" at an advanced level that were open to men and women for a fee. Undergraduates were not allowed to attend. This was the forerunner of the Graduate Department of the university, established in 1872.

60. Edward H. Clarke also waived arguments drawn from "abstract principles of right and wrong." *Sex in Education*, p. 12. Compare his asserted sources of authority with that posited here.

61. In his inaugural address Charles W. Eliot optimistically envisioned a time when, "the University offers to young women who have been to good schools as many years as they wish of liberal culture in studies which have no direct professional value, to be sure, but which enrich and enlarge both intellect and character. The University hopes thus to contribute to the intellectual emancipation of women. It hopes to prepare some women better than they would otherwise have been prepared for the profession of teaching, the one learned profession to which women have acquired a clear title. It hopes that the proffer of this higher instruction will have some reflex influence upon schools for girls—to discourage superficiality and to promote substantial education." "Inaugural Address as President of Harvard College," *Educational Reform: Essays and Addresses* (New York: Century, 1908), p. 24. By 1872 Eliot's support for coeducation eroded in the face of resistance from the Harvard faculty and the governing boards.

And what is more essential still, the scholars of the public schools live at home and are under the care and responsibility of their parents, looking to the school only for intellectual instruction. Now, it is precisely here, where the colleges differ essentially from the high schools, that we find the weak point of college discipline. It is right that a time should come when the boy shall leave home and learn to rely on himself, leaving behind him the constant and watchful control of his parents, and having in place of it only the indirect and general influence of the college. This is just what he needs *at the right time*; but it is in the impossibility of knowing in each individual case just when the right time has come that the dangers of college life chiefly consist. The boy goes from home, passes four years in the comparative freedom of college life, and leaves the college walls a man. Are we prepared to have our girls do the same thing? Many a boy is wrecked in his course, many a one stumbles and recovers himself; but a girl cannot retrace a false step as her brother can. For her, once to fall is ruin.

It is here that the peculiar difficulties of coeducation in colleges appear to reside; and it was from a consideration of these, no doubt, that Horace Mann, as we are told, insisted so strenuously upon the dormitory system as essential to success in a mixed college.[62] That is, the freedom, which young men enjoy with safety and profit will not do for young women of the same age and on professedly the same footing. In this he was probably right; a college will not undertake this peculiar responsibility for girls away from home, except by retaining a much more constant control than they care to exercise over boys.

But is not this really admitting that . . . a real equality of the sexes in college education has never been tried, [and] we are afraid to try it? If every girl lived under her father's roof, it would be different. There could then be no objection to mixed classes—none, that is, from the point we are now considering; it is in the fact that the college assumes a responsibility which it has not adequate means of maintaining that the danger lies; for we see no more harm in girls and boys meeting in the class-room and lecture-room than in sleigh rides and parties.

We have spoken only of the moral aspect of the question, and that side of it which has to do with the special dangers arising from the sexual relation; because this is the first and most essential point of view in which to regard it. . . .

---

62. Horace Mann (1796–1859), the first secretary of the Massachusetts Board of Education and the leading advocate for public education in the young United States, served as the first president of co-educational Antioch College in Ohio from 1853 until 1859. Brief writings by Mann and his wife, Mary Peabody Mann (1806–1887), a leading advocate of kindergartens, were included in *The Liberal Education of Women*, pp. 269–70.

44. James H. Fairchild, "The Experience at Oberlin" (1867)

INTRODUCTION

What may be termed the progressive argument concerning the admission of women to the B.A. course also took for granted the separate spheres ideology, but advocated offering to women the same liberal course of study provided to men. Rather than recoiling from "joint education," or coeducation, due to a fear that mixing the sexes would lead to moral transgressions, the progressive view emphasized the mutually beneficial effects of the young men and women upon each other. In particular, it was argued that young women would exert a civilizing force upon the males. As the former president of coeducational Knox College observed, "Young men would rather be fined, rusticated, expelled, any and all put together, than have the misdemeanors of which they were known to be guilty calmly discussed in chapel, where the young ladies are present."[63]

Advocates for coeducation achieved most success at state universities during the third quarter of the nineteenth century. Women generally gained access to these institutions "when parents, teachers' associations, or women's organizations, using the rhetoric of domesticity, petitioned legislatures and boards of regents to provide vocational preparation for the daughters of taxpayers."[64] Early in 1870, for example, the University of Michigan adopted co-education, and by the end of the year President Tyler asserted, "We have already ceased to fear the dangers which were apprehended from this action, and which constituted the chief argument against it—the loss of reputation and caste among universities, the decline of scholarship, and the corruption of morals."[65]

State universities thus overcame their fear of these dangers sooner than did most private, sectarian liberal arts colleges, which attended closely to students' moral formation and personal development. The outstanding exception among the private colleges was Oberlin, which in 1837 became the first college in the country to admit women to the B.A. course. The progressive view of Oberlin is discussed in the address below by President James H. Fairchild.

Born in Stockbridge, Massachusetts, James H. Fairchild (1817–1902) moved with his family in 1818 to the western reserve of Ohio, where he attended school and entered Oberlin College in 1834, a year after it opened. Graduating in 1838 at the age of 21, he then studied theology at Oberlin and became a tutor. In the antebellum tradition of the academic generalist, Fairchild was appointed professor of Greek and Latin in 1842, of mathematics in 1847, and of theology and moral philosophy in 1858. In 1866 he was elected president of Oberlin and, during the next year, delivered the following address before a meeting of college presidents in Springfield, Illinois. The forum and the address demonstrate that Oberlin had become the exemplar and test case in debates about coeducation. Fairchild's tenure as president continued until 1889, overlapping with the presidencies of his two brothers: Edward T. Fairchild at Kansas State Agricultural College (later Kansas State University) and Edward H. Fairchild at Berea College in Kentucky. James remained on the faculty until his retirement in 1898, having spent his entire career at Oberlin.

---

63. Jonathan Blanchard, "The Experience at Knox College," (1870), in *The Liberal Education of Women*, p. 261. Compare the experience at Alfred University, described in selection #39.

64. Gordon, *Gender and Higher Education*, p. 21.

65. Quoted in Moses Coit Tyler, "The Experience at the University of Michigan" (1870), in *The Liberal Education of Women*, pp. 267–8.

SELECTION[66]

After the Preparatory Department, we have two courses open to young ladies—the "Ladies' Course" and the regular "College Course." The Ladies' Course is a course of four years, requiring, as conditions of entering, a good elementary English education and a year's study of Latin. It embraces all the studies of the regular College course, omitting all the Greek and most of the Latin, omitting also the differential and integral calculus, and adding lessons in French and drawing, and some branches of natural science. Those pursuing this course recite with the college classes in the same studies. Separate classes are organized for the ladies in essay-writing until the commencement of the third year, when they are added to the junior College class in this exercise. Their training in this department is limited to reading and writing, none of the Ladies having any exercise in speaking.[67]

The great majority of our young ladies pursue this course, and it was supposed at the organization of the school that nothing farther would be required for them;[68] but in 1837 four young ladies prepared themselves for the freshman class and were received upon their own petition.[69] Since that time it has been understood that the College Course is open to young ladies. . . . The ladies in this course are under the same general regulations and discipline as in the other course, and are responsible to the lady Principal. At the termination of their course they receive the regular degree in the Arts. Eighty-four ladies have received this degree, and three hundred and ninety-five have received the diploma of the Ladies' Course. . . .

The association of gentlemen and ladies out of the classroom is regulated as experience seems to require. They sit at the same table in families and in the Ladies' Hall. Young gentlemen call on ladies in a social way at the parlors of the Ladies' Hall and of private families, between the hour for tea and half-past seven in the winter (and eight o'clock in the summer.) They walk in groups from one classroom to another, as convenience and their sense of propriety may dictate, with the help of a suggestion, if needed, from thoughtful and observing friends. Now and then the young ladies have permission to attend an evening lecture given under the auspices of the college, and in such case to accept the attendance of young men. No such association is permitted in the case of religious meetings.[70] They do not ride or walk together beyond the limits of the village, except on a holiday under special arrangements. There is no association of the sexes in literary societies or other voluntary and independent organizations. . . .

---

66. Orton, *The Liberal Education of Women*, pp. 238–56.

67. "Even women who received the A.B. degree could not read essays at commencement, the occasion where young men showed their oratorical abilities in the company of the trustees, parents, and supporters of the college. . . . Not until 1858 was an Oberlin woman allowed to read her own part in the regular commencement; not until 1874 did one cast aside her written part and orate like an Oberlin man." Barbara Miller Solomon, "The Oberlin Model and Its Impact on Other Colleges," in *Coeducation in a Changing World*, ed. Carol Lasser (Urbana: University of Illinois Press, 1987), p. 83.

68. Oberlin was originally interested in preparing women to be suitable and subordinate members of religious congregations and wives for clergymen. Lori Ginzberg, "The Joint Education of the Sexes: Oberlin's Original Vision," in *Coeducation in a Changing World*, pp. 67–80.

69. Admission of women to the "College Course" was thus not anticipated or encouraged by Oberlin. Their exclusion was not specified beforehand, and upon the petition of qualified B.A. candidates, it was thought unfair to introduce the exclusion *ex post facto*. Other colleges, put in the same situation, denied admission to qualified female applicants.

70. Association of the sexes was permitted academically and socially; why not religiously?

Among the advantages which seem to be involved in the system, as we have observed its operation, are the following

1. Economy of means and forces. The teaching force and other apparatus required in all the higher departments of study is made available to a larger number. . . . If a separate establishment were attempted for ladies, affording the same advantages, the outlay in men and means would have to be duplicated. . . .

2. Convenience to the patrons of the school. It has been a matter of interest with us to note the number of cases in which a brother is accompanied or followed by a sister, or a sister by a brother. . . .

3. Another advantage we find in the wholesome incitements to study which the system affords.[71] . . .

4. Again, the social culture which is incidental to the system is a matter of no small importance. To secure this the student does not need to make any expenditure of time, going out of his way, or leaving his proper work for the pleasure or improvement resulting from society. He finds himself naturally in the midst of it and adjusts himself to it instinctively. . . .

5. Closely connected with this influence is the tendency to good order which we find in the system. . . . This result we attribute greatly to the wholesome influence of the system of joint education. . . .

6. Nor can it be reasonably doubted that the arrangement tends to good order and morality in the town outside of the school. Evils that might be tolerated in the shape of drinking-saloons and other places of dissipation, if young men only were present, seem intolerable where ladies are gathered with them. . . .

7. It can hardly be doubted that young people educated under such conditions are kept in harmony with society at large, and are prepared to appreciate the responsibilities of life and to enter upon its work. . . .

These are among the advantages of the system which have forced themselves upon our attention. The list might be extended and expanded; but you will wish especially to know whether we have not encountered disadvantages and difficulties which more than counterbalance these advantages, and you will properly require me to speak with all frankness upon these difficulties which are commonly apprehended.

1. Have young ladies the ability in mental vigor and bodily health to maintain a fair standing in a class with young men? Do they not operate as a check upon the progress of the class and degrade the standard of scholarship? And do they not break down in health under a pressure which young men can sustain?

To this inquiry I answer [that], where there has been the same preparatory training, we find no difference in ability to maintain themselves in the recitation-room. . . . The strong and the weak scholars are equally distributed between the sexes. . . . Nor is there any manifest inability on the part of young women to endure the required labor. A breaking down in health does not appear to be more frequent than with the young men. We have not observed a more frequent interruption of study on this account; nor do our statistics show a greater draft upon the vital forces in the case of those who have completed the full college course. . . .

2. But it is held by many that ladies need a course of study adapted to their nature and their prospective work, and that it must be undesirable to bring them under the same training with

---

71. Fairchild does not directly explain how co-education produces this advantage, though he implies that "the social influence arising from the constitution of our classes" encourages every student, rather than just the top students, to study hard so as to avoid embarrassment arising from poor work.

young men. The theory of our school has never been that men and women are alike in mental constitution, or that they naturally and properly occupy the same position in the work of life. The education furnished is general, not professional, designed to fit men and women for any position or work to which they may properly he called. Even in the full college curriculum, it does not appear that there is any study that would not be helpful in the discipline and furniture of an educated lady.[72]

But only a small proportion of young ladies seeking an education will naturally require the full college course. It is not difficult to frame a suitable course parallel with the college course, made up substantially of studies selected from it, and diversified by the addition of the accomplishments supposed to be peculiarly adapted to female culture. . . . We do not find that any peculiar style of teaching is required to adapt these studies to female culture. The womanly nature will appropriate the material to its own necessities under its own laws. Young men and women sit at the same table and partake of the same food, and we have no apprehension that the vital forces will fail to elaborate from the common material the osseous and fibrous and nervous tissues adapted to each frame and constitution.[73] Except under pressure of great external violence, the female nature asserts itself by virtue of its own inherent laws. No education can make alike those whom God has made as unlike as men and women.

3. Yet apprehension is felt and expressed that character will deteriorate on one side or on the other; that young men will become frivolous or effeminate, and young women coarse and masculine. The more prevalent opinion seems to be that, while the arrangement may be desirable in its effect on young men, it will be damaging to young women. That young men should become trifling or effeminate, lose their manly attributes and character, from proper association with cultivated young women, is antecedently improbable and false in fact. It is the natural atmosphere for the development of the higher qualities of manhood—magnanimity, generosity, true chivalry, earnestness. The animal man is kept subordinate in the prevalence of these higher qualities. . . .

But, on the other hand, are not womanly delicacy and refinement of character endangered? Will not the young woman, pursuing her studies with young men, take on their manners and inspirations and aims, and be turned aside from the true ideal of womanly life and character? The thing is scarcely conceivable. The natural response of woman to the exhibition of manly traits is in the correlative qualities of gentleness, delicacy, and grace. . . .

But it is my duty not to reason, but to speak from the limited historical view assigned to me. You would know whether the result with us has been a large accession to the numbers of coarse, "strong-minded" women, in the offensive sense of the word; and I say, without hesitation, that I do not know of a single instance of such a product as the result of our system of education. It is true that in our [alumnae list] are found the names of three somewhat distinguished lady lecturers, who are sometimes referred to as belonging to this class. They pursued their studies at Oberlin from four to five years in each case. But, whatever their present position and character may be, I have personal knowledge of the fact that they came to us very mature in thought, with their views of life settled and their own plans and purposes determined and announced. Whatever help in their chosen life they derived from the advantages afforded them, they have never given us any credit for their more advanced views of woman's rights and duties. While avowing a radical dis-

---

72. This phrase shows the continuing influence of Jeremiah Day's famous phrase—"the *discipline* and *furniture* of the mind"—from the Yale Report by Jeremiah Day in selection #37.

73. This analogy that men and women differently constitute their minds out of the same studies and teaching, just as they differently constitute their bodies out of the same food is a striking example of the legitimating authority of biological metaphors in this period.

sent from those views, I can not forbear to say that I am happy to number these ladies among my friends, and to express my admiration of much that is noble and womanly in their character, and of their earnest but mistaken philanthropy. . . .[74]

4. But this view does not touch the exact point of the difficulty. It is in general admitted that the association of young men and women, under proper conditions, is elevating instead of degrading; but there is doubt whether bringing them together in a school provides for those proper associations. The wholesome association of the young requires the presence and influence of those who are mature and have experience and a sense of responsibility—more of the family influence than can be secured in a large school. Is there not danger that young men and young women thus brought together in the critical period of life, when the destructive social tendencies which draw the sexes towards each other seem to act with greatest intensity, will fail of that necessary regulative force and fall into undesirable and unprofitable relations? Will not such associations result in weak and foolish love affairs, and in such habits of communication and social life as lead to these and grow out of them? It is not strange that such apprehensions are felt, nor would it be easy to give an *a priori* answer to such difficulties; but, if we may judge from our experience, the difficulties are without foundation. . . .

5. But will not the young people form such acquaintances as will result, during the course of study or after they leave school, in matrimonial engagements? Undoubtedly they will; and if this is a fatal objection, the system will be pronounced a failure. The majority of young people form such acquaintances between the ages of sixteen and twenty-four, and these are the years devoted to a course of study. It would be a most unnatural state of things if such acquaintances should not be made in a school where young men and women are gathered in large numbers; nor is it to be expected that marriage engagements even will not be formed more or less frequently. . . .

6. But what security is there that positive immoralities may not at times occur, and startling scandals even, that shall shock the community and produce distrust of the system? Of course, such a thing might be; but it would scarce be logical to condemn the system on the ground of such possibilities or even actualities. The only pertinent inquiry is whether such immoralities are the more natural and frequent product of this than of other systems. . . . There may have been a time when one such scandal in a school for joint education would have brought reproach upon the system and overwhelmed it with popular disgust. A generation of successful trial, under a sheltering Providence, should have won for it the impartial judgment which is the right of every system. . . .

But the experiment at Oberlin, if the earliest, is by no means the only one. At least a score of schools have sprung up that have adopted essentially the same plan, and I have yet to learn that there has been any other than a uniform result in the convictions of those who have best understood these movements.

---

74. Two of the "somewhat distinguished lady lecturers" and mistaken philanthropists to whom Fairchild refers in this revealing paragraph are probably Lucy Stone (1818–1893), who graduated in 1847 and Antoinette Brown Blackwell (1825–1921), classmate of Lucy Stone and the first woman ordained to the clergy in a major Protestant denomination (Congregationalism) in the United States. The third might be Frances "Fanny" Jackson Coppin (1837–1913) who graduated from Oberlin with a B.A. in 1865 and became the first African American woman to serve as head of a college when she was named the principal of the Institute for Colored Youth in Philadelphia in 1869. She also campaigned vigorously on behalf of women's right to vote.

45. Mary Fairfax Somerville, "Testimony" (1869)

INTRODUCTION

The egalitarian view on the issue was voiced predominantly by women and distinguished by its rejection of the separate spheres ideology. One of the foremost exponents was Mary Fairfax Grieg Somerville (1780–1872), who was born in Scotland the daughter of a British admiral. Virtually illiterate until age ten, her formal education at a boarding school for girls ended at age eleven.[75] The chance discovery of an article on algebra in a fashion magazine during her teens stimulated her appetite for learning. Despite her family's opposition and the prevailing opinion that study was dangerous to women's health, Fairfax determined to become educated.

She easily mastered algebra, then taught herself enough Latin to work through Euclid's *Elements of Geometry*.[76] She read books on navigation from her father's library and solved problems in spherical trigonometry and practical astronomy. Forging ahead with her passion for mathematics, she frequently studied far into the night, worrying and bewildering her family. Her first marriage ended in the death of her husband in 1807 but produced two sons. In 1812 she remarried to a cousin, William Somerville, who recognized her genius and encouraged her studies. In 1816 they moved to London and became well known in intellectual circles, particularly in the Royal Society, the oldest scientific society in Great Britain. Because prejudice forbade Somerville even from reading her papers before the Royal Society, her husband read them instead, including one in 1826 describing the magnetizing effects of light, which established Somerville's reputation.

In the following year, she was invited to translate and condense Pierre Laplace's five-volume masterpiece *Celestial Mechanics* (1799–1825) into a popular English edition. Laplace's work presumed that the reader knew calculus, so Somerville faced a prodigious task: reworking the equations, reproving the problems, and providing illustrations and supplemental explanations of Laplace's mechanical interpretation of the solar system. Four years later Somerville finished *The Mechanism of the Heavens* (1831), which immediately became a standard authority in Britain and America, and was adopted as a textbook by universities, colleges, and schools. In later years, Somerville turned to terrestrial topics and produced her most popular work: *Physical Geography* (1848), which went through seven editions. This book, too, was widely adopted as a classroom text, as seen in the Dartmouth College catalog in selection #38. Both the British Royal Geographic Society and the Royal Society honored her with awards, but would not elect her a member.

Undaunted by these slights, she employed her fame to aid the cause for women's rights, joining the unsuccessful petition to the University of London to grant degrees to women. At age eighty-six, she was the first of 1,500 women who signed John Stuart Mill's petition to Parliament for female enfranchisement. At age eighty-eight, she published a final scientific book *Molecular and Microscopic Science*. She died in 1872, the year before James Orton compiled the selections in *The Liberal Education of Women*.

---

75. In addition to the sources listed in the bibliography, this introduction draws from Kenneth Wietzenhoffer, "The Education of Mary Somerville," *Sky and Telescope* (Feb. 1987): 138–9.

76. Compare Emma Willard's encounter with Euclid, described in selection #35. In selection #1 Plato suggests (526b–c) that engagement with the difficult study of mathematics is the best stimulus for liberal education, transcending differences of gender, race, and social class (as further illustrated by Plato in Socrates's dialogue with the slave boy in *Meno*).

SELECTION[77]

The low estimate in which our intellect has hitherto been held has been a grief and mortification to me from my earliest years. While the improvement of man's education has occupied so much attention in the present age, it is wonderful that one-half of the human race should have been comparatively so much neglected. Great duties have been demanded from us, and our minds have not been prepared by solid instruction to fulfill them. Much prejudice still exists against high intellectual education for our sex, from the mistaken idea that it would render a woman unfit for the duties of a wife and mother. A woman that would neglect her family for studies, would equally neglect them for frivolous pursuits and dissipation.

Hitherto, usefulness and duty to men have been thought the only objects worth caring for with regard to women; it would, at least, be generous to take the individual happiness of sex into consideration in the scheme of education. Thousands of women never marry, and even those that do, have many solitary hours. I can only say from experience, that the higher branches of mathematical science as well as natural history have been inestimable blessings to me throughout the whole course of my life, and more especially in extreme old age, when other resources fail. As a source of happiness as well as of intellectual strength, mathematical science and classical learning ought to be essential branches of study in the higher and middle classes of women.

Do not suppose that I undervalue accomplishments; on the contrary, I am a zealous advocate for refinement.[78] But surely the graces of life are not incompatible with solid endowments. Even if every opportunity of improvement is given, education will necessarily be subservient to the natural disposition of the child. There is no need to fear that all will be too learned, though all will be improved; but the important point is that a girl should be perfectly taught any branch of science or literature for which she shows an inclination, that she may be really learned.

---

77. Orton, *The Liberal Education of Women*, pp. 65–6. This selection, reprinted in its entirety, consists of a letter from Mary Fairfax Somerville to Josephine (Grey) Butler (1828–1906), an ardent suffragist and leading social reformer.

78. "Accomplishments" here refers to the traditional female arts. Orton noted at this point: "Mrs. Somerville is quoted as an instance alike to the highest intellectual eminence and the most faultless ménage." Bathsua Makin in selection #30 and Emma Willard in selection #35 address this point.

46. Lydia Ernestine Becker, "On the Study of Science by Women" (1869)

INTRODUCTION

The egalitarian position on the liberal education of women, with its rejection of separate spheres ideology, was expressed even more starkly by Lydia Ernestine Becker (1827–1890). Born in Manchester, England, Becker was the eldest of fifteen children; her father owned a chemical plant, and her mother died in 1855. Educated largely at home, Becker read widely on her own, wrote a treatise on elementary astronomy, and published *Botany for Novices* in 1864.

In her late thirties, she was introduced and persuaded to the idea of female suffrage, and published a prominent article on the topic in *The Contemporary Review* in 1867. In 1870 she founded the *Women's Suffrage Journal* and became a prominent figure in the movement. Despite antagonizing a branch of supporters during the 1870s and 1880s by her support for the compromise of excluding married women from suffrage, Becker continued to be a central figure in sustaining the movement during its political defeats over these decades. Meanwhile, Becker worked actively on other issues, such as the Married Women's Property Committee and the Contagious [Venereal] Diseases Act, joining Josephine Butler on the latter campaign. She also addressed the education of women and girls, serving on the Manchester School Board and publishing selection #45 in *The Contemporary Review* in 1869, which rejected separate spheres ideology and firmly supported liberal education for women. By 1889 illness prevented her from leaving home, and she died the following year, still waiting to vote in a state election.

SELECTION[79]

Male and female students, in any branch of science, must go through the same training, and have their qualifications and capacities tested by precisely the same rules; neither is there anything in these studies which is naturally more attractive or advantageous to persons of one sex than of the other. Nevertheless, the fact is indisputable that at the present time the students of science among men greatly outnumber those among women.

Some persons attribute this circumstance to an inherent specific distinction in the minds of the two sexes of man. They assume the existence of a natural distaste or incapacity for scientific pursuits among women, and they consider it neither possible nor desirable to encourage them in the successful prosecution of such studies. Others perceive in existing social and conventional arrangements which exclude women from those opportunities of cultivating their intellectual faculties which are freely enjoyed by men, a perfectly sufficient explanation of the difference in the numbers and the proficiency of persons of each sex engaged in scientific pursuits.

The last is, I think, the true solution of the question, "Why are there fewer scientific women than scientific men?" The assumed difference in the minds of the two sexes is purely hypothetical; the practical difference in the training and advantages given to each is a fact as indisputable as the one which it explains.

I do not deny the existence of distinct types or orders of mind among mankind—all I deny is the coincidence of any one of these types with the physical distinction of sex. If we take an assemblage of persons of both sexes and test the differences of thought, opinion, or capacity existing among them by putting before them any proposition on which opposite views can be held, I believe it would be im-

---

79. Orton, *The Liberal Education of Women*, pp. 67–80.

possible to find one which would range all the men on one side and all the women on the other.[80] If it were true that there is a specific difference, however slight, between the minds of men and women, it would be possible to find such a proposition, if we took one which corresponded to this distinction.

When a naturalist seeks to group a number of individuals into a distinct class, he fixes on some character or set of characters common to them all, and distinguishes them from other individuals. When he finds such a group distinctly defined, he calls it a species. But when he finds two individuals differing very widely from each other, yet so connected by intermediate forms that he can pass from one extreme to the other without a violent break anywhere in the series, he considers them to be of one and the same kind. If we apply this principle as an illustration of the variety of the human intellects, taking the conventional masculine type of mind as one end of the scale and the conventional feminine type as the other, we shall find them connected by numerous intermediate varieties distributed indiscriminately among male and female persons; that what is called a masculine mind is frequently found united to a feminine body and sometimes the reverse, and that there is no necessary nor even presumptive connection between the sex of a human being and the type of intellect and character he possesses. . . .

The existence of a difference in the intellectual powers of the sexes is a question fertile in endless disputations, which can only be satisfactorily set at rest by the test of observation and experiment.[81] Wherever this test has been impartially applied, by studies and examinations conducted without reference to the sex of the student, the honors have been fairly divided between men and women, and no line of demarcation has made itself apparent between the character of the subjects chosen, or the degree of proficiency attained. . . .

Some of the educational institutions so far recognize the existence of the other sex as to make a feeble effort to supplement their main provisions by the establishment of supernumerary "women's classes." I have not heard whether these well-meant but ill-advised efforts to combat the evil have done much good. The little I have heard leads me to the belief that the result has been what one might from the first have anticipated, and that the interest displayed in these classes has been languid. There are not a sufficient number of women as yet roused to the interest of such subjects to afford material for the promotion and continuance of such isolated classes, and the fact of their exclusion from the companionship of the other sex acts as a damper on their spirits. They would not care much for social pleasures if they were only admitted to women's balls, women's dinner parties, women's croquet parties, and women's concerts; and if they are only allowed to participate in intellectual pleasures on these exclusive terms, they will certainly not derive from them either the advantages or the healthful stimulus which these are capable of affording.[82]

It seems to me a matter for sincere regret that any effort made to promote the intellectual activity of women should be based on this system of separation and exclusion. Whatever difficulties may be thought to stand in the way of studies conducted in concert, none can exist, even in imagination, when the proposal is simply that of simultaneous and identical examinations; the placing of all the papers together for judgment and making out the class list in order of merit, with absolute impartiality and indifference as to whether the papers were the production of male or female students. The success of

---

80. Compare this argument to the late twentieth-century analysis of racial differences, holding that intraracial differences among individuals are greater than inter-racial differences. See William J. Wilson, *The Declining Significance of Race: Blacks and Changing American Institutions* (Chicago: University of Chicago Press, 1978).

81. These were the grounds upon which the debate over Dr. E. H. Clarke's *Sex in Education* and the general question of liberal education for women were resolved during the next two decades.

82. Like Mary Fairfax Somerville, Becker invokes a women's right "to participate in intellectual pleasures." This justification appears in selection #30 by Bathsua Makin and selection #35 by Emma Willard.

the local examinations in connection with [Cambridge University], where no difference of any kind is made in the examination of girls and boys, should point out the principle to be acted on in further efforts in the same direction.

The only matter for regret in respect of these examinations is the treatment of the successful students, in the invidious distinction implied in the exclusion of girls from the class lists. The boys who pass honorably have their names published; the girls who pass honorably have their names suppressed. It is just as natural for a girl as for a boy to be pleased to see her name in a list of those who have done well. The University encourages the boys by marking the proficiency they have attained as something to be proud of; it discourages the girls by implying that the acquirements they have gained are something to conceal or be ashamed of.

A still further departure from the principle of equality has been made by the University of London. They have instituted a special examination for women, to which no male student is admitted, and the recognition attached to success is a mere certificate of having passed, without the honors of a University degree.

Perhaps I ought to consider the step that has been taken by the London University not so much a departure from the principle of intellectual equality as an advance towards it. It is the pleasanter, and possibly the truer way. Certainly, before this concession was made, women were not allowed by the authorities to have any rights at all in the matter. Now that their eyes have become partly open to the needs of women in this respect, we may hope that the process will not stop till complete justice has been done.

From all that I can gather respecting the proposed examination, it is in no way inferior in what examinees call "stiffness" to that provided for the other sex. A women who passes in any subject will do quite as much as man who passes the men's examination corresponding in grade. But though she will have worked as hard and done as much as the men, she will not have equal honor. The men will say to her: "You are not on our level; you have only passed the women's examination;" and she will not be admitted as a graduate whatever the amount of intellectual power or attainments she displays. The whole arrangement proceeds on the principle that it is very womanly to work, but "unfeminine" to receive pay or reward for work. Women may be admitted to the course of study, but not to the honors or advantages to which that course of study leads men.

Debate over the "New Departure" in Liberal Education

47. Charles W. Eliot, "Liberty in Education" (1885)

INTRODUCTION

Eliot had barely assumed the presidency of Harvard in 1869 when the tuition fee rose from 104 to 150 dollars and enrollment grew from 529 to 563, yielding an increase in annual tuition income of about 30,000 dollars. Coupled with large gifts received in 1870 and 1871, "these new resources were devoted chiefly to raising salaries and increasing the number of teachers." As a result, many new courses were added to the curriculum over the next decade. Meanwhile, the faculty reduced the number of required subjects and placed them earlier in the curriculum. "Thus in 1872 all required studies had disappeared from the senior year, in 1879 from the junior year, and in 1884 from the sophomore. . . . The most important change made in the College during 1883–84 was the extension of the elective system to the freshman year. There are now no required studies in the College except rhetoric for one year, English composition (themes and forensics), German or French for one year . . . and a few lectures on chemistry and physics."[83]

That Harvard seniors, juniors, sophomores, and finally freshmen could choose most of their courses by 1884 was a scandalous abdication of intellectual and moral authority to many leaders of higher education, who attacked Eliot. In an unusual breach of collegiality in 1884 President Noah Porter of Yale publicly condemned Harvard's elimination of the requirement of Greek in the B.A. course; and in 1885 Porter published an article attacking Harvard's electivism.[84] Soon thereafter, a flock of college and university presidents joined Porter in requesting directly of the Harvard Board of Overseers that they rein in Eliot's reforms.

Meanwhile, the Nineteenth Century Club of New York City, a prominent social club, invited Porter and Princeton President James McCosh to debate Eliot publicly. Porter declined, and the debate occurred on February 24, 1885, between Eliot and McCosh and was widely noted.[85] McCosh recalled it in his farewell address as President of Princeton, and his reply was quoted approvingly by the Jesuits in their controversy with Eliot in the following decade.[86] That Eliot was concerned to defend himself and the elective system against these attacks is shown not only by his own statement in the debate, appearing below, but also by the fact that he expanded his statement into an extensive

83. Charles W. Eliot, *Annual Reports of the President and Treasurer of Harvard College 1883–1884* (Cambridge, MA: Harvard University Press, 1885), pp. 23, 5. As indicated here and below, Eliot was attentive to the financial cost of educational reforms, including electivism.

84. Noah Porter, "Greek and a Liberal Education," *Princeton Review* 2nd ser. 60 (1884): 195–218; Noah Porter, "A Criticism from Yale of the Last Harvard Educational Move—Greek and the Bachelor's Degree," *New Englander* 44 (1885): 424–35.

85. Porter may have felt dispirited because in 1884 and 1885 he was fighting and losing a battle against reformers at Yale who secured the agreement of the corporation to introduce upper-class electives. George W. Pierson, *Yale College: An Educational History, 1871–1921* (New Haven, CT: Yale University Press, 1952), pp. 80–2.

86. James McCosh, "Twenty Years of Princeton College. Being Dr. McCosh's Farewell Address, delivered June 20, 1888," reprinted in William M. Sloane, ed., *The Life of James McCosh* (New York: Charles Scribner's Sons, 1896), p. 199; Timothy J. Brosnahan, S.J., "The Relative Merit of Courses in Catholic and non-Catholic Colleges for the Baccalaureate," in *Report of the Second Annual Conference of the Association of Catholic Colleges of the United States* (Washington, DC: ACC, 1900), p. 42.

analysis of "the actual working of the Harvard elective system" and its rationale in his next annual report of 1884–5.[87]

SELECTION[88]

How to transform a college with one uniform curriculum into a university without any prescribed course of study at all is a problem which more and more claims the attention of all thoughtful friends of American learning and education.[89] To-night I hope to convince you that a university of liberal arts and sciences must give its students three things:

I. Freedom in choice of studies.
II. Opportunity to win academic distinction in single subjects or special lines of study.
III. A discipline which distinctly imposes on each individual the responsibility of forming his own habits and guiding his own conduct.

These three subjects I shall take up in succession, the first of them taking the greater part of the time allotted me.

I. Of freedom in choice of studies.

. . .There are eighty teachers employed this year in Harvard College, exclusive of laboratory assistants; and these eighty teachers give about four hundred and twenty-five hours of public instruction a week without any repetitions, not counting the very important instruction which many of them give in laboratories. It is impossible for any undergraduate in his four years to take more than a tenth part of the instruction given by the College; and since four fifths of this instruction is of a higher grade than any which can be given in a College with a prescribed curriculum, a diligent student would need about forty years to cover the present field; and during those years the field would enlarge quite beyond his powers of occupation.[90] Since the student cannot take the whole of the instruction offered, it seems to be necessary to allow him to take a part. A college must either limit closely its teaching, or provide some mode of selecting studies for the individual student.

The limitation of teaching is an intolerable alternative for any institution which aspires to become a university; for a university must try to teach every subject, above the grade of its admission requirements, for which there is any demand;[91] and to teach it thoroughly enough to carry the advanced

87. Charles W. Eliot, *Annual Reports of the President and Treasurer of Harvard College 1884–1885* (Cambridge, MA: Harvard University Press, 1886), pp. 3–49. This annual report echoes much of the language in Eliot's statement to McCosh.

88. Charles W. Eliot, "Liberty in Education" (Feb. 1885), published in *Educational Reform: Essays and Addresses* (New York: Century, 1898), pp. 125–48. This address does not seem to have been published before 1898, although parts of it appeared in Eliot's tenth annual report for 1884–1885.

89. What are the different attributes of a college and a university implied by Eliot's view?

90. At Johns Hopkins University in February, 1884, Eliot maintained, "The general growth of knowledge and the rise of new literatures, arts, and sciences during the past two hundred and fifty years have made it necessary to define anew liberal education and hence to enlarge the signification of the bachelor of arts, which is the customary evidence of a liberal education." Charles W. Eliot, "What is a Liberal Education?" *Century Magazine* 28 (June 1884): 201–12. Compare the necessity of redefining liberal education in response to the appearance of new knowledge at this time with the situation in the high middle ages when the universities originated.

91. Is Eliot answering the question of whether a university should limit or select the studies to teach, by invoking the definition that a university does not limit or select instruction?

student to the confines of present knowledge and make him capable of original research. These are the only limits which a University can properly set to its instruction except indeed those rigorous limits which poverty imposes. The other alternative is selection or election of studies.

The elective system at Harvard has been sixty years in developing, and during fourteen of these years—from 1846 to 1860—the presidents and the majority of the faculty were not in favor of it; but they could find no way of escape from the dilemma which I have set before you.[92] They could not deliberately reduce the amount of instruction offered, and election of studies in some degree was the inevitable alternative. The practical question then is: At what age, and at what stage of his educational progress, can an American boy be offered free choice of studies? Or, in other words: At what age can an American boy best go to a free university?

Before answering this question I will ask your attention to four preliminary observations.

1. The European boy goes to free universities at various ages from seventeen to twenty; and the American boy is decidedly more mature and more capable of taking care of himself than the European boy of like age.

2. The change from school to university ought to be made as soon as it would be better for the youth to associate with older students under a discipline suited to their age, than with younger pupils under a discipline suited to theirs. . . . The wise decision is to withdraw him betimes from a discipline which he is outgrowing and put him under a discipline which he is to grow up to. . . .[93]

3. A young man is much affected by the expectations which his elders entertain of him. If they expect him to behave like a child, his lingering childishness will oftener rule his actions; if they expect him to behave like a man, his incipient manhood will oftener assert itself. . . .[94] The conservative argument is: a college must deal with the student as he is; he will be what he has been, namely, a thoughtless, aimless, lazy, and possibly vicious boy; therefore a policy which gives him liberty is impracticable.[95] The progressive argument is: adapt college policy to the best students and not to the worst; improve the policy, and in time the evil fruits of a mistaken policy will disappear. I would only urge at this point that a farseeing educational policy must be based upon potentialities as well as actualities, upon things which may be reasonably hoped for, planned, and aimed at, as well as upon things which are.

4. The condition of secondary education is an important factor in our problem.[96] It is desirable that the young men who are to enjoy university freedom should have already received at school a substantial training, in which the four great subdivisions of elementary knowledge—languages, history, mathematics, and natural science—were all adequately represented. . . .

---

92. How can Eliot's dilemma be evaded: that a university must teach everything and that a single student cannot learn everything?

93. Note Eliot's appeal to the best aspects or possibilities of a student's nature.

94. Compare the strength of this rationale for electivism to that of Eliot's negative rationale that universities cannot determine what to prescribe or his positive rationale that eighteen-year-olds are wise enough to choose their studies.

95. Compare James McCosh's argument below.

96. In the subsequent decade, Eliot turned his attention increasingly to the reform and standardization of secondary schools in order to provide a smoother articulation with the universities. Specifically, "Eliot is generally credited with the first public proposal for a standardizing examination board, in 1877," which led to the founding of the College Entrance Examination Board in 1900. Hugh Hawkins, *Between Harvard and America: The Educational Leadership of Charles W. Eliot* (New York: Oxford University Press, 1972), p. 178.

With these preliminary suggestions I proceed to answer the question, At what age can an American boy best go to a university where choice of studies is free? . . .

I believe the normal age under reasonably favorable conditions to be eighteen. In the first place, I hold that the temperament, physical constitution, mental aptitudes, and moral quality of a boy are all well determined by the time he is eighteen years old.[97] The potential man is already revealed. His capacities and incapacities will be perfectly visible to his teacher or to any observant and intimate friend, provided that his studies at school have been fairly representative. . . .

Secondly, at eighteen the American boy has passed the age when a compulsory external discipline is useful. Motives and inducements may be set vividly before him; he may be told that he must do so and so in order to win something which he desires or values; prizes and rewards near or remote may be held out to him; but he cannot be driven to any useful exercise of his mind.

Thirdly, a well-instructed youth of eighteen can select for himself—not for any other boy or for the fictitious universal boy, but for himself alone—a better course of study than any college faculty or any wise man who does not know him and his ancestors and his previous life, can possibly select for him.[98] In choosing his course he will naturally seek aid from teachers and friends who have intimate knowledge of him, and he will act under the dominion of that intense conservatism which fortunately actuates civilized man in the whole matter of education,[99] and under various other safeguards which nature and not arbitrary regulation provides. . . .[100]

Every youth of eighteen is an infinitely complex organization, the duplicate of which neither does nor ever will exist. His inherited traits are different from those of every other human being; his environment has been different from that of every other child; his passions, emotions, hopes, and desires were never before associated in any other creature just as they are in him; and his will-force is aroused, stimulated, exerted, and exhausted in ways wholly his own. . . . It is for the happiness of the individual and the benefit of society alike that these mental diversities should be cultivated, not suppressed. The individual enjoys most that intellectual labor for which he is most fit; and society is best served when every man's peculiar skill, faculty, or aptitude is developed and utilized to the highest possible degree. The presumption is, therefore, against uniformity in education and in favor of diversity at the earliest possible moment.[101]

What determines that moment? To my thinking, the limit of compulsory uniform instruction should be determined by the elementary quality and recognized universal utility of the subjects of such instruction. For instance, it is unquestionable that every child needs to know how to read, write, and, to a moderate extent, cipher. Therefore primary schools may have a uniform program. . . . Only the elements of two foreign languages and the elements of algebra and geometry can be said to be generally recognized as indispensable to the proper training of all young people who are privileged to

---

97. In selection #49, William R. Harper, who advocated the "junior college," maintained that "nature has marked out the great division in education work [at about age twenty], and the laws of nature may not be violated without injury." Compare McCosh's assessment of the "laws of nature" in selection #48.

98. Is Eliot arguing that youths will choose a *good* course of study, that they choose a *better* course than anyone else, or that *no one else* can do it for them?

99. Eliot seems to presume, therefore, that the actual exercise of electivism will be more conservative than the latitude provided by the policy at Harvard.

100. These safeguards are discussed below.

101. The argument for individuation in liberal education has proceeded far, since announced in selection #25 by Pier Paolo Vergerio, in response to the scholastic belief in the uniformity of education. Here the argument is bolstered by the doctrine that pursuit of individual interest contributes to the good of the whole, which likely reflects the strong influence that the utilitarian philosophy of John Stuart Mill had upon Eliot.

study beyond their seventeenth year. There is no consent as to the uniform desirableness of the elements of natural science, and there is much difference of opinion about the selection of the two foreign languages, the majority of educated people supposing two dead languages to be preferable, a minority thinking that living languages are permissible.

The limit of that elementary knowledge, of which by common consent all persons who are to be highly educated stand in need, is therefore a narrow one, easily to be reached and passed, under respectable instruction, by any youth of fair ability before he is eighteen years old. There, at least, ceases justifiable uniformity in education.[102] There, at least, election of studies should begin; and the safest guides to a wise choice will be the taste, inclination, and special capacity of each individual. When it comes to the choice of a profession, everybody knows that the only wisdom is to follow inclination. In my view, the only wisdom in determining those liberal studies which may be most profitably pursued after eighteen is to follow inclination.[103] Hence, it is only the individual youth who can select that course of study which will most profit him, because it will most interest him. The very fact of choice goes far to secure the cooperation of his will.

I have already intimated that there exist certain natural guides and safeguards for every youth who is called upon in a free university to choose his own studies. Let us see what these natural aids are. In the first place, he cannot help taking up a subject which he has already studied about where he left it off, and every new subject at the beginning and not at the middle. Secondly, many subjects taught at a university involve other subjects, which must therefore be studied first. Thus, no one can get far in physics without being familiar with trigonometry and analytic geometry; chemical analysis presupposes acquaintance with general chemistry, and paleontology acquaintance with botany and zoology; no one can study German philosophy to advantage unless he can read German,[104] and no student can profitably discuss practical economic problems until he has mastered the elementary principles of political economy. Every advanced course, whether in language, philosophy, history, mathematics, or science, presupposes acquaintance with some elementary course or courses.[105] Thirdly, there is a prevailing tendency on the part of every competent student to carry far any congenial subject once entered upon. To repress this most fortunate tendency is to make real scholarship impossible. So effective are these natural safeguards against fickleness and inconsecutiveness in the choice of studies, that artificial regulation is superfluous.

I give, in the next place, some results of my own observation upon the working of an elective system. . . . I have never known a student of any capacity to select for himself a set of studies covering four years which did not apparently possess more theoretical and practical merit for his case than the required curriculum of my college days. Every prescribed curriculum is necessarily elementary from beginning to end and very heterogeneous. Such is the press of subjects that no one subject can possibly be carried beyond its elements; no teacher, however learned and enthusiastic, can have any advanced pupils; and no scholar, however competent and eager, can make serious attainments in any single subject. Under an elective system the great majority of students use their liberty to pursue some subject or subjects with a reasonable degree of thoroughness. This concentration upon single lines

102. Does Eliot equate "justifiable" with "common consent?" Compare the justifications for educational uniformity given by James McCosh in selection #48 and Robert Hutchins in selection #58.

103. Eliot's optimistic faith in individual inclination likely stems from Ralph Waldo Emerson, who was "the philosopher on whom he most often relied. He kept a complete set of Emerson's works in both his Cambridge home and his summer home on Mount Desert Island." Hawkins, *Between Harvard and America*, p. 143.

104. Robert Hutchins disagrees in selection #58.

105. Might these two "natural aids" provide adequate justification for a virtually prescribed curriculum or, at least, for an elective system in which a student chooses among a set of prescribed programs of study?

develops advanced teaching, and results in a general raising of the level of instruction. Students who have decided taste for any particular subject wisely devote a large part of their time to that subject and its congeners.

Those who have already decided upon their profession wisely choose subjects which are related to, or underlie, their future professional studies; thus, the future physician will advantageously give a large share of his college course to French, German, chemistry, physics, and biology; while the future lawyer will study logic, ethics, history, political economy, and the use of English in argumentative writing and speaking. Among the thousands of individual college courses determined by the choice of the student in four successive years, which the records of Harvard College now preserve, it is rare to find one which does not exhibit an intelligible sequence of studies.[106] It should be understood in this connection that all the studies which are allowed to count toward the A.B. at Harvard are liberal or pure, no technical or professional studies being admissible. . . .[107]

Two common objections to an elective system shall next have our attention. The first is often put in the form of a query. Election of studies may be all very well for conscientious or ambitious students, or for those who have a strong taste for certain studies; but what becomes, under such a system, of the careless, indifferent, lazy boys who have no bent or intellectual ambition of any sort? I answer with a similar query: what became of such boys under the uniform compulsory system?[108] Did they get any profit to speak of under that regime? Not within my observation. It really does not make much difference what these unawakened minds dawdle with. There is, however, much more chance that such young men will get roused from their lethargy under an elective system than under a required. When they follow such faint promptings of desire as they feel, they at least escape the sense of grievance and repugnance which an arbitrary assignment to certain teachers and certain studies often creates.

An elective system does not mean liberty to do nothing. The most indifferent student must pass a certain number of examinations every year. He selects perhaps those subjects in which he thinks he can pass the best examinations with the smallest amount of labor; but in those very subjects the instruction will be on a higher plane than it can ever reach under a compulsory system, and he will get more benefit from them than he would from other subjects upon which he put the same amount of labor but attained less success. It is an important principle in education, from primary school to university, that the greater the visible attainment for a given amount of labor the better; and this rule applies quite as forcibly to a weak student as to a strong one. Feeble or inert students are considerably influenced in choosing their studies by the supposed quality of the teachers whom they will meet. As a rule they select the very teachers who are likely to have the most influence with them, being guided by traditions received from older students of their sort. It is the unanimous opinion of the teachers at Cambridge that more and better work is got from this class of students under the elective system than was under the required.

---

106. Eliot evidently felt vulnerable about this issue because, in his next annual report, he devoted considerable effort to proving the point by providing 22 pages of tables conveying the program of study of each of the 350 students in the classes of 1884 and 1885. He also had three "experts" analyze these 350 programs in order to determine "whether students free to choose their studies exhibit generally in their studies some intelligible plan and a reasonable degree of consistency." *Annual Reports of . . . Harvard College 1884–1885*, pp. 35, 9–30. The experts concluded "yes."

107. What does Eliot mean here by "liberal or pure?"

108. James McCosh puts the former query to Eliot; does McCosh respond to the latter?

Having said thus much about the effects of free choice of studies upon the unpromising student, I must add that the policy of an institution of education, of whatever grade, ought never to be determined by the needs of the least capable students; and that a university should aim at meeting the wants of the best students at any rate, and the wants of inferior students only so far as it can meet them without impairing the privileges of the best.[109] A uniform curriculum, by enacting superficiality and prohibiting thoroughness, distinctly sacrifices the best scholars to the average. Free choice of studies gives the young genius the fullest scope without impairing the chances of the drone and the dullard.

The second objection with which I wish to deal is this: free choice implies that there are no studies which are recognized as of supreme merit, so that every young man unquestionably ought to pursue them. Can this be? Is it possible that the accumulated wisdom of the race cannot prescribe with certainty the studies which will best develop the human mind in general between the ages of eighteen and twenty-two? At first it certainly seems strange that we have to answer no;[110] but when we reflect how very brief the acquaintance of the race has been with the great majority of the subjects which are now taught in a university the negative answer seems less surprising.[111]

Out of the two hundred courses of instruction which stand on the list of Harvard University this year it would be difficult to select twenty which could have been given at the beginning of this century with the illustrations, materials, and methods now considered essential to the educational quality of the courses. . . . A university, while not neglecting the ancient treasures of learning, has to keep a watchful eye upon the new fields of discovery, and has to invite its students to walk in new-made as well as in long-trodden paths. . . .[112]

It may fairly be presumed that the youth will find some strenuous exercise of his faculties in following the masters into any field which it taxed their utmost powers to explore and describe. To study the conquests of great minds in any field of knowledge must be good training for young minds of kindred tastes and powers.[113] That all branches of sound knowledge are of equal dignity and equal educational value for mature students is the only hopeful and tenable view in our day.[114] Long ago it be-

---

109. Is this the appropriate standard for educational policy?

110. Eliot apparently tripped on a double negative, for it seems that he should be answering "yes." His argument here against curricular prescription resembles that made against religious prescription by John Locke, who profoundly influenced the liberal tradition that shaped Eliot's views. In his *Letters on Toleration* (1689), Locke maintained that religious toleration (or electivism) is justified because there is no way to know which sect has the truth. Agnosticism implies the absence of a criterion of selection, which implies freedom of choice. As if in confirmation of this resemblance, Eliot later wrote, "The elective system is, in the first place, an outcome of the Protestant Reformation. In the next place, it is an outcome of the spirit of political liberty." Quoted in Hawkins, *Between Harvard and America*, p. 94. The Jesuit opponents of Eliot subsequently concurred that "electivism was Protestantism applied to education." "Alumni [of the Boston College] Pleased . . . Some Speakers at Banquet Denounce Electivism . . .," *The Boston Globe* (29 June 1900).

111. Compare the interpretation of this argument made by Robert Hutchins in selection #58: "The free elective system as Mr. Eliot introduced it at Harvard . . . amounted to a denial that there was content to education. Since there was no content to education, we might as well let students follow their own bent."

112. Has this fundamental principle of Eliot been expressed previously in the liberal arts tradition?

113. "Eliot was conservative in both his emphasis on mental discipline and his faith in the trained mind as the chief social utility of education. . . . When Eliot defended the modern subjects, he generally emphasized their contributions to the student's mental training, not to his knowledge." Hawkins, *Between Harvard and America*, p. 87.

came quite impossible for one mind to compass more than an insignificant fraction of the great sum of acquired knowledge. . . .[115]

As yet we have no university in America—only aspirants to that eminence. All the more important is it that we should understand the conditions under which a university can be developed—the most indispensable of which is freedom in choice of studies.

II. A university must give its students opportunity to win distinction in special subjects or lines of study.

The uniform curriculum led to a uniform degree, the first scholar and the last receiving the same diploma. A university cannot be developed on that plan. It must provide academic honors at graduation for distinguished attainments in single subjects.[116] These honors encourage students to push far on single lines; hence arises a demand for advanced instruction in all departments in which honors can be won, and this demand, taken in connection with the competition which naturally springs up between different departments, stimulates the teachers, who in turn stimulate their pupils. The elaborate directions given by each department to candidates for honors are so many definite pieces of advice to students who wish to specialize their work. It is an incidental advantage of the system that the organization of departments of instruction is promoted by it. The teachers of Latin, of history, or of philosophy, find it necessary to arrange their courses in orderly sequence, to compare their methods and their results, and to enrich and diversify as much as possible the instruction which they collectively offer.

Many European universities, but especially the English, offer honors or prizes, or both of these inducements for distinguished merit in specialties; and the highly valued degree of Ph.D. in Germany is a degree given for large attainments in one or two branches of knowledge, with mention of the specialty. The Harvard faculty announced their system of honors in 1866-67, and they certainly never passed a more effective piece of legislation. In 1879 they devised a lesser distinction at graduation called honorable mention, which has also worked very well. To get honors in any department ordinarily requires a solid year and a half's work; to get honorable mention requires about half that time. The important function of all such devices is to promote specialization of work and therefore to develop advanced instruction. It is unnecessary to point out how absolutely opposed to such a policy the uniform prescription of a considerable body of elementary studies must be.[117]

---

114. Is Eliot's egalitarian view of academic studies justified? Compare McCosh's analysis of "dilettanti courses" at Harvard?

115. How "long ago" was this impossibility recognized in the liberal arts tradition?

116. Eliot typically associates these two points: the opportunity to win academic honor and the opportunity to specialize. In contrast, Ignatius Loyola maintains (paras. 390, 478) in selection #26 that a system of academic honors can be combined with a uniform, even elementary, curriculum. Compare the view of Frank Aydelotte in selection #60.

117. Having argued that the intrinsic appeal of pursuing individual lines of study is a key justification for the elective system, is Eliot inconsistent in arguing that the inducement of academic honor is concomitant with specialization?

III. A university must permit its students,
in the main, to govern themselves.

It must have a large body of students, else many of its numerous courses of highly specialized instruction will find no hearers, and the students themselves will not feel that very wholesome influence which comes from observation of and contact with large numbers of young men from different nations, states, schools, families, sects, parties, and conditions of life. In these days a university is best placed in or near the seat of a considerable population; so that its officers and students can always enjoy the various refined pleasures, and feel alike the incitements and the restraints of a highly cultivated society. The universities of Rome, Paris, Vienna, Berlin, Leipzig, Christiania, Madrid, and Edinburgh forcibly illustrate both of these advantages.

These conditions make it practically impossible for a university to deal with its students on any principle of seclusion, either in a village or behind walls and bars. Fifteen hundred able-bodied young men living in buildings whose doors stand open night and day, or in scattered lodging-houses, cannot be mechanically protected from temptation at the university any more than at the homes from which they came. Their protection must be within them. They must find it in memory of home, in pure companionship, in hard work, in intellectual ambition, religious sentiment, and moral purpose. A sense of personal freedom and responsibility reinforces these protecting influences, while the existence of a supervising authority claiming large powers which it has no effective means of exercising weakens them.[118] The *in loco parentis* theory is an ancient fiction which ought no longer to deceive any body. No American college, wherever situated, possesses any method of discipline which avails for the suppression or exclusion of vice. The vicious student can find all means of indulgence in the smallest village, and the worst vices are the stillest.

It is a distinct advantage of the genuine university method that it does not pretend to maintain any parental or monastic discipline over its students, but frankly tells them that they must govern themselves. The moral purpose of a university's policy should be to train young men to self-control and self-reliance through liberty. It is not the business of a university to train men for those functions in which implicit obedience is of the first importance. On the contrary, it should train men for those occupations in which self-government, independence, and originating power are preeminently needed. Let no one imagine that a young man is in peculiar moral danger at an active and interesting university. Far from it. Such a university is the safest place in the world for young men who have anything in them—far safer than counting-room, shop, factory, farm, barrack, forecastle, or ranch. The student lives in a bracing atmosphere; books engage him; good companionships invite him; good occupations defend him; helpful friends surround him; pure ideals are held up before him; ambition spurs him; honor beckons him.

---

118. Does Eliot provide any positive reason for student self-governance apart from asserting that governance by the university is impossible?

48. James McCosh, *The New Departure in College Education* (1885)

INTRODUCTION

At the time of his debate with Eliot in 1885, James McCosh (1811–1894) was seventy-four years old. Born in Scotland, he entered Glasgow University at age thirteen and graduated in 1829. He then studied theology at Edinburgh University until 1833, and was ordained and licensed as a minister in the Established Church of Scotland. In 1843 McCosh left the Established Church to become one of the founding clergymen of the Free Church of Scotland, which he served as a clergyman until 1852.

In his studies of logic and philosophy, McCosh embraced the Common Sense philosophy of fellow Scotsman Thomas Reid, who had countered empiricist skepticism by arguing that one's mind at birth is not a clean slate.[119] Rather, Reid and McCosh considered it intuitive that inherent faculties of the mind exist and yield certain essential truths which everyone knows, including the existence of God and the divine influence upon human affairs. McCosh's writings attracted widespread notice, and in 1852 he was appointed to the chair of logic and metaphysics in Queen's College, Belfast, where he taught for sixteen years and wrote and published prolifically. Meanwhile, the College of New Jersey had been declining, and in 1868 the trustees, hoping to reinvigorate the institution, offered the presidency to McCosh due to his prominence as a Presbyterian churchman and theologian. Though initially reluctant to come to the United States, McCosh accepted the appointment and reinvigorated the college, improving its finances, physical plant, and recruitment of students. McCosh also exerted a progressive intellectual influence, upgrading the faculty and academic standards and proposing to the Trustees in 1885 that the College of New Jersey change its name to Princeton University.

McCosh's exchange with Eliot therefore manifests the complexity of the various positions taken on electivism and other changes in liberal education. McCosh "had to work painstakingly for reforms at Princeton, and often against entrenched opposition. But he eased the way for change partly by presenting to the outside world an image of conservatism." Notwithstanding McCosh's reforms, Princeton was facing severe problems by the time of his debate with Eliot. In fact, "the years 1882 through 1885 were the nadir of McCosh's administration." His strict moralism was sparking student unrest; the enrollment was declining once again; conservative trustees objected to his reforms and pointedly voted down his proposal to rename the college. In addition, "somewhat to his chagrin, McCosh found that in organizing a faculty that would pursue research and scholarship, he had hired men who did just that. His professors were manifestly uninterested in the wearisome task of overseeing students and guarding their moral behavior."[120]

Worn down by these problems and his own inability to compromise, McCosh offered his resignation in 1883, but the trustees refused to accept it, and he persevered for another five years. By 1886 the situation had begun to reverse, and McCosh was able to retire in 1888 confident in his accomplishment of building a strong foundation for future growth academically, financially, and administratively. He was named president emeritus and died in 1894 at the age of eighty-four. In the following year, the trustees voted to rename their institution Princeton University, reversing the decision they had made in response to McCosh's request a decade earlier.

---

119. See the note on Thomas Reid in the introduction to selection #37.

120. Quotations are from J. David Hoeveler, Jr., *James McCosh and the Scottish Intellectual Tradition: From Glasgow to Princeton* (Princeton: Princeton University Press, 1981), pp. 234–5, 322, 324.

SELECTION[121]

Freedom is the catch-word of this new departure. It is a precious and an attractive word. But, O Liberty! what crimes and cruelties have been perpetrated in thy name! It is a bid for popularity.[122] An entering freshman will be apt to cheer when he hears the prospect is so pleasant. The leader in this departure will have many followers. The student infers from the language that he can study what he pleases. I can tell you what he will possibly or probably choose. Those who are in the secrets of colleges know how skillful certain students are in choosing their subjects. They can choose the branches which will cost them least study, and put themselves under the popular professors who give them the highest grades with the least labor. . . .[123] I am for freedom quite as much as Dr. Eliot is, but it is for freedom regulated by law. I am for liberty but not licentiousness which always ends in servitude.

I am to follow the President of Harvard in the three roads which he has taken; placing positions of mine face to face with his:

I. Freedom in Choosing Studies.
II. Freedom in Choosing Specialties.
III. Freedom in Government.

I. Freedom in Choosing Studies.

I am for freedom, but it must be within carefully defined limits. First, a young man should be free to enter a university or not to enter it. He is to be free to choose his department in that university, say Law or Medicine, or the Academic terminating in the bachelor or master's degree.[124] But, having made his choice, is he to have all possible freedom ever after? At this point the most liberal advocate of liberty will be obliged to tell the student, "We are now required to lay some restraints upon you," and the youth finds his liberty is at an end. He has to take certain studies and give a certain amount of time to them, say, according to the Harvard model, to select four topics.

He goes in for medicine: he may make his quartet physical geography, which tells what climate is; and art, which teaches us to paint the human frame; and music, which improves the voice; and lectures on the drama, which show us how to assume noble attitudes. These seem more agreeable to him than anatomy and physiology, than surgery and materia medica, which present corpses and unpleasant odors. I tell you that though this youth should get a diploma written on parchment, I would not, however ill, call him in to prescribe to me, as I might not be quite sure whether his medicines would kill or cure me. Or the intention of the youth is engineering in order to make or drive a steam engine; and he does not take mathematics, or mechanics, or graphics, or geodesy; but as unlimited choice is given him, he prefers drawing and field work when the weather is fine, and two departments of gymnastics—now so well taught in our colleges—namely, boxing and wrestling. I tell you I am not to travel by the railway he has constructed.

---

121. James McCosh, *The New Departure in College Education, Being a Reply to President Eliot's Defense of It* (New York: Charles Scribner's Sons, 1885). The text of the speech was revised for publication; a verbatim report of the actual speech is included in William M. Sloane, ed., *The Life of James McCosh* (New York: Charles Scribner's Sons, 1896), pp. 199n–202n.

122. Does Eliot's reliance upon the market of student choices to determine course offerings and teaching method amount to "a bid for popularity?"

123. Note McCosh's focus on the potential for abusing freedom of choice.

124. McCosh's viewing professional degree courses as alternatives to the liberal arts course would have disturbed Eliot who endeavored to establish the B.A. as a prerequisite to the professional degrees.

But he has a higher aim: he is to take a course in the liberal arts and expects a master's degree; but Greek and mathematics and physics and mental philosophy are all old and waxing older, and he takes French to enable him to travel in Europe, and lectures on Goethe to make him a German scholar, and a pictorial history of the age of Louis XIV and of the theater in ancient and modern times. This is a good year's work, and he can take a like course in each of the four years; and if he be in Yale or Princeton College he will in spring and fall substitute baseball and football,[125] and exhibit feats more wonderful than were ever performed in the two classical countries, Greece and Rome, at their famous Olympian Games and bull fights.

I have presented this designedly rude picture to show that there must be some limits put to the freedom of choice in studies. The able leader of the new departure, with the responsibilities of a great college upon him, and the frank and honest gentleman who has such a dread of a Fetish—the creature of his own imagination[126]—will be ready to admit that in every department of a university there should be a well considered and a well devised curriculum of study. It is one of the highest and most important functions of the governing bodies to construct such a scheme. It should have in it two essential powers or properties.

First, there should be branches required of all students who pursue the full course and seek a degree. This is done in such departments as engineering and medicine and should be done in [liberal] arts.[127] The obligatory branches should be wisely selected. They should all be fitted to enlarge or refine the mind. They should be fundamental, as forming the basis on which other knowledge is built. They should be disciplinary as training the mind for further pursuits. Most of them should have stood the test of time and reared scholars in ages past. There will be found to be a wonderful agreement among educated men of high tastes as to what these should be.

There should be included in them the eight studies on which examinations are held in order to [gain] entrance into Harvard College. These are: 1, English; 2, Greek; 3, Latin; 4, German; 5, French; 6, history; 7, mathematics; 8, physical science. This is the scheme of preparatory studies just issued by Harvard. It seems to me to require too much from our schools. It will prevent many teachers who have hitherto sent students to college from doing so any more. Teachers in smaller towns and country districts will have to look to this. If the scheme is carried out, fewer young men will come up to our colleges from such places. They will find that they cannot get French and German and physical apparatus in the schools available to them. Some of the branches had better be reserved for college, where they will be taught more effectively. . . .[128]

---

125. These sports were emerging as a major diversion of college students.

126. McCosh is referring to Charles F. Adams, Jr., (1835–1915), brother of the historian and author Henry Adams. Charles served on the Harvard Board of Overseers (1882–1906) and as president of the Union Pacific Railroad, but never held a regular academic appointment. Shortly after joining the Overseers and before McCosh's speech, Charles had written a notorious article criticizing the allegiance to the classical curriculum: "A College Fetish: An Address Delivered before the Harvard Chapter of the Phi Beta Kappa Society, June 28, 1883" (Boston: Lee and Shepard, 1883).

127. Is McCosh's analogy between professional education and the "higher" liberal arts course sound? Given that electivism in professional studies might result in graduating incompetent professionals, does it follow that electivism in liberal arts might yield incompetent graduates? What is incompetence in the liberal arts?

128. Do McCosh and Eliot differ not on electivism, but on whether obligatory studies can be completed in secondary school?

Education is essentially the training of the mind—as the [Latin] word *educare* denotes—the drawing forth of the faculties which God has given us.[129] This it should especially be in a university—in a *Studium Generale*, as it used to be called. The powers of mind are numerous and varied: the senses, the memory, the fancy, judgment, reasoning, conscience, the feelings, the will, the mathematical, the metaphysical, the mechanical, the poetical, the prosaic (quite as useful as any);[130] and all these should be cultivated, the studies necessary to do so should be provided, and the student required so far to attend to them, that the young man by exercise may know what powers he has and the mental frame be fully developed.

To accomplish this end the degrees of Bachelor of Arts and of Master of Arts were instituted. These titles have acquired a meaning. For centuries past tens of thousands of eager youths have been yearly seeking for them and the attainments implied in them. True, the standard adopted in some colleges has been low: some who have got the diploma could not read the Latin in which it is written. Still, it has a certain prestige and a considerable attractive power. It indicates as to the great body of those who possess it, that they have some acquaintance with elevated themes, that in short they have some culture. I do not wish to have this stimulus withdrawn. I have been laboring for the last twenty-two years to elevate the requirements for the degree. But let it retain its meaning and carry out its meaning thoroughly. Let it be an evidence that the possessor of it has some knowledge of literature, science, and philosophy.

I have no objection that other degrees be instituted, such as Bachelor of Literature, Bachelor of Science; but only on one condition, that examinations be deep, that they be rigid, that they imply a knowledge of the principles as well as of the details of the branches taught, that they cultivate the mind and elevate the tastes as well as fit men for professions. But let us retain in the meanwhile the old bachelor and master degrees, only putting a new life into them. They should not be given to one who knows merely English and German, or one who knows merely chemistry and physics, still less to one who knows merely music and painting. Eminence in these has no right to assume, or in fact steal, the old title. Let each kind of degree have its own meaning, and people will value it accordingly. But let A.B. and A.M. abide to attract youths to high general scholarship.[131]

Under this academic degree I would allow a certain amount of choice of studies, such as could not be tolerated in professional departments, as law or medicine.[132] But there are branches which no candidate for the degree should be allowed to avoid. There should be English, which I agree with President Eliot in regarding as about the most essential of all branches, it being taught in a scientific manner. There should be modern languages, but there should also be classic. A taste and a style are produced by the study of the Greek and Latin with their literatures which are expressively called *classic*. It may be difficult to define, but we all feel the charm of it. If we lose this there is nothing in what is called our modern education to make up for the loss.

President Eliot has a high opinion of German universities, but the eminent men in their greatest university, that of Berlin, have testified that a far higher training is given in the classical *gymnasia*

129. These lines echo McCosh's inaugural address: "What is the Idea or Final Cause of University Teaching?" in *Inauguration of James McCosh, D.D. LL.D., as President of the College of New Jersey October 27, 1868* (New York: Robert Carter, 1868), p. 40.

130. Various lists of inherent mental powers, or faculties, were proffered by advocates of the Common Sense philosophy.

131. McCosh clearly disagrees with Eliot's view that "That all branches of sound knowledge are of equal dignity and equal educational value." What are McCosh's criteria for better, higher studies?

132. McCosh now rejects the analogy between professional and liberal fields that was the basis of his argument against electivism at the outset.

than in the scientific *real schule*. There should be physical science, but there should also be mental and moral science required of all. In knowing other things our young men should be taught to know themselves. When our students are instructed only in matter, they are apt to conclude that there is nothing but matter. Our colleges should save our promising youths, the hope of the coming age and ages, from materialism with its degrading consequences. We must show them that man has a soul with lofty powers of reason and conscience and free will, which make him immortal and enable him so far to penetrate the secrets of nature, and by which he can rise to the knowledge of God.

We in Princeton believe in a Trinity of studies:[133] in language and literature, in science, and in philosophy. Every educated man should know so much of each of these. Without this, man's varied faculties are not trained, his nature is not fully developed and may become malformed.

A college should give what is best to its students, and it should not tempt them to what is lower when the higher can be had. Harvard boasts that it gives two hundred choices to its students, younger and older.[134] I confess that I have had some difficulty in understanding her catalog. I would rather study the whole cosmos. [The catalog] has a great many perplexities, which I can compare only to the cycles, epicycles, eccentricities of the old astronomy, so much more complex than that of Newton. An examination of students upon it would be a better test of a clear head than some of their subjects, such as "French Plays and Novels." As I understand it, one seeking a degree may, in his free will, choose the following course:

In sophomore year
1. French Literature of the Seventeenth Century
2. Medieval and Modern European History
3. Elementary Course in Fine Art, with collateral instruction in Water-coloring
4. Counterpoint (in music)

In junior year
1. French Literature of the Eighteenth Century
2. Early Medieval History
3. Botany
4. History of Music

The senior year
1. French Literature of the Nineteenth Century
2. Elementary Spanish
3. Greek Art
4. Free Thematic Music[135]

There are twenty such dilettanti courses which may be taken in Harvard. I cannot allow that this is an advance in scholarship.[136] If this be the modern education, I hold that the old is better. I would rather send a young man in whom I was interested to one of the old-fashioned colleges of the country, where he would be constrained to study Latin, Greek, mathematics, rhetoric, physics, logic, ethics, and polit-

---

133. Given the discussion in the paragraph above, might this be a jibe against Eliot's Unitarianism?

134. McCosh notes, "In Princeton we have nearly all the branches taught in Harvard, but we do not subdivide and scatter them as they do; we put them under compacter heads."

135. McCosh notes, "In the debate, we were told that this is a deep study; [if so,] then the degree of Master of Music (M.M.) should be given to it, but not M.A."

136. While McCosh considered these "dilettanti courses," Eliot regarded the introduction of specialized courses, such as medieval history taught by recently appointed Assistant Professor Henry Adams (1838–1918), as a great intellectual advance in the curriculum. See Henry Adams, *The Education* (1918; Boston: Houghton Mifflin, 1961), pp. 291–305. What are McCosh's criteria for scholarly rigor?

ical economy; and I am persuaded that his mind would thereby be better trained and he himself prepared to do higher and more important work in life. From the close of freshman year on, it is perfectly practicable for a student to pass through Harvard and receive the degree of Bachelor of Arts, without taking any course in Latin, Greek, mathematics, chemistry, physics, astronomy, geology, logic, psychology, ethics, political economy, German, or even English! . . .[137]

Secondly. It should be an essential feature of the course for a degree, that the attendance of the student on lectures and recitation should be obligatory. This is a very important matter. The student may have freedom in his choice, but having made his election he should be bound to attend on the instruction imparted. He should not be allowed to attend the one day and stay away the next. A professor should not be subjected to the disadvantage of only a portion of his students, say a half or a third, being present at any one lecture and of the students who attend not being the same continuously.[138] Parents living far away from the college-seat should have some security that their sons professing to be at college are not all the winter skating on the ice or shooting canvasback-ducks on Chesapeake Bay.

But it is said that if a student can stand an examination, it is no matter where he gets his knowledge. There is an enormous fallacy lurking here. I admit that a youth may make himself a scholar without being at a college or submitting to its examinations. But if he goes to college let him take all its advantages. One of these is to be placed under a continuous course of instruction in weekly, almost daily, intercourse with his professors, keeping him at his work and encouraging him in it. It is thus that the academic taste, thus that the student spirit with its hard work is created and fostered.

I have had thorough means of becoming acquainted with those systems in which there is no required attendance; and I testify that they do not tend to train high scholars. Everything depending on a final examination, the student is sure to be tempted to what is called *cramming*. A student once told me what this led to in his own experience. In five of the branches taught to his class, he spread his daily studies over the year; but in one he trusted to cramming. I said to him, "Tell me honestly, what is the issue?" He answered, "In the five branches I remember everything and could stand another examination to-day, but in the one—it happened to be botany—it is only four weeks since I was examined on it, but my mind is blank on the whole subject."

II. Specialties in Study.

Men have special talents, and so they should have special studies provided for them. They are to have special vocations in life, and college youth should so far be prepared for them. Every student should have obligatory studies, but he should also be allowed elective studies. The branches of knowledge are now so numerous and literature is so wide and varied, that no one can master it all; should he try to do so, he would only be "a jack of all trades and a master of none."

The student should have two kinds of electives provided for him. He may be allowed to take subjects which could not be required of all, such, for example, as Sanskrit, Anglo-Saxon, the Semitic tongues, and in science, histology and physical geography. No college should make these obligatory, and yet considerable numbers of students would prize them much and get great benefit from them, to fit

---

137. "The greatest flaw in the elective program at Harvard, McCosh proclaimed, was the very fact that it permitted students to avoid the new and necessary elements of learning that Eliot claimed to cherish." Hoeveler, *James McCosh and the Scottish Intellectual Tradition,* p. 236.

138. Eliot, who gave an unusual amount of detailed attention to the practice of instruction, does not seem to consider these deleterious effects of inconsistent individual attendance on the corporate instruction.

them for their farther study and life-work. Or, the student, after taking certain elementary branches, should have higher forms of the same provided for him and be encouraged to take them. Of all the rudimentary branches or cardinal studies, there should be a course or courses required of all in order to make them educated gentlemen, but there should be advanced courses—electives to produce high scholars in all branches, literary, linguistic, scientific, philosophic. . . .[139]

I may here point out the evils little noticed arising from a boy having too many choices; they say two hundred in Harvard. I believe that comparatively few young men know what their powers are when they enter college. Many do not yet know what their undeveloped facilities are; quite as many imagine that they have talents which they do not possess. Fatal mistakes may arise from a youth of sixteen or eighteen committing himself to a narrow gauge line of study, and he finds when it is too late that he should have taken a broader road. . . . A like result may follow from other unfortunate choices, as we say, from young men "mistaking their trade." . . .[140]

III. Self Government.[141]

I hold that in a college, as in a country, there should be government; there should be care over the students, with inducements to good conduct and temptations removed and restraints on vice. There should be moral teaching; I believe also religious teaching—the rights of conscience being always carefully preserved. But one part of this instruction should be to inculcate independence: independence in thinking, independence in action and self-control. The student should be taught to think for himself, to act for himself. If he does not acquire this spirit, no external authority will be able to guide and restrain him. I abhor the plan of secretly watching students, of peeping through windows at night, and listening through keyholes. Under the *spy* system, the students will always beat their tutors. The tricky fellows will escape, while only the simple will be caught.

But is there, therefore, to be no moral teaching, no restraint on conduct? Are students to be allured away from their homes, hundreds and thousands of miles away, from California, Oregon, and Florida to our eastern colleges, and there do as they please—to spend their evenings according to their inclinations, to keep no Sabbaths, and all the while get no advice, no warning from the college authorities? They see a student going into a liquor store, a dancing saloon, a low theater, a gambling-house. Are

---

139. McCosh notes, "But one in ten, or one in five, who have acquired a taste for more should be encouraged to remain in college, to take post-graduate courses, and devote themselves to special studies. We encourage this in Princeton by seven or eight endowed fellowships, and have always 30, 40, or 50 post-graduate students. In this way we hope to rear scholars."

140. As in his comments above about "teachers in smaller towns and country districts," McCosh seems more aware than Eliot of the socio-economic implications of Harvard's reforms. He notes, "President Eliot would not have students enter college till they are eighteen years of age. If this be carried out, it is evident that we shall have fewer young men taking a college education. A large number cannot afford to continue till twenty-five before they earn any money: not entering college till eighteen, continuing three or four years, and spending [an]other three years in learning a profession. In many cases many young men might be ready to enter college at sixteen, graduate at twenty, and then learn their professions. This would suit the great body of students."

141. Student conduct was much discussed at the time. See the forum of opinions by President Samuel C. Bartlett of Dartmouth College, President James B. Angell of the University of Michigan, Professor N. S. Shaler of Harvard University, President Charles K. Adams of Cornell University, President William D. Hyde of Bowdoin College, Principal J. William Dawson of McGill University, and President Horace Davis of the University of California. "Discipline in American Colleges," *North American Review* 392 (1889): 1–29.

they to do nothing? Are they precluded from doing anything? . . .[142] But my creed is, prevention is better than punishment. Surely, if we have the right to dismiss and expel (I never expelled a student), we have the liberty to instruct, to advise, to remonstrate, nay, to discipline. . . . I believe nine-tenths of the cases of discipline I have administered have ended in the reformation of the offender. I have been gratified by many fathers and mothers thanking me for saving their sons from ruin.[143] Scores of graduates, when they meet me, have said, "I thank you for that sharp rebuke you gave me; you gave it heartily, and I was irritated at the time, but now I thank you as heartily, for I was arrested thereby when rushing into folly."

It is time that fathers and mothers should know what it is proposed to do with their sons at college. The college authorities are in no way to interfere with them. They are to teach them music and art, and French plays and novels, but there is no course in the Scriptures, in their poetry, their morality, their spirituality. The President of Harvard recommends that all colleges should be in great cities. Students are to be placed in the midst of saloons, and gambling-houses, and temples of Venus; but meanwhile no officer of the college is to preach to them, to deal with them.

Suppose that under temptation the son falls. I can conceive a father saying to the head of the institution, "I sent my son to you believing that man is made in the image of God, you taught him that he is an upper brute, and he has certainly become so; I sent him to you pure, and last night he was carried to my door drunk. Curse ye this college; I 'curse ye bitterly,' [*Judges* 5: 23] for you took no pains to allure him to good, to admonish, to pray for him." I was once addressed by a mother in very nearly these words. I was able to show that her son had come to us a polluted boy from an ungodly school, and that we had dealt with him kindly, warned him solemnly, disciplined him, given notice of his conduct to his mother, and prayed for him. Had I not been able to say this conscientiously, I believe I would that day have given my resignation of the office I hold, and retired to a wilderness to take charge of myself, feeling that I was not competent to take care of others. . . .

Tell it not in the lands whence our pious fathers came that the college whose motto is *Pro Christo et Eccelesia* teaches no religion to its pupils.[144] Tell it not in Berlin or Oxford that the once most illustrious university in America no longer requires its graduates to know the most perfect language, the grandest literature, the most elevated thinking of all antiquity. Tell it not in Paris, tell it not in Cambridge in England, tell it not in Dublin, that Cambridge in America does not make mathematics obligatory on its students. Let not Edinburgh and Scotland and the Puritans in England know that a student may pass through the once Puritan college of America without having taken a single class of philosophy or a lesson in religion. But whatever others may do, *I say, I say*, let Europe know in all its universities--I wish my voice could reach them all--that in a distinguished college in America, a graduate need no longer take what the ages have esteemed the highest department of learning; and I believe that such an expression of feeling will be called forth, that if we cannot avert the evil in Harvard, we may arrest it in the other colleges of the country.

---

142. McCosh's view of students' choices reflects his experience at Princeton, where "Indiscipline among students was the bane of his administration. . . . Nonetheless, overreaction [by McCosh] was often the rule." Hoeveler, *James McCosh*, pp. 323–4.

143. Here is the policy of *in loco parentis* that Eliot considers "an ancient fiction."

144. McCosh was ironically prescient. In 1642 the Harvard board of governors apparently adopted the motto *Veritas*, but in 1693 the motto *Christo et Eccelesiae* was officially incorporated into the College seal. In 1836 the 1642 motto was rediscovered in the Harvard archives, and in 1843 a secularizing impulse led to replacing *Christo et Eccelesiae* with *Veritas*. The 1843 change was reversed in 1848 on grounds of being unchristian. In the months following McCosh's speech in 1885, a successful effort was initiated to adopt *Veritas* as the Harvard motto. Samuel Eliot Morison, *The Founding of Harvard College* (Cambridge: Harvard University Press, 1935), pp. 329-332.

Role of the Liberal Arts College

49. William R. Harper, "The Situation of the Small College" (1900)

INTRODUCTION

The renaming of the College of New Jersey as Princeton University in 1896 signified a national shift in student enrollment. "In 1890 the majority of students attended denominational colleges, the number of these colleges was still growing, and the majority of men and women students attended single-sex colleges. By 1900 none of this would still be true. The rise of universities and the pressures of standardization displaced the traditional American college from its accustomed central role."[145] Leading up to that turning point, the colleges had encountered increasing resistance from the university builders. Purely in numerical terms, the colleges' "exponential growth during the 1850s and 1860s gave way to decelerating growth in the following decades, and ceased altogether after 1893— the peak year for traditional colleges."[146] This deceleration inevitably influenced the meaning and curriculum of the liberal arts in as much as "the American college has been the exponent or the embodiment of the idea of liberal education," as the president of Johns Hopkins University observed in 1892.[147] One of the most provocative analyses of the liberal arts college was presented by the president of the University of Chicago, William Rainey Harper (1856–1906), in a speech before the National Education Association on a sultry day in Charleston, South Carolina, in July 1900.

Born to Scottish-Irish Presbyterian parents in Ohio, Harper entered Muskingum College at the age of ten and graduated four years later, presenting the salutatory oration in Hebrew, his future academic specialty. After working in his parents' dry goods store and studying languages on his own for a few years, he began graduate study at Yale University in 1873, and received his Ph.D. two years later at the age of eighteen, having completed a dissertation entitled "A Comparative Study of the Prepositions in Latin, Greek, Sanskrit, and Gothic."

After teaching briefly at Masonic College in Tennessee and Denison University in Ohio, Harper accepted an appointment in 1879 at Baptist Union Theological Seminary in Chicago to pursue his special interest in teaching Semitic languages. Undertaking this work with boundless energy, Harper earned the B.D. degree, founded two major journals in Hebrew studies, published textbooks, and established a network of correspondence and summer courses. Through this pedagogical work, he developed the inductive system of teaching languages that made him famous.[148] In 1886 Harper accepted a professorship at Yale rather than the presidency of the moribund University of Chicago. In New Haven he worked feverishly and achieved a national reputation as a teacher, lecturer, editor, and president of various learned societies.

---

145. Roger L. Geiger, "The Era of Multipurpose Colleges in American Higher Education, 1850 to 1890," *History of Higher Education Annual* 15 (1995): 51. New colleges were being founded largely due to two causes— "geographic extension largely in the West and denominational elaboration elsewhere," although "most of the foundings of the 1880s and 1890s were due to geographical extension—principally in the Dakotas (7 colleges), Texas (10), Kansas (9), Nebraska (6), Missouri (7), and Florida (5)." (p. 59.)

146. Geiger, "The Era of Multipurpose Colleges," p. 56.

147. Daniel C. Gilman, "Is It Worthwhile to Uphold Any Longer the Idea of Liberal Education?" *Educational Review* 3 (1892): 109.

148. See William R. Harper and William E. Waters, *An Inductive Greek Method* (New York: American Book, 1888).

In 1891 Harper accepted an offer to become president of the University of Chicago, which was being revitalized through the substantial financial backing of industrialist John D. Rockefeller (1839–1937). From the time of its opening in 1892, the new University of Chicago was personally associated with Harper, who characteristically participated in every aspect of its development: recruiting a brilliant faculty, building the library, defending its intellectual freedom, and advancing its stature and endowment.

In particular, he championed the strategy pursued by university builders of splitting the college into two initial years of study devoted to a range of subjects, like the German *gymnasia* and two subsequent years preparing for specialized, graduate study. Accordingly, Harper divided the four-year college into a two-year "junior" and a two-year "senior" college. By the early 1900s, however, the curriculum of Harper's junior college had been reshaped to fit the expectations of the graduate departments. This outcome intensified Harper's ambivalence about the future of the liberal arts college, that had already been voiced in selection #49. To survive, colleges had to adapt to themselves to the new regime of the university, he believed; and the separation of the two-year or junior college, as it was coming to be called, provided the best strategy for survival. Neither Harper nor Daniel C. Gilman could envision any "superior advantages of the small college" over the university that did not rest "upon grounds which are in large measure fancied or sentimental," as Harper states below.

By the late 1890s, his frenetic pace was beginning to damage his health. In 1904 his appendix was removed, and doctors discovered a cancerous tumor. Though he taught a number of large classes in the summer of 1905, Harper never recovered his full strength, and died in January 1906 in Chicago.

SELECTION[149]

In my opinion the two most serious problems of education requiring solution within the next quarter of a century are, first, the problem of rural schools, which fall within the domain of lower education; and, secondly, the problem of the small college, which lies within the domain of higher education.

This second problem, which forms the subject of our consideration here, is at the same time serious and delicate; serious, because the greatest interests, both material and spiritual, are at stake; delicate, because there are involved special and peculiar questions of privilege and right. The study of the problem is a difficult one, because it deals with data insufficiently gathered and not yet properly tabulated;[150] because, also, the territory covered is so vast and includes sections so differently situated. . . . We shall consider:

    I. Some factors which would seem to guarantee the life and the growth of the smaller institutions.

    II. Some factors which will be found to stand in the way of such development.

    III. Some changes affecting the small colleges which are to be expected and which are to be desired.

I.

Let us notice, first of all, the widely prevailing belief that the smaller institution has certain decided advantages over the larger in the character of the results produced. This belief is entertained so strongly and in so many quarters that, whether true or false, it furnishes a substantial element of strength to the cause of the smaller college. . . .

---

149. William R. Harper, "The Situation of the Small College" (1900), in *The Trend in Higher Education in America* (Chicago: University of Chicago Press, 1905), pp. 349–89.

150. Note Harper's repeated appeals to data, or lack of it, in presenting his views.

The student of the small college, it is urged, has an advantage in that he comes into closer contact with the officers of the faculty. It is certainly true, other things being equal, that the student who knows his instructor intimately and is himself intimately known by him, has a much greater chance of achieving satisfactory results than the student who has little or no personal contact with his instructor. But here two things should be noted.

First, is it a fact that in the larger institutions the student comes into less vital touch with his teachers? A study of this question, extending over several years, has convinced me that the student in the larger institutions not only comes into relationship with a greater number of instructors, but also touches in the closest possible way as many of this number, as he would have touched in the smaller college. And, second, is it a question merely of close contact, or of receiving that deep incitement which stirs the soul to its very depths? I have known instructors in both large and small institutions, close touch with whom would deaden rather than quicken any higher life; and it is only fair to say that the number of such is as great proportionately in the small as in the larger institution.

Again, the student of the small college, it is urged, has great advantages, especially in the earlier college years, because in most cases he does his work under men who have the rank of professor, while in the larger institutions he is turned over to young men who are only tutors or instructors. And yet it should be remembered that these same tutors and instructors if they were in the smaller institutions, would enjoy the rank of professor. I have in mind a university in which every man who is ranked as an assistant professor, instructor, or tutor has been offered a full professorship in a small college, and several of them the presidency of such an institution.

Further, the student of the small college, it is urged, has greater opportunity to develop responsibility; the number of students being small, each one stands out more definitely and receives greater recognition, while, at the same time, he actually counts for more in the various activities of the college life. It should be remembered, however, that the incentives to excel and the number of activities which present themselves to student ambition increase even more rapidly than the proportionate increase in numbers; and that these opportunities are higher in character and more varied in proportion to the horizon of those who find themselves in this or that environment. . . .

The point I wish to present is this: The belief in the superior advantages of the small college has taken so strong a hold upon the minds of men in general that, although it rests upon grounds which are in large measure fancied or sentimental,[151] it will serve as a strong factor in assisting to maintain and to advance the interests of the smaller as against those of the larger institutions.

A second factor which has helped the smaller institutions in the past, and one which will continue to render strong assistance, is that feeling, sometimes of awe and almost fear, at other times of jealousy and hostility, which is invariably aroused in the minds of many toward an institution that has grown large and powerful. The small college is loved and cherished, in most cases, just because it *is* small and weak; while the larger institution is hated and opposed because it is powerful. This has been the history of every institution that has become great.[152] It is the history of nearly every one of the state universities in the western states. It is the feeling with which the smaller towns or cities in a state regard the one great city of a particular region. . . .

---

151. What is Harper's evidence rebutting this "sentiment"?

152. Harper is apparently invoking the ideology of the industrialists who had arisen in the late nineteenth century and were beginning to patronize universities, including the patron of the University of Chicago, John D. Rockefeller. The influence of that ideology was reaching its apex, as described in the classic critique appearing a few decades later: Matthew Josephson, *The Robber Barons: The Great American Capitalists, 1861–1901* (New York: Harcourt, Brace, 1934).

Closely associated with this is another factor, which, through all time, will stand arrayed on the side of the small college—a strong and noble phalanx of supporters. I mean the faculty and the alumni of the institution. . . .

Another factor in the preservation and upbuilding of the small college—a factor the potency of which will increase with passing decades—is the desire of men who have been successful in accumulating wealth to do something with that wealth which will *be constructive, creative.* . . . In every section of the country, and in almost every county of every state, there are men who are disposed to use their means for the improvement of the particular locality in which their wealth has been accumulated. It is impossible to interest such men in any kind of benevolent work at a distance. . . . The small college furnishes an opportunity for these men, within their own circle, to do a work for the cause of higher education—a cause which has a peculiar fascination for many minds, in as much as it is a constructive and creative work. . . .[153]

Still another guaranty for the future of the institution under consideration is the fact that whatever may be said of the relative advantages of the small and the large institution for the average young man or woman, it cannot be denied that the small college is particularly adapted to the needs of many an individual. And yet I do not mean to say that these individuals are below the average; for many of them certainly are far above the average. I have in mind young men and women of certain peculiar temperaments, as well as those in whose case the transition from a certain mode of life to the more free and liberal atmosphere of the larger institution—the university—would prove to be too sudden. . .

Perhaps it is at this point that I may mention the economic side of student life, which controls, far more generally than perhaps we might suppose, the possibilities of higher education. . . .[154] It is evident that in large institutions the expense is more considerable than in the smaller. It is true that all of the larger universities furnish aid to many students, and that in general any deserving student is able to secure help sufficient to assist him in completing his work; but many men are unwilling to accept such assistance. Many have neither the courage nor the cleverness to secure it;[155] and if all who desire an education were to make application to the larger institutions, the funds at the command of those institutions would prove sadly inadequate. It is only because the smaller institutions, scattered throughout the country, are able to do the work for the young man or woman[156] of moderate means, that the larger institutions can, in any satisfactory way, meet the demand which is made upon them.

Only a few comparatively can gather together so large a sum as five or six hundred dollars a year for a course of college study, and yet such a sum, in most of our larger institutions, is quite small in

---

153. Bolstered by the proselytizing of industrialist Andrew Carnegie (1835–1919) in his famous essay "The Gospel of Wealth" (1889) and doubtlessly drawing upon his own experience in soliciting funds for the University of Chicago, Harper implies that it takes a "large" philanthropist to give to a "large" university. Many industrialists responded to this flattering challenge and contributed millions to their namesake universities in the closing decades of the nineteenth century: Cornelius Vanderbilt, Paul Tulane, Jonas Clark, John Creighton, Ezra Cornell, Benjamin and James Duke, Anthony Drexel, George Peabody, Johns Hopkins, William Rice, and Leland Stanford. Others gave without memorializing their name: Asa Chandler (Emory), Seth Low (Columbia), John Green (Princeton), Henry Sage (Cornell), Jay Gould (New York University), Robert Brookings (Washington University), John D. Rockefeller (Chicago).

154. As evident throughout this address, Harper, like Charles W. Eliot, attended carefully to the financial implications of his educational beliefs and plans.

155. Hence, the fittest students survive, and the "larger" students survive in the larger institutions.

156. Harper's repeated acknowledgment of providing liberal education for women indicates the burgeoning support among university leaders at the end of the nineteenth century.

view of the many and varied demands made upon the student. There must be institutions in which the man who can command only two or three hundred dollars a year may find help and guidance in his pursuit of higher education. The larger institutions, located in many cases where rents and food are more expensive, and where the demands of society compel a style of living which would not be considered necessary elsewhere, are prohibitive to the sons and daughters of families whose annual income is fifteen hundred dollars or less. . . .[157] The future of the small college is, therefore, absolutely assured. . . .

It is to be noted still further that educational tradition is peculiarly conservative. The tradition in the United States, established two and one half centuries ago, and continuing almost without change until within the last quarter of this century, has been in favor of the small college. It is only within twenty or twenty-five years that the larger institution, or the university, has been known on American soil. The tradition is deeply rooted. This fact points unmistakably to the policy of the future; and while the university idea, which has so recently sprung up among us, has before it large and unlimited possibilities, the policy of establishing small colleges here and there is one so strongly fixed that no great modification of it may be expected. . . .

One of the most important factors to be considered in any study of the small college is the religious purpose and control with which a great majority of these colleges stand connected.[158] The smaller colleges, for the most part, have been founded with a distinct and definite religious aim. . . . If men of deep religious convictions continue to cherish such convictions and to propagate them, they will find it necessary to educate those who shall hand down these same traditions. To do this with economy and certainty, there must be institutions for higher study which shall be pervaded by the spirit of the denomination desirous of maintaining and developing this growth. This factor is as strong as any that has been mentioned, perhaps strongest of all, and yet this and all that have preceded it find their basis in another factor—the last which I shall present.

The small colleges, scattered everywhere, are but the natural and inevitable expression of the American spirit in the realm of higher education. The universities of Cambridge and Oxford, as now constituted, are an expression of English aristocracy. The universities of Berlin and Leipzig, and the gymnasia of Germany, represent most fittingly the German imperial spirit. The small colleges in Ohio and Missouri, in Iowa and South Carolina, and in every state of our magnificent Union, are the expression of the democratic spirit, which is the true American spirit. . . .[159]

II.

Among the things which will be found to stand in the way of the development of the small college, first let us note the development of the high schools. . . .[160] So great a degree of perfection has been reached in the work of the high school in many quarters that even those parents who have the means prefer the public high school to the private academy or college; and by many, a great incentive to pa-

---

157. In the year 1900 about 90 percent of all American families had an annual income under $1,300. Farm laborers earned on average $247, factory workers and coal miners $435, highly skilled workers $800–1,000, and clerical workers $1,011. *Historical Statistics of the United States, Colonial Times to 1970*, pt. 1 (Washington DC: U.S. Department of Commerce, 1975), Series D, pp. 779–93.

158. Harper was renowned for having circumvented "religious purpose and control" at the University of Chicago.

159. Which of Harper's "decided advantages" of the small college are not overshadowed by the greater advantages enjoyed by large universities, in Harper's view?

160. Like many university leaders in this period, Harper was deeply interested in and well informed about the development of the schools, having served energetically on the metropolitan school board.

tronize the high school is found in the absence of a tuition fee. The requirements for admission to the high school and the length of the curriculum have been steadily increasing, and it seems quite certain that the end has not yet been reached, since satisfactory arrangements have been made in many schools for the work of the freshman year. This is a serious menace to the small college. . . .[161]

Another thing which stands in the way of the small college is the tendency toward specialism. In earlier years, when the entrance requirements were lower, it was possible for the student to give four years of time to work, the aim of which was general culture. In these latter days, when the requirements for admission are so high that they in themselves constitute an equivalent of the college course of twenty or thirty years ago, and when young men and women are unable to enter college at an earlier age than nineteen or twenty, it is impossible and undesirable to hold the student to four years of general work. Already the tendency to specialize is seen at the beginning of the third year of college work. This is a natural result of the privilege of election,[162] and also a necessary result flowing from the large number of subjects offered in the curriculum. The small college does not furnish the opportunity to follow out this tendency, and in the case of many students a longer period than is really necessary is spent on subjects which sustain no particular relation to the future work of the student. . . . Instruction higher than that of an exceedingly elementary character may not be provided in a great majority of subjects to advantage, if the college has a smaller attendance than 150 students; and yet of the 480 colleges and universities in the United States, about 160, or one-third, belong to this class— that is, 160 colleges have less than 150 students each.

As has been said, by far the larger number of our smaller colleges have had their origin in the religious spirit. In many of these even today the spirit is not simply religious, nor indeed simply Christian—it is the sectarian spirit. Even from New England one not infrequently hears the cry from denominational bosses[163] that the denominational college must be supported, its halls must be filled by students from the families of those belonging to the denomination, and the denominational ideas must be propagated, or dishonor is shown the founders of the institution and the denomination of which it is a representative. . . . With the gradual weakening of this narrow religious spirit—often confounded with the denominational spirit, but indeed something entirely separate therefrom—a great source of power and strength which has hitherto lent support to the building up of the small college will be removed. Here, then, is a further serious menace to the future of many institutions of this class. . . .

Of an entirely different character is the policy, adopted in many institutions, of allowing the college senior to substitute for regular college work the first year of the professional school.[164] This concession, brought about because of the feeling that men must enter the professional schools at an earlier age than has been the custom, is a distinct blow at the small college, where no such connection with the professional school exists, and where, consequently, such concession cannot be granted. . . .

One of the more important, perhaps the most important, of the difficulties with which the small college must contend is that of securing the strongest men to do work upon the salary that can be of-

---

161. Harper's point is demonstrated by the account in David F. Labaree, *The Making of an American High School: The Credentials Market and the Central High School of Philadelphia, 1838–1939* (New Haven, CT: Yale University Press, 1988).

162. Harper takes for granted electivism and its association with specialization, as Charles W. Eliot intended twenty years earlier.

163. What does Harper mean by these semantic distinctions and by the term "denominational bosses?"

164. This practice had become widespread, particularly at institutions seeking to require a bachelor's degree as a prerequisite to admission to their professional schools.

fered; and, further, its inability to hold such men if once they have been secured.[165] This leads to the adoption of one of two policies. In some cases the college is wise enough to be satisfied with having young instructors who are strong and vigorous, even with the consciousness that vacancies will constantly occur and thus innumerable changes be made. The disadvantage of this policy is, of course, the lack of continuity in the spirit of the institution; but in any case it is an infinitely better policy than the other one, in accordance with which men of second- or third- or even fourth-rate ability are employed, with the feeling that no other institution will cause trouble by calling away the members of the staff. On the other hand, the larger institution is able, not only to select the strongest men and to pay them salaries which will make them satisfied to remain indefinitely, but also to employ younger men, even at a lower salary than is paid by the small colleges, because the younger men see that there is always opportunity ahead. The women's college, even when a large one, labors under this same difficulty, because the strongest men will not consent to devote their lives to work in a women's college.[166] This is a serious obstacle in the way of the small college, and one the difficulties of which increase every year. . . .

The source of greatest trouble to many of our small colleges in the South, and especially in the western states, is the state university. . . .[167] The explanation of this is clear. With a political influence which naturally lends itself to the state institution; with the large number of alumni occupying the chief positions as principals and teachers in high schools; with no tuition fee, because provision has been made by the state and instruction is offered free; with excellent facilities for work in nearly every line; with fully equipped laboratories, and with libraries far more complete than any ordinary college can ever hope to possess, the state university presents an inducement to the prospective student which the smaller college cannot under any circumstances duplicate. . . .

The greatest difficulty of the small college is its lack of means with which to do the work demanded in these days of modern methods, the methods of the library and the laboratory. The number of institutions called colleges with an endowment of less than 100,000 dollars is appallingly large, and yet today the income of an endowment of 100,000 dollars may be reckoned at only four or five percent. How much opportunity does this afford for furnishing instruction of a higher grade? It should be remembered that, as has been already shown, only 66 percent of all the colleges and universities have more than 150 students. This total income is scarcely sufficient to pay the salaries of three or four men; and yet out of it must be paid expenditures for administration, for fuel and light, for circulars and catalogs, for expenses of every kind. How is it possible to do adequate work? A well-equipped academy for 250 students cannot be conducted in these days for less than 40,000 dollars a year. The cost per capita of instruction furnished the high-school students in some of our cities, even where the classes are crowded, exceeds the average cost per capita of the instruction furnished in many of our colleges.

The demands of modern methods have quadrupled the difficulty in this respect. So long as the curriculum could be restricted in large measure to the study of Latin, Greek, and mathematics, no great cost was incurred for equipment; but with the introduction of work in history, political economy, and political science the requirements for books and periodicals is very great. With the introduction of

---

165. In 1893 Harper surveyed 124 "representative" colleges and universities and concluded that $1,470 was "a very fair approximation of the actual average pay" of professors across the country. W. R. Harper, "The Pay of College Professors," *Forum* 16 (1893): 99. Compare this approximation to Harper's estimate above of the annual income required to attend a "larger institution."

166. Recall this view when reading the selections about colleges for women and African Americans.

167. The growth of state universities was fueled by the Morrill Land Grant Act of 1862, which gave to the individual states federal lands that were to be sold in order to provide revenue for founding universities in each state.

laboratory work in the various sciences the expenditures required for laboratories and for equipment are very great. Without money these demands cannot be met, and yet without meeting the demands of the present age, our colleges all over the land are graduating students who are impressed with the belief that they have been educated in accordance with modern ideas. An institution consists of the men who make up the faculty, of the buildings, and of the equipment. These, however, can be obtained and maintained only with resources of a liberal character.

These, then, are some of the difficulties which confront those who are responsible for the maintenance and development of the small college.[168]

III.

We come now to the consideration of the changes affecting the small colleges which may be expected and are to be desired. First among these will be the strengthening of some. The laws of institutional life are very similar to those of individual life, and in the development of institutions we may confidently believe in "the survival of the fittest." The severe tests, to which the life of many institutions is subjected, serve to purify and to harden these lives. The institution which has survived the trials and tribulations of early years, and, by this survival, has justified its existence, not only to its constituency, but to the world at large, deserves to live; and its subsequent life will be all the stronger and heartier because of the difficulties through which it has passed. . . .[169]

In this struggle for existence, however, some of the colleges that have already been organized, and others, the organization of which is in the future, will be compelled to limit their activity to the sphere of work known commonly as the academic, or preparatory, field. It is probable that a careful examination of the colleges now chartered in the United States would show that at least 20 or 25 percent are doing work of a character only little removed from that of an academy. . . .

Forty years ago such a college, if its small faculty had contained a few strong men, might have justified itself; but today the situation is changed, and institutions of this kind are recognized at a distance, if not at home, at their true worth. These, and, in addition, some that in times past have been more prosperous, will, in the course of educational development, come to occupy a more honest position before the world, and nothing could occur which would be more advantageous to the cause of education. Strong academies are needed side by side with the high schools of the state, just as strong colleges and universities, founded by private means, are needed to work side by side with the universities of the state.

While, therefore, 25 percent of the small colleges now conducted will survive,[170] and be all the stronger for the struggle through which they have passed, another 25 percent will yield to the inevitable, and, one by one, take a place in the system of educational work which, though in one sense lower, is in a true sense higher. It is surely a higher thing to do honest and thorough work in a lower field than to fall short of such work in a higher field.

---

168. Consider how each of Harper's "decided advantages" of the small college compares to a correlated difficulty.

169. This analysis clearly expresses Harper's belief in evolutionary progress among institutions, an ideology that pervades his statement. The phrase "survival of the fittest" was coined by Herbert Spencer, the English philosopher who popularized the extension of the idea of evolutionary progress from biology into all aspects of social life and other fields.

170. Harper's prescience is demonstrated by the similar analysis made in selection #57 drawn from John Dewey, chairman, et al., *The Curriculum for the Liberal Arts College* (1931), pt. II.

Another group of these smaller institutions will come to be known as junior colleges. I use the name "junior college" for lack of a better term, to cover the work of the freshman and sophomore years. With these may usually be closely associated the work of the preparatory department or academy. This period of six years is, I am inclined to think, a period which stands by itself as between the period of elementary education and that of the university. The work of the freshman and sophomore years is only a continuation of the academy or high-school work. It is a continuation not only of the subject matter studied, but of the methods employed. It is not until the end of the sophomore year that university methods of instruction may be employed to advantage. It is not until the end of the sophomore year that the average student has reached an age which enables him to do work with satisfaction, except in accordance with academy methods.

At present this consecutive period of preparation, covering six years, is broken at the end of the fourth year, and the student finds himself adrift. He has not reached the point when work in any of his preparatory subjects is finished. He is compelled to continue the same work under new and strange conditions, with new and strange instructors. Not infrequently the instructors under whom he is placed in the freshman year of college are inferior to those with whom he has been associated in the academy. A great waste of energy, time, and interest follows this unnatural break in the prosecution of the student's work. Nature has marked out the great division of educational work and the laws of nature may not be violated without injury.[171]

My firm conviction is that in time this difficulty will be appreciated, and that a large number, perhaps even a majority, of the colleges now attempting to do the four years of the preparatory course and the four years of college work will be satisfied to limit their work to the six years which include the preparatory training and the first two years of college life. The motive for this change will be found in its economy, and in the possibility of doing thorough and satisfactory work, where today such work is impossible. . . .

The small college is certain of its existence in the future educational history of the United States. It must, however, pass through a serious struggle with many antagonistic elements, and must adjust itself to other similar and, sometimes, stronger agencies. In the process of this struggle and adjustment some colleges will grow stronger; some will become academies; some, junior colleges;[172] the high schools will be elevated to a still more important position than that which they now occupy; while, all together, high schools, colleges, and universities, will develop greater similarity of standard and greater variety of type; and, at the same time, they will come into closer and more helpful association one with another.

---

171. In his debate with James McCosh, Charles W. Eliot, who did not advocate the junior college, assigns "the great division in educational work" to about age eighteen. Notwithstanding Harper's appeal to "the laws of nature," what is the source and justification of their different demarcation in educational maturity?

172. In sum, Harper projects that 25 percent of colleges will grow stronger, 25 percent will become academies, and 50 percent will become junior colleges.

50. Booker T. Washington, "Industrial Education for the Negro" (1903)

INTRODUCTION

In selections #1 and #3, Plato and Aristotle argued in different ways that leaders should be educated liberally, rather than practically or technically. That argument generally prevailed in the late nineteenth century, although certain university founders, such as Ezra Cornell and Leland Stanford, envisioned their namesake institutions offering vocational and technical education. But the issue was debated most forcefully among African-American educators because it entailed strategies for social uplift and for achieving racial equality in the United States. Selections #50 and #51 express sharply opposing views, though the precise point of contention requires careful consideration.

Booker T. Washington (1856–1915) was born a slave on a plantation in Franklin County, Virginia. His father was likely a white neighbor; his mother a cook. "My life had its beginnings in the midst of the most miserable, desolate, and discouraging surroundings," Washington observed, "I was born in a typical log cabin, about fourteen by sixteen feet square. . . . we slept in and on a bunch of filthy rags laid upon the dirt floor. . . . Meals were gotten by the children very much as dumb animals get theirs. It was a piece of bread here and a scrap of meat there."[173] After emancipation, Washington's family walked 250 miles to West Virginia, where he worked in a coal mine and a salt furnace, taught himself to read, attended elementary school, and learned domestic skills as a servant. In 1872, encouraged by the white mistress of the house that he served, Washington traveled 500 miles at the age of seventeen to enter Hampton Normal and Agricultural Institute, which had opened in 1868 to educate African Americans. Washington wanted to study law, but was persuaded to learn masonry while preparing to be a teacher, and graduated after three years, returning to West Virginia to teach school.

In 1879 he went back to Hampton as secretary to the principal, and in 1881 was chosen to begin a similar institution in Tuskegee, Alabama, which had been founded by southern whites and blacks. With the help of northern philanthropic industrialists, Washington's diligent effort over the next thirty-four years developed Tuskegee Normal and Industrial Institute into the foremost trade school for African Americans in the United States. The success of Tuskegee made him a prominent speaker on racial issues; and a famous speech at the Cotton States and International Exposition at Atlanta in 1893 established him—in the eyes of many whites, at least—as the leading political figure among African Americans and successor to Frederick Douglass who died in 1895. Washington's stature was further heightened when Harvard awarded him an honorary degree in 1896 and President Theodore Roosevelt invited him to dine at the White House in 1901.

By that point, however, "his views were opposed by the Negro 'intellectuals' who felt he did not sufficiently emphasize political rights, and that his stress on industrial education might result in keeping the Negro in virtual bondage. He was more interested in keeping his race worthy of the franchise . . . than in agitating for it in ways which might inflame public opinion. Looking at the controversy after a generation has passed, we can see that there was truth on both sides, but that as far as the welfare of the masses in the South was concerned, . . . he adopted the only policy which could really be effective." Such was the judgment expressed in 1936 in the *Dictionary of American Biography*.[174]

---

173. Booker T. Washington, *Up from Slavery* (New York: Doubleday, 1901), pp. 1, 3, 6.

174. Anson Phelps Stokes, s.v. "Booker Taliaferro Washington," in *Dictionary of American Biography*, ed. Douglas Malone (New York: Charles Scribner's Sons, 1936), v. 10, pp. 506–8.

The leader of the intellectuals opposing Washington was W. E. B. Du Bois (1868–1963), who assumed that role by criticizing Washington in his celebrated *The Souls of Black Folk*, published in 1903. In that same year, there appeared a volume of essays likely edited or endorsed by Washington: *The Negro Problem: A Series of Articles by Representative American Negroes of Today*. In this forum, Washington and Du Bois explicitly debated the strategic role of liberal education in improving the situation of African Americans. Their two essays appear below.

Knowing that a divided leadership would only hurt the cause of African Americans, Washington and Du Bois attempted to reconcile at a conference in 1904 but could not do so, and the rift between them widened into a chasm. Many black leaders despised Washington's accommodating approach during the oppressive era of Jim Crow segregation, Black Codes, and lynchings. In subsequent decades, Washington came to be portrayed as an unthoughtful and self-aggrandizing tool of the northern industrialists in their covert plan to maintain an efficient and docile work force for their factories. By the 1960s it was not unusual to see Washington deprecated as "that Machiavellian prince of Negroes" in comparison to W. E. B. Du Bois.[175] Washington's image declined so far that black intellectuals at the end of the twentieth century, when analyzing Du Bois's response to Washington, scarcely mention the latter who was nevertheless "the dominant political force in Negro politics" between 1895 and 1915."[176] Thus, "the ubiquitous Washington"[177] of 1903 has become virtually "the invisible man" to those striving for African American progress at the beginning of the twenty-first century.

Despite the criticism in his own time, Washington did not pause in his work on behalf of what he calls below "industrial education for the Negro." On a trip to New York in 1915 he collapsed from exhaustion, and died the day after returning to Tuskegee.

SELECTION[178]

Forty years ago my race emerged from slavery into freedom. If, in too many cases, the Negro race began development at the wrong end, it was largely because neither white nor black properly understood the case. Nor is it any wonder that this was so, for never before in the history of the world had just such a problem been presented as that of the two races at the coming of freedom in this country.

For two hundred and fifty years, I believe the way for the redemption of the Negro was being prepared through industrial development. Through all those years the southern white man did business with the Negro in a way that no one else has done business with him. In most cases if a southern white man wanted a house built he consulted a Negro mechanic about the plan and about the actual building of the structure. If he wanted a suit of clothes made he went to a Negro tailor, and for shoes he went to a shoemaker of the same race. In a certain way, every slave plantation in the South was an industrial school. On these plantations young colored men and women were constantly being trained not only as

---

175. Louis R. Harlan, "Preface [to the 1968 edition]," in Elliott M. Rudwick, *W. E. B. Du Bois: Propagandist of the Negro Protest* (1960; New York: Athenaeum, 1968), p. 8. Harlan subsequently helped reassess Washington by editing Washington's papers and authoring a multi-volume biography. See Louis R. Harlan, *Booker T. Washington* (New York: Oxford University Press, 1972–1983).

176. Henry Louis Gates, Jr., "W. E. B. Du Bois and 'The Talented Tenth'" in *The Future of the Race* by Henry Louis Gates, Jr., and Cornel West (New York: Random House, 1996), p. 119.

177. Cornel West, "Black Strivings in a Twilight Civilization," in *The Future of the Race* by Henry Louis Gates, Jr., and Cornel West (New York: Random House, 1996), p. 67.

178. Booker T. Washington, "Industrial Education for the Negro," in *The Negro Problem, A Series of Articles by Representative American Negroes of Today* (New York: James Pott, 1903), pp. 9–29.

farmers but as carpenters, blacksmiths, wheelwrights, brick masons, engineers, cooks, laundresses, sewing women and housekeepers.

I do not mean in any way to apologize for the curse of slavery, which was a curse to both races, but in what I say about industrial training in slavery I am simply stating facts.[179] This training was crude and was given for selfish purposes. It did not answer the highest ends, because there was an absence of mental training in connection with the training of the hand. To a large degree, though, this business contact with the southern white man, and the industrial training on the plantations, left the Negro at the close of the war in possession of nearly all the common and skilled labor in the South.

The industries that gave the South its power, prominence and wealth prior to the Civil War were mainly the raising of cotton, sugar cane, rice and tobacco. Before the way could be prepared for the proper growing and marketing of these crops, forests had to be cleared, houses to be built, public roads and railroads constructed. In all these works the Negro did most of the heavy work. In the planting, cultivating and marketing of the crops not only was the Negro the chief dependence [sic], but in the manufacture of tobacco he became a skilled and proficient workman, and in this, up to the present time in the South, holds the lead in the large tobacco manufactories.

In most of the industries, though, what happened? For nearly twenty years after the war, except in a few instances, the value of the industrial training given by the plantations was overlooked. Negro men and women were educated in literature, in mathematics, and in the sciences, with little thought of what had been taking place during the preceding two hundred and fifty years, except, perhaps, as something to be escaped, to be got as far away from as possible. As a generation began to pass, those who had been trained as mechanics in slavery began to disappear by death, and gradually it began to be realized that there were few to take their places. There were young men educated in foreign tongues, but few in carpentry or in mechanical or architectural drawing. Many were trained in Latin, but few as engineers and blacksmiths. Too many were taken from the farm and educated, but educated in everything but farming. For this reason they had no interest in farming and did not return to it. And yet eighty-five percent of the Negro population of the southern states lives and for a considerable time will continue to live in the country districts. . . .

Only a short time before his death the late Mr. C. P. Huntington, to whose memory a magnificent library has just been given by his widow to the Hampton Institute for Negroes, in Virginia, said in a public address some words which seem to me so wise that I want to quote them here: "Our schools teach everybody a little of almost everything, but, in my opinion, they teach very few children just what they ought to know in order to make their way successfully in life. They do not put into their hands the tools they are best fitted to use, and hence so many failures. Many a mother and sister have worked and slaved, living upon scanty food, in order to give a son and brother a 'liberal education,' and in doing this have built up a barrier between the boy and the work he was fitted to do. Let me say to you that all honest work is honorable work. If the labor is manual and seems common, you will have all the more chance to be thinking of other things, or of work that is higher and brings better pay, and to work out in your minds better and higher duties and responsibilities for yourselves, and for thinking of ways by which you can help others as well as yourselves, and bring them up to your own higher level."[180]

Some years ago, when we decided to make tailoring a part of our training at the Tuskegee Institute, I was amazed to find that it was almost impossible to find in the whole country an educated co-

179. Nevertheless, this virtual apology for slavery is what attracted the ire of many African American leaders.

180. Collis P. Huntington (1821–1900), a New England shopkeeper, moved to California and founded the Southern Pacific Railroad with Leland Stanford (1824–1893), the benefactor of Stanford University. Upon his death, Huntington left bequests to two educational institutions: Hampton Institute and Tuskegee Institute.

lored man who could teach the making of clothing. We could find numbers of them who could teach astronomy, theology, Latin or grammar, but almost none who could instruct in the making of clothing, something that has to be used by every one of us every day in the year. How often have I been discouraged as I have gone through the South and into the homes of the people of my race, and have found women who could converse intelligently upon abstruse subjects, and yet could not tell how to improve the condition of the poorly cooked and still more poorly served bread and meat which they and their families were eating three times a day. It is discouraging to find a girl who can tell you the geographical location of any country on the globe and who does not know where to place the dishes upon a common dinner table. It is discouraging to find a woman who knows much about theoretical chemistry, and who cannot properly wash and iron a shirt.[181]

In what I say here I would not by any means have it understood that I would limit or circumscribe the mental development of the Negro student. No race can be lifted until its mind is awakened and strengthened. By the side of industrial training should always go mental and moral training,[182] but the pushing of mere abstract knowledge into the head means little. We want more than the mere performance of mental gymnastics. Our knowledge must be harnessed to the things of real life. I would encourage the Negro to secure all the mental strength, all the mental culture—whether gleaned from science, mathematics, history, language or literature—that his circumstances will allow, but I believe most earnestly that for years to come the education of the people of my race should be so directed that the greatest proportion of the mental strength of the masses will be brought to bear upon the every-day practical things of life, upon something that is needed to be done, and something which they will be permitted to do in the community in which they reside.[183] And just the same with the professional class which the race needs and must have, I would say give the men and women of that class, too, the training which will best fit them to perform in the most successful manner the service which the race demands.

I would not confine the race to industrial life nor even to agriculture, for example, although I believe that by far the greater part of the Negro race is best off in the country districts and must and should continue to live there, but I would teach the race that in industry the foundation must be laid—that the very best service which any one can render to what is called the higher education is to teach the present generation to provide a material or industrial foundation. On such a foundation as this will grow habits of thrift, a love of work, economy, ownership of property, bank accounts.[184] Out of it in the future will grow practical education, professional education, positions of public responsibility. Out of it will grow moral and religious strength. Out of it will grow wealth from which alone can come leisure and the opportunity for the enjoyment of literature and the fine arts.

---

181. Washington's image of excessive "numbers" of academically educated African Americans is belied by the fact that in 1900 only a third of the 1.1 million African American children aged five to fourteen in the South attended school.

182. Du Bois concedes the converse point in similar language below: "I would not deny, or for a moment seem to deny, the paramount necessity of teaching the Negro to work, and to work steadily and skillfully; or seem to depreciate in the slightest degree the important part industrial schools must play in the accomplishments of these ends." Why did Washington and Du Bois not agree on the obvious compromise of providing liberal education for the elite and industrial education for the masses?

183. Washington's acquiescence to legal, as well as economic and social, disadvantages of African Americans, at least in the short term, attracted the wrath of his opponents.

184. Note how carefully the appeals to agrarian southerners and northern industrialists are entwined in this paragraph and above.

In the words of the late beloved Frederick Douglass:[185] "Every blow of the sledge hammer wielded by a sable arm is a powerful blow in support of our cause. Every colored mechanic is by virtue of circumstances an elevator of his race. Every house built by a black man is a strong tower against the allied hosts of prejudice. It is impossible for us to attach too much importance to this aspect of the subject. Without industrial development there can be no wealth; without wealth there can be no leisure; without leisure no opportunity for thoughtful reflection and the cultivation of the higher arts."[186]

I would set no limits to the attainments of the Negro in arts, in letters or statesmanship, but I believe the surest way to reach those ends is by laying the foundation in the little things of life that lie immediately about one's door. I plead for industrial education and development for the Negro not because I want to cramp him, but because I want to free him. I want to see him enter the all-powerful business and commercial world. . . .[187]

Early in the history of the Tuskegee Institute we began to combine industrial training with mental and moral culture. Our first efforts were in the direction of agriculture, and we began teaching this with no appliances except one hoe and a blind mule. From this small beginning we have grown until now the Institute owns two thousand acres of land, eight hundred of which are cultivated each year by the young men of the school. We began teaching wheelwrighting and blacksmithing in a small way to the men, and laundry work, cooking and sewing and housekeeping to the young women. The fourteen hundred and over young men and women who attended the school during the last school year received instruction—in addition to academic and religious training—in thirty-three trades and industries. . .[188]

It seems to me that too often mere book education leaves the Negro young man or woman in a weak position. For example, I have seen a Negro girl taught by her mother to help her in doing laundry work at home. Later, when this same girl was graduated from the public schools or a high school and returned home she finds herself educated out of sympathy with laundry work, and yet not able to find anything to do which seems in keeping with the cost and character of her education. Under these circumstances we cannot be surprised if she does not fulfill the expectations made for her. What should have been done for her, it seems to me, was to give her along with her academic education tho-

185. The ideological and personal conflict between Washington and Du Bois is revealed in their competition to claim Douglass's legacy. When a Philadelphia publishing company invited Washington to write a biography of Douglass and he did not reply, the publisher in 1903 asked Du Bois, who agreed to do so in 1904. Washington then accepted the invitation; the publisher withdrew the offer to Du Bois, and Washington published his biography in 1907.

186. Does Douglass concur with Aristotle's view in selection #3?

187. Such statements naturally endeared Washington to the philanthropic industrialists who supported his work. But does the devaluing of intellectualism necessarily imply complicity with the white power structure? Or, is it the devaluing of intellectualism that fuels intellectuals' disdain for Washington and affection for Du Bois? In 1999 Henry Louis Gates, Jr., recalled that, during the 1960s and 1970s, "Like every other black intellectual then, I was a Du Bois junkie." Quoted in *Boston Globe* (20 Jan. 1999): C1. See Robert J. Norrell, *Up from History: The Life of Booker T. Washington* (Cambridge, MA: Harvard University Press, 2009).

188. Washington's testimony of the acquisition of skills at Tuskegee has been challenged by historian James D. Anderson, who asserts that both Hampton and Tuskegee "established farms and small shops to give their teachers the manual labor experience. In these routinized work situations, however, the development of persons skilled in trades or farming was a secondary aim, seldom acquired by the students. The primary aim was to work the prospective teachers long and hard so that they would embody, accept, and preach an ethic of hard work or the 'dignity of labor'." James D. Anderson, *The Education of Blacks in the South, 1860–1935* (Chapel Hill: University of North Carolina Press, 1988), p. 34.

rough training in the latest and best methods of laundry work, so that she could have put so much skill and intelligence into it that the work would have been lifted out from the plane of drudgery. The home which she would then have been able to found by the results of her work would have enabled her to help her children to take a still more responsible position in life.

Almost from the first Tuskegee has kept in mind—and this I think should be the policy of all industrial schools—fitting students for occupations which would be open to them in their home communities. . . . Aside from the economic value of this work I cannot but believe, and my observation confirms me in my belief, that as we continue to place Negro men and women of intelligence, religion, modesty, conscience and skill in every community in the South, who will prove by actual results their value to the community, I cannot but believe, I say, that this will constitute a solution to many of the present political and social difficulties.

Many seem to think that industrial education is meant to make the Negro work as he worked in the days of slavery. This is far from my conception of industrial education. If this training is worth anything to the Negro, it consists in teaching him how not to work, but how to make the forces of nature—air, steam, water, horse-power and electricity—work for him. If it has any value, it is in lifting labor up out of toil and drudgery into the plane of the dignified and the beautiful. The Negro in the South works and works hard; but too often his ignorance and lack of skill causes him to do his work in the most costly and shiftless manner, and this keeps him near the bottom of the ladder in the economic world. . . .

I close, then, as I began, by saying that as a slave the Negro was worked, and that as a freeman he must learn to work. There is still doubt in many quarters as to the ability of the Negro unguided, unsupported, to hew his own path and put into visible, tangible, indisputable form, products and signs of civilization. This doubt cannot be much affected by abstract arguments, no matter how delicately and convincingly woven together. Patiently, quietly, doggedly, persistently, through summer and winter, sunshine and shadow, by self-sacrifice, by foresight, by honesty and industry, we must re-enforce argument with results. One farm bought, one house built, one home sweetly and intelligently kept, one man who is the largest tax payer or has the largest bank account, one school or church maintained, one factory running successfully, one truck garden profitably cultivated, one patient cured by a Negro doctor, one sermon well preached, one office well filled, one life cleanly lived—these will tell more in our favor than all the abstract eloquence that can be summoned to plead our cause. Our pathway must be up through the soil, up through swamps, up through forests, up through the streams, the rocks, up through commerce, education and religion!

51. W. E. B. Du Bois, "The Talented Tenth" (1903)

INTRODUCTION

The life of W. E. B. Du Bois moved conversely to Booker T. Washington. The latter traveled "up from slavery"—the title of his 1901 autobiography—advancing from absolute legal and political exclusion to nominal inclusion in the elite. Du Bois began as a nominal insider—"a black New England Victorian seduced by the Enlightenment ethos and enchanted with the American dream"[189]— and became progressively alienated politically and legally from the United States. At the height of his career, Washington sounded like a prudent New England shopkeeper and conferred with industrialists; Du Bois, in the end, joined the Communist Party and emigrated to Africa. In this tortuous fashion, two of the talented were racked on the legacy of slavery.

William Edward Burghardt Du Bois (1868–1963) was born and raised as part of the small African-American community in Stockbridge, Massachusetts, the town where the first liberation of slaves under due process of law had occurred in the United States. Though excelling academically, he was not offered the scholarships to northern universities that his white classmates were; so in 1885 he went to Fisk University, a black institution in Nashville, Tennessee, where he encountered more overt and vicious racism than he had previously experienced.

Graduating with a B.A. in 1888, Du Bois went to Harvard and in 1890 earned a second B.A. in philosophy and an M.A. in history in 1891.[190] The following year, he began studying the social sciences at Friedrich Wilhelm University in Berlin, where he met Max Weber, who became a friend and in 1904 participated in the annual conference on the status of the Negro that Du Bois organized at Atlanta University. Returning to the United States in 1894, Du Bois taught classics at Wilberforce University in Ohio, and completed the Ph.D. at Harvard in 1895, publishing his dissertation entitled "The Suppression of the African Slave Trade to the United States of America, 1638–1870" in 1896.

During the next year he pursued research at the University of Pennsylvania, conducting the first empirical study of a black community in the United States, which was published as *The Philadelphia Negro: A Social Study* (1897). Dedicating himself to conducting social scientific research on the condition of the African American, Du Bois then moved to Atlanta University, directed annual conferences devoted to the study of the African-American experience, and published the findings in sixteen volumes between 1889 and 1914. Meanwhile, his prolific writings in major public journals made him one of the best known African Americans in the United States. The appearance of *The Souls of Black Folk* in 1903 solidified his reputation when six printings were called for within two years.

In 1903 Du Bois established himself as the leading opponent of Washington by criticizing Washington in *The Souls of Black Folk* and in his famous essay "The Talented Tenth." After these encounters and their failed reconciliation in 1904, Du Bois founded the Niagara Movement of black leaders opposed to Washington's accommodating approach to racial prejudice. The funding for Du Bois's research then began to decline due to his encouragement of black agitation; and this decline plus his rising interest in the labor movement and socialism led him to leave Atlanta University and to help found the National Association for the Advancement of Colored People (NAACP). From 1910 to 1934 he worked full time for the NAACP, advocating racial integration and full political equality

---

189. Cornel West, "Black Strivings in a Twilight Civilization," in *The Future of the Race* by Henry Louis Gates, Jr., and Cornel West (New York: Random House, 1996), p. 57.

190. It was not uncommon for students with a B.A. from other colleges to apply to enroll in the B.A. course at Harvard College, which granted such enrollees a certain number of years of advanced study.

while editing its journal *The Crisis*. He spent the next ten years doing research at Atlanta University and then returned to the NAACP from 1944 to 1948. Drawn increasingly to Marxist interpretations of capitalist society, Du Bois began to praise the Soviet Union early in the Cold War, and was ordered to register as a foreign agent by the federal government. Upon refusing, he was indicted and denied a passport. Eventually acquitted, he traveled to China, the Soviet Union, and Africa; joined the U.S. Communist Party in 1961; and, renouncing his U.S. citizenship, emigrated to Ghana, where he died.

SELECTION[191]

The Negro race, like all races, is going to be saved by its exceptional men. The problem of education, then, among Negroes must first of all deal with the Talented Tenth;[192] it is the problem of developing the Best of this race that they may guide the Mass away from the contamination and death of the Worst, in their own and other races. Now the training of men is a difficult and intricate task. Its technique is a matter for educational experts, but its object is for the vision of seers. If we make money the object of man-training, we shall develop money-makers but not necessarily men; if we make technical skill the object of education, we may possess artisans but not, in nature, men. Men we shall have only as we make manhood the object of the work of the schools—intelligence, broad sympathy, knowledge of the world that was and is, and of the relation of men to it—this is the curriculum of that Higher Education which must underlie true life. On this foundation we may build bread winning, skill of hand and quickness of brain, with never a fear lest the child and man mistake the means of living for the object of life.

If this be true—and who can deny it[193]—three tasks lay before me; first to show from the past that the Talented Tenth as they have risen among American Negroes have been worthy of leadership; secondly to show how these men may be educated and developed; and thirdly, to show their relation to the Negro problem.

You misjudge us because you do not know us. From the very first it has been the educated and intelligent of the Negro people that have led and elevated the mass, and the sole obstacles that nullified and retarded their efforts were slavery and race prejudice; for what is slavery but the legalized survival of the unfit and the nullification of the work of natural internal leadership? Negro leadership, therefore, sought from the first to rid the race of this awful incubus that it might make way for natural selection and the survival of the fittest.[194]

In colonial days[195] came Phillis Wheatley and Paul Cuffe striving against the bars of prejudice; and Benjamin Banneker, the almanac maker. . . .[196] Then came Dr. James Derham, who could tell

---

191. W. E. B. Du Bois, "The Talented Tenth," in *The Negro Problem: A Series of Articles by Representative American Negroes of To-Day* (New York: James Pott, 1903), pp. 33–63.

192. "In 1896 [white missionary] Henry L. Morehouse became the first to use the words 'talented tenth' to describe this philosophy and program of black education. . . . Consistent with their view of the need for a well-trained black leadership, the missionaries made liberal culture rather than industrial training the chief aim of their curriculum." James D. Anderson, *The Education of Blacks in the South, 1860–1935* (Chapel Hill: University of North Carolina Press, 1988), p. 243.

193. Does Washington deny it? Is the core of the disagreement between Washington and Du Bois about the ideological influence of educational process upon students' beliefs?

194. Note Du Bois's argument that slavery violates evolutionary laws.

195. Compare the purpose and technique of the reconstructed histories of liberally educated women with Du Bois's effort here.

even the learned Dr. Rush something of medicine,[197] and Lemuel Haynes, to whom Middlebury gave an honorary M.A. in 1804.[198] These and others we may call the Revolutionary group of distinguished Negroes—they were persons of marked ability, leaders of a Talented Tenth . . . here and there in the early part of the century came other exceptional men. Some were natural sons of unnatural fathers and were given often a liberal training and thus a race of educated mulattos sprang up to plead for the black men's rights. . . .

Too little notice has been taken of the work which the Talented Tenth among Negroes took in the great abolition crusade. From the very day that a Philadelphia colored man became the first subscriber to Garrison's *Liberator*, to the day when Negro soldiers made the Emancipation Proclamation possible, black leaders worked shoulder to shoulder with white men in a movement, the success of which would have been impossible without them. . . .[199]

Where were these black abolitionists trained? Some, like Frederick Douglass, were self-trained, but yet trained liberally; others like Alexander Crummell and McCune Smith, graduated from famous foreign universities.[200] Most of them rose up through the colored schools of New York and Philadelphia and Boston, taught by college-bred men. . . .

After emancipation came a new group of educated and gifted leaders . . . Through political organization, historical and polemic writing and moral regeneration, these men strove to uplift their people. It is now the fashion of to-day to sneer at them[201] and to say that with freedom Negro leadership should have begun at the plow and not in the Senate—a foolish and mischievous lie; two hundred and fifty years that black serf toiled at the plow and yet that toiling was in vain till the Senate passed the war amendments; and two hundred and fifty years more the half-free serf of to-day may toil at his plow; but unless he have political rights and righteously guarded civic status, he will still remain the

---

196. The slave of a Boston tailor, Phillis Wheatley (1753?–1784) wrote poetry that made her famous in the American colonies and England; but she died in poverty in Boston, predeceased by her three children. Paul Cuffe (1759–1817) of Massachusetts became a wealthy merchant sailor and shipbuilder, joined the Quakers, and sponsored the emigration of African Americans to Africa, where he colonized Sierra Leone. Benjamin Banneker (1731–1806), the son of manumitted slaves who owned a farm near Baltimore, became a noted inventor, astronomer, and almanac publisher, and played a leading role in surveying and planning Washington DC.

197. Born in Philadelphia in 1762, Derham served as a physician there until he was sold to another physician in New Orleans. He learned English, French, and Spanish and, after winning his freedom, practiced medicine on his own as "the first recognized Negro physician of whom we have a record." Benjamin Brawley, *Negro Builders and Heroes* (Chapel Hill: University of North Carolina Press, 1937), p. 227.

198. Lemuel Haynes (1753–1833) fought in the battles of Lexington and Fort Ticonderoga during the Revolutionary War, became a Congregationalist minister, and served a predominantly white congregation.

199. William Lloyd Garrison (1805–1879), a radical, white abolitionist, founded the widely quoted newspaper *The Liberator* (1831–1865) and led the American Anti-Slavery Society, which split in 1839 due to disagreements over the rights of female abolitionists and the use of military force. The Emancipation Proclamation was the executive order, issued by President Abraham Lincoln on January 1, 1863, freeing the slaves in the Confederate States of America.

200. The first African American to earn a medical degree, James McCune Smith, of New York, received a bachelor's degree in 1835 and a doctorate of medicine in 1837 from the University of Glasgow and practiced medicine in New York City. Crummell (1819–1898) received a haphazard education due to racial barriers in New York and New England, was ordained a Protestant Episcopal priest in 1842, became the first African American to receive a bachelor's degree from Cambridge University in 1853, served sixteen years as a priest in Liberia, and became in 1879 the rector of St. Luke's Episcopal Church in Washington, DC.

201. Du Bois clearly addresses Booker T. Washington. Compare the rhetorical tone of each.

poverty-stricken and ignorant plaything of rascals that he now is. This all sane men know even if they dare not say it.

And so now we come to the present—a day of cowardice and vacillation, of strident wide-voiced wrong and faint hearted compromise; of double-faced dallying with Truth and Right. Who are to-day guiding the work of the Negro people? The "exceptions" of course. And yet so sure as this Talented Tenth is pointed out, the blind worshippers of the Average cry out in alarm: "These are the exceptions, look here at death, disease and crime—these are the happy rule." Of course they are the rule, because a silly nation made them the rule: Because for three long centuries this people lynched Negroes who dared to be brave, raped black women who dared to be virtuous, crushed dark-hued youth who dared to be ambitious, and encouraged and made to flourish servility and lewdness and apathy. But not even this was able to crush all manhood and chastity and aspiration from black folk.

A saving remnant continually survives and persists, continually aspires, continually shows itself in thrift and ability and character. Exceptional it is to be sure, but this is its chiefest promise; it shows the capability of Negro blood, the promise of black men. Do Americans ever stop to reflect that there are in this land a million men of Negro blood, well-educated, owners of homes, against the honor of whose womanhood no breath was ever raised, whose men occupy positions of trust and usefulness, and who, judged by any standard, have reached the full measure of the best type of modern European culture?[202] Is it fair, is it decent, is it Christian to ignore these facts of the Negro problem, to belittle such aspiration, to nullify such leadership and seek to crush these people back into the mass out of which by toil and travail, they and their fathers have raised themselves?

Can the masses of the Negro people be in any possible way more quickly raised than by the effort and example of this aristocracy of talent and character? Was there ever a nation on God's fair earth civilized from the bottom upward? Never; it is, ever was and ever will be from the top downward that culture filters.[203] The Talented Tenth rises and pulls all that are worth the saving up to their vantage ground. This is the history of human progress; and two historic mistakes which have hindered that progress were the thinking first that no more could ever rise save the few already risen; or second, that it would better the unrisen to pull the risen down.

How then shall the leaders of a struggling people be trained and the hands of the risen few be strengthened? There can be but one answer: The best and most capable of their youth must be schooled in the colleges and universities of the land. We will not quarrel as to just what the university of the Negro should teach or how it should teach it—I willingly admit that each soul and each race-soul needs its own peculiar curriculum. But this is true: A university is a human invention for the transmission of knowledge and culture from generation to generation, through the training of quick minds and pure hearts, and for this work no other human invention will suffice, not even trade and industrial schools.

All men cannot go to college but some men must; every isolated group or nation must have its yeast, must have for the talented few, centers of training where men are not so mystified and befuddled by the hard necessary toil of earning a living, as to have no aims higher than their bellies, and no God greater than Gold. This is true training, and thus in the beginning were the favored sons of the freedmen trained. . . .

Where ought they to have begun to build? At the bottom, of course, quibbles the mole with his eyes in the earth. Aye! truly at the bottom, at the very bottom; at the bottom of knowledge, down in

---

202. Does the disagreement between Washington and Du Bois stem, in part, from the conflict between American valuing of technical know-how and European valuing of cultural sophistication?

203. Might the debate between Washington and Du Bois arise partly from the conflict between democratic faith on the commoner and aristocratic confidence in elites?

the very depths of knowledge there where the roots of justice strike into the lowest soil of Truth. And so they did begin; they founded colleges, and up from the colleges shot normal schools, and out from the normal schools went teachers, and around the normal teachers clustered other teachers to teach the public schools; the colleges trained in Greek and Latin and mathematics, 2000 men; and these men trained full 50,000 others in morals and manners and they in turn taught thrift and the alphabet to nine millions of men, who to-day hold $300,000,000 of property.

It was a miracle—the most wonderful peace-battle of the nineteenth century, and yet today men smile at it, and in fine superiority tell us, that it was all a strange mistake; that a proper way to found a system of education is first to gather the children and buy them spelling books and hoes; afterward men may look about for teachers, if happily they find them; or again they would teach men Work, but as for Life—why, what has Work to do with Life, they ask vacantly.[204]

Was the work of these college founders successful; did it stand the test of time? Did the college graduates, with all their fine theories of life, really live? Are they useful men helping to civilize and elevate their less fortunate fellows? Let us see.

Omitting all institutions which have not actually graduated students from college courses, there are to-day in the United States thirty-four institutions giving something above high school training to Negroes and designed especially for this race.[205] Three of these were established in the border States before the War; thirteen were planted by the Freedmen's Bureau in the years 1864–1869; nine were established between 1870 and 1880 by various church bodies; five were established after 1881 by Negro churches, and four are state institutions supported by United States' agricultural funds. In most cases the college departments are small adjuncts to high and common school work. As a matter of fact six institutions—Atlanta, Fisk, Howard, Shaw, Wilberforce and Leland, are the important Negro colleges so far as actual work and number of students are concerned. In all these institutions, seven hundred and fifty Negro college students are enrolled.

In grade the best of these colleges are about a year behind the smaller New England colleges and a typical curriculum is that of Atlanta University. Here students from the grammar grades, after a three years' high school course, take a college course of 136 weeks. One-fourth of this time is given to Latin and Greek, one-fifth to English and modern languages, one-sixth to history and social science, one-seventh to natural science; one-eighth to mathematics, and one-eighth to philosophy and pedagogy.[206] In addition to these students in the South, Negroes have attended Northern colleges for many years. . . .

Of these graduates 2,079 were men and 252 were women; 50 percent of northern-born college men come South to work among the masses of their people at a sacrifice which few people realize;[207] nearly 90 percent of the Southern-born graduates instead of seeking that personal freedom and broader intellectual atmosphere which their training has led them, in some degree, to conceive, stay and labor and wait in the midst of their black neighbors and relatives.

---

204. Do these paragraphs, clearly aimed at the Hampton-Tuskegee philosophy of education, accurately represent Washington's viewpoint?

205. See Du Bois and Augustus G. Dill, *The College-Bred Negro American* (Atlanta, GA: Atlanta University Press, 1910), pp. 14–5.

206. These proportions reflect the conservative nature of the liberal education at the Negro colleges, as was also the case at the colleges of other marginalized populations. Curricular experimentation was especially risky for institutions fighting to establish their legitimacy. See the curricular requirements of African American colleges in selection #52 from William T. Foster, *Administration of the College Curriculum* (1911).

207. Might Du Bois have himself in mind?

The most interesting question, and in many respects the crucial question, to be asked concerning college-bred Negroes, is: Do they earn a living? It has been intimated more than once that the higher training of Negroes has resulted in sending into the world of work, men who could find nothing to do suitable to their talents. Now and then there comes a rumor of a colored college man working at menial service, etc. Fortunately, returns as to occupations of college-bred Negroes, gathered by the Atlanta Conference, are quite full—nearly 60 percent of the total number of graduates.[208] This enables us to reach fairly certain conclusions as to the occupations of all college-bred Negroes.[209] Of 1,312 persons reported, over half are teachers; a sixth are preachers; another sixth are students and professional men; over six percent are farmers, artisans and merchants; and four percent are in government service. . . .

These figures illustrate vividly the function of the college bred Negro. He is, as he ought to be, the group leader, the man who sets the ideals of the community where he lives, directs its thoughts and heads its social movements. It need hardly be argued that the Negro people need social leadership more than most groups; that they have no traditions to fall back upon, no long established customs, no strong family ties, no well defined social classes.[210] All these things must be slowly and painfully evolved. . . .

The problem of training the Negro is to-day immensely complicated by the fact that the whole question of the efficiency and appropriateness of our present systems of education, for any kind of child, is a matter of active debate, in which final settlement seems still afar off.[211] Consequently it often happens that persons arguing for or against certain systems of education for Negroes have these controversies in mind and miss the real question at issue. The main question, so far as the Southern Negro is concerned, is: What under the present circumstance, must a system of education do in order to raise the Negro as quickly as possible in the scale of civilization? The answer to this question seems to me clear: It must strengthen the Negro's character, increase his knowledge and teach him to earn a living.

Now it goes without saying, that it is hard to do all these things simultaneously or suddenly, and that at the same time it will not do to give all the attention to one and neglect the others; we could give black boys trades, but that alone will not civilize a race of ex-slaves; we might simply increase their knowledge of the world, but this would not necessarily make them wish to use this knowledge honestly; we might seek to strengthen character and purpose, but to what end if this people have nothing to eat or to wear? A system of education is not one thing, nor does it have a single definite object, nor is it a mere matter of schools. Education is that whole system of human training within and without the school house walls, which molds and develops men. If then we start out to train an ignorant and unskilled people with a heritage of bad habits, our system of training must set before itself two great aims—the one dealing with knowledge and character, the other part seeking to give the child the technical knowledge necessary for him to earn a living under the present circumstances.

These objects are accomplished in part by the opening of the common schools on the one, and of the industrial schools on the other. But only in part, for there must also be trained those who are to teach these schools—men and women of knowledge and culture and technical skill who understand

---

208. Compare DuBois's appeal to data with Washington's use of evidence.

209. Du Bois is rebutting a point made by Washington above. The certainty of the conclusions is qualified by the likelihood that the underemployed college graduates would not be found or reply and, therefore, would predominate in the missing 40 percent.

210. Is it true, then, that Du Bois "underestimated the capacity of everyday people to 'know' about life?" West, "Black Strivings in a Twilight Civilization," pp. 58, 56.

211. Note the discussion about schooling made by the university presidents in the late nineteenth century in selections #47–49.

modern civilization and have the training and aptitude to impart it to the children under them. There must be teachers, and teachers of teachers, and to attempt to establish any sort of system of common and industrial school training, without *first* (and I say *first* advisedly) without *first* providing for the higher training of the very best teachers, is simply throwing your money to the winds. School houses do not teach themselves—piles of brick and mortar and machinery do not send out *men*. It is the trained, living human soul, cultivated and strengthened by long study and thought, that breathes the real breath of life into boys and girls and makes them human, whether they be black or white, Greek, Russian or American.

Nothing, in these latter days, has so dampened the faith of thinking Negroes in recent educational movements, as the fact that such movements have been accompanied by ridicule and denouncement and decrying of those very institutions of higher training which made the Negro public school possible, and make the Negro industrial schools thinkable. . . .

I would not deny, or for a moment seem to deny, the paramount necessity of teaching the Negro to work, and to work steadily and skillfully; or seem to depreciate in the slightest degree the important part industrial schools must play in the accomplishments of these ends;[212] but I *do* say, and insist upon it, that it is industrialism drunk with its vision of success, to imagine that its own work can be accomplished without providing for the training of broadly cultured men and women to teach its own teachers and to teach the teachers of the public schools.

But I have already said that human education is not simply a matter of schools; it is much more a matter of family and group life—the training of one's home, of one's daily companions, of one's social class. Now the black boy of the South moves in a black world—a world with its own leaders, its own thoughts, its own ideals. In this world he gets by far the larger part of his life training, and through the eyes of this dark world he peers into the veiled world beyond. Who guides and determines the education which he receives in his world? His teachers here are the group leaders of the Negro people—the physicians and clergymen, the trained fathers and mothers, the influential and forceful men about him of all kinds; here it is, if at all, that the culture of the surrounding world trickles through and is handed on by the graduates of the higher schools. Can such culture training of group-leaders be neglected? Can we afford to ignore it? Do you think that if the leaders of thought among Negroes are not trained and educated thinkers, that they will have no leaders? On the contrary a hundred half-trained demagogues will still hold the places they so largely occupy now, and hundreds of vociferous busy-bodies will multiply. You have no choice; either you must help furnish this race from within its own ranks with thoughtful men of trained leadership, or you must suffer the evil consequences of a headless misguided rabble.

I am an earnest advocate of manual training and trade teaching for black boys, and for white boys, too. I believe that next to the founding of Negro colleges the most valuable addition to Negro education since the war, has been industrial-training for black boys. Nevertheless, I insist that the object of all true education is not to make men carpenters, it is to make carpenters men; there are two means of making the carpenter a man, each equally important: the first is to give the group and community in which he works, liberally trained teachers and leaders to teach him and his family what life means; the second is to give him sufficient intelligence and technical skill to make him an efficient workman; the first object demands the Negro college and college-bred men—not a quantity of such colleges, but a

---

212. In similar language above, Washington concedes the converse point: "In what I say here I would not by any means have it understood that I would limit or circumscribe the mental development of the Negro student. No race can be lifted until its mind is awakened and strengthened. By the side of industrial training should always go mental and moral training . . ." Why did Washington and Du Bois not agree on the obvious compromise of emphasizing liberal education for the elite and industrial education for the masses?

few of excellent quality; not too many college-bred men,[213] but enough to leaven the lump, to inspire the masses, to raise the Talented Tenth to leadership; the second object demands a good system of common schools, well-taught, conveniently located and properly equipped. . . .

Again, in the manning of trade schools and manual training schools we are thrown back upon the higher training as its source and chief support. There was a time when any aged and worn-out carpenter could teach in a trade school. But not so to-day. Indeed the demand for college-bred men by a school like Tuskegee ought to make Mr. Booker T. Washington the firmest friend of higher training. Here he has as helpers the son of a Negro senator, trained in Greek and the humanities, and graduated at Harvard; the son of a Negro congressman and lawyer, trained in Latin and mathematics, and graduated at Oberlin; he has as his wife, a woman who read Virgil and Homer in the same class room with me; he has as college chaplain, a classical graduate of Atlanta University; as teacher of science, a graduate of Fisk; as teacher of history, a graduate of Smith—indeed some thirty of his chief teachers are college graduates, and instead of studying French grammars in the midst of weeds, or buying pianos for dirty cabins, they are at Mr. Washington's right hand helping him in a noble work. And yet one of the effects of Mr. Washington's propaganda has been to throw doubt upon the expediency of such training for Negroes as these persons have had. . . . Education and work are the levers to uplift a people. Work will not do it unless inspired by the right ideals and guided by intelligence. Education must not simply teach work—it must teach life. The Talented Tenth of the Negro race must be made leaders of thought and missionaries of culture among their people. No others can do this work and the Negro colleges must train men for it. The Negro race, like all other races, is going to be saved by its exceptional men.

---

213. Du Bois apparently shares Washington's concern about having too many liberally educated African Americans. Do they have the same reason for this concern? Would Aristotle in selection #3 agree with either of them?

Section VIII

Experimentation and Search for Coherence, 1910s-1930s

Liberal education entered the twentieth century under a cloud of criticism, much as it would exit. "[T]he American college is on trial. Condemnation is heard on every hand," lamented the reforming president of Reed College William T. Foster in his extensive, 1911 study of the liberal arts curriculum, appearing in selection #52. Above all, critics targeted the prevailing disagreement, confusion, and uncertainty about the nature of liberal education. "The college is without clear-cut notions of what a liberal education should be," observed the president of Cornell University in 1907, "this is not a local or special disability, but a paralysis affecting every college of Arts in America."[1] In 1918 the U.S. Commissioner of Education observed, "Within the last 25 years the curricula of colleges of arts and sciences have undergone large transformations. . . . There is disagreement among college officers as to the present aim of the college of arts and sciences. There is consequently disagreement as to the principles which should govern the framing of collegiate curricula."[2] The continuing problem was identified by Abraham Flexner in 1930: "No sound or consistent philosophy, thesis, or principle lies beneath the American university of today."[3]

Both the cause and the effect of the conceptual problem lay in "the breakdown of prescribed programs through the evolution of the elective system."[4] One study of 105 liberal arts colleges found that the average number of elective credits grew from 16 percent of the total required for the B.A. degree in 1890 to 66 percent in 1940.[5] To be sure, some celebrated this development. In 1907 Louis F. Snow interpreted the history of the liberal arts curriculum in the United States as an evolution toward greater freedom and electivism for the student, and this interpretation reached an apotheosis in the 1939 treatment of R. Freeman Butts, who attributed the development to the rise of Progressive education.[6] But most college leaders affirmed with Amherst College President Alexander Meiklejohn "that a

---

1. Quoted from the president's annual report in Abraham Flexner, *The American College: A Criticism* (New York: Century, 1908), p. 7.

2. P. P. Claxton, "Letter of Transmittal," in Mabel L. Robinson, *The Curriculum of the Woman's College, Bulletin, 1918, no. 6, U.S. Bureau of Education* (Washington, DC: GPO, 1918), p. 5.

3. Abraham Flexner, *Universities: American, English, German* (New York: Oxford University Press, 1930), p. 213.

4. William T. Foster, *Administration of the College Curriculum* (Boston: Houghton Mifflin, 1911), p. v.

5. Orrin T. Richardson, "Requirements for Bachelor's Degrees, 1890–1940" (Ph.D. diss., University of Chicago, 1946), pp. 120–1, 147–50. Richardson's study examined private liberal arts colleges with enrollments under 1,000 in 1940: 11 from New England, 21 from the middle Atlantic states, 14 from the south, and 59 from the North Central Association. Roman Catholic schools were not included.

6. Louis F. Snow, *The College Curriculum in the United States* (New York: Teachers College, Columbia University, 1907); R. F. Butts, *The College Charts Its Course: Historical Conceptions and Current Proposals* (New York: McGraw-Hill, 1939).

thing is understood only so far as it is unified. . . . In so far as modern education has become a thing of shreds and patches, has become a thing of departments, groups, and interests and problems and subjects, . . . our modern teaching, our modern curriculum, is not a thing of intelligent insight."[7]

The chief mechanism for attempting to bring order to the curriculum was "systems of major and minor groups—devices for enforcing concentration and distribution of studies." In the words of W. T. Foster below, "the most conspicuous of all the plans for compulsory concentration and distribution of studies is that which went into effect with the class of 1914 at Harvard College. After more than forty years of consistent, acknowledged leadership as the modern champion of the elective system . . . Harvard College took what some believers in President Eliot's educational philosophy regard as a retroactive step. President [Abbott L.] Lowell secured the adoption of rules requiring of all students some degree both of scattering and of specialization in the choice of courses for the A.B. degree . . .." By 1932 the dean of the college at the University of Chicago observed, "In the last decade a basic theory of college education has been put before us with increasing forcefulness: though a student who enters college with a well-defined educational aim should be given opportunity and encouragement to pursue that aim from the beginning of his freshman year, the major emphasis in the junior college years should be placed upon the breadth of educational experience; and, though general education should continue in senior college, the major emphasis of the last two years should be upon concentration in . . . some particular field of thought."[8]

The concentration-distribution scheme did not, however, remedy the anomie, because the distribution requirements basically constituted an elective system with constraints. In response, proposals for "general education" began to arise in the 1920s as a means to organize the part of liberal education that was not in the concentration. Selections #53 and #54 by Lionel Trilling and Daniel Bell recount Columbia University's pioneering effort at general education, while selection #55 by Stanford University professor Edgar E. Robinson portrays the concomitant invention of the orientation or survey course. By 1940 the general education movement had thus become a "groundswell . . . in the United States."[9]

The consensus upon general education often disguised disagreement because a variety of meanings and interpretations marched under the banner of general education. Within the disputed territory known as "liberal education," the attempt to identify a coherent domain named "general education" foundered on ambiguities among three primary interpretations: education for people in general, education for life in general, and high-minded general culture.[10] The ambiguities resulted, in part, from the widespread experimentation in liberal education that occurred during the 1920s and 1930s, leading some to conclude that "the only [curricular] trend that can be clearly discerned is toward experimenta-

7. "Remarks on the Report of the Association of American Colleges Commission on the Organization of the College Curriculum," *Association of American Colleges Bulletin* 9 (1923): 79–80. On Alexander Meiklejohn, see the introduction to selection #56 by Kathryn McHale.

8. C. S. Boucher, "Current Changes and Experiments in Liberal-Arts Colleges," in McHale, et al., *Changes and Experiments in Liberal-Arts Education* (Bloomington, IL: Public School Publishing, 1932), p. 17. On this reform of the elective system, intended to provide some structure and guidance for undergraduates in the form of distribution and concentration requirements, see Julie A. Reuben, *The Making of the Modern University: Intellectual Transformation and the Marginalization of Morality* (Chicago: University of Chicago Press, 1996), ch. 8.

9. Karl W. Bigelow and Malcolm S. MacLean, "Dominant Trends in General Education," in *General Education in the American College*, ed. Guy M. Whipple (Bloomington, IL: Public School Publishing, 1939), p. 351.

10. Wayne C. Booth develops five meanings of "general education" in *The Vocation of a Teacher: Rhetorical Occasions, 1967–1988* (Chicago: University of Chicago Press, 1988), pp. 114–6.

tion."[11] In the 1930s the American Association of University Women conducted an extensive study of this phenomenon, which is summarized in selection #56 by the study's director, Kathryn McHale. There were many vectors in this experimentation; but the two major, intellectual themes were "Deweyan Progressivism" and "great books," which exercised a powerful influence on the rest of liberal education due to the strength of their conviction and the cogency of their rationales.[12] The Progressive effort is exemplified by selection #57 from the report of the Rollins College Conference on "The Curriculum for the Liberal Arts College," chaired by John Dewey in 1931. The neo-Thomist or neo-scholastic variant of the Great Books movement is expressed in selection #58 by the well-known president of the University of Chicago, Robert M. Hutchins.

11. Bigelow and MacLean, "Dominant Trends in General Education," p. 367.

12. "The 'great books' concept had as much of the flavor of the esoteric cult as Deweyan Progressivism did." Laurence Veysey, "Stability and Experiment in the American Undergraduate Curriculum," in *Content and Context: Essays on College Education*, ed. Carl Kaysen (New York: McGraw-Hill, 1973), p. 13.

52. William T. Foster, *Administration of the College Curriculum* (1911)

INTRODUCTION

Born and raised in Boston, William T. Foster (1879–1950) and his family were left destitute after his father died early in William's childhood. But he worked his way through Harvard College, graduating magna cum laude in 1901, and began teaching at Bates College in Maine. Two years later he returned to Harvard, earned an M.A. in English in 1904, and began teaching rhetoric at Bowdoin College, achieving promotion to full professor in 1905 after organizing a department of education in the college. Intrigued by the scholarly study of education (which he defends in selection #52), Foster moved to Teachers College, Columbia University, as a lecturer in 1909 and received the Ph.D. in 1911. His doctoral dissertation, "Administration of the College Curriculum," incorporated the most extensive review of data about the topic to that point, including a study of "100,000 college grades, covering the total experience of 4,311 college students under the elective system at Harvard College for fifteen years," as well as descriptions of the curriculum at two hundred colleges.[13]

In 1910 this informative study led to Foster being named the first president of Reed College, located in Portland, Oregon. Foster's mission at Reed was "to establish a college in which intellectual enthusiasm should be dominant." In his view, "if the life of the student was to be one of 'persistent and serious study,' there had to be an 'uncompromising elimination' of the activities that compete with studies—above all, of 'intercollegiate games and fraternities and sororities.'"[14] Foster's realization of this vision was, however, compromised over the ensuing decade by the declining value of the endowment, disagreement over the academic program, and disapproval of his pacifism during World War I. In 1919 Foster resigned the presidency of Reed and commenced a new career as an economist, influencing fiscal policy in the administrations of Presidents Herbert Hoover and Franklin D. Roosevelt. Foster died in 1950; his ashes were scattered over the lake on the campus of Reed College.

In the following reading, Foster's tables of data about the liberal arts curriculum are supplemented by data drawn from two contemporary and complementary sources. *The College-Bred Negro American* was published by W. E. B. Du Bois and Augustus Granville Dill as Foster was completing his dissertation and assuming the presidency of Reed College. Dill studied with Du Bois at Atlanta University, graduated in 1906, and then earned another B.A. from Harvard in 1908. Returning to Atlanta University, Dill earned an M.A. in sociology and became Du Bois's colleague.[15] The second source was *The Curriculum of the Woman's College*, which was published by the U.S. Bureau of Education in 1918 and authored by Mabel L. Robinson, who worked as a researcher at the Carnegie Foundation for the Advancement of Teaching after earning a Ph.D. from Columbia University in 1915.[16]

13. Foster, *Administration of the College Curriculum*, p. vi.

14. Burton R. Clark, *The Distinctive College: Antioch, Reed, and Swarthmore* (Chicago: Aldine, 1970), p. 96.

15. W. E. B. Du Bois and Augustus G. Dill, *The College-Bred Negro American* (Atlanta, GA: Atlanta University Press, 1910).

16. Mabel L. Robinson, *The Curriculum of the Woman's College*, Bulletin, 1918, no. 6, U.S. Bureau of Education (Washington, DC: GPO, 1918).

SELECTION[17]

Present Requirements for the A.B. Degree

The present age is one of transition in higher education: the American college is on trial. Condemnation is heard on every hand. The capital charge is preferred that there is a general demoralization of college standards, expressing the fact that, as the college serves no particular educational purpose, it is immaterial whether the student takes the thing seriously or not. The college is said to retain traces of its English origin in the familiar twaddle about the college as a sort of gentleman factory—a gentleman being a youth free from the suspicion of thoroughness or definite purpose. The college is charged with failure in pedagogical insight at each of the critical junctures of the boy's education, so that a degree may be won with little or no systematic exertion, and as a result our college students are said to emerge flighty, superficial, and immature, lacking, as a class, concentration, seriousness, and thoroughness. . . .

This confusion of ideas as to what should constitute the course of study for the Arts degree is revealed in the contradictory charges brought against the American college of today. . . . Some critics condemn the college for keeping its curriculum out of touch with the masses, and thus harboring an indolent aristocracy; others condemn the college for yielding weakly to the popular cry for more practical courses. Some deplore the desertion of culture courses in favor of courses of vocational trend; while others call the culture courses nothing but soft, wishy-washy excuses for sloth, indifference, neglect, and ill-concealed ridicule of the study and its teacher. Some critics hold that the one thing necessary is to secure concentration of each student's work in some department, while others enact complicated rules to enforce the scattering of electives among various departments. . . .

One might present an endless confusion of opinions as to what the college course should be; but altogether they would demonstrate finally only one important truth, namely, that nobody knows what the American college course should be. It is needless to tarry long with individual opinions on this subject. The resultants of thousands of such opinions can be seen at a glance in tables showing the present requirements for the degree of Bachelor of Arts in American colleges. . . .

The following table indicates the subjects required for the A.B. degree in 29 state universities. The unit used is the year-hour: one hour per week for one academic year.

---

17. William T. Foster, *Administration of the College Curriculum* (Boston: Houghton Mifflin, 1911), pp. 159–99, 304–36.

University	Latin, Greek	Modern Language	Natural Science	English, Rhetoric	Math	History	Total Required	Degree Total
Alabama	6	10	4	6	9	3.5	39.5	65
Arkansas		6		6			16	64
Colorado		7.5		5		3	18	60
Florida	6	8	3	6	8	5	38	71
Georgia	6	6	3	3	12	6	39	67
Idaho		12		8	4		26	66
Illinois		4		4			12	65
Indiana		10	2.5	2	2.5		18	60
Iowa		4		5			14	62.5
Kansas				5			9	60
Kentucky	6						11	69
Minnesota				1.5	2.5		6	62.5
Mississippi		3	3	3	2.5	1	15.5	65
Missouri	2.5	2.5	5		2.5	2.5	15	60
Nevada	7	7	4	6	3	5	37	62
New Mexico		12		3			[?]	[?]
Ohio	12		4.6	2.3	2.6	1	28	[?]
Oklahoma				3		3	10.5	62.5
Pennsylvania University		6	5	6	2	2	23	60
Pennsylvania State	15	8		6.5	4	3	51	70
South Carolina		12	3	6	6	6	38	67
Tennessee		12	3	6	3		29	60
Texas		12	6	6	3		27+	60
Utah				3			6	61
Vermont	8			6	3		21.5	58
Virginia		9	6	6	3	3	27	52+
Washington		8	4	8	2	2	32	64
Wisconsin		8	5	3	3	3	24	60
Wyoming				3			3	63

The most striking fact exhibited by the table is the total want of accepted ideas as to what subjects should be required for the A.B. degree or what proportion of the studies should be prescribed. A mere glance at the table shows the wide diversity of practice which has resulted from these attempts of many groups of men in many states to decide what is the essential core of a liberal education. Indeed, so great is the diversity of these requirements that if any one of these institutions is exactly right, all the rest must be wrong. The amount of required work ranges from three hours in Wyoming to thirty-nine and one-half hours in Alabama.[18] There is no conspicuous central tendency, and the average deviation of the individual institutions is great. . . .

The following table presents the subjects required for the A.B. degree and the number of year-hours allotted to each in certain universities under private control. The variation here exhibited is even greater than that for state universities. Here again the curriculum appears to be administered in the familiar, historical way, not according to any clearly defined and abiding principle, but according to personal [considerations] of the moment and the place.

University	Latin, Greek	Modern Language	Natural Science	English, Rhetoric	Math	History	Total Required	Degree Total
Brown		12	3	6	7	6	37	60
[City] College of New York	3	4	9	6	3	4	41.5	73
Columbia		9	7	5	3	3	28	62
Cornell		3	3	1.5	3	1.5	12	60
Harvard		3		3			6	51+
Johns Hopkins		6	5	6	1.5	3	31	60
Stanford				5			5	60
New York			1	2			6	57
Northwestern		3	4	5	3	3	21	60
Princeton	9	5	4	2	4		27	61
Rochester	10	5	5	6.6	4	3	47.3	60
Syracuse	13	3	3	3	3		26	60
Washington, St. Louis		6	3	6			15	60
Western Reserve	3			4	3		13.5	60

The following table indicates also the subjects prescribed in certain colleges for women [and for African-Americans], the most nearly uniform groups it is possible to find.[19]

---

18. The categories in the following tables have been consolidated from those presented by Foster. The number of year-hours in the "Total Required" column sometimes includes additional subjects not listed in the other columns.

19. The following table has been simplified from that presented by Foster regarding women's colleges in 1909. The data for 1916 are drawn from Robinson, *The Curriculum of the Woman's College*, pp. 62–4. The bottom half of the table has been compiled from the data in Du Bois and Dill, *The College-Bred Negro American*, pp. 20–1. The percentages there have been converted here into year-hours, assuming a sixty-year-hour college course, to facilitate comparison with the other tables. It is not possible to compute the total of all required subjects based upon the information in this source. Foster's observation about uniformity confirms the point that less experimentation and innovation occurred in colleges serving marginalized populations, which had to defend their legitimacy and could not risk appearing unorthodox academically. Hence, the curriculum of such colleges " has been marked by no particular originality" but took refuge in "the conserving power of safe imitation." Robinson, *The Curriculum of the Woman's College*, p. 108.

College	Latin, Greek	Modern Language	Natural Science	English, Rhetoric	Math	History	Total Required	Degree Total
WOMEN								
Barnard, 1916	c. 3	c. 3	c. 6	c. 6	c. 3	3	c. 30	62
Bryn Mawr, 1909		5	5	10		5	30	60
Mt. Holyoke, 1916	3	3	6	4.5	3	3	30.5	60
Pennsylvania, 1909		6	3	7	3	3	30	56
Radcliffe, 1916		3		3			6	51+
Rockford, 1909	4	4	8	6	8	3	41.5	59
Smith, 1909		6	3	2	3		21	56
Sweet Briar, 1909		6	3	6		3	25	61
Vassar, 1916	3	3	3	3	3	3	27	56
Wellesley, 1916		3	9	3	3	4	27	59
Wells, 1909	3	3	6	5	3		26.5	57.5
AFRICAN-AMERICANS								
Atlanta	11.5	8	9.5	8	5		42	60
Fisk	13	7	10.5	8	5		43.5	60
Atlanta Baptist	11.5	6	8.5	6.5	4		36.5	60
Howard	9	6	8.5	9	6		38.5	60
Spelman	12.5	3	9.5	8	5		38	60
Clark	19	7	9.5	4	6		45.5	60
Straight	14	6	8.5	6	6		40.5	60
Lane	14	5	12	2	12		45	60
Virginia Union	6	6	8.5	9	6		41.5	60
New Orleans	8	6	12	6.5	6		38.5	60
Walden	14		12	6.5	6		38.5	60
Bishop	17	4	4	5	6		36	60
Talladega	19		10	5.5	7		41.5	60
Claflin	11	5	12	11	6		45	60
Morgan	12	12	6	9	5		44	60
Wiley	8	6	12	7	7		40	60
George H. Smith	13	3	10	7	8		41	60
Bennett	14		12	7	6		39	60

The following table presents the practice of small colleges in all parts of the country. It would seem that the almost innumerable differences here revealed must shake the confidence of any faculty in the wisdom of its absolute prescriptions, and yet the table *excludes* those colleges exhibiting the greatest idiosyncrasies in their requirements. . . .

College	Latin, Greek	Modern Language	Natural Science	English, Rhetoric	Math	History	Total Required	Degree Total
Allegheny	14	4	4	5	4	3	39	60
Amherst	6			3	4		16	60
Bates	3	9		3	4		31.3	[?]
Beloit		6	3	2			12	60
Bowdoin		12		2.5			22.5	62
Butler		10	5				15	63
Carleton		8		2	4		18	65
Carroll [WS]		12	5	3		4	31	62
Colby [ME]	4	6	3	3	4		25	[?]
Colorado			3	6	4	2	23	60
Cornell [IA]		13		4	2.5		37	62
Detroit	26		10	12	6	6	72	72
Dickinson	8		1.5	6	5		[?]	[?]
Franklin and Marshall	14	6	8	6	4	4	58	58
Grinnell		10	3	3	3	3	25	60
Haverford	7	7		6	3		35	73
Hobart		12	6	6	4	3	17.5	60
Illinois		10	5	8	5	3	34	66
Kenyon			4	7		3	18	66
Knox	4	2		5	3.5	3	25	60
Lafayette	16	3	5	3.5	6.6	1	46.1	64
Lake Forest				4	3		15	62
Miami [OH]		6	4	6	3		27	60
Monmouth							4	64
Oberlin		4	4	3			13	60
Occidental			3	6	4	3	26.5	64
Pomona		4	4	6	4	4	31	64
Ripon				2			2	60
Rollins		10	9.5		5	3	56	68
Swarthmore		6	3	5	3		19.5	63
Trinity [NC]	8		9	6	6	3	35	64
Tufts		9	6	3	6		28	61
Wake Forest	5	3	9	6	5	3	37	60
Washburn		3	4	3	3		13	61
Washington and Lee				3	3		6	60
Wesleyan [CT]		3		4			7	60
William and Mary	6	6	5	7	4	3	41	60
Williams	3	3		2	5		16.5	62

College catalogs from all parts of the country tell us that "students are required to pursue those subjects that are universally regarded as essential to a liberal education." It would be pertinent to ask the writers of such statements to examine [these] tables and then name those subjects that are universally regarded as essential to a liberal education. Is there one? Even the general prescription of English is an agreement in name only; what actually goes on under this name is so diverse as to show that we have not yet discovered an "essential" course in English. And this is our nearest approach to agreement.

In most institutions the old compulsory programs of study have broken down of their own weight. Although, as the tables clearly show, nearly all colleges retain some vestige of the prescribed regime, yet in recent years most of the attempts to regulate the courses of study of individual students have dealt with systems of major and minor groups—devices for enforcing concentration and distribution of studies. Various practices of this kind we shall now consider in some detail. . . .

Present Major and Minor Requirements
Various attempts to regulate the electives of college students are summarized, as far as it is possible to summarize such diverse practices, in the following tables. . . .[20] The investigation covered two hundred of the better known colleges and universities. . . . Even these groups of colleges and universities, selected for the relative simplicity of their requirements, present great diversity and complexity as their most striking features. In the number of subjects required, in the number of year-hours unrestricted, in the proportion of work called for by the major subject, in the proportion controlled by the major adviser, in the amount prescribed for distribution, in the maximum and minimum allowances for groups, there is no uniformity, nor even any significant central tendencies.

Here, as in the attempts to prescribe "essential" subjects, the actual practices of colleges all over the country reveal no guiding principles. Most of these institutions force all students to do in general what their patchwork curriculum of a generation ago allowed no students to do. So innocent of abiding cause are these miscellaneous and contradictory regulations that the tables will be out of date, no doubt, shortly after they are printed. Indeed, such administrators as actually enforce these rules must be hard put to it for reasons, unless their students are uncommonly docile. One even wonders whether college officers can in all cases interpret their own rules. . . .

The statistics of actual student programs from various institutions . . . warrant the [conclusion] that not half of the concentration requirements in American colleges have more than a negligible effect. If compulsory specialization is preferable to complete election, then the proportion of a student's entire work required in his major subject should be more than one-fifth. Less than that is no compulsion at all, only a pretense at "safeguarding" the elective system.. . . .

The American college is on trial. . . . Yet, every year sees a larger enrollment. The total increase in seventeen years was over 150 percent, an increase out of all proportion to the corresponding gains in population. From 1902 to 1905 the registration of the small colleges in New England increased over twenty percent; and the rate continues until the question is, how much longer shall we have small colleges? Here, then, are the American public staking their sons, their daughters and their millions on their faith in the possibilities of the college, and yet agreeing, on the whole, with the verdict of the *Nation* that "the college is the least satisfactory part of our educational system and has urgent need to justify itself." This seems an anomalous condition—our colleges growing rapidly both in numbers and in popular disapproval.[21]

---

20. Foster's tables have been omitted.

21. How can one explain this anomaly, which seems to exist in the early twentieth-first century?

General Education

53. Lionel Trilling, "General Education and the American Preparatory System" (1973)

INTRODUCTION

The regulations for distribution and concentration of studies were intended to reinstate in liberal education the coherence that had disintegrated under the forces of electivism and disciplinary proliferation. But many questioned whether the desired coherence could be derived from "the central principle . . . that each student must take a considerable amount of work in some one field and that the rest of his courses must be well distributed," in William T. Foster's phrase above. Recalling the sophisticated architectures of the liberal arts in the past, some observers derided the notion of founding liberal education upon the homely aphorism of "knowing a little of everything and something well."[22]

Concentration was justified by the rationales that deep study of one field teaches understanding about the complexity of inquiry, about the limitations of expert knowledge, and about the dangerous but tempting simplicity of superficial knowledge. Distribution, though complementing concentration by providing a sense of intellectual context, is irreducibly a delimited electivism, relying fundamentally on the negative rationale underlying electivism: that the university cannot decide which subject matter is most important to study; students must choose according to their own preferences and situations. Thus, the concentration-distribution approach not only failed to provide the intellectual, moral, and psychological rationales lacking in electivism, but also incorporated a self-contradiction in as much as the superficiality exposed by concentration was embraced by distribution. While students were learning, on the one hand, about the dangerous liquor of superficial knowledge; they were being required, on the other hand, to imbibe.

Furthermore, most concentration-distribution systems had no real effect. In analyzing the new concentration-distribution system that President A. L. Lowell established at Harvard, Foster found that little change occurred from the pattern of courses chosen by students under the elective system. Regarding the impact of the distribution requirement upon the elective system in "a typical small college," such as Bowdoin in Maine, Foster concluded, "the adoption by Bowdoin of the Harvard scattering requirements would have only a negligible effect. . . . [What] the new plan for compulsory distribution of studies at Harvard aims to achieve is, in fact, already achieved under the much more restricted curriculum and the virtually unrestricted elective system of a typical small college." Moreover, "the statistics of actual student programs from various institutions . . . warrant the [conclusion] that not half of the concentration requirements in American colleges have more than a negligible effect. If compulsory specialization is preferable to complete election, then the proportion of a student's entire work required in his major subject should be more than one-fifth. Less than that is no compulsion at all, only a pretense at 'safeguarding' the elective system."[23]

Given the lack of influence, coherent or otherwise, of distribution and concentration requirements upon students' actual election of courses, colleges and universities began to formulate programs of

---

22. Lowell famously employed variations of this phrase in his inaugural address and elsewhere. See Albert L. Lowell, "Inaugural Address," *Harvard Graduates Magazine* 18 (1909): 218; Albert L. Lowell, *Annual Report of the President and Treasurer of Harvard College, 1908–1909* (Cambridge, MA: Harvard University Press, 1910), p. 9.

23. William T. Foster, *Administration of the College Curriculum* (Boston: Houghton Mifflin, 1911), pp. 190, 195. Does Foster's rule hold true today?

"general education" that would displace or, in effect, organize the distributed studies of liberal education. To be sure, the general education movement was prompted also by social forces, such as "the steady lengthening of the normal period of formal education in this country. . . . due to the increased difficulty youth had in finding jobs during the depression." Yet, for advocates of general education, the fundamental question was how to provide liberal education with coherence and structure—"a natural and significant form, with a beginning, a middle, and an end," in the words of Lionel Trilling below. Starting in the early 1920s, colleges and universities from New York to California joined the national movement toward general education. The acknowledged pioneer and leader in this effort was Columbia University, as related in the following readings by Lionel Trilling and Daniel Bell.

Born and raised in New York City, Lionel Trilling (1905–75) earned the B.A. (1925), M.A. (1926), and Ph.D. (1938) degrees from Columbia University, where he taught in the English department from 1931 until his retirement in 1970. During this period, he achieved fame as a literary critic, while evaluating literature within the social, moral, and psychological milieu of the author and the reader. Trilling's approach appears in the following account of the general education program of Columbia College. Having belonged to one of the first classes to enter the program in 1921, Trilling was well qualified to provide this retrospective commentary at a symposium on general education held at Columbia in 1973. Two years later, he died in New York.

SELECTION[24]

In 1876 the trustees had invited John W. Burgess to fill the Chair of History, Political Science, and International Law; there were big chairs in those days and presumably men big enough to fill them. It was understood that Burgess was to develop graduate study here at Columbia according to the model of the German universities. He had studied at Göttingen, Leipzig, and Berlin working under the best professors of the great German historical school. He was to establish here the ethos and the methods of these preeminent scholars, their commitment to the ideals of modern science. This being his mission, it was inevitable that Burgess should have directed toward the antiquated ideals of the undergraduate college an unremitting antagonism.[25]

It can't be said that the contempt in which Burgess held the College, and to which he presumably recruited the opinion of President Frederick A. P. Barnard,[26] was wholly unjustified. At the time when Burgess came upon the scene and for a good many years thereafter, the "College proper" was a small old-fashioned school, its curriculum limited to Latin, Greek, mathematics of an outmoded sort, a little metaphysics, a very little natural science. Burgess saw it as kept in being only by inertia and the piety of its alumni. In his view the one thing that might rationalize its existence would be its consenting to limit itself to what he called a "gymnastic" function—that is, to do the work of a German *gymnasium*, giving the pupils, by drill and rote-learning, the tools they would need as postulants either of pure scholarship or professional practice.

---

24. Lionel Trilling, "General Education and the American Preparatory System," *Seminar Reports, Program of General Education in the Humanities, Columbia University*, v. 1, no. 3 (7 Dec. 1973): 1–2. Reprinted by permission of Columbia University.

25. John W. Burgess (1844–1931) taught at Knox College, studied in Germany from 1871 to 1873, taught briefly at Amherst College, and then served on the Columbia faculty from 1876 until 1912.

26. Frederick A. P. Barnard (1809–1889) was professor of mathematics and natural science at the University of Alabama (1837–1854) and then at the University of Mississippi (1854–1856), where he served as president (1856–1861). During his presidency at Columbia (1864–1889), the institution grew tenfold, adding many departments and associated schools.

In 1894 the "College proper" found its champion, and Burgess met his legendary opponent, in John Van Amringe, who in that year was appointed Dean of the College. For Van Amringe no claims of intellectual distinction can be made. He had wanted to be Professor of Latin and Greek in the College, and when that ambition was frustrated, he accepted the professorship of mathematics. In both fields he was a sincere scholar of no originality whatever. He seems to have had no particular respect for intellectual achievement and to have favored athletes over serious students. But he thought that the "College proper" did an important thing—the College, he said, did a job of "making men." . . .[27]

When he spoke of the College "making men," he meant that it did not concern itself to make specialist scholars or practitioners of the professions, but that it set its students on the way to knowing the good when they saw it and to being disposed to choose it, that it aimed to teach them to look before and after, and in general to use their minds in ways which are appropriate to civil existence. In all his annual reports Van Amringe asserted his belief that this aim was forwarded by liberal undergraduate education and he resisted all efforts to curtail its scope.

Of such efforts there were many during the term of Van Amringe's service as Dean of the College, and despite his resistance they were mostly successful. In the early years of this century the idea of the undergraduate college fell into disrepute with many serious Americans. Some decades earlier the tendency had gone the opposite way and the professional schools of the first rank had insisted upon graduation from college as a requirement for admission. Now this came to be thought supererogatory and even harmful.

In 1902 Nicholas Murray Butler, in his presidential report, expressed his belief that "four years is too long a time to devote to the College course as now constituted, especially for students who are to remain in University residence as technical or professional students."[28] And in his report of 1903, President Butler advocated that there be set up in the College a two-year course as an option along with the usual four-year program. In 1905 he was able to announce with pride the establishment of the plan of "professional option," the so-called "Columbia plan," by which a student after two years of College might go on to one of the University's professional schools. Butler summed up the meaning of the new arrangement in the following words: "The Faculty of Columbia College say explicitly that to prescribe graduation from a four-year college as a *sine qua non* for the professional study of law, medicine, engineering, or teaching is not to do a good thing but a bad thing." Why was it not a good thing but a bad thing? Butler was in no doubt about the reason. In those days what we now call liberal education went under the name of "culture" and Butler said flatly that "any culture that is worthy of the name . . . will be increased, not diminished, by bringing to an end the idling and dawdling that now characterize so much of American higher education . . .."

No sooner had "idling and dawdling" been curtailed by cutting down the number of college years through the "professional option," than Butler began to wonder whether he after all quite liked the new efficiency. In his report of 1909, . . . it seems to him that young men are in much too much of a hurry to become lawyers, doctors, engineers, teachers; and he reflects nostalgically that the four-year undergraduate college did after all make possible what he now calls the "generous and reflective use of leisure."

---

27. Compare this account of Van Amringe (1835–1915), who graduated from Columbia College in 1860 and served as professor of mathematics (1865–1910) and dean (1894–1910): "As a teacher he was clear, quick, and incisive; having a perfect mastery of his subject, he expected and demanded hard work of his students, and was intolerant of inattention or neglect. Keen to detect a fault and sharp to reprimand, he was equally ready to recognize a good work and anxious to do strict justice." J. B. Pine, Memorial to John H. Van Amringe, *Columbia Alumni News* (5 Nov. 1915), sec. 2, p. 192.

28. Nicholas Murray Butler (1862–1947) held the office of president of Columbia University from 1902 to 1945.

Despite Butler's change of heart about the four-year college course, the plan of professional option remained in force into the 1920s. But in that decade there was a mounting opposition to the conception of Columbia College as what came to be called a "service institution," having no other goal than that of readying young men for their professional training. The plan of professional option fell into disrepute and was ultimately abolished. More and more boldly the College asserted that its existence was defined by a particular function, which was not to be discharged in less than four years. And these four years were not to be thought of in their more linear consecutiveness but as having a natural and significant form, with a beginning, a middle, and an end. The College course was to be conceived of as a whole—could be conceived of in no other way since its purpose was to make whole men.

From the 1930s through the 1940s and the 1950s, the life of Columbia College was informed with a sense of educational purpose which, in the cogency of its conception of liberality and generality and in the firmness of its commitment to this ideal, was unequaled in its time.

54. Daniel Bell, *The Reforming of General Education* (1966)

INTRODUCTION

Like Trilling, Daniel Bell (1919-) was born and raised in New York City and pursued a career as a writer and professor, though in a different field. After completing the B.S. in 1939 at City College of New York, Bell worked as managing editor of *The New Leader* during World War II and taught social science at the University of Chicago from 1945 to 1948. For the next ten years he wrote on social and political topics as labor editor for *Fortune*. Returning to Columbia, he received the Ph.D. in 1960 and taught as professor of sociology from 1960 until 1969, when he moved to Harvard University, retiring in 1990.

Over the course of his career, Bell published a number of significant books, including *Marxian Socialism in America* (1952), *The Radical Right* (1963), *The Coming of Post-Industrial Society* (1973), and *The Cultural Contradictions of Capitalism* (1976). Selection #54 is drawn from a report by Bell's "committee of one," appointed by the dean of Columbia College, to the faculty at Columbia concerning the reform of general education at that institution. Bell's report became a landmark book on the course of the noted general education program at Columbia University: *The Reforming of General Education: The Columbia College Experience in Its National Setting* (1966).

SELECTION[29]

Columbia College has always been proud of its role as the pioneer of general education in the United States. . . . For a program that has had such extraordinary influence, general education at Columbia was the result of a curious mixture of parochial, sociopolitical, and philosophical motives.[30] Within Columbia College, if I have read the history correctly, there were three impulses: the College's struggle against the German tradition of the university, with its "professional" emphasis, which had been favored by Professor John W. Burgess and President Nicholas Murray Butler; the abandonment of a sterile classicism symbolized by the Latin entrance requirement, which aped the English model; and the changing character of the student body, particularly as the children of immigrants began to predominate intellectually, if not in numbers, in Columbia College. . . .

The stand against professionalism, thus was one of the shaping elements of what would become, in the post-World War I years, the new Columbia College. A second was the abandonment of an emphasis on the classics as the basis for the bachelor of arts degree. In 1897 the College had abolished the Greek entrance requirement, but retained Latin as a basic requirement for admission. Those who sought a bachelor of arts degree had to demonstrate proficiency in Greek or Latin. But the trustees, in order to maintain the emphasis on the classics, voted in 1905 to give a bachelor of science degree to those who preferred subjects alternative to the classics. For a decade the College offered both the B.A. and the B.S. degrees, but . . . a large number of the students who were candidates for the bachelor of arts degree found the Latin requirement burdensome and oppressive. In 1916 the faculty voted to abolish the Latin requirement for those entering and seeking the B.A., and this decision was accepted by the trustees. . . .[31]

---

29. Daniel Bell, *The Reforming of General Education: The Columbia College Experience in Its National Setting* (New York: Columbia University Press, 1966), pp. 12–26. Reprinted by permission of Columbia University Press.

30. Compare the motives of Cicero, who advocated general education in selection #4.

31. This paragraph, and the following four, are displaced from Bell's order.

One of the chief consequences of this action—one that the College was mindful of in making the move—was to change the ethnic and social composition of the College. In the emphasis on Latin, students from the public high schools, where Latin was often either not taught or taught poorly, were at a disadvantage against those from private preparatory schools. The abolition of the Latin requirement made the public high school more important as a source of student supply. The result was that it helped bring a new kind of student into Columbia.

The change in the character of the Columbia student body—the third parochial element that shaped the new college—was . . . "a social diversity which is a factor often unappreciated in college life."[32] "Social diversity," in this context, was a euphemism for Jews, and with his characteristic courage Keppel confronted the question directly. "One of the commonest references that one hears with regard to Columbia," he wrote, "is that its position at the gateway of European immigration makes it socially uninviting to students who come from homes of refinement. The form which the inquiry takes in these days of slowly dying race prejudice is, 'Isn't Columbia overrun with European Jews who are most unpleasant persons socially?'" Columbia, said Keppel, is not "overrun with Jews." But he defended their admission.

Not only were the Jewish students intellectually stimulating, but Columbia, he said, had a public duty to aid the ambitious but socially maladroit child of immigrants. "What most people regard as a racial problem is really a social problem," he wrote, "The Jews who have had the advantages of decent social surroundings for a generation or two are entirely satisfactory companions. Their intellectual ability, and particularly their intellectual curiosity, are above the average, and the teachers are unanimous in saying that their presence in the classroom is distinctly desirable. There are, indeed, Jewish students of another type who have not had the social advantages of their more fortunate fellows. Often they come from an environment which in any stock less fired with ambition would have put the idea of higher education entirely out of the question. Some of these are not particularly pleasant companions, but the total number is not large, and every reputable institution aspiring to public service must stand ready to give to those of probity and good moral character the benefits which they are making great sacrifices to obtain."[33]

It was this social diversity—not just the Jewish students but the transformation of Columbia from a genteel New York College to a national school—that was to give Columbia its cosmopolitanism and intellectual vigor in the two decades following World War I. . . .

These three elements were inherent in the proposal by John Erskine, in 1917, to set up a General Honors course that would read and discuss one classic a week.[34] The intention in reading the "great

---

32. Bell does not provide specific citations for his quotations. This one is from *Columbia* (New York: Oxford University Press, 1914), pp. 179–81, by Frederick P. Keppel (1875–1943), who received the B.A. from Columbia College in 1898, served as dean from 1910 to 1917, and held the office of president of the Carnegie Corporation of New York from 1922 to 1941.

33. Compare Keppel's view of good companionship to John Van Amringe's idea of "making men" described in selection #53 by Lionel Trilling.

34. "Erskine's famous General Honors course, in which students read and discussed one classic a week, became the prototype of humanities courses later given on a hundred campuses." Henry D. Aiken, *Predicament of the University* (Bloomington: Indiana University Press, 1971), p. 139. Raised in New York City and tutored by governesses, John Erskine (1879–1951) received a classical diploma from Columbia Grammar School, the B.A. from Columbia College (1900), and the Ph.D. (1903) from Columbia University. He taught English at Amherst College (1906–1909), and then at Columbia (1916–1928). From 1928 until 1937, he was president of the Julliard School of Music in Boston.

books" was to inculcate in the student a humanistic rather than a professional orientation;[35] to force him to confront a great work directly, rather than treat it with awe reserved for a classic; and, in the contemporary jargon, "to acculturate" a student whose background and upbringing had excluded him from the "great traditions."

Within the larger American society there were two important influences, more general in nature, upon the shape of the new education. One, which universities were struggling to assimilate, was the great rush of knowledge coming out of empirical investigations in recently developed disciplines like institutional economics and sociology.[36] The second influence, and perhaps more important, was World War I. When the United States entered the war the country was divided in its feelings, and the government had set up some organizations to propagandize, indoctrinate, and educate the country about America's war aims. On behalf of the Student Army Training Corps, which had been established in colleges throughout the country, the government asked Columbia to prepare a course in "War Issues." . . . After it was approved in Washington, the course was given at Columbia and at all other Student [Army Training] Corps centers. While the "War Issues" course was in progress, various faculty members . . . felt that there should be a course devoted to "Peace Issues."[37] These two influences resulted in a course, offered in the fall of 1917, entitled "Contemporary Civilization"; it was required of all freshmen and was conducted five days a week. . . .

Thus, the Erskine course on the "great books" and the course in War Issues shared in the ancestry of general education, both at Columbia and elsewhere. Yet the yoking of these two produced tensions and paradoxes that were not always evident to the practitioners of general education: The Erskine program, with its emphasis on the classics of Western thought, constituted, as Lionel Trilling has put it, "a fundamental criticism of American democratic education," while the Contemporary Civilization course was an open and frank acknowledgment of the direct responsibility of the College to the stated democratic needs of society. . . .[38]

The tradition of the liberal arts at Columbia was embodied in the idea of three broad courses—Contemporary Civilization, the Humanities, and the Sciences—which would be required of all students. These courses evolved slowly.[39] Contemporary Civilization, at the start a one-year course, in

---

35. In a footnote, Bell quotes these words of Lionel Trilling: "One opposition to the plan came from men who were concerned to protect what they conceived to be the scholarly integrity of their subject. To some scholars who had spent a lifetime in the study of certain authors of certain books, it seemed sacrilegious that undergraduates should be presumed able to read them with understanding in a single week. Erskine replied that every book had to be read at some time for the first time, that there was a difference between a reading acquaintance with great authors and a scholarly investigation of them."

36. Bell notes parenthetically, "In 1910, for example, Amherst College . . . set up a general course entitled "Social and Economic Institutions" to 'unify' or 'integrate' social studies."

37. See Herbert E. Hawkes, "A College Course on Peace Issues," *Educational Review* 58 (1919): 143–50. Mentioned below as Dean Frederick Keppel's successor, Hawkes (1872–1943) attended Yale, receiving the B.A. in 1896 and the Ph.D. in mathematics in 1900. After teaching at Yale, he came to Columbia as a professor of mathematics and served as dean of Columbia College from 1918 onward.

38. Another "tension and paradox . . . not always evident to the practitioners of general education" was that, while Erskine devoted his course to studying primary texts, "from the beginning [Contemporary Civilization] has based itself largely on materials written or edited by members of the staff: a carefully wrought educational venture needs specially devised instruments." Justus Buchler, "Reconstruction in the Liberal Arts," in *A History of Columbia College on Morningside*, ed. Dwight C. Miner (New York: Columbia University Press, 1954), pp. 102–5

39. See Robert L. Belknap and Richard Kuhns, *Tradition and Innovation: General Education and the Integration of the University* (New York: Columbia University Press, 1977).

1929 became a two-year sequence, the first year dealing primarily with the intellectual traditions and institutional development of Western society, and the second year, with changing emphases, focusing on contemporary socioeconomic problems. The two-year Humanities sequence (the first year initiated in 1937, the second in 1947) concentrated in the first year on the masterpieces of literature and philosophy, from Homer to the nineteenth century, and in the second year on the masterpieces of music and the plastic arts.[40]

Though in principle the College was committed to a parallel organization in the Sciences (successive committees called for a "specially constructed and well-integrated two-year course in the natural sciences" and courses "to stress inclusive organizing principles of the sciences rather than special techniques for mastering specialized subject matters"), institutional and staffing difficulties confounded the various efforts to create such general education science courses.[41] From 1934 to 1941, a two-year course, Science A and B, was offered as an option to the specialized science courses, but this ended during the war. Since World War II the Science requirement has remained simply two years of any science courses, a requirement that can be fulfilled by any selective combination of two one-year or one two-year course in any of a half-dozen fields.

This idea of a foundational "tripod" led logically to the conception, which was formalized in 1936, of a "lower college," where the commonality of work would be emphasized, and an "upper college," where students would be able to pursue their individual interests. . . .

The interest in general education, which had emerged just before World War II, along with the reconsideration of curriculum made necessary by the social upheavals of the war, led [the Dean] to appoint a Committee on College Plans, which in 1946 carried out a thoroughgoing review of the curriculum. The committee reaffirmed Columbia's original commitment to the liberal arts. "It is no lip service to tradition to declare once more that the liberal arts program should be the heart of our interests and aims as a college. In the meaning of liberal arts we include all studies that contribute to the art of living, as distinct from the channeled preparation for making a living." The committee found that "our objects with respect to the purpose of the first two years have now been realized through the courses in Contemporary Civilization, Humanities, and the Sciences. [It] feels that the plan of the freshman and sophomore work has plainly demonstrated its fitness for contemporary needs. It feels quite as strongly, however, that the important effort of the next few years must be the working out of plans for upper-class instruction."

The problem of upper-college instruction grew largely out of the "professional option" plan that had been instituted in 1905, whereby a student at the end of his third College year might enter one of the university's professional schools (or an approved medical or dental school) and after his first year there receive the A.B. degree from the College. Many students were pre-professional in their basic outlook, if not in their specific career choice, when they entered the College. The work in the lower college emphasized disinterested and liberal study. But competitive pressures for admission to professional school, the rising costs of education, and the likelihood of military service, all served to sharpen the undergraduates' vocational consciousness, and for a considerable number of students a year of professional study replaced the fourth year of college work. At a time when four years of college had

---

40. Erskine describes the beginning and development of these courses in *The Memory of Certain Persons* (Philadelphia: J. B. Lippincott, 1947), pp. 342–4; and in *My Life as a Teacher* (Philadelphia: J. B. Lippincott, 1948), ch. 12.

41. Frank Aydelotte implies in selection #60 that the Swarthmore College faculty encountered most difficulty in designing honors courses for the sciences.

become the norm before one could enter professional school, the Columbia system was serving as an inducement to accelerate college work. . . .[42]

Columbia College has counted itself, justly, as the pioneer of general education among American colleges. But it is necessary to point out, in discussing the traditions of this idea, that Columbia College has never had a doctrinal commitment, like Chicago's and Harvard's (at least in theory, if not always in practice) to a single theory or substantive formulation of educational philosophy.[43]

This has been due to three factors. One of them was the influence of John Dewey, with his emphasis on the *process* of learning and the *continuity* of experience, rather than on an unvarying curriculum based on a conception either of "eternal verities"—a hierarchy of knowledge, the specification of a major tradition of thought—or of a body of great or fundamental ideas or "great books" as the organizing conception of the courses. . . .

The second factor was the proposition, enunciated specifically by Dean Herbert E. Hawkes in 1922, that "the student is the focus of the undergraduate college." It was Hawkes's theory that in the graduate school the subject is paramount; in the college it is the student. Thus the College sought primarily to be aware of the individual person whose capacities it was trying to develop. . . .[44]

Third (though the point is rarely made explicitly in the theoretical and philosophical discussions of the College and its curriculum) has been the institutional structure of the university itself, in which the locus of attention and power has come to be "the department," rather than any larger entity. Though the College has a distinct identity and ethos, the content of the courses—although less so in the basic lower-college courses—has been defined by the departments and not by the College administration or the College faculty as a whole. Whether this is vice or virtue, the consequence has been that the interests, slants, and prejudices of the departments, rather than any central or unified source, have shaped the curriculum. . . .

[W]ithin the broad rationale supplied by Dewey's ideas (a philosophy that was more explicit in the original construction of the general education courses than it has been in the last decade and a half) a number of diverse intellectual tendencies—Marxism, historicism, existentialism, analytic philosophy, the new criticism—have, in varying degree, subsequently influenced the successive formulation of the courses and are examples of the receptivity to experience and experiment which is the fundamental tradition of Columbia College. While in a sense, again because of the nature of institutional structure, this has served to make a virtue out of necessity, the sensitivity of the College to the nature of continuing inquiry has led not only to the acceptance of broad intellectual diversity as a practice, but to a willing endorsement of this diversity as a general principle of liberal education.[45]

---

42. Compare William R. Harper's analysis of this acceleration in selection #49.

43. Bell must have in mind the views of Robert Hutchins, which were ambiguously related to the liberal education at Chicago, as discussed in selection #58. Regarding Harvard, Bell is apparently thinking of *General Education in a Free Society* (Cambridge: Harvard University Press, 1945), a report of a committee of the Faculty of Arts and Sciences at Harvard University, which is discussed in the introduction to Section IX.

44. Does a university then require two distinct faculties with different purposes?

45. Does this intellectual diversity undermine Columbia's project in general education, notwithstanding Bell's apology?

Citizenship

55. Edgar E. Robinson, "Problems of Citizenship," Stanford University (1929)

INTRODUCTION

While Columbia College pioneered general education and "Contemporary Civilization" was "probably the most famous course ever in the American curriculum,"[46] other institutions were only a step behind. By 1920 Dartmouth College in the east and Stanford University in the west had plans underway to offer similar courses that were both named "Problems of Citizenship." Five years later, as Edgar Robinson observes in selection #55, "there were a dozen institutions" engaged in the effort, including Williams College with its "American National Problems" course and the University of Missouri with its "Problems of American Citizenship." By 1928 "nearly sixty institutions will give work of this general character to freshmen," Robinson maintains.

The terminology about "citizenship" in the titles of these courses demonstrate, on the one hand, the widespread concern with inculcating American democratic ideology in the wake of World War I. On the other hand, the prevalence of terminology about "problems" reveals a factor discussed above by Daniel Bell: the widespread influence of John Dewey, whose writing in the previous two decades had given currency to "the meaning of the word *problem*" or "a *problematic* situation" in discussion about thinking and teaching.[47] The organization of these courses in the "Problems of Citizenship" borrowed from "a new type of course called an 'orientation,' or 'survey,' course," identified by the Dean of the College at the University of Chicago.[48] Orientation or survey courses were often taught by lecture because they intended to synthesize information and convey a cogent and persuasive argument. This was the purpose of the citizenship courses, demonstrated by the following selection from Edgar Robinson's introductory lecture to "Problems of Citizenship" at Stanford University.

Born in Wisconsin, Robinson (1887–1977) graduated with the A.B. from the University of Wisconsin in 1908. While earning the M.A. (1910), he taught history at Wisconsin, then served as an instructor at Carleton College before joining the faculty of Stanford University as an assistant professor of American history in 1911. In 1923, without having earned a Ph.D., he was appointed a full professor and director of the newly instituted "Problems of Citizenship" course at Stanford.

In the late 1910s Stanford deemed its system of concentration and electivism inadequate for liberal education, and a faculty committee proposed the "Problems of Citizenship" course. First offered in the 1923–24 academic year as a requirement for all freshmen, the course was directed for the next twelve years by Edgar Robinson, who delivered the opening and closing lectures. In 1935 the faculty voted to introduce "The History of Western Civilization" as a substitute for "Problems of

46. W. B. Carnochan, *The Battleground of the Curriculum: Liberal Education and American Experience* (Stanford, CA: Stanford University Press, 1993), p. 71. The following account of Stanford's course is drawn from ch. 6.

47. John Dewey, *How We Think* (Lexington, MA: D.C. Heath, 1910), p. 9; John Dewey, *Logic: The Theory of Inquiry* (New York: Henry Holt, 1938), p. 107.

48. C. S. Boucher, "Current Changes and Experiments in Liberal-Arts Colleges," in Kathryn McHale, et al., *Changes and Experiments in Liberal-Arts Education* (Bloomington, IL: Public School Publishing, 1932), p. 18. Karl W. Bigelow and Malcolm S. MacLean, "Dominant Trends in General Education," in *General Education in the American College*, ed. Guy M. Whipple (Bloomington, IL: Public School Publishing, 1939), pp. 367–8.

Citizenship,"[49] and the latter was redesigned as "Introduction to Social Problems" and included among the optional courses in economics, philosophy, political science, psychology, and sociology within a scheme of distribution. In 1946 "Introduction to Social Problems" became "Introduction to Social Service" and then expired in 1951. Robinson continued writing and teaching at Stanford nearly to the end of his life in 1977.

SELECTION[50]

You have entered Stanford University as freshmen, and you are now enrolled in the course in Problems of Citizenship, a course of lectures, readings, and discussions which will continue throughout the year. . . . As you begin this year to lay the foundations for work in your special field of interest, built as they are upon still earlier foundations, so too you are called upon to build carefully and to prepare thoughtfully for your work as a citizen. For citizenship, as Thomas Arnold pointed out long ago, is the second calling of every man and woman.[51] You will observe as we go forward that our constant endeavor will be to relate what we do and say to the facts of the world from which you came and in which all of you will live, and to correlate the various aspects of the modern scene, so that it will appear that citizenship is not a thing apart, something to be thought of only occasionally or left to the energies of a minority of our people, but that its proper understanding is at the very root of our daily life. It is a personal matter, just as all education is a matter for the individual. We begin our labor this year with an old conviction, so sorely tried in the speed and impersonality of the present day, that there is a possibility of insisting upon standards of personal conduct, in public affairs as in private life, powerful enough to bring into existence, and to continue in existence, an honest, effective, and purposeful world.

Some of you may be familiar with the fact that when Senator and Mrs. Stanford prepared the Founding Grant of this University they declared that its object was "to qualify its students for personal success and direct usefulness in life, and its purposes to promote the general welfare by exercising an influence on behalf of humanity and civilization, reaching the blessings of liberty regulated by law, and inculcating love and reverence for the great principles of government as derived from the inalienable right of man to life, liberty, and the pursuit of happiness."[52] . . . We may assume that they had in mind a preparation for citizenship as a problem in education, rather than the development of a technique in Political Science, Economics, or Law. . . .

You are right in expecting that in the intervening years there has been some thinking, as well as other forms of activity, touching upon this work at Stanford. . . . [M]ost of all in the shift of interest to a consideration of man's relation to his environment, his capacity to feel and to think, his powers of discrimination, his dependence upon public opinion, his intelligence; altogether his capacities as a thinking man. Thus it is that in seeking an alert, intelligent, and efficient citizenry we do not confine

49. On the subsequent events concerning "The History of Western Civilization" at Stanford, see selection #66 by Mary Louise Pratt.

50. Edgar E. Robinson, "Citizenship in a Democratic World" (1929), reprinted in W. B. Carnochan, *The Battleground of the Curriculum: Liberal Education and American Experience* (Stanford, CA: Stanford University Press, 1993), pp. 131–44. Reprinted by permission of Stanford University.

51. Thomas Arnold (1795–1842) was a British historian, evangelical educator, and the father of the literary scholar Matthew Arnold (1822–1888).

52. Leland Stanford (1824–1893) was one of the founders of the Union Pacific Railroad, served as a U.S. Senator from 1885 to 1893, and endowed the Leland Stanford Junior University as a memorial to his son.

our attention to the structure and functions and theories of government. We are dealing first of all with man himself. . . .[53]

At Stanford as freshmen you are to devote about a fourth of the time of your first year to this work. Despite the reasons which have just been given, it has appeared to many that this was a great deal of time to spend on a subject not directly related to preparation for a business or a profession. It has been seriously maintained by parents and students, as well as by some members of the faculty, that there is no time for such "extras" now that the student has entered college. This is an old cry with which educators have long been familiar. Said an eager father to James A. Garfield, then president of Hiram College, "My boy hasn't any time for all these studies. Get him through quickly." "Well," replied Garfield, "it all depends upon what you want. When God wants to make an oak He takes a hundred years, but He takes only two months to make a squash."[54] We must begin to realize that there is a difference between the freedom to choose an objective and the ability to choose the proper way to reach that objective.

The desire to hurry over these college years is not so prevalent as it once was.[55] Indeed the emphasis in recent years has been upon an enlargement and improvement of the groundwork taken in the first two years of the college course. There is an agreement that every university has the means of giving all of its students certain elementary principles, both in social and natural sciences, and that it has a duty to do so. When Stanford first undertook to do this six years ago it was a pioneer. At Dartmouth College and at Columbia University experiments of a similar order were going forward, but little elsewhere. Three years ago there were a dozen institutions giving serious attention to the problem. In a recent compilation it is reported that nearly sixty institutions will give work of this general character to freshmen this year. . . .

You are entering college at a time when there is growing acceptance of the view that in the social sciences there should be analysis and criticism not alone by the experts in those fields but by those who, as educated men and women, are to have an adequate comprehension and a trustworthy technique in handling the affairs of government and country. Such a view asks that men turn away from traditional ways of thinking and acting when they are shown to be irrational, and undertake to establish new procedures based upon facts scientifically established. It is not enough just to point out past mistakes and present fallacies. "Reason must take the field to criticize our institutions" as Meiklejohn has said.[56]

Just now at Stanford this course is prescribed for all students, because it is designed to prepare all to do what they can in community effort. It is impossible to think accurately, vote intelligently, participate productively in public affairs without a preparation in the make-up of society. To do this effectively, it is necessary to construct a considerable background. We must be sure we know what American objectives are and have been. We must be sure we have a reliable method of procedure. In a university many departments are concerned with public affairs, but certain departments are more directly interested than others. In particular is it the work of the social sciences, the departments of economics, political science, sociology, philosophy, and history. From these departments and from others

---

53. Carnochan regards the two prior sentences as "illustrating attitudes that eventually converted "Problems of Citizenship" to "History of Western Civilization." *The Battleground of the Curriculum*, p. 130.

54. James A. Garfield (1831–1881), who graduated from Williams, served as head of the forerunner of Hiram College (1857–1861), became President of the United States in 1881, and was assassinated enroute to his twenty-fifth college class reunion.

55. See the discussion of Columbia University's "professional option" plan in selection #53 by Lionel Trilling.

56. On Alexander Meiklejohn, see the introduction to selection #56 by Kathryn McHale.

will come the men who are to develop the problems of citizenship in the lectures given during the year. . . .

Courses like this one and movements elsewhere throughout the country to draw attention to public affairs are symptomatic of the growth of the belief that it is dangerous to let things drift. We found that particularly true at the time when the United States entered the war. We were not only physically unprepared for war but also mentally unprepared for the implications of that war. As long as man lived in comparative isolation it made little difference to him what happened in adjacent, and certainly in distant, areas; but with the increase in the means of communication that have bound the world in the last thirty-five years, the actual world is growing smaller and smaller, and we are not free to ignore what takes place in the next state or the next nation, or anywhere in the world.

When we speak of an educated man we mean educated not only in the sense of the possession of facts, but the ability to use them, or in a phrase of David Starr Jordan's "to arrange facts so they mean something."[57] The educated man listens and reads, and then he does what the mass of men do not yet do, he reasons about it. The educated classes in England and in Scotland are excellent examples of this, and it is probable that the success of the English in government, in executive efficiency, popular control, and individual freedom, may be traced to the fact that many educated Englishmen do more than listen and read: they proceed to the point of thought and reason in advance of action. Take, for example, an impending coal strike in America. The man we are considering cannot be content to take the statements of operators or miners. Much less would he be content to take only one of these. He must get a various information and he must get it from many sources. He must know something of costs of transportation, of methods of mining, of living conditions of the workers, of the state of the financial market, if he is to get at a contribution in the public interest. It is hard in the midst of a world in which self-interest and hurry are dominant notes to get at the facts or to get the time to use those facts. It is apparent that only a few educated men and women can be counted upon to do it.

The hope of democracy from the point of view of men and women of education lies in the use and development of the instrumentalities that they find ready for use. The road to a more and more satisfactory state of affairs lies in perfecting the instrumentalities which our forefathers have left to us. . . .[58] In America, as it developed into a nation, there was always a reminder of the price of democracy. As Dr. Hadley succinctly says: "A liberal education is an education for liberty, the kind of education needed by a free man."[59]

---

57. David Starr Jordan was president of Stanford from 1891 to 1916 and died in 1931. The source has not been identified.

58. "The advance of civilization means that a larger number of natural forces and objects have been transformed into instrumentalities of action, into means for securing ends." John Dewey, *Democracy and Education* (1916; New York: Free Press, 1966), p. 36.

59. This apparently refers to Arthur T. Hadley (1856–1930), who had served as president of Yale from 1899 to 1921. The source of this quotation has not been identified.

Experimentation, Progressivism, "Great Books"

56. Kathryn McHale, "Future Possibilities in Liberal-Arts Education" (1932)

INTRODUCTION

The early twentieth-century curricular innovations, such as distribution requirements, general education programs, and orientation courses, gave rise to an era of full-scale change and experimentation in liberal education during the second quarter of the twentieth century. The period of transformation and exploration was epitomized by the career of Alexander Meiklejohn (1872–1964), who had the pedigree of an English upbringing, an A.B. from Brown University, and a Ph.D. from Cornell University in philosophy and logic. After serving as president of Amherst College (1912–24), Meiklejohn assumed the leadership of the Experimental College at the University of Wisconsin for the five years of its existence from 1927 to 1932,[60] then of the School for Social Studies in San Francisco, and finally of the American Association for Adult Education by 1944. Meiklejohn was known as an eclectic thinker, but his migration from a tradition-minded college into experimental liberal education was not atypical during the 1920s, 1930s and 1940s.[61]

Already in 1928 the directors of the National Society for the Study of Education (NSSE), located at the University of Chicago, were discussing the possibility of devoting an NSSE yearbook to the developments in the curriculum of the liberal arts college. Meanwhile, the American Association of University Women (AAUW) was planning a "Cooperative Study of Changes and Experiments in the Liberal-Arts College," prompted by the fact that "those intimate with the four-year liberal college know that more changes and experiments have been introduced in higher education in the last five years than in the previous twenty-five years. . . . Almost all four-year colleges of arts, literature, and science are making contributions to improve their educational offerings."[62]

The AAUW study was directed by Kathryn McHale (1890–1956), who was born in Indiana and earned the B.S. from Columbia University at the age of twenty-nine. McHale completed the Ph.D. at Teachers College, Columbia University, in 1926, writing a dissertation on "Comparative Psychology and Hygiene of the Over-weight Child," which was published in 1926 and reissued in 1975. She subsequently published more than forty-five pamphlets and articles on the psychology and education of children, though she never married or had children of her own. In 1920 McHale began teaching in the education department at Goucher College in Baltimore and was promoted to full professor in 1927. Taking a leave in 1929, she assumed the position of general director of the AAUW and director of the "Cooperative Study of Changes and Experiments in the Liberal-Arts College." This study divided the country into nine geographical regions, established a research committee for each, and examined the developments at nearly a hundred colleges and universities. The NSSE devoted its yearbook of 1932 to reporting the results, which identified "One Hundred Twenty-eight Outstanding

---

60. Alexander Meiklejohn, *The Experimental College* (New York: Harper and Brothers, 1932).

61. See Adam R. Nelson, *Education and Democracy: The Meaning of Alexander Meiklejohn, 1872–1964* (Madison: University of Wisconsin Press, 2000). Meiklejohn's influence is discussed in selection #58 by Robert Hutchins.

62. Kathryn McHale, "Introduction," in McHale, et al., *Changes and Experiments in Liberal-Arts Education* (Bloomington, IL: Public School Publishing, 1932), pp. 1–2.

Changes and Experiments" in liberal arts colleges and universities throughout the country.[63] Kathryn McHale's reflections appear in selection #56.

Following the publication of the report, McHale continued as general director of the AAUW and became a "non-resident professor" at Goucher College. She was awarded honorary doctorates by Brown University, Russell Sage College, and MacMurray College. In 1950 McHale was appointed as the only female member of the United States Subversive Activities Control Board and conducted the lengthy investigation of the Veterans of the Abraham Lincoln Brigade, which she formally condemned for its left-wing activities in the Spanish Civil War, though her judgment was not endorsed by the Board.[64] McHale continued as a member of the Board until her sudden death in 1956.

SELECTION[65]

The content of the foregoing chapters affords a sampling of the experimentation and changes that may be found in the liberal-arts college. . . . There may be those who observe that, after a consideration of current changes and experiments, we do not know which is the best plan;[66] or that it is a misnomer to talk of experimentation at the college level, since, in a bona fide experiment all the factors are counted, isolated, and controlled, the processes are watched, and the results quantitatively measured; or that the vitality of a college cannot be measured in terms of its administrative machinery. There are others who regard such observations as indicative of unprogressive and deterrent attitudes, who believe that, the tendency to give up educational experimentation is a dangerous one. They say that we must believe in it, we must go on venturing, using the best techniques known, if progress is to be made, even though we seem at times to be in contradiction with one another. . . .

The colleges are prone to work alone and, as a rule, independently of educational units that come before and after college. This precipitates many inconsistencies as well as opposed concepts and practices in college educational work. As a consequence, we have some interesting examples of the things colleges do which are not consistent, as for example, the honors course demands prerequisites of secondary schools in which methods are emphasized that do not prepare the honors student; again, both the secondary school and the college are working on admissions, but in opposite directions;[67] the se-

---

63. Frances Valiant Speek, "One Hundred Twenty-eight Outstanding Changes and Experiments," in McHale, et al., *Changes and Experiments in Liberal-Arts Education*, pp. 43–156.

64. United States Subversive Activities Control Board, *Herbert Brownell, Jr., U.S. Attorney General, petitioner v. Veterans of the Abraham Lincoln Brigade, respondent*, Recommended decision by Kathryn McHale, Board Member (18 May 1955) Docket, pp. 108–53.

65. Kathryn McHale, "Future Possibilities in Liberal-Arts Education," in McHale, et al., *Changes and Experiments in Liberal-Arts Education*, pp. 231–6. Reprinted by permission of the National Society for the Study of Education.

66. Thus, in Robert Hutchins's contemporaneous selection #58, "the heart of [the] indictment of the higher learning in America lies in the charge of 'confusion,' 'chaos,' or 'disorder.'" Harry D. Gideonse, *The Higher Learning in a Democracy, A Reply to President Hutchins's Critique of the American University* (New York: Farrar and Rhinehart, 1937), p. 5.

67. Among the "current changes and experiments in liberal-arts colleges" the Dean of the College at the University of Chicago listed first the appearance of "selective admissions" arising from a belief on the part of some "too many persons are going to college." As a result, "institutions with highly selective requirements will get the type of students they desire . . . and will have a homogeneous student body, while institutions that, because of state law or financial pressure, are forced to take any and all applicants will have a most heterogeneous student body, including many who are anything but satisfactory and promising students." C. S. Boucher, "Current Changes and

minar in college as an instructional method is stimulating to the teachers, but the tutorial method as a practice is in the ascendant; the abolition of the course credit without the development of the proper type of comprehensive examination is current, or the external examination is used with a board which should, but does not, include some technicians [in educational measurement.]

The naïveté of some of our experimentation indicates that our faculty and administration groups could profit from more information on the fundamentals of educational experimental methods.[68] The graduate schools may in the future make provisions which will allow them to recommend "no doctor of philosophy for a college position unless he has given clear proof of his aptitude and equipment for conducting college classes" and for educational experimentation in phases of collegiate education pertinent to the organization and administration of his major professional field.[69] Cooperative research on the part of a college faculty into problems of college education should eventuate in a more critical evaluation of the best possible techniques of investigation and produce more effective experimentation. . . .

The probable future trends in American liberal-college education are in many respects difficult to forecast. . . . [P]erhaps we may expect more widespread and important changes with respect to the care and direction of the individual student. There is an increasing interest in such needs. Interest in putting meaning into college work is centered at present on special considerations of the top stratum of our student body,[70] but emphasis is shifting, by way of suggestion and example, to a modification of such provisions for the entire student body. There is apparent also a tendency to stress preventive, rather than remedial, measures with respect to all types of students. The college's interest in youth is growing more comprehensive, and we may expect the college of the future to set as its standard a completely integrated personality in which every aspect of adolescent growth and development will receive adequate attention.[71]

One could only hazard a guess as to what exactly will constitute the curriculum ten years hence or in what way learning will be guided. It may be safe, however, to assert as general characteristics of the future that the curriculum will integrate fields of learning; that both curriculum and method will be individualized (differentiated in terms of individual capacity, interest, and future needs); that teaching will be more exact but more informal; and that the student will be socialized through contacts with many more life situations and will be able to learn more completely by living more completely.

There will be a great deal more study of, and experimentation with, such phases of organization and administration as articulation [with other levels of education], selection [of students], alumni education, college or educational finance, the support and the making and administration of the budget, the tuition and scholarship systems and the cost of instruction, administrative machinery, the faculty sabbatical, research provisions, etc.

These represent practically uninvestigated problems in need of study. We have concerned ourselves primarily with the more important problems relating directly to the students. When their salient needs are better understood, the problems of organization and administration will no doubt receive

---

Experiments in Liberal-Arts Colleges," in McHale, et al., *Changes and Experiments in Liberal-Arts Education,* pp. 10–1.

68. McHale's unqualified enthusiasm for applying experimental method to educational questions reflects the prevailing, contemporaneous view at Teachers College and other schools of education.

69. McHale quotes from William S. Gray, *The Training of College Teachers* (Chicago: University of Chicago, 1930), pp. 230–3.

70. See selection #60 by President Frank Aydelotte of Swarthmore College.

71. To what extent is this standard realized or desirable?

more attention. The problem of educational finance is the most complex and difficult of these and directly circumscribes the progress of the changes that depend upon money for their development; so, obviously it is a major and immediate one for solution.

The outlook for changes and experiments in liberal education will be determined largely, however, by the spirit of all interested in the future of American education. . . . They will help to predict trends of study of the liberal-arts college and offer working hypotheses to be tested in an experimental way.[72]

57. John Dewey, et al., *The Curriculum for the Liberal Arts College* (1931)

INTRODUCTION

John Dewey (1859–1952) was born and raised in Burlington, Vermont, where he attended the public schools and graduated from the University of Vermont (1879). After earning a Ph.D. in philosophy at Johns Hopkins University (1884), he taught philosophy and psychology at the universities of Michigan and Minnesota over the next decade. Moving to the University of Chicago in 1894, Dewey became chair of the Department of Philosophy, Psychology, and Pedagogy, which he developed into the leading center of progressive educational thought.

In 1904 Dewey resigned after a series of disagreements with President William R. Harper, and became a professor of philosophy at Columbia University. Drawing upon the insights of philosopher Charles S. Peirce (1839–1914) and psychologist William James (1842–1910), Dewey articulated at Columbia "the theory of the method of knowing which . . . may be termed pragmatic"[73] and which he sometimes called "experimentalism" because he viewed all inquiry and education as conforming to the pattern of experimental method. After retiring in 1930, he continued to write prolifically, ultimately publishing some 44 books and 800 articles. "When Dewey died in 1952, he was widely regarded as the preeminent philosopher in the United States and the twentieth century's foremost American intellectual," and today many still consider him "the most important twentieth-century American thinker."[74]

Commensurate with this stature, Dewey exercised significant influence upon liberal education during the 1920s, 1930s, and early 1940s, when his philosophical influence was at its peak. During these decades, college leaders subtly—but self-consciously and significantly—changed the terminology about liberal education in ways that carried distinctly Progressive overtones. One such change, heralded by President Alexander Meiklejohn of Amherst College, was displacing the traditional term "liberal-arts college" with "liberal college."[75] In 1924 Dewey took note of this

---

72. In his review of the McHale volume [*The Journal of Higher Education* 3 (1932): 397–8], Dean Herbert E. Hawkes of Columbia College (mentioned above in Daniel Bell's selection #54) expressed greater confidence in the ideas of individual college leaders than in the "One Hundred Twenty-eight Outstanding Changes and Experiments" institutionalized in the liberal arts colleges.

73. John Dewey, *Democracy and Education* (1916; New York: Free Press, 1966), p. 344.

74. Quotations are from Bruce Kuklick, *Churchmen and Philosophers: From Jonathan Edwards to John Dewey* (New Haven, CT: Yale University Press, 1985), pp. xv–xvi; Robert B. Westbrook, *John Dewey and American Democracy* (Ithaca, NY: Cornell University Press, 1991), p. ix.

75. See Alexander Meiklejohn, *The Liberal College* (Boston: Marshall Jones, 1920).

preference for "liberal college," observing that "today the word liberal is applied to an educational institution to denote opposition to the reactionary and the ultraconservative, not to denote just preoccupation with intellectual and ideal matters. The word has taken on economic and political significance in connection with the human struggle for economic independence and political emancipation."[76] By 1930 "the term 'The Liberal College.' . .[wa]s preferred by many in the Association of American Colleges" to "the term 'The Liberal-Arts College.'"[77] The trend was extended further by 1944, when Dewey noted approvingly, "Nothing is more striking in recent discussions of liberal education than the widespread and seemingly spontaneous use of liberating as a synonym for liberal."[78]

Another change in terminology was the introduction of "Progressive College" to refer to the dozens of colleges and universities conducting various curricular experiments in the 1920s and 1930s, including Wittenberg, Hamline, Grinnell, Wells, Swarthmore, Franklin and Marshall, Brown, and Johns Hopkins.[79] In particular, however, the term "Progressive College" or even "Progressive Education College" was applied to a subset of the "experimental colleges": the newly founded, refounded, or rejuvenated institutions that were organizing their entire program around particular conceptions of liberal education. The Progressive Education Colleges included Sarah Lawrence College in New York, Reed College in Oregon, Antioch College in Ohio, Bennington College in Vermont, Black Mountain College in North Carolina, and Rollins College in Florida.[80] Though widely divergent in character, these colleges generally endorsed Dewey's criticism that "upholders of 'cultural' education" were neglecting students' interests in designing liberal education.[81]

Many were critical of this Progressive influence, interpreting Dewey and his colleagues as defining liberal education in terms of its "direct application to immediate needs" of students, in the words of the President Mary E. Woolley of Mount Holyoke College.[82] In 1937 Norman Foerster at the State University of Iowa anathematized "our prevailing philosophy of education, for which John Dewey and Teachers College are largely responsible" and "in consequence [of which] . . . the liberal college is threatened with extinction."[83] Adopting the criticism into his historical interpretation, George Pierson of Yale University maintained that "the Progressive Education movement . . . developed by the followers of John Dewey" was "naturally anti-religious, anti-disciplinary, anti-theoretical and anti-humanistic in emphasis. [It] criticized the liberal arts, scorned the tradition of liberal education, and prided itself on being realistic and present-minded."[84] Similarly, historian

---

76. John Dewey, "The Prospects of the Liberal College" (1924), reprinted in Jo Ann Boydston, *John Dewey, The Middle Works, 1899–1924* (Carbondale: Southern Illinois University Press, 1983), v. 15, p. 200.

77. Kathryn McHale, et al., *Changes and Experiments in Liberal-Arts Education* (Bloomington, IL: Public School Publishing, 1932), p. 1n.

78. John Dewey, "The Problem of the Liberal Arts College," *The American Scholar* 33 (1944): 391.

79. "Some Progressive College Projects," *Association of American Colleges Bulletin* 17 (1931): 312–21, 480–7; McHale et al., *Changes and Experiments in Liberal-Arts Education*, p. 2.

80. See Donald P. Cottrell, "General Education in Experimental Liberal Arts Colleges," in *General Education in the American College*, ed. Guy M. Whipple (Bloomington, IL: Public School Publishing, 1939), pp. 198–9, 201.

81. Dewey, *Democracy and Education*, p. 162. Compare this statement about the relationship between "liberal" and "intellectual" with Dewey's observation in 1924, quoted above.

82. Quoted in McHale, et al., *Changes and Experiments in Liberal-Arts Education*, pp. 244–5.

83. Norman Foerster, *The Future of the Liberal College* (New York: A. Appleton-Century, 1938), p. v.

84. George W. Pierson, *Yale, The University College, 1921–1937* (New Haven, CT: Yale University Press, 1955), pp. 482, 483.

Laurence Veysey's distaste for "the adherents of the Dewey persuasion" and their "ritual formulas of low intellectual caliber" led him to delimit the historical influence of pragmatism and progressivism to "colleges which . . . usually happened to be either girls' schools or else truly obscure."[85]

Notwithstanding this criticism, "most educators' definition of the liberal arts was considerably broadened in the 1920s and 1930s" due, in part, to "the ready acceptance of John Dewey's philosophical concept of pragmatism"; and many of the specific curricular reforms "bear his unmistakable imprint,"[86] reflecting "efforts to transpose progressive education's central tenets to the college level."[87] Such efforts were exemplified by the 1931 conference "The Curriculum of the Liberal Arts College," in which "a group of progressive educationists gathered at Rollins College . . . to construct a liberal arts curriculum within the framework of progressive educational principles. It proved to be a landmark conference because important luminaries in progressive education for the first time wrestled with the issue of an appropriate 'progressive' liberal arts curriculum, and at the end of the conference produced a statement on 'progressive' liberal arts."[88] That statement, sent by Rollins to over one hundred colleges, appears in selection #57.

SELECTION[89]

I. The Function of the Liberal Arts College.

The purpose of the college of liberal arts is to discover and achieve the values and significance of life, individual and social, through:

A. The organization, transmission, extension and application of knowledge.

B. The awakening, developing, enlarging, disciplining and harmonizing of interests, appreciations, and attitudes.

C. The inspiring of the students, the faculty, and the officers to consecrate their unique personalities to the common good.

These general purposes involve:

1. A realizing sense of the controlling importance of continuity in the human quest and the integration of personal aims with that quest.

---

85. Laurence Veysey, "Stability and Experiment in the American Undergraduate Curriculum," in *Content and Context: Essays on College Education*, ed. Carl Kaysen (New York: McGraw-Hill, 1973), p. 11.

86. David O. Levine, *The American College and the Culture of Aspiration* (Ithaca, NY: Cornell University Press, 1986), pp. 97, 101.

87. Judith Sealander, "'Forcing them to be Free': Antioch College and Progressive Education in the 1920s," *History of Higher Education Annual* (1988): 60. See Bruce A. Kimball, "Toward Pragmatic Liberal Education," in *The Condition of American Liberal Education*, ed. Robert Orrill (New York: The College Board, 1995), pp. 3–122. See Dewey's influence upon Columbia's pioneering program of general education, discussed above by Daniel Bell in selection #54.

88. Jack C. Lane, "The Rollins Conference, 1931 and the Search for a Progressive Liberal Education: Mirror or Prism?" *Liberal Education* 70 (1984): 297.

89. John Dewey, et al., *The Curriculum for the Liberal Arts College, Being the Report of the Curriculum Conference Held at Rollins College* (Winter Park, FL: Rollins College, 1931), pp. 8–14. The 850-page, stenographic record of the conference is reposited in the Rollins College Library as *Proceedings, Curriculum Conference, Rollins College* (Winter Park, FL: Rollins College, 19–24 Jan. 1931). Reprinted by permission of Department of College Archives and Special Collections, Olin Library, Rollins College.

2. An increasing understanding and control of the physical world, and the achievement and maintenance of a favorable physical environment.

3. An increasing understanding of the nature of man in his human relations, and the realization of social harmony.

4. An increasing knowledge and control of the biological nature of man and of eugenic processes.[90]

5. A search for the nature and significance of meanings, ends, and values in human experience, through inquiry and through personal emotional experience of such values.

6. Helping the individual to find his appropriate life-work and stimulating him toward mastery therein.

7. Helping to realize the importance of the intelligent use of leisure, including the lifelong development through education of new interests and capacities as these emerge, and the fostering of interest in nature and the various fine arts and handicrafts.

8. The development of wholesome physical and mental habits, the development of ideals, the education of the will and of the emotions as well as of the intellect, the harmonizing of the elements of personality, both innate and acquired, and the stimulation and increase of creative powers.

II. Place of the Liberal Arts College in Education . . .

The place of the liberal arts college in the educational system must be a growing and an ever-changing one.[91] At the present moment, several types of organization are in competition and conflict. The newest of these is the junior college, followed by the professional or graduate school. In recent years there have been organized a great many junior colleges, which ordinarily include the last two years of high school and the first two years of college. Most professional schools accept suitably prepared students from the junior college. Some universities have eliminated the freshman and sophomore college years, and accept junior college graduates for graduate and professional work. This development tends to reproduce in America the general structure of the educational system of continental Europe. It is the most rapidly growing element in American higher education today,[92] and, in so far as it prevails, the liberal arts college as we know it may disappear.[93]

A second type of educational organization is the parallel existence, often within a single institution, of the liberal arts college and of undergraduate professional schools, teachers colleges, schools of engineering and of business, colleges of chemistry, and other departments, which receive students directly from the secondary school for four years of undergraduate professional work. The liberal arts

---

90. Eugenics refers to the much debated effort to improve inherited characteristics of human beings through the study and control of human genetics. This fourth point likely stemmed from Antioch President Arthur Morgan who attended the Rollins Conference and later addressed the American Eugenics Society, in *American Eugenics . . . the Proceedings of the Annual Meeting . . . of the American Eugenics Society . . . New York City, May 7, 1936* (New York: American Eugenics Society, [1936?]).

91. Or should the place of the liberal arts college be a stabilizing and conserving one?

92. "[M]any educators, particularly those at large public universities, formally divided the first two and last two years of college. In the junior college, a broad general education was required; in the senior college, the student had the opportunity to pursue an area of special interest. . . . During the 1920s this innovation was widely adopted; by 1930 55 percent of the independent colleges, 80 percent of the endowed universities, and 90 percent of the state universities [according to one survey] had established junior and senior colleges." Levine, *The American College*, p. 99.

93. Compare selection #49 by William R. Harper (part II).

college in such a university is seen as an alternative to these professional schools and, to some degree, as in competition with them. The undergraduate professional schools tend to attract those who have definite vocational purposes in their fields, while the liberal arts college tends to attract those without definite vocational purposes, especially women;[94] also those whose aims are primarily cultural and scholarly; those whose chief aim in going to college is to receive the advantages of social contacts; and those preparing for graduate professional schools.

A third general type of educational organization is the historic four years of liberal arts college, followed by professional schools of law, medicine, architecture, etc., or graduate work in arts or sciences, or entrance into the business world.

A fourth type of organization, now emerging, would eliminate so far as possible the separation into undergraduate and graduate education, or into liberal and professional education, and would provide an integrated program beginning probably with the last one or two years of secondary education and continuing to the completion of professional preparation. In such an organization of higher education, the college of liberal arts cannot be delineated and identified as such, but will be integrated with the whole, and will condition and qualify the entire process. Cultural courses will extend through the whole period of higher education, and professional or vocational courses will begin whenever the student is ready for them through maturity and definition of vocational aim.

One of the limitations of the liberal arts college has been a tendency to deny worth to economic and other practical issues and to assume the old classical attitude that usefulness and dignity are in conflict. For the liberal arts college to survive it must recognize the unity and equal dignity of all necessary human concerns, and must endeavor to include and synthesize them all. This is the lesson the liberal arts college must learn from the institutions which seem to threaten its existence. Insofar as the liberal arts college stands for a perpetuation of the traditional conflict between vocation and culture, it seems doomed to play a constantly decreasing role in education.[95]

In a day when most of the occupations of men involved little more than manual skill and the repeated application of a few rule-of-thumb formulae quickly learned by the apprentice method, the concept of vocational as illiberal may have had some basis. With the modern applications of all the sciences and arts to vocations, and the successful scientific search for principles within the operations and purposes of the vocations themselves, it can be no longer true. It is rapidly becoming a fact that study within one's vocational preparation is an important means of freeing and liberalizing the mind. This being true, the inevitable trend in education is toward the rapid thinning of the traditional educational wall between vocational and cultural.[96] The liberal arts college will survive and render service in proportions as it recognizes this fact and brings its course of study and administrative set-up into effective conformity with it.

The liberal arts college has been one of the chief agencies in America for broadening and deepening cultural traditions, and for introducing young men and women to great accomplishments in literature, art, history, and science. It has been the chief means by which American youth have had contact with cultivated and disciplined minds, and have come to undertake similar development in themselves. American graduate [students] are largely recruited from small liberal arts colleges where intellectual interests have been aroused.

---

94. See selection #59 on "'Experimental' Liberal Education for Women, 1939–1947" at Purdue University.

95. Where has this "traditional conflict" been evident in the past?

96. This paragraph was inserted at the insistence of President Arthur Morgan of Antioch College. Would Aristotle agree that greater sophistication of vocational knowledge implies "the rapid thinning of the traditional educational wall between vocational and cultural?"

For millions of young Americans the liberal arts college has been almost the sole opportunity for escaping from provincialism, and for achieving the intellectual, ethical and social outlooks and interests of cultured men and women. It is chiefly through the influence of the liberal arts college that American business has to some degree escaped from the traditional petty shrewdness and sordidness of the trader, and is taking its place among the older professions as a form of enlightened human service.

Probably more than half of all liberal arts college students during the past twenty-five years have been the first in their immediate family line to receive the benefits of a liberal education.[97] The college therefore has served not simply to perpetuate existing family culture, but has been a major influence in creating a new American culture.

Chief among all our educational institutions, the liberal arts college has been dedicated to the principle that man does not live by bread alone. To curtail or to eliminate its influence in favor of a predominantly utilitarian education, either by substituting undergraduate professional schools or by crushing it between the upper and nether millstones of the junior college and the professional school would be an irreparable loss. This would be particularly true at the present time when America is emerging from economic deficit and is achieving a condition of general economic surplus, and when education for the use of surplus and of leisure is most necessary. Changes in the educational system should come, not by surrendering the peculiar values of the liberal arts college, but by suffusing through the whole educational structure the liberalizing spirit and outlook that have characterized the liberal arts college at its best. This will be accomplished in different institutions in different ways through the recognition by all education of the aims of the liberal arts college.

III. On Student Interest[98]

While a great deal of attention has been given to the subject of teaching, singularly little has been devoted to the process of learning. Granting that this is still highly mysterious, the Conference feels assured that an indispensable element in real learning is interest on the part of the learner—whatever its source or motivation. We would emphasize the primacy of the doctrine of interest on the part of the student as fundamentally controlling in the building and administration of any scheme of education. . . . . It is the first business of the college to ascertain with respect to each individual student, whether interests exist, what they are, upon what they are founded, how motivated, and, generally, the interplay of interest and aptitude. . . .

It is, therefore, the second business of the college to assist the student in examining and appraising these supposed "interests," and their background. Probably in most cases—certainly in very many—that background, including the student's whole nexus of experience, from his birth and the heritage behind it, will be found not merely inadequate, but narrow, disproportionate, biased—ill adapted to supply any sure footing upon which to choose either life-work or the means of making life itself personally satisfactory or socially effectual. . . .

This obligation upon the college includes that of recognizing and enlarging those interests, and, still more, of awakening new and possibly more rewarding ones.[99] Of the ways in which this may be

---

97. Due to the increasing number of secondary school students and to the more systematic articulation between secondary and higher education that developed in the first two decades of the twentieth century, the numbers of students attending college rose dramatically after World War I.

98. At the conference, "the major topic of interest proved to be the doctrine of individual interest. . . . Since [Dewey] had formulated the concept of the primacy of interest, progressive educators had been attempting (many thought unsuccessfully) to define and evaluate the meaning of the concept in the educational process. . . . The conferees debated this question almost daily." Lane, "The Rollins Conference, 1931," pp. 299–300.

done, best of all is the natural growth and spread of existing interests into broad new channels by a continuous self-directing process, aided by the guidance of the excellent teacher. There may be a readjustment of bias or removal of obstruction by wise and sympathetic psychological counsel. When required courses exist, there is special responsibility upon the teacher to make them so evidently worth while that the student may find them highly rewarding, and may derive from them enduring interests of which he had been unaware.

IV. Organization of Material: Curriculum

1. The scope of knowledge has become so vast that it is impossible for the student to cover it all and a selection must be made. The problem is to determine the basis for such selection.

2. There should be less emphasis on the acquisition of mere facts and more emphasis upon generalization, thinking, application of knowledge and awareness of gaps in knowledge.

3. There should be different introductory courses for those who plan further work in a field and for those who do not. . . .

4. In the first part of the college student's career there should be more emphasis on breadth; while in the latter part there should be more emphasis on specialization. . . .

5. More emphasis on the development of the individual rather than on a sort of machine production should characterize the college. . . .

6. Vocational names should not be given to lines of study that do not give very definite vocational training.

7. Each college should make a careful study of the vocations for which its students might desire or endeavor to prepare themselves and should consider the feasibility of giving at least initial direction to the student in a larger number of vocations.

8. At the terminal point of his college career, in addition to accomplishment in his chosen field, the student should have a reasonable acquaintance with the subject matter and skill, together with interest and appreciation, with respect to: the world in which we live, including both organic and inorganic, animate and inanimate; the realm of personal and social relationships; the literary, linguistic and artistic products by our civilization; and the tools necessarily involved in the acquisition of these. He should also demonstrate an effective mastery in a special field of interest.

9. We recognize the value in the student's understanding of the relationship of each portion of education on the one hand to the life situation in which it functions and on the other hand to the organized body of subject matter of which it is a part. . . .

10. One question that was referred to the Committee was: "How shall we determine what shall go into the curriculum of a liberal arts college? What weight should be given to: (i) the present interests of the student; (ii) the problems of civilization; and (iii) the traditional classifications of knowledge? Is a creative synthesis from these sources possible?" The Committee feels it impossible to answer in mathematical terms the question as it is worded, but feels that integration of these three items is necessary and possible.

11. It is recognized that so-called extra-curricular activities are really a part of the educational offerings of the college and should be subjected to the same critical analysis, selection and guidance desirable in other phases of the curriculum.

12. We feel that there is some tendency to give to students schedules that are too crowded to permit the most genuine intellectual growth.

---

99. The fact that some interests are "supposed," that some are "more rewarding" than others, and that new ones may be "awakened" by proper teaching implies a hierarchy of actual and potential interests. Does this hierarchy belie the individual's autonomous role in identifying interests to pursue?

13. We believe that prerequisites for entrance and within the college have been too rigid, too formal and not fully justified. . . .

14. In general, the committee favors the extension of methods of individual guidance through advisers and faculty committees and the recognition of such methods as an important function of a college faculty.[100]

V. . . . Administration

Similar things may be said of educational administration. The present trend toward making college administration a matter of business processes is to be deplored. The president of a college, the deans and all the other officials having to do with student interests, including registrars and recorders, should consider their work primarily from the standpoint of its educational bearings. That faculties should permit registrars or recorders to determine matters of educational procedure on terms of convenience to their filing systems is absurd.[101]

The dean who is not primarily a teacher, student of the actualities of psychology, and disinterested counselor of the young is an anachronism. Provision must be made by training on the job, and in universities, for the broadest education of deans and other administrative officials, when men and women fit for such positions are found. Much more important than the present counseling and selection of students is the discovery, selection and preparation—on lines of the broadest social intelligence—of officials who will become wise selectors and counselors of students.[102]

58. Robert M. Hutchins, *The Higher Learning in America* (1936)

INTRODUCTION

Aside from the Progressivist program, the other most deeply rationalized approach to liberal education that emerged from the roiling debate and experimentation in the second quarter of the twentieth century was that of "great books" and neo-scholasticism. To be sure, the orientation courses, general education programs, concentration-distribution formulae, and junior-senior college divisions persevered; but these were essentially organizing strategies intended to impose structure upon the anomie left by electivism. Advocates of "Deweyan Progressivism" and "neo-Thomism and the 'great books'" exercised a powerful influence on the rest of liberal education due to the strength of their conviction and the cogency of their rationales.[103] Beyond that, the two approaches were virtually adversarial, as seen in the noted exchange between the chief authority for progressive liberal

---

100. Compare Lionel Trilling's assessment of Dean John Van Amringe at Columbia College.

101. Why is this trend to be deplored so vehemently?

102. The first dean of students in the United States was appointed by Harvard College in 1891 in order to relieve the President and deans of academic units of this responsibility.

103. Laurence Veysey, "Stability and Experiment in the American Undergraduate Curriculum," in *Content and Context: Essays on College Education*, ed. Carl Kaysen (New York: McGraw-Hill, 1973), p. 13. See the discussion of Veysey in the introduction to Section VIII.

education, John Dewey, and the most prominent spokesman for "great books" and the associated neo-scholasticism, Robert M. Hutchins.[104]

Born in Brooklyn, New York, Hutchins (1899–1977) moved at the age of eight to Oberlin, Ohio, with his parents, both of whom were college educated and committed to evangelical Protestantism. After spending two years at Oberlin College (1915–1917), where his father was a theology professor, Hutchins joined the U.S. Ambulance Service and served in Italy during World War I. Upon returning, he entered Yale College, received the B.A. in 1921, and taught school for two years. In 1923 he entered Yale Law School, and was appointed Secretary to the Yale Corporation by his mentor, President James R. Angell, who had run the psychology laboratory for John Dewey at the University of Chicago. Graduating in 1925 with the LL.B., Hutchins continued as Secretary and became an instructor in the Law School. In 1927 he was made a full professor and acting dean of the Law School, and in 1929 the meteoric ascent of his career culminated in his appointment as president of the University of Chicago.

Over the next six years, Hutchins brought to Chicago a group of acquaintances with whom he tried to reorganize the liberal arts education at the university. In 1930 he recruited Mortimer Adler, an iconoclastic intellectual who was co-leading the General Honors "great books" course at Columbia. In 1934 he enlisted Richard McKeon, who was teaching medieval and Renaissance philosophy at Columbia. In 1935 Hutchins appointed as visiting professors Scott Buchanan and Stringfellow Barr to lead the Committee on the Liberal Arts at Chicago. All four of these figures were deeply committed to the philosophies of Aristotle and Thomas Aquinas and to organizing the curriculum around reading "great books." Their efforts to reorganize liberal education failed, however, due to disagreements among the four and to bitter resistance from the Chicago faculty.[105]

In 1937 Barr and Buchanan left to resuscitate St. John's College in Maryland, where they established "a four-year, all-required curriculum based on the study of the great books of Western civilization from the Greeks to the present and including rigorous training in mathematics and laboratory science," as Barr later wrote.[106] Stridently asserting their commitment amid "the major experimenting in general education" that surrounded them,[107] both "Barr and Buchanan continued to resist the portrayal of the [St. John's] program as experimental. . . . In an address in August 1937 on 'Reviewing the Ancient Purpose of Education,' Barr stated, 'True liberal education is one of the few things in life that can never be called an experiment.'"[108] Meanwhile, Hutchins composed the educational manifesto that he had intended to serve as a justification for the program that the Committee on the Liberal Arts at Chicago had been expected to establish. Delivered as the Stowe

104. John Dewey, "President Hutchins's Proposals to Remake Higher Education," *Social Frontier* 3 (Jan. 1937): 103–4; Robert M. Hutchins, "Grammar, Rhetoric, and Mr. Dewey," *Social Frontier* 3 (Feb. 1937): 137–9; John Dewey, "The Higher Learning in America," *Social Frontier* 3 (Mar. 1937): 167–9.

105. See Donald N. Levine, "Preface" (1992), in *The Idea and Practice of General Education: An Account of the College of the University of Chicago* (1950; Chicago: University of Chicago Press, 1992); Mary Ann Dzuback, *Robert M. Hutchins: Portrait of an Educator* (Chicago: University of Chicago Press, 1991).

106. Quoted in Stanley Kunitz and Howard Haycraft, *Twentieth Century Authors: A Biographical Dictionary of Modern Literature, 1st Supplement* (New York: H.W. Wilson, 1955), s.v. Stringfellow Barr. See selection #65 on St. John's College.

107. Malcolm S. MacLean, et al., "The General Colleges," in *General Education in the American College*, ed. Guy M. Whipple (Bloomington, IL: Public School Publishing, 1939), p. 135.

108. Quoted in J. Winfree Smith, *A Search for the Liberal College: The Beginning of the St. John's Program* (Annapolis, MD: St. John's College Press, 1983), p. 25.

Lectures at Yale, *The Higher Learning in America* rapidly gained widespread attention, bolstered by the attention attracted by St. John's College, whose leaders explicitly endorsed Hutchins's book.

Although the Committee on the Liberal Arts disintegrated at Chicago, the legacy of Hutchins and his colleagues included not only founding the highly influential exemplar of St. John's College, but also launching in 1952 the famous fifty-four volume series entitled *Great Books of the Western World*, published by Encyclopedia Britannica. The central metaphor of the project—and of studying Great Books—was the "Great Conversation," as Hutchins wrote in the first paragraph of the first volume, entitled, *The Great Conversation: The Substance of a Liberal Education*: "The tradition of the West is embodied in the Great Conversation that began in the dawn of history and that continues to the present day. . . . The goal toward which Western society moves is the Civilization of the Dialogue. The spirit of Western civilization is the spirit of inquiry. . . . Nothing is to remain undiscussed. Everybody is to speak his mind. No proposition is to be left unexamined."[109]

Meanwhile, the years until Hutchins left the University in 1951 were generally difficult for the young president. He "could hardly have chosen a less congenial setting [in] which to sally forth on his mission of reform. The University of Chicago exemplified the American research university in the 1920s and 1930s."[110] Neither the institutional nor the intellectual context at Chicago was thus receptive, and, despite his charisma and eloquence, Hutchins's leadership style caused difficulties. After leaving Chicago, Hutchins served as an associate director at the Ford Foundation from 1951 to 1954, and then became president of the Ford-sponsored Fund for the Republic. From 1959 to 1974 he was president of the Center for the Study of Democratic Institutions located in Santa Barbara, California, where he died in 1977.

SELECTION[111]

My excuse for devoting one chapter to general education in a series on the higher learning is the relation between the two. We can never get a university without general education. Unless students and professors (and particularly professors) have a common intellectual training, a university must remain a series of disparate schools and departments, united by nothing except the fact that they have the same president and board of trustees.[112] Professors cannot talk to one another, not at least about anything important. They cannot hope to understand one another.[113]

We may take it for granted that we shall always have specialists; yet neither the world nor knowledge of it is arbitrarily divided up as universities are. Everybody cannot be a specialist in every field.

---

109. Robert M. Hutchins, *The Great Conversation: The Substance of a Liberal Education*, v. 1 of *Great Books of the Western World*, ed. Robert Maynard Hutchins (Chicago: Encyclopedia Britannica, 1952), p. 1. What were the goals and the spirit that characterized liberal arts curricula in the past that required reading classic books?

110. Benjamin McArthur, "Revisiting Hutchins and 'The Higher Learning in America,'" *History of Higher Education Annual* 7 (1987): 19.

111. Robert M. Hutchins, *The Higher Learning in America* (New Haven, CT: Yale University Press, 1936), pp. 59–87. Reprinted by permission of Yale University Press.

112. Amherst College President Alexander Meiklejohn apparently concurred: "Our question is how we can get unity in the curriculum. . . . [for] a thing is understood only so far as it is unified. . . . In so far as modern education has become . . . a thing of departments, groups, and interests and problems and subjects, . . . our modern teaching, our modern curriculum, is not a thing of intelligent insight." "Remarks on the Report of the Association of American Colleges Commission on the Organization of the College Curriculum," *Association of American Colleges Bulletin* 9 (1923): 79–80.

113. Is "a common intellectual training" necessary to communicate and understand each other?

He must therefore be cut off from every field but his own unless he has the same basic education that other specialists have. This means more than having the same language and the same general interest in advancing knowledge. It means having a common stock of fundamental ideas. This becomes more important as empirical science advances and accumulates more and more data. The specialist in a narrow field has all he can do to keep up with the latest discoveries in it. Other men, even in his own department, struggling to stay abreast of what is happening in their own segments of the subject, cannot hope to keep up with what is happening in his. They may now expect to have some general understanding of what he is doing because they all have something in common; they are in the same department. But the day will shortly be upon us when even this degree of comprehension will be impossible, because of the infinite splitting of subject matters and the progressive submergence of any ideas by our insistence on information as the content of education. . . .[114]

In this chapter I should like to talk about content, not about method. I concede the great difficulty of communicating the kind of education I favor to those who are unable or unwilling to get their education from books.[115] I insist, however, that the education I shall outline is the kind that everybody should have, that the answer to it is not that some people should not have it, but that we should find out how to give it to those whom we do not know how to teach at present. You cannot say my content is wrong because you do not know the method of transmitting it. Let us agree upon content if we can and have faith that the technological genius of America will solve the problem of communication. . . .

Please do not tell me that the general education I propose should not be adopted because the great majority of those who pass through it will not go on to the university. The scheme that I advance is based on the notion that general education is education for everybody, whether he goes on to the university or not. It will be useful to him in the university; it will be equally useful if he never goes there. I will admit that it will not be useful to him outside the university in the popular sense of utility. It may not assist him to make money or to get ahead. It may not in any obvious fashion adjust him to his environment or fit him for the contemporary scene. It will, however, have a deeper, wider utility: it will cultivate the intellectual virtues. . . .

In short, the intellectual virtues are habits resulting from the training of the intellectual powers. An intellect properly disciplined, an intellect properly habituated, is an intellect able to operate well in all fields. An education that consists of the cultivation of the intellectual virtues, therefore, is the most useful education, whether the student is destined for a life of contemplation or a life of action. . . .

I shall not be attentive when you tell me that the plan of general education I am about to present is remote from real life, that real life is in constant flux and change, and that education must be in constant flux and change as well. I do not deny that all things are in change. They have a beginning, and a middle, and an end.[116] Nor will I deny that the history of the race reveals tremendous technological advances and great increases in our scientific knowledge. But we are so impressed with scientific and technological progress that we assume similar progress in every field. We renounce our intellectual heritage, read only the most recent books, discuss only current events, try to keep the schools abreast or even ahead of the times, and write elaborate addresses on Education and Social Change. . . .

---

114. Does "advancing knowledge" through specialized research mean "accumulating more and more data" or imply viewing "information as the content of education?"

115. One reason for "the great difficulty of communicating" between Hutchins and his critics was that Hutchins took for granted premises, such as the dualistic distinction between subject matter and method, that others, such as Dewey, denied. See "The Unity of Subject Matter and Method," in John Dewey, *Democracy and Education* (1916; New York: Free Press, 1966), pp. 164–70.

116. Is the assertion that things "have a beginning, a middle, and an end" the same as saying that "real life is in constant flux and change?"

Our erroneous notion of progress has thrown the classics and the liberal arts out of the curriculum, overemphasized the empirical sciences, and made education the servant of any contemporary movements in society, no matter how superficial. In recent years this attitude has been accentuated by the world-wide depression and the highly advertised political, social, and economic changes resulting from it. We have been very much upset by all these things. We have felt that it was our duty to educate the young so that they would be prepared for further political, social, and economic changes. Some of us have thought we should try to figure out what the impending changes would be and frame a curriculum that embodied them. Others have even thought that we should decide what changes are desirable and then educate our students not merely to anticipate them, but also to take part in bringing them about. One purpose of education is to draw out the elements of our common human nature. These elements are the same in any time or place. The notion of educating a man to live in any particular time or place, to adjust him to any particular environment, is therefore foreign to a true conception of education.[117]

Education implies teaching. Teaching implies knowledge. Knowledge is truth. The truth is everywhere the same. Hence education should be every where the same.[118] I do not overlook the possibilities of differences in organization, in administration, in local habits and customs. These are details. I suggest that the heart of any course of study designed for the whole people will be, if education is rightly understood, the same at any time, in any place, under any political, social, or economic conditions. Even the administrative details are likely to be similar because all societies have generic similarity.

If education is rightly understood, it will be understood as the cultivation of the intellect. The cultivation of the intellect is the same good for all men in all societies. It is, moreover, the good for which all other goods are only means. Material prosperity, peace and civil order, justice and the moral virtues are means to the cultivation of the intellect. So Aristotle says in the *Politics*: "Now, in men reason and mind are the end towards which nature strives, so that the generation and moral discipline of the citizens ought to be ordered with a view to them."[119] An education which served the means rather than their end would be misguided.[120]

I agree, of course, that any plan of general education must be such as to educate the student for intelligent action. It must, therefore, start him on the road toward practical wisdom. But the question is what is the best way for education to start him and how far can it carry him. Prudence or practical wisdom selects the means toward the ends that we desire. It is acquired partly from intellectual operations and partly from experience. But the chief requirement for it is correctness in thinking. Since education cannot duplicate the experiences which the student will have when he graduates, it should devote itself to developing correctness in thinking as a means to practical wisdom, that is, to intelligent action. . . .

---

117. Does Hutchins infer the existence of permanence and unity in the universe from his preference for that above change and plurality? Compare Plato's view on these matters in selection #1.

118. These are the most frequently quoted lines from *The Higher Learning in America*. Hutchins adds here a note quoting Thomas Aquinas: "It is therefore evident that, as regards the general principles whether of speculative or practical reason, truth or rectitude is the same for all, and is equally known by all." *Summa Theologica*, pt. II, ques. 94, art. 4.

119. Hutchins does not provide the citation, which is *Politics* VII 1334b15–17.

120. Hutchins's presupposed and repeated distinction between ends and means was denied by John Dewey: "Every means is a temporary end until we have attained it. Every end becomes a means of carrying activity further as soon as it is achieved." *Democracy and Education*, pp. 106, 323.

A modern heresy is that all education is formal education and that formal education must assume the total responsibility for the full development of the individual. The Greek notion that the city educates the man has been forgotten. Everything that educated the man in the city has to be imported into our schools, colleges, and universities. We are beginning to behave as though the home, the church, the state, the newspaper, the radio, the movies, the neighborhood club, and the boy next door did not exist. All the experience that is daily and hourly acquired from these sources is overlooked, and we set out to supply imitations of it in educational institutions.[121] The experience once provided by some of these agencies may be attenuated now; but it would be a bold man who would assert that the young person today lived a life less full of experience than the youth of yesterday. Today as yesterday we may leave experience to other institutions and influences and emphasize in education the contribution that it is supremely fitted to make, the intellectual training of the young. The life they lead when they are out of our hands will give them experience enough. . . .

If there are permanent studies which every person who wishes to call himself educated should master; if those studies constitute our intellectual inheritance, then those studies should be the center of a general education. They cannot be ignored because they are difficult, or unpleasant, or because they are almost totally missing from our curriculum today. The child-centered school may be attractive to the child, and no doubt is useful as a place in which the little ones may release their inhibitions and hence behave better at home. But educators cannot permit the students to dictate the course of study unless they are prepared to confess that they are nothing but chaperones, supervising an aimless, trial-and-error process which is chiefly valuable because it keeps young people from doing something worse.[122] The free elective system as Mr. Eliot introduced it at Harvard and as Progressive Education adapted it to lower age levels amounted to a denial that there was content to education. Since there was no content to education, we might as well let students follow their own bent.[123] They would at least be interested and pleased and would be as well educated as if they had pursued a prescribed course of study. This overlooks the fact that the aim of education is to connect man with man, to connect the present with the past, and to advance the thinking of the race. If this is the aim of education, it cannot be left to the sporadic, spontaneous interests of children or even of undergraduates. . . .

It cannot be assumed that students at any age will always select the subjects that constitute education. If we permit them to avoid them, we cannot confer upon them insignia which certify to the public that they are in our opinion educated. In any field the permanent studies on which the whole development of the subject rests must be mastered if the student is to be educated.[124]

The variations that should be encouraged fall not in the realm of content but in that of method. Allowances for individual differences should be provided for by abolishing all requirements except

---

121. Consider Hutchins's point in light of the increasingly expansive and expensive "co-curricular" programming for undergraduates in colleges and universities. Compare the argument of Jeremiah Day in selection #37 that schools and colleges need not be responsible for teaching everything.

122. Hutchins appears to have Progressive schools in mind, but John Dewey emphasized the importance of education having an aim, asserting "that acting with an aim is all one with acting intelligently." But he also said, "To talk about an educational aim when approximately each act of the [student] is dictated by the teacher, when the only order in the sequence of his acts is that which comes from the assignment of lessons and the giving of directions by another, is to talk nonsense." *Democracy and Education*, pp. 103, 101–2. Hence, the disagreement between Hutchins and "Progressive Education" on this point was not whether there should be aims. What is the source of their disagreement?

123. Does Eliot deny that there is content to education in selection #40 or #47?

124. James McCosh in selection #48 and Hugh of St. Victor in selection #15 likewise argue that all students should study all the subjects of liberal education.

the examinations and permitting the student to take them whenever in his opinion he is ready to do so. The cultivation of independent thought and study, now almost wholly missing from our program, may thus be somewhat advanced. . . .

By insisting on the permanent studies as the heart of a general education, I do not mean to insist that they are the whole of it. We do not know enough to know whether certain technological work, for example, may not have a certain subsidiary value in general education for some students. Nor do I overlook the fact that since by hypothesis general education may be terminal for most students, it must connect them with the present and future as well as with the past. It is as important for them to know that thinking is still going on as it is for them to know what has been thought before.

The question whether certain technical work shall be allowed to be a part of general education is rather a question of method than of content, a question how to teach rather than what. Technology as such has no place in general education. If it can be justified at all, it can only be because we discover that certain principles can best be communicated through technical work. The question of present thought is largely answered by saying that it is impossible to think of a teacher who contented himself with elucidating the thought of the past without intimating that these ideas have a history running to the present day. . . .

Let us avoid all questions of administration and method. Let us assume that we have an intelligible organization of education under which there is a four-year unit, beginning at about the beginning of the junior year in high school and ending at about the end of the sophomore year in college. Let us assume that we are going to try to teach in that unit everybody who can learn from books. Let us assume further that the conclusion of their work in this unit will mark the end of formal instruction for most students. They will not go on to the university. Nevertheless we must have a curriculum which will, in the main, do as well for those who are going on as those who are not. What shall this curriculum be?

We have excluded body building and character building. We have excluded the social graces and the tricks of trades. We have suggested that the curriculum should be composed principally of the permanent studies. We propose the permanent studies because these studies draw out the elements of our common human nature,[125] because they connect man with man, because they connect us with the best that man has thought, because they are basic to any further study and to any understanding of the world. What are the permanent studies?

They are in the first place those books which have through the centuries attained to the dimensions of classics. Many such books, I am afraid, are in the ancient and medieval period. But even these are contemporary. A classic is a book that is contemporary in every age. That is why it is a classic. The conversations of Socrates raise questions that are as urgent today as they were when Plato wrote. In fact they are more so, because the society in which Plato lived did not need to have them raised as much as we do. We have forgotten how important they are.

Such books are then a part, and a large part, of the permanent studies. They are so in the first place because they are the best books we know. How can we call a man educated who has never read any of the great books in the western world? Yet today it is entirely possible for a student to graduate from the finest American colleges without having read any of them, except possibly Shakespeare. Of course, the student may have heard of these books, or at least of their authors. But this knowledge is gained in general through textbooks, and textbooks have probably done as much to degrade the American intelligence as any single force. If the student should know about Cicero, Milton, Galileo, or Adam Smith, why should he not read what they wrote? Ordinarily what he knows about them he learns from texts which must be at best second-hand versions of their thought.

---

125. At the beginning of the twenty-first century, the diversity of individuals and cultures is emphasized. Do people and cultures share a "common human nature" that liberal education could or should cultivate?

In the second place these books are an essential part of general education because it is impossible to understand any subject or to comprehend the contemporary world without them. . . . If every man were educated—and why should he not be?—our people would not fall so easily a prey to the latest nostrums in economics, in politics, and, I may add, in education.[126]

You will observe that the great books of the western world cover every department of knowledge. *The Republic* of Plato is basic to an understanding of the law; it is equally important as education for what is known as citizenship. The *Physics* of Aristotle, which deals with change and motion in nature, is fundamental to the natural sciences and medicine, and is equally important to all those who confront change and motion in nature, that is, to everybody. Four years spent partly in reading, discussing, and digesting books of such importance would, therefore, contribute equally to preparation for specialized study and to general education of a terminal variety. Certainly four years is none too long for this experience. It is an experience which will, as I have said, serve as preparation for advanced study and as general education designed to help the student understand the world. It will also develop habits of reading and standards of taste and criticism that will enable the adult, after his formal education is over, to think and act intelligently about the thought and movements of contemporary life. It will help him to share in the intellectual activity of his time.

In order to read books one must know how to do it. The degeneracy of instruction in English grammar should not blind us to the fact that only through grammatical study can written works be understood. Grammar is the scientific analysis of language through which we understand the meaning and force of what is written.[127] Grammar disciplines the mind and develops the logical faculty. It is good in itself and as an aid to reading the classics. It has a place in general education in connection with the classics and independently of them. For those who are going to learn from books learning the art of reading would seem to be indispensable. . . .

I add to grammar the rules of reading, rhetoric and logic, or the rules of writing, speaking, and reasoning. The classics provide models of excellence; grammar, rhetoric, and logic are means of determining how excellence is achieved. We have forgotten that there are rules for speaking. And English composition, as it is commonly taught, is a feeble and debased imitation of the classical rules of writing, placing emphasis either on the most trivial details or on what is called self-expression. Self-expression as here understood is, of course, the exact reverse of the discipline which rhetoric in all ages up to the present was used to give. Logic is a statement in technical form of the conditions under which reasoning is rigorously demonstrative. If the object of general education is to train the mind for intelligent action, logic cannot be missing from it.

Logic is a critical branch of the study of reasoning. It remains only to add a study which exemplifies reasoning in its clearest and most precise form. That study is, of course, mathematics, and of the mathematical studies chiefly those that use the type of exposition that Euclid employed. In such studies the pure operation of reason is made manifest. The subject matter depends on the universal and necessary processes of human thought. It is not affected by differences in taste, disposition, or prejudice.[128] It refutes the common answer of students who, conformable to the temper of the times, wish to

---

126. Is Hutchins successful in linking a democratic rationale to the argument for a high culture and a curriculum of great books?

127. Hutchins's view of grammar here fits closely the "science of grammar" that was developed by the medieval scholastics and that contrasted with the literary grammar advanced by Renaissance humanists.

128. Hutchins is here agreeing with Aristotle that the conceptual foundation and system of every science resembles that of axiomatic geometry. By the time Hutchins was writing, however, the discovery of non-Euclidean geometries in the nineteenth century, leading to the general theory of relativity in the 1910s, had undermined the universality of "the type of exposition that Euclid employed."

accept the principles and deny the conclusions. Correctness in thinking may be more directly and impressively taught through mathematics than in any other way. . . .[129]

We have then for general education a course of study consisting of the greatest books of the western world and the arts of reading, writing, thinking, and speaking, together with mathematics, the best exemplar of the processes of human reason. If our hope has been to frame a curriculum which educes the elements of our common human nature, this program should realize our hope. If we wish to prepare the young for intelligent action, this course of study should assist us; for they will have learned what has been done in the past and what the greatest men have thought. They will have learned how to think themselves. If we wish to lay a basis for advanced study, that basis is provided. If we wish to secure true universities, we may look forward to them, because students and professors may acquire through this course of study a common stock of ideas and common methods of dealing with them. All the needs of general education in America seem to be satisfied by this curriculum.

What, then, are the objections to it? They cannot be educational objections; for this course of study appears to accomplish the aims of general education. One objection may be that the students will not like it, which is, as we have seen, irrelevant. But even if it were relevant, it is not true. Since the proposed curriculum is coherent and comprehensible, and since it is free from the triviality that now afflicts our program, students will respond to it if the teachers will give them a chance to do it.

It may be said that the course of study is too difficult. It is not too difficult for students who can read or who can be taught to do so. . . . No, the students can do the work if the faculties will let them.

Will the faculties let them? I doubt it. The professors of today have been brought up differently. Not all of them have read all the books they would have to teach. Not all of them are ready to change the habits of their lives. Meanwhile they are bringing up their successors in the way they were brought up, so that the next crop will have the habits they have had themselves. And the love of money, a misconception of democracy, a false notion of progress, a distorted idea of utility, and the anti-intellectualism to which all these lead conspire to confirm their conviction that no disturbing change is needed.

The times call for the establishment of a new college or for an evangelistic movement in some old ones which shall have for its object the conversion of individuals and finally of the teaching profession to a true conception of general education. Unless some such demonstration or some such evangelistic movement can take place, we shall remain in our confusion; we shall have neither general education nor universities; and we shall continue to disappoint the hopes of our people.

---

129. In notes, Hutchins quotes from Plato's *Republic* (526b, 527a). See selection #1.

Section IX

The "Emerging Curricular Blueprint" of the Mid-Twentieth Century

During the 1940s and 1950s, much of the energy that had animated the experimentation and reform in liberal education in previous decades was siphoned away by the Great Depression, the Second World War, and the associated recovery. Rather than pursuing or debating innovation, advocates of liberal education in the mid-twentieth century were reduced to arguing for survival, because "higher education of any kind, but particularly that which has no specific vocational aim, is always threatened in time of war."[1] Responding to this threat, leaders of "liberal colleges," such as the President of Carleton College, persistently advocated "The Preservation of Liberal Education in Time of War."[2] In selection #60, President Frank Aydelotte of Swarthmore College elaborates this defense.

Apart from the perception that liberal education has no technical application, another significant factor contributing to the threat was the decline in enrollments in the liberal arts. Young men, who traditionally dominated enrollments in liberal education, were entering the military instead. Yet, this factor presented an opportunity and responsibility for women, suggested the president of Sweet Briar College, because "what women get in their education now may largely determine . . . the ideals and attainments of the next generation. . . . [W]omen, who are not primarily absorbed into war activity, keep alive the long-time values of learning and culture which belong to all generations."[3] Although this aspiration was generally unrealized due to the exclusion or marginalization of women by most institutions that traditionally championed liberal education, the suggestion that liberal education pursued by women during the war would determine that for men after the war was confirmed in a few instances. One such case was the "experimental" liberal education for women instituted at Purdue University between 1939 and 1947, as described in selection #59 by Sarah Barnes.

Meanwhile, the Association of American Colleges (AAC), comprising some 550 institutions throughout the country, issued a report in 1943, "The Nature and Purpose of Liberal Education," which was summarized in a news release sent to 1,894 newspapers; condensed in a booklet distributed to nearly 7,000 educational organizations, journals, elected officials, and heads of schools, colleges, and universities; and sold, in 6,000 copies, to institutions of higher education, many of which were revising their curricula.[4] Despite all this effort, the report exercised little influence, for it drew from nearly every viewpoint arising in the experimentation of the early decades of the twentieth century. In the "nature" of liberal education, the report included physical, intellectual, aesthetic, moral, and spiri-

1. Robert E. Spiller, "Higher Education and the War," *The Journal of Higher Education* 13 (1942): 287.

2. Donald J. Cowling, "The Preservation of Liberal Education in Time of War," *Association of American Colleges Bulletin* 29 (1943): 187–91.

3. Meta Glass, "How Shall the College Curriculum be Adjusted to Wartime Conditions and Needs?" *Association of American Colleges Bulletin* 28 (1942): 554. Glass was speaking at the National Institute on Education and the War, held in Washington, DC in August, 1942, under the auspices of the United States Office of Education.

4. James P. Baxter III, "Commission on Liberal Education Report," *Association of American Colleges Bulletin* 29 (1943): 269–74.

tual training whose "purpose" was to inculcate individual freedom, personal fulfillment, intellectual discipline, and social responsibility, as well as the "skills and abilities . . . to use intelligently and with a sense of workmanship some of the principal tools and techniques of the arts and sciences."[5]

This eclecticism was no embarrassment to the Commission because the tendency to blend and reconcile different viewpoints characterized many statements on liberal education during the middle of the twentieth century. The earlier, distinctive proposals from Progressive Colleges or Robert M. Hutchins gave way to eclectic statements, such as *General Education in a Free Society*, a report of a committee of the Faculty of Arts and Sciences at Harvard University. Declaring that "general and liberal education have identical goals," *General Education in a Free Society* endorsed conviction while respecting tentativeness of conclusions, honored heritage and tradition while admitting a modern emphasis on process and change, recommended "unity conditioned by difference," promoted "tolerance not from absence of standards but through possession of them," and reconciled "Jeffersonianism and Jacksonianism."[6] Though the "now famous Harvard report" attracted a great deal of comment,[7] it was never adopted by the Harvard faculty and widely thought to be self-contradictory or unsystematic.[8]

Amid this eclecticism, the most significant innovation appearing in the middle decades of the twentieth century was the introduction of honors work. The honors idea recalled the critique of democratic culture associated with John Erskine's strain of Great Books, as discussed by Daniel Bell in selection #54. But the leading spokesman for the full-fledged movement in subsequent decades was Frank Aydelotte, whose explanation and justification for honors study is found in selection #60. Honors work thus became the most innovative aspect of "the emerging curricular blueprint devot[ing] the first two years of the undergraduate course to general education in fundamental liberal arts subjects and the last two to more specialized, often frankly professional, training," in the words of Willis Rudy. This blueprint, described in selection #61, was instituted throughout the country between 1925 and 1960.

The following two decades presented "as volatile a period of educational reform as America has ever experienced," including widespread social and political protests on American campuses.[9] Amid that upheaval, some reformers attempted to tear up the curricular blueprint and radically reform liberal arts in the United States. The conceptual relationship between liberal education and liberatory movements, including political or social liberalism, is debated by Harold Taylor and Paul Kristeller in selections #62 and #63. The prominent attempts at curricular reform are analyzed by sociologists Gerald Grant and David Riesman in selection #64.

---

5. "The Post-War Responsibilities of Liberal Education: Report of the Committee on the Re-Statement of the Nature and Aims of Liberal Education," *Association of American Colleges Bulletin* 29 (1943): 275–99.

6. *General Education in a Free Society* (Cambridge, MA: Harvard University Press, 1945), pp. 27–35, 42–53, 66, 76–8, 92ff.

7. Gordon K. Chalmers, "Report on a Work in Progress: Education, the Redefinition of Liberal Education," *Association of American Colleges Bulletin* 32 (1946): 60.

8. See George E. Ganss, *Saint Ignatius's Idea of a Jesuit University* (Milwaukee, WI: Marquette University Press, 1954), p. 269; George N. Shuster, "Introduction," in *The Idea of a University*, by John Henry Newman (New York: Doubleday, 1959), p. 39; Paul Hirst, "Liberal Education and the Nature of Knowledge," in *Philosophical Analysis and Education*, ed. Reginald A. Archambault (New York: Humanities Press, 1965), pp. 116–21; John S. Brubacher and Willis Rudy, *Higher Education in Transition: A History of American Colleges and Universities, 1636–1976*, 3d ed. (New York: Harper and Row, 1976), p. 303.

9. Gerald Grant and David Riesman, *The Perpetual Dream: Reform and Experiment in the American College* (Chicago: University of Chicago Press, 1978), p. 183.

59. Sarah V. Barnes, "'Experimental' Liberal Education for Women, 1939–1947"

INTRODUCTION

Between 1939 and 1947 an "experiment" in liberal education was conducted at Purdue University, one of the land-grant universities that was founded under the Morrill Act of 1862 and dedicated to providing training in "agriculture and the mechanical arts." The Purdue experiment was not only to offer liberal education, but to offer it to women. The stimulus to attempt either venture arose out of the upheaval and reorganization caused by World War II. Due to its success, the experiment was ultimately co-opted by men. Nevertheless, the women's program determined post-war liberal education at Purdue, and thereby demonstrates that "women were sometimes at the center, rather than on the periphery, of fundamental developments in liberal education," as discussed in selection #59.

Among the 109 women who completed the program in "Liberal Science" was Virginia MacDonald Menke, whose reflections provide some of the data for this selection. Menke's daughter, Sarah V. Barnes, is the author of this selection. Born in Wisconsin in 1961, Barnes's interest in the topic was peaked partly by the experience of her mother, but also by her undergraduate studies at Williams College, which, she says, "kindled my profound belief in the value of a liberal education." After graduating with a B.A. in history in 1984, Barnes studied at Northwestern University, completing a Ph.D. on the comparative history of Modern Britain and the United States. She has taught at Northwestern University, Southern Methodist University, University of Colorado, Colorado State University, University of Hong Kong, and Texas Christian University. She is now a professional horse trainer in Colorado. Citations have been excised from this selection, except for quotations.

SELECTION[10]

A female student entering Purdue University in the late 1930s found her options rather limited. If not one of the two or three women to enroll in Engineering or Agriculture, she could either join the majority of her peers in the School of Home Economics or tackle a technical degree in Science. For President Edward C. Elliott and a handful of others on campus, this was a less than satisfactory state of affairs. . . . As was true of other land-grant institutions, the university's historic mission to offer training in "agriculture and the mechanical arts" dictated a commitment to providing the citizens of the state, men and women alike, with preparation for careers in an expanding array of scientific and technical fields. The university's aim for its male students seemed clear: equip them to be scientists and engineers. But as the number and variety of employment options for women began to increase, and as more and more female students arrived on campus, not all of whom sought highly technical careers, or careers at all for that matter, nor wished to major in home economics, administrators struggled with how best to prepare these young women for the future.

At the same time, the perennial debate about the broader purposes of higher education within American society was in the midst of a particularly contentious phase. Faced with rising enrollments and the arrival on campus of an increasingly diverse and vocationally-minded student body, individual institutions sought some effective means of reconciling an ever-more specialized and fragmented curriculum with the traditional claims of the liberal arts. Even at Purdue, the long-standing land-grant commitment to training scientists and engineers began to seem problematic. For many schools, the

10. Sarah V. Barnes, "The 'Experimental' Liberal Education for Women at Purdue University, 1939–1947" (unpublished typescript, 2000). Printed by permission of the author.

solution appeared in the form of general education, an approach which aimed to provide students with a broad foundation of cultural knowledge before allowing them to equip themselves with the specific skills needed to earn a living.

Amid these contentious debates, a unique program for female students flourished at Purdue from 1939 until 1947. Beyond recovering some memory of the program's existence, one purpose in recounting the story is to add to our understanding of the experiences of women in liberal education during a period of unusual opportunity that soon passed. In addition, this story illustrates that women were sometimes at the center, rather than on the periphery, of fundamental developments in liberal education and it is important to recognize the significance of their presence.

Purdue in the 1930s did represent, in many respects, the typical Midwestern land-grant institution. Like its regional neighbors Iowa State and Michigan State, the university—located in West Lafayette, Indiana, along the banks of the Wabash River—concentrated primarily on instruction in engineering, agriculture, and other vocational subjects. Hoosiers seeking a less technical degree went either to Indiana University in Bloomington or to one of the state's numerous small private liberal arts colleges. Undergraduate enrollment was rising throughout the second half of the decade, from 4,381 in 1935 to 6,669 in 1939, as the economy recovered from the Depression and higher education became more and more central to American life.

Not surprisingly, men outnumbered women at Purdue by more than four-to-one.[11] Yet although always a distinct minority on campus, the number of women attending Purdue during these years increased in both absolute and relative terms, from 744 or 17 percent of the student body in 1935, to 1,272 or 19 percent in 1939. More than two-thirds of these women graduated from the School of Home Economics; most of the rest, slightly more than a quarter, earned B.S. degrees from the School of Science, while the majority of the remainder graduated in pharmacy.[12] Of the men, two-thirds earned engineering degrees; the rest were mainly in either agriculture or science, with a handful in pharmacy. Of the largest divisions on campus—Engineering, Agriculture, Science and Home Economics—only the School of Science enrolled a substantial number of both male and female students. Here the ratio was approximately two-to-one.

As was true of Purdue's other schools, the School of Science concentrated on preparing students for technical or teaching careers, in this case primarily in the fields of chemistry, physics and biology. In addition, Science provided a home for the departments of English, Mathematics, History, Government, Economics and Modern Languages, whose collective purpose was mainly to offer basic courses required by the other schools for graduation. In addition to a minimum of such general requirements, graduation from the School of Science itself involved numerous hours of laboratory work in the hard sciences, even for those students seeking careers in a non-technical field. Restricted by a "gentleman's agreement" with Indiana University, Purdue at the time offered only B.S. degrees.

Thus, a female student entering the university in the late 1930s found her options limited, particularly if she did not want a degree in home economics. Administrators were not unmindful of the dilemma. President Elliott, himself the father of two teenage daughters, demonstrated his concern in a

---

11. Purdue's first class of students in 1874 included no women. The following year the institution became coeducational, although it was not until 1920 that women represented more than 10 percent of the student body. Beginning in the early 1920s, land-grant institutions (in this case including state universities) were relatively hospitable toward women, both as students and faculty. Susan B. Carter, "Academic Women Revisited: An Empirical Study of Changing Patterns of Women's Employment as College and University Faculty, 1890–1963," *Journal of Social History* 14 (1981): 675–97.

12. By the late 1930s a handful of women were enrolled in Agriculture and Engineering. One woman earned a B.S. in Agriculture in 1939, and by 1943 two women had earned engineering degrees.

number of ways, including two significant faculty appointments, both made in 1935. . . .[13] One was Amelia Earhart, who made several trips to Purdue over the course of the 1935–36 academic year, living in the women's residence hall, meeting with students, and generally causing quite a stir on campus during her stays. Besides inspiring Purdue's co-eds to flaunt fashion etiquette by wearing slacks in public, she challenged them to believe in their potential as women to succeed at a wide range of vocations. Meanwhile, with the help of Purdue engineers, she prepared for her ill-fated flight around the world.[14]

Perhaps less newsworthy but of more enduring significance was Elliott's other major female faculty appointment, Lillian Moller Gilbreth. With a Ph.D. in psychology and a successful career as an industrial engineer, Gilbreth joined Purdue's engineering faculty in 1935 as a visiting full professor, a position she retained until 1948. While her interactions with students in this capacity involved men as well as women, she was always especially supportive of the handful of women in Purdue's engineering program, as well as female students generally. As the only female full professor outside of the School of Home Economics who was not primarily serving in an administrative capacity, she represented an important role model.[15] In particular, she influenced many female graduates of Purdue to pursue careers in industrial management and personnel.

Yet while the presence on campus of these two accomplished women reflected President Elliott's efforts to foster a positive atmosphere, difficulties remained. More and more women were coming to Purdue, but not necessarily because of its reputation in agriculture, engineering, science, or even home economics. Some were the daughters of faculty or alumni, others had older brothers already enrolled, some were simply from West Lafayette and wanted to attend school close to home. Whatever the reason, they arrived on campus but found little in Purdue's existing curriculum that appealed to them. Dean of Women Dorothy Stratton in particular lamented the university's lack of a bachelor of arts program, which she felt would have served the needs of this growing population. At her urging, President Elliott in 1937 appointed a committee to consider the problem.[16]

Over the course of the next two years, the Committee on the Education of Women met under the leadership of Helen Hazelton, professor and head of women's physical education and, like her colleague Dean Stratton, a forceful and articulate advocate of the interests of female students.[17] The

13. Born in Chicago, Elliott (1874–1960) earned a B.S. and an M.A. in chemistry at the University of Nebraska. After serving as a teacher and administrator in Colorado public schools from 1897 to 1903, he pursued graduate work at Teachers College, Columbia University, for two years. He then became professor of education at the University of Wisconsin (1905–1916); chancellor of the University of Montana system (1916–1922); and president of Purdue University (1922–1945).

14. Born in Kansas, Amelia Earhart (1897–1937), the famed aviator, disappeared over the Pacific Ocean, attempting to fly solo around the world in 1937.

15. Lillian Moller Gilbreth (1878–1972), born in Oakland, California, earned a B.A. at the University of California, Berkeley, in 1900 and a Ph.D. in psychology from Brown University in 1915. In 1939 Purdue had twenty-four female faculty members at the rank of assistant professor or above and twenty-four female instructors. Including both categories, women represented 8 percent of the total faculty.

16. Raised in Missouri, Dorothy C. Stratton (1907–2006) earned a B.A. at Ottawa University, Kansas, an M.A. in education from the University of Chicago, and a Ph.D. at Teachers College, Columbia University. In 1933 President Elliott brought her from teaching high school in California to become the second Dean of Women at Purdue.

17. After graduating with the B.A. from Mount Holyoke College, Helen Hazelton received professional training in the Department of Hygiene at Wellesley College and taught for four years at Northwestern University. In 1929 Hazelton completed an M.A. at Teachers College, Columbia University, and was appointed Professor and Director of Physical Education at Purdue.

committee's first report, submitted in February 1938, began by dividing the question under consideration into three areas: 1) the problem of training for vocations, 2) the problem of training for marriage and family life, and 3) the problem of the kind of general education appropriate to women students. . . .

In reference to "that possibly increasing group of women who are not particularly concerned with a specific vocation, but come to Purdue for a general education," the committee asked, "What education should they have that will fit them to be intelligent members of the community and, what is more important, give them the background of personal culture, in the broadest sense?" Noting that many of these students ended up in the School of Science, where they were frustrated by required laboratory classes designed for specialists, as well as by the lack of a broad range of courses in the humanities, the committee bluntly observed "that what many of these women students seem to want is, in good part, the subject matter commonly associated with the B.A. degree."[18]

Purdue could not offer a B.A. because of its agreement with Indiana University, but the committee did not consider advising these women to go elsewhere. The reasons for this were probably threefold: 1) the women were there already, drawn by family ties, convenience and cost; 2) Purdue wanted to do more for women students generally; and 3) adapting the curriculum promised to attract larger numbers of women to the university. Given the heavily skewed gender ratio, the economics of increased enrollment and the fact that every high school graduate from the State of Indiana, male or female, represented a potential Purdue student, finding a way to attract more women constituted a reasonable priority. . . .

The committee proposed combining two years of general education in the School of Science with further specialized work in whichever departments of the university would best serve the individual student's vocational ambitions. Instead of meeting the traditional freshman and sophomore requirements in the School of Science, the women would enroll in a specially planned series of four survey courses in physics, math, chemistry and biology aimed at presenting science as an area of knowledge and inquiry rather than as a basis for technical skill. . . . A fifth survey, devoted to the history of civilization, would serve in similar fashion to introduce the fields of knowledge covered by the social sciences and humanities. Finally, the committee proposed fewer credit hours be demanded for graduation, allowing students to devote more study time to the surveys and later to pursue specialized subjects in greater depth. . . .

Consequently, as the statement on the proposed curriculum concludes, "it was agreed that these new courses should first be given to an experimental group and that this procedure be considered as an experiment."[19]

---

18. On the contemporaneous situation of women seeking a B.A. course but being forced to choose among vocational programs, see selection #57 from John Dewey, et al., *The Curriculum for the Liberal Arts College* (1931), pt. II.

19. The fundamental objectives of the experimental curriculum were stated as follows: "The program is designed to train select groups of young women for intelligent leadership in whatever communities, large or small, urban or rural, they may be placed after college. Since science plays so predominant a part in molding the modern world, a keen interest in scientific problems and a sensitive appreciation of the part which the contributions of scientists play in our daily lives are deemed essential for such leadership. . . . Moreover, if these young women are to be influential members of their respective communities, they must be trained in the science and art of human relations. That implies possession of sympathetic understanding of their fellow human beings, with an ability to present their own ideas in an effective fashion. College should prepare students for a life of personal satisfaction as well as for effectiveness as members of society. The cultured person turns to literature and the arts as a sure source of pleasure. Every normal individual derives satisfaction from a vocation for which he feels himself well fitted. Included among the chief objectives of this program are the development of esthetic [*sic*] appreciation and the intelligent choice of a vocation."

Accordingly, in April of 1939, the university's Executive Committee approved the recommendation of the Committee on the Education of Women that a group of about forty young women be permitted to register in the School of Science, that survey courses as outlined in the committee's report be established for this group, and that a qualified female faculty member be hired to direct the program and act as an advisor to the students. Assured by President Elliott of the administration's moral and financial support, the committee began to prepare for the arrival of the program's first class of students in September.

Despite its small number, the group's presence on campus was portentous, marking a trial effort at serving students with a different set of needs than Purdue was accustomed to accommodating. Although sponsored by a committee ostensibly concerned only with the education of women, the program symbolized an attempt to widen and shift the mission of the university as a whole, with ramifications for students of both genders. As demonstrated by the committee's difficulty in confining itself to its stated mandate, the issue of general education and the problems involved in the education of women proved virtually inseparable, particularly within the context of a traditionally male-dominated, technically-oriented land-grant university.[20] Herein lies much of the significance of Purdue's experimental curriculum.

In addition, particularly for the actual women involved, the program's significance lay also in its implications for their own educational experience. Between 1939–40 and 1946–47, the last year in which only women were admitted, 109 students completed the experimental curriculum. As a whole, they were a select group, chosen on the basis of outstanding high school records, test scores and recommendations, as well as personal interviews. Dean Stratton, Prof. Hazelton and Prof. Dorothy Bovée, who arrived half-way through the first year to direct the program, were determined to admit only young women capable of meeting the rigorous academic standards which they felt must be maintained if the program were to prove its educational worth.[21] The students themselves, referred to in campus publications as "the guinea pigs," chose the experimental curriculum primarily because it offered a distinctive approach to education in the sciences, as well as the opportunity to take a broad range of classes from any school in the university. Most were explicitly not interested in home economics or technical scientific training, yet had other reasons for attending Purdue, including family connections and financial considerations. Others who wanted a liberal education and normally would not have considered Purdue, learned of the curriculum and decided to attend. Clearly, then, the program was serving the constituency for which it had been planned.

Once enrolled, the women's response to the experimental curriculum was overwhelmingly enthusiastic. The survey courses, they found, were both challenging and stimulating, taught by outstanding faculty members who welcomed the chance to develop the new courses and work with a group of such able and dedicated students. The professors themselves seemed curious about how the young women would react to the material, which presented fundamental scientific principles from an historical and philosophical perspective, and then raised questions about the role of science in contemporary life. Yet while they might have been unaccustomed to classrooms full of female faces, the science faculty

20. In the words of its report, "The Committee found that it was practically impossible to consider separately the needs of women as different from men when it came to general education, but proceeded to limit the study to women at Purdue, since that was the original assignment."

21. Dorothy A. Bovée received her B.S. (1921), M.S. (1930), and Ph.D. (1943) from the University of Minnesota. During her tenure at Purdue, she married a younger man, shocking the conservative communities of Purdue and West Lafayette. In about 1948 Dr. Bovée left with her husband for California, and by the early 1950s was serving as an associate professor and chairperson of the department of education at Mills, a women's college near San Francisco, where she retired in 1964.

involved in the program clearly respected their students' intellectual capacities and expected them to use their minds. . . .

Above all, students in the experimental curriculum were encouraged to think of themselves as leaders—leaders with an awareness and understanding of the critical role of science in modern life, a clear perception of present-day social, economic and political problems, and the resolve to confront and solve those problems in an objective and democratic fashion. In the words of an alumna, "while statistics said that somewhere around 95 percent of us would marry and stay home to rear our children, the Liberal Science environment told us we were valuable citizens and just as important to society as any man on the engineering campus. . . . "

Certainly the women in the program felt special. As one of them recalled, "my classmates were the cream of the crop. . . . We had the very best professors, small classes, could head in our own directions academically after studying the broad core curriculum." "It was like being in a small college inside a huge university," remarked another. Competition among the guinea pigs could sometimes be fierce, as everyone strove to do well in demanding classes, but mainly the women felt privileged to be part of a rather elite group. If they did perceive any obstacles as women at Purdue, it was only in their junior and senior years, when they found themselves in upper-level courses surrounded by male students and taught by a different set of male professors, some of whom were unaccustomed to sharing the classroom with such sharp and self-confident co-eds. More often than not, however, the women were unaware of gender discrimination in the classroom, and continued to compete and succeed academically alongside their male peers.

They also participated avidly in a wide range of student activities, from sororities to student government to the year book and newspaper, and in this manner were part of the regular student body. . . . Nevertheless, throughout their time at Purdue, women in the experimental curriculum consistently earned top scholastic honors and also tended to be over-represented in the leadership positions of various extracurricular activities, indicating the degree to which they were indeed a special group, both inside the classroom and out. . . .

Following graduation, many of the women did go on to pursue a variety of careers for which the program's combination of liberal education and vocational training had prepared them. In 1948, a survey of the first 109 graduates found 20 had gone on to graduate school, 14 were teachers and 13 were in personnel or industrial management (reflecting the influence of Lillian Gilbreth). Of the remainder, most had jobs in a wide variety of fields ranging from journalism, radio, and advertising, to social work, business, law, and scientific and economic research. Of course in 1948 many of these women had only been out of college for a few years, and many subsequently left their jobs to raise families. Nevertheless, as another survey conducted in 1996 revealed, many alumnae of the experimental curriculum either combined work and family throughout their careers, or returned to work later in life. . . .

Judging from the experiences and testimony of these women, then, the experimental curriculum seems to have been a success. Its goal, "to train select groups of young women for intelligent leadership in whatever communities, large or small, urban or rural, they may be placed after college," was surely met. Nonetheless, by the fall of 1947 the focus of the program was beginning to shift. Indeed, some changes had already been made as early as 1944–45, when the experimental curriculum officially lost its "experimental" designation and became known instead as "Liberal Science." In the same year two new required courses, open only to Liberal Science students, were added. The first, entitled "Science and Technology in Present-Day Life," was to be taken junior year. The second, open to seniors, was "Women and Women's Work." . . .

Liberal Science was increasingly becoming recognized as a distinctive program within the university. Indeed, the Liberal Science curriculum, with its selective standards for admission, small class sizes and demanding courses, opportunities for individually-directed work, outstanding faculty and stellar students, had begun to take on the characteristics of a four-year general education honors program.

Given the experiment's success, it is perhaps not surprising that the decision soon followed to admit men. The first group, selected according to the same criteria as the women, joined the program at the beginning of the 1947–48 academic year. Undoubtedly many factors were involved in the change. First, from a philosophical standpoint, the Committee on the Education of Women, which originally developed the experimental curriculum, had always believed the program's objectives and methods applied to men as well as women. From the beginning, the experiment was viewed as one in which the results might eventually become more widely applicable. Secondly, from a practical standpoint, Purdue by 1947 was being overrun with veterans returning to college on the G.I. Bill. The School of Science was particularly taxed by the jump in enrollments, not only because of rapid growth within the school itself, but because students in all the other schools in the university took at least some courses in the School of Science. Indeed, Liberal Science was the only department within the School of Science not offering at least one course required by another school. Under the circumstances, maintaining an elite and rather expensive program in the sole interests of a small group of women students, however smart, seemed hard to justify. Finally, male students were clamoring to get in. In the words of one of the last women to go through the program before it was integrated, "the men saw they were missing a good thing."

The admission of men, however, was only the beginning of fundamental changes in the status of "Liberal Science" at Purdue, changes which were tied not to the special interests of women but instead to major post-war imperatives affecting all of American higher education. The land-grants, in particular, faced a major reassessment of their mission in the wake of the shattering experiences of a war between democracy and totalitarianism, in which technological capacity seemed to have so far outstripped moral judgment. Even before the war, land-grant leaders had begun to question the impact of proliferating course offerings and increasingly fragmented curricula, so that the experience of war itself only added to concerns about their institutions' tendency to produce narrowly specialized scientific knowledge at the expense of a broader understanding of basic human values. . . .

For Elliott, an educational program designed particularly to meet the needs of women served the wider purpose of helping to elevate Purdue's status as a "true university," meaning an institution committed to some form of liberal learning, as well as to its historic mission of scientific and technical training. The role of gender as an agent in redefining the university's identity in these terms was instrumental. Women were literally the guinea pigs. Yet extending the results of the experiment beyond the laboratory remained a problematic process, not least in regard to its implications for the guinea pigs themselves.

It was a problem with which Purdue officials began seriously to grapple during the early years of the war, when a committee was established to consider the "Functions of the University in the Post-War World." . . . Seeking to clarify the goals of the new curricula, the committee went on to list eight major objectives of general education, including: 1) the ability to read with understanding and to express thoughts clearly and accurately in oral and written English; 2) an understanding of the major factors in the historical development of American institutions and international relations; 3) an understanding of the major phases of contemporary social and economic life along with the ability to read with discrimination and to arrive intelligently at opinions on social and economic problems; 4) an understanding of human behavior as a means of attaining a) sound personal adjustment and b) the ability to deal intelligently with problems of human relationships; 5) an appreciation of the major forms of expression of the culture as evidence in literature, the fine arts, and music; 6) an understanding and appreciation of the basic principles of science, the scientific method, and the part science and technology play in the modern world; 7) the understandings and abilities necessary to maintain health and physical fitness on both an individual and community basis; and 8) an understanding and appreciation of the ethical and social concepts necessary for a satisfying personal philosophy.[22]

Fulfilling these objectives, in the committee's view, was central to the mission of American higher education in the post-war world, especially at the land-grants. . . . Beginning in the fall [of 1947], all entering students were to meet a series of core requirements consisting of specified courses in the sciences, humanities and social sciences. . . . Although the report spoke of such courses as being in the process of development, with no mention of the existing Liberal Science curriculum, the assignment of course numbers, as well as the catalog descriptions, indicate the "new" survey courses were simply taken over from Liberal Science. . . .

A comprehensive program in general education which in effect fundamentally transformed the character of the university was thus built upon the foundation provided by the Liberal Science curriculum for women. In the process, however, many of the curriculum's unique features, particularly those which made it most valuable to women, were lost. These included a female academic administrator devoted particularly to the interests of female students. Not long after men were admitted to the program in 1947 and just as the curriculum revision process in the School of Science was getting underway, the director of Liberal Science, Dorothy Bovée, resigned. . . .[23]

The values of general education thus gained ascendancy within Purdue's School of Science, yet at a price. Women qualified for the Liberal Science program lost not only an advocate, in the person of Dr. Bovée, but also the opportunity to enroll in demanding classes composed of above-average students who were expected to excel regardless of gender. Indeed, to the extent that Liberal Science functioned in its last year as an honors program for both men and women, its demise represented a loss for any student in the School of Science capable of exceptional achievement. This fact was recognized by members of the university's Committee on Students of Superior Ability, who campaigned for the program's preservation while questioning the ability of the average Purdue student actually to benefit from the type of courses instituted under the revised curriculum. . . . [H]owever, the expression of such views merely provoked a hostile response from those who viewed them as symptomatic of an academic elitism which had no place at Purdue, given the land-grant institution's populist ethos. . . . Unfortunately for talented women, of whom little enough was often expected anyway, supplanting Liberal Science with general education meant that the affirmation involved in being selected to participate in an elite program, along with the liberating effects of the educational experience itself, were both sacrificed.

---

22. Compare this 1945 committee report to the 1943 report "The Nature and Purpose of Liberal Education" from the Association of American Colleges and the 1945 committee report of the Faculty of Arts and Sciences at Harvard University, *General Education in a Free Society*, both of which are discussed in the introduction to Section IX.

23. Barnes observes, "Although no record exists of the reasons for her departure, one can speculate that Dr. Bovée, who had not participated in the original planning stages of the program, did not agree with the decision to admit men."

60. Frank Aydelotte, *Honors Work in American Colleges and Universities* (1944)

INTRODUCTION

Raised in Indiana, Frank Aydelotte (1880–1956) earned a B.A. from Indiana University in 1900; and, after teaching English in college for two years, completed an M.A. in English at Harvard University in 1903. He then taught for two more years at Louisville Boys High School in Kentucky, and was named a Rhodes Scholar in 1905 to study at Oxford University. In 1907 Aydelotte married and therefore had to resign the scholarship, but he remained at Oxford to complete the B.Litt. in 1908, at which point he became Associate Professor of English at Indiana University. He was named professor of English at Massachusetts Institute of Technology in 1915 and acquired a national reputation through his work with the Rhodes Trust. In 1921 he accepted the presidency of Swarthmore College, a small relatively undistinguished institution that had been founded by Quakers. In selection #60, Aydelotte describes his arrival at Swarthmore and the genesis and nature of the honors work that earned Swarthmore renown and stimulated a national movement in liberal education.

Although Aydelotte attributes the origins of his own conception of honors education to the colleges of Oxford, the selections in Section VIII indicate that certain American movements informed honors work in the United States. The focus on elite intellectual education had precursors in John Erskine's honors seminar in great books at Columbia University, as well as in the commonly expressed view in the 1920s "that more colleges should adopt a rigorously selective plan of admission, because too many persons are going to college."[24] In addition, the honors impetus toward individual autonomy, personal fulfillment, and opposition to regimentation were rooted in educational Progressivism. Hence, when the Master of Balliol College, Oxford, visited Swarthmore in 1930, "what struck him about our honors plan was not so much its resemblance to Oxford as its differences."[25]

In 1939, his last year at Swarthmore, Aydelotte began to write a summative book reporting developments in honors work occurring at 130 colleges and universities throughout the country. By the time Aydelotte completed the book in 1943, he observed that "many plans for honors work have had to be curtailed or suspended because of the war and the absorption of college faculties in the educational programs prescribed by the Army and Navy." (p. xiii.) With this in mind, Aydelotte wrote the first chapter addressing the preservation and role of liberal education in a time of war. Meanwhile, in 1940 Aydelotte had resigned the presidency of Swarthmore to become the second director of the Institute for Advanced Study at Princeton, NJ. He succeeded Abraham Flexner (1866–1959), the prominent commentator, researcher, and reformer of education, who had known Aydelotte since they taught high school together in Louisville, Kentucky. After a turbulent tenure as Director, Aydelotte retired in 1947 and died in Princeton, NJ, in 1956.

24. C. S. Boucher, "Current Changes and Experiments in Liberal-Arts Colleges," in McHale, et al., *Changes and Experiments in Liberal-Arts Education* (Bloomington, IL: Public School Publishing, 1932), pp. 10–1.

25. Aydelotte, *Breaking the Academic Lock Step*, pp. 36–7.

SELECTION[26]

Liberal Education in the Post-War World

All times of strain, such as war or depression, tend to shake men's faith in liberal education. When danger threatens, competence to perform immediate practical tasks is at a premium and the expert takes precedence over the philosopher. Freedom of the mind then seems less useful than the habit of faithfully obeying instructions. Defense calls for efficiency. Too much emphasis on freedom of thought and the unrestricted development of the individual seems to make society less efficient, more wasteful of human resources, less manageable, less subject to planning and discipline. The miraculous achievements which flow from individual initiative and free enterprise are, when all is said, unpredictable, and do not appeal to men who, in the face of catastrophe, desire above all else to be secure. On the other hand, the very foundation of our democracy is our conception of liberal education and the freedom of the mind which that implies. Upon the broad liberal training of youth in our high schools and colleges our future will depend. This fact is widely realized and it is not surprising that men everywhere are discussing anxiously in these days the future of liberal studies.

There is another subject, however, about which men in general are even more anxious; that is security—military security, political security, and economic security. Not merely the war, but also the depression which preceded it, show how fragile is our twentieth-century civilization and how easily our supposedly inalienable rights to life, liberty, and the pursuit of happiness may be swept away. The soldiers and sailors and aviators who are fighting this war and the laborers who are supporting them at home will demand as their reward security not merely against military aggression, but also against unemployment.

There is a real conflict between these ideals. Liberal education is an adventure, both for the individual and for society: for the individual because its first aim is not to enable a man to make a living but rather to teach him how to live; for society because when able young men and women are trained to think for themselves and are left in freedom to do so, no one can predict the result. Security in war and prosperity in time of peace seem, on a superficial view, to depend more upon technical training than upon liberal knowledge.

Some degree of regimentation in war time is inevitable. Education is perforce restricted and it is the liberal element which is the first to be curtailed. That fact is strikingly illustrated by the changes brought about in American education by the present war. College students are called into military service often before their higher education is more than well begun. For those that remain programs must be altered in accordance with military needs. In the curricula prescribed by the Army and Navy there is and must be strong emphasis upon technical subjects at the expense of liberal studies, and this fact has aroused widespread apprehension as to the future of the liberal college. The cruel test of war brings out in sharp relief what seem to be the manifold inefficiencies of liberal education.

This is a war of physicists and engineers. The day has gone by when it was sufficient training for a soldier to teach him to shoot straight with a rifle and lunge effectively with a bayonet, to develop his physical strength and courage, and to give him the discipline needed to make him behave well in combat. The soldier of today must learn to handle intelligently many kinds of intricate mechanical devices. He must be a specialist in the operation of tanks, airplanes, artillery, radio, and other precision instruments of great complexity. He needs at least an elementary understanding of mathematics,

---

26. Frank Aydelotte, *Breaking the Academic Lock Step: The Development of Honors Work in American Colleges and Universities* (New York: Harper, 1944), pp. 1–19, 32–4, 42–4. Reprinted by permission of HarperCollins Publishers.

physics, navigation, meteorology, and other scientific subjects. The training of soldiers and sailors demands vast schemes of practical scientific and mechanical instruction.

The manufacture of the implements of war likewise calls into play all the resources of our physicists, chemists, engineers, inventors, and skilled mechanics, and all the resources of industrial management. Never before in history have we had so close a relationship between abstruse theoretical research by the physicist in his laboratory, scientific mass production of heretofore unprecedented accuracy, and practical use of scientific instruments of warfare on the battle field, on the high seas, and in the air above. Our strength in battle seems to depend not so much on broad liberal education as upon highly specialized technical skill.

The question has arisen in many minds whether the postwar period, which will confront us with a different though no less severe test, may not produce a similar demand for the revamping of our entire educational program along more practical lines.[27]

In the first place all the accelerated scientific discoveries and mechanical improvements made under the stimulus of war will contribute to the amelioration of human life in time of peace. Nothing is more fascinating than the romantic predictions, which sound like fairy tales but which will doubtless some day be sober reality, of the marvelous gadgets we shall all have to play with when the war is over, and we are able once again to beat our scientific swords into mechanized and automatic ploughshares. There will be no end to the wonderful toys and useful tools which we shall make out of the newly developed instruments of war-tanks, battle planes, radio equipment, new alloys, and plastics. Health will be improved and sickness eased by new discoveries in connection with nutrition and newly developed medical and surgical techniques. All of these contributions to human welfare depend upon science and technology and will inevitably enhance the importance of technical training in the post-war world.

In the second place there are signs which point to a parallel enhancement of the importance of the techniques of the social sciences, especially economics. The last quarter of a century has been a period of daring economic experimentation in many countries. War and depression have revolutionized traditional methods in public finance and private trade. Economic problems—unemployment, social security, international trade and finance—have become increasingly technical and complex. They are in many respects too difficult for the layman and tax the knowledge of the expert. The so-called brain trust is the logical answer. Governments and large industrial organizations depend more and more upon expert knowledge in the fields of trade and finance just as they have done in the past in the field of public health.

The war has witnessed for the first time in history the mobilization of the total economic strength of all the great nations engaged, at the price, for the most part willingly paid, of national regimentation and the substitution of specialized technical training for broad liberal education. The question inevitably arises whether this strength cannot similarly be mobilized for the purpose of realizing peaceful ends, to free the world from want, and whether if this is done it will not demand similar regimentation and similar emphasis upon technical skill at the expense of liberal values.

It is such considerations as these which cause men to fear that this war may mark a turning point in the development of our system of higher education, away from the liberal arts to technical training of experts in the natural and social sciences. Men fear that nations and individuals in the post-war world will be so poor, will feel so insecure, that they will be compelled to study how to get a living at the expense of how to live. The demand for security—economic security, political security, and what one might call ideological security—will be strong in this and every other country. We shall be in

---

27. The neglect of liberal education during war-time is caused by necessity. What are the motives, implied by Aydelotte, for neglecting liberal education after the war?

danger, in the search for security, of curtailing the life of freedom and adventure which is the condition of all high achievement. It is not only in the sphere of politics and international relations that timidity is fatal and "security mortal's chiefest enemy."[28] It may be also that weariness and want will make men and nations fearful of freedom of economic enterprise, freedom of scientific invention, and freedom of speculation in the realm of pure intellect. Regimentation of the human spirit in one direction may lead to its regimentation in all forms of activity. . . .

One cannot but feel that such a shift in emphasis in our education would be a moral and spiritual calamity, that no measure, however full, of material comfort and security would justify. Even if human life has been insecure—solitary, nasty, poor, brutish, and short,[29] it has been better than the life of Leacock's man in asbestos.[30] To abandon the ideals of liberal education would mean that in winning the war we had given up all that we are fighting for, and it would be furthermore a tragic misreading of the lesson which we ought to learn from the issue of the conflict. This war is a contest between individualism and totalitarianism. And just as freedom and individualism, despite a late start and despite many errors and inefficiencies, are now beginning to show themselves strong enough to prevail in the struggle, we may hope that they will be strong enough to prevail in the post-war world. We must not allow ourselves to forget that freedom—political freedom and freedom of the mind—has been our greatest asset in the present war. The totalitarian powers had a long start in technical preparation. What they do not have and cannot develop is the courage which free men show in meeting adversity and in struggling against odds. The problems of the war and of the peace are fundamentally not technical but moral, philosophical, and religious. They can be solved only by men into whose education has been infused a liberal element which makes the man so trained, not a mere tool ready to be turned to the service of any power above him, ready to do his job regardless of whether the consequences of his work are good or evil, but rather a thinking being, a citizen, morally responsible, who will take into consideration not merely means but also ends.[31]

It is upon these considerations that we are entitled, in my opinion, to put our faith in the continuity of the liberal tradition.[32] No abstruse arguments will be needed to drive home that point. The lesson will be plain for all to read. We may even expect in the enthusiasm of victory a reaction in the direction of those liberal studies which alone can give victory its true meaning and guide us in the building of the brave new world of our dreams. It is not without significance for the future that many college professors find that their Army and Navy students are keenly interested in those liberal subjects which have been included in the military curriculum. But this is not the time for those of us who believe passionately in the value of liberal studies to be complacent. It is rather a time to examine critically our whole plan for liberal education, to define our aims, to abolish the wasteful and stupid routines which are sometimes the product of traditional methods too long continued, and to avoid, on the other hand, the fads and aberrations into which men fall in the mistaken belief that any change is an improvement.

---

28. Aydelotte does not provide citations to his quotations or references, many of which are drawn from Elizabethan literature, his scholarly specialty. This quotation is from Shakespeare, *MacBeth*, act 3, sc. 5, l. 35.

29. This phrase comes from the description of life in a state of war by English philosopher Thomas Hobbes (1588–1679) in *Leviathan*, ch. 13, pt. 9.

30. Stephen Leacock (1869–1944), a Canadian economist and political scientist who received his Ph.D. from the University of Chicago in 1903 and taught at McGill University (1903–1936), became famous for writing humor, which began to appear in *Literary Lapses* (1910).

31. Compare Plato's and Aristotle's analyses of means and ends in education to that of Aydelotte.

32. Many advocates of liberal education do not associate it with "freedom and individualism." Does Aydelotte's defense for liberal education require this association?

If our liberal education is to meet the needs of the post-war world we must clarify its aims and improve its quality. Energetic and effective efforts to do both have been the most encouraging fact of our educational situation during the last twenty years. As to aims, it is already becoming clear that the central purpose of liberal education cannot be restricted to the study of any particular subject or combination of, subjects. It is not a problem of requiring every student to take courses in Latin and Greek. Nor is it a problem of resisting the claims of science, which for students with any aptitude for it must be an important ingredient in the liberal education of the future. Liberal knowledge is not a formula; it is a point of view.

The essence of liberal education is the development of mental power and moral responsibility in each individual. It is based upon the theory that each person is unique,[33] that each deserves to have his own powers developed to the fullest possible extent—his intellect, his character, and his sensitiveness to beauty—over against merely learning some useful technique.[34]

There is no such sharp distinction between liberal education and technical education as prejudice, even learned prejudice, sometimes believes. Instruction in the plays of Shakespeare may be strictly technical, while electrical engineering or law may be liberal, according to the point of view from which each is studied. An educational system based on belief in the value of liberal knowledge will infuse a liberal element into all training, even the most technical, while exclusive preoccupation with techniques, with means as opposed to ends, may deprive the study of literature, or philosophy, or history, or religion, of any liberal element.[35]

When peace comes the need for making the most of our best brains for the service of democracy will be not less but more insistent than ever. The tasks which will confront this and every country will be unprecedented in their difficulty and importance, and in the performance of these tasks we shall have to face the choice between regimentation and the voluntary efforts of free men and women. We must choose between the calculable but mediocre results of planning imposed from without and the brilliant but incalculable results of individual initiative working in freedom.

Only our best brains and our highest idealism, trained in freedom and working in freedom, can solve the appalling economic and political problems which we shall face. The democracies have for a long time failed to build into their institutions of government and industry the best ideas of their ablest thinkers. They have not always done so even in education. They must do so in every department of the democratic way of life, if that life is to persist. No merely defensive attitude will meet the need. Only by a democratic attack, worldwide in scope, as daring as are the dreams of the dictators, upon the evils of ignorance and selfishness and want, can the world be made a fit place to live in. Such an attack must involve the public spirit which places the common welfare above private ends in time of peace, as men so naturally do in time of war. It must be as intelligent as campaigns of conquest are stupid. Its aim must be to utilize the resources of nature and the achievements of science to raise the standard of living, material and spiritual, everywhere, and to utilize the resources of intelligence and good will to deal justly with all men and nations. Civilization in one country or one part of the world is meaningless unless its aim is to make all men civilized. Modern industry has unified the world, modern science has made all men neighbors, and we are false to all our ideals unless we treat them as such. This war will mark the beginning of a new and better age than we have ever had before or it will mark the beginning of the end of our civilization. . . .

---

33. Or, has the theory been that all people share a common nature?

34. Is "the theory that each person is unique" the same as "the theory . . . that each deserves to have his own powers developed to the fullest possible extent?"

35. What is Aydelotte definition of "technical" education?

If we strive, as we must, to realize these high aims, we can do so only by improving the quality of the liberal education offered in our high schools and colleges. The greatest defect of that education is the regimentation of individuals of different levels of ability into the same program. We offer to our students in high school and college bewildering freedom as to the subjects they should study. But once they have made their choice we set up a common standard of achievement for the poorest, the average, and the best. The converse of this policy would produce better results. With some knowledge of the ambitions and aptitudes of a given individual, older heads may well be wiser as to the subjects which he should study. But once the plan of study is determined it is obvious that, each individual should be required to come up to the highest standard of excellence of which he is capable.[36] This can never be the case if individuals of all levels of ability are taught in the same classes and set the same examinations. That is the common practice. It constitutes a kind of academic lock step, bad for the poorest and wasteful for the best. We must eliminate that waste if we are to have a liberal training adequate to the needs of the post-war world. While seeing to it that individuals of each level of ability have the training best suited to them, we must realize that the future of our country depends upon what happens to the best. It is from the ablest young men and women, given the proper training, that we may hope for the leadership without which democracy cannot survive.

The immense increase in the enrollment in high schools and colleges at the end of the last war first made educators generally aware of the vast range of individual differences. As a result, during the last twenty years energetic and promising measures have been taken to make education individual and selective. Following the example of the English universities, whose greatest contribution to democratic education is a workable solution of this problem, most of the leading colleges and universities of the United States have put into operation programs for students of unusual ability and ambition which, instead of holding them back to the average pace, allow them to go forward as far and as fast as they can. . . .

It requires courage in a democracy like ours, which considers each man as good as his neighbor, if not a little better, to put into operation what seems to many an aristocratic method of education. But we must learn to see the error in that superficial interpretation of democracy which assumes that all men are equal in intellectual ability. We must understand that in recognizing individual differences we are paying the truest homage to the worth of all individuals.[37] Universities and colleges and schools which are today facing the problem of giving to undergraduates of each level of ability opportunities suited to their needs are fulfilling their function in our democracy. They are keeping up their communications with the future. They are ensuring the training of citizens who can make their greatest contribution to all the offices of peace and war, whether as loyal followers or as leaders of courage and insight. The ideal for democratic education good enough to meet the needs of the post-war world must be not security but excellence.

The Academic Lock Step

American students are as individuals extraordinarily free. They have their own self-government associations, they manage their own college activities, they take almost complete responsibility for their personal conduct. But the methods of mass education, which are all but universal even in small colleges, effectively deny them the opportunity of taking the same kind of responsibility for their intellectual development. The system of instruction which forms the subject of this book might be de-

---

36. According to Aydelotte, what is excessively regimented and what is excessively free in liberal education? And what should be regimented and what free, instead?

37. Is Aydelotte persuasive in attempting to reconcile democracy and honors education?

scribed as an extension of undergraduate freedom from the personal to the intellectual sphere. It is essentially a system for selecting the best and most ambitious students, prescribing for these students a more severe program than would be possible for the average, and allowing them freedom and opportunity to work out that program for themselves.

The instruction of the average American student has been standardized beyond the point where uniformity has value. This is perhaps the natural result of the immense increase in numbers of college students during the last half-century. We have in our colleges and universities as many students as we had in the high schools two generations ago. The standardization of the instruction of these masses has been carried to a point where it resembles the Federal Reserve system. If a student has a certain number of hours of academic credit in a certain recognized college, he can cash in this credit at any other recognized college just as he might cash a check through a Federal Reserve bank. Intellectual values cannot be correctly represented by this system.

The system assumes that all college students are substantially alike, that all subjects are equal in educational value, that all instruction in institutions of a certain grade is approximately equal in effectiveness, and that when a student has accumulated a certain specified number of credit hours he has a liberal education. All these assumptions are of course false.[38] All courses of instruction are not equally effective; all subjects are not equal in educational value; our students are extraordinarily different in their interests and intellectual capacity; and it is only by qualitative, not quantitative, standards that liberal knowledge can be recognized and measured.

Our ordinary academic system is planned to meet the needs of that hypothetical individual—the average student. It does not pay him the compliment of assuming that his ability is very great or that he has any consuming interest in his studies. Its purpose is to make sure that he does a certain amount of carefully specified routine work. He can get a degree without undergoing any profound intellectual transformation; he can even get a degree without doing much work; but he cannot escape conformity to a prescribed academic routine. He must faithfully attend classes, hand in themes and exercises, undergo frequent tests and quizzes, follow instructions, and obey regulations, which are the same for all. He is treated not as an individual, but as a member of a group. . . .

Our college activities are organized on a different theory. Whereas in studies the virtue most in demand is docility, in extra-curricular clubs, teams, and societies the undergraduate has a chance to plan for himself, to exercise his own initiative, to succeed or fail on his own responsibility. It is not surprising that many students feel that they get the best part of their education outside the classroom and that employers often look more keenly at the young graduate's record in activities than they do at his grades. Docility has its uses but independence and initiative are virtues of a higher order.[39] The man who will do what he is told at the time he is told to do it has a certain value in the world, but the man who will do it without being told is worth much more. Consequently when one faces the problem of providing a more severe course of instruction for our abler students, one sees immediately that it is not sufficient merely to provide more of the same kind of work. The work must be different; it must not only be harder but must also offer more freedom and responsibility, more scope for the development of intellectual independence and initiative. . . .

The free elective system and the profusion of courses offered give each individual an embarrassing range of choice as to what he shall study. But the amount and difficulty of the work required in

---

38. This standardization emerged at the end of the nineteenth century to provide students access to a wide variety of colleges and universities across the country and allowed students to move between institutions, once enrolled. Are these benefits outweighed by the problems that Aydelotte attributes to standardization?

39. What is the proper role of extracurricular activities in liberal education? Do these activities, in fact, cultivate "independence and initiative" more than academics?

each course are rigidly standardized to the capacity of the average. It is not feasible to fail more than a small proportion of the members of each class, and this fact effectively limits the difficulty of the work required to what all or nearly all can do. The assignments or reading must not exceed in character or amount the capacity and interests of the student of average ability. The lectures and class discussions must not be over his head. The result is that the student of unusual ability suffers in many ways: he may become an idler, or he may devote his spare time to a wide variety of extra-curricular activities on which he tends to set an entirely fictitious value. In too many cases, comparing himself with his duller colleagues, he tends to rate too highly his own ability and achievements.

The student who is below the average standard, on the other hand, becomes discouraged and disheartened in the vain attempt to perform tasks which are too much for him. For a longer or shorter time he drags along, looking eagerly for easy courses, seeking help from private tutors, trying to catch up by attending summer schools, endeavoring by expedients which are sometimes pathetic and sometimes heroic to gain the coveted A.B. degree. A few succeed, but many are forced to confess themselves failures and to drop out, which is partly the reason why in many universities not more than one-fourth of the entering freshmen are able to graduate with their class. If one thinks in terms of education and not merely of the degree, it is obvious that the solution for both groups is to set them tasks adjusted to their mental capacity, their previous preparation, and their intellectual interests. . . .

Fifty years ago the limitations set by custom and interest upon entrance to college produced a student group of much more homogeneous character. Now our undergraduates are a cross section of the nation. It was, only when the number of college students increased so remarkably at the end of the last war that the menace to standards began to be widely recognized. By that time we were faced not merely with the difficulty of the average versus the superior student, but also with, a large and increasing group for whom even the average standard was too high.[40]

In the state universities, to which any high school graduate must be admitted on the basis of his diploma, and in many small colleges where need for students prevents the enforcement of any higher qualification for entrance, the standards of the average are beginning to be pulled down by the students who are below the average in ability or preparation. The number of these below-average students (roughly speaking those who graduate in the lower half of their class in high school) is constantly on the increase. These students are frequently not adapted to the subjects included in the ordinary program of study and they cannot keep up with the level of achievement of the average college student, modest as is that standard. They deserve nevertheless that their needs should be understood and met. It is important that the subjects they study be suited to their interests and that they should not learn to think of themselves as failures simply because they are set to perform tasks in which they are not interested and to which they are not equal. It is still more important that, just as the average student should not be allowed to pull down the level of the best, so these below-average individuals should not be allowed to become a threat to the standards of work of the average. Taken all in all, the variation in levels of ability of our undergraduates is the most serious problem confronting American higher education today. . . .[41]

The most serious of these hindrances is the confusion of thought inherent in our theories of democracy. To many people democracy means equality, and equality means uniformity. Our people wear the same clothes, eat the same food, drive the same cars, see the same movies, listen to the same radio programs. Why should they not have the same education? The fact that we do not all do the same kind of work, read the same books, look at the same paintings, or listen to the same music is for

---

40. Should the "standards" of liberal education be constant or change to fit the nature of the student population?

41. How is this "most serious problem confronting American higher education today" related to the overarching problem of the "academic lock-step"?

the moment forgotten. It is also forgotten that one of the purposes of democracy is to provide each individual with the opportunity that is best for him and that our society needs services of increasing variety and complexity. The end of democracy should be not to make men uniform, but rather to give them freedom to be individuals.

The confusion in the aims of democracy between uniformity and individualism comes home with special force to education: and it may well be that our colleges and universities, in solving the problem of the best treatment for students of different levels of ability, will contribute something to the solution of one of the central problems of the democratic way of life. We must guard against the temptation to think that a man's worth as an individual or his value to society can be measured by his aptitude for mathematics or languages. We must recognize that there are diversities of gifts, but whether it be plumbing or Plato that is in question, a society that is not to be condemned to mediocrity must demand the best of each. . . .

The Swarthmore Plan

From the beginning, as I have said, we . . . planned each honors course in co-operation between two or three related departments so as to give the student a program which would be clearly organized and focused upon a particular field, but not so narrowly specialized as would be the case were his work confined to a single department.

We soon decided upon the seminar method of teaching as opposed to individual tutorials. From the start we decided that for honors students the course and hour system should be abolished, that attendance at lectures and classes should be entirely voluntary, and that the honors degree should depend upon the student's success in a series of examinations, written and oral, conducted by external examiners. Our most important and most difficult task was to decide upon the content of these examinations.

The question as to what the student should be expected to know in order to qualify for a degree was a novel one, and the members of the faculty had no answers ready. . . . At the end of six months or so of constant work by various committees only two honors courses were sufficiently agreed upon to make it possible for students to begin the next year—English literature and the social sciences.[42] Accordingly, volunteers were called for in those two fields. . . .

The work, which was planned for two years, we subdivided into four parts for the four semesters, and the part for each semester into weeks, thus making a kind of program of reading and discussion for each seminar. The topic for a single meeting was usually split up into four or five subtopics corresponding to the number of students, and each undergraduate prepared a paper on one of these questions. In addition, all the students concerned were held responsible for a common background of reading which would enable them to discuss intelligently each other's papers. For the first few years it was our practice to have two members of the faculty attend each seminar. Often there were more. . . .

Twenty years of honors work at Swarthmore have produced extraordinary changes in the atmosphere of the college. Of all the changes produced the most intangible and most important is the improvement in morale of students and members of the faculty alike. This seems to me fully as important from the point of view of building character as for its intellectual value. The best index of character is the sincerity and honesty and faithfulness with which an individual does his work. If an educational institution can be induced to put first things first, to subordinate everything else to its main business of education and scholarship, it will be sincere in a way that it cannot be if its principal

---

42. Similarly, Columbia University "was committed to a parallel organization in the Sciences," but "institutional and staffing difficulties confounded the various efforts to create such general education science courses," as reported in Daniel Bell's selection #54.

pride is in its athletic teams or in some other irrelevant activity. That sincerity will make it a better place in which young people can live and grow. . . .

Something of the same kind has happened in the case of social activities. The complaint that in American academic life the side-shows seem to the students more important than the main performance may be due to the fact that the main performance has too often not been sufficiently difficult and adventurous to demand the best effort from the best. When that is corrected, when the academic program demands the utmost effort of the ablest students, all the other activities of college life fall into their rightful place. No negative regulation is necessary. Point systems and other devices for limiting the participation of students in extra-curricular activities are no longer needed. The best students, who set the pace and start the fashions, will make the right choices, and the atmosphere of the college will change from that of a country club to that of an educational institution.[43]

61. Willis Rudy, *The Evolving Liberal Arts Curriculum* (1960)

INTRODUCTION

Willis Rudy (1920–2004) was born and raised in New York City, where he graduated with a B.S. from the City College of New York in 1939. He then taught at his alma mater until completing his Ph.D. at Columbia University in 1948. After teaching as an instructor at Harvard University, Rudy joined the faculty of the state teachers college in Worcester, Massachusetts, in 1953 and co-authored with John S. Brubacher what became a standard history of American higher education: *Higher Education in Transition: An American History, 1636–1956*. In 1956 the Carnegie Corporation of New York invited Rudy to undertake a national study of college catalogs in order to determine the formal changes that had occurred in the liberal arts curriculum during the first half of the twentieth century. Rudy's research was part of a large project, located at Teachers College, Columbia University, examining undergraduate professional education, which had grown from ancillary parallel courses in the nineteenth century into the predominant component of the undergraduate curriculum by the 1950s. In 1960 Rudy's study was published, and in 1963 he became a professor of history at Farleigh Dickinson University, where he remained for the rest of his career.

In selection #61, Rudy sketches what he considered to be the "emerging curricular blueprint" for the liberal arts, which incorporated a growing number of departments and courses at nearly all colleges and universities. This "vast expansion and diversification of liberal arts college course offerings" eventually contributed to the "looseness" in academic regulation observed by Gerald Grant and David Riesman in selection #64.

SELECTION[44]

In order to carry forward a detailed study of college curricula into the twentieth century, institutions were selected and their catalogs were examined at ten-year intervals, beginning in 1905 and proceed-

---

43. See *An Adventure in Education*, by the Swarthmore College Faculty (New York: Macmillan, 1941), chs. 10, 12.

44. Willis Rudy, *The Evolving Liberal Arts Curriculum: A Historical Review of Basic Themes* (New York: Teachers College Press, 1960), pp. 39–47, 85–114. Reprinted by permission of Teachers College Press. The wording in this selection has been adapted at points.

ing through the year 1955. . . . The exact proportions and extent of change in terms of two measurable items—namely, the number of separate, functioning departments of instruction and the number of semester courses offered—can be determined through a study of the college catalogs. The data thus collected reveal notable increases in both categories during the period from 1905 to 1955.

What generalizations can we draw from these data? One obvious trend is the vast expansion and diversification of liberal arts college course offerings. In response to the demands of an increasingly complex social order, vocations such as business and finance, journalism, public health, music, architecture, the theater, and fine arts were gaining entrance to the college curriculum as fields with distinct intellectual content. Charles W. Eliot of Harvard observed in 1917 that these undertakings had "become to a much greater extent than formerly an intellectual calling, demanding good powers of observation, concentration, and judgment." Eliot, leader in the campaign for a completely free elective system, remarked that it was no longer the principal business of the colleges to train scholarly young men for the service of church, state, and bar. Now they were increasingly called upon "to train young men for public service in new democracies, for a new medical profession, and for finance, journalism, transportation, manufacturing, the new architecture, the building of vessels and railroads, and the direction of great public works which improve agriculture, conserve the national resources, provide pure water supplies, and distribute light, heat, and mechanical power."[45]

As specialization advanced, the areas of elective study in the college curriculum expanded with equal rapidity. . . . The emerging curricular blueprint devoted the first two years of the undergraduate course to general education in fundamental liberal arts subjects and the last two to more specialized, often frankly professional, training. Upper-division specialization of this kind fostered a growing departmentalization of the college curriculum. An analysis of the college catalogs reveals the sweeping nature of this trend between 1905 and 1955, as seen in the table of representative institutions on the following page.

Many college presidents, as, for example, William Rainey Harper of the University of Chicago, saw academic specialization as valuable in its own right. Specialization was encouraged by rewarding productive specialists on the faculty with promotions and by seeking only specialists for staff vacancies. It was recognized more and more by academic careerists that in order to make one's mark professionally and advance in one's calling, it was necessary to specialize.[46]

---

45. Charles W. Eliot, "The Case against Compulsory Latin," *Atlantic Monthly* (Mar. 1917): 360–1. Eliot's views reflect the development that the various fields of engineering began to require a bachelor's degree at this time.

46. See C. Wright Mills, *White Collar, The American Middle Classes* (New York: Oxford University Press, 1951), pp. 131.

Table: Departments and Courses in Selected Colleges and Universities, 1905–1956

Institution	1905–6	1915–16	1925–26	1935–36	1945–46	1955–56
Allegheny University						
depts.	23	22	24	28	27	24
courses	169	236	280	301	351	406
Amherst College						
depts.	22	22	21	21	24	30
courses	154	172	214	286	—	401
University of Colorado						
depts.	22	32	26	30	29	30
courses	218	386	344	451	NA	570
Davidson College						
depts.	14	21	24	27	22	24
courses	82	123	170	257	268	287
Georgetown University						
depts.	5	16	15	15	13	17
courses	77	108	183	176	112	294
Haverford College						
depts.	19	21	19	23	23	24
courses	197	198	203	260	291	299
University of Iowa						
depts.	21	25	28	29	37	31
courses	476	—	985	1,059	1,299	1,310
Macalester College						
depts.	19	22	21	22	26	32
courses	128	229	306	380	421	694
University of Notre Dame						
depts.	5	7	13	18	19	23
courses	190	227	244	463	582	633
University of North Carolina						
depts.	14	18	18	18	27	33
courses	232	339	440	552	647	1,107
University of Oregon						
depts.	16	21	19	20	18	19
courses	369	508	811	771	941	1,126
Pomona College						
depts.	18	28	29	25	33	30
courses	129	391	452	380	451	588
Vanderbilt University						
depts.	15	19	18	18	23	25
courses	110	164	259	693	542	603
College of William and Mary depts.	10	19	26	21	23	25
courses	92	109	376	451	549	602
University of Wisconsin						
depts.	32	33	29	30	32	33
courses	725	879	1,117	1,073	1,624	1,457

Reflecting this new emphasis, college faculties were reorganized on the basis of specialized departmental areas of scholarly and professional interest.[47] Closely paralleling this increasingly atomistic faculty organization was a compartmentalization of the curriculum in terms of carefully demarcated areas of college instruction. In 1931 President William L. Bryan of the University of Indiana described the situation as one which "tempts every department in the college to become primarily a breeding place for specialists, each department after its kind." . . . This, Bryan believed, had completely transformed the nature of the American liberal arts college.[48]

The number of such specialized departments in the average college was increased also by the demands of newer fields of study for recognition. Fields such as experimental psychology, sociology, anthropology, modern literature, speech and drama, and various subdivisions and specialties in the natural sciences were pushing their way forward and laying claim to a place in the sun.

While professional specialization was thus becoming the watchword of the liberal arts college from one end of the nation to the other, there was considerable variation in the way this approach was actually implemented. Perhaps the most popular solution of the problem was some form of the "major-minor" system. In accordance with this pattern, all undergraduates followed a prescribed program of general studies during their first two years in college and then majored or concentrated in some one subject-matter area during the last two. At the same time, they were expected to select one or two minor subjects and distribute most of their remaining upper-division credits among these fields. A variant of the major plan was the "area study" type of concentration, under which a student specialized on an interdepartmental basis in the civilization of one of the main regions of the world, such as Latin America or the Near East.

In the years following the first world war undergraduate specialization was also advanced by the introduction of systems of independent study and honors work in the junior and senior years of many liberal arts colleges.[49] Increasingly, it became clear that whatever else their purpose, such honors courses on the undergraduate level made possible the early training of persons who were pointing toward Ph.D.s and careers as research specialists or college professors. Departmental statements in the annual catalogs of many institutions made no attempt to conceal this objective. They frankly admitted that undergraduate specialization by means of individual honors or independent study programs would serve as a valuable preliminary to later professional specialization in graduate school.[50]

What were some of the other means by which professional specialization was entering into the college curriculum? In nearly every institution we have selected for study an established feature came to be the offering of special pre-professional course sequences preparing directly for admission to schools of medicine, law, theology, dentistry, medical technology, engineering, nursing, social welfare, and public service. Invariably, the bulk of this special pre-professional work came in the third and fourth undergraduate years. Closely related to this type of program was the so-called "combined

---

47. This theme became central in Christopher Jencks and David Riesman, *The Academic Revolution* (New York: Doubleday, 1968), which provides the background for selection #64 by Gerald Grant and David Riesman.

48. William L. Bryan, "The Liberal Arts College in the State University," *Association of American Colleges Bulletin* 17 (1931): 128–9.

49. A study of 105 liberal arts colleges from across the country found that only one had established some form of independent study in 1910. By 1940, however, more than one-third of the total had provided such options. [Orrin T. Richardson, "Requirements for Bachelor's Degrees, 1890–1940" (Ph.D. diss., University of Chicago, 1946), pp. 34–5.] Rudy observed that "a similar trend may be noted in the colleges which we have surveyed for the period 1905–1955."

50. The vocationalism that Rudy regards here and below as the predominant motive for the flourishing of honors work is distinguished from honors work by Frank Aydelotte in selection #60.

course" under which students dovetailed the semi-professional work of their senior year in college with the equivalent of the first year's work of a professional school.

This system, most often found in liberal arts colleges which were affiliated with large, multi-unit universities, made it possible for students to shorten by at least one year the time of their combined academic and professional training, while securing both a bachelor's degree and a professional degree. Combined courses were offered most frequently in fields such as law, medicine, and engineering. In these callings, the system had made its appearance even before the advent of the twentieth century.

Still another feature in many liberal arts colleges was the partial or terminal programs of a frankly professional nature which were made available to students during their junior and senior years. These offerings ranged over fields as varied as journalism, public health, physical education, geology, library science, petroleum engineering, applied and manual arts, forestry, social work, business administration, chemical engineering, and radio, drama, and the dance. And nowhere did the colleges under review more universally recognize a professional aim than in their programs preparing teachers for the secondary schools. Nearly all had education departments which offered specific sequences of professional courses in education in order to equip their students to teach and to meet state certification requirements.

As more and more professional programs were introduced in the liberal arts colleges, many new kinds of academic degrees were established and the traditional baccalaureate came to acquire new meanings. Richardson's study of private liberal arts colleges during the period 1890 to 1940 resulted in findings very similar to our own. Among the 105 institutions included in his survey, many new types of bachelor's degrees were discovered to be splitting off from the original B.A. and B.S. . . .[51]

Although the professionalizing movement affected to some degree every liberal arts college in our group, there was some variation in the completeness with which adjustment was made to it. Vocational or utilitarian emphasis was most pronounced in those liberal arts colleges which were component parts of a larger university structure, especially those affiliated with state universities. It was there that the tendency had the freest reign to give the twentieth-century American public what it demanded in special training for utilitarian fields. Indeed, Pierson has asserted that, in so doing, the western state universities practically discarded the liberal arts college ideal altogether, replacing it with a series of undergraduate departments specializing in vocational subjects.[52] In a similar vein, Edwards concludes from his study of the college curriculum in 20 state universities that by 1930 the college of liberal arts in its traditional sense no longer existed in such institutions.[53]

In contrast to this development the smaller independent liberal arts colleges did not move as far or as fast to adjust themselves to the new dispensation. But within this independent group, minor differences existed, mainly following regional lines. A few nationally renowned liberal arts colleges in the northeast and southeast were slower to convert their curricula to meet the demands for specialized and professional programs than were other independent colleges, particularly those in the midwest and far west. Similarly, Roman Catholic institutions in the main seem to have been somewhat less sweeping in their acceptance of the new trends in higher learning than non-Catholic ones.

---

51. Richardson, "Requirements for Bachelor's Degrees, 1890–1940," p. 16.

52. George W. Pierson, *Yale College: An Educational History, 1871–1921* (New Haven: Yale University Press, 1952), pp. 44–5.

53. Harry E. Edwards, "Trends in the Development of the College Curriculum within the Area of the North Central Association, 1830–1930" (Ph.D. diss., University of Indiana, 1933), pp. 514–5.

Liberalism and Liberal Education

62. Harold Taylor, "Individualism and the Liberal Tradition" (1958)

INTRODUCTION

The social and political liberalism of the United States certainly fostered "the vast expansion and diversification of liberal arts college course offerings" that Willis Rudy identified in 1960. But whether the social and political ideology of the time—and liberalism, in particular—should determine the "curricular blueprint" of the liberal arts has been disputed. In 1958 Harold Taylor argued strongly in favor of the shaping influence of liberalism in a lecture at Swarthmore College.

Born in Toronto, Harold Taylor (1914–1993) earned a B.A. at the University of Toronto in 1935 and a then a Ph.D. in philosophy at the University of London in 1938. After teaching philosophy at the University of Wisconsin from 1939 to 1945 and working in the U.S. Office of Scientific Research and Development during the second half of World War II, he became the youngest college president in the country when he was chosen in 1945 to lead Sarah Lawrence College.[54]

Founded among the experimental colleges for women during the Progressive college movement between the World Wars,[55] Sarah Lawrence gave no grades and required each student to develop an independent course of study and to contribute labor to maintain the college. Taylor extended these progressive policies by pressing for racial integration at the predominantly white college and by championing academic freedom against McCarthyism at a time when "opposition to [McCarthy's] version of academic freedom was limited. . . . A few academic leaders spoke out. Harold Taylor . . . insisted that a professor should be judged by his actions, not his affiliations. He offered the standard civil libertarian objection to firing Communists: 'If we begin excluding Communists, we will end by excluding anyone who says anything provocative, unorthodox, or interesting.'"[56] Near the end of his presidency, Taylor gave the following lecture, advocating "the progressive idea" or "pragmatic thesis" of liberal education.[57] Taylor's civil libertarianism and pragmatic view, hardened by McCarthyism, naturally influenced his presentation of the history of liberal education.

Upon retiring from Sarah Lawrence in 1959, Taylor taught at the New School for Social Research and City University of New York.[58] He also lectured for the U.S. Department of State both in the United States and abroad and served as chairman of the Peace Strategy Committee of the National Research Council from 1959 to 1968. During the 1970s he chaired the United States Committee for the United Nations University. Taylor died in 1993 in New York City.

54. Bruce Lambert, "Harold Taylor, Novel Educator and College President, Dies at 78," *New York Times* (10 February 1993).

55. See the introduction to the selection by John Dewey et al. in selection #57, as well as Taylor's account in "The Philosophical Foundations of General Education," pp. 21–45, in *General Education, Part I, The Fifty-First Yearbook of the National Society for the Study of Education*, ed. Nelson B. Henry (Chicago: NSSE, 1952).

56. Ellen W. Schecker, *No Ivory Tower: McCarthyism and the Universities* (New York: Oxford University Press, 1986), p. 109.

57. Willis D. Weatherford, Jr., "Introduction," in *The Goals of Higher Education*, pp. 3–5.

58. The New School for Social Research was founded in 1919; its first director was historian James Harvey Robinson (1863–1936), who participated in the 1931 conference on progressive liberal education at Rollins College described in selection #57.

SELECTION[59]

The idea of liberalism and of liberal education is a fairly recent one and a local one. It has its origin in the Western world, in political and social changes which began in the seventeenth century with the discovery of a new universe and a new world, with a new mercantile class and the growth of common law. Liberalism as a social philosophy grew in the eighteenth century through the organization of new political forms and social classes. It exploded the nineteenth century with a series of revolutions against the regimes of church, royalty, aristocracy, and state. It emerged into the twentieth century to face its greatest test in two world wars, a world depression, and any number of minor wars and current conflicts and revolutions. There are those who look at this short history and say that liberalism is now bankrupt, that individualism is dead, and that a liberal democracy cannot stand up against authoritarian systems, either in international affairs or in the development of internal strength. What is needed is said to be a stronger and more ordered political doctrine and stronger social controls, including the control of education.

Liberal education is the intellectual and cultural instrument through which the basic ideas of liberalism are transmitted and developed. This kind of education began with the clusters of scholars and students who joined together to study, examine, and revise the known ideas of Greek society, religion, and classical thought. Throughout the history of Western society, liberal education has been both the institutional expression of liberalism as a philosophy and the intellectual force which helped to create the political and social changes of liberalized societies.[60]

The central idea of liberal education is therefore the idea of individualism and individual freedom.[61] Its tradition is that of the liberal revolt against state authority, religious dogma, and all the elements of the old regime. It is allied to the Protestant movement in its assertion of the individual conscience and the individual reason against church doctrines and church control.[62] It is part of the tradition of the enlightenment and the age of reason. It is centrally concerned with the struggle of reason against ignorance, moral values against brute force, freedom against tyranny.

---

59. Harold Taylor, "Individualism and the Liberal Tradition" (1958), pp. 9–12, 24–5, in *The Goals of Higher Education*, ed. Willis D. Weatherford, Jr. (Cambridge, MA: Harvard University Press, 1960). Reprinted by permission of the President and Fellows of Harvard College.

60. John Dewey, the Pragmatist philosopher whose ideas informed both Sarah Lawrence College and Harold Taylor, dated the association between liberalism and liberal education to the 1920s, observing, "Today the word liberal is applied to an educational institution to denote opposition to the reactionary and ultraconservative, not to denote just preoccupation with intellectual and ideal matters. The word has taken on economic and political significance in connection with the human struggle for economic independence and political emancipation." John Dewey, "The Prospects of the Liberal College" (1924), reprinted in Joann Boydston, *John Dewey, The Middle Works, 1899–1924*, vol. 15 (Carbondale: Southern Illinois University Press, 1983): 200. A similar view is expressed by President Hamilton Holt (1872–1951) of Rollins College, another progressive liberal arts college, in "Liberalizing a Liberal Education," in Kathryn McHale, et al., *Changes and Experiments in Liberal-Arts Education* (Bloomington, IL: Public School Publishing, 1932), pp. 221–8.

61. Or is it the case that "education is not a practice which concerns the individual alone: it is essentially a function of the community." Werner Jaeger, *Paideia: The Ideals of Greek Culture* (1933), tr. Gilbert Highet, 2nd English ed. (New York: Oxford University Press, 1945), v. 1, pp. xiii–xiv.

62. Hence, in their battle against the electivism of Harvard President Charles W. Eliot, leaders of Catholic colleges maintained that "electivism was Protestantism applied to education." Rev. J. J. Howard of the College of the Holy Cross, in "Alumni Pleased," *Boston Globe* (29 June 1900): 1.

The tradition of liberalism and of liberal education does not lie solely within the arts and the humanities; it has to do with the doctrines of social progress and the disciplines of science. For it was the combination of liberal social theory and scientific thinking which infused Western society with a spirit of discovery and the idea of change. The universe itself had been considered a static entity; space was a local affair; society was fixed and unchangeable. The scientific spirit, with its insistence on rational proof and objective evidence, was the driving force in the seventeenth century which released intellectual and social energies into new dimensions of thought and action.

The characteristic of the modern movements in philosophy, the movements which began in the nineteenth century and set the framework for the twentieth, is the scientific basis on which they stand. In the nineteenth century, the scientific disciplines, when applied to the study of nature, society, and man, produced discoveries in all fields from physics to psychology. The idea of evolutionary change affected the concept of religion, of society, of art, of human nature; the philosophies of Bergson, Russell, Whitehead, Dewey, and Santayana, for example, are based on the facts of science and their interpretation by scientists and philosophers.[63] The new emphasis on psychology as a science came from the application of philosophical theory and the scientific method to individual case studies of human nature, culminating in the work of Freud, Jung, and Adler, among others.[64] New attitudes to the individual found their way into twentieth-century literature, poetry, painting, sculpture, and the arts. From Martha Graham to Dylan Thomas, from the surrealist poets to the experimental novelists, from Bauhaus design to Frank Lloyd Wright, new forms, new traditions, new philosophies emerged in the first half of this century.[65] The central core of the new aesthetic was a philosophy of individualism.

On the other hand, the central idea of modern philosophy came to be that of a profusion of unfolding possibilities emerging from the development of the universe and everything in it through billions of years. If the world is a huge organism, alive, changing, moving toward an expanding goal whose ultimate point is unknown, then everything in it is in a state of change. Everything in it is in the process of becoming something else. The teeming birth of cells, the constant unfolding of new forms of life were all considered to be demonstrations of the creative energy which lies within nature.

William James, to come closer to our present world, accepted a philosophy of creative evolution and accepted the idea of creativity as a basic concept in his system of thought. The human mind, for William James, was continually creating its own knowledge out of the day-to-day run of human experience. "All the while," said James in his *Principles of Psychology,* "the world *we* feel and live in will be that which our ancestors and we, by slow cumulative strokes of choice, have extricated out of this, like sculptors, by simply rejecting certain portions of the given stuff. Other sculptors, other statues from the same stone. Other minds, other worlds from the same monotonous and inexpressive chaos."[66]

The essence of the modern movement in education is the idea of creative experience and its liberating effects on the individual. The modern movement is in fact a fundamental shift in attitude

---

63. Henri Bergson (1859–1941), French philosopher; Bertrand Russell (1872–1970), English philosopher; Alfred North Whitehead (1867–1947), English philosopher; George Santayana (1863–1952), United States philosopher.

64. Sigmund Freud (1856–1939), Austrian founder of psychoanalysis; Carl G. Jung (1875–1961), Swiss psychiatrist; Alfred Adler (1870–1937), Austrian psychiatrist.

65. Martha Graham (1895–1991), leader and performer of modern dance in the United States; Dylan Thomas (1914–1953), Welsh poet; Frank Lloyd Wright (1869–1959), United States architect.

66. Taylor does not provide a reference, but the point, if not the quotation, comes from the concluding chapter addressing the nature of "experience" in William James, *Principles of Psychology*, 2 vols. (New York: Henry Holt, 1890), v. 2, ch. 28.

toward life itself. It refuses to accept the conventional forms in which life is presented to us and looks for fresh ways of interpreting facts, for new forms of art, of architecture, of scientific discovery, of literature, of society. It refuses to accept the fatalism of the classical philosophy, or the classical tone of reconciliation to things as they exist, or the warning to mankind that everything which is done has already been done before and that everything will pass away and return to nothingness. The modern movement believes in the reality of novelty and discovery; it believes in progress toward goals which man has made and which he can remake as he goes along. . . .

First, then, the content of the curriculum, particularly in the freshman year, should be drawn from original materials in the fields of politics, social science, philosophy, psychology, the arts, literature, and science, dealing with issues and questions which can evoke genuine concern in the students. Courses should be planned which are not summaries and outlines of fields of subject matter but which deal with fresh and interesting ideas about man and nature, society and the individual.[67] The purpose of the course is not to cover ground but to plunge the student into a world of ideas with which he can become truly concerned. He will cover ground once he becomes involved with the ideas. Give the freshman or the sophomore some room to move among fields of his choice; do not restrict him only to required courses; give him the largest chance he can have to work at the things he wants to know.

Secondly, the lecture system, the academic credit system, the conventional examination system must be replaced by a combination of discussion methods, independent study, tests of achievement, and a greater freedom and responsibility for the individual student.

Thirdly, programs of study should be planned to individual needs, allowing those with the ability to go as far and as fast as their capacities can take them in those areas to which their aims, motives, and interests drive them. This need not involve the complete rearrangement of present college structures but only a change in the attitude of educators toward their students by which their individual differences are respected in the development of educational programs.

Fourthly, the value of immediate experience must be recognized as a prime educational force. Such recognition would mean that students could paint, sculpt, compose, act; write plays, poetry, novels, short stories; carry out research projects and experiments as a regular part of their academic program. The whole life of the college campus is thereby enriched, and the spirit of the creative arts infuses the community with ideas and values which are simply not available from other academic sources.

These are the dimensions of an approach to learning which seeks to maintain the central tradition of liberal education—the tradition of individualism and humanism. It is an approach which gives promise of developing in the generations of the young an open and active mind, a capacity for further growth, and a concern for those ideals of liberalism which can transform a mass of human beings into a community of interesting citizens.

---

67. Survey and orientation courses had been introduced some three decades earlier, as described in the introduction to Edgar Robinson's selection #55.

63. Paul O. Kristeller, "Liberal Education and Western Humanism" (1976)

INTRODUCTION

Two decades after Harold Taylor spoke, Paul O. Kristeller expressed a contrary view at a symposium on "Liberalism and Liberal Education" held at Columbia University. In fact, he maintained more generally "that education and culture are autonomous . . . and are not merely the by-products of social and political forces that happen to prevail at a given time."

Kristeller (1905–1999) was born in Berlin and earned a Ph.D. in philosophy from the University of Heidelberg in 1928. After postdoctoral study at the universities of Berlin and Freiburg, he lectured at universities in Italy between 1935 and 1938. In 1939 he came to Yale University as an instructor, then moved to Columbia University where he was made professor of philosophy in 1956 and retired in 1973. During his academic career, Kristeller spent several years at the Institute for Advanced Study at Princeton University, studying Renaissance philosophy, his academic specialty. In fact, Kristeller "is responsible for establishing Renaissance philosophy as a particular field of enquiry, at least among English-speaking scholars." Kristeller wrote more than 800 books and articles, including his seven-volume *Iter Italicum*, begun in the 1930s and published between 1963 and 1996. This "Italian Journey" is a catalog and guide to Italian Renaissance documents and manuscripts held in libraries around the world.[68] Kristeller died in his Manhattan home in 1999.

SELECTION[69]

I should like to begin with a few remarks about liberalism, which is mentioned in the title of our series though not in the title of my paper. Liberalism is a political concept, and its meaning has been rather fluid, as all political concepts are—especially in times of trouble, according to a famous passage in Thucydides.[70] I gladly leave the thankless task of defining liberalism to the political theorists. The title of our series might suggest that liberalism and liberal education are related or interdependent. In my opinion, this is not the case. Liberal education in a broad sense existed for many centuries before political liberalism was even heard of.[71] Liberal education did not produce liberalism, but flourished under many different political systems that were not at all liberal. Conversely, liberal education is not a necessary product of liberalism, and it may actually decline and disappear in a politically liberal society. For those of us who favor both liberalism and liberal education, as I think I do at least in some sense, the question must be put differently: How can liberal education be adapted to liberalism and be made to promote liberalism, and how can liberal education be defended and maintained in a liberal society? My assumption is that education and culture are autonomous, have their own

68. Material in this biography is drawn "Paul Oskar Kristeller," *Boston Globe* (11 June 1999): E15. The quotation is from C. B. Schmitt, "The Philosophical Mode," *Times Literary Supplement* (25 July 1980): 856.

69. Paul O. Kristeller, "Liberal Education and Western Humanism," *Liberalism and Liberal Education*, vol.5, no.1, *Seminar Reports, Program of General Education in the Humanities, Columbia University* (Fall 1976), pp. 15–22. Reprinted by permission of Columbia University.

70. Thucydides (c. 460–c. 400 B.C.), Greek historian of Athens, wrote about the Peloponnesian War.

71. A contrasting view addressing liberalism in general, various kinds of liberalism in particular, and liberal education, as well as their inter-relationships, may be found in the companion essay: Charles Frankel, "Intellectual Foundations of Liberalism," *Liberalism and Liberal Education*, pp. 3–11.

traditions, and are not merely the by-products of political and social forces that happen to prevail at a given time.[72]

The topic I am supposed to treat, as I understand it, is different and more specific: What is the history of liberal education in the western world, and what is the place of humanism, and especially of Renaissance humanism, in this history? In using the terms humanism and humanistic education, I do not refer to the vaguely moral connotation that these terms have assumed in recent years, but to the very specific meaning that the terms humanist and humanities, if not humanism, received in the Renaissance and retained up to the early decades of our century. In other words, I am referring to the learned humanism of the fifteenth, and not to the unlearned humanism of the twentieth century. The humanities in documents of the fifteenth century are listed as grammar, rhetoric, poetry, history, and moral philosophy,[73] and the way to teach and study them is to read and interpret the Greek and Latin classics in their original text. The humanistic school was, and until recently has been, based on a classical curriculum. I am myself the product of a *Humanistisches Gymnasium* which involved, among other things, nine years of Latin and six years of Greek, six hours or more per week. In order to understand this phenomenon, let us go back to classical Antiquity.

The Greeks developed a system of general, as distinct from professional, education that emphasized grammar and the reading of Homer and the other great poets, and later added rhetoric and the study of the great prose writers, the orators, the historians, and the philosophers. In late ancient and Byzantine times, this also involved the careful study of the classical literary language from which the spoken language had moved further and further away. The Romans also studied the grammar and literature of their own language, but as pupils and later as rulers of the Greeks they also studied the language, grammar, and literature of the Greeks. The main Latin writers, including Cicero and Vergil, came comparatively late. They belonged to the first century B.C.—after the time the Romans had adopted many features of Greek civilization—and obtained their place as school authors only during the imperial period.

In the early Middle Ages, Greek disappeared from the schools of Western Europe and Latin grammar assumed a crucial role, since Latin had ceased to be the spoken language of the population while remaining the language of the Church, of law, of administration and diplomacy, of learning and instruction. The core of the curriculum were the so-called seven liberal arts: grammar, rhetoric, logic, arithmetic, geometry, astronomy, and music. They were all taught on a very elementary level, and grammar was by far the most important of them. During the twelfth century, learning expanded through the translation of many philosophical and scientific texts from the Greek and Arabic, through the rise of the cathedral schools and universities, and through an increased curiosity for knowledge and logical skill. The reading of the classical Latin authors flourished, and there was for a while a rivalry between the arts and the authors (the liberal arts and the great authors).[74] In the thirteenth century, the arts prevailed—that is, the disciplines of philosophy, theology, law, and medicine that had by then been firmly established at the universities. The secondary schools which were supposed

---

72. Compare the views expressed by Elizabeth Kamarck Minnich and Jane Roland Martin in the Introduction and by Mary Louise Pratt in selection #66.

73. See the introduction to Section IV and selection #25 by Pier Paolo Vergerio and selection #26 by Ignatius Loyola.

74. This rivalry is the subject of the thirteenth-century poetical ballad: Henri d'Andeli, *The Battle of the Seven Arts: A French Poem by Henri d'Andeli*, tr. Louis J. Paetow (Berkeley: University of California Press, 1914).

to prepare their students for the universities were left with the task of teaching the old liberal arts, and especially grammar, including the Latin language.[75]

With the fourteenth and even more with the fifteenth century, especially in Italy, the study of the Latin classics expanded, both in the secondary schools and at the universities, and a number of long-neglected authors, including Lucretius and Tacitus, were discovered and more widely studied. Moreover, the study of Greek language and Greek classical literature was introduced from the East and favored by the influx of many Byzantine scholars both before and after the Turkish conquest of Constantinople in 1453. This reform of education, and especially of secondary education, is what constitutes an important facet of the humanistic movement in the Italian Renaissance, and it was sustained by the firm and widespread belief that a classical education, the study of Greek and Latin literature, was the best way to train future rulers and citizens, professionals and scholars. While there was some resistance on the part of theologians, classical education was on the whole victorious, and it functioned not as a substitute for but as an important supplement to religious, Christian education.

The formal aspect of learning how to write well and elegantly in prose and in verse was given great emphasis, and it seemed obvious that the study and imitation of the classical models was the best way to attain this goal. As to content, the classical historians provided instruction in ancient history and institutions, and supplied models of imitation and warning examples for future rulers, statesman, and generals. . . . The reading of classical poets and orators, as well as of other prose writers, was not only enjoyable, as it undoubtedly is, but also useful as an exercise to imitate and master their language and their style, thus enabling the student to learn how to write well in prose and verse. The reading of the ancient philosophers also provided moral education and some instruction in philosophy.[76]

Once the products of the humanist grammar school became university students, scholars, and professionals, the newly gained classical learning bore its fruits in their own specialized disciplines. The scholars of the late fifteenth and sixteenth century spoke and wrote a better Latin, to be sure, but above all, the jurists acquired a better knowledge of the meaning and historical context of Roman law which was still the basis of much continental law, and even made new advances during this period. The physicians, mathematicians, astronomers, and geographers still enhanced their knowledge by a study of the more advanced Greek treatises on their subjects—particularly Hippocrates and Galen, Archimedes and Diophantus, Ptolemy and Strabo, of whom this period produced either new or first translations.[77] The philosophers improved their understanding of Aristotle and acquired for the first time a comprehensive knowledge of the Aristotelian commentators, of Plato and the Neoplationists, of Stoic, Epicurean, and Skeptic philosophy, and of the large body of Greek popular thought represented by such writers as Lucian or Plutarch—all sources not accessible in the Middle Ages in the West. Finally, the theologians applied classical knowledge to a textual study of the Greek New Testament, of the Greek and Latin Church Fathers, and occasionally of the Hebrew Old Testament.

When the humanist movement and the humanist school spread from Italy to the rest of Europe, mainly during the sixteenth century, the same beliefs and interests were at work and the theological aspect was especially important. In Catholic Europe (and Latin America), humanist education was adopted by the Jesuits and other religious orders. In Protestant Europe, especially Germany, the Low Countries, and England, new humanist schools were founded that served in part the purpose of training future ministers who would be able to interpret the Word of God from the original text of the

---

75. See "Rules for Men and Women Teaching in Grammar Schools" (c. 1357) in selection #22.

76. Kristeller's account is demonstrated by *On the Method of Instruction* (1511), composed by Desiderius Erasmus (c. 1466–1536), Dutch scholar and humanist.

77. Diophantus (c. A.D. 250) Greek algebrist; Strabo (c. 63 B.C.–c. A.D. 20) Greek geographer.

Bible and of the Church Fathers. This was also true of early America, and in Protestant Germany some of the best humanist schools even in my time traced their origin to the period of the Reformation.

Yet through the sixteenth century, the study of Latin served very important practical purposes which gradually disappeared afterwards and which we are likely to forget. Latin was and remained to our time the language of the Catholic Church, of its liturgy and administration, and to some extent of its theological literature and instruction. Latin was the language of much international law and diplomacy; it yielded but slowly and partly to Italian in the late sixteenth, to French in the mid-seventeenth, and to English in the twentieth century. Latin was the language of much law and medicine. Latin was the language of practically all university instruction until the late eighteenth century, and of all scholarly and learned literature for students and professionals, as against the popular literature for laymen. When Galileo, Descartes, Newton, and Leibniz wrote for their colleagues, they wrote in Latin; and when they wrote in Italian, French, or English, they wrote for the general public. It was only in the seventeenth century that Italian, French, and English began to be used as scholarly languages, and German followed only in the eighteenth century. Finally, there was a great output of Latin poetry and prose literature, some of it excellent and influential, during the sixteenth and down to the eighteenth century.

The result of all this is easily forgotten: European culture down to the seventeenth and even eighteenth century is a bilingual culture that found its expression in two languages, Latin and the respective national language. It was only in the nineteenth century that the literature in Latin became negligible, except in classical philology, and perhaps with the exception of Hungary and the Slavic countries where the natural languages were slower in asserting themselves. In other words, up to the eighteenth century, a classical education, and especially the knowledge of Latin, was not only a cultural asset or a status symbol, but a useful training indispensable for a number of professional activities. It was indispensable for the future university student, diplomat and administrator, let alone for the university-trained jurist, theologian, physician, scientist, or scholar. . . .[78]

The classical school persisted to the eighteenth century very much as it had been since the fifteenth and sixteenth, while it gradually lost some, though by no means all, of its practical usefulness, and certainly none of its educational and literary appeal. By 1800, the school was ready for reforms and changes which were bound to come. . . . New subjects were added, such as the sciences, medieval and early modern history, and the national and other modern languages and literatures. Also, the classical core subjects of Greek were modified under the impact of their diminishing practical use and the new developments in classical philology, history, and archaeology. The classical authors were now read with the help of modern classical scholarship in which the teachers had been trained and to which they themselves made important contributions. There was less and less emphasis on the ability to write—let alone to speak—Latin, since the practical use for these skills had rapidly declined and disappeared.

The classical school of the nineteenth and early twentieth century—at least the type of school in which I was brought up—thus conveyed many other skills, such as some modern mathematics and physics, German literature and composition, French (and some English) language and literature; but it also gave us a good reading knowledge of classical Greek and Latin, and an acquaintance with some of the best ancient poets and prose writers, presented in the light of the best classical scholarship then available. Other subjects were missing or poorly represented. Religious instruction was optional. There was some calisthenics but no sports. Instruction in music was poor and elementary, and there

---

78. Bathsua Reginald Makin in selection #30 and Emma Willard in selection #35 note the import of this indispensability for women.

was no art history or philosophy, no social or political studies, no contemporary history or literature—not to speak of home economics or family living, typing, or driving. Yet the idea was that the tough subjects, such as languages and composition and mathematics, required study and instruction, whereas other subjects could be more easily pursued outside of school.

My teachers did not think that I was unfamiliar with contemporary German literature because I didn't have such courses in school. They thought I could do that without guidance, and I did. I also pursued a lot of music and art history, modern history, and literature on my own in the time free from class hours and homework. These studies and pursuits were encouraged and respected by my parents and teachers. It just did not occur to them that every conceivable field of interest should be pursued as a part of the school curriculum or that a young person should not learn anything except what was taught to him in school.[79] School instruction was limited to the subjects that were considered essential and required hard work.[80] I must admit with some embarrassment that I thoroughly enjoyed my work in school, as well as many other things besides, and that it never occurred to me to question its value or to rebel against its discipline.[81]

During the present century, criticism of the classical school became increasingly vocal, and especially in this country, but also in Europe, humanistic education has lost more and more ground and is now rapidly disappearing. . . . The liberal arts college, of which so much has been said and written, and especially the programs in the humanities and western civilization at Columbia College and elsewhere, have obviously been designed as a substitute for the classical school that has vanished.[82] The program does teach classical literature and civilization and this is a great merit. Yet it teaches them in a hurry, and in English translations rather than in the original languages, and this is by no means the same thing. (I do not believe in translations, or in their ability to replace the original texts, although many people nowadays comfortably assume this as a dogma.[83]) I consider this program valuable, and am glad that it is continuing at Columbia. It is better than nothing, for it is better for a young person to read Homer and Plato quickly and in a translation than not at all. Yet even this substitute, known as the humanities or the liberal arts, is now under attack and has disappeared from most colleges, though fortunately not from Columbia.

---

79. This point is echoed by Robert Hutchins in selection #58 and Jeremiah Day in selection #37. What should be the relationship between liberal education and contemporary culture?

80. Compare Plato's rationale in his selection (526c) in Section I for putting mathematics at the core of the liberal arts.

81. Compare Kristeller's personal experience with Harold Taylor's view of liberal education above.

82. Lionel Trilling in selection #53 and Daniel Bell in selection #54 recount the inception of general education at Columbia University.

83. Compare the views of Robert Hutchins in selection #58 and of Charles Eliot, addressing the study of German philosophy, in selection #40.

64. Gerald Grant and David Riesman,
Reform and Experiment in the American College (1978)

INTRODUCTION

By 1970 not only was the remnant of classical or humanistic education "under attack" even in the liberal arts college, as Paul Kristeller lamented, but the liberal arts curriculum had been thoroughly "reorganized on the basis of specialized departmental areas of scholarly and professional interest," as Willis Rudy described. These developments resulted because "the research universities were producing the faculties for collegiate institutions and . . . competition among the colleges led them to imitate the major university model," as stated in selection #64 drawn from *The Perpetual Dream: Reform and Experiment in the American College*. Authored by Gerald Grant and David Riesman, this book examines the counter-reaction in undergraduate curriculum, which occurred amid the liberalizing social and political movements of the late 1960s and early 1970s.

Born in Philadelphia, David Riesman (1909–2002) graduated from Harvard College in 1931 and from Harvard Law School in 1934. After clerking for U.S. Supreme Court Justice Louis D. Brandeis, he practiced law in Boston and then was appointed professor of law at the University of Buffalo in 1937. During the Second World War he worked in industry, and in 1946 became a professor of social sciences at the University of Chicago and engaged in field work leading to his acclaimed analysis of the urban upper class: *The Lonely Crowd* (with Reuel Denney and Nathan Glazer) in 1951. In 1958 Riesman was appointed Henry Ford II Professor of the Social Sciences at Harvard University, where he remained until his retirement in 1980. Gerald P. Grant (1938–) was born in Syracuse, New York, and received his bachelor's degree from John Carroll University in 1959. After earning a master's degree from Columbia University and serving in the U.S. Marine Corps, he joined the staff of the *Washington Post* in 1961. He became a Nieman fellow at Harvard University in 1967 and earned his Ph.D. in sociology in 1972. Grant then accepted a faculty appointment at Syracuse University, and was named Hannah Hammond Professor in 1993 and Distinguished University Professor in 1998.

Grant and Riesman chose *The Perpetual Dream* for their title because "the campus has been a kind of dreamscape for utopian as well as practical reformers, some projecting their notions of an ideal community on the curriculum and extracurriculum, and others seeing the diversity of undergraduate experience as an epitome of the American dream that education can change one's life, at whatever age. These yearnings, so ingrained in a nation that believes deeply in a second (and often a third) chance for everyone, are never fulfilled but endlessly renewed." (p. 1) *The Perpetual Dream* was awarded the Borden Prize as the Outstanding Book in Higher Education for 1978 by the American Council on Education.

SELECTION[84]

The Telic Reforms

[W]e restricted the scope of our inquiry to "merely" 3,000 formally constituted institutions of higher education and focused most of our efforts on what the experimenters themselves claimed to be reforms. Through a variety of methods, we began to investigate these claims and to attempt to under-

---

84. Gerald Grant and David Riesman, *The Perpetual Dream: Reform and Experiment in the American College* (Chicago: University of Chicago Press, 1978), pp. 15–37, 179–91, 204–13, 216. Reprinted by permission of the University of Chicago Press.

stand the intentions of the reformers. Some of the reforms have a large resonance, representing attempts not only to change the university but to set forth new ideals. We call these telic reforms, reforms pointing toward a different conception of the ends of undergraduate education, to distinguish them from the more popular reforms of the last decade which have brought about a general loosening of the curriculum. The telic reforms approach the status of social movements or generic protests against contemporary American life. . . . [but] we have not constructed anything grand enough to be called either a sociological or an educational theory. Rather, in the more usual way of inductively oriented social scientists, we have looked at some cases, compared them, and arranged them in [a] typology of reform movements. . . . In this chapter, we explain that typology and attempt to place the telic reform movements in historical perspective.

In Chapter 6, we discuss the popular reforms as partially a response to the meritocratic discontents that came to characterize student life in the most selective colleges and universities. By the early 1960s, the expansion of the American system of higher education had led to fierce competition for admission to elite colleges and greatly intensified academic pressures for undergraduates who, once admitted, continued to compete for choice graduate-school opportunities. Students sought relief in a wide range of popular reforms that gave them a considerably greater degree of autonomy and resulted in dramatic changes in their relationships with teachers. Students were freer than before to pick and choose their way through the curriculum and to move at their own pace without penalty. The most popular of these reforms—student-designed majors, free-choice curricula, the abolition of fixed requirements—sought not to establish new institutional aims, but to slow the pace and expand the avenues of approach. While these reforms began in the elite academic institutions, they spread to other colleges and universities. They were adopted in part out of misconceived notions that they would serve to quench campus revolts as well as out of genuinely educational motives on the part of a new generation of faculty who wished to change the processes of education in significant ways. The popular reforms modified the means of education within the constraints of the existing goals of the research-oriented university.[85]

The telic reforms, on the other hand, embody a significantly different conception of the goals of undergraduate education. To some degree, they represent an attack on the hegemony of the giant research oriented multiversities and their satellite university colleges. In one sense, these telic reforms could be thought of as counterrevolutionary, that is, as counter to the rise of the research-oriented universities that Christopher Jencks and David Riesman described in *The Academic Revolution*. By "revolution," Jencks and Riesman meant the crescent hegemony of the academic professions over previously influential parties: trustees and legislators, students, administrators, religious denominations.[86] That book, like others of its genre, noted that the research universities were producing the faculties for collegiate institutions and took for granted the way in which competition among the colleges led them to imitate the major university model. But because of their resentment and later disaffection with the aims of the academic vanguard, many faculty members trained under its auspices have shown resistance to the model; and their ambivalence, as well as lack of resources, limited the momentum with which it could be imitated. Until the 1920s, the university college model . . . was neither strong enough at the center nor extensive enough at the periphery of American higher education

---

85. Why do Grant and Riesman call these "popular reforms" given that they arose "in the most selective colleges and universities?"

86. Christopher Jencks and David Riesman, *The Academic Revolution* (New York: Doubleday, 1968).

to incite rebellions that might establish contrasting models of higher education other than those affi-liated with denominational groups.[87]

But in the 1930s, two of the telic movements—in our typology the neo-classical and the aesthetic-expressive—arose in opposition to the university college model, and they were followed later by what we have called the communal-expressive and activist-radical. By telic reforms, then, we mean to sig-nify those reforms that emphasize ends and purposes that are different from, if not hostile to, the goals of the regnant research universities. . . . Essentially, the typology contrasts different models of under-graduate education, which can be translated into ideas about the purposes of such an experience, the values it should embody, and the forms of authority on which it ultimately rests, Each offers a distinc-tive vision of an educating community. . . .[88]

Neo-classical

St. John's College is the ideal-typical example of what we call the neo-classical college since it has sought to restore the classical curriculum with new intensity and purity.[89] Like the other anti-university experiments, it was basically dominated by a moral imperative: a vision of human unity, of the good life in a Platonic mode. And like Plato's Socratic dialogues, the mode of discourse at St. John's is aporetic:[90] "The argument either leads nowhere or it goes around in circles."[91] Beginning with the Socratic dialogues in the first year, and progressing through the 100-odd Great Books which have come to characterize the program, St. John's teaches that "one dogma and doctrine is not to be compromised: the assertion that learning is first and last for its own sake."[92] The idea of "dogma" in its Greek sense of "a formulated belief" is not foreign at St. John's, a community that believes educa-tion should not be instrumental to some other end, but should itself be an end. Thus the college should model the forms of life of liberally educated men, enabling students to join in this process and to ex-perience it as its own reward. The object is to create a great conversation about the great questions. At root, these are connected with intellectual and moral virtue, and with all the Socratic paradoxes about whether and in what ways virtue is "teachable." . . .

The neo-classicals regarded and still regard the universities and the conventionally departmenta-lized colleges as vulgar and technocratic. They envisage the universities as sterile, exploiting know-ledge for merely technical ends and preparing students not for the "calling" of life, but for superficial, though profitable, vocationalism. They underestimated the diversity of what later came to be called the multiversity, and also its incremental inventiveness.

---

87. Jencks and Riesman introduced the term "university college" in *The Academic Revolution* to denote colleges whose faculties had adopted the values and mores of the faculty at the research universities.

88. What is the conceptual distinction between the "popular" and "telic" reforms?

89. On the founding of St. Johns, see the introduction to selection #58.

90. *Aporia* is the state of doubt, or perplexity, that one enters upon encountering a problem or puzzle that cannot be resolved. Socrates was said to reduce his interlocutors to *aporia* through his relentlessly probing questions.

91. Quotation is from Hannah Arendt, "Thinking and Moral Considerations: A Lecture," *Social Research*, 38, no. 3 (Autumn 1971), who makes a point in this essay that would find great favor at St. John's: "Could the activity of thinking as such, the habit of examining and reflecting upon whatever happens to come to pass, . . . be of such a nature that it 'conditions' men against evil doing?" p. 148.

92. Eva Brann, "What are the Beliefs and Teachings of St. John's College?" *The Collegian, St. John's College* (May 1975): 10. See selection #65 from the 2007–2008 catalog of St. John's, introduced by Eva Brann.

Students were invited to come to St. John's College not for certification or entry into a meritocratic elite, but in order to become more civilized, in order to join an aristocratic great chain of being, stretching back through the medieval university to Plato's Academy. The graduates of St. John's College, an institution which in Scott Buchanan's words was designed to produce cultural misfits, are not rendered unemployable but have, in fact, done well in law, teaching, business, and other fields. . . .

Aesthetic-Expressive

In the 1920s to learn the performing arts, one's best bet was probably at a conservatory or an art institute. A few liberal-arts colleges had, so to speak, musical appendages, such as Oberlin with its Conservatory. Some of the great state universities, such as Indiana, Illinois, Michigan in music, and Iowa in creative writing, were diverse enough and flexible enough to get away from traditional scholarly canons as to what is appropriate in a university setting.[93] In a way, they followed the land-grant model. Just as they had prepared people who wanted to teach home economics, they prepared people who wanted to teach music or to enter "commercial" callings in the graphic arts as well as those who aspired to the fine arts.

But the creation of colleges whose main emphasis lay in the aesthetic dimension was mirrored by the founding of a kind of second generation of institutions devoted to the education of women. Vassar, Bryn Mawr, Smith, and Mount Holyoke had established that women could equal men in cognitive facility. Now Scripps and, later, to a lesser degree, Mills on the West Coast and Bennington and Sarah Lawrence on the East Coast, took advantage of the somewhat sheltered status of upper-class women to give freer rein to acknowledged creativity in the arts. . . . Along with Black Mountain College, [they] embodied what we have here termed the aesthetic-expressive ideal. . . . [C]reative expression lay at the core of the enterprise. . . .

Although the arts did not flourish on American campuses before World War II, major gains were made in the 1960s. More than 80 campuses, three-fourths of them public institutions (UCLA is the largest, awarding 232 fine-arts degrees in a recent year), now award degrees in art. Among the private institutions which have sizable programs are Brigham Young University, Wellesley College, Boston University, and Northwestern University; but no private institutions are among the first twenty in numbers graduated; and, with the exception of Stanford, no elite private university awards more than twenty-five art degrees annually. And as more students are trained in the arts, pressure is created for such programs to move downward as graduates seek jobs in the lower schools. . . .

Viewed from the perspective of the discipleship that characterized both Black Mountain and the early Bennington, the new palaces of the arts rising in some of the public universities would be seen as corrupting in their giantism. Those early pioneers in education in the arts might also view the Carnegie Commission's recent anointing of the arts as somewhat of a curse.[94] One consequence of the imitation by the broader academic culture is that the colleges founded to give form to the aesthetic impulse have had perhaps an even harder time surviving than the other offbeat enterprises we are discussing here. For one thing, the polarization in terms of sex which relegated creative expression to the female domain has greatly moderated; with men encouraged to develop what would once have been thought "feminine" aspects of themselves, colleges specializing in aesthetic expressivity for women have had to reconsider their mandate. . . .[95]

---

93. Syracuse University, which in 1873 established the first degree-granting professional school of art, was an early exception to this pattern.

94. See Clark Kerr, "The Carnegie Commission Looks at the Arts," *Arts in Society* 11 (1974): 190–97.

95. On this point, see the discussion of Jane Roland Martin in the Introduction.

Communal-Expressive

As higher education spread and as the specifically religious impulse waned [in the twentieth century], it is understandable that a few institutions of higher education began to see themselves as the principal expression of the values of community, even though they also operated as peripheral members of a system valuing competition and cognitive rationality. Community was one theme at Black Mountain College, along with the emphasis on the arts; and like other utopian communities, Black Mountain suffered a series of schisms in its search for wholeness. Schisms, in fact, seem to be part of the "natural history" of communal-expressive ventures. Such institutions generally begin with a charismatic leader who is often not good at balancing either books or interests and is subsequently expelled.

The full flowering of the communal-expressive movement in the several colleges that have been dominated by it occurred only with the growing influence of humanistic psychology. Much of the literature of humanistic psychology, including the journal of that name, focuses less on expressing its own particular ethos, than on differentiating itself from such major currents in psychology as behaviorism and traditional Freudian psychoanalysis. Its view of man tends to be Rousseauistic. Carl Rogers, Abraham Maslow, and a more distant and more intellectual mentor, Norman O. Brown, provided the movement with an ideology about the importance of the affective life. . . .[96]

Some of the spirit that animated Johnston College at its founding was also present at the birth of Evergreen State College several years later, but it is considerably attenuated now. However, the communal-expressive impulse was widespread, even though it was often short-lived and seldom established as the dominant metaphor of an entire institution. Seeds of the so-called human potential movement found life at the College Within at Tufts University, the Inner College of the University of Connecticut, at an Esalen-like Center at the University of Oregon, Bensalem College at Fordham University, and a variety of "living-learning" experiments from Old Westbury to Fresno State. Rochdale College, though not actually a degree-granting institution, was set up in an apartment house near Toronto University where resident members were required to contribute labor and hire their own teachers and administrators. The College of the Person in Washington, DC, advertised itself as a center for encounter, bodily awareness exercises, and Gestalt therapy "that will provide for emotional involvement and support, an opportunity to share feelings, perceptions, insights, love and concern." . . .

In the late 1960s, the seminar table began to resemble the family dinner table.[97] Affective relations came to outweigh intellectual competition, although students as well as their teachers were often ambivalent about awarding academic credit for such explorations. The purest realization of the Communal-Expressive style that we have encountered is . . . Kresge College at the University of California at Santa Cruz, which opened in 1970. Kresge appealed to students as "a living learning community which concerns itself with the human as well as the intellectual needs of its members." . . .

Kresge strikes us as an experiment of integrity that deserves the careful attention of those who would hope that a better balance can be struck between feeling and intellect, and who believe that we have a great deal to learn about how to be more cooperative without sacrificing essential human diversity.

---

96. Carl Rogers (1902–1987), humanistic psychologist who developed client-centered counseling; Abraham Maslow (1908–1970), founder of humanistic psychology; Norman O. Brown (1913–2002), classicist and philosopher who wrote on psychoanalytic themes.

97. This analogy is drawn from Craig Eisendrath's and Thomas J. Cottle's discussion in *Out of Discontent: Visions of the Contemporary University* (Cambridge, MA: Schenkman, 1972), pp. 56–8.

Activist-Radical

If the communal-expressive colleges have identified principally with the counterculture, the colleges dominated by political activism in the 1960s have been at odds with the counterculture's softness, its emphasis on consensus. They sought change in the society, less consciously in themselves. In the early days of Students for a Democratic Society, the two currents were fused, and often confused; members sought expressive comradeship as well as specific political mobilization and change.

Even now, with the receding wave of protest, departments at many universities, eminent and nonelite alike, are dominated by faculty who were "radicalized" in the 1960s, often, of course, with leadership from the few charismatic elders.[98] As Carnegie Commission surveys of faculty attitudes show, there are dramatic differences among fields, with sociology at one extreme and engineering or veterinary medicine at another. But if one asks not about enclaves within major institutions, but rather about colleges founded by or dominated by activist-radicals, then the list is short indeed. . . .

The 1920s saw the founding of the college which was to become in the 1960s the most visible and highly charged base for political activism of any college in America. Antioch College (as it was later reconstituted by Arthur Morgan) represents an ideal-typical instance of the activist-radical college. Its commitment to extramural action began in the 1920s with its focus on the co-op program by which Antioch students spent alternate terms on and off campus in work programs. These programs were not, as were those designed for non-affluent students at Northeastern University or University of Cincinnati, designed to help them finance their education; in fact, their education at parental expense was in effect prolonged in order to help immerse them more fully in the dilemmas and contradictions of American life. Although the work program even to this day has not been fully integrated into the Antioch curriculum, the ideology of the program under the aegis of Arthur Morgan reflected an attempt to get away from bookishness, to provide mentors for students other than scholarly faculty, for whom, in fact, Arthur Morgan had an almost philistine lack of respect.[99]

Antioch was neither founded by radicals originally, nor was it in fact refounded by them during the era of Arthur Morgan. But it has been committed to social, political, and curricular change since that refounding, and in the 1960s it experienced with particular intensity the commitment of a large part of its faculty and student body to using the college for the political ends of the far left. Antioch expanded early, as a few other colleges did, to serve minority groups and had a small cadre committed to expressive-communitarian ideals that were now avowedly political. The college was never wholly "radicalized," but the largest single unit on the campus, although not formally a department, came to be the Marxist-oriented Institute for the Solution of Social Problems. . . .[100]

---

98. For accounts by various hands of the impact of student protest on an array of more or less prominent colleges and universities, see David Riesman and Verne Stadtman, eds., *Academic Transformation: Seventeen Institutions under Pressure* (New York: McGraw-Hill, 1972); Seymour M. Lipset, *Rebellion in the University* (Boston: Little, Brown, 1971).

99. Arthur E. Morgan (1878–1975), a civil engineer, became a trustee of Antioch in 1919, when it was on the brink of bankruptcy. Appointed to lead the reorganization committee to find a new president, he assumed the position himself in 1920 and became president of the Progressive Education Association in the following year. Disappointed in the faculty's reluctance to follow his vision for thoroughgoing experiential and vocational education, Morgan stepped down in 1933, and worked in a number of domestic and international public service and advocacy roles until his death.

100. Given that Antioch College went bankrupt and closed in 2008, it may be asked whether any of these telic reforms are financially viable.

Antioch's complex metamorphoses have outrun our own ability to keep pace. Although we had prepared a chapter on Antioch for this volume, we later decided that the College for Human Services would be in some ways a better illustration of the activist-radical model. CHS, as nearly everyone refers to it, was founded on the lower West Side of New York in 1965 by an extraordinary woman, Audrey Cohen. . . . As at Antioch, students sometimes find it more tempting to try to change the college than the world outside, and the College for Human Services suffered a series of strikes in the early 1970s. But, perhaps because neither student nor faculty rebels had any tenure at CHS, and because Audrey Cohen did not hesitate to show some the door, the experiment not only survived but grew stronger. The curriculum, under development for more than a decade, demands a dedication approaching sainthood from its students. But it is also one of the most ingenious we have seen in terms of engaging students in a carefully articulated series of practical challenges.[101]

Antioch and the College for Human Services illustrate different strains of the activist radical movement. Antioch, in its Marxist Institute for the Solution of Social Problems, was more grandly revolutionary for a brief time, but was not grounded in any stern tradition of radicalism. There has never been any very powerful endemic Socialist movement in America. . . . The College for Human Services is closer to the impulses of Jane Addams and the early settlement-house leaders than it is to Marxist or more specifically radical political movements. . . .

Comparison

Our typology emphasizes the differences among the telic reforms. But the commonalties are also striking. Each of these experiments has a sense of mission. We suspect that many faculty who are attracted to them are not only dissatisfied with competitive life in the multiversity but yearn for a sense of identity and esprit. They want to join an institution that is capable of evoking the deep loyalties of the whole self and of engendering all-out efforts. They want to believe. A visitor is immediately aware of the basic choices participants have exercised. Bridges have been cut; commitments have been made, and ideals are continually tested, including those of the visitor.

A spirit of vocation and intensity about teaching permeates these communities, partly as a result of the jettisoning of research and publication norms, but also from the growth of a new sense of mission. Of course, new ideals may fade for individuals if not institutions, and faculty who have sacrificed much in their own conversion often hide even from themselves the hurt they feel when their offerings are rejected by the intended acolytes. Yet there is some protection against such wounds since the expertise of the teacher is de-emphasized. In all these radical experiments, teachers and students are seen as co-learners: at St. John's students and tutors puzzle out the great texts together and at Black Mountain they joined others in creating paintings and poems. The egalitarian spirit does not deny to teachers all authority, although the grounds of that authority do not lie in disciplinary expertise in the way that they do in the university colleges. . . .

What does mark these colleges off from most modern universities is the devotion to community. Bonds of community are nourished by reinforcing participation in the full round of life, whether at the Friday night lecture at St. John's or the kin-group meeting at Kresge. At three of these institutions, there are no departments to compete for students. The important judgments have to do with whether

101. See Audrey Cohen, "The Founding of a New Profession: The Human Service Professional" (New York: unpublished paper, 19 June 1974), Educational Resources Information Center doc. #ED136171.

students measure up to the ideals of the college, not whether they perform well according to the traditional standards developed by a departmentally organized faculty.[102]

Like the popular reforms, the telic experiments are bound together in their aversions to the multiversity model, but their arena is wider than that of the enemy—their hope is to create some notion of the good life whether in the Platonic or the Rogerian mode.

It is in this deepest sense that these institutions are "trans-disciplinary," i.e., there is some notion of an end or a good to which academic disciplines are subordinate. Their sense of mission is reflected in the forms of teaching, too. At St. John's there is the belief that disciplines serve as falsifying lenses through which students preconceive and are likely to misconceive the "natural articulations of the intellectual world. . . . This college chooses to overcome these institutionalized prejudgments by substituting fundamental books for departments and elementary skills for disciplines."[103] The mixed-media event was born at Black Mountain, where poets, musicians, dancers, actors—and on occasion stray dogs—joined together to create productions. At Kresge, the disciplines were viewed as subordinate to the task of building community, and at CHS, subordinate to the aim of discovering the generic competencies of the "humane professional." . . .

In the telic reforms, disciplines in the narrow sense are subordinate to—and usually exist in uneasy tension with—the broad authority that establishes "the moving spirit of the whole group."[104] That authority defines the relation between the student and the community into which he is being inducted. In what we have called the neo-classical model, the authority rests in the wisdom of the Socratic elders as interpreters of the texts of the liberal tradition. The young tutor who questions the selection of any particular reading or its relations to other aspects of the St. John's program is told to be patient: in time he will come to see the wisdom of the choice in the larger scheme of things. For the aesthetic-expressive model, the authority lies in submission to the sensibilities of the master artists. They determine what counts as art and what kind of community discipline will best sustain the tradition of artistic innovation. In the communal-expressive case, the authority derives from the charisma of the founding prophet or guru, the one who can win the devotion of followers to a particular notion of a nurturing community. . . .

The activist-radical model is grounded in an agenda of social or political reform, and the discipline lies in the experience of learning to effect change. The student at the College for Human Services must perform "constructive actions" that result in benefits to clients. The authority attaches to the one who creates a vision of a better society and who acts to bring about change in the desired direction. In the extreme case it is the author of the revolution; in democratic situations it is the one whose program of reform wins the most adherents or votes. Challenges to the authority of the activist-radical inevitably turn on the question of whether one is trying to understand the world or to change it, and at the College for Human Services the curriculum is based on the idea that one will understand it best by trying to change it.

---

102. Yet, to the extent that such a judgment of the "whole" student reflects an "ideal," it can be deeply wounding, especially if the idealistic judgment leads to exclusion from the group. Departmental verdicts based on "traditional" academic standards can be discounted to some extent.

103. Eva Brann, "What are the Beliefs and Teachings of St. John's College?" p. 9.

104. Grant and Riesman draw these words of John Dewey from Kenneth D. Denne, "Authority in Education," *Harvard Educational Review* 40 (1970): 385–410—"whose analysis of the authority of rule and authority of the expert helped us to clarify these distinctions." A fundamental source for the analysis of authority in charismatic, sect-like, or other such "transcendent" communities is: Ernest Troelstch, *The Social Teaching of the Christian Churches*, tr. Olive Wyon, 2 vols. (New York: Macmillan, 1931).

We speak of the transcendent, and even this brief overview hints at the utopian strains that run through these reform movements. The utopian impulses are strong, representing a search for a more perfect union that, as we have noted, often leads to disunion and schism. Because the founders have made radical choices, not leaving many options open in the way that the contemporary university does, the alternative to opposition is withdrawal. . . .

Meritocratic Discontents and Popular Reforms

In contrast to our discussion of the telic reforms, our effort here is to suggest the major lines of the popular reforms that have brought widespread changes in curriculum and extracurriculum during the last dozen years. These do not involve a radical reorientation of institutional goals but affect the relations between students and faculty, the processes of education, and the context in which it takes place. . . .[105] Only a very few institutions have stood unequivocally unaltered during the period of change that overtook both American society and its educational institutions in the 1960s and thereafter. While both individual students and institutions have been unevenly affected by these changes, there is no doubt that almost everywhere requirements have been relaxed, the paths toward a degree have been made more multiple and open, and the gold standard of academic currency (in some cases more nominal than real) has been diluted by grade inflation. . . .

Only a very small proportion of faculty and students ever spent their time in protest meetings, rallies, and demonstrations, even on the more agitated campuses. Yet a small proportion of a very large base can still be a sizable—and threatening—number, and since many activist students were also among the more talented and dramaturgical, their activities had a stunning impact. . . . Students got onto boards of trustees (or invaded their meetings), drafted reports proposing educational reforms, and campaigned ceaselessly in fiery columns in the student papers for alterations in the established ways of conducting academic business.

The changes brought about in this manner are those we are terming "popular reforms." They included changes in curriculum, which not only introduced black and other ethnic studies and later women's studies, but also provided opportunities for credit for off-campus work. . . . Among the new institutions founded during the sixties, some had no traditional departments and emphasized interdisciplinary programs or contract-based individuated learning. Evergreen State College in Olympia, Washington; New Jersey's Stockton State and Ramapo Colleges; the College of Old Westbury in the State University of New York system; Hampshire College; the University of Wisconsin, Green Bay, were all non-departmental in original structure. Johnston College of the University of Redlands, Sterling University in Ottawa, Kansas, and many others emphasized nontraditional learning for what Patricia Cross has termed the "new students."[106] Adults and especially older women returning to or finishing college were given the opportunity to participate in individuated programs at places like Empire State College of the State University of New York or Minnesota Metropolitan University.

Yet these new colleges and new programs did not drive out the old. . . . What has happened in fact is that the college curriculum has been expanded. At some colleges, for example, black and other ethnic studies have been added as the result of student and often faculty and administration pressures; often these are organized in new departments, though they may draw on the knowledge base and faculty of existing departments. Women's studies, both within established departments such as history, sociology, psychology, economics, and as separate departments and majors, have spread with extraordinary speed, and are served by a whole new outpouring of texts and scholarly journals. Environmen-

---

105. Is the distinction between the "telic" and "popular" reforms consistent?

106. See K. Patricia Cross, *Beyond the Open Door* (San Francisco: Jossey-Bass, 1976).

tal studies (around which the University of Wisconsin at Green Bay and the College of the Atlantic initially organized their entire curricula) have been seen as a way to respond to interest in the environment; and law schools have added courses in environmental law, medical schools in environment-related subjects, and schools of education, adopting a different focus, have added departments of "learning environments." The interest in the environment has been seen by natural scientists as a way of attracting students with "relevant" subject matter.

It is clear that to an uneven extent the major or field of concentration has lost, however, a good deal of its earlier rigidity. In fields like mathematics and chemistry, sequences remain. But in less technical departments, students can fulfill academic requirements in a greater variety of ways than before: with courses in related departments; with so-called experiential off-campus learning; or with self-paced courses, in which, according to the Carnegie Council survey, 30 percent of the nation's students have participated. The pass/no credit option, favored by a majority of the students in 1969, is now favored by only a third, but the surveys report that nearly half have made use of it. Still the major stands as the focus of the average student's academic experience, in part because of the increasing vocational pressures felt by undergraduates in recent years. What has dramatically changed is the place of any kind of general education or core curriculum; in all but a few institutions, the hold of the curriculum as a set of more or less systematic pathways toward a baccalaureate degree has become attenuated. Grade inflation and the loosening of requirements have weakened the role of faculty members and departments as gatekeepers of the degree (and whatever honors may be bestowed along with it). In the language of the student movement, students have "gained control over the decisions which affect their own lives"; in the language of the market, the student consumer has become king. . .

We state at the outset our tentative conclusion: that the most widespread and significant impact of the educational upheaval of the sixties was to bring about a considerably greater degree of autonomy for students.[107] They were free to plan their courses of study in a way they had never done before. The most important change was the virtual or complete abolition of fixed requirements in many departments and of mandatory distribution requirements, whether of breadth or depth, including class attendance and the time, mode, and kinds of credits needed to secure a baccalaureate degree. . . .[108] With the end of the draft, the "stop-out" again became a possibility for male students, and upper middle-class women liberated enough to be on their own often followed suit. Even in the selective residential institutions, the notion of a curriculum built around four consecutive years began to seem almost archaic. . . .

It should be noted in this connection that central to these reforms is what we might term the sanitized transcript, which erases all incompletes, tentatives, and failing grades, and records only successes. However, the pass/no credit option has in the last few years become increasingly less satisfying, or is used by diligent students to provide leeway for even harder work, for example, on essential pre-med courses.[109] The Buckley Amendment, which permits students to see their own files and what has been written about them, only carried further the institutionalization of the sanitized transcript. . . .

---

107. Is this greater degree of autonomy beneficial or not? Has the autonomy diminished subsequently?

108. There remain a few traditional, usually small, liberal-arts colleges run by Protestant denominations (although virtually none that are Catholic) where class attendance is still required, where the very small size of the faculty can be used to limit options, and where curricular coherence has remained relatively "unliberated."

109. The Carnegie Council studies show that, in 1969, 50 percent of undergraduates agreed strongly or with reservations that undergraduate education would be improved if grades were abolished; in 1975, 32 percent did. (Faculty percentages over the same period dropped from 34 percent to 19 percent.) See Martin Trow, *Aspects of American Higher Education, 1969–1975: A Report for the Carnegie Council on Policy Studies in Higher Education* (1977), table 3, p. 14.

As with many empirically based typologies, it is far from easy to draw a line between the telic reforms and the nationwide sweep of what we have termed the [popular] movement toward an over-optioned life. One way of looking at the latter group of changes is to see them as bringing to the smaller institutions, such as regional state or local private colleges, some of the benefits as well as some of the drawbacks of the multiversity. In educational units within the multiversity, as in the deregulated liberal-arts colleges, the options sought and retained by students vary greatly, as does the holding power of institutions against the inevitable lessening of loyalty on the part of both students and faculty. . . .

Political protests—particularly on those leading campuses that were for a time under siege—no doubt also affected faculty dispositions. . . . Thus the pedagogical left, like the political left, was not just a student movement. A sizable percentage of the faculty were convinced of the need for relaxations in the curriculum that would permit more experiment and innovation. And many believed that student-directed education was the best kind of education. . . .

[A]dded to the curriculum were not only new subjects based on scientific developments and on student pressures, but also new opportunities for work in the performing arts (a necessity in the men's colleges which went coed) as well as credit in liberal arts colleges for activities once considered vocational, such as preparation for schoolteaching, or, within sociology departments, for field work in social agencies or probation departments. Still, if one compares catalogs of today with those of a dozen years ago, in general one sees the same departments along with the new additions, and, notably and advantageously, some movement away from a too exclusive emphasis on the Western World. . . . It should be clear that these changes, though offensive to traditionalist faculty, are not invariably changes for the worse. . . .

[W]e conclude that the popular reforms of the sixties are here to stay, even though enthusiasm for them has greatly ebbed. . . . What remains is the patternless multiversity where such coherence as exists is intradepartmental and where, as a result of the popular reforms, the minority of students who want to create their own individuated program find neither help nor hindrance in doing so.

Section X

Approaching the Past in the New Millennium

Discussion about the liberal arts at the turn of the millennium was remarkably similar to that of a century earlier, inasmuch as those involved in liberal education sharply disagreed over what to teach, how to teach, and why to teach, as Aristotle also commented about his epoch in selection #3. These controversies reached a crescendo during the "culture wars" in the closing decades of the twentieth century. The acrimony was reassuring in some respects. Although "the patternless multiversity" had become normative, although "the student consumer ha[d] become king," and although the faculty had abdicated intellectual authority to the students to plan much of their academic program with "neither help nor hindrance in doing so,"[1] many members of the academy still cared deeply about the meaning and nature of liberal education. Among the many issues in the dispute, the subject most fitting for the concluding section of this documentary history is, perhaps, the controversy over the role of tradition and historical sources in the liberal arts.[2]

At one end of the continuum of opinion stood the "Great Books" program, exemplified at St. John's, a liberal arts college that might have been expected to enter the controversy at full tilt, but which continued to read and discuss its canon relatively oblivious to the tumult. Representing either the cardinal sin or the last best hope in the minds of many disputants, St. John's quietly persevered in the eye of the hurricane, pursuing what Eva Brann, in selection #65, calls its "slow, reflective, fundamental, time-divorced inquiry." In this way, St. John's contributed to the debate simply because its fidelity strengthened the resolve of many professors at other institutions in arguing for core requirements in reading some classic texts, knowing that their proposals were modest compared to "the list of Great Books" at St. John's. But what exactly is the St. John's program? Proponents and opponents often debated a virtually hypostasized "Great Books" program without knowing how the exemplar actually worked. In selection #65, Eva Brann's introduction and the catalog of St. John's explain this program of liberal arts that, almost uniquely, "did not attempt to find the students' level or to be relevant to their immediate interests."

At the other end of the continuum was the disaggregating counter-movement that came to be known as "multiculturalism" during the closing decades of the twentieth century. Multiculturalism challenged not only the uniform requirement to read a canon of classics, but also the criteria identifying a book as "great," and even the principles of universalism and idealism that undergirded those criteria. In the extreme, multiculturalism went beyond calling for "equal representation" of different viewpoints and voices, to claim that all knowledge was politically and socially "constructed." Knowledge, in this view, was "cultural capital," as Mary Louise Pratt states in selection #66. One of the most prominent debates prompted by the multiculturalist challenge to core requirements in "Great

---

1. Quotations are drawn from Grant and Riesman, *Reform and Experiment in the American College*, in selection #64.

2. An excellent source, unusually informed by extensive data, assessing liberal education within the institutional and social context of the late twentieth century is: Francis Oakley, *Community of Learning: The American College and the Liberal Arts Tradition* (New York: Oxford University Press, 1992).

Books" occurred at Stanford University in the late 1980s, and participant Mary Louise Pratt recounts the events and the arguments on both sides, as well her own conviction that a list of Great Books normally "not only lays down a Eurocentric paradigm, but also embodies a very restricted sense of Europe."

By the late 1990s most proponents of liberal education were debating not whether to incorporate multiculturalism, but how it could be accommodated with prescribed reading in a canon of classic texts. Meanwhile, both canonism and multiculturalism contributed to renewing attention to the goal of fostering civic virtue through liberal education. In 1997 philosopher Martha Nussbaum published a widely acclaimed book that appealed to Socrates for a philosophical justification of multiculturalism and to Socrates and the Stoics to justify the prevailing concerns of moral and civic education as part of the liberal arts. Drawn from that book, selection #67 by Nussbaum thus presents a notable argument for accommodating multiculturalism, canonism, and civic virtue within liberal education.

Apart from the conceptual problem of reconciling traditional texts with modern epistemological challenges, liberal arts faculty teaching "core texts" often find that undergraduates early in the twentieth-first century resist this approach due to "two major and interrelated obstacles: relativism and relevance." In selection #68 philosopher Nancy du Bois Marcus proposes a strategy both to overcome these obstacles and to engage current undergraduates by teaching modern classics that build upon and therefore lead to traditional classics. Still another strategy similar to that of Nussbaum is drawing upon the traditional canon to critique the canon. In selection #69, English professor Christopher Metress of Samford University employs St. Benedict's monastic rule of silence to challenge the metaphor of the "Great Conversation" that has predominated in discussion about teaching "great books" or "core texts" over the past century.

Are there additional philosophical resources that could justify the accommodation of multiculturalism, canonism, and civic virtue within liberal education—resources that are closely associated with American culture and history? Selection #70, authored by political theorist David Paris and historian Bruce Kimball, proposes that philosophical Pragmatism provides a rationale and historical explanation. In their view, Pragmatism explains and justifies theoretically the "overlapping consensus" among proponents of liberal education that liberal education should be multi-perspectival and provide civic and moral education. In addition, the grounding of Pragmatism in United States' culture and its resurgence in the late twentieth century account historically for the fact that these points have arisen in American debates over liberal education at this time. Whether Socratic or Pragmatic, such philosophical analyses may still be challenged by multiculturalists on the grounds that they present a "Eurocentric" view.[3] Nevertheless, Paris and Kimball propose below that Pragmatism, notwithstanding its origins, "provides a perspective . . . consistent with a kind of pluralism that is the foundation of liberal democratic societies." This kind of debate will not soon be resolved, but what is clear is that discussion about the nature of liberal education in the twenty-first century continues to interweave claims about the meaning and import of its past.

---

3. Shirley Hune, "Pragmatism, Liberal Education, and Multi-culturalism: Utilizing the 'Master's Tools' to Restructure the 'Master's House' for Diversity," in *The Condition of Liberal Education*, ed. Robert Orrill (New York: College Entrance Examination Board, 1995), pp. 163–9.

65. St. John's College, "Statement of the Program" (2007)

INTRODUCTION

The "great books" movement of the second quarter of the twentieth century, described in selection #58, found its home and champion in 1937 at St. John's College in Annapolis, Maryland. At the beginning of the twenty-first century the college maintains the program essentially in its original form. To accommodate growth, the college opened another campus at Santa Fe, New Mexico, in 1964, and has about 440 students on each campus.

From the outset, the founders asserted that the program was in no way experimental. Speaking in August 1937 on "Reviewing the Ancient Purpose of Education," Stringfellow Barr stated, "True liberal education is one of the few things in life that can never be called an experiment."[4] Critics objected to these assertions,[5] but they have been of fundamental importance to the survival of the program: It had no criteria for failure, and it had a cast of conviction. It did not attempt to find the students' level or to be relevant to their immediate interests. Instead it trusted to the attractive power of the books and subjects to carry the students beyond themselves. In this spirit, the program was and still is almost completely required; there are no electives, and all students each year read the same primary books, and study the same material, which is chosen and organized not by contemporary university disciplines but by the traditional seven liberal arts.

The notion of a "great book" is an essential ingredient in this attitude: the conviction that there are books (and studies) that are worthy and will not fail to capture the attention of almost all students. Critics have pointed out that the students of this program are self-selected for this interest. That is an undeniable but double-edged fact: the students are primarily *self*-selected, but that is possible only because criteria for admission are very flexible. Alumni and tutors (the title of professor is eschewed) say that the approach is exceedingly successful in engaging students. The college freely admits that students do not gain specialized and cutting-edge knowledge; the emphasis is on slow, reflective, fundamental, time-divorced inquiry. The college is thus responsible for showing that such inquiry is possible, and that is a topic under constant debate, even while the program is functioning.

From its inception the program has been faulted for being elitist. Insofar as this charge refers to the small number of its participants, it is undeniable. Moreover, the program has not succeeded in propagating itself, the chief reason being the deeply entrenched departmental character of higher education.[6] Intellectually speaking the program is, in fact, markedly egalitarian and democratic in its ethos. It is predicated on the "a cat may look at a king" principle. Students are expected to challenge books of great standing and to regard their tutors as co-learners rather than professing authorities. They are expected to listen and respond respectfully to others' opinions. The rigid structure of the program itself is intended to give students the liberty of thought that comes from not having been

---

4. Quoted in J. Winfree Smith, *A Search for the Liberal College: The Beginning of the St. John's Program* (Annapolis, MD: St. John's College Press, 1983), p. 25.

5. Sidney Hook, "Ballyhoo at St. John's College," *The New Leader* 27 (27 May 1944): 8–9; 27 (3 June 1944): 8–10.

6. While a number of colleges, such as St. Mary's College of California, have modeled part of their curriculum upon St. John's, only Thomas Aquinas College at Ojai, California, has a long-surviving, full-scale St. John's-derived curriculum. While St. John's is, however, strictly secular, Thomas Aquinas College is an orthodox Catholic school that puts a theology tutorial at its center. Many programs on a smaller scale have come and gone. A large number of St. John's style seminars for executives, professionals, and the general public are mounted or advised by the college.

allowed to avoid harsh but necessary learning matter. The teachers are chosen above all for their capacity to learn and teach with intelligence and imagination in all parts of the program. Publication is not a criterion for tenure. Since tutors are eventually acquainted with all parts of the program they are competent to judge curricular revisions, which are continual.

The chief issues facing St. John's College in the twenty-first century, are, besides the funding problems common to all small colleges, these: The intellectual renewal of a faculty continually learning beyond the limits of its professional preparation; the integration of the scientific advances of the late last century, for example in scientific computer applications and biology, into the curriculum; and the college's role in justifying liberal education to an increasingly vocation-driven educational world.[7] Meanwhile, St. John's is the sad beneficiary of the lack of definition and the precipitous decline of the liberal arts in American higher education, as shown in rising admission figures and retention rates at the college.

SELECTION[8]

St. John's College is a community dedicated to liberal education. Liberally educated human beings, the college believes, acquire a lifelong commitment to the pursuit of fundamental knowledge and to the search for unifying ideas. They are intelligently and critically appreciative of their common heritage and conscious of their social and moral obligations. They are well equipped to master the specific skills of any calling, and they possess the means and the will to become free and responsible citizens.

St. John's College is persuaded that a genuine liberal education requires the study of great books—texts of words, symbols, notes, and pictures—because they express most originally and often most perfectly the ideas by which contemporary life is knowingly or unknowingly governed. These books are the most important teachers. They are both timeless and timely; they illuminate the persisting questions of human existence, and they bear directly on the problems we face today. Their authors can speak to us almost as freshly as when they spoke for the first time, for what they have to tell us is not of merely academic concern or remote from our true interests. They change our minds, move our hearts, and touch our spirits.

The books speak to us in more than one way. In raising the persisting human questions, they lend themselves to different interpretations that reveal a variety of independent and yet complementary meanings. And while seeking the truth, they please us as works of art with a clarity and a beauty that reflect their intrinsic intelligibility. They are, therefore, properly called great, whether they are epic poems or political treatises, and whether their subject matter is scientific, historical, or philosophical. They are also linked together, for each of them is introduced, supported, or criticized by the others. In that sense they converse with each other. They draw the readers to take part, within the limits of their abilities, in a large and continuing conversation.[9]

---

7. See Eva T. H. Brann, "The American College as *the* Place for Liberal Learning," *Daedalus* (Winter 1999): 151–71.

8. St. John's College, "Statement of the St. John's Program, 2007–2008" (Annapolis, MD; Santa Fe, NM: St. John's College, 2007). This document serves as the catalog of St. John's College, and is reprinted by permission of St. John's College. The introduction is adapted from an unpublished typescript by Eva T. H. Brann (1929–), who earned a B.A. (1950) from Brooklyn College in history, an M.A. (1951) from Yale University in Classics, and a Ph.D. (1956) from Yale in archaeology. She joined the St. John's faculty as a Tutor in 1957, served as Dean from 1990 to 1997, and became a Tutor once again.

9. Martha Nussbaum's criticizes the idea of "great books" in the fourth point of "Socratic Liberal Education" in selection #67.

This conversation, however, is unavoidably one-sided. The great books can only repeat what they have to say, without furnishing the clarifications that we desire. To remedy this defect is the goal of the St. John's seminar. Here a number of students of varied backgrounds, faced with a text that may present unfamiliar thoughts, attempt to discuss it reasonably. It is presupposed that the students are willing to submit their opinions to one another's questions. The demands of the individual and those of the group are in continuous interplay, setting limits within which the discussion moves with the utmost possible freedom. The discussion may concern itself primarily with trying to establish the meaning of a poem or the validity of an argument. On the other hand, it may concern itself with more general or with very contemporary questions that thrust themselves forward. The students bring to the seminar the assumptions they have derived from their experience in the contemporary world. Through discussion they acquire a new perspective, which enables them to recognize both the sameness of a recurrent problem and the variety of its historical manifestations.

Principally, however, the aim is to ascertain not how things were, but how things are—to help the students make reasonable decisions in whatever circumstances they face. And it is the ultimate aim of the program that the habits of thought and discussion thus begun by the students should continue with them throughout their lives.[10]

Most of the teaching at St. John's takes the form of a discussion. The conversational methods of the seminar are carried over into the tutorials. As much as possible, the actual instruction in all classes and laboratories is made to depend on the activity and initiative of the students. The tutors function as guides, more intent on listening to the students and working with them than imposing upon them their own understandings.

St. John's seeks to restore the true meaning of a liberal arts education. The primary function of the liberal arts has always been to bring about an awareness of the forms that are embodied in combinations of words and in numbers so that they become means of understanding. Traditionally, the liberal arts were seven in number: grammar, rhetoric, logic—the arts of language; and arithmetic, geometry, music, and astronomy—the arts of mathematics. In more contemporary terms, the liberal arts bring to light what is involved in the use of words and numbers in all kinds of discursive thought, in analyzing, speaking, and writing, and also in measuring, deducing, and demonstrating.[11]

There are many ways to develop these arts. The curriculum emphasizes six of them: discussion, translation, writing, experiment, mathematical demonstration, and musical analysis. Whatever methods are used, they all serve the same end: to invite the students to think freely for themselves. By these means, students will be able to envisage actual situations, to deliberate by articulating clear alternatives with the hope of arriving at a proper choice. The acquisition of these intellectual skills will serve the students who have learned them throughout their lives.

Knowledge advances and the fundamental outlook of humanity may change over the centuries, but these arts of understanding remain in one form or another indispensable. They enable men and women to win knowledge of the world around them and knowledge of the themselves in this world and to use that knowledge with wisdom. Under their guidance, men and women can free themselves from the wantonness of prejudice and the narrowness of beaten paths. Under their discipline, men and women can acquire the habit of listening to reason. A genuinely conceived liberal arts curriculum cannot avoid aiming at the most far-reaching of all human goals.

---

10. Is it also presumed that not only these habits, but the content of the "great books" provides insight into "how things are" today?

11. Has this always been "the primary function of the liberal arts?"

The Seminar

The heart of the curriculum is the seminar—a discussion of assigned readings from the books of the program. In each seminar seventeen to twenty-one students work with two members of the faculty who serve as leaders. The group meets twice a week, on Monday and Thursday evenings, *for two hours*—or sometimes *longer* if the topic under discussion has aroused a sustained and lively conversation. The assignment for each seminar amounts, on the average, to around eighty pages of reading, but may be much shorter if the text happens to be particularly difficult.

The seminar begins with a question asked by one of the leaders. Thereafter the seminar consists mostly of student discussion. Students talk with one another, not just to the leaders. They do not raise their hands for permission to be heard, but enter the discussion or withdraw from it at will. The resulting informality is tempered by the use of formal modes of address. Once underway, the seminar may take many forms. It may range from the most particular to the most general. The reading of Thucydides, for example, is almost certain to elicit a discussion of war and aggression and to bring to the surface the students' opinions and fears about the wisdom or error of national policies. Homer and Dante prompt reflections on human virtues and vices and on humanity's ultimate fate. Sometimes a seminar will devote all its time to an interpretation of the assigned reading, staying close to the text; at other times the talk may range widely over topics suggested by the reading, but bearing only indirectly on the text itself in the minds of the participants. In the coffee shop after seminar, students from different groups compare the points made in their discussions.

Except for the requirements of common courtesy, there are only two rules: first, all opinions must be heard and explored, however sharply they may clash; second, every opinion must be supported by argument—an unsupported opinion does not count.[12] In a freshman seminar the students may tend to express their opinions with little regard for their relevance to the question or their relation to the opinions of others. Gradually, in their interplay with one another, the students learn to proceed with care, keeping to the topic and trying to uncover the meanings of the terms they use. They learn, gradually also, that to some extent the procedure of the seminar varies with the kind of reading under study; poetry is not philosophy, and it can require a different approach. Such progress in learning together may be crowned by sudden insights on the part of a few of the seminar members, or by occasions when the seminar as a whole achieves illumination.

The course of the discussion cannot be fixed in advance; it is determined rather by the necessity of "following the argument," of facing the crucial issues, or of seeking foundations upon which a train of reasoning can be pursued. The argument does not necessarily lead to the answer to a question. More often than not the question remains open with certain alternatives clearly outlined. The progress of the seminar is not particularly smooth; the discussion may sometimes branch off and entangle itself in irrelevant difficulties. Only gradually can the logical rigor of an argument emerge within the sequence of analogies and other imaginative devices by which the discussion is kept alive. A seminar may also degenerate into rather empty talk, without being able for some time to extricate itself from such a course. At its best, the seminar may reach insights far beyond the initial views held by any of its members.

Under these circumstances, the primary role of the leaders is not to give information, nor is it to produce the "right" opinion or interpretation. It is to guide the discussion, to keep it moving, to raise objections and to help the students in every way possible to understand the author, the issues and themselves. The most useful instrument for this purpose is the question; perhaps the most useful de-

---

12. Compare Martha Nussbaum's description of a Socratic "community that can genuinely reason together about a problem" in selection #67.

vice of all is the question "Why?" But the leaders may also take a definite and positive stand and enter directly into the argument. If they do so, however, they can expect no special consideration. Reason is the only recognized authority. Consequently, all opinions must be defended with reason, and any single opinion can prevail only by general consent. The aim is always to develop the students' powers of reason and understanding, and to help them arrive at intelligent opinions of their own. Every freshman, sophomore, and junior submits an essay on some theme suggested by the seminar readings . . . The essay is not a research paper with extensive footnotes and a bibliography, but rather an attempt on the part of the students to set out in writing, as clearly as they can, their own thoughts on some aspect of the liberal arts. . . .

The Tutorials

The seminar cannot suffice as the only setting for liberal education. By its very nature, the seminar does not give the students an opportunity to cultivate the habits of methodical and careful study and of persistently precise discussion and writing. Other learning devices must therefore support it; these are the tutorials in language, mathematics and music. For each of four years, a student attends one language and one mathematics tutorial three times a week. Sophomores also attend a music tutorial.

In the tutorials, around a table, about thirteen to sixteen students study and learn together under the direct guidance and instruction of a tutor. The tutorial provides conditions for a small group to work together toward a careful analysis, often through translation or demonstration, of an important work. As in the seminar, students talk freely with one another and with the tutor, but the discussion focuses sharply on assigned tasks. There are opportunities for all students to contribute their measure of instruction and insight to their fellows. Other tutors often attend, seeking to learn about a particular subject that they may later teach.[13] Writing assignments are normally made in all classes: mathematics, music, and laboratory sections, as well as in language tutorials. The students are thus called upon continually to articulate and organize their thinking in both the written and spoken forms.

The Language Tutorial

Specialization in higher education has led to a profound neglect of language skills. As country is separated from country by the barrier of language, so profession is separated from profession by technical jargon. Primarily, the language tutorial attempts to remedy this condition by training in the means of precise communication. In a broad sense, it may be thought of as a present-day restoration of the traditional studies of grammar, rhetoric, and logic. The tutorial seeks to foster an intelligent and active grasp of the relations between language on the one hand and thought and imagination of the other. To do this, it must direct attention to the fundamental ways in which words can be put together; to the modes of signifying things; to the varied connotations and ambiguities of terms; to the role of metaphors, analogies and images; and to the logical relations that connect propositions.

The study of foreign languages (Greek in the first and second years, and French in the third and fourth years) provides an effective means to these ends. By studying these languages, by translating from them into English, and by comparing them with each other and with English, the students learn something of the nature of languages in general and of their own in particular. During the four years, then, they study language as the discourse of reason, as the articulation of experience, and as the medium of the art of poetry; and both directly and indirectly, through the intermediary of foreign tongues, they study their own language. They discover the resources of articulate speech and learn the

---

13. Note that faculty attend as learners in the tutorials for students.

rules that must govern it if it is to be clear, consistent and effective—if it is to be adequate and persuasive. . . .

The Mathematics Tutorial

Mathematics is a vital part of education; that this is true or ought to be is suggested by the word itself, for it is derived from a Greek word meaning "to learn."[14] It is regrettable, then, that students should come to dislike mathematics or to think of themselves as unmathematical. It is equally regrettable that competent mathematicians are often unaware of the philosophical assumptions upon which mathematical equations and formulas are based.[15] Mathematics at St. John's is studied as a liberal art, not artificially separated from what have come to be called the humanities. When mathematics is taught at an unhurried pace in an atmosphere of reflective inquiry, and from treatises chosen not only for their matter but also for their elegance and imagination, as it is at St. John's, mathematics becomes not only the most readily learnable liberal art but also one that provides ready access to others and significant analogies with them.

There are two main reasons for studying mathematics. First, it pervades our modern world, perhaps even defines it. Therefore anyone who means to criticize or reform, to resist or cooperate with this world, not only must have some familiarity with the mathematical methods by which it is managed, but also must have thought about the assumptions that underlie their application. It is the task of the mathematics tutorial and the laboratory together to help students to think about what it means to count and measure things in the universe. The second main reason for studying mathematics concerns the mathematics tutorial more specifically. Since mathematics has, as its name implies, a particularly close connection with the human capacity for learning,[16] its study is especially useful in helping students to think about what it means to come to know something.[17]

To prepare themselves for such reflection, students study artfully composed mathematical treatises, demonstrate propositions at the blackboard, and solve problems. By doing this over four years, they learn a good deal of mathematics and they gain noticeably in rigor of thought, nimbleness of imagination, and elegance of expression. But while they are practicing the art of mathematics in all its rigor, they are continually encouraged to reflect on their own activity. Scores of questions, of which the following are examples, are raised during the four years:

Why and how do mathematical proofs carry such conviction? What is a mathematical system and what are its proper beginnings and ends? What is the relation of logic to mathematics? What do "better" and "worse," "ugly" and "beautiful" signify in mathematics? Do mathematical symbols constitute a language? Are there "mathematical objects"? How might the discoverer of a particular theorem have come to see it? By means of such questions, which grow out of the daily work and which excite the intellect and the imagination at the same time, a discussion is initiated in the mathematics tutorial that is easily and often carried over into the larger sphere of the seminar. . . .

---

14. Compare Isidore of Seville (bk. III) in selection #11; Hugh of St. Victor (bk. II, ch. 3) in selection #15.

15. Compare the point of Mary Louise Pratt below that "it proved extremely difficult to communicate the [curricular] issues to [scientists]" in the debate at Stanford University.

16. See Plato's comment (526b) on this point in selection #1.

17. Compare these two reasons with those found in the selections by Plato, Augustine, Cassiodorus, Isidore, Hugh of St. Victor, and Pier Paolo Vergerio.

The Music Tutorial

One of the aims of the St. John's program has been to restore music as a liberal art to the curriculum. The study of music at St. John's is not directed toward performance, but toward an understanding of the phenomena of music. The ancients accorded music a place among the liberal arts because they understood it as one of the essential functions of the mind, associated with the mind's power to grasp number and measure. The liberal art of music was based, for them, on the ratios among whole numbers.

In particular, the music program at St. John's aims at the understanding of music through close study of musical theory and analysis of words of musical literature. In the freshman year, students meet once a week to study the fundamentals of melody and its notation. Demonstration takes place primarily by singing, and by the second semester the students perform some great choral works. In the sophomore year, a tutorial meets three times a week. Besides continuing the singing, the music tutorial reflects two different but complementary aspects of music. On the one hand, music is intimately related to language, rhetoric and poetry. On the other, it is a unique and self-sufficient art, which has its roots deep in nature.

The work of the tutorial includes an investigation of rhythm in words as well as in notes, a thorough investigation of the diatonic system, a study of the ratios of musical intervals, and a consideration of melody, counterpoint, and harmony. None of these are done apart from the sounding reality of good music. The inventions of Bach, the songs of Schubert, the masses of Palestrina, the operas of Mozart, and the instrumental works of Beethoven are the real textbooks. In the second semester, at least one major work is analyzed closely. . . .

The Laboratory

Three hundred years ago, algebra and the arts of analytic geometry were introduced into European thought, mainly by Rene Descartes.[18] This was one of the great intellectual revolutions in recorded history, paralleling and in part determining the other great revolutions in industry, politics, morals, and religion. It has redefined and transformed our whole natural and cultural world. It is a focal point of the St. John's program and one that the college takes special care to emphasize. There is scarcely an item in the curriculum that does not bear upon it. The last two years of the program exhibit the far-reaching changes that flow from it, and these could not be appreciated without the first two years, which cover the period from Homer to Descartes.

Modern mathematics has made possible the exploration of natural phenomena on an immense scale and has provided the basis for what is known to us as the laboratory. The intellectual tools of the laboratory are the consequence of the vast project of study conceived by the great thinkers of the seventeenth century. They are based on a mathematical interpretation of the universe, which transforms the universe into a great book written in mathematical characters.

Liberal learning is concerned with the artifices of the human mind and hand that help us to relate our experiences to our understanding. For this purpose, St. John's has set up a three-year laboratory in the natural sciences, wherein characteristic and related topics of physics, biology, and chemistry are pursued. There is the art of measurement, which involves the analytical study of the instruments of observation and measurement; crucial experiments are reproduced; the interplay of hypothesis, theory,

---

18. René Descartes (1596–1650), French philosopher and mathematician, developed a highly rationalistic philosophy that provided a bridge from scholastic to modern philosophy.

and facts has to be carefully scrutinized. All of this is supported by the mathematics tutorial, which provide the necessary understanding of mathematical techniques.

The task, however, is not to cover exhaustively the various scientific disciplines, to bring the student up to date in them, or to engage in specialized research. . . . The laboratory program is largely determined by three considerations relevant to the liberalization of the study of science: (1) The formally scheduled experimental work must be combined with a full and free discussion of the instruments and principles involved in it. (2) The content of the work should be so chosen as to enable the students to trace a scientific discipline to its roots in principle, assumption and observation. Thus certain integrated wholes of subject matters are to be selected as problems in which the roles of theory and experimentation can be distinguished through critical study. (3) The schedule of laboratory work should give opportunity for leisurely but intensive experimentation. The students must have time to satisfy themselves as to the degree of accuracy their instruments permit, to analyze procedures for sources of error, to consider alternative methods, and on occasion to repeat an entire experiment. Only thus can they come to a mature understanding of the sciences called "exact." . . .

The Formal Lecture

The curriculum as described so far calls for student participation at every active stage of the work. On Friday evenings, however, a different form of instruction occurs. The formal lecture is the occasion when the students have an opportunity to listen steadily and attentively. The subject may be closely connected with seminar readings or it may open up a new field of interest and test the student's readiness to absorb new information and to follow arguments in unfamiliar fields: in anthropology or space science, in painting or architecture. The lecturers are often visiting scholars, but not infrequently they are members of the St. John's faculty. Visitors may be from the academic world or from the arena of public affairs; they may be poets or artists. Sometimes a concert replaces a lecture.

The lecture is followed by a discussion. Here the lecturers submit themselves to prolonged questioning by the students, with the faculty participating. Often the discussion turns into a seminar. Thus the formal lecture serves two purposes: It inculcates in the students the habit of listening and following the exposition of a subject they may not be familiar with, and it also provides them an opportunity, in the discussion period, to exercise their dialectical skills in a setting very different from the classroom. It is here that they can test the degree of their understanding and the applicability of what they have learned. . . .

St. John's List of Great Books

The list of [c. 200] books that serves as the core of the curriculum had its beginnings at Columbia College, at the University of Chicago, and at the University of Virginia. Since 1937, it has been under continuous review at St. John's College. The distribution of the books over the four years is significant. More than two thousand years of intellectual history form the background of the first two years; about three hundred years of history form the background for almost twice as many authors in the last two years.

The first year is devoted to Greek authors and their pioneering understanding of the liberal arts; the second year ranges from the Hebrew Bible to the sixteenth century seeds of modernity; the third year has books of the seventeenth and eighteenth centuries, most of which were written in modern languages; the fourth year brings the reading into the nineteenth and twentieth centuries. The chronological order in which the books are read is primarily a matter of convenience and intelligibility; it does not imply a historical approach to the subject matter. The St. John's curriculum seeks to convey to students an understanding of the fundamental problems that human beings have to face today and at all times. It invites them to reflect both on their continuities and their discontinuities. The list of books that constitute the core of the St. John's program is subject to review by the Instruction Committee of the faculty.

[Authors and works include:]

Freshman Year. Homer, Aeschylus, Sophocles, Thucydides, Euripides, Herodotus, Aristophanes, Plato, Aristotle, Euclid, Lucretius, Plutarch, Nicomachus, Lavoisier, Harvey, Archimedes, Fahrenheit, Avogadro, Dalton, Cannizzaro, Virchow, Mariotte, Driesch, Gay-Lussac, Spemann, Stears, J. J. Thomson, Mendeleyev, Berthollet, J. L. Proust.

Sophomore Year. Hebrew Bible, New Testament, Aristotle, Apollonius, Virgil, Plutarch, Epictetus, Tacitus, Ptolemy, Plotinus, Augustine, St. Anselm, Aquinas, Dante, Chaucer, Machiavelli, Copernicus, Kepler, Rabelais, Palestrina, Montaigne, Viete, Bacon, Shakespeare, Marvell, Donne, Descartes, Pascal, Bach, Haydn, Mozart, Beethoven, Schubert, Monteverdi, Stravinsky.

Junior Year. Cervantes, Galileo, Hobbes, Descartes, Milton, La Rochefoucauld, La Fontaine, Pascal, Huygens, Eliot, Spinoza, Locke, Racine, Newton, Leibniz, Swift, Hume, Rousseau, Molière, Adam Smith, Kant, Mozart, Austen, Dedekind, Articles of Confederation, Declaration of Independence, U.S. Constitution, The Federalist Papers, Twain, Wordsworth, Young, Taylor, Euler, D. Bernoulli, Orsted, Ampère, Faraday, Maxwell.

Senior Year. U.S. Supreme Court opinions, Goethe, Darwin, Hegel, Lobachevsky, Tocqueville, Lincoln, Frederick Douglass, Kierkegaard, Wagner, Marx, Dostoevsky, Tolstoy, Melville, O'Connor, William James, Nietzsche, Freud, Baudelaire, Booker T. Washington, Du Bois, Husserl, Heidegger, Einstein, Millikan, Conrad, Faulkner, Flaubert, Woolf, Yeats, T. S. Eliot, Wallace Stevens, Rimbaud, Faraday, J. J. Thomson, Millikan, Minkowski, Rutherford, Davisson, Schrodinger, Bohr, DeBroglie, Heisenberg, Mendel, Boveri, Sutton, Morgan, Beadle and Tatum, Sussman, Watson and Crick, Jacob and Monod, Hardy.

66. Mary Louise Pratt, "The Western Culture Debate at Stanford" (1992)

INTRODUCTION

Though rarely adopted in full, the approach to general education requiring study of a canon of classical texts was strongly challenged toward the end of the twentieth century by the pluralistic counter-movement known as multiculturalism. Entering academic parlance in the 1980s, the term multiculturalism "acquired a vast range of significations. For example in the university milieu, multiculturalism is often presented . . . as both a liberal and liberatory movement in its inclusiveness of differences, be they social, ethnic, or sexual. In other more politically conservative quarters, the multiculturalist rhetoric is viewed with suspicion as a strategy to legitimate Affirmative Action policy."[19] In addition, multiculturalism challenged the premise that study in "the classics" of Western Civilization constitute the surest route to liberal education. According to this challenge, this canon and these classics represent partial and self-interested view points of culture and do not fully account for the developing, multi-dimensional, and organic nature of culture.[20]

The most prominent debate over the multiculturalist challenge to general education requirements of reading in the classics of Western Civilization occurred at Stanford University. Originally instituted in 1935,[21] Stanford's requirement that freshman study the history of Western Civilization was dropped in 1969, following the recommendations of a University Committee that "general education, as epitomized by . . . the Columbia two-year sequences in Humanities and Contemporary Civilization, is dead or dying." The committee called for "a new kind of general education" because "the University cannot in any event impress upon its students the total content of present knowledge, and it is impossible to choose what exactly it is that every student should know. . . ."[22]

The demise was short-lived. In 1980, in line with the reaction against the loosening of curricular requirements described by Gerald Grant and David Riesman in selection #64, Stanford restored a two-semester History of Western Civilization course, or "Western Civ," as it was commonly termed, and again required it for all incoming students. "Western Civ" rapidly encountered criticism that the course focused mostly on individuals and texts, that it was too Eurocentric in its outlook, finally, that it was restrictive in its approach to new scholarly research. In 1988, after an internal review and intensive debate, described below, the university dropped "Western Civ," switching instead to a new course called Culture, Ideas, Values (CIV). This switch attracted widespread attention in the academic and popular media.

At the time of the debate, Mary Louise Pratt (1948–), an associate professor of Spanish and Portuguese and Comparative Literature at Stanford, criticized the "Western Civ" course and published her views in an essay, from which selection #66 is drawn. A native of Canada, Pratt received her B.A. in Modern Languages and Literatures in 1970 from the University of Toronto, an M.A. in Linguistics in 1971 from the University of Illinois, and her Ph.D. in 1975 from Stanford in Comparative Literature. Currently, she is a Professor of Social and Cultural Analysis at New York University.

---

19. Jean-Francois Fourny and Marie-Paule Ha, "Introduction: The History of an Idea," in *Research in African Literatures: Multiculturalism* 28 (1997): 1, 1–7.

20. Lawrence Levine, *The Opening of the American Mind: Canons, Culture, and History* (Boston: Beacon Press, 1996), p. 160.

21. On the origins of Stanford's "History of Western Civilization" course, see the introduction to selection #55.

22. Steering Committee of the Study of Education at Stanford, *The Study of Education at Stanford* 10 vols. (Stanford, CA: Stanford University Press, 1968), as quoted in Levine, *The Opening of the American Mind*, p. 66. Compare the view of Charles Eliot in selection #47.

SELECTION[23]

The debate which took place at Stanford during the winter of 1988 and the resulting reform of the Western Culture requirement received a great deal of national attention, largely due to the involvement of then U.S. Secretary of Education William Bennett, who chose to use the Stanford case as a platform to advocate his views, quite literally making a federal case out of it. Perhaps because of Bennett's own partisanship, the account of the Stanford debate in the national press had a shape somewhat different from the local experience. As other institutions face similar struggles, fuller accounts of the workings of change at Stanford may be helpful. At the same time, there is an urgent need to formulate the concerns that so unexpectedly made freshman book lists an object of wide public concern. What nerves had been touched?

Histories of Western culture curricula in the United States point to the Western civilization course instituted at Columbia University in 1919 as a main antecedent for such courses all over the country. One recent account, however, notes that the Columbia course had a direct antecedent of its own, a War Issues course instituted in 1918 at various universities, including Columbia.[24] . . . Current struggles over Western culture curricula—both challenges to them and reactionary attempts to reassert them—also emerge from urgently felt national imperatives. Among these is an imperative to reimagine cultural and civic identity in the United States in the wake of vast changes produced by the decline of its global hegemony,[25] the rapid internationalization of capital and industry, the immigrant implosion of the "third world" onto the "first," and the democratization of American institutions and political processes that occurred in the two decades prior to 1980. The question can be posed in Pierre Bourdieu's sometimes helpful language: What is to count as "cultural capital" in a culturally plural nation and a globalized human world? How will that capital be constructed and deployed, how will people be asked to identify with it? How might the United States project itself into the future as a cultural and political entity? . . .

The world is full of multicultural, multi-ethnic, multilingual nations, so there are plenty of models around. Indeed, Bloom, Bennett, Bellow, and the rest (known by now in some quarters as the Killer B's) are advocating one of them: to create a narrowly specific cultural capital that will be the normative *referent* for everyone, but will remain the *property* of a small and powerful caste that is linguistically and ethnically unified.[26] It is this caste that is referred to by the "we" in Saul Bellow's astoun-

---

23. Excerpted from Mary Louise Pratt, "Humanities for the Future: Reflections on the Western Culture Debate at Stanford," *South Atlantic Quarterly* 89 (1990): 7–25. Reprinted by permission of Duke University Press.

24. See selection #54 by Daniel Bell; Gilbert Allardyce, "The Rise and Fall of the Western Civilization Course," *American Historical Review* 87 (1982): 695–743.

25. How might the decline (or rise) of this global hegemony be related to debates over general education courses in "Western Civ"?

26. At the time, William Bennett (1943–) was U.S. Secretary of Education and had recently written *To Reclaim a Legacy: A Report on the Humanities in Higher Education* (Washington, DC: National Endowment for the Humanities, 1984). Allan Bloom (1930–1992) was a professor at the University of Chicago who published *The Closing of the American Mind: How Higher Education Has Failed American Democracy and Impoverished the Souls of Today's Students* (New York: Simon and Schuster, 1987), which spent thirty-one weeks on *The New York Times* bestseller list and sold over 800,000 copies. Saul Bellow (1915–2005) was a noted author and professor at the University of Chicago who won the 1976 Nobel Prize for literature.

dingly racist remark that "when the Zulus have a Tolstoy, we will read him."[27] Few doubt that behind the Bennett-Bloom program is a desire to close not the American mind, but the American university, to all but a narrow and highly uniform elite with no commitment to either multiculturalism or educational democracy. Thus while the Killer B's (plus a C—Lynne Cheney, the Bennett mouthpiece now heading the National Endowment for the Humanities) depict themselves as returning to the orthodoxies of yesteryear, their project must not be reduced to nostalgia or conservatism. Neither of these explain the blanket contempt they express for the country's universities. They are fueled not by reverence for the past, but by an aggressive desire to lay hold of the present and future. The B's act as they do not because they are unaware of the cultural and demographic diversification underway in the country; they are utterly aware. That is what they are trying to shape; that is why they are seeking, and using, national offices and founding national foundations.

Many citizens are attracted to Bloom's and Bennett's pronouncements, on the other hand, out of fairly unreflected attachments to the past (including their own college experience), and simply have trouble seeing how good books could possibly do any harm. Many people are perfectly ready for change but remain deeply anxious about where it is all supposed to be heading. . . .

Stanford adopted its first Western civilization course in 1935, and, like many other universities, abolished it around 1970. Efforts to restore a requirement began around 1975 on the part of a group of senior faculty in literature, classics, and history. By 1978 a two-year pilot program had been approved and in 1980 a new year-long required course began for all incoming students. It consisted of several tracks corresponding roughly to different departments and schools, and sharing a core reading list that became the focus of the controversy. It is interesting to note that the notorious reading list was not part of the original proposal for the requirement. The list evolved during the pilot program out of desire to guarantee a "common intellectual experience," a phrase that acquired great importance in the subsequent debate without acquiring any greater specificity of meaning. . . .[28]

Participants in developing the course say that in its specifics the list was not intended to be written in stone. It represented a series of compromises rather painfully hammered out by a committee, inevitably through some of the crudest kind of horse-trading—Catholics for Protestants, poets for scientists, Italians for Germans. In the end, ironically, the difficulty of negotiating the list was one source of its permanence: the process had been so painful and so lacking in intellectual integrity that no one expressed the slightest desire to repeat it.

In any case, regardless of its specific content, the list did the job of shaping the requirement in, for many people, unnecessarily narrow ways. Indeed, its extreme narrowness clearly contributed to the breakdown of the program at Stanford. Most conspicuously, the list installed a specific historical paradigm: one quarter for ancient world, one for medieval-renaissance, and one for the past five hundred years. Implicit in the sequence was the canonical narrative of origins deriving the present from clas-

---

27. By Pratt's account, Bellow's words deny the existence of such a literary masterpiece and associate him with "a small and powerful caste that is linguistically and ethnically unified." Bellow's comment is more reliably reported to have been: "Who is the Tolstoy of the Zulus? The Proust of the Papuans? I'd be glad to read him." Wil Haygood, "In Pursuit of Saul Bellow," *Boston Globe* (16 Nov. 2000): D5. To what extent do scholars on both sides of the debate adhere to rigorous standards of scholarship in evidencing and arguing their views in this debate over multicultural liberal education?

28. The much-discussed list included these authors or works: *Ancient World.* Required: Hebrew Bible, Plato, Homer, a Greek tragedy, New Testament. Recommended: Thucydides, Aristotle, Cicero, Virgil, Tacitus. *Medieval and Renaissance.* Required: Augustine, Dante, More, Machiavelli, Luther, Galileo. Recommended: Boethius, Aquinas, Shakespeare, Cervantes, Descartes, Hobbes, Locke. *Modern.* Required: Voltaire, Marx and Engels, Freud, Darwin. Recommended: Rousseau, Hume, Goethe, nineteenth-century novel, Mill, Nietzsche.

sical Greece via the Italian Renaissance and the Franco-German Enlightenment, a narrative that begins and ends with European lettered high culture. (Where is America?) Clearly, teachers of the course could question that implicit narrative, and some did. But to do so in a consistent or structured way involved teaching against the grain of the syllabus, an extremely difficult pedagogical task that often confused students more than it empowered them.

Second, the list not only lays down a Eurocentric paradigm, but also embodies a very restricted sense of Europe. France and even England are barely represented in the required readings; Iberia, Eastern Europe, and Scandinavia not at all. Only "high" culture is represented, an exclusion that has long been under challenge not just by the Black Students' Union, but by whole schools of mainstream literary and historical scholarship. One thinks of the scholars at Princeton's Center for European Studies, or the Berkeley-based new historicism, movements that are in no way radical or critical of the West, but which refuse to give "high" culture or belles lettres a monopoly on cultural understanding. Many Stanford scholars were troubled by the fact that the course organized itself around authors and orthodoxies rather than around problematics or issues, and that it therefore took as orthodoxies matters that were actually under serious debate in their fields. . . .[29]

Third, the list implicitly suggests a monumentalist attitude to the texts as great works whose interest and value were *sui generis*.[30] Again, teachers were of course not forbidden to adopt a critical attitude, but to do so required teaching from the negative position of a counter-discourse or a heresy. What you couldn't do was embark positively on a different project or way of thinking, even one that was equally celebratory and equally Eurocentric. An attempt was made to set up a critical track, a course titled "Conflict and Change in Western Culture." In many ways this course was extremely successful, but its founders were constantly hampered by the structure of center and periphery into which they were locked. To bring in other texts was always to bring in "Other" texts. In the end, this structure of otherness comprises, depending on your perspective, the main *obstacle* or the main *bulwark against* relational approaches to culture. "The notion of a core list," argued one teacher in the history track, "is inherently flawed, regardless of what kinds of works it includes or excludes. It is flawed because such a list undermines the critical stance that we wish students to make toward the materials they read. . . . A course with such readings creates two sets of books, those privileged by being on the list and those not worthy of inclusion. Regardless of the good intentions of those who create such lists, the students have not viewed and will not view these separate categories as equal. . . ."[31]

Many critics felt that the Western culture program set a tone for the humanities as a whole at Stanford, in the words of one Latin Americanist, making "second-class citizens out of faculty whose work focuses on non-European literatures, on noncanonical writers, on European literatures not included in the core, or on the West in dialogue with other parts of the world." In terms of faculty, in the

---

29. Might the intellectual critiques of a core list of readings represent the professional and departmental interests of academic disciplinarians?

30. Compare the definition of a great book by Eva Brann in the introduction to selection #65.

31. In a review of the volume in which Pratt's article was reprinted, John Searle criticized this reasoning that the canonical readings of "Western Civ" are inappropriate because they are "monumentalist" and "privileged," because this view "would argue against any set of required readings whatever; indeed, any list you care to make about anything automatically creates two categories, those that are on the list and those that are not." However, "it is not the aim of education to provide a representation or sample of everything that has been thought and written, but to give students access to works of high quality. . . . [E]ducation is by its very nature 'elitist' and 'hierarchical' because it is designed to enable and encourage the student to discriminate between . . . what is intelligent and what is stupid, what is true and what is false." John Searle, "The Storm Over the University," *New York Review of Books* (6 Dec. 1990): 34–9, 42. How would Pratt respond?

years the Western culture program was in place, classics outgrew all the departments of modern languages and literatures; a Europeanist comparative literature department was founded; the English department continued to boast four medievalists while African, African-American, and Caribbean literatures in English were represented by a single half-time faculty member (whose tenure was hotly contested), and so-called "Commonwealth" literature not at all. The curriculum in French continued to include not a single course in Franco-African or even Quebecois literature. The number of Chicano faculty remained the same in 1988 as it was in 1972. . . .

The chronology of the reform process ran roughly as follows:

1. In the spring of 1986 the dean of undergraduate studies, a European historian and the first woman to hold the position, appointed a task force to review the Western culture requirement and produce recommendations for the faculty senate's Committee on Undergraduate Studies. . . .

2. Throughout the 1986–87 academic year the task force met regularly, speaking with all the relevant parties and anyone else who wished to address them. In the spring of 1987 they released an interim report calling for a reconception and restructuring of the requirement. This trial balloon provoked a great deal of discussion and response that was quite polarized.

3. In the late autumn of 1987, believing it had the support of all relevant parties, the task force released a revised report and recommendations to the Committee on Undergraduate Studies. . . . The report recommended a modified requirement called Culture/Ideas/Values (CIV) structured around a series of ground rules rather than a core list. Four instructional objectives were proposed which can be summarized as follows: increasing understanding of cultural diversity and interaction within the United States and elsewhere; engaging students with works that have intellectual importance "by virtue of the ideas they express, their mode of expression, or their influence"; developing critical thinking; and increasing skills in reading, reasoning, arguing, and analyzing texts. Requirements for social, geographical, and historical diversity would mean courses designed to "confront issues relating to class, ethnicity, race, religion, gender, and sexual orientation; to include the study of works by women, minorities, and persons of color"; to study works from at least one European and at least one non-European culture in their own historical and cultural context; and to involve at least six to eight centuries of historical depth.

4. In January of 1988 the new recommendations headed for the floor of the faculty senate with committee approval. At this juncture, opponents of the reform surprised many by introducing counter-legislation which retained the status quo but added one woman and one black writer to the core list for the third quarter of the course. This polarizing move set the stage for the debate that went on through the winter and into the spring. . . .

It would be absurd to summarize the untold hours of meetings, statement writing and reading, corridor talk, cynical maneuvering, and brutal negotiating sessions that followed. . . .

[Against the reform]: Education is an exercise of modesty, a process whereby we give up some of ourselves to gain an understanding of that which is not ourselves, an understanding of things still shaping us. It's a kind of surrender; we learn that some things are superior in consequence to us, even to our particular gender, to our particular ethnic heritage, to all the parochialisms to which we are subject. Then the apparent foreignness of the past, its record of people seemingly *unlike* ourselves, becomes much less foreign and those people much less strange and irrelevant.

[For the reform]: The famous texts of the past cannot continue to live for us if we simply place them on a pedestal and teach our students to worship them. Only if we see them as engaged with the stuff of history, both of the times in which they were written and of those later times, can we give a continuing life to these texts and to our cultural tradition as a whole. Only if we understand how the idea of a Western culture took shape in differing ways over the centuries and how it defined itself in relation to other forms of culture, can we justify giving it the prime consideration. . . . to our students.[32]

[Against the reform]: As a historian of the United States I would be the last person to deny the ethnic, racial, and cultural complexity of American society. But, from the same perspective, I find it puzzling, if not troubling, to learn that some of the dominant and influential ideas in modern America are to be seen [in the new legislation] as originating outside the West. Few historians of the United States believe that the culture of this country has been seriously influenced by ideas from Africa, China, Japan or indigenous North America. . . . There is no direct connection between the dominant ideas and institutions in American culture and the cultures of Africa or Eastern Asia. [The roots of American culture], if one is talking about ideas and institutions, are derived overwhelmingly from Europe. To contend otherwise, I think would cause American historians to scratch their heads in amazement.

[For the reform]: A "liberal education" for our time should expand beyond the culture-bound, basically colonialist, horizon that relies, albeit subtly, on the myth of the cultural superiority of the "West" (an ill-defined entity, in any event, whose borders are ludicrously artificial). . . . Does the new, integrated vision of Area One entail our teaching the Greek Hermes and Prometheus alongside the North American Indian Coyote or the East African Anansi and Legba as paradigms of trickster heroes, or Japanese Noh alongside Greek drama or Indian philosophy alongside Plato? If the answer is yes, so much the better.

[For the reform]: I was never taught in Western Culture the fact that the Khemetic or "Egyptian" Book of the Dead contained many of the dialectic principles attributed to Greece, but was written three thousand years earlier, or the fact that Socrates, Herodotus, Pythagoras, and Solon studied in Egypt and acknowledged that much of their knowledge of astronomy, geometry, medicine, and building came from the African civilizations in and around Egypt. . . . I was never told that algebra came from Moslem Arabs, or numbers from India. I was never informed when it was found that the "very dark and wooly haired" Moors in Spain preserved, expanded, and reintroduced the classical knowledge that the Greeks had collected, which led to the "renaissance." . . . I read the Bible without knowing St. Augustine looked black like me, that the Ten Commandments were almost direct copies from the 147 negative confessions of Egyptian initiates, or that many of the words of Solomon came from the black pharaoh Amen-En-Eope. I didn't learn that Toussaint L'Ouverture's defeat of Napoleon in Haiti directly influenced the French Revolution or that the Iroquois Indians in America had a representative democracy which served as a model for the American system. . . ."[33]

In the end, the reform legislation was passed, with some substantial amendments. One, for instance, required courses to "include treatment of ancient and medieval cultures"; another required faculty teaching in the program to agree each spring on a set of "common elements" which all tracks would share the following year. The latter amendment, which finally broke the deadlock, is a very big loophole. It leaves open the unlikely possibility of faculty agreeing to restore the entire core list, or of the whole battle being fought over in miniature every spring. At the moment, it seems more likely that the parties will learn to understand each other better through this compulsory conversation.

---

32. On this point, Barbara Herrnstein Smith agrees that canons are determined by standards based upon a particular time and cultural setting. A canon therefore needs to be "refreshed" in order to "represent the changing nature of culture, beliefs and values" and "reflect the best quality that a canon should by rights contain." "Introduction: The Public, the Press, and the Professors," in *The Politics of Liberal Education*, ed. Darryl J. Gless and Barbara Herrnstein Smith (Durham: Duke University Press, 1992), pp. 1–11.

33. Some of these asserted facts are disputed, to say the least.

The actual consequences of the reform remain uncertain, however. With only minor alterations, the standard Great Books course can continue to exist at Stanford, and nobody is being required to reeducate him or herself. You can certainly talk about gender without challenging sexism, or race without challenging racism, or class without challenging classicism. On the other hand, a space has been made for much greater change by those who desire it. Tracks constructed around other understandings of culture and broader perspectives on the West are now possible. Their existence and survival depends, however, on the presence of sufficient faculty to teach them, and the hiring and tenuring of such faculty is not possible without the acquiescence of those who opposed the reform. It is no accident that the final amendment passed by the senate deleted a phrase calling for the recruitment of minority faculty to teach in the new program. In the larger national picture, it seems fair to say that the new program puts Stanford in the vanguard of the rear guard, for other schools have long since left our modest reform behind. . . .

The final amendments-to-the-amendments on the Stanford reform were resolved in the last week of May 1988. In the days that followed, a series of local events suggested with unexpected clarity the need for the experiment Stanford had embarked on. A student was expelled from his dormitory after a year of disruptive activity directed especially toward a gay resident assistant, culminating in an assault on the resident and the vandalizing of the dormitory lounge. The following evening, ten fraternity brothers, in defense of the expelled student's freedom of speech, staged a silent vigil at midnight outside the dormitory lounge wearing masks and carrying candles, a gesture that seemed to deliberately invoke the customs of the Ku Klux Klan. The reactions of black students who assembled at the site ranged from terror to outrage, and the action was treated by the university as a serious racial and homophobic incident. The ten demonstrators, however, claimed complete ignorance of the associations their vigil invoked. They did not know, they said, that masks and candles at midnight had any connotations – it is just what they thought a vigil was. The following day a group of sorority women, as part of a rush ritual, performed a mock "Indian dance" around a fountain which happened to stand in the doorway of the native American student center. Asked to stop, they refused, later saying they did not intent to offend, or see the dance as offensive. It was just a tradition.

Many people did not believe these students' pleas of ignorance. But either way, the call for educational change was reinforced. If it is possible for young adults to leave the American educational system ignorant of the history of race relations in the United States (not part of standard Western culture curricula), then something needs to change. And if a person who knows the history of race relations and their symbolizations feels free to reenact racist rituals of mockery or intimidation, something needs to change. At the same time, blame must be placed where it belongs. In pleading ignorance, the students were following the example of many of the country's own leaders, for whom ignorance had become an acceptable standard of public life. Throughout their high school and college years these students had looked to a president who consistently showed himself to be both ignorant and utterly comfortable with his ignorance. (The Stanford incidents coincided with (president Ronald Reagan's extraordinary remarks in Moscow about the "coddling" of Native Americans.) For many of us exhausted by conflict that spring, these discouraging incidents reminded us of what we were fighting for. . . .

67. Martha C. Nussbaum, *A Classical Defense of Reform in Liberal Education* (1997)

INTRODUCTION

Martha Craven (1947-) was born in New York city where her father was a lawyer and her mother a homemaker. After attending Wellesley College for two years, she completed the B.A. at New York University in 1969, and married Alan J. Nussbaum, whom she later divorced. Moving to Harvard University to pursue a doctorate in philosophy, she became in 1972 the first woman to be awarded a Junior Fellowship, the most prestigious award given by Harvard to graduate students or junior scholars. Upon receiving her Ph.D. in philosophy in 1975, Nussbaum began to teach in Harvard's philosophy department and continued until 1983. At that point, she became professor of philosophy, classics, and comparative literature at Brown University and in 1995 moved to the University of Chicago, where she is now Ernst Freund Professor of Law and Ethics at the Law School, with affiliations in the programs of philosophy, classics, gender, and Southern Asia, as well as in the Divinity School. As suggested by the last two academic appointments, Nussbaum has learnedly addressed a broad spectrum of topics in more than ten books, plus an equal number that she has edited.

Selection #67 is drawn from *Cultivating Humanity: A Classical Defense of Reform in Liberal Education* (1997), which was awarded the Frederic W. Ness Prize for 1999 by the Association of American Colleges and Universities. This book draws both upon her experience as a Phi Beta Kappa Visiting Lecturer in which she "visited ten campuses for three days each, in each case teaching three or four undergraduate classes as well as giving public lectures to students and faculty and holding many informal office hours." (p. ix) These two different kinds of sources inform the thesis of her book that "the ancient debate between Socrates and his enemies is of value for our present educational controversies" concerning liberal education.

SELECTION[34]

Socratic Self-Examination

The Old Education, in Aristophanes's portrait, acculturated young citizens to traditional values.[35] They learned to internalize and to love their traditions, and they were discouraged from questioning them. As Aristophanes sees it, the most dangerous opponent of this Old Education is Socrates, whose questions subvert the authority of tradition, who recognizes no authority but that of reason, asking even the gods to give a reasoned account of their preferences and commands. Socrates's "Think-Academy" is depicted as a source of civic corruption, where young people learn to justify beating their parents. [Aristophanes's] fictional attack fed a real suspicion of the Socratic way of life. Athenian leaders, unsettled at the idea that young people would search for arguments to justify their beliefs rather than simply following parents and civic authorities, blamed Socrates for the cultural disharmony they sensed around them. Charged with corrupting the young, he eventually forfeited his life.

The ancient debate between Socrates and his enemies is of value for our present educational controversies. Like Socrates, our colleges and universities are being charged with corruption of the

---

34. Martha C. Nussbaum, *Cultivating Humanity: A Classical Defense of Reform in Liberal Education* (Cambridge, MA: Harvard University Press, 1997), pp. 1–42. Reprinted by permission of the President and Fellows of Harvard College.

35. In *Clouds* the Athenian dramatist Aristophanes (c. 446–c. 386 B.C.) presented an account of the Old Education as part of a satirical portrayal of Socrates.

young. Seeing young people emerge from modern "Think-Academies" with many challenges to traditional thinking—about women, about race, about social justice, about patriotism—social conservatives of many kinds have suggested that these universities are homes for the corrupt thinking of a radical elite whose ultimate aim is the subversion of the social fabric.[36] Once again an education that promotes acculturation to the time-honored traditions of "Western Civilization" is being defended against a more Socratic education that insists on teaching students to think for themselves. At institutions of the most varied sorts, students are indeed asking questions and challenging the authority of tradition. . . .

In colleges and universities around the country, students are following Socrates, questioning their views to discover how far they survive the test of argument. Although Socratic procedures have been familiar for a long time in basic philosophy courses, philosophy is now reaching a far larger number of students than it did fifty years ago, students of all classes and backgrounds and religious origins. A philosophy, which at one time was taught as a remote and abstract discipline, is increasingly being linked to the analysis and criticism of current events and ideas.[37] Instead of learning logical analysis in a vacuum, students now learn to dissect the arguments they find in newspapers, to argue about current controversies in medicine and law and sports, to think critically about the foundations of their political and even religious views.

To parents in contemporary America, as to parents in the time of Socrates, such developments can appear very unsettling. Argument seems like a cold strange invader into the habits of the home. . . . The Socratic emphasis on reason seems not only subversive but also cold. To kind and affectionate people, it can seem insulting to demand an argument for some political belief that they have long held and have taught to their children. It can appear that their cherished traditions must now undergo scrutiny from the point of view of an elite intellectual world that is strange to them. It is not surprising that the proliferation of "applied ethics" courses, and of philosophy generally, in our colleges and universities should alarm many parents.

Tradition is one foe of Socratic reason. But Socrates has other enemies as well. His values are assailed by the left as well as by the right. It is fashionable today in progressive intellectual circles to say that rational argument is a male Western device, in its very nature subversive to the equality of women and minorities and non-Western people. Socratic argument is suspected, here again, of being arrogant and elitist—but in this case the elitism is seen as that of a dominant Western intellectual tradition that has persistently marginalized outsiders. The very pretense that one is engaged in the disinterested pursuit of true can be a handy screen for prejudice. Such critics would look askance [at minority students studying Western philosophy]: as powerless, marginalized people, they are allowing themselves to be co-opted by the dominant liberal tradition when they devote their energies to rational argument in the Socratic tradition.

But Socrates's opponents on the left make the same error, as do his conservative opponents, when they suppose that argument is subversive of democratic values. Socratic argument is not undemocratic. Nor is it subversive of the just claims of excluded people. In fact, as Socrates knew, it is essential to a strong democracy and to any lasting pursuit of justice. In order to foster a democracy that is reflective and deliberative, rather than simply a marketplace of competing interest groups, a democracy

---

36. Nussbaum cites Roger Kimball, *The Tenured Radicals* (New York: Harper and Row, 1990).

37. In the middle of the twentieth century, the teaching of ethics and the consideration of social issues and human behavior were given little attention by philosophy departments, due to their engagement in decontextualized logical analysis. This was also a time when enrollments in philosophy declined dramatically. See Douglas Sloan, "The Teaching of Ethics in the American Undergraduate Curriculum, 1876–1976," in *Ethics Teaching in Higher Education*, ed. Daniel Callahan and Sissela Bok (New York: Plenum, 1980), pp. 1–60.

that genuinely takes thought for the common good, we must produce citizens who have the Socratic capacity to reason about their beliefs. It is not good for democracy when people vote on the basis of sentiments that they have absorbed from talk-radio and have never questioned. This failure to think critically produces a democracy in which people talk at one another but never have a genuine dialogue. In such an atmosphere bad arguments pass for good arguments, and prejudice can all too easily masquerade as reason. To unmask prejudice and to secure justice, we need argument, an essential tool of civic freedom.

Liberal education in our colleges and universities is, and should be, Socratic, committed to the activation of each student's independent mind and to the production of a community that can genuinely reason together about a problem, not simply trade claims and counterclaims.[38] Despite our allegiances to families and traditions, despite our diverse interests in correcting injustices to groups within our nation, we can and should reason together in a Socratic way, and our campuses should prepare us to do so. By looking at this goal of a community of reason as it emerges in the thought of Socrates and the Greek Stoics, we can show its dignity and its importance for democratic self-government. Connecting this idea to the teaching of philosophy in undergraduate courses of many sorts, we shall see that it is not Socratic education, but its absence, that would be fatal to the health of our society. . . . The distinctive contribution of Socrates was to bring sustained unrelenting philosophical argument to bear on these issues of communal concern—as Cicero later put it, bringing philosophy from the heavens down to earth.[39] His activity did not please everyone who encountered it.

Socrates walks up to a leading politician—a person who "seems knowing and clever to many people, and especially to himself."[40] He engages him in questioning about his alleged expertise, asking him no doubt, as Socrates does so often, for a coherent contradiction-free account of some central legal and political concepts, concepts such as equality, justice, and law. The expert proves unable to answer Socrates's questions in a satisfactory way. Socrates professes surprise. He goes away, concluding that he is after all a little more knowing than this expert, since he at least knows how difficult the concepts are, and how much his own understanding of them stands in need of further clarification, whereas the expert lacks not only an adequate understanding of the concepts but also knowledge of his own inadequacy. Socrates concludes that he is a very useful figure for democratic government to have around—like a stinging gadfly on the back of a noble but sluggish horse.[41]

When intellectuals behave this way, the people they intend to benefit are not always happy. Socrates proposes that he should be given a salaried position for life at the city's expense. The citizens of Athens had a different idea. To people who are deeply immersed in practical affairs, especially in a democracy, the questioning intellectual—especially, perhaps, the philosopher—is always a slightly suspect character. Why is this person so detached? What is his field of empirical expertise? What gives him the right to walk up to people and question them, as if he had the right to tell them what was wrong with them? Today too, when our campuses "sting" students into rethinking their values, there is likely to be anxiety and resentment. It is very natural to feel that the faculty who are causes of this rethinking must be a self-appointed radical elite, detached from and insensitive to popular values. . . .

We might wonder how much questioning could bring a practical benefit. When a skeptical culture looks at today's campuses from a distance, it is easy to judge that people who question convention are rude and disrespectful, rootless and hedonistic. Their Socratic tendency to ask for reasons and argu-

---

38. Compare the Seminar at St. John's College, described in selection #65.

39. Cicero, *Tusculan Disputations* V iv 10.

40. Plato, *Apology* 20c.

41. Plato, *Apology* 30e–31a.

ments makes them insolent without making them wise. But if we look more closely at Plato's account of Socratic questioning, we will begin to understand how it could be beneficial to democracy; and we will begin to recognize some of those same benefits in our colleges and universities. . . .

Socrates's inquiry opens up questions that are, and already were, of urgent importance for a culture committed to justice. These questions are still with us, when doctors try to decide how to balance patients' rights against patients' interests, asking what conduct justice requires; when judges try to decide when it is appropriate to use their own discretion in criminal sentencing or in constitutional or statutory interpretation, asking when the codified principle needs to be supplemented, extended, or even revised in the light of judgment about the complexities of a case. Should I, as a doctor, tell the truth to a terminally ill patient, even though such news, removing hope, will blight the remaining time this person has to live? Should I, as a judge, exercise discretion in the direction of leniency to do justice to the particular character of this criminal offender's history and conduct?

A lawyer or doctor . . . who had never attempted to systematize his or her intuitions about the just and the right—would be ill equipped to reach an adequate decision in such circumstances. He or she would no doubt make some decision; but it is unlikely that such decisions would be consistent and evenhanded, reflecting a well-considered policy about the practice of his or her profession. That is why medical schools and law schools are increasingly supplementing their technical education with courses in ethics that pose just such questions and show students how difficult, and how urgent, they are. Such courses, like Socrates, do not impose anything from outside in that sense they are highly respectful of the content of traditional ethical beliefs. But they do demand reflective sorting-out and consistency; and they claim that in so doing they are bringing a practical benefit.

Socrates's dialogue with Polemarchus[42] and its modern counterparts show us something else as well: that progress can be made through a reflection that seeks the common good. Sorting these issues out does make it possible to give a more precise and adequate analysis of a medical or legal dilemma. Such an analysis, in turn, can help powerless people defend their claims against those in power. Progress needs clarity; it needs concepts and arguments. Distinguishing patients' rights from patients' interests, for example, as reflection about Socrates's example helps us to do, proves crucial in organizing people to oppose the excessive control of a professional medical elite and to vindicate their autonomy.

Socrates questions generals about courage, friends about friendship, politicians about self-restraint, religious people about piety. In every case he demands to know whether they can give good coherent reasons for what they do, and in every case they prove to have been insufficiently reflective. Socrates shows them that the demand for reasons has a bearing on what they will actually choose. This demand now begins to seem not an idle luxury in the midst of struggles for power, but an urgent practical necessity, if political deliberation is ever to have a dignity and consistency that make it more than a marketplace of competing interests, that make it a genuine search for the common good. Or, as Socrates himself says, "Remember that it is no chance matter we are discussing, but how one should live." . . . [43]

Socrates—unlike Plato—holds that the capacities it takes to become a good reflective citizen are in all citizens, or at least all who are not in some unusual degree deprived of the ordinary ability to reason.[44] Unlike Plato, who holds that a high level of mathematical and scientific expertise is required of the potential judge and legislator, Socrates, like the later Stoics, demands only the sort of moral capacity that ordinary people have and use in their daily conduct. What he asks is that this capacity be

---

42. See Plato, *Republic* 331d-336c.

43. Plato, *Republic* 352d.

44. Compare the view of Edgar Robinson in selection #55.

trained and sharpened so as to realize itself more fully. Nor did Socrates propose that democracy should be replaced by aristocracy or tyranny if people proved resistant to his demands. In fact, in prison just before the end of his life—an end brought about, it would seem, by the irrational behavior of the democracy—he continued to hold that democracy was the best form of government. He believed, it seems, that his demands needed to be met if that noble but sluggish horse would ever be able to realize its potential fully.

But even in its semi-somnolent state it did better than the more repressive forms of government—perhaps because, more than other forms, it gave most respect to the powers of reasoning and moral judgment that reside in each and ever citizen. It is perfectly obvious that the best educational system in the world will not make all our citizens rational in the Socratic way. The sources of irrationality in human life are many and profound. Thus, there is room in democracy for non-majoritarian institutions, such as the judiciary. It also seems good that in our democracy, unlike many others, fundamental rights and liberties cannot be abridged by a majority vote. But rights belong to everyone, and this should mean that the development of reason belongs to everyone. This successful and stable self-realization of democracy such as ours depends on our working as hard as possible to produce citizens who do examine tradition in the Socratic way. The successful integration of previously excluded groups as citizens with equal respect depends on realizing their capacities for rational autonomy and Socratic self-examination. Our institutions of higher education have a major role to play in this project.

The case for preferring democracy to other forms of government is weakened when one conceives of democratic choice as simply the clash of opposing interests. It is very much strengthened by conceiving of it in a more Socratic way, as the expression of a deliberative judgment about the overall good.[45] Socrates prefers democracy because democracy is noble, and he thinks it noble because it recognizes and respects powers of deliberation and choice that all citizens share. His case for democracy cannot easily be separated from his conception of what democratic choice is, and his respect for the moral faculties that are involved in these choices, if not for their current level of development.

That is why education seems to him so urgently required in democracy. That is why it seems to him so irrational to turn the most important things over to people whom you then fail to educate. If your children were colts or calves, he says to a prominent citizen, you would make sure that you found a really high-quality trainer for them. Why, then, do you neglect the education of your children, turning it over in a haphazard manner to any slick operator who happens along?[46] These questions would not matter so much in an aristocracy—except for the elite. And they would not matter in a democracy either, if we really thought that democratic choice was and should be simply the clash of uninformed interests. It is because we share with Socrates a richer conception of democratic deliberation—one that the [nation's] founders derived from their own reading of ancient Greek sources—that we need to take Socrates's demand to heart.

Socratism and Liberal Education: The Stoics

Socrates depicted "the examined life" as a central educational goal for democracy. But he gave few indications of how this abstract ideal might be realized in formal education programs. It is from the writings of the Greek and especially the Roman Stoics that we begin to see the curricular implications of Socrates's example. Stoicism began in the third century B.C. at Athens; it continued to exercise enormous influence, in both Greece and Rome, at least through the second century A.D. Its leading

45. On 'deliberative democracy' and its roots in Madison, see, for example, Cass R. Sunstein, *The Partial Constitution* (Cambridge, MA: Harvard University Press, 1993), pp. 133–45, 162–94. Nussbaum's note.

46. Plato, *Apology* 20a–b.

participants including figures of enormous political influence—including Seneca, who was regent and tutor to the young emperor Nero, and thus effectively ruler of the Roman Empire during that time. . . .[47] Since these thinkers left copious writings behind, as Socrates did not, and since they were actively engaged in the design of educational and other institutions, we can learn a good deal from them about the practical realization of Socratic goals. It is from their writings that we derive our modern conception of liberal education—or, rather, two distinct ideas of liberal education, which they carefully distinguished but we sometimes do not.[48]

The central task of education, argue the Stoics following Socrates, is to confront the passivity of the pupil, challenging the mind to take charge of its own thought. All too often, people's choices and statements are not their own. Words come out of their mouths, and actions are performed by their bodies, but what those words and actions express may be the voice of tradition or convention, the voice of the parent, of friends, of fashion. This is so because these people have never stopped to ask themselves what they really stand for, what they are willing to defend as themselves and their own. They are like instruments on which fashion and habit play their tunes, or like stage masks through which an actor's voice speaks. The Stoics hold, with Socrates, that this life is not worthy of the humanity in them, the capacities for thought and moral choice that they all possess.

According to the Stoics, critical argument leads to intellectual strength and freedom—by itself a remarkable transformation of the self, if the self has previously been lazy and sluggish—and also to a modification of the pupil's motives and desires. . . . Reason, in short, constructs the personality in a very deep way, shaping its motivations as well as its logic. Argument doesn't just provide students with reasons for doing thus and so; it also helps to make them more likely to act in certain ways, on the basis of certain motives. In this very deep way, it produces people who are responsible for themselves, people whose reasoning and emotion are under their own control.

It is difficult, in a traditional culture, to devise an education that promotes rational freedom. Seneca addresses this problem in his famous letter on liberal education. The letter is addressed to Seneca's friend and constant correspondent Lucilius, a middle-aged political man whose questions about various aspects of philosophy, and of life, serve Seneca as occasions to develop his own views in an intimate and particularized way, while engaging in the give-and-take of argument. Lucilius has asked for Seneca's opinion on the traditional "liberal studies," or *studia liberalia*. This was an education by acculturation to the time-honored values and practices of the Roman upper classes; it included grammar, music and poetry, some math and science, and the use of rhetoric in public life—all taught in a way that emphasized uncritical assimilation of tradition. The word *liberalis* in the traditional phrase meant "suited for the freeborn gentleman." Seneca begins his letter by announcing that he will call that understanding of the term into question. For the only kind of education that really deserves the name *liberalis*, or, as we might literally render it, "freelike," is one that makes its pupils free, able to take charge of their own thought and to conduct a critical examination of their society's norms and traditions. He then proceeds to examine this notion. Combining his discussion here with material taken from elsewhere in Stoic writings, we may extract five claims about Socratic education.[49]

1. Socratic education is for every human being.

From the Socratic idea that the unexamined life is not worth living for a human being, together with their belief that a certain sort of critical and philosophy-infused education is both necessary and (if well done) sufficient for a Socratic examined life, the Stoics derive the conclusion that this sort of

---

47. On Seneca and on Lucilius, mentioned below, see selection #5.

48. What does Nussbaum consider to be "our modern conception of liberal education?"

49. Nussbaum actually lists only four claims. Compare these to Seneca's views in selection #5.

education is of essential importance for every human being. Since they also hold that it has prerequisites, such as literacy, basic logical and mathematical capability, and a good deal of knowledge about the world, they tend to think of this as a kind of higher education and to defend the view that higher education is an essential part of every human being's self-realization. . . .

There is an intimate connection between the conception of what liberal education involves and the conclusion that it must be extended to all citizens alike. For if higher education were conceived of as the calling of a select view to a life of theoretical contemplation—as it is sometimes conceived, for example, in Plato—it would be impossible, as Plato in fact argues, to extend it broadly. We would have to search for an elite with special powers of mind, and only these should be admitted to the higher curriculum. Indeed, trying to admit all to this form of study would lead to large-scale social problems. For this contemplative life, as Plato imagines it, is not compatible with a daily active pursuit of political and familial duties. But then, who will there be left to attend to the practical functions of life? Thus Plato's conception of contemplation entails political elitism in more than one way.[50] The Socratic/Stoic conception, by contrast, supports and is supported by democracy. It is because higher education is the development of powers of practical reasoning that every citizen is believed to have that it can be universalized; and it is because it is intimately connected with citizenship and the family that its universalization does not threaten, but promises to strengthen, the democratic political community.

2. Socratic education should be suited to the pupil's circumstances and context.

If education is understood in the Socratic way, as an eliciting of the soul's own activity, it is natural to conclude, as Socrates concludes, that education must be very personal. It must be concerned with the actual situation of the pupil, with the current state of the pupil's knowledge and beliefs, with the obstacles between that pupil and the attainment of self-scrutiny and intellectual freedom. Socrates therefore questions people one by one. The Stoics, concerned with the broad extension of education to all, are not always able to do this. But they insist that individualized instruction is always, in principle, the goal. Education, they say, is to the soul what the medical art is to the body. As doctors do well only if they are sufficiently sensitive to their patients' actual conditions and symptoms, so too with the teacher. This they show in practice in many ways; these include refusing to recommend a universal curriculum, and writing philosophical works exemplifying Socratic attentiveness to the particular situation of the student.[51]

In recent debates on higher education, the tendency has been to ask whether a "great books" curriculum or certain types of core or distribution requirements are good things in general. All too rarely does anyone ask about the circumstances and background of the students for whom requirements are being designed. If we have in mind a general shared goal but, like the Stoics, acknowledge that our students approach the goal from many different starting points, we will naturally conclude that many different curricular approaches are required.

3. Socratic education should be pluralistic, that is, concerned with a variety of different norms and traditions.

There is no more effective way to wake pupils up than to confront them with difference in an area where they had previously thought their own ways neutral, necessary, and natural. Exploring the way in which another society has organized matters of human well-being, or gender, or sexuality, or eth-

---

50. Compare Plato's view presented in selection #1.

51. Can a uniform curriculum be personal and attentive to the particular situation of the student, as the statement from St. John's College maintains in selection #65?

nicity and religion will make the pupil see that other people in viable societies have done things very differently. In our complex world, Socratic inquiry mandates pluralism.[52]

There is a widespread fear—reflected, for example, in the argument of Allan Bloom's book *The Closing of the American Mind*—that critical scrutiny of one's own traditions will automatically entail a form of cultural relativism that holds all ways of life to be equally good for human beings and thereby weakens allegiance to one's own. This was the deep fear, too, that led Athenians to charge Socrates with corruption of the young, and led Aristophanes to associate him with father-beating. But of course this is not what Socratic scrutiny implies. Rather, it implies that we should cling to that which we can rationally defend, and be willing to discover that this may or may not be identical with the view we held when we began the inquiry. . . .

4. *Socratic education requires ensuring that books do not become authorities.*

It is an irony of the contemporary "culture wars" that the Greeks are frequently brought onstage as heroes in the "great books" curricula proposed by many conservatives. For there is nothing on which the Greek philosophers were more eloquent, and more unanimous, than the limitations of such curricula. . . .[53] Socrates himself wrote nothing at all. If we are to believe the account of his reasons given in Plato's *Phaedrus*, it was because he believed that books could short-circuit the work of active critical understanding, producing a pupil who has a "false conceit of wisdom." Books are not "alive." At best, they are reminders of what excellent thinking is like, but they certainly cannot think. Often, however, so great is their prestige that they actually lull pupils into forgetfulness of the activity of mind that is education's real goal, teaching them to be passively reliant on the written word. Such pupils, having internalized a lot of culturally authoritative material, may come to believe that they are very wise. And this arrogance undercuts still further the motivations for real searching. Such people are even less likely than ignorant people to search themselves, looking for arguments for and against their culture's ways of doing things. So books, when used in education, must be used in such a way as to discourage this sort of reverence and passivity. . . .

Books, including some of the great texts from the past of one's own culture, can indeed tone up the slack mind, giving it both the information it needs to think well and examples of excellent argument. Literacy, including cultural literacy, confers both strength and independence,[54] if viewed as a kind of essential training and nourishment, not as itself the goal. Working through the arguments contained in great books can make the mind more subtle, more rigorous, more active. It guarantees that the mind will confront a wide range of options on important questions, and confront them in a challenging presentation, even where popular culture is diffuse and superficial. All this the Stoics knew already; it is even more important for our time.

But . . . books are all too likely to become objects of veneration and deference, sitting in the mind without producing strength in the mind itself. This is, of course, especially likely to happen if they are introduced as cultural authorities, as in curricula titled "Western civilization" or "The Great Books." If we were to use a more Senecan title, such as "Some useful and nourishing books that are likely to help you think for yourself," . . . then we would be on the right track. Everyone involved would be on

---

52. How is the second claim conceptually distinct from this third claim?

53. This "ironic" approach to teaching Great Books arose early in the twentieth century out of the effort to unify the philosophical and literary traditions of liberal education. See Bruce A. Kimball, *Orators and Philosophers: A History of the Idea of Liberal Education* (New York: College Board, 1995), pp. 186–190.

54. "See E. D. Hirsch, Jr., *Cultural Literacy* (Boston: Houghton Mifflin, 1987), who uses the term *cultural literacy* to denote a basic grasp of cultural information that proves necessary to decode other information." Nussbaum, 306n23.

notice that there is no substitute for thinking things through, and the hope for a quick fix for compli-cated problems would no longer be held out.[55] We would see the truth on which Seneca's letter on liberal education ends: that we live in a messy, puzzling, and complicated world, in which there is absolutely no substitute for one's own active searching.

Socratic Reason and Its Enemies

We have not produced truly free citizens in the Socratic sense unless we have produced people who can reason for themselves and argue well, who understand the difference between a logically valid and logically invalid argument, who can distinguish between the logical form of an argument and the truth of its premises. Logical reasoning, like speaking one's native language, comes naturally to hu-man beings; no doubt it is part of the equipment we evolved in order to survive. Work with young children has shown repeatedly that they can master all the basics of logic readily, through the use of simple examples. But, like mastery of one's native language, it needs help from teachers, at many dif-ferent levels of education. Most students don't immediately spot fallacious forms of reasoning in a complicated text—or in a political argument they hear on television. Most people carry around inside themselves lots of ill-sorted material, beliefs they have never examined for logical consistency, infe-rences they have never examined for validity. . . .

Socratic reason is not unopposed on today's campuses. It faces two different types of opponents. The first is a conservative opposition, who suspect that Socrates's dedication to argument will subvert traditional values. This opposition is stronger outside the academy than within it, but we can also find it at some institutions. . . . More often, however, Socratic goals encounter a different type of resis-tance, from challenges to truth and reasons associated with postmodernists literary theory. Even logic itself is not immune from attack. It is often alleged—not only by bigoted or unsympathetic people but often also by champions of race and sex equality—that logical argument is not for women or not for African-Americans. Some left-wing opponents of Socrates think that logic is all right in its place but impotent as a critical tool, next to the entrenched realities of power. In that sense it is not worth spending one's time on it or investing hope in it.

This cynical position, like that of Thrasymachus, can best be refuted by showing what reason can do and has done in the struggle for justice, and by pointing out that if the game is merely power, the powerless will always lose out.[56] Reason has a special dignity that lifts it above the play of forces, and it is only to the extent that reason is respected in a society that minorities will be able to make their just but unpopular claims heard. In Plato's vivid image, reason is a soft golden cord, sometimes pushed around by the iron cord of greed and envy and fear (in operating the imaginary marionette that is the human being), but sometimes prevailing, and always shining with a dignity of its own. It is dif-ficult to imagine how bogus arguments against the equality of women, or of ethnic or religious or ra-cial minorities, could be unmasked without a reliance on the distinction between prejudice and reason; such unmasking will prove futile unless the democratic community as a whole shares that distinction. Cynicism of the Thrasymachean sort is the best recipe for continued oppression of the powerless.[57]

---

55. In what specific ways does Nussbaum's Senecan approach differ from the defense and use of "great books" in the catalog from St. John's College above?

56. Thrasymachus (c. 400s B.C.), Greek sophist, presented this highly cynical position in a debate with Socrates in the Plato's *Gorgias*.

57. Arriving at Harvard in 1969 merely six years after the University first began awarding Ph.D.'s to women, Nussbaum experienced the residual attitudes of that exclusion. "As a Jew (in fact a convert from Episcopalian Christianity), I knew that my husband and I would have been forbidden to marry in Harvard's Memorial Church, which had just refused to accept a Jewish wedding. As a woman I could not eat in the main dining room of the faculty club, even as a member's guest. Only a few years before, a woman would not have been able to use the

Some left-wing opponents of Socrates, however, make a still stronger attack on logic: they charge that the central forms of logical argumentation don't suit the minds of women, or minorities, or non-Western people. Although these views are sometimes put forward by people who wish to deny full political equality to minorities or to women, their influence in the academy derives from the fact that they are also put forward in a progressive spirit, as if we cannot help disadvantaged groups to make progress unless we recognize the "fact" that logic itself is patriarchal or a tool of colonial oppression. But we do not respect the humanity of any human being unless we assume that person to be capable of understanding the basic issues of consistency and validity and the basic forms of inference. We sell that person short as a human being unless we work to make that person's potentiality for logical thought into an active reality. Such criticisms typically show ignorance of the logical traditions of non-Western peoples and a condescending attitude to the logical abilities of women and racial minorities. There is no sound evidence for such claims, and it is counterproductive for allegedly progressive thinkers to speak as if there were. . . .[58]

Socrates in the Modern Curriculum

How can an undergraduate liberal arts education follow Socrates's example? The most important ingredient of a Socratic classroom is obviously the instructor. No curricular formula will take the place of provocative and perceptive teaching that arouses the mind. And a dedicated instructor can enliven the thinking of students in almost any curricular setting. Socratic activity can take place in virtually any humanities or social science course, in connection with readings of many different kinds, as long as the instructor knows a good deal about the particular nature of the student body and strives to develop each individual's capacity to reason.

Although in principle any humanities course might teach Socratic reasoning, many such courses do not focus intensively on critical argument. But such a focus, characteristic of the professional philosopher, is necessary to teach students how to analyze the arguments that they and others make. Given the tremendous importance, for citizenship and for life, of producing students who can think clearly and justify their views, a course or courses in philosophy play a vital role in the undergraduate liberal arts curriculum. If philosophy presents itself as an elite, esoteric discipline pre-occupied with formal notation and with questions of little evident human interest, it will not be able to play this role. But professional philosophy has increasingly, over the past twenty years, returned to the focus on basic human interests that it had in the time of John Dewey and William James. Questions about justice and rights, questions about love, fear, and grief, questions of medical and legal and business ethics—all these are now not at the margins of the profession but at its heart. The profession is once again, like Socrates, bringing philosophy from the heavens down to the earth.

---

undergraduate library. In 1972 I became the first female to hold the Junior Fellowship that relieved certain graduate students from teaching so that they could get on with their research. At that time, I received a letter of congratulations from a prestigious classicist saying that it would be difficult to know what to call a female fellow, since "fellowess" was an awkward term. Perhaps the Greek language could solve the problem: since the masculine for 'fellow' was *hetairos*, I could be called a *hetaira*. *Hetaira*, however, as I knew, is the ancient Greek word not for 'fellowess' but for 'courtesan' [in contradistinction to *porné*, meaning 'common prostitute']. In a setting in which such exclusions and such 'jokes' were routine, is it any wonder that the academic study of women's history, of literature written by women, of the sociology and politics of gender—that all these perfectly normal and central topics were unavailable for serious study?" Nussbaum, pp. 6–7.

58. Does Nussbaum's argument refute the opponents of the Stanford Western Civilization course, described in selection #66?

68. Nancy D. Marcus,
"Three Philosophical Heroes: King, Boethius, and Socrates" (2008)

INTRODUCTION

For St. John's College, "the notion of a 'great book'" implies "the conviction that there are books (and studies) that are worthy and will not fail to capture the attention of almost all students," as stated above by Eva Brann. Nevertheless, liberal arts faculty teaching "core texts" often find that undergraduates early in the twentieth-first century resist this approach. Apart from the "rigid structure" and "harsh but necessary learning matter" that "great books" may entail at St. John's or elsewhere, this resistance arises from "two major and interrelated obstacles: relativism and relevance" that are addressed in this selection by philosopher Nancy du Bois Marcus.

Born in Illinois, Nancy du Bois (1968–) grew up in Seneca, South Carolina and attended The University of the South, in Sewanee, Tennessee. In 1990 she graduated as valedictorian with honors in philosophy, and, in order to continue her liberal arts education, embarked on a Ph.D. program in the history of philosophy at Emory University. Her dissertation examined the philosophical relationship between Giambattista Vico (1668–1744) and Plato, whom Vico regarded as a primary source of inspiration.[59] She has taught Spelman College and Oglethorpe University and currently resides in Atlanta. Selection #68 describes a core course, Human Nature and the Social Order, that Marcus taught at Oglethorpe and exemplifies another kind of Socratic effort made by teachers of classic works to "capture the attention of almost all students" early in the twenty-first century by "bringing philosophy from the heavens down to the earth."

SELECTION[60]

"The less familiar is to be inferred through the more familiar."[61]

In Plato's *Crito*, Socrates states that "the most important thing is not life, but the good life."[62] The place of core texts can be constructively imagined as the place where perennial human questions such as what constitutes the good life or human happiness can be discussed. But there are obstacles to entering such a place for undergraduates today. What are the greatest obstacles to philosophical conversations about human happiness and the good life in today's classrooms? How can they be overcome? How can the classic works of ancient, medieval, and modern philosophy be brought to life? These questions motivate my approach to teaching the core course, Human Nature and the Social Order. . . .

Teaching Plato's *Crito* at the end of this course is the most rewarding moment, but only because the students have been carefully prepared to read it through a descent from modern to medieval to ancient philosophy. For such a journey, the students need guides. I chose a prison narrative from each period: Martin Luther King, Jr. for modern, Boethius for medieval, and Socrates for ancient philoso-

---

59. See Nancy du Bois Marcus, *Vico and Plato* (New York: Peter Lang, 2001).

60. Nancy D. Marcus, "Three Philosophical Heroes: King, Boethius, and Socrates," in *The Place of Core Texts, Selected Papers from the Ninth Annual Conference of the Association of Core Texts and Courses*, ed. Patrick Malcolmson et al. (Lanham, MD: University Press of America, 2008), pp. 55–60. Reprinted by permission of the University Press of America.

61. Aristotle, *Topics* 159b15.

62. Plato, *Crito* 48b.

phy. The key to the success of this intellectual archaeology is its starting point in King's "Letter from Birmingham Jail," which serves as a palimpsest for the Western philosophical tradition.[63] The three philosophical heroes, King, Boethius, and Socrates, bring to life the ideas of each period, and their integrity and courage make a memorable impression on the students.

The required core texts for this course are selections from Aristotle's *Nicomachean Ethics* and *Politics*, Augustine's *City of God*, Aquinas's *Summa Theologiae*, and Locke's *Second Treatise of Government*. Why not simply read the texts chronologically? And how could it possibly help to add more reading? The reverse chronological method is the means of clearing away the two major and interrelated obstacles: relativism and relevance. Undergraduates taking core classes often complain that core texts are boring. I suggest that "boring" means "not relevant to me, personally." How could the truths that great minds have discovered about the human condition not be relevant to them as human beings?

Facing Aristotle's *Nicomachean Ethics* for the first time, for example, many students resist what they call with self-righteous disdain his "assumptions," such as the possibility of a definition of happiness true for all human beings. If one digs a little deeper behind the symptoms of "boring" and "not relevant," one finds the illness of relativism. This relativism is not a sophisticated epistemology but a vague prejudice against universal truth, arising from an unexamined belief that all truth is culturally relative and a misguided application of the desire to be tolerant. Such relativism prevents students from asking the questions of what is human happiness or justice because they believe that such questions are illegitimate. Texts such as Aristotle's *Ethics* or Plato's *Republic* that "assume" there is a human nature and universal truth are irrelevant to their intellectual lives because those texts violate their axiom that truth is relative.

This obstacle is not a new one; Plato and Aristotle both knew that relativism had to be cleared away before philosophy could begin. If we do not clear away this obstacle, students will read Aristotle's *Ethics* and think that is true for Aristotle, but not for them, and the same for the other authors. How can we help students discover that these texts are talking about and to them also? As teachers, we must show that these texts are relevant, not by compromising the texts to make them relevant, but by changing the students so that they can engage the texts as they were intended by their authors. The "Letter from Birmingham Jail" by King is the most effective way that I have found for initiating this change.[64]

When students read King's "Letter," they discover that they are not really relativists. They agree with King that "injustice anywhere is a threat to justice everywhere" and that all human beings have rights. King reinforces their positive (though at this point unexamined) beliefs in universal justice and human rights, and at the same time shows them that relativism is incompatible with these beliefs. To defend breaking an unjust law, which is why he is in prison, King says, "I would agree with St. Augustine that 'an unjust law is no law at all.'" King articulates the difference between a just and an unjust law as follows:

A just law is a man-made code that squares with the moral law or the law of God. An unjust law is a code that is out of harmony with the moral law. To put it in the terms of St. Thomas Aquinas: An unjust law is a human law that is not rooted in eternal law and natural law.[65]

---

63. A palimpsest is writing material that can be erased, or scraped, in order to write on it repeatedly, such as a tablet or blackboard.

64. Compare Nussbaum's approach to initiating this change and clearing away the obstacle of relativism.

65. Quotations are drawn from Martin Luther King, Jr. "Letter from Birmingham Jail," in *Why We Can't Wait* (New York: Penguin, 2000), pp. 65, 70.

The just is not relative to the legal, but instead depends on the universal reality of justice that transcends all human laws. In his eloquent defense of breaking an unjust law, King describes the consequences for moral judgment of being a legal positivist. To refute this kind of relativism, King argues that: "we should never forget that everything that Adolph Hitler did in Germany was 'legal' and everything the Hungarian freedom fighters did was 'illegal.' It was 'illegal' to aid and comfort a Jew in Hitler's Germany."[66] King's examples are moral smelling salts. One cannot be a relativist and still hold that genocide is morally wrong and simply unjust regardless of one's culture, and that holds for slavery as well. Once the students see that relativism is incompatible with their more passionately held beliefs in justice, human rights, and freedom, most (though not all) students jettison relativism with a sense of shame that they ever entertained it.

Reading King's "Letter" has another pedagogical advantage beyond the cure for relativism; it addresses any lingering doubts about the relevance of core texts. The students are surprised when they read King's "Letter" that he mentions by name Socrates, Augustine, and Aquinas, and their dread of reading these authors changes into curiosity and the joy of discovery. King read these authors and integrated them into his thinking so that even in prison he could quote their ideas. Just beneath the surface of the "Letter," the students can discern the layer of modern philosophy. Although King does not mention Locke directly, he does quote the *Declaration of Independence*: "We hold these truths to be self-evident, that all men are created equal." Students see, when they read Locke's *Second Treatise*, that King is steeped in Lockean ideas, which means that if they agree with King, then they also are standing on King's foundation in Locke. Not only King's ideas, but also the ideas in the *Declaration of Independence* have a history of which they have been ignorant. The history of philosophy becomes personal and relevant. The recognition of their previous ignorance of the origins of their ideas opens them to examining these beliefs, and asking what they really mean when they use the words "justice," "freedom," and "rights." The pain of *aporia* motivates the inquiry to move beyond the comfort of the familiar.[67]

Next, the students see that not only are they standing with King on Locke's modern philosophical foundation, but also on Locke's own foundation in the medieval philosophy of Augustine and Aquinas. Locke defines human rights as those rights that we all have by nature, from natural law rather than civil law. This unfamiliar idea of natural law is the necessary condition of the more familiar idea of human rights. The students are eager to unearth the next layer in order to discover exactly what King meant when he quoted Augustine and Aquinas on what makes a law just. King's summary of Aquinas provides a meaningful, relevant context for reading Aquinas's original questions on the four types of law. Working through King to Locke to the foundation of justice and rights in medieval natural law has opened the door for the idea of human nature itself, previously closed by relativism.

Once the students can think in terms of human nature with respect to human rights, they can take the next step to human happiness. Boethius's *Consolation of Philosophy* crystallizes the medieval ideas on happiness and provides a bridge to ancient philosophy. Boethius's eloquence draws the students into thinking in terms of what constitutes the good life for a human being. Students are able to think about questions such as whether bad fortune could be better than good fortune for human beings, as Boethius argues, even though he is unjustly facing execution. Boethius sets up Aristotle's dis-

---

66. King, "Letter from Birmingham Jail," p. 72.

67. *Aporia* is the state of doubt, or perplexity, that one enters upon encountering a problem or puzzle that cannot be resolved. Socrates was said to reduce his interlocutors to *aporia* through his relentlessly probing questions. Compare the definition of "aporetic" discussions in selection #64 by Grant and Riesman in regard to "neoclassical" reforms in liberal education.

cussion of the necessity of virtue for happiness, the role of external goods in happiness, and "true friends" as "the most precious of riches."[68] When the students read Aristotle's *Nicomachean Ethics*, they are ready to think about human nature and happiness in a way that they would not have been if the course had been arranged chronologically.[69]

When the students finally meet Socrates, they are in a place intellectually where they can learn from his example. King's "Letter" is used as a tether for a final time. We have arrived at the origin of Western philosophy, the deepest layer of the palimpsest, and the students see why Socrates is King's hero.[70] Socrates's statement that "the most important thing is not life, but the good life" is the origin of Aristotle's idea that virtue is the key to happiness, which was already familiar from Boethius. Socrates is Aristotle's man of practical wisdom (*phronimos*) and embodies each of the cardinal virtues. Socrates's refusal to do the unjust act of escaping from prison because he would no longer be able to be Socrates inspires the students to have more integrity themselves. If Socrates can maintain his beliefs under the most extreme conditions, how much more so should they be able to resist peer pressure?

Socrates knows what is right, desires what is right, and does what is right. His courage, fearing what ought to be feared (harming the soul through injustice), and not fearing what ought not to be feared (the physical death of the body), awakens in the students a desire to do what they know is right. The students are inspired not merely to be continent by desiring the wrong thing but doing the right thing, but to achieve temperance (*sophrosyne*) like Socrates and genuinely to desire to do the right thing. Socrates's constancy motivates students to practice what they preach, to embody their own principles, as each of the three heroes did. Socrates shakes them into asking themselves, what principles would they die for rather than betray? A desire "not to know what virtue is, but to become good," Aristotle's stated goal of the study of ethics, wells up in the students.[71] Reading Plato's *Crito* inspires the students to take what they have learned from Aristotle and our other authors and become better human beings. At this moment, the students have fully entered the transformative place of core texts.

The place of core texts is a place where students have to be drawn into, educated into. We were some time ago educated into this same place by our teachers. Facing directly the contemporary obstacles to entering that place and introducing authors who can be guides and heroes bring the core texts to life for the students. The image in many college catalogues of students sitting with their teacher on a sunny quad may convey more than admission staffs intend. That is the place where we need to take our students, out of the cave and into the sunlight. There, questions such as the good life are not sneered at, but instead are responded to with an awareness of ignorance, an intense desire to know, and an admiration of heroic individuals who have asked those questions and died rather than betray the answers that they found.

---

68. King, "Letter from Birmingham Jail," pp. 76, 77. See selection #9 by Boethius.

69. See selection #20 by Thomas Aquinas.

70. King, "Letter from Birmingham Jail," pp. 67–8, 74.

71. Aristotle, *Nicomachean Ethics* 1103b30.

69. Christopher Metress,
"A Place for Silence: Benedict's *Rule* and the Great Books Dialogue" (2008)

INTRODUCTION

While Martha Nussbaum recommends reading the classic works of Socrates and Seneca in order to deepen understanding of "present educational controversies" and Nancy Marcus employs a contemporary palimpsest of Great Books to demonstrate their truth and relevance for liberal education today, this selection offers a somewhat paradoxical strategy of endorsing the "Great Conversation" about "Great Books" by challenging it.

Christopher Metress was born in New York in 1963 and raised in Fairfax County, Virginia. He earned his B.A. from St. Mary's University in San Antonio and his Ph.D. in English from Vanderbilt University in 1991. After teaching for three years as a visiting assistant professor at Wake Forest University, he moved to Samford University in Birmingham, Alabama, where he now serves as Professor of English and Director of the University Fellows Program. In 1997 he served as Samford's professor-in-residence in London, and in the fall of 2003 a visiting professor of humanities at Kalmar University in Sweden. In addition to publishing articles on American and British literature, he has edited three books: *The Critical Response to Dashiell Hammett* (1995), *The Lynching of Emmett Till: A Documentary Narrative* (2002), and *Emmett Till in Literary Memory and Imagination* (2007). He is currently working on a book about white southern writers and the civil rights movement.

SELECTION[72]

All of us who champion the benefits of a core text curriculum stand firmly within the legacy of Mortimer J. Adler, Robert Maynard Hutchins, and gospel of great ideas they established at the University of Chicago in the 1930s.[73] As heirs to that legacy, we may respectfully dissent from their selection of specific core texts, but one thing we are all likely to agree on is that there exist great books—and if not great books, then very important books—and that assigning some of those books to all our students will help us help them get the liberal education they deserve. It is not surprising, then, that in adopting the grand idea of one of the original core text programs—the idea of great books—we would also adopt its grand metaphor: that of the "Great Conversation." . . .Certainly not a day goes by during the school year that some professor somewhere teaching in some core course does not talk to his or her students about "putting texts in dialogue with each other." When we use such language, we embrace an inherited metaphor, one that Hutchins was keen to establish as the central metaphor for the Western experience. . . .

> The tradition of the West is embodied in the Great Conversation that began in the dawn of history and that continues to the present day. . . . No other civilization can claim that its defining characteristic is a dialogue of this sort. . . . The goal toward which Western society moves is the Civilization of the Dialogue. The spirit of Western civilization is the spirit of inquiry. . .

---

72. Christopher Metress, "A Place for Silence: Benedict's *Rule* and the Great Books Dialogue," in *The Place of Core Texts, Selected Papers from the Ninth Annual Conference of the Association of Core Texts and Courses*, ed. Patrick Malcolmson, et al. (Lanham, MD: University Press of America, 2008), pp. 61–6. Reprinted by permission of the University Press of America.

73. Is the idea that liberal education means studying and discussing Great Books, in fact, a twentieth-century innovation?

. Nothing is to remain undiscussed. Everybody is to speak his mind. No proposition is to be left unexamined.[74]

Unfortunately, whereas we always seem willing to spend endless committee energy calling into question which great books we ought to place into this conversation, we rarely challenge the metaphor that has been handed down to us by the founders of the great books programs, a metaphor that not only shapes our syllabi but also defines the way that we tell our students that knowledge is best acquired and the mind best engaged. I am not arguing here that conversation or dialogue is not an efficacious means for structuring the substance of the liberal education. Rather, I want to suggest that it is not the only way to think about structuring the substance of that education.

In this essay, I want to explain how I use *The Rule of Saint Benedict* in my own freshmen core text course at Samford University to challenge the centrality of dialogue to the Western experience. Benedict's *Rule*, and the monastic tradition that the *Rule* both emerged from and helped to establish, can encourage us to find a place for silence within the great books conversation. The *Rule*, with its recommendation of silence alongside of fasting, poverty, humility, and compassion, can serve as a provocative countercultural text, one that challenges not only the values that rule of our society but also, more revealingly, the assumptions the dominate our syllabi.

At Samford the two-semester, interdisciplinary core text course for freshmen runs from Socrates to Shakespeare in the fall and from Luther to the present in the spring. Each semester has a set of core texts around which all professors build the course, adding other texts to enhance these core readings. I begin each semester with a lengthy discussion of Socrates' allegory of the cave in Book VII and his conception of justice in Books I–IV of Plato's *Republic*. Here, I set out to establish the value of dialogue as a means of ascertaining truth and constructing the just self and just society. Although later I will question this construct, I encourage my students to start thinking of Western civilization as, in Hutchins' phrase, "the Civilization of the Dialogue." While I want my students to take away many ideas from this opening unit, it is important that they grasp the spirit of Socrates' warning, "Don't let us be *misologues*, hating argument as misanthropes hate men; the worst disease one can have is to hate arguments."[75]

After then teaching core selections from Vergil's *Aeneid*, the *New Testament*, and Augustine's *Confessions*, I am now ready to challenge the great conversation metaphor. A "set up" text on monasticism—either Athanasius' *St. Antony of the Desert* or Thomas Merton's *Wisdom of the Desert*—gets this discussion going. In Merton's collection of wisdom sayings, for instance, students encounter koan-like narratives or instructions instead of lengthy syllogistic arguments. As one representative "misologic" wisdom saying intones:

An elder said: Cut off from yourself rash confidence, and control your tongue and your belly. . . . And if anyone speak to you about any matter do not argue with him. But if he speaks right, say: Yes. If he speaks wrongly say to him: You know what you are saying. But do not argue with him about the things he has said. Thus your mind will be at peace.[76]

---

74. See the introduction to Robert Hutchins in selection #58. Metress quotes from the opening paragraph of Robert M. Hutchins, *The Great Conversation: The Substance of a Liberal Education*, v. 1 of *Great Books of the Western World*, ed. Robert Maynard Hutchins (Chicago: Encyclopedia Britannica, 1952), p. 1.

75. Plato, *Republic* 494.

76. Thomas Merton, *The Wisdom of the Desert: Sayings of the Fourth Century Desert Fathers* (New York: New Directions, 1960), p. 29. Merton (1915–1968) was a Catholic scholar and monk.

Or, as another saying states even more succinctly, "Any trial that comes to you can be conquered by silence."[77]

The *Rule* opens up with the command to "Listen," and Benedict makes much of the idea of "obedience," a word that is rooted in the Latin verb for "to hear."[78] Many students are initially put off by such calls for obedience and the silence that must attend any act of hearing. They can appreciate the practice of other monastic virtues—such as poverty, fasting, humility, and compassion—because these virtues have, at least, some larger individual and social utility (eat less, and save the planet while you lose weight). But it is difficult, at first, to persuade students that silence is a good and desirable thing. This is especially so since the first six weeks of the semester have been devoted to reading the spirited dialogues of Plato, the evangelical epistles of Paul, and the ruminative confessions of Augustine. Add to this the fact that their teacher has been energetically practicing the give and take of the Socratic method in the classroom, and it is no wonder that when Benedict quotes approvingly Psalm 39, which proclaims, "I have guarded my speech. I held my peace and humbled myself and was silent, even from speaking good things,"[79] such talk strikes the students as strange, unprofitable, and downright out of place on the syllabus.

It must be remembered, however, that the *Rule* is just that, a rule for living, and as teachers, we are often obliged to meet texts on their own terms in order to make their virtues accessible to our students. This is easy to do with, say, *Republic*, because we can meet Plato on his own terms by employing in our classrooms the Socratic method he wants to cultivate in all of us. The challenge presented by Benedict's *Rule*, of course, is that one of the text's chief virtues, silence, simply cannot be practiced in the classroom. That is why the week after teaching the *Rule* I use the following exercise.

I cancel class for the week. I remind students of the six monastic virtues (silence, solitude, poverty, fasting, humility, and compassion), and every day for the next seven days the class is required to practice those virtues. Although I change the details of the assignment each semester, I make it difficult enough that students must adopt the very Benedictine attitude of "monitor[ing] one's actions ceaselessly."[80] In order to practice the silence component of the exercise, students must build their day around silence. Four times a day, for fifteen minutes at a time, they must sit quietly. They cannot read or write or engage in any other activity that would be considered "useful." They are asked to clear their minds and think about either one of the wisdom sayings from Merton or one of Benedict's favorite Psalms.

As you may well suspect, some students simply ignore the assignment. But most students do not, and many have discovered that they can learn as much about themselves through a half hour of silence as they can during two weeks of class discussion. Although different students learn different things about themselves, they share one universal experience: they understand how much the university culture and, of course, the larger culture as whole, disdains silence. After just one week of trying to cultivate silence in their lives, and failing more times than not, students come to understand that silence is not, as they first thought, doing nothing. Rather, it is hard work, something hard to find and then even harder to maintain once one has found it. More often than not, they are relieved to return to the great conversation because the sounds they hear in silence are more challenging to their sense of self than any idea they will hear in class.

---

77. Merton, *The Wisdom of the Desert*, p. 55.

78. In Latin, *audire* means "to hear" and also carries the sense of "to listen to" and "obey."

79. *The Rule of St. Benedict*, tr. Anthony C. Meisel and M.L. del Mastro (New York: Image Books, 1975), p. 56.

80. *The Rule of St. Benedict*, p. 53.

It is hard to give up a week of class when there is so much to teach. It is even harder to resist the temptation to think that when I'm not leading the great conversation I'm not doing my job. But here again I can turn to Benedict, who reminds me, "Let no one do what is best for himself, but rather what is best for others."[81] I do not doubt that my students need the great books, and they need even more to see themselves as part of the great conversation, both in my classroom and throughout their lives. But as much as Western civilization is the "Civilization of the Dialogue," it is also the culture of distraction. And our students may be the worst victims of this culture, for they are not only too often distracted but they are also, as T. S. Eliot reminds us, "distracted from distraction by distraction."[82] Good, intelligent conversation about what is right and just and true is one way to combat the noise of our culture and the overwhelming barrenness of our busy lives. But so too is silence, and our students deserve to discover that part of their intellectual heritage as well. When I look at my syllabus and see that blank week with no great book, that blank week when nothing appears to be going on, I know this is not what the founders of the great conversation envisioned. But that's fine. There may not be any great books listed on week eight of my syllabus, but that empty space on the page still promotes one of Western culture's great ideas.

70. David C. Paris and Bruce A. Kimball, "Liberal Education: An Overlapping Pragmatic Consensus" (2000)

INTRODUCTION

While acrimonious disputes over the merits of competing approaches to liberal education dominated the 1990s, the College Board convened a conference in 1994 at which twenty-five academic leaders considered a paper by Bruce Kimball, proposing that a new consensus was emerging about the understanding of liberal education in the United States at the end of the twentieth century. Kimball suggested that the longstanding twofold tradition of liberal education with its shifting emphases and accommodations between "orators" and "philosophers," was being transformed into a new "American tradition of liberal education . . . deeply rooted in the resurgent intellectual tradition of Pragmatism."[83] The "culture wars," in his view, were now giving way to a new consensus around a Pragmatic understanding of liberal education.

Kimball maintained that the emerging Pragmatic consensus involved seven tenets, that liberal education should: "first, become multicultural; second, elevate general education and integration, rather than specialization; third, promote the commonweal and citizenship; fourth, regard all levels of education as belonging to a common enterprise; fifth, reconceive teaching as stimulating learning and inquiry; sixth, promote the formation of values and the practice of service; seventh, employ assessment."[84] Kimball also proposed that these tenets of liberal education were made coherent and

81. *The Rule of St. Benedict*, p. 105.

82. T. S. Eliot, "Burnt Norton" in *The Norton Anthology of American Literature: Shorter Fourth Edition*, ed. Nina Baym, et. al. (New York: W. W. Norton, 1995), 1896.

83. Bruce A. Kimball, "Toward Pragmatic Liberal Education," in *The Condition of Liberal Education*, ed. Robert Orrill (New York: College Board, 1995), p. xxiii.

84. Kimball, "Naming Pragmatic Liberal Education," in *Education and Democracy* ed. Robert Orrill (New York: College Board, 1997), p. 47.

legitimated by the American philosophy of Pragmatism that was attracting renewed scholarly attention in the final third of the twentieth century.

Kimball's proposal was strongly criticized on a number of grounds. Some, such as Alan Ryan of Princeton University, Ellen Harris of the Massachusetts Institute of Technology, and Northeastern University President Richard Freedland asserted that the thesis was "implausible" because there was "no consensus in sight."[85] Moreover, some suggested that even proposing such a consensus was wrongheaded, because it implied the exclusion of some groups and viewpoints.[86] Paradoxically, an opposite kind of criticism came from others who contended that the consensus was obvious and old news. For example, June Phillips of Weber State University maintained that "faculty and administrators . . . in the public sector of higher education . . . [were] startled by Kimball's characterization of Pragmatic liberal education as a destination not yet reached," because "developments identified by Kimball as reflective of Pragmatic liberal education constitute the core of initiatives underway at many of the nation's public four-year colleges and universities."[87] Thus, Kimball's thesis purporting to describe and explain the course of liberal education at the end of the twentieth century and the beginning of twenty-first was simultaneously characterized as wrong, unjust, or perfectly obvious.[88]

Subsequently, political scientist David C. Paris proposed that Kimball's consensus thesis might be helpfully understood by comparing it to John Rawls's idea of an "overlapping consensus."[89] Paris and Kimball therefore collaborated on an essay analyzing the Pragmatic nature of the new consensus on liberal education and of the seven tenets. In this way, they suggested that a new intellectual framework was providing coherence and legitimacy for liberal education at the beginning of the twenty-first century.

SELECTION[90]

In 1985 John Rawls offered an interpretation of his theory of justice that he characterized as "political, not metaphysical."[91] In what seemed to be a departure from previous formulations of his views,

---

85. Quotation is from Alan Ryan, "No Consensus in Sight," p. 238. See Ellen Harris, "Prognostication and Doubt," p. 254; Richard Freedland, "Pragmatism Won't Save Us But It Can Help," p. 158, all found in *The Condition of Liberal Education*.

86. Shirley Hune, "Pragmatism, Liberal Education, and Multi-culturalism: Utilizing the 'Master's Tools' to Restructure the 'Master's House' for Diversity," in *The Condition of Liberal Education*, pp. 163–9.

87. June Phillips, "Pragmatic Missions and the Struggle for Liberal Education in State Colleges and Universities," in *The Condition of Liberal Education*, pp. 151, 154.

88. See also essays in *Education and Democracy*.

89. See John Rawls, "The Idea of an Overlapping Consensus," *Oxford Journal of Legal Studies* 7 (1987): 3–4. Cf. David C. Paris, "The Theoretical Mystique: Neutrality, Plurality, and the Defense of Liberalism," *American Journal of Political Science* 31 (1987): 909–39; Paris, "Moral education and the Tie That Binds in Liberal Political Theory," *American Political Science Review* 85 (1991): 875–901.

90. David C. Paris and Bruce A. Kimball, "Liberal Education: An Overlapping Pragmatic Consensus," *Journal of Curriculum Studies* 32 (2000): 145–58. Reprinted by permission of Taylor and Francis, Ltd. This introduction is adapted from that of the original article, written by David C. Paris, who was born in Rochester, NY, in 1949. After graduating from Hamilton College in 1971, he studied political science at Syracuse University and was awarded the Ph.D. in 1975. During the subsequent four years, Paris taught at Virginia Polytechnic Institute and State University, and in 1979 joined the faculty of his undergraduate alma mater, where he is currently James S. Sherman Professor of Government.

Rawls claimed that his two principles of justice (of equal liberty, for just distribution)[92] represent "the kernel of an overlapping consensus" in the liberal democratic tradition. Both principles are or could be agreed to by "each of the opposing comprehensive moral doctrines influential in a reasonably just democratic society." Even though proponents of such doctrines might interpret the two principles in various ways, they could still agree to them as a "political charter" for a liberal democratic society. In short, the opposing doctrines overlap on these two cardinal principles.

Rawls presents two reasons for appealing to a political consensus. First, he doubts that a deeper philosophical rationale for his or other principles is achievable, because the "diversity of doctrines—the fact of pluralism—is . . . a permanent feature of the public culture of modern democracies."[93] Second, staying "on the surface, philosophically speaking," and confining our attention to shared political principles, as opposed to seeking "truth about an independent . . . order," better serves what Rawls sees as the "task of political theory."[94] Namely, political theory should provide principles that form the basis for a shared, workable order among groups that hold different and even incommensurable positions on philosophy, morality, and politics. Thus the appeal to consensus combines a Pragmatic skepticism about deeper philosophical argument with a Pragmatic criterion of warranted belief arising from the need for shared recognition of some workable principles in a liberal democracy.

There are at least two ambiguities in Rawls appeal to consensus that are important for both his argument and Kimball's discussion of a Pragmatic consensus on liberal education. The first is whether an appeal to consensual principles is primarily descriptive/empirical or normative/rhetorical. Such a claim might be taken as a descriptive report of what "we" (most or all of "us") believe to be basic, shared principles about justice—or, similarly, about liberal education. Alternatively, such a claim might be seen as a persuasive definition of shared principles; if we think about our beliefs, these are the principles we should endorse. Certainly, these two conceptions are related to one another. It would make little sense to try to persuade others of the consensual nature of certain principles if they bore no discernible relationship to common, existing understandings. Nonetheless there remains some, perhaps inevitable, tension about the descriptive and normative aspects of the purported consensus.

The second ambiguity involves the effective role such principles might play. They may be understood as being either strong or weak, as respectively either guides or boundaries to political debate. On a strong interpretation, the principles serve as guides, clear criteria for judging political (or educational) practices and institutions—as Rawls puts it, "a publicly recognized point of view [of] . . . what are recognized . . . as valid and sufficient reasons." Alternatively, consensual principles may be understood weakly as constraints or boundary conditions on argument and institutions. Principles of justice (or of liberal education) allow a plurality of interpretations—as they must in a liberal democratic society—but that plurality is not unbounded. Some shared principles set the parameters within which a plurality of views, sometimes even incommensurable views, are discussed and explored. On either

91. John Rawls, "Justice as Fairness: Political not Metaphysical," *Philosophy and Public Affairs* 14 (1985): 223–51; Rawls, "The Idea of an Overlapping Consensus," pp. 1–25.

92. The two principles are: "1. Each person is to have an equal right to a fully adequate scheme of basic rights and liberties, which scheme is compatible with a similar scheme for all. 2. Social and economic inequalities are to satisfy two conditions: first, they must be attached to offices and positions open to all under conditions of fair equality of opportunity; and second, they must be to the greatest benefit of the least advantaged." John Rawls, *A Theory of Justice* (Cambridge, MA: Harvard University Press, 1971), p. 60.

93. Rawls, "The Idea of an Overlapping Consensus," pp. 3–4.

94. Rawls, "Justice as Fairness," p. 230.

understanding, disagreements are dampened because they are discussed on the basis of consensual principles or "theorems, as it were, at which their several views coincide." . . .[95]

Any argument appealing to consensus—concerning principles of justice or liberal education—will, beyond answering obvious questions of descriptive accuracy, need to clarify the form and function of the consensus it claims to describe. To achieve this clarification, any argument appealing to consensus must put together delicate combinations of descriptive accuracy and persuasive argument, of rhetorical significance and interpretive leeway. The elements of a purported consensus must be easily recognized as reflecting "our" beliefs and principles, even as the presentation goes beyond description to persuade us that these principles should govern institutions and policies. Similarly, the consensus such an argument describes or captures must have some significance; it must have more force than merely providing a listing of vague generalities. At the same time, it cannot seem to impose excessive constraint upon arguments or dissent; it must leave open room for competing interpretations of consensual principles. Given that liberal democratic societies and institutions within them (and particularly educational institutions) tolerate and even encourage considerable disagreement, an argument that appeals to consensus must steer a middle course between a largely symbolic sharing or values and principles and a fairly strict understanding that threatens to impose limits or constraints upon interpretations or dissent.[96]

Rawls and Kimball negotiate the ambiguities of arguments from consensus and answer questions about the form and function of consensus in different ways. Rawls attempts to answer these questions in what might termed a "theoretical" way. That is, consensual principles are treated like a scientific theory in which a small number of axioms provide inferences that cover a range of phenomena. Rawls's argument mimics scientific theory in that his two principles, ordered by their priority, claim to capture our most basic sentiments of justice and provide a vantage point from which to view political questions; if we observe the various positions on justice we will find that the two principles underlie them. Though Rawls claims to be advancing a "political" account of his principles, he retains certain philosophical or theoretical expectations about the nature of that consensus. Consensus consists of a small number of principles ("theorems") that guide or bound political commitments. Particular commitments, policies, practices, and institutions are fully justified when they can be shown to be consistent—if not required by—these principles. Thus these principles regroup and even "trump" the various other principles or viewpoints that they are claimed to capture and thus supersede.

But this strategy leads to some serious problems in Rawls's account and illustrates some of the differences and advantages of Kimball's account of an emerging consensus about liberal education. The key problem in Rawls's account is that the "overlapping consensus" in a liberal democratic society is not reducible to this theoretical form. Rather what "overlaps" is a set of tenets or values (ideals) that vary in their relationship to one another depending upon historical circumstance and particular contexts. That is, the various values (liberty, equality, rule of law, etc.) lack the form of a theory in that they are not organized theoretically as precisely ordered axioms. For example, in the liberal tradition there may be some deep consensus about the importance of rights but not about their absolute priority over considerations of consequences. There may be procedural or other values that are fundamental and consensual as well, and some communitarian philosophers have suggested that there are other ideas (about duty, virtue) that have a similar status.[97] Similarly, our shared principles do not

---

95. Quotations are from Rawls, "Justice as Fairness," pp. 229, 247.

96. Paris, "Moral Education and the Tie That Binds in Liberal Political Theory," pp. 877–82.

97. See Stephen Macedo, *Liberal Virtues: Citizenship, Virtue, and Community in Liberal Constitutionalism* (New York: Oxford University Press, 1990); William A. Galston, *Liberal Purposes: Goods, Virtues, and Diversity in the Liberal State* (New York: Cambridge University Press, 1991).

function as axioms or "theorems" in some straightforward way that yields specific conclusions. Agreed upon policies and practices are seldom subjected to theoretical exploration, since there are many areas of consensus in policy and practice. Political disagreement typically involves problems concerning how principles, though widely shared, need to be applied in specific circumstances or cases in which they seem to be in conflict with one another.

The consensus about liberal education that Kimball describes, on the other hand, does not take the theoretical form of Rawls's proposal. It more resembles the political consensus in liberal democratic societies, and it functions in much the same way. Kimball's "tenets" defining the consensus are less abstract and more numerous than Rawls's "principles"; and the tenets are not described as having any prioritized relationships to one another. Similarly, each individually provides some kind of prescription ("should become multicultural") but in a way that leaves open differing interpretations. To put the matter more generally, Kimball offers what is primarily a descriptive account of an emerging consensus whereas Rawls's account has a much stronger normative component. Rawls tries to distill from an existing multifaceted and less structured consensus what he believes ought to be its underlying normative structure whereas Kimball tries to provide a more accurate description of a set of tenets that form a less theoretically organized "overlapping consensus." Descriptively at least, Kimball's account stays more "on the surface, philosophically speaking."

These differences favor Kimball's account and show why the nature of an "overlapping consensus" should be understood and described in the latter fashion. First, as an empirical matter, it is doubtful that the basic beliefs about justice in a liberal democracy are reducible to Rawls's two principles; indeed, one of these principles (the second, "difference" principle) might not even be widely shared. It is more likely that the overlapping consensus in a liberal democracy is a far less structured and more complex mix of libertarian and utilitarian beliefs.[98] The consensus concerning liberal education that Kimball describes, on the other hand, does not attempt to reduce our notions of liberal education to one or two prioritized principles. Besides being more numerous, the principles that Kimball puts forth are more flexible than those offered by Rawls in that they are not assigned some theoretical priority or position. This explains why there seems to be less dispute about whether Kimball has accurately described some widely shared principles and more about whether these add up to a meaningful, comprehensive consensus.

This review of appeals to an overlapping consensus also suggests why there have been such very different reactions to Kimball's analysis. On the one hand, some observers, such as Alan Ryan and Ellen Harris, have a more theoretical expectation for a strong consensus and therefore do not see that one exists.[99] Continuing disagreements about the interpretation of generally shared principles is taken as evidence that there is no consensus. But, when Kimball's seven tenets are understood as an overlapping consensus, these concerns are seen to be misplaced. A consensus does not mean the absence of disagreement; again, for example, Americans share a political consensus, but disagree about many things. On the other hand, those, like June Phillips, who see Kimball's account as "old news" are confident that there is such a consensus, but wonder what the value is in describing what is already known to exist. Such a description, as Richard Freedland implies, does not tell us how to deal with situations when the interpretation of principles is in doubt, when the several principles conflict, and so on. But these objections likewise miss an important point about overlapping consensus as setting out boundaries or parameters, providing a vocabulary, and directing attention, rather than determining specific practices. Kimball's proposed consensus includes many things but not everything, and it di-

98. G. Klosko, "Rawls's Political Philosophy and American Democracy," *American Political Science Review* 87 (1993): 348–59.

99. Ryan, "No Consensus in Sight," pp. 244–9; Harris, "Prognostication and Doubt," pp. 253–8.

rects our attention to some things and not others. Likewise, that these principles are not organized in some theoretical form does not mean they are useless. Rather they provide a frame of reference for discussing and debating proposals and practices in liberal education.

Certain approaches to liberal education are generally outside this consensus. Some traditional "great books" approaches or programs with a fairly strict religious program eschew many, and even most, of the elements of the consensus Kimball describes. Similarly, some programs that might emphasize some elements of the consensus to the exclusion of the others would have difficulty accepting the overlapping consensus. For example, at least some who regard themselves as multiculturalists view with suspicion the notion of consensus in general and this consensus in particular as being insufficiently activist in its orientation or Eurocentric in its origins.[100] Finally, for those who believe that liberal education ought to be distinguished by its opposition to preprofessional or otherwise "useful" courses of study, the tenets that Kimball articulates point to a reconnection of liberal education with a number of ongoing social concerns: social diversity, citizenship, the other parts of the educational system, and so on.

The explication of the nature and boundaries of an overlapping consensus—suggesting tenets that "overlap" and those that do not—leads the discussion from the nature of an overlapping consensus to its content. Describing the nature of an overlapping consensus whose tenets set parameters, direct attention, include or exclude things, does not tell us substantively how we should understand what is being attended to, included or excluded, etc. and why. A listing of tenets as an emerging consensus invites the question of what, if anything, ties these tenets together and indeed why we should accept these tenets as opposed to some others. This takes the argument beyond the nature of the emerging consensus as overlapping, hence, Pragmatic, to its substantive character as Pragmatic. Specifically, Kimball suggests that the (overlapping) consensus is best understood as converging with Pragmatism. Pragmatism is both an apt characterization of the nature of the consensus and a philosophy or meta-rationale that fits with its content. Thus, a fuller account of the emerging overlapping consensus on liberal education must also address the relationship of the tenets of that consensus to Pragmatism.

Why a "Pragmatic" Consensus?

As with the idea of consensus, a number of critics of Kimball's formulation took very different and even conflicting positions with respect to the claim that the tenets of the consensus were "Pragmatic." Some suggested that Kimball had misunderstood and misappropriated Pragmatism to his cause. For example, David Steiner of Vanderbilt University argued that a more penetrating discussion of what Pragmatism might mean for education would lead to a "depth Pragmatism" that would raise some fundamental issues, particularly about public education, but "the new Pragmatism of the academy has little patience with such issues."[101] Others claimed that the appeal to Pragmatism is so loose as to be meaningless. It becomes a catchall rationale, Eva Brann of St. John's College suggested, that "exists in a mist in which all cats are gray."[102] Finally, some argued that it was unclear that Pragmatism was causally or even logically related to the consensus. As Robert Westbrook of the University of Rochester put it, "some advocates of the sort of liberal education he [Kimball] describes are speaking Pragmatism (some knowingly), but . . . most are not."[103] Westbrook went on to suggest that the seven te-

---

100. See Hune, "Pragmatism, Liberal Education, and Multi-culturalism," pp. 163–9.

101. David Steiner, "Funeral Rites," in *The Condition of Liberal Education*, p. 236.

102. Brann, "Four Appreciative Queries," in *The Condition of Liberal Education*, p. 172.

103. Robert Westbrook, "Wishful Thinking: On the Convergence of Pragmatism and Liberal Education," in *The Condition of Liberal Education*, p. 229.

nets might fit the philosophy of G. W. F. Hegel, and Edmund Gordon of Yale University suggested Jean-Paul Sartre.[104] Thus again, the critics come at odd angles. For some the consensus is not properly characterized as Pragmatic, or it is the wrong kind of Pragmatism, while for others, the consensus may be Pragmatic but, ironically, it does not matter that it is.

Before answering these objections, it is important first to clarify what it means to say that the consensus is "Pragmatic" both in its overlapping nature and in its substantive tenets. As described above, an overlapping consensus is one in which a variety of doctrines or ideologies overlap on a set of ideas or tenets that give guidance for understanding and evaluation in a certain area. Although there may be some presumptive priorities among these ideas, they do not necessarily form a theoretical structure— precisely because they are the (shared) parts of other theoretical structures, of other (overlapping, but varied) viewpoints. For example, the principles of justice in a liberal democratic society are more numerous and related in more complex ways than Rawls proposed reduction of them to two prioritized primary principles; they overlap in ways that defy this reduction because they encompass varied viewpoints on shared values such as liberty, justice, and so on. The consensus concerning liberal education that Kimball has described takes an overlapping form in that the seven tenets describe a set of commitments that are widely shared by academic leaders of diverse viewpoints. While this consensus does not yield precise practical guidance it does, as noted previously, set out some boundaries and parameters for discussion, directs attention to some things rather than others, and so on.

Similarly, Pragmatism as a school of thought or philosophy also takes the form of an overlapping consensus in that it is usually described as an "approximation" of the shared beliefs of a number of important thinkers who have called themselves Pragmatists. These beliefs or characteristics are not always consistently maintained or described by all those who call themselves Pragmatists, but they do set a context and direction for philosophical discussion. The characteristics Kimball notes include: that all belief and meaning are fallible; that experimental method is employed in all inquiry; that belief and truth depend upon the context and judgment of the community in which they are formed; that experience involves the close interrelation of thought and action; that problem solving is intrinsic to all inquiry; and that judgments of fact are not different than judgments of value. These characteristics are derived from a putatively empirical assessment of the actual way human beings think. The fundamental outcome of Pragmatism is to recommend a scientific, experimental method in addressing experienced problems, with the community as the ultimate, yet fallible, arbiter of how such problems are resolved. The warrant of the community determines what we know and ought to do, and in this way science and democracy are closely intertwined. Thus, Pragmatism itself involves a kind of overlapping consensus among several different versions or presentations of this philosophy. . . .

The question then becomes what it means to say that the emerging (overlapping) consensus about liberal education is a Pragmatic consensus. Most simply put, it means there are substantive (logical, historical) connections between the emerging consensus about liberal education and an "approximation" of Pragmatism. Pragmatism provides a philosophical framework for rationalizing the tenets of liberal education in the emerging consensus.

The relationship between the overlapping consensus concerning liberal education and Pragmatism, then, is not limited to a similarity in nature or form. . . . The seven tenets of the emerging consensus are a Pragmatic response to some of the ongoing problems of defining liberal education and justifying it as we move into the twenty-first century. As a conceptual matter, this is fairly easy to see. For example, multiculturalism reflects a communitarian and contextual view of knowledge, while the recently emphasized movements toward service learning and citizenship education comport with the interrelation of thought and action as well as fact and value. The recent demands for assessment also

104. Westbrook, "Wishful Thinking," p. 229; Edmund Gordon, "Response to Bruce Kimball's 'Toward Pragmatic Education'," in *The Condition of Liberal Education*, p. 190.

fit well with the experimental attitude of Pragmatism, namely that postsecondary education must test its results empirically and show that in fact it is effective in doing what it claims to do. Indeed, the "fit" illustrated by these connections between the tenets of the consensus and Pragmatism could be drawn out at length.

It is important to note here that "fit" here is neither strict logical inference—the tenets are uniquely justified by Pragmatism as a philosophy—nor direct historical causation—the development of Pragmatism caused these tenets to emerge. Describing the consensus as Pragmatic means that the consensus has deeper philosophical roots that support it and that historically Pragmatism has provided (and will provide) an available rationale for understanding liberal education. That the consensus is thus "rooted" in Pragmatism suggests that there are both philosophical and historical reasons for linking the two. The emerging consensus "fits" Pragmatism in a coherent way, and the longstanding and resurging interest in Pragmatism provides a historical context for understanding why these tenets might be popular.

Many of the objections to characterizing the emerging consensus as Pragmatic set expectations for defining Pragmatism or explaining its relationship to the consensus that are too demanding. Just as Rawls attempts to provide a "theoretical" version of an overlapping consensus, so too critics often demand that the understanding of Pragmatism and the claimed relationship of the consensus to Pragmatism meet some test of precise definition, logical or justificatory inference, or clear historical causation. They set "theoretical" expectations that are inconsistent with a Pragmatic orientation and the kind of consensus it supports. . . .

Pragmatism is more consistent with the emerging consensus than other possible meta-rationales. It is, conceptually, more supportive of an accommodation between the "philosophical" and "oratorical" in liberal education that shifts some emphasis from the former to the latter. Other philosophies, such as Hegelianism or Marxism, are hardly as open-ended or as consistent with liberal education in a democratic society. Still others such as existentialism might be plausibly related to at least some of the tenets of liberal education that Kimball describes, but that relationship is less congenial. For example, existentialism is at least as likely to be associated with a kind of disengagement from the world that would be less sympathetic to the concern with citizenship and service learning. If the question is, "What might Pragmatism imply for liberal education"? then Kimball's principles certainly have a Pragmatic cast to them. If the words "Marxism" or "existentialism" or any other "ism" are substituted in the question, it is not clear that the same answer would emerge, that the conceptual fit is as clear or tight.

Logical fit is not historical causation, and it might be argued that, as an empirical matter, there is not a great deal of evidence that Pragmatism has played a direct role in the emerging consensus. For instance, it is not clear that those who speak about multiculturalism are speaking the language of Dewey instead of Foucault or Derrida. However, here again the point is not that there is some neat historical pattern of one set of philosophical ideas causing people to adopt certain tenets concerning postsecondary education. Rather, the claim that the consensus is rooted in Pragmatism is simultaneously descriptive and prescriptive. Descriptively, Pragmatism is and has, historically, been available to provide an orientation toward liberal education and the current consensus illustrates one way in which this United States' tradition is now playing itself out. Pragmatism has always had something of a pride of place in American philosophy generally and with regard to education (at all levels) in particular. What Kimball is suggesting by the "heuristic naming" of the consensus as "Pragmatic" is that Pragmatism can serve as a means of understanding certain developments in postsecondary education, as it often has been in the past. . . .[105]

---

105. See selection #54 by Daniel Bell.

Pragmatism has been and continues to be "historically available" as setting a philosophical context for liberal and general education in ways that are logically consistent with the emerging consensus. In fact, the concurrence of the emerging consensus and the resurgence of Pragmatism suggest that each development is mutually reinforcing.

"What Difference"?

In the end the dialectic of objection and rebuttal must give way to the process of examining what might be gained by acknowledging and endorsing the consensus and its link to Pragmatism. As one college president asked Kimball at a convocation at Nichols College in 1997, what difference would it make if you're right that this Pragmatic consensus is emerging? The difference is twofold. First, as a matter of legitimation, "if we are seeing changes in liberal education converging with a sophisticated, philosophical rationale that is historically grounded in United States' culture, then it follows that the changes are likely to persevere for some time."[106] This convergence with Pragmatism imparts legitimacy to the emerging changes in liberal education, which will therefore likely continue into the foreseeable future. For example, multiculturalism has emerged from a marginal issue in liberal education into a widely accepted policy. Even those who have been critical of it in the past are willing to acknowledge its legitimacy in higher education; "We are all multi-culturalists now," as Nathan Glazer asserts.[107] However much changing demographics may have stimulated this development, it is certain that its perseverance as a policy depends upon it being warranted, or legitimated, by a widely held meta-rationale in American culture. Similarly, changes in patterns of curricular reform, faculty development, programs in service learning, and assessment are all prominent and generally accepted features of liberal education that are warranted or legitimated by Pragmatism. . . .

To summarize, the nature of the emerging consensus on liberal education suggested by Kimball is best understood as an overlapping consensus, which is both similar to and different from John Rawls's claimed consensus about his theory of justice. Kimball has described and, in the process of describing, recommended for endorsement a set of tenets that embody liberal education as currently practiced and discussed. These tenets take the form of an overlapping consensus, as does Pragmatism as a philosophical orientation. Both involve ideas and tenets that set a context and direction for discussion and evaluation. Substantively, the emerging consensus is Pragmatic, and Pragmatism as a philosophy provides a historically available meta-rationale for the consensus. Pragmatism's substantive commitments—to the interrelationship of thought and action, the centrality of problem solving, a communitarian criterion of truth, and so on—are supportive of the emerging consensus concerning liberal education. The emerging consensus and Pragmatism mutually reinforce each other. The value of the "heuristic naming" of a Pragmatic (overlapping) consensus concerning liberal education, and seeing its fit with Pragmatism, lies in warranting, or legitimating, the tenets of the consensus, as well as providing a perspective from which to evaluate current practices and new developments in liberal education.

---

106. Kimball, "Naming Pragmatic Liberal Education," pp. 48–9.

107. Nathan Glazer, *We Are All Multi-culturalists Now* (Cambridge, MA: Harvard University Press, 1997).

Glossary of Names

Names in bold face signify authors whose writing appears in this anthology.

ABELARD, Peter (1079–1142) early scholastic logician and teacher

ACHILLES, legendary Greek hero, fought in the Trojan War (c. 1200s B.C.) and is portrayed in the *Iliad* of Homer

AESCHYLUS (525–456 B.C.), Athenian poet and early dramatist

AGASSIZ, Louis (1807–73), prominent zoologist and Harvard professor

AGAMEMNON (c. 1200s B.C.), legendary Greek hero and leader of the Greek army in the Trojan War

ALBERT the Great (1206–1280), Dominican theologian and teacher of Thomas Aquinas

ALEXANDER the Great (356–323 B.C.), Macedonian general and king, tutored by Aristotle

ALEXANDER of Villedieu (c. 1170–c. 1250) author of a metrical verse grammar, the *Doctrinale*, that displaced the standard textbooks of Donatus and Priscian

AMBROSE (c. 340–397), theologian and bishop of Milan and mentor of Augustine

ANAXAGORAS of Clazomenae (c. 500–428 B.C.), Greek philosopher and scientist and teacher of Socrates, fled from Athens for fear of persecution in 450s B.C.

AQUINAS, Thomas (1225–1274), Dominican theologian at the University of Paris

ARISTOPHANES (c. 446–c. 386 B.C.), Athenian comic and satiric playwright

APOLLO, Greek god of the arts, muses, medicine, and prophecy

ARCHIMEDES (287–212 B.C.), Greek physicist and mathematician, who lived in Syracuse

ARISTOTLE (384–322 B.C.), Greek philosopher and student of Plato

ASCHAM, Roger (1515–1568), English humanist and tutor to Queen Elizabeth I

ATHANASIUS of Alexandria (293–373), Christian theologian and bishop of Alexandria

ATHENA, Greek goddess of wisdom and learning and of war and peace, also called Pallas and, in Latin, Minerva

AUGUSTINE (354–430), Christian theologian and bishop in North Africa

AUGUSTUS, Caesar (63 B.C.–A.D. 14), Roman emperor, ruled from 31 B.C. to A.D. 14.

AVERROËS, *see* Ibn Rushd.

AYDELOTTE, Frank (1880–1956), president of Swarthmore College and advocate of honors education

BACON, Francis (1561–1626), English statesman and philosopher of science and author of the *Advancement of Learning* (1605)

BECKER, Lydia Ernestine (1827–1890), author of scientific textbooks and advocate of women's rights

BELL, Daniel (1919–), sociology professor at Columbia University and Harvard University

BENEDICT of Nursia (c. 480–c. 547), Italian monk, founder of a monastery at Monte Cassino and author of the predominant rule of Western monasticism

BERNAL, Martin (1937–), British scholar of Chinese studies and ancient Middle Eastern history who taught at Cornell University

BOCCACCIO, Giovanni (1313–1375), Italian writer and poet

BOETHIUS (c. 480–525), Latin scholar and imperial administrator

BUTLER, Nicholas Murray (1862–1947), founding president of Teachers College at Columbia University (1886–1891) and later the president of Columbia University (1902–1945)

CAESAR, Julius (c. 102–44 B.C.), Roman general and statesman.

CALVIN, John (1509–1564), French theologian and Protestant reformer

CARMENTIS, learned Italian woman and legendary inventor of the Latin alphabet, called Nicostrata in Greek

CAPELLA, Martianus (c. A.D. 420), encyclopedist of the liberal arts

CASSIODORUS, (c. 485–c. 585), Latin scholar and administrator

CATHERINE, learned Christian woman of the fourth century and patron saint of the medieval faculty of the liberal arts

CATO the Elder (234–149 B.C.), Roman statesman and writer on moral themes

CATO the Younger (95–46 B.C.) Roman statesman and great grandson of Cato the Elder

CERETA, Laura (1469–1499), Italian feminist writer

CHRISTINE de Pizan (1365–c. 1430), feminist poet and essayist

CICERO (106–43 B.C.), Roman statesman, orator, and author

CLARKE, Edward H. (1820–1877), a professor of Harvard Medical School who opposed educating women in the liberal arts

COPERNICUS, Nicholas (1473–1543), Polish astronomer, advanced the heliocentric view of the solar system

CORAX, legendary Sicilian rhetorician of the sixth or early fifth century B.C.

CORNELIA, name of several prominent women: wife of the Roman statesman Pompey, stepdaughter of Emperor Augustus, and mother and teacher (c. 180–c. 105 B.C.) of her sons, the Gracchi, the leading social reformers in the Roman Republic

de la CRUZ, Juana Inéz (1648–1695), Mexican poet and scholar

CURTIUS, Ernst R. (1886–1956), German scholar of Romance languages and literatures

CYPRIAN (c. 200–258), patrician, teacher of rhetoric, and bishop of Carthage

DANTE, Alighieri (1265–1321), Italian poet, wrote the *Divine Comedy*

DAY, Jeremiah (1773–1867), president of Yale College

DEMOCRITUS (c. 460–c. 370 B.C.), Greek philosopher and scientist, first posited the thoroughly mechanistic view that the universe was composed of atoms

DEMOSTHENES (c. 384–322 B.C.), Athenian orator

DESCARTES, René (1596–1650), French philosopher and mathematician, developed a highly rationalistic philosophy that provided a bridge from scholastic to modern philosophy

DEWEY, John (1859–1952), United States philosopher of Pragmatism

DIOGENES (412–323 B.C.), Greek moral philosopher

DONATUS, Aelius, (c. A.D. 350s), author of an influential Latin grammar, later divided into the *Lesser Art* or *First Art* (addressing the eight parts of speech) for novices and the *Greater Art* or *Second Art* for advanced students

DOUGLASS, Frederick (1817–1895), abolitionist and editor, was a leading voice of African Americans in the late nineteenth century

DU BOIS, W. E. B. (1868–1963), African-American leader and advocate of liberal education

EDWARDS, Jonathan (1703–1758), American theologian who served briefly as president of the College of New Jersey

ELIOT, Charles W. (1834–1926), president of Harvard University from 1869 to 1909

ELIZABETH I (1533–1603), ruling queen of England from 1558 to 1603

ELYOT, Thomas (c. 1490–1546), English author, published the first Latin-English dictionary in 1538, as well as *The Boke Named "The Governour"* in 1531.

EMERSON, Ralph Waldo (1803–1882), Transcendentalist philosopher and essayist

EMPEDOCLES (c. 490–c. 430 B.C.), Greek philosopher theorized that all matter is composed of earth, air, fire, and water

EPICURUS (341–270 B.C.), Athenian moral philosopher, taught that pleasure was the supreme good and the guiding principle of conduct

ERASMUS, Desiderius (c. 1466–1536), Dutch scholar and humanist

ESTHER (400s B.C.), Jewish maiden who became queen of Persia and persuaded the king to reverse an edict authorizing the annihilation of all the Jews in the Empire

EUCLID (200s B.C.), Greek mathematician and teacher in Alexandria, who wrote the *Elements of Geometry*

EURIPIDES (c. 480–406 B.C.), Athenian tragedian

EUSEBIUS of Caesarea (c. 263–c. 339), bishop of Caesarea and historian of the Christian church

EVRARD of Bethune (c. 1210), author of a Latin grammatical textbook in metrical verse, *Graecismus*, that displaced the standard textbooks of Donatus and Priscian

FAIRCHILD, James H. (1817–1902), president of Oberlin College and advocate of coeducation

FOSTER, William T. (1879–1950), president of Reed College and economist

FRANKLIN, Benjamin (1706–1790), American journalist, scientist, and statesman

GALEN (c. 130–c. 200), Greek physician, lived in Italy and wrote treatises on physiology and medicine

GALILEO, Galilei (1564–1642), Italian mathematician and astronomer

GILMAN, Daniel C. (1831–1908), first president of Johns Hopkins University

GOETHE, Johann Wolfgang von (1749–1832), German writer, philosopher, and polymath

GORGIAS (c. 485–c. 380), prominent Athenian sophist and teacher of rhetoric

GREY, Lady Jane (1537–1554), learned English woman and great granddaughter of King Henry VII, enthroned by reformist Protestants as queen of England for nine days

HARPER, William R. (1856–1906), reforming president of the University of Chicago

HELÖISE (c. 1100–c. 1163) nun, writer, and lover of Peter Abelard

HERCULES, legendary Greek hero and son of Zeus

HERODOTUS (c. 484–c. 425 B.C.), Greek historian of the wars between Persia and the Greek city-states

HESIOD, Greek poet of the eighth century B.C.

HIPPOCRATES (c. 460–c. 370 B.C.), Greek physician

HOMER (c. 800 B.C.), Greek composer of the oral epics *Iliad* and *Odyssey*.

HORACE (65–8 B.C.), Roman lyric poet

HUGH of St. Victor (1096–c. 1141), scholar and teacher of the liberal arts near Paris

HUTCHINS, Robert M. (1899–1977), president of the University of Chicago

HUXLEY, Thomas Henry (1825–1895), English naturalist and advocate of evolution, who gave the inaugural address at the opening of Johns Hopkins University in 1876

ISIDORE of Seville (c. 560–636), Spanish churchman and encyclopedist of the liberal arts

ISIS, legendary Queen of Egypt and Egyptian nature goddess, whose cult became widespread in the Roman empire

ISOCRATES (c. 436–338 B.C.), Athenian teacher of rhetoric

JAEGER, Werner (1888–1961), influential German classicist who emigrated to the United States in 1936

JAMES, William (1842–1910), American philosopher and founder of psychology in the United States

JEFFERSON, Thomas (1743–1826), third president of the United States from 1801 to 1809

JEREMIAH (c. 628–586 B.C.), Hebrew prophet

JEROME (c. 347–c. 420) Christian scholar and editor

JOHN OF SALISBURY (c. 1115–1180), English scholar and statesman

JORDAN, David Starr (1851–1931), president of Indiana University (1885–1891) and Stanford University (1891–1916)

JUNO (Hera, in Greek), wife of Jupiter and queen of the gods

JUPITER (Zeus, in Greek), the lord and father of the Roman pantheon

JUVENAL (c. 100s A.D.), Roman satiric poet

KANT, Immanuel (1724–1804), German philosopher

KRISTELLER, Paul O. (1905–1999), professor of Renaissance philosophy at Columbia University

LEIBNIZ, Gottfried Wilhelm (1646–1716), German philosopher, mathematician, and polymath

LIVY (59 B.C.–A.D. 17), Roman historian

LOCKE, John (1632–1704), English philosopher

LOUIS XIV (1638–1715), king of France and patron of arts

LOWELL, A. Lawrence (1856–1943), president of Harvard University (1909–1933)

LOYOLA, Ignatius (1491–1556), Catholic evangelist and founder of the Society of Jesus

LUCAN (A.D. 39–65), Roman epic poet

LUCIAN (c. 125–c. 180), Greek writer of satiric dialogues

LUCRETIUS (c. 99–c. 55 B.C.), Roman poet and Epicurean philosopher

McCOSH, James (1811–1894), Scottish theologian and President of the College of New Jersey, later Princeton University

McHALE, Kathryn (1890–1956), education professor at Goucher College and scholar with the American Association of University Women

MACROBIUS (c. A.D. 400), Latin author of a commentary on Cicero's *Dream of Scipio* that was a major source of information about Plato through the Middle Ages

MADISON, James (1751–1836), fourth president of the United States and co-author of *The Federalist Papers*

MAKIN, Bathsua Reginald (c. 1608–c. 1675), English feminist educator

MANTO, legendary prophetess of ancient Greece and Rome

MARCUS, Nancy D. (1968-), United States philosopher

MARTIAL (c. A.D. 40–c. 104), Roman poet of Spanish origin

MARTIN, Jane Roland (1929–), United States feminist philosopher of education

MEIKLEJOHN, Alexander (1872–1964), leader of several American educational institutions

MERCURY, (in Greek, Hermes) messenger god in Greek and Roman mythology

MILL, John Stuart (1806–1873), English philosopher and logician

MILTON, John (1608–1674), English poet

MINERVA, *see* Athena

MINNICH, Elizabeth Kamarck (1943–), United States feminist philosopher and scholar of Women's Studies

NAKOSTEEN, Mehdi (1906–), American historian and philosopher of middle eastern education

NEWMAN, John Henry (1801–1890), English theologian, educator, and essayist

NEWTON, Isaac (1642–1727), English mathematician and physicist

NICOSTRATA, *see* Carmentis

NUSSBAUM, Martha C. (1947-), United States philosopher and essayist

ORPHEUS, mythological musician of ancient Thrace

OVID (43 B.C.–A.D. 17), Latin lyric poet

PARMENIDES (b. c. 515 B.C.), Greek monistic philosopher and teacher of Zeno of Elea

PAUL (d. c. 64), Christian evangelist and martyr, wrote many of the letters in the *New Testament*

PEIRCE, Charles S. (1839–1914), seminal American philosopher of Pragmatism

PERICLES (c. 495–429 B.C.), Athenian statesman and orator

PERSIUS (A.D. 34–62), Roman satiric poet, highly popular in the Middle Ages

PETER Lombard (1100–c. 1160), Italian theologian and bishop of Paris

PETRARCA, Francesco (1304–74), Italian poet and humanist

PLATO (c. 427–c. 348 B.C.), Athenian philosopher and student of Socrates

PLINY the Elder (c. A.D. 23–79) author of an encyclopedic treatise on the natural world

PLUTARCH (c. 46–c. 120), Greek essayist and biographer

POMPEY (106–48 B.C.), Roman general and statesman

PORPHYRY (c. 232–c. 304), Greek Neo-platonic philosopher and author of a standard medieval textbook on Aristotle's epistemology

PORTER, Noah (1811–1892), philosopher and president of Yale College (1871–1886)

PRIESTLEY, Joseph (1733–1804), British chemist and Unitarian clergyman

PRISCIAN (c. A.D. 500s), author of a standard medieval grammar conventionally divided into Books 1–16, known as *Greater Priscian*, and Books 17–18, known as *Lesser Priscian*

PTOLEMY, Claudius (c. 100s A.D.), Greco-Alexandrian geometer and astronomer

PYTHAGORAS (c. 582–c. 507 B.C.), Greek philosopher and mathematician

QUINTILIAN (c. 40–c. 100), Roman teacher of rhetoric

REID, Thomas (1710–1796), Scottish philosopher, advocating Common Sense philosophy

REMIGIUS of Auxerre (c. 841–908), late Carolingian scholar and commentator

ROBINSON, Edgar E. (1887–1977), American historian and founder of "Problems of Citizenship" course at Stanford University

ROUSSEAU, Jean-Jacques (1712–1778), French political theorist and essayist

RUSHD, Ibn (1126–1198), Spanish-Arabian philosopher and commentator on Aristotle, known as Averroës in the Latin West

SALLUST (86 B.C.–34 B.C.), Roman statesman and author of histories about Rome

SAPPHO (c. 500s B.C.), Greek lyric poetess

SATURN, father of Jupiter, lord of the gods, in Roman mythology

SENECA the Younger (c. 3 B.C.–A.D. 65), Roman official, tragedian, and Stoic philosopher

SHAKESPEARE, William (1564–1616), English playwright and poet

SMITH, Adam (1723–1790), Scottish political economist and author of *An Inquiry into the Nature and Causes of the Wealth of Nations* (1776)

SMITH, Samuel Harrison (1772–1845), United States political journalist

SOCRATES (c. 329–399 B.C.), Athenian philosopher and teacher of Plato

SOLON (c. 639–c. 559 B.C.), Athenian statesman

SOMERVILLE, Mary Fairfax (1780–1872), British mathematician and scientist and advocate of women's rights

SOPHOCLES (c. 496–c. 406 B.C.), Greek tragedian

SPENCER, Herbert (1820–1903), English philosopher and advocate of idea of evolutionary development in all fields

SPINOZA, Benedict (1632–77), Jewish Dutch philosopher

STILES, Ezra (1727–1795), president of Yale College

STURM, John (1507–1589), Protestant scholar and founder of famous school in Strasbourg

SUETONIUS (c. A.D. 69–c. 140), Latin author of surviving biographies of prominent Romans

SWIFT, Jonathan (1667–1745), English essayist and satirist

TACITUS (c. A.D. 55–c. 117), Roman biographer and historian

TAYLOR, Harold (1914–1993), president of Sarah Lawrence College and civil libertarian

TERENCE (c. 190–c. 159 B.C.), Roman playwright of realistic humorous dramas

THEODORIC (c. 454–526), king of the Ostrogoths and conqueror of Italy in about 490

THEOPHRASTUS (c. 370–c. 287 B.C.), Greek philosopher and Aristotle's successor as head of the Lyceum

THRASYMACHUS (c. 400s B.C.), Greek sophist

THUCYDIDES (c. 460–c. 400 B.C.), Greek historian of Athens and the Peloponnesian War

TRILLING, Lionel (1905–75), literary critic and English professor at Columbia University

VARRO, Marcus Terentius (116–c. 27 B.C.), Roman scholar and author of lost influential encyclopedia of the disciplines

VERGERIO, Pier Paolo (1370–c. 1445), Renaissance humanist and educator

VERGIL (*also* Virgil), (70–19 B.C.), Latin author of classic epic poem of Roman culture, the *Aeneid*

VICTORINUS, Marius (c. 285–c. 370), Roman grammarian, Neo-Platonic philosopher, and convert to Christianity

WASHINGTON, Booker T. (1856–1915), African American leader and advocate of industrial education

WAYLAND, Francis (1796–1865), reforming president of Brown University

WHITE, Andrew D. (1832–1918), founding president of Cornell University

WILLARD, Emma Hart (1787–1870), feminist educator and author of *A Plan for Improving Female Education*

XENOPHON (c. 430–c. 355 B.C.), Greek historian of Socrates and of the Persian Wars

ZENO of Elea (c. 490–c. 430 B.C.), Greek philosopher and student of Parmenides

ZEUS (in Latin, Jupiter), lord and father of the Greek pantheon

Index